First Alabama Cavalry
U.S.A.

★ ★ ★ ★ ★ ★ ★ ★ ★ ★ ★ ★ ★ ★ ★ ★

Homage to Patriotism

Glenda McWhirter Todd

HERITAGE BOOKS
2006

HERITAGE BOOKS
AN IMPRINT OF HERITAGE BOOKS, INC.

Books, CDs, and more—Worldwide

For our listing of thousands of titles see our website
at
www.HeritageBooks.com

Published 2006 by
HERITAGE BOOKS, INC.
Publishing Division
65 East Main Street
Westminster, Maryland 21157-5026

International Standard Book Number: 978-0-7884-1198-5

CONTENTS

FORWARD

Several years ago, a friend asked me to join the United Daughters of the Confederacy. My response to her was something like this, "Sure, no problem, my great, great grandfather, Andrew Ferrier McWhirter, from Marion County, Alabama was in the Civil War", thus inaugurating the quest for my heritage. Much to my surprise (and dismay, I might add) I found him buried in the Nashville National Cemetery along with one of his sons, nineteen-year old George Washington McWhirter. A few months later, I was able to uncover the fact that another son, Thomas A. McWhirter, also joined the First Alabama Cavalry Volunteer Union army, was captured and held prisoner several times but lived to return home to north Alabama where he faced the wrath and persecution of his southern neighbors.

At this point, I became so intrigued and had so many questions milling around in my mind as to why these men from the "heart of Dixie" would join the Union army, every spare moment was spent researching every piece of material available on the Southern Unionists.

The few books that had been written about the First Regiment, Alabama Volunteer Cavalry, U.S. were written by Confederate sympathizers and were not very kind to the Union cause and had portrayed these Unionists as "hill people", "poor, often underprivileged people who had been isolated on their rocky highlands", etc.

The more I studied these men and their cause, the more determined I became to "tell their story" to the world and it is a story that is long overdue. Rather than being the cowards that some had portrayed them, they were brave men who stated their grandfathers fought too hard and suffered too much during the Revolutionary War for them to turn against their country and they refused to fire on "Old Glory", the flag of their forefathers.

This book is dedicated to my great, great grandfather, Andrew Ferrier McWhirter and all of the other brave men of the First Alabama Cavalry Volunteer Union army whose conscience and dedication to their country, led them to a fate that no man should ever have to endure.

This so called Civil War was anything but civil and did not end at the war's end but continued for many years throughout northwest Alabama.

Glenda McWhirter Todd

INTRODUCTION

Microcopy Number 276 of the National Archives Microfilm Publications contains 10 rolls of microfilm which include the compiled service records of volunteer Union soldiers belonging to the First Regiment of Alabama Cavalry. This regiment is the only organization of Union troops from Alabama for which the National Archives has separate compiled service records, except those organizations redesignated as U. S. Colored Troops. These records consist of a jacket-envelope for each soldier, labeled with his name, rank and the unit in which he served and typically containing (1) card abstracts of entries relating to the soldier as found in original muster rolls, returns, hospital rolls, and descriptive books; and (2) the originals of any papers relating solely to the particular soldier. There are cross-references for soldiers' names that appeared in the records under more than one spelling.

The compiled service records for the First Regiment of Alabama Cavalry, contain information relating to soldiers belonging to the "old" and the "new" companies of the regiment. Originally the regiment was composed of Companies A - H and L, which were formed between December 1862 and September 1863 to serve for 1 year. In August 1862, two companies of 3-year men, I and K, were added to the regiment to complete its organization. These two companies formerly were Companies D and E of the First Middle Tennessee Cavalry. On May 15, 1863, The Adjutant General of the Army authorized the filling of the command at the expiration of the terms of the 1-year men; thus, as the "old" Companies A - H and L were discharged between December 1863 and September 1864, they were replaced by "new" companies that were formed to serve for 3 years. Because the "old" and the "new" companies served together under the same commanding officer and were entered on the same returns, the compiled service records for the two companies are filed together.

The compilation of service records of Union soldiers was begun in 1890 under the direction of Captain Fred C. Ainsworth, head of the Record and Pension Division of the War Department. Abstracts were made from documents in the custody of the War Department and from muster, pay, and other rolls borrowed from the Second Auditor of the Treasury. The abstracts made from the original records were verified by a separate operation of comparison, and great care was taken to ensure that the abstracts were accurate.

The compiled service records of soldiers belonging to the First Regiment of Alabama, Cavalry, are arranged alphabetically by soldiers' surnames.

Preceding the jacket-envelopes for the individual soldiers there are some envelopes containing record-of-events cards giving the stations, movements, or activities of the regiment or a part of it, and sometimes information relating to its organization or composition. In addition, there is an envelope containing a general notation card giving information relating to the regiment that was not placed on the card abstracts.

There also is a name index to certain original numbered documents filed with regimental papers that are among another series of records of The Adjutant General's Office in the National Archives. These numbered documents, which are not filmed in this microcopy, are similar to the original records (personal papers) filed in the jacket-envelopes of individual soldiers, except that each appears to contain information relating to two or more soldiers and therefore could not be filed with the records of any one soldier. A few of these documents, which were not indexed or numbered, are among the index cards.

Following the series of jacket-envelopes for the individual soldiers are separate series of card abstracts and personal papers that are not in jacket-envelopes. These series were accumulated by the War Department to be interfiled with the regular series of compiled service records but were not iterfiled, for one reason or another. The usual reason was that the information was insufficient or contained discrepancies and could not be positively identified with any soldier for whom there was a compiled service record. Other reasons were that no compiled service record had been established on the basis of regular service records and that the item did not provide enough evidence to justify establishing one. The series of card abstracts and personal papers are arranged in alphabetical order.

There is a card index that may be used to locate the compiled service record of a Union soldier from Alabama. This index, reproduced as Microcopy 263, contains the names of Alabama soldiers for whom there are regular compiled service records. An index card gives the name of the soldier, his rank, and the unit in which he served; sometimes there is a cross-reference to his service in other units or organizations. The separate series of card abstracts and personal papers are not indexed.

The compiled service records reproduced in this microcopy and the index referred to above are part of a body of records in the National Archives designated as Record Copy 94, Records of The Adjutant General's Office.

The compiled service record of a volunteer Union soldier from Alabama may not appear in this microcopy for several reasons. First, he may have served in a unit from another State or in the Regular Army. Second, he may have served under a different name or used a different spelling of his name. Third, proper records of his service may not have been made; or, if made, they may have been lost or destroyed in the confusion that often attended the initial mobilization, subsequent military operations, and disbandment of troops. Fourth, the references to the soldier in the original records may be so vague that it is not practicable to determine his correct name or the unit in which he served.

The National Archives has other records that may contain information relating to Union soldiers from Alabama. Other series of compiled service records for volunteer soldiers are (1) an alphabetical series of records of Union staff officers, (2) medical records for volunteer Union and Mexican War soldiers, and (3) records for non-State rganizations, such as U.S. Sharp Shooters, Signal Corps, U.S. Colored Troops, and 'eterans Reserve Corps. Information relating to soldiers who served in the Regular \rmy is recorded in Registers of Enlistments in the U.S. Army, 1798-1914 reproduced as Microcopy 233), and in other records of The Adjutant General's)ffice. If an application for a pension was made, additional information about the oldier may be found among the pension application files of the Veterans \dministration in Record Group 15. Sometimes supposed Union military service is hown by the records to have been civilian service as a scout, guide, or spy. :vidence of such service may be among the records of the Provost Marshal General n Record Group 110.

ranscribed from National Archives Microfilm Publications Microcopy Number 76.

Col. George E. Spencer
Courtesy of U.S.A. Military History Institute
Credit to: Roger D. Hunt Coll.

Capt. Jerome J. Hinds
Courtesy of Col. Gerald R. Jefferson

Capt. Frank Cortez Burdick
Courtesy of Sallie Cox

Major Miciah F. Fairfield

John Jarman Wilhite
Courtesy of Anne Miller

Corp. John B. Hughes
with grandchildren, Jack Willis Tuck & Mable Tuck Allen
1907/08
Courtesy of Charles A. Tuck

Doctor Tandy Boyd

Thomas K. Cook
Courtesy of Gary W. Long

George W. Whitehead & 2nd wife, Jane Herren
Courtesy of Joel Mize

Pvt. Hugh W. Logan
Courtesy of U.S.A. Military History Institute
Credit to: Mrs. Hoyt O. Smith Coll.

James Dill
Courtesy of James Quinn

Lewis & Elizabeth Hood Kelley
Courtesy of Dan Sniffin

Major J.H. Shurtleff
Courtesy of Charles & Lil Shurtleff

William Mack Guess

Joseph Pinson Byers

Pvt. Isaac A. Mize
Courtesy of Robert P. Lindley, Jr.

Margaret Davis & Stephen A. Scott

Alexander Campbell Williams
Courtesy of son, Waldemar Williams

Pvt. John D. Linley
Courtesy of Robert P. Lindley, Jr.

Robert Henry Logan

Corp. Thomas M. Lindley
Courtesy of Robert P. Lindley, Jr.

Lt. John A. Spaulding

Lt. Oliver H. Fishback

Capt. Phillip A. Stemburg

Maj. Francis L. Cramer

Lt. Richard J. Turrentine

Lt. Francis Tupper

Maj. Micajah F. Fairfield

Lt. James C. Swift

Lt. Joseph H. Hornbach

A.B. Stuart, Surgeon

Colonel George E. Spencer

Capt. Ephraim B. West

Capt. Alonson W. Edwards

Capt. Mortimer Flint

Lt. James H. Lukins

CHAPTER I

Abbreviated History of Northwest Alabama

Life, at best, in the 1840's northwest Alabama region was difficult. This is when Andrew Ferrier McWhirter and his wife, Sarah Harper, along with several of their friends decided to hitch up their wagons, leave Warren County, Tennessee, where they had been married in 1841[1], and try to find a better life. They settled, at first, in Walker County, Alabama. By 1850, they had settled in Marion County, Alabama.[2] What lay in store for them, their family and many of their friends is somewhat of a horror story.

Before continuing with this story, let me first give you a brief history of the area up to the time of the Civil War. The scenic beauty of northwest Alabama is probably what drew the pioneer settlers to the area. On March 3, 1817, the Alabama Territory was by law formed from the approximate eastern one-half of the long existed Mississippi Territory. It was in 1817, that Mississippi became a State of the Union as Alabama began to function as a Territory. Marion County was created by the Alabama Territorial Legislature on February 13, 1818, drawing its name from the great Southern Revolutionary War General, Francis Marion.[3] Initially the county encompassed land along the Tombigbee River that now makes up parts of Monroe and Lowndes counties in the state of Mississippi. In fact, before 1821, the first two county seats were located on the Tombigbee in what is now Mississippi. All lands east of the Tombigbee and Southeast of Gaines' Trace had been considered Alabama Territory until the state line was officially determined in 1820-21. Thus, when first formed in 1818, greater Marion County stretched half the North-South length of the Alabama Territory along the Tombigbee to its convergence with the Warrior River. In the initial description of the county drawn up by the Alabama Territorial Legislature in 1818, Marion was the largest Territorial county. Then, by 1819-1820 the county was reduced in size by the Legislature and the establishment of the Mississippi state line. However, the county remained extensively large into 1824, retaining most of present day Walker, Winston, Fayette and Lamar Counties within its boundaries.

All the lands that were at one time encompassed in Marion County initially served as "hunting grounds" of the Chickasaw Indian Domain before the vast Indian Cessions across the Alabama region in 1816. The Chickasaws were one of the three "civilized tribes" of the South and played a key role in the pioneer settlement of the county; providing corn to establish new immigrants, and trade goods for early county seats.

A key Indian location is marked by three large mounds on the Buttahatchee River just south of Hamilton, Alabama, at the so-called "Military Ford", where Andrew Jackson's Military Road crossed that river. Indian arrowheads, grinding stones, and pottery are found throughout the county.

By the winter of 1817-18, just prior to county creation, approximately 1000 pioneer settlers had arrived in what would become "greater Marion County". This sparse settlement was thus scattered throughout what became Marion, Fayette, Lamar, Walker and Winston Counties Alabama; and most of Monroe and Lowndes Counties Mississippi. Most early settlers came from Tennessee, but sizable numbers came from Kentucky, Georgia and the Carolinas. By the mid 1850's an extensive number of settlers came especially from Georgia. The earliest initial settlement in what was considered Marion County was along the Tombigbee River, but the hill country received numerous pioneers in the 1820's. Indeed, in the early ante-bellum years, Alabama was considered a part of the Western frontier where Federal lands could be obtained by grant and reasonable purchase prices, thus settlement came fast.[4]

It was this original county that provided as many troops for the Union army as for the Confederacy.

Marion County's second seat of justice was located just north of present-day Columbus, Mississippi which was on the lower Buttahatchee River near where it empties into the Tombigbee. Thus, in 1819-20, the community of Columbus (now Mississippi) became the first real town in Marion County, Alabama and basically served as the Marion Court Town. However, before Marion's first official Post Office could be established there in 1820 the Federal Government determined the town was located on the Mississippi side of the Alabama state line, and designated Marion's first projected official Post Office as Columbus, Mississippi.[5] The establishment of the present day Alabama/Mississippi state line in 1820-21, deprived Marion County of all its "Tombigbee bottoms", making most of the county "hills and valleys" of Northwest Alabama.

The next chosen site for the county seat was Pikeville which was surveyed in 1821. Pikeville was destined to become the historical focus of the county in the Ante-bellum period. However, being located on a rather narrow and isolated ridge along the Military Road among rather poor lands, it would not attract many settlers or many nearby farming ventures. By 1860, it contained no more than 15 business establishments and 20-30 homes. The primary businesses from the 1820's through the 1880's were tan yards or leather tanning and products such as shoes and saddles. Pikeville was also noted for beaver hat production and several good hotels/taverns and saloons. Pikeville's society was led by Judge John Dabney Terrell, Jr.

After Pikeville's village status led to rapid community dissipation, its viable central location and usefulness as a County Seat was diminished. The formation of Lamar County from Marion and Fayette Counties in 1867-68 left no choice, but to choose a more centrally located county town.

Hamilton was eventually selected as the county seat of Marion County and the Court House was built in 1882-83, however, it burned in 1887, destroying valuable records collected in the county since the 1820's.[6]

Chapter II

The Reason Why

An extremely important decision had to be made by Andrew Ferrier McWhirter, his sons and many of their friends in northwest Alabama and it was a decision that would affect thousands of people for the rest of their lives. There was considerable talk in the area about secession and war. Many of these people saw no need to fight and die in someone else's conflict which was viewed as "the rich man's war and the poor man's fight." The talk escalated and day by day, sides were taken and battle lines were drawn. They were about to be faced with what men of all times had faced, the endurance of war.

The decision was difficult and it had ceased to be safe to even whisper a word against secession. While they did not want to fight against their neighbors and sometimes family, they did not want to go against their government. They stated their grandfathers fought too hard for this country and suffered too long during the American Revolution, for them to ever engage against the "Stars and Stripes",[7] and the thought of them firing on "Old Glory", the flag of their forefathers, was a thought that was very troubling to them. All things considered, they had only one of two choices - resistance or submission.

The first public voice in America for disolving all connection with Great Britain, came not from the Puritans of New England, the Dutch of New York, nor the planters of Virginia, but from Scotch-Irish Presbyterians.[8] This passion of loyalty was born and bred in our ancestors who chose to preserve our Union.

Andrew Ferrier McWhirter's great grandfather came to this country in the early part of the 18th Century from Scotland and Ireland, where they had faced religious persecution. The McWhirters were happy in America and loved their country of choice. His grandfather, George Marlin McWhirter, was the first teacher of "the classics" in Tennessee, teaching Greek and Latin in Wilson County.[9] They were educated people and leaders in their communities. On May 30, 1889, the *Marion County Herald* printed the following story:

A REMARKABLE FAMILY

"Marion County has one of the most remarkable families within her borders, probably, that exists within the limits of the State. It is the family of Andrew F. McWhirter.

Some 50 years ago Mr. McWhirter moved to Marion County, from Tennessee, and settled near Goldmine, where he lived to the date of his death which occurred during the war. At the time of his death he had 5 children, 4 boys and 1 girl. The daughter married Mr. Harbin and lives near the old homestead. The boys are all temperate men, two of them never even drank a cup of coffee and not one of them use tobacco. The combined weight of the four men is over 800 pounds. The four have 22 living children and 7 dead. Three of them are farmers and one a preacher. The oldest, T.A. is a farmer and is 47 years of age; W.H. is a farmer and 35 years old; and A.J., (the author's great grandfather) who is the baby, is 30 years old, and weighs 211 pounds. He also is a farmer and holds the office of county commissioner, and by the way he is one of the best commissioners in the State. They are highly respected and gentlemen of moral worth and men of which any county might well be proud."

This paints a very different picture of these men than that portrayed by the few Southern sympathizers who have written about the First Alabama Cavalry, USA, and stated they were poor, uneducated, "hillbilly" type traitors. I, as thousands of other Southerners, had ancestors who wore the Gray as well as the Blue and I am equally proud of them all. However, the men of the 1st Alabama Cavalry, USA had a story to tell and I am pleased to tell it more factually than it has ever been told.

Thousands of people across the South expressed their opposition to secession. This was not an isolated problem in northwest Alabama. While Alabama furnished over 2,500 white Alabamians and many blacks to the Federal cause, western Virginia furnished over 31,000 while eastern Tennessee had 30,000 to join the Union.

The chances for peace diminished with the opening shot of the Civil War when it was fired from Fort Johnson in South Carolina on Fort Sumter at 4:30AM on April 1, 1861. **The guns had spoken!** Talk of the Civil War escalated in Alabama and the draft was imminent. The men who wished to remain loyal to their country met at Houston, the county seat of Winston County, and decided to round up the Union sympathizers to decide what action should be taken for them to pursue their position of neutrality. A meeting was scheduled at Looney's Tavern in Winston County for July 4, 1861, to discuss the situation. Six men set out in six different directions all over northwest Alabama to apprise the men of the meeting. It was allegedly attended by more than 2,500 people who came on mules, horseback and covered wagons and camped out over the week-end to decide their fate. A committee was appointed and the resolutions that were drawn up were approved. Two points were clear to all of these men - they could not fight against their country out of respect for their heritage, believing that the union had been cemented by the blood of their forefathers and that it must be preserved. They also believed it was best to keep their views to themselves. They knew their country and their flag must be defended and defend it they did!

One resolution drawn up at the meeting states, in part: "We agree with Jackson that no state can legally get out of the Union; but if we are mistaken in this, and a state can lawfully and legally secede or withdraw, being only a part of the Union, then a county, any county, being a part of the state, by the same process of reasoning, could cease to be a part of the state."

Another resolution concerned their wishes for neutrality: "We think that our neighbors in the South made a mistake when they bolted, resulting in the election of Mr. Lincoln, and that they made a greater mistake when they attempted to secede and set up a new government. However, we do not desire to see our neighbors in the South mistreated, and therefore, we are not going to take up arms against them; but on the other hand, we are not going to shoot at the flag of our fathers, "old Glory," the Flag of Washington, Jefferson, and Jackson. Therefore, we ask that the Confederacy on the one hand, and the Union on the other, leave us alone, unmolested, that we may work out our political and financial destiny here in the hills and mountains of northwest Alabama."

Their attempt to defeat secession failed and their wishes of neutrality branded them as "traitors". Then on April 16, 1862, the Conscription Act was passed by the Confederate Congress which made every able-bodied white man

4

between the ages of eighteen and thirty-five subject to the military service of the Confederate States. It was at this point that the Union sympathizers of northwest Alabama, fled to the hills and caves to keep from fighting against the country they so loved, the country that had embraced their forefathers as they searched for a place to worship in peace.

The people who wished to secede from the Union formed a band of Home-Guards and Partisan Rangers to hunt down these men and force them to join the Confederacy. This was the beginning of the bloodiest battle of guerrilla warfare ever fought in the South or on American soil.

As the Confederates combed the hills searching for Union loyalists, they captured several each day and forced them to join the Confederate army "or be shot". Many of them managed to escape, find their way to the Union lines and join their country's army. Others who managed to remain hidden soon ran out of food and became extremely tired and weary.

Charles Christopher Sheats spoke to a group of Unionists on July 14, 1862, urging them to fight side-by-side for a cause they believed in and put down the rebellion. He stated that the time had come to either fight in an army for which they had no sympathy and in a cause for which they hated, or join the army of the United States for a cause they loved and put down the rebellion so peace would again prevail. His closing statement was, "tomorrow morning I am going to the Union army, I am going to expose this fiendish villainy before the world. They shall hear from me. I have slept in mountains, in caves and caverns, till I am become musty; my health and manhood are failing me, I will stay here no longer till I am enabled to dwell in quiet at home."[10]

Typically of the Southern Unionists, one-by-one took a stand and risked their lives traveling, in some cases, hundreds of miles to join the Union Army. Within three days of the urging of C.C. Sheats, one-hundred and fifty men joined the Union Army. On July 24, 1862, Andrew Ferrier McWhirter along with two of his sons and many neighbors, joined the Union army in Huntsville, Alabama.[11] They had managed to escape the Confederate soldiers still scouring the woods for these Southern Unionists.

Colonel Abel D. Streight, Commander of the Fifty-first Indiana Regiment stationed at Decatur, Alabama, stated, *"I wish to say a word in relation to the condition of these people. They are mostly poor, though many of them are, or rather were, in comfortable circumstances. They outnumber nearly 3 to 1 the secessionists in portions of Morgan, Blount, Winston, Marion, Walker, Fayette, and Jefferson Counties; but situated as they are, surrounded by a most relentless foe, mostly unarmed and destitute of ammunition, they are persecuted in every conceivable way, yet up to this time most of them have kept out of the way sufficiently to avoid being dragged off by the gangs that infest the country for the purpose of plunder and enforcing the provisions of the rebel conscription act. Their horses and cattle are driven off in vast numbers. Every public road is patrolled by guerrilla bands, and the Union men have been compelled to seek protection in the fastnesses of the mountainous wilderness. They cannot hold out much longer. This state of things has so disturbed them that but very little attention has been paid to farming, consequently many of them are not destitute of food of their own and are living off their more fortunate neighbors. Such examples of patriotism as these people have set are worthy of being followed. One old lady, Mrs. Anna Campbell, volunteered to ride 35 miles and return, making 70 miles,*

5

with about 30 recruits, within 36 hours. *When it is taken into consideration that these people were all hid to avoid being taken by the rebels and that the country is but sparsely settled, this case is without a parallel in American history. I have never witnessed such an outpouring of devoted and determined patriotism among any other people.*"[12]

In a letter dated July 16, 1862, from Col. James B. Fry in camp near Mooresville, Alabama, he stated: *"SIR: While in command at Decatur there were several small parties of loyal Alabamians who came into our lines begging me to give them protection and a chance to defend the flag of our country. The tale of suffering and misery as told by each as they arrived was in itself a lamentable history of the deplorable condition of the Union people of the South. Notwithstanding the oft-repeated assertion that there was a strong Union sentiment in portions of the cotton States, I had long since given up all hopes of finding the people entertaining it; hence I was at first incredulous as to what they said and even suspicious that they were spies belonging to the enemy, but as their numbers increased, each corroborating the story of the other, I at last became convinced that the matter was worthy of notice.*

About this time (10th instant) I was informed by a courier that there was a party of about 40 men some 5 or 6 miles toward the mountain trying to come to us and about the same number of the enemy's cavalry were between them and Decatur trying to intercept and capture them. As my orders were to defend the town only I did not feel at liberty to send out assistance to the Union men without further orders, and there being no telegraphic communication with you I at once informed General Buell by telegraph of the circumstances, whereupon I received the following reply:

Send out what force you deem sufficient to assist the Union men in and drive off the rebel cavalry, and see that they are not playing a trick to draw you out by these reports.[13]

Col. Streight wrote the following letter: *SIR: I have the honor to report to you that the party of Alabama volunteers has just arrived and 40 of them have been mustered into the service of the United States. Their accounts of the hardships endured are sufficient to enlist the sympathies of the hardest heart. They report that there are several hundred who would come but for the danger of passing from the foot of the mountains here, some 25 miles distant......*[14]

Col. Streight went on to say: *"Never did people stand in greater need of protection. They have battled manfully against the most unscrupulous foe that civilized warfare has ever witnessed. They have been shut off from all communication with anybody but their enemies for a year and a half, and yet they stand firm and true. If such is not to be rewarded, if such citizens are not to receive protection, then their case is deplorable indeed."* Colonel Streight had requested permission to return to the foot of the mountains and recruit enough of the "brave mountaineers" to protect the Union sympathizers in the region.

These men truly embodied everything that loyalty and patriotism were all about!

Not only were these loyal Americans driven from their homes, forced to hide in the deep gorges, coves and caves, being pursued by their angry neighbors

6

who were determined to force them to enlist in the Confederate army or shoot them to keep them from joining the Union army, they were now, not being taken seriously by the very people they wanted to serve! Col. Streight was finally given permission to go after them but the mission was not without incident.

Several accounts have been written about the sons of Solomon Curtis, three of whom were killed by the Confederates and/or Home Guards. Joel Jackson Curtis was supposedly killed in 1862 in Jasper, AL for refusing to join the Confederate Army. George Washington Curtis was shot and killed in 1863, in front of his wife and three small children, while attempting to elude the Home Guards. Tom Pink Curtis, who was Probate Judge of Winston Co., AL, was tortured, hung, shot and thrown over a bluff by some of the same men who killed his brothers, for aiding the Union Loyalists. Jim Curtis was the only brother to survive the war and allegedly vowed to kill every rebel who participated in the death of his brothers. This is only one of the many stories of the harassment endured by the loyal Americans whose wish was to remain neutral in a war where they were forced to make a choice they did not wish to make.

Their country and its flag were of prodigious importantance to these patriotic soldiers, this flag that led them into a bloody battle in the defense of the most glorious nation in the world. They believed, as did Abraham Lincoln, that "A nation divided against itself cannot stand". They believed the red on the flag stood for courage, the white for purity and the blue stood for justice and steadfastness. The flag was indicative of God's Heaven under which it flew. To them, America had been built on a dream. A dream of their forefathers, where they could bring their families and be free to worship their God in the church of their choice without fear of persecution. To them, "Old Glory" stood for freedom, the freedom for which their forefathers had already shed their blood. A freedom for which they, themselves must continue to defend and protect.

So call them "tories" if you like, or "bluecoats" or "home-made Yankees" - even call them "traitors", if you must but we have the proof that they loved their God and they loved their Country and they loved "Old Glory", the Flag of their forefathers, to the extent they were willing to sacrifice their lives, families and homes for these beliefs and in many cases, lost it all!

So rest in peace, you loyal, courageous, soldiers. We love you and we know and understand the cause for which you stood and we thank you for the noble legacy you left us. You have taught us what loyalty and patriotism are all about. We salute you and will keep your memory and your legend alive. You gave your **all** to save our Union.

7

CHAPTER III

REGIMENTAL HISTORY
Company K

Many of the men had enrolled in the Union army in Huntsville, Alabama on July 21 & July 24, 1862 when Special Order Number 155, dated September 8, 1862 stated the following:

> *The companies of Alabama Troops lately organized at Huntsville, Ala. are transferred to the 1st Middle Tenn Regiment of Cavalry, and will report to Col. Stokes, Commanding, without delay.*

> By Command of Maj. Gen. Buell
> W.H. Sidell
> Major 15th U.S. Inf.
> A.A.A.G.[15]

Company Muster Roll dated October 31, 1862 at Camp Campbell in Nashville, TN stated "K Co. 1st Regt. Ala. Cav. (New)" was now Company E, 1st Regiment Middle Tennessee Cavalry.

> *"Company organized at Huntsville, Ala. under Special Orders No. 106, Hd. qrs. Army of the Ohio dated July 18, 1862. Company organized July 24, 1862 at Huntsville, Ala. and designated Co. B, 1st Ala. Volunteer Infantry Aug. 31, march from Huntsville by order of Capt. Lytle Sept 5 to arrive at Nashville Tenn Sept 8. Co. transferred to 1st Middle Tenn Cavalry by Sp O No 155 dated Nashville Tenn Sept 8, 1862 Hd qrs Army of the Ohio, Co reported to Col. Stokes for duty."*

The Springfield Research Service states that no arms were reported issued to the 1st AL Cav. until the 1st quarter of 1863, and then only Company A reported arms (19 Hall's carbines and 29 muskets). This probably means that they relied on private weapons before that. They have documented about 5 weapons for the 1st AL Cav., the latest being a Smith's carbine issued to Madison Barton of Company L. The Smith's carbines were issued in the 3rd quarter of 1863. They have also documented a Smith's carbine issued to Pvt. David Shobert, which is currently in the possession of one of his descendants.

The Regimental Return dated March, 1863, Glendale, Mississippi states that from the first formation the regiment had been engaged in scouting in NE Mississippi and it was due to the fact that the men were so familiar with the country that they had been so universally successful.

From April 14th to April 17th, 1863, the regiment was engaged under the command of General Dodge in an expedition toward Decatur, AL. They were engaged in battle on April 17th and skirmishing at other times with arms unfit for that branch of service.

From May through October, the Field & Staff were in camp at Glendale, MS; in November, December and January, at Camp Davies, MS; in February, 1864, they were reported in Memphis, TN; March & April, they were in Mooresville, AL, and from June through November they were in Rome, GA where the regiment was on duty every day scouting the country around Rome, GA, skirmishing with Wheeler's "Rebel" Cavalry, until November 11th when they broke camp and moved in the direction of Atlanta, GA. They arrived in Atlanta the evening of November 14th where they were assigned to duty with the 17th A.C. They took advance of the corps and moved on the 15th in a South-easterly direction and kept the advance. They had several brisk skirmishes with the enemy, the hardest of which was at Oconee River on the 23rd where they stated they drove the enemy at every point with slight loss and then continued in the advance of the corps until the last of November.

In December 1864, they were stationed at Fort Thunderbolt, GA. The regiment left Millen, GA on December 1st, moving down the Georgia Central Rail Road in advance of the 17th A.C. They had a brisk skirmish on the 4th at Buck Head Creek and continued skirmishing each day until the 9th when they arrived at the Confederate outer works at Savannah, GA where they drove them two miles over a road where torpedoes were buried. These wicked land mines contrived by the Confederates, took a toll on the 1st Alabama Cavalry (US) as they were the escorts and the first to set off the explosions which scattered bodies and horses in all directions.

As Gen. Sherman reached the mangled bodies of his soldiers, he gazed at Lt. Francis Tupper, whose right foot had been blown off and his knee and hand were mutilated. It was with shock and pain that he could offer little help to the young soldier who had been in the army for three years and his time had been up the previous week.

Sherman quickly ordered the Confederate prisoners, they had captured along the way, to go on ahead and clear the road of the land mines. As they screamed in disbelief that an order like that was inhumane, the General ordered them to look at Lt. Tupper and asked if that was humanity. Six other men were wounded and six horses were killed during the land mine explosion.

They continued to drive the enemy to their main works, destroyed the Gulf Rail Road and returned to camp on the 21st. They arrived in Savannah on December 22nd and camped four miles South of the city at Thunderbolt Battery. The men were without rations and the animals were without forage. The weather was cold and rainy and the soldiers had waded through the icy swamps until their clothes were frozen on their aching bodies. Water was frozen in their canteens and they had lived on a diet of rice for over a week. They were suffering extremely.

The regiment was camped at Thunderbolt until the 17th when it moved to Little Ogeeche River, having been transferred to General Kilpatrick's Division of Cavalry. From there they moved to Sister's Ferry, GA, arriving there on the 29th and remaining until the last of the month.

From Sister's Ferry, GA, they began their campaign through the Carolinas often working all night crossing the numerous and almost impassable swamps and streams, skirmishing with the enemy at various points, *"conducting themselves in all their arduous duties in the most noble and creditable manner"*.[16]

While General Sherman was sympathetic to the civilians and ordered his men not to destroy any private property or hurt any women or children, he blamed the South Carolina secessionists for starting the country's Civil War so it was not expected that he would spare anything in his path through South Carolina. However, he was blamed for burning Columbia when in essence, the fire was started by the Confederates. Gen. Wade Hampton, deciding his troops were no match for the Union army, ordered them out of Columbia before Sherman arrived. Upon leaving, his troops set fire to the cotton and as the winds picked up that evening, the flames spread to other buildings and had become a raging holocaust by the time Sherman and his troops arrived. Sherman, himself, tried to help extinguish the fires.

The regiment continued the march through South Carolina with the 3rd Brigade, 3rd Cavalry Division, crossing the Pedee River in North Carolina on March 6th, skirmishing with the enemy at Rockingham. On the morning of the 10th their camp was surprised by an overwhelming force of the enemy. *"We fought most desperately and held possession of the camp sustaining a loss of four killed, 27 wounded and 41 prisoners. The defeat of the enemy on this occasion was due to the personal bravery and gallantry of the officers and men which cannot be too highly appreciated."*[17]

They arrived at Fayetteville, NC on the 11th where they remained until the 15th when they crossed the Cape Fear River, encountering the enemy the same evening. On the 16th, they had a battle *"of some note"*, and again they encountered the enemy on the 18th.

They were present at the Battle of Bentonville, NC on the 19th, 20th & 21, holding a position on the left flank of the army but not actively engaging. They then moved to Faison's Depot, NC where they arrived on the 24th and remained until the last of the month. *"The officers and men are ever ready to do every duty and have in their various duties and hardships evinced a species of patriotism and valor worthy of the noble cause in which we are engaged."*[18]

To continue with Company K, the Company Muster Roll dated July & August, 1863, Nashville, Tennessee records the following events:

"July 1/63, on the march near Manchester, Tenn, at Decherd from the 2nd till the 6th and Winchester from the 6th till the 10th when marched for Fayetteville. 12th marched for Pulaski, 13th had a skirmish at Pulaski, 15th marched to Elkton, 16th arrived at Fayetteville, 17th arrived at Huntsville, Ala., 20th marched to Fayetteville, arrived at Pulaski 23rd, 26th marched to Shelbyville, Tenn., arrived 27th. Received order from War Dept. Sp. O. No. 281 dated June 25/63, Aug 9th proceeded to Nashville, arrived 10th. Remained at Nashville under Sp. O. No. 44 Hd. qrs. Dist. of the Cumberland temporarily under the command of Col. Pickens, 3rd E Tenn Cavalry."

"July 1, 1863, Co. on the march near Manchester, Tenn, at Decherd from the 2nd till the 6th and at Winchester from the 6th till the 10th when marched for Fayetteville, Tenn. Left Fayetteville for Pulaski the 13th, arrived 15th, had a skirmish with rebels, marched to Elkton 16th and back to Fayetteville 17th & proceeded to Huntsville, Ala., arrived there the 20th. Returned to Pulaski, Tenn. via Fayetteville, arrived 23rd, marched to Shelbyville 26th, arrived 27th. Rec'd Special Order No. 281, War Dept. dated June 25/63. Proceeded to Nashville Aug. 9th, arrived there Aug. 10th. Remained at Nashville under Special Order No. 44. Hd qrs Army of the Cumberland temporarily under command of Col. Pickens 3rd E. Tenn. Cav. Sep 7 (or 17)/63 left Nashville & proceeded to Glendale, Miss via Louisville, Cairo & Memphis. Arrived at Glendale Sep. 23/63. Oct. 19/63 Co. marched with 1st Ala. Cav. on an expedition into Walker Co., Ala. Oct. 26/63, Co.

in the skirmish at Vincents Cross Roads, Miss. On arriving at the 1st Ala Cav. the letter of the Co. was changed from E to K. "

In November and December 1863, Company K was stationed at Camp Davies, Mississippi.

Company Muster Roll for January & February 1864 shows Company K to be in Memphis, Tennessee and records the following events:

"Jan. 23, 1864, Co. marched with the Regt. from Camp Davies, Miss to Lagrange, Tenn. on cars Jan. 30, 1864, moved to Memphis, Tenn. by R.R. In camp since to date."

The next Company Muster Roll for K Co. was dated July & August 1864 showing the company to be stationed in Rome, Georgia and records the following events:

"On the first day of July the Co. was stationed at Rome, Ga. 3rd & 4th on a scout to Opossum Snout, Ga. Six men of the Co. under Capt. West went to Randolph Co., Ala. 19th, 20th, 21st & 22nd on a scout to Wills Valley, Ala 29th & 30th on a scout to Summerville, Ga."

Company Muster Roll for September and October 1864 shows them stationed in Rome, Georgia.

In November and December 1864 the Company Muster Roll shows Co. K to be stationed at Thunderbolt, Georgia and records the following events:

"On the 11th of Nov. 1864 the Co. marched with the Regt. from Camp at Rome, Ga. in advance of the 17th A.C. In a skirmish at Oconee Bridge, Ga. Central R.R. Nov. 30/64. Burned Oconee Bridge Ga. Central R.R. Nov 30/64. In a skirmish near Millen, Ga. Dec 2nd/64. In a skirmish near Savannah, Ga. Dec. 9/64. Dec. 17th/64 marched on a scout towards Altamaha (?) Bridge, Dec 21st arrived at Camp 10 miles west of Savannah, Ga. Dec 22nd marched into Savannah. Dec 23rd went into camp at Thunderbolt, Ga."

Company Muster Roll dated December 31, 1864 to April 30, 1865 shows Company K stationed at Durham's Station, North Carolina and records the following events:

"Jany 16th/65 Co. moved with the Regt. from Thunderbolt, Ga. to Camp at Ogeechee 10 miles West of Savannah, Ga. Jan. 28 marched on Gen. Sherman's Carolina Campaign being in Genl Kilpatrick's 3rd Brig. Feby 10th in battle near Ackin, S.C. Mch 10th in battle at Monroes Crossroads N.C. 1 sgt killed. 1Lt. & 6 men wounded & 5 captured. Mch 15th in battle near Averysboro N.C., 16th same, Mch 18th, 19th & 20th in battle near Bentonville N.C. Arrived at Durham's Station N.C. April 16, 1865."

The Sgt. referred to as being killed was William C. Boling. Other members of the 1st Regiment of Alabama Cavalry, USA killed in action at Monroe's

Crossroads were Archie Bowen, Pvt., Co. D; James R. Mize, Pvt., Co. E; and John J. Vines, Pvt., Co. D.

General William Tecumseh Sherman referred to Brigadier General Hugh Judson Kilpatrick, better known as "Kill Cavalry" Kilpatrick, as "a hell of a damn fool" which was proven to him at Monroe's Cross Roads, North Carolina by Kilpatrick's disobedience of orders and carelessness. Sherman had, however, personally requested Kilpatrick to command his cavalry in the March to the Sea, because he was so headstrong, and stated "he is just the sort of man to command my cavalry on this expedition".

On March 4, 1865, Sherman had sent a message to Kilpatrick ordering him to Fayetteville, North Carolina, warning him that his primary mission was to protect the army's left flank and that under no circumstances was he to confront the Confederate cavalry in battle! In the mean time, Kilpatrick learned that Lt. Gen. Wade Hampton's force would be advancing along either the Morganton Road, Chicken Road or Yadkin Road and decided to send some of his men out, including Colonel George E. Spencer and his 1st Alabama (Union) Cavalry, to intercept Hampton's force.

Spencer's Brigade had arrived at Monroe's Cross Roads (Solemn Grove, North Carolina) about 2:00 PM while the other Brigades arrived a few hours later. Late in the evening of March 9th, Kilpatrick was reportedly riding in a wagon with two lady friends behind his personal guards and they were led into the hands of the 5th Kentucky who managed to capture 30 prisoners without firing a single shot. Kilpatrick, however, escaped the Confederates.

After Hampton was apprised of the situation he decided to attack Kilpatrick the next morning and ordered his men to follow the tracks of Spencer and his men to locate their camp. While Kilpatrick had men sent out in three directions, attempting to surround the Confederates, he was actually cut off by them, therefore only about one-third of his men wound up at Monroe's Cross Roads. Another grave mistake by Kilpatrick was failing to post pickets to guard his encampment from the rear. Col. Spencer and part of his 1st Alabama Cavalry were among the approximately 1,500 men in this camp which adjoined a swamp.

General Joe Wheeler arrived on the scene early the next morning and ordered an attack on the Federal camp. While the Federal soldiers were still asleep and just as Kilpatrick stepped out of the farmhouse in his underwear, the Rebels rode into the camp firing their weapons. Many of the men tried to escape to the large swamp but most were run down by the Confederates. Kilpatrick, however, did manage to escape into the swamp partially dressed but had to leave his pistol, sword, coat, hat, and pants behind.

This attack failed to stop the Federals and after they regrouped they positioned themselves behind trees and began firing on the Rebels killing and wounding many of them, thus ending the Battle of Monroe's Cross Roads.

In Kilpatrick's report to Sherman he stated he lost "4 officers killed and 7 wounded, 15-19 men killed and 61-75 severely and several slightly wounded, and 103 officers and men taken prisoner." He also stated the enemy left upward of 80 killed, including many officers and a large number of men wounded. Twenty-seven of the Union soldiers are buried in three graves on the grounds of Fort Bragg, North Carolina.

Continuing with Company K, the Muster Roll dated May and June 1865 shows them stationed in Huntsville, Alabama and records the following events:

"May 4th/65 Co. marched with the Regt from Durhams Station, N.C. June 14/65 arrived at Huntsville, Ala. Encamped near Davis Spring, Huntsville, Ala."

> J.H. Hornback
> 1st Lieut. 1st Ala. Cav.
> Comdg. Co. K.

The men of this company, who survived the war, were mustered out October 20, 1865 in Huntsville, Alabama.

COMPANY A (Old)

Company A was recruited in Alabama in September and October, 1862, for the cavalry service and assigned temporarily to the 12th Regiment, Illinois Infantry.

In November and December, 1862, they were on general duty as scouts and guides and were in action near Tuscumbia, Alabama December 12, 1862.

January and February, 1863, company was on active duty as guides and scouts and on expedition in Alabama from February 5th - 13th and also from February 15th to 28th.

March and April, 1863, on active duty as guides and scouts and with the expedition through Alabama from April 15, 1863 to May 2, 1863.

May and June, 1863, company was on active duty as guides and scouts and on raid to Pikeville, Alabama from May 3-12, 1863. May 21-27, 1863, they were on a raid to Fulton, MS and from June 5-11, 1863, on raid from Tuscumbia, Alabama. June 17-23, they were on raid to Barnesville, Alabama.

July-October 1863, they were in camp at Glendale, Mississippi.

COMPANY A (New)

New Company A was recruited at Camp Davies, Mississippi during the months of December 1863 and January 1864 by Lt. Hinds, Lt. Files, and Sgt. Emrich. On January 23, 1864, it was ordered aboard the cars (train) and moved to LaGrange, Tennessee where it went into camp on January 27th. On January 29th, it went aboard "the cars" and was moved to Memphis, Tennessee and on January 30th, it went into camp about one mile east of Memphis.

On February 5, 1864, the company was mustered into the U.S. Service by Capt. Williams, Co. M, 16th A.C. and were armed with Smith's Carbines.

In March and April, 1864, "Co. A, 1st Reg't. Ala. Vols. Cav'y since last muster remained at Memphis, Tenn. the 27th of Mar. at which time we moved in company with the regt. by water to Nashville, Tenn. landing there on the 5th of April from thence we moved by Rail Road to the present encampment, (Mooresville, Alabama), arriving here Apr 12/64 where we have been doing duty with the reg't up to the present date."

May and June, 1864, "Co. A, 1st Reg't. Cav. Ala. Vols. marched from Mooresville, Ala. on the morning of the 1st of May 1864 for Chattanooga, Tenn. From there we marched to Snake Gap, Ga. where we joined left wing 16 A.C. under command of Gen'l Lodge (?). Remained with that command until 21st of June at which time we were ordered to Rome, Ga. Was at the time of our departure in front of Kennesaw Mountain, have been on duty here since our arrival the 26th of June."

July and August, 1864, "Co. A of the 1st Regt. Cav. Ala. Vols. commanded by Capt. J.J. Hinds has been on duty with the reg't during the past 2 months at Rome, GA, have not changed their encampment since last muster. The duty performed by them is scouting the country in its various directions from the post of Rome, Ga."

September and October, 1864, "This Co. has been on duty with the reg't since last muster at Rome, Ga. where we are stationed at present. Nothing transpired out the line of regular duty, had no close engagement with the enemy, quite a number of skirmishes not amounting to any great deal of importance. Received quite a number of recruits."

November and December, 1864, "A Co. of the First Reg't. Cav. Ala. Vols. has been on duty with the Reg't. since last muster. Had the good Fortune of being able to bare their part well in the campaign through Georgia and against Savanah. Participated in destroying the Gulf Rail Road, returning to Savanah going in to camp at Fort Thunderbolt 5 miles east of Savanah where we are today."

January through April, 1865, the company was shown as "In the Field, S.C."

May and June, 1865, stationed at Huntsville, Alabama.

July & August, 1865, stationed at Moulton, Alabama.

COMPANY B (Old)

January through August, 1863, Old Company B was stationed at Glendale, Mississippi. (September and October does not state where they were.)

November and December, 1863, stationed at Camp Davies, MS. The Record of Events states the following: *"Nov. 26th the company marched South with the Cav. Brig. Nov. 27th when near Tupelo, Miss. turned about and marched North and East. Returned to camp on the night of Nov. 29th. Distance traveled about 100 miles."*

April 13 to October, 1864, New Company B was stationed at Rome, Georgia. *November and December, 1864,* New Company B was stationed at Thunderbolt, Georgia. Record of Events states the following: *"Since laster muster Co. B left Rome, Ga. with the regiment. Nov. 11th joined the main body of the army at Atlanta*

15

Nov. 15 taking the advance of the 15th Corps in the Campaign through the State of Georgia. The company was engaged at the Battle of Balls Ferry on the Oconee River, losing 1 man killed, 1 captured and 6 wounded. We were engaged again at the Battle at Station No. 1 on the Central R.R. We arrived at our present encampment Thunderbolt, Ga. 5 miles south of Savannah on the Sav. River completing a march of about 300 miles on the 23 of Dec. 1864 where we have remained ever since."

January and February, 1865, in the field in South Carolina, March and April, 1865, they were stationed at Durham, NC and in May, June, July and August, 1865, in Courtland, Alabama.

COMPANY C (Old)

From enlistment to February 28, 1863, Old Company C, stationed at Glendale, Mississippi. From May through December, 1863, still camped at Glendale.

From enlistment to April 30, 1864, New Company C was stationed at Mooresville, Alabama.

June through October, 1864, they were stationed at Rome, Georgia.

November and December, 1864, stationed at Savannah, GA.

January and February, 1865, stationed "In the Field, S.C."

March and April, 1865, stationed at Durham, North Carolina.

May and June, 1865, stationed at Moulton, Alabama still remaining in Moulton August 31, 1865.

COMPANY D

From April through October, 1863, Company D was stationed at Glendale, Mississippi and November and December, 1863, they were at Camp Davies, Mississippi.

January and February, 1864 , Evacuated Camp Davies, Miss. Jan 24, burned gov't. Buildings and proceeded to Corinth, Miss. Evacuated Corinth 25th, burned all gov't Buildings. Moved to LaGrange, Tenn., arrived 27. This Regt. remained at Lagrange until all others left. Started for Memphis 30th, 3 A.M. Arrived at Memphis 11 A.M. 31/64. Bef. 1, men were paid for the months of Nov. & Dec. Stopped pay on officers because some were behind on ordnance returns. Ordnance returns of this co. have been made promptly and are all up. Ordered on scout Feb. 5 under command of Maj. Fairfield, went to Hernando, captured (?) prisoners, then moved out on the Hernando and Memphis Road 3 1/2 miles and stopped for the night.

16

A detachment of this Co. and H Co. under command of Capt. Shurtleff went dismounted one mile east of the planta.... to Mr. ....beth, there captured a decoying party, took 9 prisoners , wounded Capt. Taylor of _orksay in C.S. army. Took 15 horses & equipments. Arrived in Memphis the 6 at 11 a.m. Detachment of this Regt. was ordered out with 5 days rations on the 7. This company reenlisted, joined and reported to Col. McCreden (?) comdg. Regt. of Infantry at Hernando 23 miles south of Memphis. That night the 8 moved southwest and skirmished at Sanatobia, Miss. On the 9 this co. lost one man captured by the enemy, had skirmishing 10, 11, 12 and up to 15 then proceeded home by the way of Collierville. Arrived at Memphis on the 18. Distance marched 200 miles."

March and April, 1864, "This Co. with the Regt. broke camp at Memphis, Tenn. on the 26 of March and shipped on board the Steamer Wetmoreland for Nashville. Left Memphis on the 27 Mch. arrived at Nashville on the 3 of Mch. (April ?). Marched across the country to this farm, arrived at Decatur on the 14 of April 1864.

　　　May and June, 1864 Company Muster Roll shows them stationed at Rome, Georgia, June 30, 1864 where they remained through October, 1864.

November and December, 1864, stationed at Savannah, Ga. Dec. 31/64. Record of Events states the following. " Co. on duty with Regmt. at Rome, Ga. up to Nov. 11th scouting the country and skirmishing with Hoods (rebels) every day. Co. moved with Regmt. on the 11th in direction of Atlanta, Ga. arriving there the evening of 14th. Regt. assigned to duty there with 17th Army Corps and moved the 15th in direction of Macon, Ga. Regt. lead the advance of the Corps through Ga. to Savannah where we arrived Dec. 10th. Co. had a brisk skirmish at Oconee River on the 23rd Nov. Regt. burned the R.R. bridge on the Oconee River. Co. had a skirmish at little Ogeehe(?) River Dec. 4th with enemy. One man severely wounded.

January and February, 1865, Company D in the field. (Does not state where.)

March and April, 1865, stationed at Durham, S.C. (?), April 30/65.

May and June, 1865, stationed at Huntsville, Alabama 6/30/65.

July and August, 1865, stationed at Moulton, Alabama, August 31, 1865.

COMPANY E

　　　Company Muster Roll dated February 28, 1863, shows Company E stationed at Glendale, Mississippi and Record of Events states: "Company on Genl. duty as scouts. Portion of Co. in action near Tuscumbia, Ala. February 12/63. Company in action near Bear Creek March 3/63."

March and April, 1863, company stationed at Glendale, MS, and in action near Tuscumbia, Alabama April 17, 1863.

May through August, 1863, stationed at Glendale, MS.

September and October, 1863, company stationed at Glendale, MS and records the following events. *"Co. on general Scouting duty. Co. engaged with the Regt. at Vincent's Cross Roads Ala. with the enemy October 26, 1863. In this engangment Capt. Chandler was killed immediately, also Mr. M. Byrd* (Marshall Byrd) *was killed and 9 men missing.*

November and December, 1863, Company E was stationed at Camp Davies, Mississippi and records the following events: *"Nov. 26th Co. went on Scout towards Tupelo, Miss, had several skirmishes with enemy. Returned Nov. 29/63, distance marched 120 miles. Dec. 20 Co. went on Scout towards Jackson, Tenn. to attack Gen. Forest (Rebel). Returned to Corinth Miss Dec. 28/63 and left next day for Lagrange, Tenn."*

January and February, 1863, company stationed at Memphis, TN. Left Camp Davies, MS on January 23, 1864 and arrived in Memphis January 29, 1864.

March and April, 1864, company stationed at Mooresville, Alabama.

May and June, 1864, company stationed at Kingston, Georgia.

June and July, 1864, company stationed at Rome, GA where we remained through October.

November and December, 1864, company stationed at Fort Thunderbolt, Georgia.

January and February, 1865, company on Gen. Sherman's Raid in North Carolina and records the following events: *"Started from Sa (Savannah), Ga. with 3rd Brig 3 Cav. Div M.D. M (?) 28 June 1865 having marched since last muster about 400 miles. Constantly skirmishing with the enemy during which time several details of 4 & 5 men of my Co. were scouting inside the enemies lines by order Gen. Kilpatrick which had a very unfavorable effect on the good diciplin of my men ...ing a desire for straggling."*

March and April, 1865, company was stationed at Durham's Station, North Carolina having marched about 500 miles, having skirmishes with the enemy with one man killed and one wounded.

May through August, 1865, company was stationed at Moulton, Alabama.

COMPANY F

June through August, 1863, Company F was stationed at Glendale, Mississippi and from September through December, 1863, stationed at Camp Davies, MS.

January and February, 1864, stationed at Memphis, TN.

April 30, 1864, stationed at Mooresville, Alabama.

From the end of June through October, 1864, Company F was stationed at Rome, Georgia.

November and December, 1864, stationed at Savannah, GA.

January and February, 1865, stationed at Moulton, Alabama. Record of Events states the following: *"Were stationed at Fort Thunderbolt, Ga. until Jany 18 when we moved to and joined 3rd Brig, 3rd Cav. Div. Md. Gen. Kilpatrick comdg on the Ogeechee River. Moved from there Jany 28 at which time began our March through the Carolinas continually skirmishing with the enemy with no serious results. Marched about 350 miles."*

March and April, 1865, company stationed at Durham Station, North Carolina having been engaged with the enemy several times, marching about 400 miles since last muster.

May and June, 1865, company stationed at Moulton, Alabama having marched about 600 miles since last muster and remained at Moulton through August.

COMPANY G

Company Muster Roll for Company G, dated November 27, 1862 to June 30, 1863, shows company at Chewalla, TN and Record of Events states: *"This company has been engaged with the 18th Indiana M. Vols. in scouting the country adjacent to the Post of Chewalla."*

July and August 1863, stationed at Glendale, Missississippi. (There is no station shown for September and October and nothing else shown until April 1864 stating they were at Mooresville, Alabama.)

March 1 to June 30, 1864, Company G stationed in Rome, Georgia. Record of Events states the following: *"I hereby certify on honor that Leiut. Edward Godfrey of Co. "M" was detailed from Co. "M" to take com'd of Co. "G" Apr 15/64."*

(Signed) G.L. Godfrey
Lt. Col. Comdg.

Company G was shown as being stationed in Rome, Georgia until the end of October, 1864.

November and December 1864, stationed at Fort Thunderbolt, Georgia.

January and February 1865, *"In the field in South Carolina"*.

March and April 1865, stationed at Durham Station, North Carolina. Record of Events states the following: *"Company G has been in the campaign in the Carolinas under Gen'l Killpatrick and has borne an honorable part in every engagement in which the reg't. was engaged. It was engaged in the fight at White Pond, Aikins, Williston and Munroe Cross Roads on the 10th of March 1865."*

May and June 1865, stationed near Decatur, Alabama Record of Events *states: "This company has marched over six hundred miles since the 4th day of May/65. Leaving Durham Station N.C. on the 4th of May and reaching Decatur, Ala. on the 20th of June."*

The last Company Muster Roll was for July and August 1865 and shows them still at Decatur, AL.

COMPANY H

September and October 1863, Company H was stationed at Glendale, Mississippi and November and December, at Camp Davies, MS.

January and February 1864, stationed at Memphis, Tennessee. The Record of Events states the following: *"Stationed at Camp Davies Miss, evacuated, barracks destroyed by order of Gen. Stevenson Comdg Dist of Corinth Jan 24/64. Marched to Memphis Tenn reaching this place Sun Jan 31/64."*

March and April 1864, stationed at Decatur, Alabama and May through October, in Rome, Georgia. (There is no record of events for this company at Rome and no other Muster Roll for them until March 1865, when they were shown stationed at Huntsville, Alabama through June.)

July and August 1865, stationed in Blountsville, Alabama. (This was the last muster roll for Company H.)

COMPANY I

November 30, 1862, Company I stationed with Co. D, 1st Middle Tennessee Cavalry and stationed at Camp Campbell in Nashville, Tennessee.

November and December 1862, stationed at Murfreesboro, Tennessee. December 31, 1862, the Record of Events states the following: *"The company engaged in action near Murfreesboro Tenn Dec 30th. In another Dec 31st 1862."* (This would have been the Battle of Stone's River.)

Company Muster Roll for December 31, 1862 to June 30, 1863 was dated June 30th and shows them stated at that time near Manchester, Tennessee. The Record of Events states: *"The Co. (D) engaged in action near Murfreesboro Jan 5th/63. On detached duty from April 8th 1863 under command of Col. Straight. Captured by Gen'l Forrest at Cedar Bluff, Ala May 3rd 1863. Exchanged and returned to duty June 15th 1863 near Murfreesboro Tenn. Marched from Cripple Creek near Murfreesboro June 24th 1863. Engaged in an action at Shelbyville Tenn June 27th 1863."*

July and August 1863, stationed at Nashville, Tennessee. (There were no events recorded.)

June 30, 1863 to October 31, 1863, stationed at Glendale, Mississippi. It shows following Record of Events: *"Company D 1st Mid Tenn Cavalry having been transferred by the secretary of war to the 1st Ala Cavalry on the 15 of June 1863 upon the reception of the order (Aug 8) the Co. left Shelbyville Tenn and proceeded to Nashville. Arrived at Nashville Aug 10. Was detained there by order of Gen Granger until Sept 17. It arrived at Glendale Miss Sept 23 having travelled about 1000 miles. By order of the Col. comd'g 1st Ala. Cav. the letter of the Co. was changed from D to I. The Co (I) engaged in an action at Vincennes* (Vincent's) *Cross Roads Miss Oct 26/63. On a scout from the 17th of October to the 26th through the Northern Counties of Ala."*

November and December 1863, Company I at Camp Davies, Mississippi. It gives the following Record of Events: *"November 22nd in an engagement with detachment of Rebel Cavalry near Camp Davies, Miss. Lost one man captured & one wounded. On scout from 26th day of Nov. to 29th toward Okalona Miss. On scout from Dec 21st to present time toward Jackson Tenn. In an engagement near Jackson Tenn Dec. 24th lost 3 (men) killed."* (The three men killed at Jack's Creek, Tennessee on December 24, 1863 were: James H. Murphree, William Pell, and Henry C. Welch.)

January and February 1864, Company I stationed at Memphis, Tennessee. The following Record of Events states: *"Moved from Corinth Miss Dec. 29/63 by Rail to Lagrange Tenn. On scout from Lagrange to Coldwater Miss and return to Lagrange Jan 2nd .64. From Lagrange by Rail to Corinth Jan. 3 .64. Distance marched 170 miles. On scout from Camp Davies Miss to White Sulphur Springs Tenn from Jan. 12 to 14. Distance marched 60 miles. Marched from Camp Davies Miss. Jan. 25th arrived at Memphis Tenn Jan 31. Distance 100 miles. On scout from Memphis to Talahatchee River from Feb. 7th to Feb. 17th. In engagement February 11th at Jantobio Miss. In skirmish near Memphis Feb. 20th 64."*

March and April 1864, stationed at Mooresville, Alabama and May and June 1864, stationed at Rome, Georgia.

July and August 1864, Company I still stationed at Rome, Georgia. It records the following events: *"Company I was out on a scout from Rome Ga to the town of Possum Snout/Shout. Captured one horse, mule and goose. Got the goose yet turned the mule loose. On another toward Ceader Bluff said by Frank Tupper to be d-d route. On short scouts too many to mention. Short trips not worthy of attention."*

September and October 1864, Company I was still at Rome, Georgia.

November and December 1864, company was stationed at Savannah, Georgia. It recorded the following events: *"(21) Twenty one men under command of Lieut D.R. Snelling detached as escort to Maj. Genl W.T. Sherman 1st Nov. 1864. (24) Twenty four men under command of 2nd Lieut. J.H. Day along with the Regiment skirmished almost daily with the enemy on the march from Atlanta Ga to Savannah Ga. Whole distance marched from Rome Ga to Savannah Ga 350 miles."*

COMPANY E, 1ST MIDDLE TENNESSEE CAVALRY
(COMPANY K, 1ST ALABAMA CAVALRY)

Company Muster Roll dated October 31, 1862 shows company stationed at Camp Campbell, Nashville, Tennessee and records the following events: (A portion of this information was reported previously, but by a different officer.) *"Company organized at Huntsville Ala. under Special Orders No. 106. Hd. Qrs. Army of the Ohio dated July 18, 1862. Company organized July 24, 1862 at Huntsville Ala. and designated Co B 1st Ala Volunteer Infantry. Aug 31 march from Huntsville by order of Capt. Lytle. Sept. 5 Co. arrived at Nashville Tenn. Sept 8 Co. transferred to 1st Middle Tenn Cavalry by Sp O No. 155 dated Nashville Tenn Sept 8, 1862. Hd Qrs Army of the Ohio. Company reported to Col. Stokes for duty.*

November and December 1862, company was stationed near Murfreesboro, Tennessee.

January 1, 1863 to June 30, 1863, company stationed in Camp near Winchester, Tennessee. The Record of Events states the following: *"Co detached from regt Apr 7th to accompany Col. Straights expedition to Ala. Co. surrendered with the whole command of Col. Straight near Rome, Ga May 3/63. Sent to Richmond and exchanged May 13/63. Arrived at Camp Chase Ohio May 22/63. Remained till June 9th & started to Nashville Tenn. Arrived at Camp at Cripple Creek Tenn. June 15/63. Put on duty immediately. June 27th in the battle of Shelbyville Tenn."*

July and August 1863, (New) Company K was stationed at Nashville, Tennessee. It recorded the following events: *"July 1/63, on the march near Manchester, Tenn., at Decherd from the 2nd till the 6th and at Winchester from the 6th till the 10th when marched for Fayetteville. 12th marched for Pulaski, 13th had a skirmish at Pulaski, 15th marched to Elkton, 16th arrived at Fayetteville, 17th arrived at Huntsville, Ala., 20th marched to Fayetteville, arrived at Pulaski 23rd, 26th marched to Shelbyville, Tenn., arrived 27th. Received order from War Dept. Sp. O. No. 281 dated June 25/63. Aug. 9th proceeded to Nashville, arrived 10th. Remained at Nashville under Sp. O. No. 44, Hd Qrs. Dist. of the Cumberland. Temporarily under the command of Col. Pickens 3rd E. Tenn. Cavalry."*

Another Company Muster Roll for (New) Company K, 1st Ala. Cav. was dated for June 30 to Oct. 31, 1863 shows them stationed at Glendale, Mississippi and states the following which is, for the most part, a repeat of the last Muster Roll but contains additional information: *"July 1, 1863, Co. on the March near Manchester Tenn at Decherd from 2nd till the 6th & at Winchester from the 6th till the 10th when marched for Fayetteville Tenn. Left Fayetteville for Pulaski the 13th arrived 15th had a skirmish with rebels. Marched to Elkton 16th & back to Fayetteville 17th & proceeded to Huntsville, Ala. Arived there the 20th. Returned to Pulaski Tenn via Fayetteville. Arrived 23rd. Marched to Shelbyville 26th, arrived 27th. Rec'd Special Order No. 281 War Dept. dated June 25/63 Aug 8th & proceeded to Nashville Aug. 9th. Arrived there Aug 10th. Remained at Nashville under Special Order No 44. Hd Qrs Army of the Cumberland temporarily under command of Col. Pickens 3rd E. Tenn. Cav. Sep. 17/63 left Nashville & proceeded to Glendale Miss via Louisville, Cairo & Memphis. Arrived at Glendale Sep. 23/63.*

Oct. 19/63 Co. marched with 1st Ala Cav. on expedition into Walker Co. Ala. Oct. 26/63 Co. in the skirmish at Vincents Cross Roads, Miss. On arriving at the 1st Ala. Cav. the letter of the Co. was changed from E to K." (This was probably when Co. E, 1st Middle Tennessee Cavalry was changed back to Co. K, 1st Alabama Cavalry.)

November and December 1863, company was stationed at Camp Davies, Mississippi.

January and February 1863, Co. K was stationed at Memphis, Tennessee. It recorded the following events: *"Jan. 23, 1864, Co. marched with the Regt. from Camp Davis, Miss. to Lagrange, Tenn. on cars. Jan. 30, 1864, moved to Memphis, Tenn. by R.R. In camp since to date."*

March and April 1864, Company Muster Roll shows Co. K to be stationed at Mooresville, Alabama and Record of Events states the following: *"Company left Memphis Tenn March 26, 1864 by the river on Steamboat Westmoreland. Arrived at Nashville, Tenn Apr 3, 1864. Marched from Nashville Tenn April 9/64 & arrived at Moresville Ala place of present muster April 14, 1864 and went into camp."*

May and June 1864, company was stationed at Rome, Georgia. The following Record of Events states: *"I hereby certify upon honor that I was in command of the Co. and was responsible for Ordnance, Ordnance Stores and Company property from Oct 31st 1863 to Mch 26, 1864".* (Signed J.H. Hornback, 1st Lieut. 1st Ala Cav.)
I hereby certify upon honor that was in command of the Co. and was responsible for Ordnance, and Ordnance stores, and Company property from March 26/64 to Apl. 30/64." (Signed Francis W. Tupper, 1st Lieut, 1st Ala. Cav.)

July and August 1864, company still stationed at Rome, Georgia. It records the following events: *"On the first day of July the Co. was stationed at Rome Ga, 3rd & 4 on a scout. 12th & 13th, 14 & 15 on a scout to Opossum Snout, Ga. Six men of the Co under Capt. West went to Randolph Co. Ala. 19th, 20th, 21st & 22nd on a scout to Wills Valley Ala. 29th & 30th on a scout to Summerville Ga."*

September and October 1864, New Company K still stationed at Rome, Georgia.

November and December 1864, New Company K was stationed at Thunderbolt, Georgia and recorded the following events: *"On the 11th of Nov. 1864 the Co. marched with the Regt. from Camp at Rome, Ga in advance of the 17th A.C. In a skirmish at Oconee Bridge Ga Central R.R. Nov. 30/64. Burned Oconee Bridge Ga. Central R.R. Nov. 30/64. In a skirmish near Millen Ga. Dec. 2nd/64. In a skirmish near Savannah Ga Dec. 9/64. Dec 17th/64 marched on a scout towards Allamaha Bridge. Dec 21st arrived at Camp 10 miles west of Savannah Ga. Dec 22nd marched into Savannah. Dec 23rd went into camp at Thunderbolt, Ga."*
December 31, 1864 to April 30, 1865, New Company K was stationed at Durham's Station, North Carolina and recorded the following events: *"Jany 16th/65 Co. moved with the Regt from Thunderbolt Ga. to Camp at Ogeechee, 10 miles*

West of Savannah, Ga. Jan 28 marched on Gen. Sherman's Carolina Campaign being in Genl Kilpatricks 3rd Brig. Feby 10th in battle near Aikins S.C. Mch 10th in battle at Monroes Crossroads N.C. 1 sgt killed, 1 Lt. & 6 men wounded & 5 captured. March 15th in battle near Averysboro N.C. 16th same. Mch 18th, 19th & 20th in battle near Bentonville N.C. Arrived at Durhams Station N.C. Apl 16th 1865."

May and June 1865, New Company K was stationed at Huntsville, Ala. and Record of Events states the following: *"May 4th/65 Co. marched with the Regt from Durhams Station N.C. June 14/65 arrived at Huntsville Ala. Encamped near Davis Spring Huntsville Ala."* (Signed by J.H. Hornback, 1st Lieut. 1st Ala. Cav. Comdg. Co. K.)

COMPANY L

From September 25, 1863 to October 31, 1863, Company L was stationed at Glendale, Mississippi and Record of Events states the following: *"Co. L, 1 Ala Cav. was organized Sept 25, '63. Was recruited by Lieut. Tramel in Ala - 116 men being collected and brought from within the rebel lines - from among Union citizens at a distance of 160 miles from the Federal lines in 14 days from the time of leaving camp. Entered upon duty with the regiment immediately and lost severely in action shortly thereafter. Has marched over 400 miles during the month."*

November 1863 and December 1863, company was stationed at Camp Davies, Mississippi and recorded the following events: *"Left Camp Dec 20, 1863. Joined Brigade at Corinth. Marched for Tennessee. Met the enemy at Jack's Creek Dec. 24. This Co. in advance with orders to dive in the enemy's pickets and then into line if possible. Drove in their pickets. They ambushed us. Charged them and was compelled to fall back with the loss of one man killed. Was reinforced and drove the enemy camped on the field during the night."*

January 1864 and February 1864, Company L was stationed at Memphis, Tennessee. It recorded the following events: *"Evacuated Camp Davies, Miss. Sunday. 24 Jany. 1864. Co L rear guard had the honor of firing the fort & seeing it fall. Evacuated Corinth the 25 Jan. Burned barracks there. Moved to LaGrange by land, last troops out of LaGrange the 30 Jany. 1864. Arrived in Memphis the 31 late. Paid on the first Feby for Nov & Dec. 63 Officer's pay stopped on a/c some officers being behind in ordnance returns. The return of this co has always been sent promptly and it's rather hard for us. Ordered on scout. Reg. under command of Maj. Fairfield on the 5 Feby. 1864. Went to Hernando, Miss, returned the 6 inst. 11 prisoners captured at a dance, on the 6 ordered out with 5 days rations 15 miles south. Overtook & reported to Col. McMillian, 95 Ohio Inf. Comdg Brigade, Maj. Godfrey comdg our regt. Co. L took the advance of the Inf into Hernando. Crossed the Coldwater the 9. Had cav. fight the 11 inst at San Atruba, Miss. Our regt lost 1 prisoner (?) enemy 7 men 1 Lt mortally wounded & 13 horses. Genl. Long Smith complimented the 1st Ala Cav for their fighting qualities. Skirmished the 12 & 13 & 14. On the 15 fought the enemy under Forrest at Wyath, Miss. while Genl. Smith crossed the Tallahatchie at New Albany, Miss. Returned to camp by way of Collierville arriving the 18 inst. Have had hard scouting since last muster. Used up nearly 50 horses."*

December 31, 1863 to April 30, 1864, Company Muster Roll shows company stationed at Mooresville, Alabama and records the following events: *"26 Mar '64 ordered on board steamer Westmoreland at Memphis, Tenn. and reach Nashville April 4/64 during which time disease raged severly among the men owing to disagreeable weather and no way of cooking rations."*

March and April 1864, company stationed at Mooresville, Alabama.

May 1864 and June 1864, company stationed at Rome, Georgia.

July 1864 and August 1864, shows company still stationed at Rome, Georgia. It records the following events: *"Company was on a scout with one Battl 1 Ala Cav. Maj Cranver comdg. to Buchanan, Ala. Absent from the 13 to 15 Aug. inclusive. Had several severe skirmishes, repulsing the enemy in each. Co L had one man missing in action on the 14. Marched one hundred and fifty miles. Also on a scout with entire Regt. Col. Spencer comdg. to Lebanon, Ala. leaving camp on the 19 Aug and returning on the 23, having marched 200 miles. Have been almost constantly engaged during the last two months in scouting the country surrounding Rome."*

September 28 1864, stationed at Rome, Georgia. "Subsistence furnished to and including the 30 day of Sept. 1864. Transportation to be furnished by the 2 M. Det to Nashville, Tenn. (Signed J.D. Davis, 1st Lt. 52nd Illinois Inf. A.C.M., 4th Div. 15th A.C. and H.L. Bolton, 2nd Lt. Comd. Co. L, 1st Ala. Cav.

September and October 1864, Company Muster Roll shows Company L to be stationed at Rome, GA and states the following: *"This Co. has been on duty with the regiment at Rome, Ga. since last muster. Has scouted considerable and participated in several slight skirmishes but no general engagement."*

November and December 1864, company stationed at Savannah, Georgia. The Record of Events states the following: *"This Co. has been on duty with the Regt since last muster. During the last campaign through Ga maintained the advance of the 17 A.C. on the march. The Co. participated in the skirmishes at Balls Ferry Station No. 2 and numerous other light skirmishes. The Co. also assisted in the destruction of the Gulf R.R."*

January and February 1865, stationed in the field in South Carolina. The Record of Events states: *This Co. has been on duty with the Regt since last muster. The Regt was attached to the 3rd Brig, 3rd Cav. Div (Kilpatricks) on the 12th of June/65 and thus far have participated in several slight skirmishes on our campaign through S. Carolina."*

March and April 1865, stationed at Durham, NC; May and June 1865, stationed at Huntsville (or Courtland), Alabama; July and August 1865, stationed at Moulton and Pikeville, Alabama.

COMPANY M

January and February 1864, Company M was stationed at Memphis, Tennessee and Records of Events states the following: *"This company was recruited by Capt. John Lomax at Chewalla Tenn and at Glendale & Camp Davis Miss. It was mustered into service on the 29th day of December 1863. On the 24th day Jan/64 we broke up camp and moved into Corinth and on the 25th we started for Memphis, Tenn and marched three miles beyond Chewalla Tenn. On the 26th the Co. marched to Saulsbury Tenn and on the 27th to Lagrange Tenn where we remained until the 29th when we moved on toward Memphis reaching this place on the 31 of Jan/64. On the 7th of Feb part of the Co. under command of the 1st Lieut. started on a march. They were gone eleven days and were in two or three light skirmishes with the enemy and on each occasion bore themselves with credit. Since then the Co. has been on several scouts and marches with out any incidents worthy of note. The Co. is armed with Smith's Carbines and Colt's Remington's Revolvers and hope soon to be mounted on good horses."*

When the war was over, the men in the First Alabama Cavalry Union army had marched thousands of miles, traveled almost 2,000 miles by steamboat and over 1,000 miles by train. They had fought with AND against their fathers, brothers, sons and other relatives and seen hundreds of them die in battle and of disease.

CHAPTER IV

REPORTS FROM THE FIELD

The following reports from the field, written by some of the officers and found in various volumes of the Official Records of the Civil War, are included to give the reader a more enlightened view of some of the more significant battles in which the First Alabama Cavalry Volunteer Union Regiment was engaged.

Report of Brig. Gen. Grenville M. Dodge, U.S. Army, commanding expedition to Courtland, Alabama April 15-May 2, 1863, and Streight's raid. Official Records of the Civil War, Series I, Volume XXIII, (p. 246-250)

CORINTH, MISS.,

May 5, 1863

SIR: I have the honor to submit the following report of the expedition up the Tuscumbia Valley to Courtland, Ala. The intention and plan of the movement was to cover a raid by Colonel Streight, of Major-General Rosecrans' command, into Georgia to break up the Atlanta and Chattanooga Railroad. Colonel Streight was to meet me with his brigade at Eastport, on Thursday, April 16.

I moved from Corinth with the Second Division, Sixteenth Army Corps, Wednesday, west of Great Bear Creek, and made my preparations to cross, the rebels holding the opposite side.

Friday morning, April 17, I made a feint at Jackson and Bailings' Fords, and under the cover of my artillery, threw the most of my force across at Steminine's Ford.

The cavalry, under Colonel Cornyn, and mounted infantry, under Lieutenant-Colonel Phillips, made the crossing and pushed forward. My instructions were for them to go forward 3 1/2 miles, and await my coming. Colonel Cornyn, meeting the enemy about a mile out, commenced fighting them, they falling back rapidly. Hearing of Colonel Roddey commanding a force of the enemy on my left flank, I sent orders forward for the command to halt; but before the messenger got to him, Colonel Roddey had got between the cavalry and infantry. The Third Brigade being in advance, commanded by Colonel Bane, who, ascertaining this fact, pushed forward and fell upon their rear, but not until Colonel Roddey had taken two pieces of artillery, 22 men, and one company of mounted infantry, who were guarding it, which, through neglect, had been allowed to fall 3 miles in the rear of the advance.

Colonel Cornyn hearing firing in the rear, immediately fell back, and with the First Alabama Cavalry, charged the rebels and retook the artillery and caissons, with the exception of one gun, which the enemy succeeded in getting off with.

The charge of the Alabamians with muskets only, and those not loaded, is creditable, especially as they are all new recruits and poorly drilled. In this charge, Captain

27

Cameron, the commanding officer of the Alabama cavalry, a deserving and much lamented officer, was killed.

Colonel Bane, on his arrival, disposed of his troops admirable. Colonel Cornyn advanced with his cavalry as a feint, and the rebels advanced to meet him. He fell back to the rear of the infantry, which was posted under cover and out of sight on both flanks of the cavalry. On the appearance of the enemy, the infantry opened a heavy and destructive fire, which caused the rebels to fall back in confusion, utterly routed.

This day's work brought us 13 miles in advance of the main force. Colonel Streight not arriving, I fell back with the advance to Great Bear Creek, where the rest of the command was posted, to await his coming.

Sunday afternoon, Colonel Streight commenced landing his force at Eastport, but came poorly prepared for his contemplated movement. He had 2,000 infantry and about 1,000 mules. At least 400 of them were unserviceable, and in unloading them, through the carelessness of one of his officers, 200 strayed away. He was under the impression that he would find plenty of stock in the valley to mount the rest and replace those broken down.

During Monday and Tuesday we scoured the country, and gathered all we could.

Tuesday night, Colonel Fuller's brigade, from Corinth, joined me. Wednesday morning, I advanced with all the force, and came up with the enemy at Rock Cut, 5 miles west of Tuscumbia; planted my batteries and drove them out of it, taking the line of Little Bear Creek that night. The enemy's position was a very strong one, and there was but one way to flank it. The enemy fell back as soon as I brought the Infantry to bear upon them.

Thursday we moved, crossing at three places, throwing my cavalry, by the Frankfort and Tuscumbia road, into the enemy's rear; but during the night, anticipating this movement, the enemy fell back. We reached Tuscumbia about noon, and after slight skirmishing, took possession of the city. I immediately dispatched Lieutenant-Colonel Phillips, with two squadrons of mounted infantry, two squadrons of the Fifteenth Illinois Cavalry, and a section of Welker's battery, to take Florence. They refused to surrender, when Colonel Phillips immediately opened on the town. A few shell brought them to terms, and we occupied the place. At the same time I ordered Colonel Cornyn forward toward Courtland, to fell the enemy. He came up with their rear some 2 miles beyond Leighton. The command consisted on our part of the Tenth Missouri and Seventh Kansas Cavalry, about 800 in all, driving the enemy 8 miles. The rebel force was 3,500, beside one battery. The fighting of the cavalry against such odds is beyond all praise.

The next morning cavalry fell back to Tuscumbia, to await the advance of the main column.

Finding it impossible to obtain stock to mount Colonel Streight's command, I took horses and mules from my teams and mounted infantry, and furnished him some 600 head, mounting all but 200 of his men. I also turned over all my hard bread, some 10,000 rations, and he left me at midnight on the 26th instant, with the intention of going through Russellville, Moulton, and Blountsville to Gadsden, then divide, one force to strike Rome and the other Etowah Bridge.

I moved forward Monday morning, and drove the enemy across Town Creek that night, and ascertained that they were in force, under Forrest, on the opposite bank. That night I communicated with Colonel Streight, at Mount Hope, and ascertained that he was all right.

Tuesday morning, the creek rose 10 feet, and the current was so swift that neither horse nor man could cross. I immediately made disposition to cross at three points, to cover the railroad bridge and throw across foot bridges.

The resistance of the enemy was very strong, and their sharpshooters very annoying. The artillery duel was very fine, parts of Welker's, Tannrath's, Richardson's, and Robinson's batteries taking part in it. The practice on both sides was excellent. The Parrott guns drove the enemy away from their pieces, disabling and keeping them away for two hours, but the fact of my being unable to cross infantry prevented our securing them.

About noon I crossed the railroad bridge with the Eighty-first Ohio and Ninth Illinois Infantry, and soon after crossed the rest of my force, except the artillery, on foot bridges, and drove the enemy within 3 miles of Courtland, when they, hearing of the force at Moulton, fled to Decatur. I followed up, and then returned to camp at Town Creek that night, being unable to cross any of my artillery.

Colonel Streight reached Moulton Tuesday night, and commenced crossing the mountains Wednesday, having got nearly two days' start of them.. They supposed he was making for Decatur, and only discovered Wednesday that he was crossing the mountains toward Georgia.

Having accomplished fully the object of the expedition, and drove the enemy, which was 5,500 strong, to Decatur, and having been on half rations for a week, I fell back to Tuscumbia, in order to communicate with transports, to obtain rations and ammunition. On arriving there, I received information that the gunboats had gone down the river, taking the transports with them, a part of Van Dorn's force having made their appearance on the north side of the Tennessee River, and shelled South Florence that day at 4 p.m. They also planted a battery at Savannah and Duck River; but my precaution in destroying all means of crossing the river on my advance, prevented him getting in my rear, and the gunboats, to save the transports, left the day before, having a short engagement at Savannah and Duck River. Van Dorn's force then moved toward Decatur. That was the last we heard of them.

On my return, I burned all provisions, produce, and forage, all mills and tan-yards, and destroyed everything that would in any way aid the enemy. I took stock of all kinds that I could find, and rendered the valley so destitute that it cannot be occupied by the Confederates, except provisions and forage are transported to them. I also destroyed telegraph and railroad between Tuscumbia and Decatur, and all the ferries between Savannah and Courtland.

I have no doubt but that Colonel Streight would have succeeded had he been properly equipped, and joined me at the time agreed upon. The great delay in an enemy's country necessary to fi_ him out gave them time to throw a large force in our front. Although Colonel Streight had two days' start, they can harass him, and perhaps check his movements long enough for them to secure all their important bridges. If he could have started from Bear Creek the day I arrived there, then my movements would have been so quick and strong that the enemy could not have got their forces together.

The animals furnished him were very poor at the start. Four hundred of them were used up before leaving me, and those furnished him by me were about all the serviceable stock he had, though I hear he got 200 good mules the day he left me, in Moulton Valley.

On my return, I sent Colonel Cornyn, with the Tenth Missouri, Seventh Kansas, and Fifteenth Illinois Cavalry, and Ninth Illinois Mounted Infantry, to attack the force congregated at Tupelo and Okolona. He came up with the enemy on Wednesday, and immediately attacked them, they being some 3,000 strong, under Major-General Gholson and Brigadier-General Ruggles. Brigadier-General Chalmers, with 3,500 men, was at Pontotoc, but failed to come to Gholson's aid, though ordered to.

Colonel Cornyn fought so determinedly and so fast that he soon routed the force in his front, driving them in all directions, killing and wounding a large number and taking 100 prisoners, including some 7 officers; also a large number of arms and 150 horses, saddles, &c.

The enemy fled toward Okolona and Pontotoc, and Colonel Cornyn returned to Corinth.

The expedition, so far, can be summed up as having accomplished the object for which it started, the infantry having marched 250 miles and the cavalry some 400, and fought six successful engagements, driving the enemy, 3,000 strong, from Bear Creek to Decatur taking the towns of Tuscumbia and Florence, with a loss not to exceed 100, including 3 officers. Destroyed 1,500,000 bushels of corn, besides large quantities of oats, rye, and fodder, and 500,000 pounds of bacon. Captured 150 prisoners, 1,000 head of horses and mules, and an equal number of cattle, hogs, and sheep; also 100 bales of cotton, besides keeping the whole command in meat for three weeks. Destroyed the railroad from Tuscumbia to Decatur; also some 60 flat-boats and ferries in the Tennessee River, thereby preventing Van Dorn, in his move, from crossing to my rear; also destroyed five tan-yards and six flouring mills.

It has rendered desolate one of the best granaries of the South, preventing them from raising another crop this year, and taking away from them some 1,500 Negroes.

We found large quantities of shelled corn, all ready for shipment, also bacon, and gave it to the flames.

I cannot speak too highly of the conduct of the officers and troops under my command. They were guilty of but one disobedience of orders - in burning some houses between Town Creek and Tuscumbia; on the discovery of which I issued orders to shoot any man detected in the act. After that nothing was burned except by my order.

The fighting of the cavalry was excellent. The Tenth Missouri Seventh Kansas, Fifteenth Illinois, and First Alabama all did themselves credit; they invariably drove the enemy, no matter what their force.

The disposition of the troops at Lundy's Lane, by Colonel Bane, Fifteenth Illinois, was very creditable, and the management of the right, by General Sweeny, at the Rock Cut, also deserves mention. Lieutenant-Colonel Phillip's handling his men in action drew the commendation of all. Colonel Cornyn, of the cavalry brigade, made some fine charges, and his fighting cannot be excelled. His advance on the first day was injudicious, and against my instructions, and came very near causing trouble; otherwise he managed his command very creditably.

The Pioneer Corps, under Captain Tiedemann, built two bridges across Bear Creek, and also several minor ones. Their long marches and night work deserve to be mentioned.

To my staff I am indebted for valuable service. Captain Spencer, assistant adjutant-general; Captain Dodds, acting assistant quartermaster; Captain Carpenter, commissary of subsistence; Captain Hanna; Major Stone, chief of artillery; Lieutenant Barnes, aide-de-camp, and Dr. Marsh, medical director, all accompanied me.

Reports of killed and wounded have already been forwarded.

I am, very respectfully, your obedient servant,

G.M. DODGE
Brigadier-
General

Report of Colonel Abel D. Streight's raid from Tuscumbia, Alabama, toward Rome, Georgia, April 26 - May 3, 1863. Official Records of the Civil War, Series I, Volume XXIII, (p. 285-293)

HEADQUARTERS FIFTY-FIRST INDIANA VOLUNTEERS

Chattanooga, Tenn., August 22, 1864

SIR: I have the honor to report that since my return to duty, June 1 last, I have been endeavoring to obtain the necessary information, from the several regiments that composed my command, to enable me to render you an accurate report of my expedition in April, 1863; but, owing to the absence of most of my officers (who are still confined as prisoners of war) and the scattered condition of the men, I have been unable to collect as many of the particulars as I had intended.

On April 7, 1863, I received orders from General Rosecrans to proceed with the Provisional Brigade--about 1,700 officers and men, composed of my regiment (the Fifty-first Indiana), Seventy-third Indiana, Colonel Hathaway; Third Ohio, Colonel Lawson; Eighteenth Illinois, Lieutenant-Colonel Rodgers, and two companies of the First Middle Tennessee Cavalry, Capt. D.D. Smith <The First Middle Tennessee Cavalry was the unit to which the 1st Alabama Cavalry was assigned upon arriving in Nashville> - to Nashville, and to fit out as speedily as possible for an expedition to the interior of Alabama and Georgia, for the purpose of destroying the railroads and other rebel property in that country. I was instructed to draw about half the number of mules necessary to mount my command, at Nashville, and to seize in the country through which I passed a sufficient number of animals to mount the balance. On arriving at Nashville, I organized the following staff, to wit: Capt. D.L. Wright, Fifty-first Indiana Volunteers, to be acting assistant adjutant-general; Maj. W.L. Peck, Third Ohio, to be brigade surgeon; Lieut. J.G. Doughty, regimental quartermaster Fifty-first Indiana Volunteers, to be acting assistant quartermaster; Captain Driscoll, Third Ohio, to be acting assistant inspector-general; Lieut. J.W. Pavey, Eightieth Illinois Volunteers, to be ordnance officer, and Lieut A.C. Roach, Fifty-first Indiana Volunteers, to be aide-de-camp.

As soon as possible all hands were at work to supply the command with the necessary clothing, ordnance, and equipment for an expedition of this kind, and on the afternoon of the 10th I received orders from General Garfield, chief of staff, to embark at once on steamers then at the landing and proceed down the river to Palmyra, land my command there, and march across the country to Fort Henry, and to seize all the horses and mules I could find in the country. Everything was speedily put on board, although it was late in the evening before the mules were brought to the landing for shipment. I was temporarily absent at the time, attending to some business affairs preparatory to starting; consequently did not see them.

As soon as everything was ready we proceeded down the river to Palmyra, where we arrived on the evening of the 11th, and disembarked at once. I sent the fleet, consisting of eight steamers, around to Fort Henry, under the command of Colonel Lawson, Third Ohio, and furnished him with four companies of the Fifty-first Indiana Volunteers ad guard. He had orders to stop at Smithland and take on a quantity of rations and forage for General Dodge's command.

As soon as it was light the next morning all hands were set at work to catch and saddle the mules. I then for the first time discovered that the mules were nothing but poor, wild, and unbroken colts, many of them but two years old, and that a large number of them had the horse distemper; some 40 or 50 of the lot were too near dead to travel, and had to be left at the landing; 10 or 12 died before we started, and such of them as could be rode at all were so wild and unmanageable that it took us all that day and part of the next to catch and break them before we could move out across the country; but in the mean time I had sent out several parties to gather in horses and mules, and they had been successful in getting about 150 very good animals, but mostly barefooted.

On the 13th, the command left Palmyra and marched about 15 miles in a southwesterly direction, and encamped on Yellow Creek. My scouting parties did not succeed in finding many horses or mules. The people had got warning of our movements, and the stock was mostly run off.

Early the next morning we resumed our march, and arrived at Fort Henry about noon on the 15th. We had scoured the country as far south as it was safe, on account of the proximity of a large force of the enemy, under Woodward, and although about 100 of the mules gave out and had to be left behind on our march, yet when we reached Fort Henry our animals numbered about 1,250. Those that we had collected in the country were mostly in good condition, but were nearly all barefooted. Contrary to my expectations the boats had not arrived, nor did they reach there until the evening of the 16th, having been delayed in getting the rations and forage above referred to.

General Ellet's Marine Brigade and two gunboats accompanied the fleet to Fort Henry, and informed me that they were ordered to proceed with me as far as Eastport, Miss. General Ellet assumed command of the fleet, and we embarked as soon as possible; but the pilots declared that at the existing low stage of water it would be unsafe to run at nights; hence we did not start until the morning of the 17th, when we steamed up the river, but, despite all my efforts to urge the fleet ahead as fast as possible, we did not reach Eastport until the afternoon of the 19th.

As soon as we arrived at Eastport, I left Colonel Lawson in command, with orders to disembark and prepare to march, while I went to see General Dodge, who, with his command (some 8,000 strong), I returned to Eastport about midnight, and was informed that a stampede had occurred among the animals, and that some of them had got away.

Daylight the next morning revealed to me the fact that nearly 400 of our best animals were gone. All that day and part of the next was spent in scouring the country to recover them, but only about 200 of the lost number were recovered; the remainder fell into the hands of the enemy.

The loss of these animals was a heavy blow to my command, for besides detaining us nearly two days at Eastport and running down our stock in searching the country to recover them, it caused still further delay at Tuscumbia, to supply their places. Quite a number of the mules drawn at Nashville had to be left at Eastport, on account of the distemper before mentioned; several died before we left.

We left Eastport on the afternoon of April 21, and reached General Dodge's headquarters the following morning about 8 o'clock. We then proceeded in rear of General Dodge's forces, which were continually skirmishing with the enemy as they advanced as far as Tuscumbia, Ala., scouring the country to the river on the left and to the mountains on our right, and collected all the horses and mules that could be found.

We arrived at Tuscumbia about 5 p.m. on April 24. Here General Dodge furnished me some 200 mules and 6 wagons to haul ammunition and rations. I ordered my surgeon to carefully examine my command, and send back to Corinth with General Dodge all men who were not fit for the arduous duties before us. This reduced my command to 1,500 men.

General Dodge informed me that there was no doubt but Forrest had crossed the Tennessee River, and was in the vicinity of Town Creek; hence he agreed to advance as far as Courtland, on the Decatur road, and, if possible, drive the enemy in that direction, but if they (the enemy) turned toward Moulton, our cavalry, under General Dodge, was to be sent in pursuit.

With this understanding, I marched from Tuscumbia at 11 p.m. on the night of the 26th instant in the direction of Moulton via Russellville. It was raining very hard, and the mud and darkness of the night made our progress very slow. One hundred and fifty of my men had neither horses nor mules, and fully as many more had such as were unable to carry more than the saddles; hence fully 300 of the men were on foot.

It was expected when I left General Dodge that the greater part of my command would be able to reach Moulton, some 40 miles distant, by the next night, but, owing to the heavy rains and consequent bad condition of the roads, it was impossible; consequently I dispatched a messenger to General Dodge, stating that I would halt at Mount Hope and wait for the portion of my command who were on foot to come up.

We continued to scour the country for horses and mules, but so many of those drawn at Nashville were continually failing, that, although we were successful in collecting a large number, still, many of the men were without anything to ride.

On the night of the 27th, at Mount Hope, I received word from General Dodge, stating that he had driven the enemy, and that I should push on. My command had not all come up yet, nor did they until about 10 a.m. the next day, when we proceeded to Moulton, where we arrived about dark. Up to this time we had been skirmishing occasionally with small squads of the enemy, but I could hear of no force of consequence in the country. All of the command but about 50 men were now mounted.

We started from Moulton, in the direction of Blountsville, via Day's Gap, about midnight on April 28. The two previous days it had been raining most of the time, and the roads were terrible, though on the evening of the 28th it bid fair for dry weather, which gave us strong hopes of better times.

We marched the next day (the 29th) to Day's Gap, about 35 miles, and bivouacked for the night. Every man now was mounted, and although many of the animals were very poor, nevertheless we had strong hopes that we could easily supply all future demands. We destroyed during the day a large number of wagons belonging to the enemy, laden with provisions, arms, tents, &c., which had been sent to the mountains to avoid us, but luckily, they fell into our hands. We were not in the midst of devoted Union people. Many of Captain Smith's men (Alabamians) were recruited near this place and many were the happy greetings between them and their friends and relations. I could learn nothing of the enemy in the country, with the exception of small squads of scouting parties, who were hunting conscripts.

We moved out the next morning before daylight. I will here remark that my men had been worked very hard in scouring so much of the country, and unaccustomed as they were to riding, made it still worse; consequently, they were illy prepared for the trying ordeal through which they were to pass. I had not proceeded more than 2 miles, at the head of the column, before I was informed that the rear guard had been attacked, and just at that moment I heard the boom of artillery in the rear of the column. I had previously learned that the gap through which we were passing was easily flanked by gaps through the mountains, both above and below; consequently I sent orders to the rear to hold the enemy in check until we could prepare for action. The head of the column was at the time on the top of the mountain. The column was moving through the gap; consequently the enemy was easily held in check.

I soon learned that the enemy had moved through the gaps on my right and left, and were endeavoring to form a junction in my advance; consequently I moved ahead rapidly until we passed the intersecting roads on either flank with the one we occupied. The country was open, sand ridges, very thinly wooded, and afforded fine defensive positions. As soon as we passed the point above designated (about 3 miles from the top of the mountains), we dismounted and formed a line of battle on a ridge circling to the rear. Our right rested on a precipitous ravine and the left was protected by a marshy run that was easily held against the enemy. The mules were sent into a ravine to the rear of our right, where they were protected from the enemy's bullets. I also deployed a line of skirmishers, resting on our right and left flanks encircling our rear, in order to prevent a surprise from any detached force of the enemy that might approach us from that direction and to prevent any straggling of either stray animals or cowardly men.

In the mean time I had instructed Captain Smith, who had command of our rear guard (now changed to our front), to hold his position until the enemy pressed him closely, when he should retreat rapidly, and, if possibly, draw them on to our lines, which were concealed by the men lying down immediately back of the top of the ridge. The lines were left sufficiently open to permit Captain Smith's command to pass through near the center. I had two 12-pounder mountain howitzers, which were stationed near the road (the center). They were also concealed. We had hardly completed our arrangements when the enemy charged Captain Smith in large force, following him closely, and no sooner had he passed our lines than our whole line rose up and delivered a volley at short range. We continued to pour a rapid fire into their ranks, which soon caused them to give way in confusion; but their reenforcements soon came up, when they dismounted, formed, and made a determined and vigorous attach. Our skirmishers were soon driven in, and about the same time the enemy opened upon us with a battery of artillery.

The enemy soon attempted to carry our lines, but were handsomely repulsed. During their advance they had run their artillery to within 300 yards of our lines, and as soon as they began to waver I prepared for a charge. I ordered Colonel

Hathaway, Seventy-third Indiana, and Lieutenant-Colonel Sheets, Fifty-first Indiana, on the left, to make a charge, in order to draw the attention of the battery, and immediately threw the Third Ohio, Colonel Lawson, and the Eightieth Illinois, Lieutenant Colonel Rodgers, forward rapidly, hoping to capture the battery. The enemy, after a short but stubborn resistance, fled in confusion, leaving two pieces of artillery, two caissons, and about 40 prisoners, representing seven different regiments, a large number of wounded, and about 30 dead on the field. Among the former was Captain Forrest, a brother of General Forrest. Our loss was about 30 killed and wounded, among the latter Lieutenant-Colonel Sheets, Fifty-first Indiana (mortally), a brave and gallant officer, and one that we were illy prepared to lose, and Lieutenant Pavey, Eightieth Illinois (on my staff), severely.

It was now about 11 o'clock, fighting having continued since about 6 o'clock in the morning. I had learned, in the mean time, that the enemy were in heavy force, fully three times our number, with twelve pieces of artillery, under General Forrest in person; consequently I was fearful that they were making an effort to get around us and attack in the rear of our position; hence I decided to resume the march. Everything was soon in readiness, and we moved out, leaving a strong guard (dismounted) in the rear, to check any immediate advance the enemy might make previous to the column getting in motion. We were not too soon in our movements, for the column had hardly passed a crossroad, some 6 miles from our first battle-ground, when the enemy were discovered advancing on our left. Sharp skirmishing commenced at Crooked Creek, which is about 10 miles south of Day's Gap, and finally the enemy pressed our rear so hard that I was compelled to prepare for battle. I selected a strong position, about 1 mile south of the crossing of the creek, on a ridge called Hog Mountain. The whole force soon became engaged (about one hour before dark). The enemy strove first to carry our right; then charged the left; but with the help of the two pieces of artillery captured in the morning and the two mountain howitzers, all of which were handled with good effect by Major Vanada, of the Third Ohio, we were able to repulse them.

Fighting continued until about 10 p.m., when the enemy were driven from our front, leaving a large number of killed and wounded on the field. I determined at once to resume our march, and as soon as possible we moved out. The ammunition which we had captured with the two guns was exhausted, and being very short of horses, I ordered the guns spiked and the carriages destroyed. I had ordered the Seventy-third Indiana (Colonel Hathaway) to act as rear guard, and I remained in the rear in person, for the purpose of being at hand in case the enemy should attempt to press us as we were moving out. We had but fairly got under way when I received information of the enemy's advance.

The moon shone very brightly, and the country was an open woodland, with an occasional spot of thick undergrowth. In one of these thickets I placed the Seventy-third Indiana, lying down, and not more than 20 paces from the road, which was in plain view. The enemy approached. The head of his column passed without discovering our position. At this moment the whole regiment opened a most destructive fire, causing a complete stampede of the enemy. I will here remark that the country from Day's Gap to Blountsville (about 40 miles) is mostly uninhabited; consequently there is nothing in the country for man or beast. I had hopes that by pushing ahead we could reach a place where we could feed before the enemy would come up with us, and by holding him back where there was no feed, compel him to lay over a day at least to recuperate. I had learned that they had been on a forced march from Town Creek, Ala., a day and two nights previous to their attacking us. We were not again disturbed until we had marched several miles, when they attacked our rear guard vigorously. I again succeeded in ambuscading them, which caused them to give up the pursuit for the night. We continued our march, and reached Blountsville about 10 o'clock in the morning. Many of our mules had given out, leaving their riders on foot, but there was very little straggling behind the rear guard.

At Blountsville we found sufficient corn to feed our tired and hungry animals. Ammunition and rations were hastily distributed to the men, and the remaining ammunition was put on pack mules and the wagons burned, as it was now understood that it would be impossible to take them over the roads before us. After resting about two hours, we resumed our march in the direction of Gadsden.

The column had not got fairly under motion before our pickets were driven in, and a sharp skirmish ensued between Forrest's advance and our rear guard, under Captain Smith, in the town of Blountsville. The enemy followed closely for several miles, continually skirmishing with the rear guard, but were badly handled by small parties of our men stopping in the thick bushes by the side of the road and firing at them at short range, and when we reached the East Branch of the Black Warrior River the ford was very deep and the enemy pressed so closely that I was compelled to halt and offer him battle before we could cross. After some maneuvering, I advanced a heavy line of skirmishers, who drove the enemy out of sight of my main line, when I ordered the troops, except the skirmishers, to cross the river as rapidly as possible. After all had crossed, except the skirmishers, they were rapidly withdrawn, under cover of our artillery, and a heavy line of skirmishers thrown out on the opposite bank for that purpose. It was about 5 p.m. when the last of the command crossed the East Branch of the Black Warrior. We proceeded in the direction of Gadsden without further interruption, with the exception of small parties who were continually harassing the rear of the column, until about 9 o'clock the next morning, May 2, when the rear guard was fiercely attacked at the crossing of Black Creek, near Gadsden. After a sharp fight the enemy was repulsed. I had learned in the mean time, through my scouts, that a large column of the enemy was moving on our left, parallel with our route, evidently with the intention of getting in our front, which made it necessary for us to march all night, though the command was in no condition to do so, and, to add still more to my embarrassment, a portion of our ammunition had become damaged in crossing Will's Creek, which, at the time, was very deep fording. I only halted at Gadsden sufficiently long to destroy a quantity of arms and commissary stores found there, and proceeded on. Many of our animals and men were entirely worn out and unable to keep up with the column; consequently they fell behind the rear guard and were captured.

It now became evident to me that our only hope was in crossing the river at Rome and destroying the bridge, which would delay Forrest a day or two and give us time to collect horses and mules, and allow the command a little time to sleep, without which it was impossible to proceed.

The enemy followed closely and kept up a continuous skirmish with the rear of the column until about 4 p.m., at which time we reached Blount's plantation, about 15 miles from Gadsden, where we could procure forage for our animals. Here I decided to halt, as it was impossible to continue the march through the night without feeding and resting, although to do so was to bring on a general engagement. Accordingly, the command was dismounted, and a detail made to feed the horses and mules, while the balance of the command formed in line of battle on a ridge southwest of the plantation.

Meanwhile the rear guard, in holding the enemy in check, had become severely engaged and was driven in. The enemy at once attacked our main line, and tried hard to carry the center, but were gallantly met and repulsed by the Fifty-first and Seventy-third Indiana, assisted by Major Vananda, with two mountain howitzers. They then made a determined effort to turn to our right, but were met by the gallant Eightieth Illinois, assisted by two companies of the Third Ohio.

The enemy, with the exception of a few skirmishers, then fell back to a ridge some half a mile distant, and commenced massing his force, as if preparing for a more determined attack. It was becoming dark, and I decided to withdraw unobserved, if possible, and conceal my command in a thicket some half a mile to our rear, there to lie in ambush and await his advance. In the mean time I had ordered Capt. Milton Russell (Fifty-first Indiana) to take 200 of the best mounted men, selected from the whole command, and proceed to Rome, and Hold the bridge until the main command could come up.

The engagement at Blount's plantation revealed the fact that nearly all of our remaining ammunition was worthless on account of having been wet. Much of that carried by the men had become useless by the paper wearing out and the powder sifting away. It was in this engagement that the gallant Colonel Hathaway (Seventy-third Indiana) fell, mortally wounded, and in a few moments expired. Our country has seldom been called upon to mourn the loss of so brave and valuable an officer. His loss to me was irreparable. His men had almost worshipped him, and when he fell, it cast a deep gloom of despondency over his regiment which was hard to overcome.

We remained in ambush but a short time when the enemy, who by some means had learned of our whereabouts, commenced a flank movement, which we discovered in time to check. I then decided to withdraw as silently as possible, and push on in the direction of Rome, but as a large number of the men were dismounted, their animals having given out, and the remainder of the stock was so jaded, tender-footed, and worn down, our progress was necessarily slow; yet, as everything depended on our reaching Rome before the enemy could throw a sufficient force there to prevent our crossing the bridge, every possible effort was made to urge the command forward. We proceeded without interruption until we reached the vicinity of Centre, when one of my scouts informed me that a force of the enemy was posted in ambush but a short distance in our front. I immediately threw forward a line of skirmishers, with orders to proceed until they were fired upon, when they should open a brisk fire on the enemy, and hold their position until the command had time to pass.

The plan worked admirable, for, while my skirmishers were amusing the enemy, the main column made a detour to the right, and struck the main road some 3 miles to the rear of the enemy. As soon as our main force had passed, the skirmishers withdrew and fell in the rear of the column. I was then hopeful that we could reach Rome before the enemy could overtake us. My principal guide had thus far proved reliable, and I had made particular inquiries of him as to the character of the road and the country the evening before, and he assured me that there were no difficult streams to cross and that the road was good; hence we approached the Chattanooga River at the ferry without any information as to the real condition of things. Captain Russell had managed to ferry the last of his command across about one hour previous to my arrival, but the enemy had seized and run off the boat before we reached there.

I then ascertained that there was a bridge some 7 or 8 miles up the river near Gaylesville, and procured new guides and pushed on as rapidly as possible in order to reach the bridge before the enemy should take possession of it. We had to pass over an old coal chopping for several miles, where the timber had been cut and hauled off for charcoal, leaving innumerable wagon roads running in every direction, and the command was so worn out and exhausted that many were asleep, and in spite of every exertion I could make, with the aid of such of my officers as were able for duty, the command became separated and scattered into several squads, traveling in different directions, and it was not until near daylight that the last of the command had crossed the river. The bridge was burned, and we proceeded on and passed Cedar Bluff just after daylight. It now became evident that the horses and mules could not reach Rome without halting to rest and feed. Large numbers of the mules were continually giving out. In fact, I do not think that at that time we had a score of the mules drawn at Nashville left, and nearly all of those taken in the country were barefooted, and many of them had such sore backs and tender feet that it was impossible to ride them; but, in order to get as near as possible to the force I had sent ahead, we struggled on until about 9 a.m., when we halted and fed our animals. The men, being unaccustomed to riding, had become so exhausted from fatigue and loss of sleep that it was almost impossible to keep them awake long enough to feed. We had halted but a short time, when I was informed that a heavy force of the enemy was moving on our left, on a route parallel with the one we were marching on, and was then nearer Rome than we were. About the same time I received this information our pickets were driven in. The command was immediately ordered into line, and every effort made to rally the men for action, but nature was exhausted, and a large portion of my best troops actually went to sleep while lying in line of battle under a severe skirmish fire. After some maneuvering, Forrest sent in a flag of truce, demanding the surrender of my forces. Most of my regimental commanders had already expressed the opinion that, unless we could reach Rome and cross the river before the enemy came up with us again, we should be compelled to surrender. Consequently I called a council of war. I had learned, however, in the mean time, that Captain Russell had been unable to take the bridge at Rome. Our condition was fully canvassed. As I have remarked before, our ammunition was worthless, our horses and mules in a desperate condition, the men were overcome with fatigue and loss of sleep, and we were confronted by fully three times our number, in the heart of the enemy's country, and, although personally opposed to surrender, and so expressed myself at the time, yet I yielded to the unanimous voice of my regimental commanders, and at once entered into negotiations with Forrest to obtain the best possible terms I could for my command, and at about noon, May 3, we surrendered as prisoners of war.

We were taken to Richmond, Va. The men were soon sent through the lines and exchanged. My officers and myself were confined in Libby Prison, where we remained until the night of February 9 last, when four of my officers and myself, together with several other prisoners, succeeded in making our escape, and reached Washington in safety about March 1. The balance of my officers, or nearly all of them, are still confined as prisoners or have died of disease, the result of long confinement, insufficient food, and cruel treatment at the hands of the enemy.

I am unable to report the exact number of casualties in the command, but from the best information I have been able to obtain, there were 15 officers and about 130 enlisted man killed and wounded. It was a matter of astonishment to all that so much fighting should occur with so few casualties on our side; but we acted purely on the defensive, and took advantage of the nature of the country as best we could. From actual personal observation where we had driven the enemy from the field, and from what my surgeons, left with our wounded, learned in relation to the loss of the enemy, I am convinced that we killed more of his men than we lost in both killed and wounded.

Previous to the surrender, we had captured and paroled about 200 prisoners, and had lost about the same number in consequence of the animals giving out, and the men, unable to keep up, broke down from exhaustion, and were necessarily picked up by the enemy; but in no case was the enemy able to capture a single man in any skirmish or battle within my knowledge.

I deem it proper to mention the barbarous treatment my wounded received at the hands of the enemy. Owing to the nature of the service we were performing, we were compelled to leave our wounded behind. I provided for them as best I could by leaving them blankets and such rations as we had, and two of my surgeons remained behind to attend them; but no sooner did the enemy get possession of our hospitals than they robbed both officers and men of their blankets, coats, hats, boots, shoes, rations, and money The medical stores and instruments were taken from the surgeons, and my wounded left in a semi-naked and starving condition, in some instances many miles from any inhabitants, to perish.

Many thanks to the Union ladies of that country, for they saved many a brave soldier from a horrible death. In reviewing the history of this ill-fated expedition, I am convinced that had we been furnished at Nashville with 800 good horses, instead of poor, young mules, we would have been successful, in spite of all other drawbacks; or if General Dodge had succeeded in detaining Forrest one day longer, we would have been successful, even with our poor outfit.

In conclusion, I will bear testimony to the bravery and uncomplaining endurance of both officers and men of my command during those trying days and nights. To my staff I owe much for their good example and constant labors.

I have the honor, sir, to be, your obedient servant,

A.D. STREIGHT
Colonel Fifty-first Indiana Veteran
Volunteer Infantry

Brig. Gen. WILLIAM D. WHIPPLE,
Chief of Staff, Department of the Cumberland

Report of Col. Florence M. Cornyn, concerning the expeditions to Courtland, Alabama April 15, 1863 - May 2, 1863 and Tupelo, Mississippi, May 2-8, 1863. Official Records of the Civil War, Series I, Volume XXIII, (p. 251-258)

HEADQUARTERS
CAVALRY BRIGADE
Corinth, May 16, 1863

Captain, I have the honor to submit for consideration the following report of the transactions of the cavalry brigade which I had the honor to command on the recent expeditions in which it was engaged.

On the receipt of news from Glendale, and in pursuance of instructions from Headquarters District of Corinth, Department of the Tennessee, this command, consisting at that time of the Tenth Missouri Cavalry, Lieutenant-Colonel Bowen, and the Fifteenth Illinois Cavalry, Major Gilbert, proceeded on Tuesday, April 14, to the above place, to assist in repelling the enemy, who was said to be making an attempt upon that post. On our arrival there, we found that the enemy, variously estimated as to strength had been repelled, and that the First Alabama Cavalry, under Captain Cameron, had started in pursuit. I, with my command, determined to start also in pursuit. At Glendale we were joined by the Ninth Illinois Mounted Infantry, commanded by Lieut. Col. J.J. Phillips, who reported to me, and joined in the chase. We drove the enemy through and beyond Burnsville, overtaking at this place the First Alabama Cavalry, where we left them, under orders to repair a bridge over Yellow Creek, and guard a forage train that was expected to arrive at that point during the night. The balance of the command pushed on in close pursuit after the flying rebels, pausing only at nightfall, and going into camp about 4 miles west of Iuka (Mississippi).

It might not be improper here to remark that but for the fact that the almost impassable condition of the roads at some points prevented the moving as fast as desirable of the howitzers attached to the Tenth Missouri Cavalry, we would have come up with the enemy's force on that day, and driven him to or beyond Great Bear Creek.

On the following day (Wednesday, the 15th) we moved through Iuka, to Cook's farm, on the Memphis and Charleston Railroad, and went into camp, to await orders.

41

About 10 o'clock that night we were joined by the First Alabama Cavalry. On the afternoon of Thursday, the 16th, the whole of the command of Brig. Gen. G.M. Dodge came up and encamped on the same plantation. In pursuance of orders, the next morning, being Friday, the 17th, the whole command moved from its encampment and proceeded to Great Bear Creek, this brigade leading the advance. At the creek a halt was made, and after some shelling of the opposite shore, the cavalry were ordered to ford, which was immediately done, and with alacrity. The Ninth Illinois Mounted Infantry still formed a portion of the cavalry brigade, which, at this time, consisted of the Tenth Missouri Cavalry, the First Alabama Cavalry, the Fifteenth Illinois Cavalry, and the Ninth Illinois Mounted Infantry, amounting, in all, to about 1,050 fighting men.

The creek was crossed without any opposition, our batteries still shelling the opposite side, and many of them falling amongst this command; but, fortunately, no one was hurt. I immediately started out on the road to Tuscumbia, having previously ordered two squadrons of the Tenth Missouri Cavalry and a company of the Ninth Illinois Mounted Infantry to take a road leading off to the left and north of the main road, to develop the enemy, should it turn out that he had taken that route, as some of his flying pickets had moved off in that direction. Deploying skirmishers on my right and left flanks, and throwing out vedettes to my front, I moved on rapidly toward Tuscumbia, and, at a distance of about 1 1/2 miles, my advanced skirmishers came up with a small squad of the enemy, and drove them on down the road for a distance of about 4 miles. The enemy frequently showed himself in line across the road directly in front of us, but always out of range for our rifles until we arrived at Dickson, and a little beyond that point, he engaged our advance guard; and in order to gain time to close up my column, let down the fence, and deploy to the right and left of the road, I ordered Captain Tannrath, of the First Missouri Light Artillery, who had reported to me with a section of his battery, to open on them with shell, which he did, with good execution. Here Lieut. N.B. Klaine, of the Tenth Missouri Cavalry, was hit in the neck by a glancing ball, but very slightly hurt. Several of the rebel force were wounded at this point, and one of them, left upon the field, was found by us severely wounded in the leg by a shell. He afterward died.

After a few rounds from the battery the enemy hastily retired, closely pursued by us, until he reached Buzzard Roost, where he reformed across the road, his right and left flanks extending into the woods, and his left flank was massed in considerable force. Here we threw a few shell and scattered his left flank into the woods. I ordered Lieutenant-Colonel Phillips to dismount and deploy his command to the left of the road as skirmishers, to dislodge the enemy's right. Great praise is due to Lieutenant-Colonel Phillips for the manner in which he executed this order, he himself acting with commendable coolness and courage, and his officers and men exhibiting all the characteristics of true bravery. They advanced to within short musket-range of the enemy, and by their cool and deliberate firing, succeeded in driving him on. He was immediately pursued by the cavalry, with slight skirmishes, beyond Barton Station, and on to within a short distance of Caney Creek, where the command halted in a clover field to rest our animals and men. In the mean time the two squadrons of the Tenth Missouri Cavalry, commanded by Capt. P. Naughton and Lieut. H.C. McCullough, and the company of mounted infantry under Lieut. R.B. Patterson, proceeded by the route already indicated, and came upon a force of the enemy, and drove them to and beyond what was said to be the camp of the rebel Colonel Roddey, whose force then was estimated at about 600 men. In driving them, owing to the greater distance they had to make, they forced them out on to the main road and into our rear. Here an unfortunate affair occurred, which, as it could not be helped, can only be deplored. Just after the skirmish at Buzzard Roost, Captain Tannrath reported to me that he was out of ammunition. I directed him to send back word for his caissons to come up with a supply, and in the mean time for the guns to fall to the rear, to keep them from being in the way of the cavalry, intending that he should move immediately in the rear of the column. Either owing to the misunderstanding of my order or to the fatigue of the horses, the guns, instead of following up directly behind, fell to the rear, to the distance of nearly 2 miles, and when the flying rebels that were being driven by Captain Naughton's command came upon them, the guns, which were under the charge of Lieutenant Brunner, of the battery, were charged and after all the resistance that could be opposed to them by a company of the Ninth Illinois, which had been ordered to guard them, they were taken, together with the most of the gun support. The whole number of men lost by us here amounted to 43, including Lieut. Edward Krebs, who commanded the company guarding the pieces.

While my animals and men were resting as already stated, word came to me of the attack upon our rear and the taking of the guns. I immediately ordered the First Alabama Cavalry, Captain Cameron, to move down the road to our rear and attack the rebels, and recapture, if possible, the guns. Ordering the Fifteenth Illinois Cavalry, Major Gilbert, and Captain Bruns' squadron of the Tenth Missouri Cavalry to follow, and leaving Lieutenant-Colonel Bowen, to protect the front, I moved out on the road, and soon came in sight of the enemy, with the two guns, when I ordered a charge by the First Alabama Cavalry, which I am sorry to say, was not obeyed with the alacrity it should have been. After charging to within short musket-range of the enemy, they halted for some cause I cannot account for, and the enemy escaped to the woods with one of the pieces and _____ of the other, it having been previously thrown down the railroad excavation. Here Captain Cameron was killed, and a private of the Tenth Missouri Cavalry and one of the First Alabama Cavalry, but not until after they had desisted from the charge, when the enemy turned and poured a perfect hail of lead into our ranks. About this time 6 men of the Tenth Missouri, that I had stationed, by order of General Dodge, to the woods, kept up such a constant fire upon us that I ordered Captain Bruns, with his squadron and the Fifteenth Illinois Cavalry, into a field, with instructions to move toward the edge of the woods, and return the fire. I also ordered the howitzer squadron into the same field to shell the woods, which was done with great credit to the officers and men, doing fine execution. In order to prevent any movement of the rebels from dividing my command, as they outnumbered us nearly three to one, I ordered that portion of my command which I had left on the front to close in on the balance, and moved back down the road nearly a mile, so placing the enemy once more on my front. Here I halted, and ordered my command to move into a field in column of squadrons. This had hardly been accomplished when the enemy was seen in line of battle on the brow of a hill about a mile distant from us and moving toward us. I at once ordered out my force into a field immediately to the east of the one occupied by us, with orders to form and wait the demonstrations of the enemy. Here allow me to say that it has been erroneously reported that at this juncture I sent back for re-enforcements. I did not do so, for at no time did I feel that my force was inadequate to beat the rebels, and, on the contrary, I had the fullest confidence in my officers and men, and felt that I could hold my ground, and even drive the enemy with them should I choose to do so.

At this juncture of affairs, Colonel Bane arrived with a portion of his brigade, when I requested him to order Captain Welker, First Missouri Light Artillery, to open on the rebels with a section of his battery, my own guns being of too short range to reach them. While getting his guns into position, Captain Welker's movements must have been observed by the enemy, for he immediately began to move to the right and left. A portion of my command immediately charged them and drove them to their usual shelter - the woods. All my command was moved simultaneously toward the enemy, the mounted infantry on the north side of the railroad and the cavalry on the south side. Here a brisk firing was kept up by musketry on both sides, until I ordered the mountain howitzers to move up in range and shell the brush, which was obeyed promptly, and I had the satisfaction of seeing the enemy's fire slacken and in a few minutes quit altogether. Moving my command still farther to the east, and facing the enemy, I consulted with Colonel Bane for a few moments, and it was decided to fall back beyond a slight hill to our rear, so as to conceal our force, leaving the Ninth Illinois Mounted Infantry and a regiment of Colonel Bane's command concealed in ambush, the former on the north side of the railroad, and the latter in the woods lately occupied by the enemy, on the south side. At the same time the artillery, consisting of Welker's and Richardson's batteries, with their horses concealed behind the hill, was to be placed in battery just on its brow. At this time, and while the preliminaries were being arranged, the enemy opened on us with a piece of artillery. However, the arrangements agreed on were carried out, and in about half an hour, after all had settled down in quietness, the enemy made an attempt to move toward us, when the two infantry regiments, which had been left concealed, opened on them, emptying many saddles and driving them in dismay. Night was now coming on, when we were joined by the balance of General Dodge's command, and went into camp for the night, the two regiments of infantry already spoken of remaining in their concealment all night.

The casualties happening to my command were very few. Our killed were Captain Cameron and 2 privates. In the unfortunate matter of the capture of the guns, we lost 45, taken prisoners, including Lieutenant Krebs, commanding the guard. The loss of the enemy was heavy, but I have no official means of getting at the exact number.

On Saturday, April 18, in pursuance of instructions from General Dodge, my command was moved out toward Caney Creek, but did not proceed beyond the clover field mentioned in the report of the transactions of the day before, and, after halting a short time, I received orders to fall back to Bear Creek, which I did, reaching that place and going into camp about nightfall.

On the following day, Sunday, 19th, on the receipt of orders from Headquarters, I started with my command, now reduced by the loss of the First Alabama Cavalry, which had been ordered to report to Colonel Bane, and Captain Ford's squadron, of the Fifteenth Illinois Cavalry, which was doing orderly duty for General Dodge, and, taking a guide, moved by an unfrequented road around to Buzzard Roost Creek, hoping by this means to take the enemy in the rear. Owing, however, to the high stage of water in the creek, I was not able to cross it at the point desired, and by that means I emerged from the woods directly in the enemy's front, and near the Widow Barton's plantation. Here, in a field and in the road, the enemy were drawn up to receive us. I sent forward the Fifteenth Illinois Cavalry, Maj. F.T. Gilbert, to skirmish with the enemy, and ordered Lt. Col. Phillips to dismount his command and deploy to the right and left as skirmishers, supporting him on the left by the Tenth Missouri Cavalry, Lieutenant-Colonel Bowen, at the same time directing Major Gilbert to move gradually to the right, to support him on that flank. We gradually moved on the enemy, driving him to Buzzard Roost, and on the summit of the hill he made a halt. I at once ordered all hands to charge, which was done with a yell, the enemy retiring even more rapidly than we advanced. He again showed himself in line at the edge of a wood, nearly a mile distant. Here I ordered a halt, and after several ineffectual attempts to draw him out, I concluded to fall back to camp. On our way back, we found the dead bodies of 5 rebels, lying at the place of our first encounter. We also captured a prisoner, the bearer of dispatches.

On Monday, the 20th, my command lay all day in camp at Bear Creek. On this day, the Seventh Regiment of Kansas Cavalry reported at my headquarters for duty.

Tuesday and Wednesday, the 21st and 22d, we remained in camp awaiting orders. On Tuesday, the Ninth Illinois Mounted Infantry was taken from our command.

On Thursday, the 23d, this brigade, with the whole of the command, moved from our camp at Great Bear Creek, and marched toward Tuscumbia, taking the advance, and driving small squads of the enemy before us, until about 1 p.m., when we went into camp, by order, about 2 miles west of Little Bear Creek, where we lay all night.

On Friday, the 24th, still taking the lead of the main force, we moved off toward Tuscumbia, until within about a half a mile from the ford on Little Bear Creek, when, by order of General Sweeny, we moved off to the right and south of the main road, and took a by-road, which led across an upper ford and into the Frankfort Road, with instructions to march by that route on Tuscumbia, the Fifteenth Illinois Cavalry and two squadrons of the Seventh Kansas proceeding, by the main route, in advance of the main column. Owing to the difficult nature of the road and the greater distance traveled, my command did not reach Tuscumbia until after the infantry and the main body of our force. Here I received instructions to move on through the town, taking with me the two squadrons of the Seventh Kansas that had preceded the command, and pursue the enemy toward the east, the Fifteenth Illinois Cavalry having gone, with the Ninth Illinois Mounted Infantry, toward Florance. I was also instructed to destroy as much of the railroad as possible, and return by night. In pursuance of the above orders, with my command, consisting at this time of the Seventh Kansas and Tenth Missouri Cavalry, numbering in all about 800 men, I moved out toward Leighten, on the Memphis and Charleston Railroad. About 1 mile from Tuscumbia we came upon the enemy's trail, and distinctly saw traces of artillery. Moving on rapidly in pursuit, following the trail across several plantations until about 4 miles east of Tuscumbia, we struck the enemy himself. He rapidly retired, we pursuing. I here deployed the Seventh Kansas, under Lieutenant-Colonel

Herrick, to the left of the road, dismounting his revolving-rifle squadrons as skirmishers, and the Tenth Missouri, with the exception of the howitzer and three other squadrons, to the right, in line of battle, under Lieutenant-Colonel Bowen. These last-named squadrons I kept in the center, under my own immediate command, to use, when occasion required, as chargers.

The enemy retired a distance of about a mile, toward Leighton, and here, on the edge of a wood, to the right of the road, he had placed a piece of artillery, which opened on us the moment we got in range, his line of battle extending some distance to the right and left. At this juncture I ordered my left to move through and around the woods on the left of the road that lay between it and the enemy, which was obeyed with alacrity; perceiving which, the rebels, after a few rounds of musketry from us, retired. About a mile from this point, they reformed across the road, and opened on us with musketry and several pieces of artillery. I moved up the mountain howitzers close enough to give them range, and opened with shell and case-shot upon their battery, my right and left wings steadily advancing all the time. I soon had the satisfaction of seeing them draw off their artillery, just previous to which, however, a charge was made by a squadron on my left, belonging to the Seventh Kansas, around a clump of woods that partially concealed them from the enemy. The success of this charge was frustrated by the commanding officer, Capt. L.H. Utt, receiving a severe wound in his foot from a shrapnel from one of the enemy's guns. After drawing off his artillery, he retired it a distance of about 500 yards, and, placing it behind some deserted negro quarters, again opened on us, with redoubled fury. Ordering a dismounted squadron of the Seventh Kansas and a squadron of the Tenth Missouri to Support them, I moved my howitzers to the front, and opened a steady fire upon their battery, from a very short range, and soon succeeded in silencing every one of their guns. This artillery duel lasted from twenty to thirty minutes, and, in the mean time, my right flank was steadily approaching the enemy's line, and exchanging shots with it. While the cannonading was going on, a corporal of the Seventh Kansas was killed by a shell, and a corporal of the Tenth Missouri Cavalry was wounded severely in the foot. After the enemy ceased firing from his artillery, he rapidly withdrew it from the field, and retired from his position, on to within a short distance of Leighton, where he again formed, many of his men massed in the road, and his wings extending far to the right and left. Here a charge was made by my right wing upon the enemy's line, which was formed in a field immediately behind a fence. They charged up close to the enemy and within short pistol-range, and succeeded in driving and wounding several of them.

In this charge Lieut. John S. Hazard, of the Tenth Missouri Cavalry, was severely wounded in the left arm. In the mean time, on the road, our battery had approached to within range, and sent a few shell into the enemy's dense column on the road, putting it to a rapid retreat. From this on he retreated rapidly, moving through Leighton in apparent dismay. At this place I learned the approximate force of his command. It consisted of Forrest's, Roddey's, Baxter's, and Julian's commands, amounting, as I am informed, to about 3,500 men. The enemy did not pause until about 4 miles east of Leighton, where he formed in line of battle at the extreme eastern edge of an immense plain, some 3 miles square. Here his line of battle seemed to extend from horizon to horizon. It having now approached toward sunset, and the enemy in full sight, I did not deem it prudent to return to Tuscumbia, but sent back a message to General T.W. Sweeny, stating my position and asking for re-enforcements and some heavier artillery, and, placing my pickets, went into camp for the night, the men sleeping on their arms.

At early daybreak next morning (Saturday, the 25th), a portion of the Ninth Illinois Mounted Infantry, Colonel Mersy, came up to us with orders for us to fall back at once to Tuscumbia, which order I obeyed, reaching there about 10 a.m. Here we remained in camp until the following day (Sunday, the 26th), when, in pursuance of orders, with the Tenth Missouri and Seventh Kansas, I proceeded to Bainbridge, on the Tennessee River, with orders to destroy any means of crossing that stream that I should find. Nothing of this kind, however, was found, and we returned to Tuscumbia, reaching there just after nightfall.

On Monday, the 27th, taking the advance of the main force, we marched from Tuscumbia to Town Creek, our advance guard skirmishing with the enemy at that point. Arriving on the clear field on the bank of the creek, I formed my command in line of battle, and slowly approached its edge, and went into camp along a line of fence close to it. I was compelled, however, to withdraw from that camp and fall back, as the enemy opened on us with their artillery, throwing shell amongst us.

On the following day (Tuesday, the 28th), nothing was done by my command except to send scouting parties in various directions; and on Wednesday, the 29th, sending out two squadrons of the Seventh Kansas to the north, and the Fifteenth Illinois to the south, to destroy all the forage that could be found, and covering the return march of the main body, we moved toward Corinth. That night we encamped at Little Bear Creek.

Thursday and Friday, the 30th of April and 1st of May, were occupied in marching as far as Burnsville, where I received orders to take ten day's rations and march the following day from that point toward Tupelo, for the purpose of forming a junction with Colonel Hatch, who, it was supposed, would meet us at that point. Here four companies of the Ninth Illinois Mounted Infantry were added to my command, which, with the addition amounted to about 900 effective men. On Saturday we started on the march to Tupelo, which place we reached on the following Tuesday, passing through Jacinto, Booneville, Cartersville, Baldwyn, and Guntown, frequently skirmishing with the enemy's scouting parties.

As already stated, we arrived at Tupelo on Tuesday, May 5, and here we fought the best contested fight of the whole expedition. Just before entering the town of Tupelo, and to the east of the railroad, it is necessary to cross a dense and almost impassable swamp, on the western edge of which runs Old Town Creek. We had almost reached the western edge, and were approaching, as well as the nature of the swamp would permit, the bridge over this creek, when the enemy, entirely unseen by us, opened upon us with musketry. I immediately threw out to my right and left several squadrons of the Tenth Missouri who succeeded in dislodging the enemy, and securing an easy passage of the bridge for the balance of the command. Still keeping my skirmishers out to my right and left, and an advance guard in the front, I moved down a lane to the left and south of the town, and massed my command in an open field, about 600 yards from the southern border of Tupelo. Here word was brought

47

me from one of my skirmishing squadrons that the enemy were drawn up in line on their front, to the number of 600. I ordered two squadrons of the Seventh Kansas, that were armed with Colt's revolving rifles, to dismount and attack them on foot, supporting them with two squadrons of the Tenth Missouri (mounted), under Lieutenant-Colonel Bowen, with orders to charge with the saber as soon as the enemy's line should break. This order, I am proud to say, was well obeyed and gallantly executed by both the mounted and dismounted soldiers, for the enemy retired, and for a few minutes all was silent along the lines. In about half an hour from the first attack, sharp firing was heard on my front, and the enemy was advancing toward us with yells. I immediately moved my whole force to the rear and west of the village, and, placing my mountain howitzers upon the brow of a hill, I sent forward all the cavalry except one squadron of the Fifteenth Illinois, which I ordered to dismount and support the battery. Lieutenant-Colonel Phillips, commanding the Ninth Illinois Mounted Infantry, having been detailed for that purpose early in the morning, acted as the rear guard and guard for the train, and, knowing that the rear was in such good hands, I felt no anxiety on that account; and this important trust was well sustained. As soon as my front had become fully engaged with the enemy, who fought with considerable determination, I ordered the battery to shell the woods from which the enemy was emerging. This fire was effective, and from that moment the battle became general. At one time two regiments of mounted infantry, commanded by the rebel General Ruggles, forced their way between my fighting column and my reserve, but were suddenly induced to retire much more rapidly than they came. My left at one time fell back toward the battery, which then poured charge after charge of canister into the rebel ranks, with considerable effect, forcing them to retreat, rapidly followed by the cavalry. The enemy had scarcely begun to waver when his whole force fled in dismay, throwing away their arms, coats, and hats.

Our loss amounted to 1 killed, 5 wounded, and three missing.

We took from the enemy 81 prisoners, including 3 commissioned officers. On the field, the scene of the battle, immense quantities of arms, coats, and blankets were found and destroyed by us. I had no means of ascertaining the enemy's loss in killed and wounded, but from the evidence of the battle-field it must have been heavy.

His force consisted of Inge's command, 400 strong, Barteau's Second Tennessee Cavalry, 600 strong, and Smith's command, 1,000 strong. These were commanded by General Gholson. Also two regiments of mounted infantry and a number of irregular conscripts, commanded by General Ruggles, which made the enemy's force amount to about 3,500 men. The whole fight, from the skirmishing in the swamp until the retreat of the enemy, lasted about two hours and a half.

That same night, after consultation with my field officers, and hearing no reliable news from Colonel Hatch, I started back toward Corinth, marching the whole of that night, all of the next day, and until a late hour at night, when I went into camp at Parson Yates' plantation.

On the morning of Thursday, the 7th, Maj. J.C. Smith, in command of the Fifth Ohio Cavalry, met us with orders to return immediately to Corinth. That night we encamped at Booneville, and on the following day we reached Corinth, having been almost constantly in the saddle twenty-five days. The fruits of our expedition were 81 prisoners taken and about 600 head of horses and mules captured.

My officers and men are all entitled to great praise for their bravery and the unmurmuring patience with which they bore the fatigue, hardships, and privations of the march. My thanks are due to Lieutenant-Colonel Bowen, Lieutenant-Colonel Phillips, and gallant assistance. Of the rest of the officers I must say that they all acted like heroes, and it would be invidious to name any of them in preference to others.

The following is a list of the casualties happening to the command on the whole expedition.

Command.	Killed.	Wounded.	Prisoners
10th Missouri Cavalry	1	9	14
7th Kansas Cavalry	1	5	..
15th Illinois Cavalry	..	..	2
9th Illinois Mounted Infantry	..	5	43
1st Alabama Cavalry	2	..	..
Total	**4**	**19**	**59**

I remain, your obedient servant,

FLORENCE   M.

CORNYN

Cavalry Brigade

Colonel Tenth Missouri Cavalry, Commanding

Capt. GEORGE E. SPENCER
   Assistant Adjutant General

Report of Col. George E. Spencer, First Alabama Cavalry, commanding Third Brigade of operations January 28-March 24, 1865.   Official Records, Series I - Volume XLVII, (p. 891-893)

HEADQUARTERS   THIRD   BRIGADE, CAVALRY COMMAND,

DIVISION OF THE MISSISSIPPI,

Faison's Depot, North Carolina, March 30, 1865

MAJOR: I have the honor to report that, in obedience to orders received from your headquarters, on the 28th of January last, this command, consisting of the First Alabama Cavalry, Major Cramer commanding; Fifth Kentucky Cavalry, Maj. C.T. Cheek commanding; and the Fifth Ohio Cavalry, Major Rader commanding, and

Lieutenant Stetson, commanding section of the Tenth Wisconsin Battery, broke camp on the Little Ogeechee River, Ga., ten miles from Savannah, and marched to Sister's Ferry, Ga., arriving there on the following evening. We remained at Sister's Ferry, waiting for the completion of the pontoon bridge over the Savannah River and the causeway on the opposite side until the afternoon of the 2d of February, when we again resumed our line of march.

Nothing of interest occurred until the morning of the 6th of February, when we left Allendale and marched on the left flank of the division at Barnwell Court-House. This day we skirmished considerable with Crews' brigade, of Wheeler's command, and drive them to our left.

We captured during the day five prisoners without loss ourselves. On the morning of the 8th we broke camp at Blackville four hours in advance of the balance of the division and marched to Williston, the First Alabama having the advance. After marching about five miles we struck a force of the enemy and our advance engaged them and had no difficulty in driving them in and through the town of Williston. Being ordered to go into camp there I commenced putting the command into camp, when the picket-post on the Aiken road was attacked. I immediately re-enforced the post with two squadrons of the First Alabama Cavalry, under Captain Latty, with orders to feel of the enemy and endeavor to ascertain what force was in the vicinity, and I cease further preparations for going into camp for the present. The firing in the advance becoming quite heavy, I ordered Major Cramer to take the balance of Major Tramel's battalion of the First Alabama and go to the support of Captain Latty, with instructions to crowd the enemy (the other battalion of the First Alabama Cavalry then being with General Slocum on the road from Sister's Ferry). I then ordered Major Cheek, with the Fifth Kentucky Cavalry, and Lieutenant Stetson with his section of battery, without the caissons, to move out to the support of Major Cramer. I then directed Major Rader to leave one battalion of his regiment with the transportation of the brigade and caissons and in charge of the town, and to take the two other battalions of his regiment and move slowly out on the Aiken road in support of the force already sent. By this time Major Cramer had driven the enemy about one mile and a half into a strong line of battle, in a strong position in timber, with one flank resting on a large pond and a large open field in their front. I ordered Major Cramer to deploy his men in a skirmish line and the Fifth Kentucky in a line of battle and to charge, which was done by both commands in the most gallant manner, the enemy stopping to fire but one volley. Then commenced one of the most thorough and complete routs I ever witnessed. The ground was completely strewn with guns, haversacks, &c. Five battle-flags were captured, including the brigade and four regimental flags, and a large number of horses and over thirty prisoners. After a charge of about seven miles from this point the enemy dispersed and went in every direction through the woods and swamps. I then ordered the chase to be discontinued and brought the command back to camp at Williston. The force we had the encounter with proved to the Alabama brigade, of Allen's division, Wheeler's cavalry corps, commanded by Colonel Hagan, and consisting of the First, Third, Fifth, Ninth, Twelfth, and Fifty-first Regiments Alabama Cavalry.

The next morning we again resumed our line of march and proceeded to Windsor, the next station toward Augusta, where we remained till the next morning, when we again moved still farther on the Augusta road to Johnson's Station without incident, where we went into camp and remained till the next morning, when the Second Brigade, General Atkins commanding, moved in the direction of Aiken. Soon hearing heavy firing in the direction of the Second Brigade, I put my command in line of battle behind rail barricades and awaited further developments. After a time the Second Brigade returned, followed closely by the enemy. The enemy then made a few slight demonstrations along my line, but made no attack. We remained in this position the remainder to the day and till the second afternoon, when I moved north to Pine Log Bridge on the South Edisto River, which I found burned, and impossible to build without a delay of at least three days. The next morning I moved down the river to Guignard's Bridge, twelve miles, and crossed at that point, General Jeff C. Davis kindly giving me permission to cross in advance of his corps, when I moved eight miles in a northwest direction and went into camp for the night. Nothing of interest occurred for several days, and not till after we had crossed the Saluda, Broad, and Wateree Rivers, when we reached the town of Lancaster, SC., and went into camp two miles and a half north of the town on Camp Creek and found a heavy force of the enemy immediately in my front with their pickets on the opposite side of the creek from mine......................

We again resumed our line of march in an easterly direction, my brigade marching fifteen miles upon the left flank of the division; raining very hard and the roads being almost impassable. The next day we again marched upon the left flank, but did not, on account of the horrible state of the roads, make more than eight miles. The following day we again marched upon the left of the division, and camped near the North Carolina line, three miles north of Blakeny's, in Chesterfield District, South Carolina.

On the morning of the 3d of March we resumed our line of march on the left through a clay country with horrible roads and traveled a distance of ten miles when we went into camp in Anson County, North Carolina, about three miles from the State line. We had hardly placed our pickets out when they were driven in by General Hampton's cavalry. The command was quickly thrown into position and we awaited an attack. A small force of the enemy attempted to charge the extreme right of our line, when a few shells from Lieutenant Stetson's section quickly scattered them. We remained in position, expecting an attack, till next morning, when we again resumed our line of march without further incident till after we had crossed the Great Pedee River at Sneedsborough and passed Rockingham, North Carolina. On the 9th of March we moved in advance of the division from the headwaters of Lumber River, in Moore County, North Carolina to Solemn Grove, reaching there about 2 p.m., some five hours in advance of the other two brigades. We there ascertained that General Hardee had passed that point the day before with his corps of infantry, and was marching as speedily as possible to Fayetteville. We also learned from our scouts and foragers that the enemy's cavalry was several miles upon our left flank, also moving toward the same point. We remained in position at Solumn Grove till 5 p.m., waiting for the balance of the command to join us, when we received orders to move with the major-general commanding toward Fayetteville to Monroe's Cross-Roads, a distance of twelve miles. Before leaving Solumn Grove we were joined by Lieutenant-Colonel Way, commanding the dismounted man, and having in charge about 150 prisoners and the headquarters wagons of the division and ordnance train.

In obedience to orders we moved to Monroe's Cross-Roads, it raining terribly during the entire march, and went into camp there at 9 p.m. In obedience to instructions we picketed carefully the country in the direction of Fayetteville, leaving Lieutenant-Colonel Way, whose command was immediately in the rear of my brigade, to picket the rear. Simultaneously on the morning of the 10th of March with our reveille the camp of the dismounted men and our camp was charged by three divisions of the enemy's cavalry, viz, Butler's, Hume's and Allen's, General Hampton personally leading the charge of Butler's division and General Wheeler leading the charge on the right with Hume's division. The camp of the dismounted man was instantly captured; also the headquarters of the division and brigade, and with the wagons and artillery. In the cavalry camp the firing became very severe, and for a time the enemy gained and held nearly two-thirds of their camp, when, by desperate fighting behind trees, the men succeeded in driving the enemy entirely out of camp and partially away from the headquarters. About this time Lieutenant Stetson succeeded in creeping stealthily to his section of artillery and unlimbered one of his guns and fired upon the enemy. This was a rallying signal for the entire command, and immediately a sufficient force was placed in support of the battery and withering and deadly fire of grape and canister was opened upon the enemy. Three successive charges were made by the enemy to recapture our artillery, but each charge was unsuccessful and cost them dearly.

About 7:30 the enemy retreated in confusion, leaving their dead and wounded in our hands. One hundred and three of the enemy's dead were left on the field, also a large number of wounded and about thirty prisoners. Our men were too much exhausted and fatigued to follow the enemy, and nearly all were out of ammunition. For two hours and a half three small regiments, numbering in the aggregate less than 800 men, had successfully resisted the oft-repeated charges of three entire divisions, numbering not less than 5,000 men. We remained on the field of battle till 3 p.m., burying the dead and taking care of the wounded, when we moved about five miles in the direction of Fayetteville, and joined the other two brigades and camped for the night. Our loss at the battle of Monroe's Cross-Roads was 18 killed, 70 wounded, and 105 missing.

Among the killed and wounded were some of the best officers of the command. Adjutant Mitchell of the Fifth Kentucky, was killed. The First Alabama Cavalry lost eight officers, including both of its field officers, Major Cramer being both wounded and a prisoner.

It is impossible for me to speak in too high terms of the conduct of the officers and men of my command in this fight, and it would be invidious to mention any, although I cannot let the gallant conduct of Lieutenant Stetson go without mention, who, unaided and alone, crept through the ranks of the enemy and unlimbered and fired one of his guns. To this fact, more than to any other, I ascribe a terrible disaster turned into a brilliant victory.

Nothing of further interest occurred until the 16th of March, when we struck Hardee's command on the Raleigh road near Averasborough, between the Cape Fear and Black Rivers. I was ordered to place my brigade on the left of the infantry and to advance upon the enemy. I placed the Fifth Ohio, Major Rader commanding, in front and in line of battle, the Fifth Kentucky and First Alabama in support, when we advanced skirmishing quite heavily up to within 200 yards of their works, when we were relieved by General Jackson's division of infantry of the Twentieth Army Corps, and moved to the extreme right. We lost 3 men wounded and several horses, and captured 18 prisoners.

Nothing further of interest occurred till the battle of Bentonville on the 19th, 20th, and 21st, when we were engaged guarding part of the time the left flank, which was done without loss. On the 24th instant we reached this point and went into camp after a campaign of fifty-five days, during which time I marched over 700 miles, crossing seven large rivers on pontoon bridges and an innumerable number of smaller streams and swamps that under ordinary circumstances would be considered impassable. At times I found the road in such a condition that even a mile an hour could not be averaged by the command.

My especial thanks are due and are here tendered to Capt. Andrew Offutt, of my staff, who took charge of the pioneer corps of the brigade. To him we are indebted for any number of hastily constructed bridges, and also that our wagons and artillery were not often abandoned in the almost impassable swamps of the two Carolinas.

My thanks are also tendered to my entire staff for their bravery, perseverance, and patience in executing each and every order during this long, laborious and tedious campaign. I also tender my thanks to each of the regimental commanders for their faithful observance of each and every order, and their energy and zeal upon every occasion, and through them to their brave commands.

We subsisted almost entirely upon the country for rations for the men and entirely for forage for animals. For fifty days my brigade drew only five days' partial rations from the commissariat. I herewith forward the reports of the regimental commanders, and also Lieutenant Stetson's report. This command captured during the campaign 207 prisoners.

I have the honor to be, very respectfully, your obedient servant.

GEO. E. SPENCER,
Colonel First Alabama Cavalry, Commanding
Third Brigade.

Maj. L.G. Estes,
Asst. Adjt. Gen., Third Cav. Div., Mil. Div. of the Miss.

Report of Maj. Sanford Tramel, First Alabama Cavalry, of operations January 28 - March 24, 1865 - The Campaign of the Carolinas. O.R. Series I - Volume XLVII, (p. 896-898)

LIEUTENANT: I have the honor to report that, in obedience to orders received from your headquarters, my regiment, under command of Maj. F.L. Cramer, numbering 18 officers and 292 men for duty, broke camp near Savannah, Ga., on the

28th day of January, 1865, and moved with the brigade on the Springfield road leading to Sister's Ferry on the Savannah River. We arrived at Sister's Ferry on the evening of the 29th, and camped two miles from the river, where we remained until the 3d day of February, when we crossed the river and commenced our march in South Carolina in the direction of Lawtonville.

On the 4th Capt. J.J. Hinds, commanding Second Battalion, was ordered back to Sister's Ferry to report to Major-General Slocum, in obedience to orders from the colonel commanding brigade. This left only one battalion of 170 men in the regiment. On the 6th we had some skirmishing with Crews' brigade, of Wheeler's command, capturing some prisoners. On the 7th assisted in destroying Charleston and Augusta Railroad. On the 8th we moved from Blackville on the road to Williston, my regiment in advance. I, with two squadrons, was ordered in the advance, and came to the rebel pickets just before reaching the village. We routed and drove them through the town, and established a picket-post half a mile west of the village, awaiting the arrival of the command. The regiment soon arrived, and as we were about to establish camp the picket-post was attacked. Captain Latty, in command of two squadrons, was immediately ordered forward with instructions to ascertain, if possible, the force the enemy had in the vicinity. As he advanced the firing became rapid, and I, with the remaining three squadrons, was ordered to Captain Latty's assistance. We drove them one mile and a half, where we found they had established a strong line. Major Cramer was soon on the ground and took command of the main body in the center, while I, with twenty men, and Captain Latty with the same number, moved on each flank of the enemy, Major Cramer advancing with the center. This movement routed them. We drove them half a mile, where they had another line. This we broke, also, and halted for a short time, when Colonel Spencer, commanding brigade, re-enforced us with the Fifth Kentucky Cavalry. We were then ordered to resume the chase, and on advancing found the enemy in a strong position in the woods near White Pond. On being ordered, we charged them, when followed the most complete rout I ever witnessed. Guns, sabers, canteens, haversacks, saddle-bags, hats, and everything which would impede the flight of the affrighted and flying enemy were abandoned and completely strewn over the ground. We continued the pursuit over five miles, capturing quite a number of prisoners, with five stand of colors. We were then ordered to abandon the pursuit, and returned to camp at Williston. We ascertained we had been contending against a greatly superior force of the enemy.

The conduct of the officers and men of my regiment on this occasion was praiseworthy in the highest degree. The loss of the regiment was four men wounded, one mortally, who afterward died.

On the 10th of February Captain Hinds joined us with his battalion, and the regiment was present at the fight near Aiken, but took no active part, except to build a barricade and hold a position on the right. On the 11th we again resumed our march with the brigade, and participated in all the different scenes through which it passed, crossing the Edisto, Saluda, Broad, Wateree, and Great Pedee Rivers, via Lexington, Alston, Black Stocks, Lancaster, and Sneedsborough, nothing of special importance occurring. After crossing the Great Pedee River and going into camp at 9 o'clock on the evening of March 6, I was ordered to take fifty men and proceed to Rockingham,

N.C., about twelve miles distant, and, if possible, take the place and secure the mail. I advanced to within three miles of the place without meeting any opposition. I there found the road strongly picketed by the enemy, and immediately ordered my men to charge, which they did in a gallant manner, driving the enemy from post to post until we reached the edge of the village, where we found a line too strong for us to break with the small force at my command; consequently I ordered the men to fall back slowly, which they did in good order. I then returned to camp, arriving there at 4 a.m. on the 7th. We again moved with the brigade on the 7th, via Rockingham and Solumn Grove, and on the evening of the 9th camped at Monroe's Cross-Roads, having marched during the day in close proximity with the enemy. At the sounding of reveille on the morning of the 10th instant, we were aroused from sleep by the whistling of bullets and the fiendish yelling of the enemy, who were charging into our camp. Then followed a most bloody hand-to-hand conflict, our men forming behind trees and stumps and the enemy endeavoring to charge us (mounted) with the saber.

While gallantly cheering his men Maj. F.L. Cramer was wounded and taken prisoner.

The fighting was most desperate for an hour, when we succeeded, in connection with the Fifth Kentucky and Fifth Ohio Volunteer Cavalry, in driving the enemy away from our camps.

During the fight I was captured by the enemy and held as prisoner until the 14th instant, when I succeeded in making my escape, and after three days lying in the swamps and traveling nights I succeeded in rejoining my command.

After my capture Capt. J.J. Hinds took command of the regiment and retained it until my return, and I am indebted to him for the gallant manner in which he handled the command during the remainder of that severe and terrible fight.

Captain Peek deserves special mention for his gallant daring and coolness during this struggle. The loss of the regiment in the affair was 4 men killed, 27 wounded, and 41 missing.

My regiment moved with the brigade, and was present when the cavalry encountered the enemy on the evening of the 15th, also in the fight of the 16th instant, but sustained no loss as it held a position on the left. We next encountered the enemy in strong force on the 18th, but evaded him by taking a road leading more to the right, while a portion of the Fifth Kentucky Cavalry attracted his attention at a certain point. We encountered the enemy again same day, but he was easily repulsed and driven away. My regiment continued with the brigade; was present and assisted in guarding the left flank of the army during the hard battles of the 19th, 20th, and 21st instant. The enemy then being routed and the campaign ended, my regiment moved with the brigade to Faison's Depot, where we arrived on the 24th instant and have remained in camp since that time.

During the campaign my regiment has captured something over 100 prisoners and over 200 horses.

The regiment has lost during the campaign: Maj. F.L. Cramer, severely wounded and a prisoner; afterward paroled on account of wounds. Capt. John Latty, Company C; First Lieut. George W. Emerick, Company A; First Lieut. Joseph H. Hornback, Company K; Second Lieut. George C. Jenkins, Company M, wounded severely; Surg. J.G.C. Swaving and First Lieut. John P. Moore, Company E, captured. Moore afterward escaped. Four enlisted men killed, 28 wounded (2 or 3 mortally, who afterward died), 46 captured; 215 horses---some by being captured, others by being worn out and abandoned.

I have the honor to be, lieutenant, very respectfully, your obedient servant.

S. TRAMEL
Major First Alabama Volunteer Cavalry, Comdg. Regiment

Report from Brevet Major-General Judson Kilpatrick on Operations in North and South Carolina, January, February and March, 1865. Official Records Series I, Volume XLVII, (p. 786-787)

HEADQUARTERS CAVALRY COMMAND,
In the Field NC on Chicken Road, Eleven miles from
Fayetteville, March 11, 1865
Maj. L.M. DAYTON
Asst. Adjt. Gen., Military Division of the Mississippi

Major: You will remember that I stated in my last communication from Solemn Grove that Hardee was marching rapidly for Fayetteville, but that Hampton and Wheeler were still in rear, and that I would endeavor to cut them off. The information was correct. Hampton, however, was found to be moving upon two roads - the Morganton road and a road three miles farther to the north, and parallel to it, just south and east of Solemn Grove. I posted upon each road a brigade of cavalry, and learning that there was a road still farther north, upon which some of the enemy's troops might move, I made a rapid night march with Colonel Spencer's little brigade of three regiments and 400 dismounted men and one section of artillery, and took post at the point where the road last mentioned intersected the Morganton road. During the forepart of the evening I left General Atkins and joined Colonel Spencer with my staff and actually rode through one of General Hampton's divisions of cavalry, which by 11 o'clock had flanked General Atkins and was then encamped within three miles of Colonel Spencer. My escort of fifteen men and one officer was captured, but I escaped with my staff. General Atkins and Colonel Jordan discovered about 9 o'clock that, while the enemy was amusing them in front, was passing with his main force on a road to his right. These officers at once pulled out and made every effort to join me before daylight but failed to do so, owing to the bad roads and the almost incessant skirmishing with the enemy, who was marching parallel to him, and at some points not a mile distant. Hampton had marched all day, and rested his men about three miles from Colonel Spencer's position at 2 o'clock in the morning, and just before daylight charged my position with three divisions of cavalry - Humes', Allen's and Butler's. Hampton led the center division - Butler's - and in less than a minute had driven back my people, had taken possession of my headquarters, captured my artillery, and the whole command was flying before the most formidable cavalry charge I have ever witnessed. Colonel Spencer and a large portion of my staff were virtually taken prisoners. On foot I succeeded in gaining the cavalry camp, a few hundred yards in rear, and found the men fighting with the rebels for their camp and animals, and we were finally forced back some 500 yards farther to a swamp impassable to friend or foe.

The enemy, eager for plunder, faded to promptly follow us up. We rallied, and at once advanced upon the enemy. We retook the cavalry camp, and, encouraged by our success, charged the enemy, who was endeavoring to harness up my battery horses and plundering my headquarters. We retook the artillery, turned it upon the enemy about my headquarters, not twenty steps distant, and finally forced him out of my camp. We re-established our lines, and for an hour and a half foiled every attempt of the enemy to retake it. At about 8 o'clock General Mitchell, with a brigade of infantry, came within supporting distance, having rapidly marched to my assistance across the country from the plank road. He at once moved up into position and remained with me until 1:30 o'clock, rendering me every assistance possible. The enemy did not, however, make it necessary for the infantry to fire a single shot. General Mitchell has my thanks and deserves great credit for the rapid march over a broken country, the soldierly feeling displayed, and anxiety to assist me. We lost 4 officers killed, 15 men, and 61 severely wounded, and several others slightly wounded, and 7 officers wounded, and we have lost in officers and men about 100. I do not think it will exceed that number, and may fall short of it. The enemy left in my camp upward of 70 killed, including many officers and a large number of wounded. The enemy made nothing by the attack, save some 25 or 30 valuable horses about headquarters. We captured about 30 prisoners during the day and about 150 horses and equipments, which the enemy were forced to abandon in a swamp into which he was driven by a charge made by the Fifth Kentucky Cavalry. (Note P.S. at end of letter.) We held the only road upon which the enemy could move to Fayetteville without moving across the country to a road about five miles distant. I find, however, a portion of Hampton's cavalry passed during the night upon a road running between my present position and Little River. The main portion of his force, however, has not yet passed. I have written you in detail, that you may fully know all that has taken place. Prisoners taken from Allen's, Humes', and Butler's divisions differ as to the movements of Cheatham's command. Some say that it is moving upon the railroad, others that it is moving after Hardee, and will probably take a road north of Little River. The information is not, however, reliable. We have marched over the worst roads I ever saw, and have had scarcely forage for the past two days, Hardee having taken nearly everything in the country. My command very much needs rest.

I am, with great respect, your obedient servant,

J. KILPATRICK,
Brevet Major-

General

57

P.S. Colonel Spencer informs me that it was a charge made by Captain Hinds' First Alabama Cavalry, and not Fifth Kentucky Cavalry, which drove the enemy into the swamp, resulting in the capture of their horses and animals.

J.K.

CHAPTER V

GENERAL WILLIAM TECUMSEH SHERMAN

William Tecumseh Sherman (named after the Shawnee Indian Chief, Tecumseh, whose strategy was diplomacy first and bloodshed second) was probably the most misunderstood General of the Civil War. Martin Luther once said: "Great soldiers make not many works, but when they speak the deed is done." This could very well apply to Generals Sherman and Grant. Sherman was ranked second only to General Ulysses S. Grant as the greatest Northern commander in the Civil War. He was born February 8, 1820 in Lancaster, Ohio. His father was an Ohio Supreme Court Judge who died when William was nine years old, leaving him to be raised by Thomas Ewing, an influential friend who was eventually able to get William an appointment at West Point Military Academy.

The military service seemed to be "Billy's" calling and he studied hard at West Point, graduating sixth in his class. His excessive deportments for his dress kept him from graduating fourth. His intellectual standing was excellent, however, he had a difficult time conforming to the West Point dress codes. Drawing was his best subject and he loved to paint. He stated that painting was so fascinating it was painful for him to lay down his paint brush. He spent the next thirteen years in the military but decided to marry Thomas Ewing's daughter, Ellen, and settle down. This private life of law, banking, etc. did not suit him very well so he took a job as superintendent of the Louisiana Military Academy (later became Louisiana State University) which is where he was when the Civil War broke out. Although he was a Southern sympathizer, he did not believe in secession. He loved his country and stated he would do no act, breathe no word, or think no thought hostile to the government of the United States.

Sherman felt that his life was dull and was just waiting for an opportunity to serve his country in war. After Louisiana seceded from the Union, he left his job at the academy and went to Washington where he turned down a commission as brigadier general from Abraham Lincoln because he did not want to be obligated to him, stating he had rather earn his stars and he began the next segment of his military career as Colonel. Although he was involved in many battles and skirmishes, his "march to the sea" would bring him immortal fame. Part of his strategy was to make war so terrible that the rebels would never again take up arms against the United States of America.

By September 1864, Atlanta had been taken and Sherman had a plan. Being the brilliant strategist that he was, he closely studied the agriculture census of the areas where he was to march, to determine which areas would provide the most needed food for his men and their horses and mules. He then mapped out the route for his march to the sea and holding history in his hands, set out for the Atlantic Ocean with approximately 80,000 Union troops who lived off of the land while foraging the countryside. (His troops have been estimated as low as 62,000 up to 100,000.)

General Sherman had disciplinary problems among his soldiers from the beginning of the march. He had given strict orders not to burn any private homes or bother any women or children, and especially the poor people. In one of Sherman's orders to Kilpatrick, he stated, "Spare dwellings that are occupied and teach your men to be courteous to women; it goes a great way, but take all provisions and forage you need." He ordered them to only destroy the things that would aid the enemy. As the soldiers branched out in an eighty-mile wide range, some of them went out on their own, looting, burning and harassing the citizens. A few cases of rape were reported. Sherman found it more and more difficult to control all of the 80,000 or so soldiers under his command. The Civil War seemed to foster drinking and no matter how stringent the orders, nothing could prevent the thirsty soldiers from inventing all of their ingenious ways to obtain whiskey. They, at times, even concocted their own bootleg whiskey which they called "oh, be joyful". The more they drank, the more out of control they became.

Am I condoning the destructive acts of the Union soldiers? Certainly not! Were they the only ones who committed these destructive acts? Absolutely not! Both sides destroyed and burned anything they thought might aid the enemy following them.

Upon their arrival in Savannah, Sherman was treated with "Southern Hospitality" because the residents were afraid of what the troops would do to their fine city. Sherman was kind in return and rested there for about one month. While Savannah had been defended by 10,000 Confederate troops, they decided they would be no match for Sherman and his army so they retreated and moved on ahead into South Carolina. After Sherman and his troops left Savannah for South Carolina, they skirmished almost daily with the Confederates. The trip took its toll on the Union soldiers, the country was not as plentiful as had been Georgia and they went without rations for long periods of time. The country was marshy, the water icy and it was difficult to maneuver. Sometimes the horses became stuck in the mud and had to be left. Many nights they worked all night crossing the almost impassible swamps and streams. Sherman later wrote Grant that the roads would have halted almost any other body of men he ever heard of.

General Hugh Judson "Kilcavalry" Kilpatrick, still commanding Sherman's 3rd Division, was skirmishing with General Joe Wheeler and Lt. Gen. Wade Hampton almost daily.

After crossing the Savannah River, they proceeded to Williston when they ran into several regiments of Wheeler's cavalry, and four of the First Alabama Cavalry Union soldiers were wounded in a skirmish and one later died. Sherman had no sympathy for the South Carolinians since he credited them with starting the rebellion that he was having to fight so diligently to put down. He thought of South Carolina as the "hellhole of secession". He still, however, ordered his men not to bother the women, children and private dwellings. As they approached Columbia, South Carolina, he ordered that nothing in Columbia except public buildings and war supplies should be burned. The Confederates, already in Columbia, decided again that they were no match for Sherman's army and evacuated the city, setting fire to the cotton as they rode out. The wind had spread the flames to other buildings and by the time

Sherman's men arrived, the city was nothing less than an inferno. Sherman, himself, tried to help put out the flames but the slaves had met the Union soldiers with large vessels of wine and whiskey and the more they drank, the harder they fanned the flames, consequently, Sherman was blamed for burning Columbia.

Upon entering North Carolina, Sherman told Gen. Kilpatrick: "Deal as moderately, and fairly by North Carolinians as possible...." The Federal troops had to build pontoon bridges in order to cross the Pee Dee River on the border of the Carolinas and at which time a skirmish began between Kilpatrick's troops and Hardee's rear guard. The Federals pushed on toward Fayetteville, finally making camp on March 9th, next to a swamp. The area was called Monroe's Crossroads. While Kilpatrick was in the farmhouse visiting with his lady friend, Wade Hampton was planning how best to attack the Union forces and early the next morning, about daybreak, Hampton's Confederate squadron, with a loud rebel yell, carried out his plans and for a few minutes, they were successful. However, Hampton's success was short lived although several of Kilpatrick's men, including many First Alabama Cavalry soldiers, had been killed, including eight officers, and several were wounded while many others had been captured. After Lt. Stetson made his way to one of the guns and fired on the enemy, the rest of the Federal troops collected their strewn artillery and began firing. The enemy finally retreated about 7:30, leaving one hundred and nine dead Confederate soldiers scattered around the camp and swamp. This was according to a report written by Col. George E. Spencer. The numbers varied by other accounts. This would be the last major battle in which the First Alabama Cavalry Union soldiers would have to participate.

After recovering from the battle, burying their dead and tending to the wounded, Kilpatrick and his men gathered the scattered blankets and supplies and continued their march to Raleigh, via Fayetteville. They would soon learn that the Confederates had blocked the road to Raleigh between the Cape Fear and Black rivers which were surrounded by swamps, and another skirmish erupted. After Kilpatrick's men had again reigned over the Confederates, he was being scolded by Confederate Colonel Rhett who exclaimed, "I was taken by my own fool mistake, but you damned Yankees won't have it your way for long, we've got 50,000 fresh men waiting for you in South Carolina." To which Kilpatrick replied, "Yes, and we'll have to hunt every swamp to find the damned cowards."

During the march, Sherman was called "Uncle Billy" by his soldiers, "Messiah of the Lord" by some while others called him the "devil reincarnate". Whatever he was, history tells us he was a brilliant soldier, commander, and master of modern warfare. He did what he thought he had to do in order to end the rebellion. He wrote from his headquarters in Goldsboro, NC, *"I do not believe a body of men ever existed who were inspired by nobler impulses or a holier cause than they who compose this army"*. Sherman loved his men and had become very attached to them. He hated to discipline his soldiers because he felt that no military leader could be successful by quarreling with his troops.

Sherman died February 14, 1891, in New York City. His cap and sword rested on his coffin while thousands of people viewed his remains, tears streaming down the old soldiers' faces. Over 30,000 young and old soldiers had come to bid their

General farewell. Bells tolled all around while one of the many military bands played "Marching Through Georgia". His body was taken by train to St. Louis, Missouri where he was buried. After the bugler blew taps, the muskets began to fire across his grave, thus ending the saga of the notorious General. The tombstone which he had designed, himself, was eventually erected.

Sherman had been baptized as a young lad and considered himself a Christian. In one of his last speeches he stated, "When Gabriel sounds his trumpet I shall be ready". The trumpet had sounded and the great General had finally gone to meet his God.

CHAPTER VI

SOME NATIONAL CEMETERIES WITH INTERMENTS OF FIRST ALABAMA CAVALRY SOLDIERS

CHATTANOOGA NATIONAL CEMETERY

One of the most picturesque of America's National Cemeteries is located near the heart of the city of Chattanooga. One hundred twenty acres of gently rolling hills, landscaped meadows and intriguing rock formations surround a round knoll rising some 100 feet. Graves of over thirty-one thousand veterans and their dependents are on the gentle slopes below a memorial area. The Chattanooga National Cemetery is a lasting tribute to the defenders of our Nation.

The original need for the cemetery was created by furious Civil War battles fought at Chickamauga, Chattanooga, Lookout Mountain, and Missionary Ridge from September to November 1863. It was established by General George H. Thomas, known to history as the "Rock of Chickamauga," in General Order No. 296, Headquarters, Army of the Cumberland, dated December 25, 1863. By 1865, more than twelve thousand Union soldiers had been buried; about five thousand were unknown. However, the cemetery was not officially designated a National Cemetery until 1867 when Congress passed "An Act to Establish and Protect National Cemeteries."

A daring and famous escapade of the Civil War is commemorated in this cemetery. It is the story of the "General," a locomotive, commandeered by James Andrews. Andrews' Raiders attempted a daring sabotage mission to destroy the rail line between Atlanta and Chattanooga. Tried as spies, Andrews and seven of his men were hanged. Their final resting places are at the base of the monument.

Chattanooga National Cemetery, 1200 Bailey Avenue, Chattanooga, TN 37404. (423)855-6590/91.

CITY POINT NATIONAL CEMETERY

The existence of military burial grounds at City Point and the subsequent establishment of City Point National Cemetery in 1866 reflects another aspect in the struggle for the capital city of the Confederacy. Here at City Point on the James River the Union army established a great supply depot for receipt of troops and vast quantities of all manner of material of war in preparation for another try for Richmond. General Grant's objective was the capture of Petersburg, a vital communication center, and then to advance upon Richmond from south of the James River. From June 1864 to April 1865 heavy siege action by the forces of the Union and desperate and stubborn defense tactics by Lee's Army of Northern Virginia characterized the campaign which brought Grant's forces to Petersburg and ultimately into the streets of Richmond.

Coincident with this all-out thrust for the capital of the Confederacy were the war casualties - the dead and the wounded. A large army general hospital at City Point cared for some of the sick and the wounded. The death rate from wounds and disease was high, and many of the combatants of the 1864-1865 siege of Petersburg and Richmond were interred in burial grounds near the hospital. Following cessation of hostilities, this burial ground became a part of City Point National Cemetery, a site on the bank of the Appomattox River. Today this cemetery is a part of the City of Hopewell, Virginia with entrance gate located at 500 North 10th Avenue.

1,423 unknown soldiers from the Civil War, 115 Confederate soldiers and Veterans from 7 wars were interred here. It is located on the site of a depot field hospital during the Civil War. The number of identifiable remains initially interred exceeds the number of unknown remains initially interred. Initial interments made in the cemetery numbered 3,753 known remains and 1,403 unknown remains. In 1955, the remains of 17 unknown soldiers of the Civil War were discovered during an excavation of some vacant lots in Hopewell, VA (apparently the site of an abandoned cemetery). Buttons from both Union and Confederate uniforms were found in some of the graves uncovered at that time. Reinterment of these remains was made in City Point National Cemetery. In 1959, two remains determined to be those of unknown Union soldiers were recovered from shallow graves in the path of Interstate Route 95. These remains were reinterred in the national cemetery on 12 August 1959. Some of these remains were found at Point of Rocks in Chesterfield County and Harrison's Landing in Charles City County. In 1982, the skeletal remains of yet another Union soldier were discovered near Hopewell, VA and reinterment was made on Memorial Day 1982. In August, 1990 a box of original burial documents from the depot field hospital was discovered in an attic in the maintenance building at this cemetery. The documents date back to 1864.

City Point National Cemetery, 10th Avenue & Davis Street, Hopewell, Virginia 23860.
(Address of for location only, correspondence should be addressed to: Richmond National Cemetery Complex, 1701 Williamsburg Road, Richmond, VA 23231. (804)222-1490.

COLD HARBOR NATIONAL CEMETERY

There is a mass grave with the remains of 889 Union soldiers gathered from the battlefields nearby, buried in this cemetery. (It has not been proven that any of the soldiers from the 1st Alabama Cavalry, USA are buried here.) It is located on the actual battle site of the campaign in July, 1862. Across the street from the cemetery is the Garthright House which was used as a field hospital by General Ulysses S. Grant during the Civil War. It is reported the blood seeped through from the second floor of the house onto the food and belongings below. Blood stains are still evident along with bullet holes throughout the frame. A wagon would be parked under the window of the second floor so that amputated arms, legs, etc. would be thrown into it for disposal. About a mile down the road from the cemetery is the Watt House which was used in 1862 during the Battle of Gaines' Mill. Today, this house is occupied by a Park Ranger. He and his family have witnessed the presence of a Confederate soldier in this house. Nearby neighbors have also stated that at night you can hear the sound of the fife and drum corps in the open fields across from the cemetery.

This little cemetery is truly a battlefield cemetery. A portion of the fighting of two Union campaigns to reach Richmond occurred in this area. General George R. McClellan's Peninsula Campaign to reach Richmond virtually collapsed as a result of the fighting of the Seven Days' Battles of June 26 - July 2, 1862. The fighting at Gains' Mill (Cold Harbor) on June 26-27 has been described as the most costly and vicious of the Seven Days' battles with heavy losses inflicted on both Union and Confederate forces. Then again in early June 1864, a mighty army under General Ulysses S. Grant met General Robert E. Lee's forces, fewer in number but strongly entrenched, at Cold Harbor, a strategic crossroad guarding the approaches to Richmond. Here during June 1-3, 1864, the security of Richmond was purchased for another 10 months, but only at the cost of tremendous casualties for both Union and Confederate forces. Writing of the operations at Cold Harbor during those hot days of early June, General Lee's biographer, Douglas Douthall Freeman, states that Lee *"had won his last great battle in the field."*

Cold Harbor National Cemetery, Rt. 156, North, Mechanicsville, Virginia 23111. (Address is for location only and correspondence should be addressed to Richmond National Cemetery Complex, 1701 Williamsburg Road, Richmond, Virginia 23231.

MARIETTA NATIONAL CEMETERY

Established July 31, 1866, Marietta National Cemetery has represented the sacrifices of servicemen and women for more than 120 years. This 23.2 acre cemetery was donated to the government by Henry Cole, a Marietta resident (formerly from Chenango County, NY, who hoped to soothe the bitterness between the North and the South after the Civil War, by providing a sacred burial ground for the casualties from both the Union and the Confederacy. The people of the South could not, however, accept the offer, and consequently a separate Confederate Cemetery was established in Marietta, adjacent to the Marietta National Cemetery, where the original Cole family members were interred. It is located approximately twenty miles northwest of Atlanta and the records are now housed at the Chattanooga National Cemetery.

The natural beauty of the cemetery with its gently rolling terrain and graceful curving roadways is further enhanced by a dignified and beautiful white marble rostrum, erected in 1940 and located in the center of the cemetery near the flag pole. A flagstone walk from the flag pole to the rostrum passes underneath a wisteria arbor, the brick pillars of which were part of an earlier rostrum used prior to the erection of the present structure. Near the rostrum is the Wisconsin Monument, a 12' shaft of Wisconsin granite erected by the State of Wisconsin to honor the memory of four hundred and five soldiers from the state who died in defense of the Union and are interred in the Marietta National Cemetery.

The initial burials (9,973) in the cemetery were reinterments from original burial places around the Atlanta area, such as Kennesaw Mtn, Ezra Chapel, Allatoona,

Peachtree Creek, Big Shanty, Jonesboro, Lovejoy Station and New Hope Church, as well as Alabama and as far east as Augusta, Georgia.

Twenty three states are represented from the Civil War. They are Ohio (1609), Illinois (1239), Indiana (867), Wisconsin (405), Iowa (352), New York (274), Michigan (215), Kentucky (214), Pennsylvania (191), Missouri (147), New Jersey (82), Tennessee (72), Minnesota (42), Connecticut (41), Maine (20), Alabama (19), Massachusetts (16), Kansas (6), Georgia (4), West Virginia (3), Louisiana (1), Vermont (1) and North Carolina (1).

In addition to the Civil War burials in the National Cemetery, there is one from the Indian Wars (Cherokee War - 1836), two from the Revolutionary War, and from the Persian Gulf, and several representatives from the Spanish American War, WWI, WWII, Korean War, Vietnam, Lebanon, and the Sinai Peninsula.

The individual from the Indian War is S. Wilder, a Private who was killed in 1836 (originally buried at Fort Butler, SC). One of the Revolutionary War veterans interred is John Clark, who was a Major General during the war and a two time Georgia State Governor. The other is John Hames who was 112 years old when he died in 1860.

Most of the men who died while being held prisoners of war at Cahaba Prison in Alabama were later moved to the Marietta Cemetery.

Marietta National Cemetery, 500 Washington Avenue, Marietta, GA 30060.

MEMPHIS NATIONAL CEMETERY

The National Cemetery at Memphis, Tennessee was established in 1867, then comprising an area of 32.62 acres and was at that time about seven miles northeast of the city of Memphis. It was at one time known as the Mississippi River National Cemetery which was a most appropriate designation in recognition of the fact that a very large number of the initial burials in the cemetery were the remains of members of the Union forces who participated in the battles and engagements during the early years of the war, which contributed to eventual control of the Mississippi River by the forces of the United States. Following the close of the war, reinterments were made in the national cemetery at Memphis from wartime burial sites along the Mississippi from Hickham, Kentucky to Helena, Arkansas including New Madrid, Island No. 10, and Fort Pillow.

The location of the city of Memphis, as one of the great commercial centers on the Mississippi River, was of considerable strategic importance to the Confederacy following Tennessee's secession from the Union in 1862. Strong Union land and river forces combined to deprive the Confederacy of this important city when Memphis came under United States control on 6 June 1862. Prior to this, in April 1862, New Orleans had fallen to United States Navy forces under command of Flag Officer David G. Farragut. Thus the Confederacy was severely pinched by invasions from both ends of the Mississippi valley, through complete domination of the "Father of Waters" was not to come until after the fall of Vicksburg in early July 1863. During all of this period, riverboats of the United States Navy played an effective and important role. Interred here at Memphis National Cemetery are the identified remains of nearly 200 crew members from many ships of this great river flotilla, including many of the victims, known and unknown, who perished in one of the nation's most tragic maritime disasters - the explosion and burning of the Mississippi River steamboat, *U.S.S. Sultana*, during the night of 26 April 1865. This ship, a well known river craft, had limited cabin space for from 75-100 passengers, and by law could carry 376 persons including crew. The ship left New Orleans on 21 April 1865 with stops scheduled upriver at Vicksburg, Memphis, Cairo, Evansville, Louisville, and Cincinnati. At Vicksburg a huge throng of Union soldiers lately released from Confederate prison camps anxiously awaited the arrival of the *Sultana* which was to take them to Cairo, Illinois, from which point they would make their way to their respective homes. An estimated 1,800-2,000 crowded on board the ship. The men were so eager to go on board that the authorities decided to delay making out muster rolls until after the ship had left Vicksburg. A leaking boiler had been hastily repaired at Vicksburg, and the overloaded steamer pressed on upriver towards Memphis, bucking river currents reinforced by heavy spring rains. Memphis was reached the evening of 26 April. Some of the returning soldiers disembarked there and went out to view the sights of the town while the ship was readied for the trip upriver. A few of the men missed the boat when it set out after more repairs had been made to the boilers. As the *Sultana* pushed on through the night to a point above Memphis near a group of islands known as the Hen and Chickens, the overburdened and weakened boilers exploded. Fire broke out on the ship, and the hundreds of helpless passengers were forced to jump into the swift and hostile current of the dark Mississippi. Some were drowned outright; others were rescued and taken to various Memphis hospitals where many died as a result of burns, exposure to the elements, and as a result of weakened physical stamina brought about by long incarceration as prisoners of war in Confederate prison camps. The death toll of this Mississippi River tragedy has been estimated at more than 1,700 persons.

By 1870, Memphis National Cemetery had become the burial site for the remains of some 13,965 Civil War decedents. Some five hundred and thirty-seven Civil War regiments are represented among the honored dead. Some 8,866 unknown soldiers, the second largest number of unknowns in any of the national cemeteries presently under the jurisdiction of the Department of the Army, are buried here.

Memphis National Cemetery, 3568 Townes Avenue, Memphis, Tennessee, 38122

NASHVILLE NATIONAL CEMETERY

Roll of Honor, No. XXII dated July 31, 1869, submitted to Quartermaster General's Office, U.S.A., Washington, D.C. recorded the graves of 16,485 Union soldiers interred in the Nashville National Cemetery and remains as a part of the cemetery's historical records. Original burials, 16,489 of which number thirty-eight officers, ten thousand three hundred white soldiers, fourteen hundred and forty-seven colored soldiers, and seven hundred and three employees are known and three thousand ninety eight white soldiers, four hundred and sixty-three colored soldiers, and twenty nine employees are unknown. All have been gathered from an extensive region of country, along the Cumberland River from Carthage on the east to Clarksville on the west; from the line of the Louisville and Nashville railroad as far as Mumfordsville, Kentucky; from the Nashville and Northwestern Railroad to the Tennessee River at Johnsonville; from the Edgefield and Kentucky and the Memphis branch of Louisville and Nashville Railroad; from Bowling Green to Clarksville; from the Nashville and Chattanooga Railroad to Lavergne; and from all intermediate and adjacent country; from the Nashville battlefield, and many of the skirmish grounds in Southern Kentucky, comprising those originally collected and buried at Thompkinsville.

The number of distinct burial places from which these bodies were taken is two hundred and fifty-one. A very large proportion of the dead in this cemetery, however, were transferred from the hospital burial grounds in and around the city of Nashville and remains of those moved from temporary burial grounds around general hospitals in Nashville and nearby battlefields of Franklin and Gallatin, Tennessee. Reinterments were also made from Bowling Green and Cave City, Kentucky. As a matter of information, during the Civil War, if marked at all, graves of those who died in general hospitals, in the battlefields, or as prisoners of war were marked by wooden headboards with the names and identifying data painted thereon. Many of these headboards deteriorated through exposure to the elements. The result was that when the remains were later removed for burial to a national cemetery, identifications could not be established, and the gravesites were marked as unknown.

Nashville National Cemetery, 1420 Gallatin Road South, Madison, Tennessee 37115 (615)736-2839.

RICHMOND NATIONAL CEMETERY COMPLEX

Slightly more than one hundred miles separated Richmond, Virginia and Washington, D.C., respective capitals of the Confederacy and of the United States. Yet, it was only after four long years of hard fought campaigns, exceeding in intensity, in property damage and in loss of life any conflict experienced on the North American continent, that the capital of the Confederate States was besieged by the forces of the Union with the fall of Richmond and a few days later on April 9, 1865, the surrender of General Robert E. Lee's Army of Northern Virginia at Appomattox Court House, the guns were silenced and a great war passed into history.

Six national cemeteries located in the Richmond area offer mute and eloquent testimony of the intensity of the struggle that was waged during the war years to obtain control of the capital of the Confederacy. These cemeteries--City Point, Cold Harbor, Fort Harrison, Glendale, Richmond and Seven Pines National Cemeteries-- are now under the jurisdiction and care of the Veterans Administration, all established in 1866. None of these six cemeteries is a large cemetery. Four contain approximately two acres. City Point and Richmond, largest of the six, have an area of approximately 7 and 10 acres respectively.

5,706 unknown soldiers from the Civil War are interred here. One unknown Confederate soldier was interred with full military honors on 7 April 1978. An employee of a local radio station was relic hunting near the banks of Beaverdam

Creek in Hanover County and discovered the remains. There were several minie balls, at least four he presumed, had struck the soldier. There were buttons and a belt buckle among the items that had triggered the alarm on his metal detector. The remains were found under a foot of dirt roughly 80 feet from the creek. A knife, pewter bayonet scabbard and canteen also were among items that led Les Jensen of the Museum of the Confederacy to verify that the soldier was indeed a Confederate.

Richmond National Cemetery Complex, 1701 Williamsburg Road, Richmond, Virginia 23231. (804)222-1490.

STONES RIVER NATIONAL CEMETERY

After the battle of Stones River at Murfreesboro, TN, most of the dead were buried on the field. When the National Cemetery was established in 1865, the Army reburied the Union dead from this and other battles here. Of the more than 6,100 Union burials, 2,562 were not identified. Most of the Confederate dead were taken to their home towns or the nearest southern community. Some, however, were buried in a mass grave south of town and later reinterred in another mass grave in Evergreen Cemetery in Murfreesboro.

The Stones River National Battlefield encompasses only a small part of the original battlefield.

Thanks to Fortress Rosecrans on the battlefield, the Union army was able to launch a successful attack on the Confederate rail center in Chattanooga and complete the wedge through the Confederacy along the transportation routes running southeastward through Tennessee. It was abandoned in April 1866, a year after the Civil War ended. Today Lunettes Palmer and Thomas and Curtain Wall No. 2 are among all that remain of the original 14,000 feet of earthworks. Of the original four interior forts, only Redoubt Brannan survives.

Stones River National Battlefield, 3501 Old Nashville Highway, Murfreesboro, TN 37129. (615)893-9501.

(Above information was taken from brochures from respective national cemeteries.)

OTHER BURIAL GROUNDS

In only fourteen months, almost 13,000 Union soldiers had died while prisoners of war in the hands of the Confederates at Andersonville Prison, which was probably the most deplorable of all prison camps. It housed thousands more men than it was originally designed to house. The prisoners had no way of hiding their bodies from the hot summer sun nor keeping it warm during the frigid winters. The ones who were fortunate enough to have any clothes at all, were buried naked when they died so others could use their garments. Their food was rancid and they were fed vermin infested meat. The water supply was not adequate for even half of the soldiers. Due to the vast numbers of soldiers dying each day, they were buried in long, narrow, shallow trenches. Due to the efforts of Private Dorance Atwater, Second New York Cavalry, who was a prisoner at Andersonville, many of the names of the dead were preserved and have been identified with grave markers. Several of the soldiers of the First Alabama Cavalry, U.S.A. are buried there.

Of those who died at Libby Prison, 6,276 are buried in a cemetery in Henrico County, Virginia, southeast of Richmond, two miles from the city and one and a half miles from the James River. Of the 6,276 graves, only 817 of the soldier's names are known. [19]

CHAPTER VII

SOME PLACES OF DEATHS OF 1ST ALABAMA CAVALRY SOLDIERS

ADAMSVILLE, TN

Ham, James F.   8/27/63   (died at home)

AIKEN, SC

Tate, William   2/12/65

ANDERSONVILLE, GA

Name	Death Date	Grave #
Barton, William H.	9/1/64	#7524
Beard, Alfred	12/1/64	
Bell, Robert	8/3/64	#4622
Berry, James M.	6/17/64	#2111
Bice/Price, John C.	9/11/64	#8425
Booker, William W.	8/13/64	#5505
Guthery, Isaac	9/8/64	#8147
Henry, Peter	6/26/64	#2514
Johnson, Columbus	6/15/64	#1996
Jones, James F.	5/10/64	#996
Mitchell, John D.	8/4/64	#4715
Panter/Painter, Rufus	8/15/64	#5763
Patterson, William A.	8/26/64	#6886
Perrett, John	6/26/64	#2504
Pounders, James B.	8/8/64	#5077
Redmond, William A.	10/13/64	#10900
Sisson, Oliver B.	9/13/64	#8728
Stubbs, W.	8/4/64	#4731

ATHENS, AL

Tune, James A.   6/1/64   (while in military prison)

ATLANTA, GA

Wall, John   11/15/64
Wooly, William T.   9/28/64

ALEXANDRIA, VA

| Phillips, William L. | 5/21/65 | #3035, US Military Cemetery |

ANNAPOLIS, MD

Price, Gabriel	1/1/65	
Smith, David D. (or P.)	4/18/65	
Tittle, James S.	12/16/63	
Vanhouse, Lewis	6/5/65	

BALL'S FERRY, GA

| Davis, William | 11/23/64 | KIA |

BEAR CREEK, ALABAMA

| Johnson, James | 7/25/63 | KIA |

BEAUFORT, SC

| Smalling, George | 1/4/65 | 53-6357, Beaufort National Cemetery |

BENTON BARRACKS, MO

| James Reed | 7/29/63 | 6-68, Jefferson Barracks, MO |

BETHEL (?)

| McCall, Thomas (Corp.) | 7/11/63 | |

BRIDGEPORT, AL

Hill, Richard G.	5/4/64	H-10930, Chattanooga National Cemetery *
Mauldin/Madlin, William	5/14/64	H-496, Chattanooga National Cemetery
Riggs, George	5/14/64	H-577, Chattanooga National Cemetery
Wooten/Whorton, Charles W.	5/25/64	H-10904, Chattanooga National Cemetery*
Shopton/Sharpton, Joel T.	5/18/64	H-548, Chattanooga National Cemetery
Snelson/Smelser, Adam	5/21/64	H-604, Chattanooga National Cemetery
Williams, George B.	5/15/64	H-578, Chattanooga National Cemetery
Wooten, Charles	5/25/64	H-479, Chattanooga National Cemetery

(* These records were from the Chattanooga National Cemetery. The Roll of Honor states Richard G.W. Hill was buried in Grave H-505 and Charles Whorton in H-479)

CAHABA PRISON, AL

Blackstock, Thomas W.	2/1/64
Reed, David B.	1/26/64
Reed, Francis M.	7/29/63

CAMP CHASE, OH

Russell, Josiah	6/11/63
Williams, Riley	1/25/64

CAMP DAVIES, MS

Adams, James, M.	11/28/63	
Bishop, David H.	1/11/64	
Brunson, David A.	12/28/63	
Collins, Volney	1/15/64	
Cook, William	12/1/63	
Dillard, Smith	3/14/63	
Entrican, John W.	12/20/63	B-3495, Corinth National Cemetery
King, Samuel D.	1/19/64	B-3362, Corinth National Cemetery
Mabry/Maberry, Alberry	1/4/64	
Mitchell, Eldon C.	1/17/64	B-3494, Corinth National Cemetery
Parker, John	12/1/63	
Prentice, James	1/8/64	
Reid, Jonathan	1/18/64	
Thomas, William	1/16/64	
Tittle, James S. (Sgt.)	12/16/63	
Worthom, James H.	1/11/64	

CAVE SPRINGS, GA

Lambert, William J.	7/7/64 (or 7/15)

CHARLESTON, SC

Childress, M.	10/13/64
Dikes/Dykes, Thomas L.	10/2/64

CHATTANOOGA, TN

Castlebury, Robert B.	6/28/64	E-11506, Chattanooga National Cemetery

Ford, John A.	9/17/64	E-220, Chattanooga National Cemetery
Tuck, Robert	7/2/64	

COLUMBIA, TN

Lewis, Isaiah	10/22/64

COOSAVILLE, GA

Johnson, Mitchell	8/20/66, KIA	F-991, Marietta National Cemetery

CORINTH, MS

Barraun, George L.	11/6/63	
Boyer, Thomas H.	11/13/63	B-3357, Corinth National Cemetery
Boyd, Joseph	8/25/63	
Clements, Curtis	6/25/63	
Con/Crow, John W.	2/27/63	
Cooksey, Enoch C.	2/22/63	B-3425, Corinth National Cemetery
Creekmore, Brison C.	2/27/63	
Douthit, William G.	2/17/63	
Faulkner, Frank	3/20/63	
Fowler, Isreal	7/28/63	A-2190, Corinth National Cemetery
Fowler, William	7/4/63	
Franks, James M.	2/5/63	
Green, Joseph	3/2/63	
Hammonds, Robert	3/3/63	
Harper, Robert	3/8/63	
Hays, Mansfield	2/28/63	
Henson, Andrew T.	11/27/63	
Hood, John	2/24/63	
Hunter, Thomas T.	8/31/63	A-2131, Corinth National Cemetery
Inman, Arthur	3/36/63	
Johnson, Alex	7/23/63	
Johnson, Noah	9/20/63	
Kingsley, William J.	3/20/63	
Lambert, Wilson	12/1/62	
Lewis, Peter	4/15/63	
Logan, Alexander	2/11/63	
Lovett, Andrew J.	3/19/63	A-2069, Corinth National Cemetery
Lovett, Archibald B.	3/4/63	A-2067, Corinth National Cemetery

Matthews, James	10/21/62 (or 9/8/62)	
Mathis, Jesse	9/19/63	
McDonald, Miles	5/11/63	
McGough, Joseph	1/25/63	
Miles, Benjamin R.	4/27/63	
Miles, William W.	5/26/63	
Neal, Charles B.	6/24/63	
Nichols, James F.	2/17/63	
Osborn, Fountain W.	7/10/63	
Osburn, William	6/26/63	
Osborn, William L.	9/25/63	
Rayborn, Thomas C.	4/12/63	
Reed, Thomas	3/16/63	
Richards, John G.	5/3/63 (or 4/27/63)	
Robinson, George	11/19/63	
Rogers, Augustus P.	6/16/63	
Sitton, Mikiel	11/18/63	
Smith, Henry H. (or M.)	2/10/63	
Spence, Julius	9/16/63	
Stewart, Michael	11/15/63	
Stout, John M.	11/15/63 (or 12/11/63)	
Stover, Abraham	12/18/63	
Sutton, M.	11/15/63	
Thornton, Henry M.	12/3/63	
Weaver, James R.	6/10/63	
Settlemire, Jacob G.	9/14/63	

COURTLAND, AL

Pool, Thomas	7/24/65	B-131, Corinth National Cemetery

DECATUR, AL

Carter, John	10/1/64	
Dickenson, John	5/1/64	
Ernest, William	12/?/6?	A-1979, Corinth National Cemetery
Estell, William L.	6/1/65	
Green, Samuel	7/7/64	B-3241, Corinth National Cemetery
Blankenship, William W.	4/29/64	
Holt, Isaac M.	5/21/64	
Milligan, James M.	4/28/64	B-3230, Corinth National Cemetery
Patterson, David	5/2/64	
Sides, John M.	6/6/64	
Sides, John R.	5/23/64	
Smith, Henry F.	6/25/64	(died at home)

Smith, James	7/6/64	B-3225, Corinth National Cemetery
Statum/Statom, James A.	5/18/64	
Sterling, Josiah	4/24/65	B-3235, Corinth National Cemetery
Taver/Tarrer, John	4/8/64	B-3299, Corinth National Cemetery
Taylor, Warren	5/19/64	
Tidwell, Micajah	6/24/64	(buried in soldier's cemetery at the post)
Uttley, George W.	6/25/64	(died at home)
Wright, Joseph B.	4/8/64	B-3231, Corinth National Cemetery
Young, John W.	9/14/64	

DU QUOIM, IL

Turrentine, Martin J.	7/21/63

FAISON'S STATION, NC

Cantrell, John S.	6/18/64
Newland, Hugh	3/31/65

FT. DONELSON

Willis, William	4/18/64

FRANKLIN CO., AL

Cantrell, John S.	6/18/64

GLENDALE, MS

Adams, John Q.	6/18/63
Bishop, Robert W.	8/3/63
Brown, Robert M.	9/17/63
Byram, William T.C.	8/6/63
Cantrell, William	2/20/63
Carpenter, Frazier E.	8/9/63
Chafin, William M.	6/28/63
Dillard, Smith	3/14/63
Dugan, Richard S.	9/27/63
Forman, Elijah	6/4/63
Freeman, Robert D.	9/29/63
Ganns, David	4/12/63
Gentry, John L.	6/6/63
Gibson, John H.	5/26/63

Green, John J.	7/25/63	A-2067, Corinth National Cemetery
Houston, S.T.	9/4/63	
Jackson, Joseph M.	7/5/63	KIA
James, Joseph	6/24/63	
Jones, Joshua	5/27/63	A-2334, Corinth National Cemetery
Lerock, P.	5/1/63	
McCullough, Joseph	6/12/63	
Mitchell, Francis M.	7/31/63	A-2063 Corinth National Cemetery*
Nichols, David	7/3/63	
Nichols, General Morgan	4/3/63	
Osburn, Chesley	3/14/64	
Parker, Pleasant A.	8/5/63	
Parsons, Raymond	4/2/63	
Reddish, Thomas J.	5/29/63	
Sparks, Coleman	6/24/63	
Taylor, John R.	8/9/63	
Thompson, Nathan	10/20/63	
Wardlow, Joseph	7/10/63	

(*Roll of Honor states Grave A-96)

GOLDSBORO, NC

Pollard, William	5/11/65	

HILTON HEAD, SC

Gordon, Samuel J.	12/27/64	53-6346, Beaufort National Cemetery, SC
Guttery, Henry	12/9/64	23-2070, Beaufort National Cemetery, SC
Smalling, George W.	1/4/65	53-6337, Beaufort National Cemetery, SC

HUNTSVILLE, AL

Abbott, Israil P.	6/18/65	L-554, Chattanooga National Cemetery
Brooks, George	6/17/65	
Campbell, George B.	2/15/65	
Ellison, William J.	5/22/65	L-558, Chattanooga National Cemetery
Gaines, Charles W.	3/8/65	
Griffin, Franklin	2/10/65	
Halcomb, Wiseman	8/23/62	Maple Hill Cem., Huntsville
Lowry, James C.	4/15/65	KIA
Lowrimore, James	8/3/64	

Moody, Samuel	7/31/65	L-504, Chattanooga National Cemetery
Mooney, George W.	5/1/65	(died at Madison Station)
Nichols, Edward	5/1/65	
Pierce, Uphratus C.	5/29/65	(killed by train)
Ray/Roy, Alex/Clemond R.	5/17/65	L-543, Chattanooga National Cemetery
Sansing, James	2/5/63	
Scott, John B.	5/28/65	L-528, Chattanooga National Cemetery
Woody, Daniel	8/16/65	

According to the Maple Hill Cemetery Record Book in Huntsville, AL, there were countless unmarked graves of "Union soldiers who died in Huntsville during occupation in the Civil War....By 19 November 1862, 180 Union soldiers had been buried here but only the names of those interred during the month of August, 1862 have been determined through research....Most of the bodies are believed to have been removed to the Chattanooga National cemetery in 1867 or claimed by relatives."

JACK'S CREEK, TN (Near Jackson, TN)

Files, Jesse L.	12/24/63	
Murphree, James H.	12/24/63	
Pell, William	12/24/63	A-327, Corinth National Cemetery
Welch, Henry C.	12/24/63	
Welch, William	12/24/63	

JACKSON, TN

Robinson, James	6/15/63
Robinson, John	5/15/63

JEFFERSON BARRACKS, MO

Box, Francis E.	5/17/64
Glenn, John W.F.	6/11/64
McRay, John H.	3/14/64

JEFFERSONVILLE, IN

Nichols, Jasper	6/14/65
Vest, Jonathan	1/19/65

LIBBY PRISON, VA

Barnett, Job	3/18/64	Buried in Richmond National Cemetery, VA

Clements/Clemens, Edward	1/25/64	Buried in Richmond National Cemetery, VA
Cook, Charles	2/23/64	Buried in Richmond National Cemetery, VA
Glenn, James H.	2/24/64	Buried in Richmond National Cemetery, VA
McCullough, Thomas D.	2/26/64	
Pike, John F.	1/31/64	Buried in Richmond National Cemetery, VA
Russell, John F.	5/19/63	Buried in Richmond National Cemetery, VA

LOUISVILLE, KY

Hallmark, James W.	2/26/63 (or 8/17/64)
Henson, John	6/11/64
Wilhite, John/James P.	1/6/63

MADISON STATION, AL

Mooney, George W.	5/1/65

MEMPHIS

Adams, Levi	2/2/64	B-1342, Memphis National Cemetery
Armstrong, James	12/9/63	B-1355, Memphis National Cemetery
Austin, Jessie W.	3/15/64	
Blevins, Nathaniel	3/1/64	B1364, Memphis National Cemetery
Bookout, Abel	12/18/63	B-1363, Memphis National Cemetery
Byford, Quiller J.	3/1/64	B-1365, Memphis National Cemetery
Byrom, Cavaller	4/21/64	B-1367, Memphis National Cemetery
Cain, James	3/26/64	B-1375, Memphis National Cemetery
Cheek, Edmond/Elijah S.	2/6/64	B-1378, Memphis National Cemetery
Cotton, James H.	1/27/64	B-1343, Memphis National Cemetery
Dodd, Franklin	4/15/64	B-1349, Memphis National Cemetery
Eaton, Lewis	11/19/63	B-1356, Memphis National Cemetery

Ezell, Thomas L.	3/10/64	B-1333, Memphis National Cemetery
Gann, Newton	2/11/64	B-1381, Memphis National Cemetery
Godwin/Goodwin, Henry K.	12/9/63	B-1382, Memphis National Cemetery
Green, Samuel	2/29/64	
Green, William	2/25/64	B-1335, Memphis National Cemetery
Guin, Levi	4/7/64	B-1362, Memphis National Cemetery
Guin, Michael	3/22/64	B-1372, Memphis National Cemetery
Harbin, John H.	3/16/64	B-1350, Memphis National Cemetery
Harbison, David	5/3/64	
Hightower, Wilburn	3/29/64	B-1337, Memphis National Cemetery
Johnson, James W.	3/1/64	B-1347, Memphis National Cemetery
Jones, Matthew	4/2/64	B-1353, Memphis National Cemetery
King, Berryman	3/11/64	
Knight, Benjamin P.	2/21/64	
Little, C.	3/20/64	
Maloy, Hugh	4/1/64	B-1354, Memphis National Cemetery
Mattox/Maddox, Henry	5/6/64	B-1360, Memphis National Cemetery
McDonald, William	3/14/64	
McKinney, Thomas	4/10/64	B-1357, Memphis National Cemetery
Mills, Stephen H.	4/3/64	B-1361, Memphis National Cemetery
Morbin, John H. (Sgt.)	3/16/64	
Moore, James	4/11/64	B-1358, Memphis National Cemetery
Norris, George W.	4/17/64	B-1371, Memphis National Cemetery
Norris/Morris, Phillip	3/11/64	B-1368, Memphis National Cemetery
Pace, Andrew J.	2/12/64	B-1336, Memphis National Cemetery
Patrick, William	3/21/64	B-1348, Memphis National Cemetery
Penn, George W.	3/14/64	B-1345, Memphis National Cemetery
Price/Prince, John A.	5/10/64	B-1352, Memphis National Cemetery

Pugh, George W.	3/19/64	B-1359, Memphis National Cemetery
Ricard/Rikard, John H.	2/28/64	B-1338, Memphis National Cemetery
Reavis, John J.	2/9/64	B-1376, Memphis National Cemetery
Redus, George F.	3/14/64	
Sanderson, John/James M.	6/14/64	B-1366, Memphis National Cemetery
Stroud, Charles/Carroll D.	3/30/64	B-1374, Memphis National Cemetery
Swim, Aaron H.	3/12/64	B-1351, Memphis National Cemetery
Tittle/Little, Clinton	3/20/64	B-1344, Memphis National Cemetery
Trotter, Josiah	3/28/64	B-1380, Memphis National Cemetery
Truelove, George A.	11/17/63	
Tucker, Daniel	3/11/64	B-1341, Memphis National Cemetery
Walker, William H.	2/27/64 (?)	B-1340, Memphis National Cemetery
Ward, William H.	3/18/64	B-1339, Memphis National Cemetery
West, Green B.	3/19/64	Memphis National Cemetery
Williams, Daniel	1/7/64	B-1370, Memphis National Cemetery
Williams, George W.	3/29/64	B-1377, Memphis National Cemetery
Wilson, Charles M.	2/19/64	

Grave numbers courtesy of John W. Cothern.

MONROE'S CROSS ROADS, NC

Bowen, Archie	3/10/65
Mize, James R.	3/10/65
Vanhoose, Robert F.	3/10/65
Vines, John J.	3/10/65

MOORESVILLE, AL

Evans, Edmund R.	2/5/65
Thacker, Thomas F.	4/22/64

MORGAN CO., AL

Taylor, Joseph P.	8/8/64

MOULTON, AL

Jordon, William T.   7/24/65

MURFREESBORO, TN

Hefner, William H.   2/12/63
Henry, John R., Jr.   4/13/63
Kennedy, Artemus   3/30/63   O-5634, Stone's River
                                                  National Cemetery
Oden, William D.   3/20/63
Penn, Pleasant   2/7/63

NASHVILLE, TN

Bain, Alfred A.D.   11/8/62
Bain, John D.H.   12/30/62
Blevins, Dillard   10/17/62
Blevins, John (#2)   2/4/63   E-0436, Nashville National
                                                  Cemetery
Bowlin/Bowling, William   4/6/64
Brooks, John A.   11/7/62   A-5186, Nashville National
                                                  Cemetery
Brown, Elijah   10/30/62   B-6968, Nashville National
                                                  Cemetery
Brown, William   12/13/62   B-6102, Nashville National
                                                  Cemetery
Calvert, Ralphord   11/7/62
Campbell, Adam   10/22/62   A-5062, Nashville National
                                                  Cemetery
Campbell, Alexander   12/5/62   B-5628, Nashville National
                                                  Cemetery
Canady, Isaac A.   11/22/62
Crumbley, Thomas   2/12/65   H-09225, Nashville National
                                                  Cemetery
Davis, Archibald   11/12/62   A-4340, Nashville National
                                                  Cemetery
Davis, Jesse   10/19/62   A-5045, Nashville National
                                                  Cemetery
Davis, Robert   1/27/63   B-6554, Nashville National
                                                  Cemetery
Downum/Donner, James H.   4/13/64
Durm, John   8/15/63
Edwards, James   1/28/63   B-5674, Nashville National
                                                  Cemetery (I.C. Edwards)
Felton, Abraham   12/22/62
Finerty, Thomas W.   10/20/62

Goode, James	3/6/63	E-0850, Nashville National Cemetery
Guthrie, Calvin	4/19/64	H-09834, Nashville National Cemetery
Hallmark, George N.	11/3/62	
Harper, Tennessee Polk	12/9/63	C-7159, Nashville National Cemetery
Hendon, Henry H.	1/15/65	
Hightower, Monroe	12/6/62	
Huey, Thomas	7/21/64	J-13787, Nashville National Cemetery
Inman, Henry	12/1/62	
Jaggers, Benjamin F.	10/16/62	A-4518, Nashville National Cemetery
James, William H.	7/13/64	H-09946, Nashville National Cemetery
Jett, Isaac	12/13/62	C-7114, Nashville National Cemetery
Jones, John B.	1/28/63	B-5921, Nashville National Cemetery
Jones, McDonald (Thos.)	9/9/62	A-4010, Nashville National Cemetery
Lawrence, William F.A.	9/26/62	A-5018, Nashville National Cemetery
Lentz, John P.	10/21/62	
Logan, James M.	12/24/62	
Lott, Simeon H.	10/23/62	
Martin, Daniel	11/12/62	
Martin, Nathaniel G.	12/26/62	B-6418, Nashville National Cemetery
McColloch, Leroy	11/22/62	B-5863, Nashville National Cemetery
McCulloch, Samuel	10/23/62	B-6986, Nashville National Cemetery
McWhirter, Andrew F.	10/23/62	B-6918, Nashville National Cemetery
McWhirter, George W.	10/8/62	A-4367, Nashville National Cemetery
Miles, William H.	10/15/62	B-5659, Nashville National Cemetery
Milligan, William K.	12/1/62	A-4351, Nashville National Cemetery
Mitchell, John C.	10/8/62	A-4566, Nashville National Cemetery
Mooney, Peter	11/17/62	
Nelson, Thomas M.	10/29/62	B-5786, Nashville National Cemetery
Oden, Andrew J.	1/6/63	G-8013, Nashville National Cemetery

Perrett, Isaac R.	4/12/64	
Pettus, Egbert L. (or J.)	11/27/62	C-7060, Nashville National Cemetery
Pitts, John B.	4/14/64	H-10019, Nashville National Cemetary
Rhone, John	10/15/62	
Riggs, James A.	12/13/62	B-6201, Nashville National Cemetery
Russell, George W.	11/23/62	A-5223, Nashville National Cemetery
Russell, James J.	10/27/62	C-7110, Nashville National Cemetery
Self, Allen J.	9/3/62	
Self, Allen R.	10/10/62	A-4186, Nashville National Cemetery
Self, Martin D.	10/27/62	A-4671, Nashville National Cemetery
Self, Matthew G.	10/28/62	A-4768, Nashville National Cemetery
Senyard, Henry C.	8/24/64	
Shaffer, William H. (or B.)	4/26/63	E-0248, Nashville National Cemetery
Sharpton, Daniel	9/9/64	F-3616, Nashville National Cemetery
Sheets, John	10/1/62	F-3616, Nashville National Cemetery
Shehon/Shellborne, David	6/7/64	Nashville National Cemetery
Smith, Allen	10/15/62	A-4748, Nashville National Cemetery
Smith, John M.	10/31/62	
Smith, Matthew J.	10/28/62	A-5227, Nashville National Cemetery
Speegle, Carroll K.	10/8/62	A-4707, Nashville National Cemetery
Speegle, Thomas C.	11/2/62	B-6921 Nashville National Cemetery
Stanton, Elijah A.	11/9/62	
Stanton, John	10/26/62	A-4359, Nashville National Cemetery
Stephenson, Joseph	11/17/62	A-5124, Nashville National Cemetery
Stewart, Andrew J.	10/27/62	C-7088, Nashville National Cemetery
Stokes, John W.	4/25/64	J-13610, Nashville National Cemetery
Stringer, James	10/30/62	B-6771, Nashville National Cemetery
Swan, Lambert	11/7/62	
Tedford, Thomas	11/22/62	

Thornton, Martin V.	11/10/62	B-5715, Nashville National Cemetery
Turrentine, Martin F.	12/19/62	B-5931, Nashville National Cemetery
West, John B.	6/29/64	
Woodall, William E.	10/3/62	A-4999, Nashville National Cemetery
Wood, Joseph R.	10/17/62	A-4280, Nashville National Cemetery
York, Marion L.	12/2/62	A-4868, Nashville National Cemetery

* Some of these were taken from the Roll of Honor and grave numbers may have changed. Other grave numbers taken from Nashville National Cemetery Records.

NEW ALBANY, IN

Cagle, Enoch	5/3/64

PADUCAH, KY

Speegle, Andrew	12/5/62

PERRY CO., IL

Glenn, James F.	8/10/63

RICHLAND, NC

Boyd, Elisha F.	4/1/65

RICHMOND, VA

Pike, John F.	1/31/64	Richmond National Cemetery
Wicks, Thomas	3/2/64	

RICHMOND, NC

Gleen, J.	3/9/64

RIPLEY, MS

Holden/Halden, Archibald, J.	8/3/63	KIA

ROME, GA

Bell, John	8/17/64	C-1234, Marietta National Cemetery

Bolton, John	8/7/64	C-1630, Marietta National Cemetery
Comer, Lewis	9/6/64,	KIA
Dillenger, John	7/18/64	C-1275, Marietta National Cemetery
Harbison, Matthew D.	7/15/64	
Ingle, Murray	7/31/64	C-296, Marietta National Cemetery*
Johnson, John	7/31/64	C-276, Marietta National Cemetery*
Lansford/Lunsford, Michael	8/15/64	C-170, Marietta National Cemetery*
Lewis, Noah	11/1/64	
Osborne, Elick/Alex	7/1/64	C-1505, Marietta National Cemetery
Taylor, Simeon	7/30/64	C-53, Marietta National Cemetery*
Tyler, Wiley S.	8/30/64	C-1226, Marietta National Cemetery
Wood, William A.	10/28/64	C-1448, Marietta National Cemetery

* Taken from Roll of Honor and grave number may have changed. Others taken from Marietta National Cemetery Records stored in Chattanooga, TN.

SAVANNAH, GA

Gordon, Samuel J.	12/27/64	Sec. 53, Grave 6346 Beaufort Nat. Cem., SC
Guttery, Henry	12/9/64	Sec. 23, Grave 2070 Beaufort Nat. Cem., SC
Holmes, John M.	3/27/65	Sec. 23, Grave 2072 Beaufort Nat. Cem., SC
Lovin/Lovoon, William W.	2/18/65	
Milam, Jesse	1/20/65	
Smalling, George W.	1/4/65	Sec. 53, Grave 6337 Beaufort Nat. Cem., SC
Wallace, Robert L.	2/12/65	

STEVENSON, AL

Homan/Homes, Andrew J.	5/21/65
Phillips, Thomas	4/1/65
Self, James T.	12/3/64
Tolbert, Silas	3/25/65

SUMMERVILLE, AL

Powell, Joshua	5/2/63

VICKSBURG, MS

Dickinson/Dickenson, James	2/15/64	
Goode, John M.	3/3/64	

VINCENT'S CROSS ROADS, MS

Byrd, Marshal H.	10/26/63	
Chandler, Erasmus D.	10/26/63	C-9, Corinth National Cemetery
Cooper, James Mack 10/26/63)	12/15/63	(Died from wounds received
Morphis, James K.	10/26/63	
Perry, James	10/26/63	
Stenberg/Sternburg, Phillip A.	10/26/63	C-8, Corinth National Cemetery
Swift, James C.	11/2/63	
Tyler, William G. (or J.)	10/26/63	(J.Tyler buried B-264, Corinth Nat. Cem.)

WILLETT'S POINT, NY

Guyse, Enoch M.	4/17/65	

WINSTON CO., AL

Mayfield, Milton	3/10/65	

YELLOW CREEK, MS

Murphy, William M.	7/5/63	KIA

UNKNOWN

Beach, John	4/19/63	
Blanchard/Blanchitt, Wm. C.	11/11/63	
Blankenship, Robert S.	Unknown	(R.R. accident in Giles Co., TN)
Bumper, David A.	12/18/63	
Bumper, William H. (Corp.)	12/9/63	
Conaway, John E.	1/15/64	
Dudley, Dean	6/3/63	
Files, James L.	12/24/63	(Died in TN)
Funderburk, Christopher C.	2/21/64	(While POW)
Gutherie, John	Unknown	(Died at home in AL)
Guttery/Guthrie, Marion M.	4/20/64	(Could be Baltimore, MD)
Hawkins, Jackson (Corp.) 10/9/63		
Mabry/Mayberry, Alberry W.	1/4/64	

Ringsley, William J.	4/1/63	
Smith, David	7/10/64	(Died at home)
Stevenson, William	9/15/63	
Stuart, J.M.	11/15/63	
Swift, James E. (Lt.)	11/2/63	
Taylor, Hiram	1/10/64	
Thompson, W.L.	10/19/63	
Waldrep/Waldress, Pinckney	7/14/64	F-5439, Marietta National Cemetery
Ward, John W.	5/1/65	
Whitehurst, Simeon A.	1/16/64	
Willis, William	4/18/64	
Wyatt, William	5/1/65	
West, John	6/29/64	

CHAPTER VIII

CIVIL WAR DIARY OF FRANCIS WAYLAND DUNN

The following diary is from the Francis Wayland Dunn Papers, Bentley Historical Library, University of Michigan and while it covered the period of September 1, 1862 through November 12, 1864, only the period he spent with the First Alabama Cavalry, U.S.A. is included. It was transcribed by Ken Baumann of Milan, Michigan who has so graciously offered it to be included in this book. Mr. Baumann spent many hours in the library transcribing the diary as it could not be photocopied. His generosity and untiring effort to keep the memory of Union soldiers alive, is very much appreciated.

According to Mr. Baumann, Francis Wayland Dunn was born in Wayne, Astabula County, Ohio on January 29, 1843. His father, Ransom Dunn, was a New England born preacher and missionary of the Free Will Baptist Church and was instrumental in founding Hillsdale College at Hillsdale, Michigan. He also taught at the college. Wayland and his older brother, Newell Ransom Dunn, were both graduated from Hillsdale College in June of 1862. They enlisted in the 64th Illinois Infantry in September of 1862. On May 16, 1863, Wayland became Sergeant Major of the 1st Alabama Cavalry, U.S.A. and I will include the portion of his diary he wrote during the time he served with this regiment. His brother had already died with typhoid fever and he had shipped his body back home to his father.

Camp Life, 1863

May 16 - Went out to Burnsville with Sampson. Had a talk with Miss Phelps and eat dinner at a Union mans house. Pretty good time. When I got back Conger took me out and said that he had a chance of recommending a man for a commission in a negro regiment that General Thomas was forming at Corinth. I could have had my choice but before telling him anything I went over to see Walt about the application for sergeant major. It had been sent in and after talking the thing over I concluded the cavalry (1st Alabama Union) offered the best chance. There are four or five more companies yet that can be made up and I think the chance is pretty good for a commission. If I can get one here I should like it better than at Corinth. Then I can get out at the end of the year and shall probably be in a better location as far as health is concerned.

May 17 - Applications went up today. I'm afraid I've not done the best thing. Nothing going on. Kennedy goes as captain. _____ and _____ from Company F and B as lieutenants and Sampson as orderly.

May 18 - On guard in the field. Major Stewart wanted me to go into the negro regiment, expect I ought to have gone. Kennedy came out to the post at night and told me that an order had come by telegraph for my detail. Got a letter from Avis Thomas and Miss Fisher, pretty good.

May 19 - Frank came over in the morning and told me to leave and I went over to the cavalry (1st Alabama Union). Eat dinner with the officers and am to mess with they for awhile. Pleasant enough for the present.

May 20 - Wrote to the girls. Made out some reports and the like. Wrote to father.

May 21 - Got a letter from father and one from Pratt. The batallion were cut out in the assignment of officers to the negro regiment but they will be good for the next cut. There is some talk of ours that the new officers in the cavalry not being mustered out or transfered, but I don't think there is any truth to that or at least it can be got around for they will not keep men in a detail to perform these duties for such a time. A fellow was down from Corinth picking up the negros, a perfect blowhard.

May 22 - Passed like the rest. Wrote a letter to Pratt. General Dodge sent for our tent and we had to unfurl about the middle of the afternoon. Major is getting some better. I'm in hopes that tomorrow I can get a horse. I want to be on the next scout without fail.

May 23 - Today we moved into the doctors tent.

May 24 - Took a wash in the evening. I am getting into the rigamarole of camp duty.

May 25 - Eat breakfast over to the old camp. Got a letter from Dick Baker and one from father. Directed or intended for mother. In the afternoon set up tents for major and ourselves. This tent is much better than the other, two feet larger each way, convenient (in) every way. in the evening drank two or three glasses of beer with mess one.

May 26 - Put brush around the tents. An order came at noon for (us to be) ready for (a) move. Three days rations. Got a horse from Gray, saddle from same, saddle and bridle from Booth, pistol from major, sabre from same, belt from Trammell. Got everything all ready and start at night at sundown. There may be some danger but it can't be wrong however it may come out.

May 27 - Last night we rode till almost day and reached the railroad about three miles this side of Bear Creek. I lost my blanket before I had gone ten rods from (the) picket post. Two companies were sent over to the fords and just after daybreak we heard some firing. Major Stuart went to the front and in a little while sent for us. We went up to the ford and he deployed the men and they advanced to the creek. The Rebels on the other side than gave a volley but hurt no one. Summers company was sent down to a lower ford and Shurtliff to an upper (one). I rode down near the creek and all of us stopped in a little flat a few rods from the bank. Their bullets whistled over our heads some twenty feet or more. All the forenoon from daylight they were firing back and forth but not a man was hurt. At twelve the major sent word to the other two companies to fall back. We went to within one and one-half miles of Iuka and then turned east and north looking for feed until we came to within two miles of the ford where we were in the morning. Here (we) fed horses and made supper. I milked a cow and Steve made coffee and we made a good one. The boys hooked chicken, two bee hives, eggs and everything they could find. The horses were tied to the trees in his orchard because it wouldn't be safe to leave them in the lane. Walt and I slept on the piazza of the old mans house.

May 28 - Took the rest of the old man's corn and saddled up just before daylight. Had a good breakfast with some of the honey and chicken that the boys had stolen the night before. Major Stuart and Walt helped eat it. We went back to the creek again but did not try to cross and did not meet any Rebels. When we came into the road where we halted yesterday morning, I was riding with Trammell in front. Day had stopped for a drink with two scouts two or three rods ahead of us. Just as we were coming to the top of a little knoll I saw some men standing by a house to the left of us, across a field, and spoke to Trammell "Is that not a squad of them?". He did not answer but started off on the run on a left hand road that led to where they were. When he got ten or twelve rods he turned his head around and called for part of us to come that way. I tried to turn my horse to call to the men, but before I got him around the company had all taken the direct road after the scouts. Day came up and we went on three men going with Trammell. The Rebels skedadled and we had a run for nothing. (We) waited until Shurtliff came up and then went on into Iuka. The people told us that Captain George had gone along the night before with seventy five men. We had heard yesterday that he had crossed the creek. We followed the track into Iuka and Walt and I went in on the run with Trammel's company but no signs of Rebels. They found the direction again and came in two or three miles. Walt and I with a couple of sergeants were out ahead of the column quite aways and stopped to let our horses rest until the men came up. Two men rode up in the road and halted and Walt took them to be the advance of George's men coming back, so we got onto our horses and walked them back, the men following slow. When we got most to our men Walt told me to ride ahead and tell the men to mount up. I did so and one of the men just as soon as I left struck off into the brush. This one was a soldier, the other one said he was a citizen. We ran across one man in the same way but no sign of any company. Got into camp about four o'clock. Enjoyed it pretty well.

May 29 - Today rested from the trip. Captain Sherman brought in six men taken out in the country. Colonel Cornyn has gone into Tennessee and our expedition was to cover that.

May 30 - Nothing of any consequence today. The major is getting better. There is a great deal of sickness in the cavalry. Three men died within a week.

May 31 - No church today but things were quiet and still it seemed like Sunday. The pickets brought in three horses that the theives around the camps had stolen but they did not succeed in getting them. These are not soldiers but take from citizens and everyone. It is terribly lonesome. Every evening just as soon as it begins to grow dark I seem to forget everything but Ransoms death and I can hardly endure it. I want to cry but can't. Everything about it seems so strange and unreal. This life appears more and more like a stopping place where a man is obliged to halt against his own wishes. I can't pray at such times, all I can do is look up at the sky and say, "Oh God", there is such a longing for something to lean upon. Friends will not answer and if they would I have none there who can enter into these feelings. If God was only something material that I could see, a person that I could take by the hand and talk to. (It) seems to me it would be easy but my faith is so low. It is easy enough to believe that God is near and that he answers our requests but to feel it is not so easy. Heaven is now the only thing that is pleasent in my future. I have no heart to enter into the affairs of the time. All that makes them good and desirable seems to have been taken out for the amusements of camp although I join in them more than ever. There is no relish, the zest gone. It seems to me it is growing worse. I try not to be melancholy and succeed in appearing cheerful, but there is not an enjoyment that I don't think of his being absent. While we were out on the trip to Tuscumbia I could not help thinking how he (Ransom) would enjoy this thing or that and imagine him asking questions and talking of the ride with the confidence and trust that can be found only between brothers and although I <u>know</u> that he is enjoying a life as much higher than this as can be considered yet for all that on all these occasions I miss the companionship of a brother and I believe I always shall and it will throw a dark shadow over every pleasure in the future. There never was a brother that loved another as he did me. Oh God, it is so lonesome and I am so weak and sinful and mean and doubting, how can I lean on the promises in the Bible and trust them as I ought to. If father was here I think I should feel better. There is nothing that would give me so much pleasure as to hear that this war was closed. Talking with him and being with him I think I could grow into a more even and a better life. It is not often that I write this way but there is not a day passes without my having these thoughts. There was a deadness at first; I could not make it seem real to me. That is gone now and every day I have to suffer and choke back feelings that I hope I never shall again. I never can but once. I pray (to) God daily that that day may be as distant as possible. If father was gone I do not think I should be worth anything and would be like a ship without a rudder. There is no ambition in me to be free and for myself I would much rather be always under his guidance. I am perfectly willing to trust it.

June 1 - Some saddles came today and I think I can get one of the lot. Cornyn got over a hundred prisoners, 200 cattle, 100 horses, and 200 negros but came very near being taken. (They) would have been if he had not got back to the Tennessee under cover of the gun boats.

June 2 - Made a bunk and moved over. Walt began to be sick today.

June 3 - Walt worse. I sat up the first part of the night. It's typhoid fever. I had to make out the reports alone.

June 4 - Walt went to (the) hospital at (the) Sharpshooters. The noise in camp troubled him considerably. He will have (a) good place there.

June 5 - Monthly returns for April came in today for correction. I sent back for blanks, got them today and made a new return. Made inspection reports.

June 6 - Sent out report to inspector and at noon he came down himself. He said the report would be all right.

June 7 - Made out rolls. Muster in and muster out for the major and Doctor Gray helped me at night.

June 8 - The monthly had to be made out again. They had only marked part of the mistakes. Walt must have got a previous month and entered it for April. I straightened it (out) as well as I could and got ready to send (it) back. News came in that the Rebels were advancing on all sides and all the companies were sent out. At noon a flag of truce came in ostensibly to see about exchanging prisoners but really to find out the position. No one hurt.

June 9 - Company A went on a scout and Company E. Rained like fun. Fullerton sent back the tri-monthly. I fixed it to suit him but think it was right in the first place. Major said it was.

June 10 - Company C went to Burnsville in the afternoon and found plenty of the Rebels. They fired a few rounds and then fell back into camp. They put the number at two hundred. General Dodge sent a telegram - Send out all your cavalry. It was dark as any night could be and on the whole it was a risky piece of business. Captain Burdick was in command. He said he did not care about my going and I staid. He only expected to go out a few miles and wait till morning. I did not like the night trip anyway and thought I could stay in and go out in the morning.

June 11 - Sent out my semi-weekly. Found Murdock was going out to the columns with some men. I saddled my horse and went with him. I was all in a hurry and Murdock had already started and although I intended to speak to Major Fairfield about it I neglected to do it. We found the regiment coming in. Met them just beyond the picket post. Murdock said he would go on and reconoiter a little and I went with him. Just as we got across Patrick's cleared field where we could be seen for half a mile I saw a man on a horse ride out from behind a grainry and then ride back. I spoke to Murdock - "Isn't that a Rebel on that horse?". "Mabey it is a citizen". I had hardly said it when we turned the corner and there was a whole line facing us, thirty-five or fifty men at least. We were twelve. Murdock says they were a lot dismounted. They had their guns all ready and as soon as we turned the corner they fired. I could see each puff of smoke plain as light as it burst out of the gun. My horse whirled and when he came down he went most to his knees. This threw me out the neck. I grabbed both hands into his mane and was getting back when he fell again. This time it threw me off. I fell under his feet and he jumped over me (and) struck me on the legs with both feet. Neal could not manage his horse and was behind me. His (horse) came over me too before I could get out of the way. The Rebels charged full tilt right after the boys and passed me as I was getting up from the road; someone in the rear called to catch that fellow but they had to turn their horses around and dismount before they could get after me and by that time I was out of sight. Murdock says they called on me to surrender. I heard them yelling but thought it was their usual charge yell. I hid in the bushes and heard them coming and got up and changed locations. The woods were like this. The dotted spaces are woods. Their line was formed behind the houses and our boys retreated west up the hill.

(Map drawn and inserted at this point.)

I took into the woods in the south and then they followed into the little corner in the field. While I was there I saw one of them come back leading a horse. From here I crossed the road and went east for I could not go west without being seen. I stopped twice and rested and then lay down in the corner of the fence expecting to hear the column go by. At noon I heard eight shots fired but what they meant I could not tell. I kept quiet an hour longer and then started to find my way out. Once I came up to a creek, pulled the bushes apart, stepped out and in the other side not eight rods from the creek and in plain sight were four butternuts on the ground playing some game or other. I turned back tolerably quick. Another time I came to some women picking berries but heard them talking and avoided them. I struck the road and kept down it a little ways but thought it not quite safe and went off. I had not been in the brush three rods when I heard a man cross the bridge a few rods back. I went up to the fence of the field and saw the butternut. He went around the field. He might have been looking for me but perhaps only hunging cattle. I turned back and just as I struck the road again a man came from the other way. I went into the brush and missed them. After a couple of hours I got around to the same log that I had been on twice before. Then the sun came out and I got the direction and came on to the railroad just west of Scattertown three miles from camp. I was very tired as the vines, blackberries and woods were thick and matted so that sometimes I had to crawl on my hands and knees. I was pretty sore in several (places) where the horses hoofs had struck me. When I fell off I lost my hat, sabre, and spurs. I kept sheath and pistols and brought them in. Everybody was glad to see me when I came in. Shook hands with colonel, major and all of them. Five horses were lost and five boys taken. Most of them had to take to the woods and one by the name of Neal lay by the side of the road within reach of them as they passed him three or four times. They picked his gun up within four feet of him. Another running his horse over a bridge got his horse's leg broken off and sent him whirling into the brush and mud. I was mud and water all over and (my) hands (were) scratched all to pieces. Old Bacon had started a story that they called to me to surrender and Murdock told me to come on but I pulled up my horse and gave them my sabre and pistols. I soon fixed that story. There was some rumor of attack at night but nothing (came) of it. It was by all odds the most risky place I was ever in and the hardest days work I ever did. The hills were little short of mountains and the swamps full of vines. I did not feel afraid any of the time and at the last I was mad enough not to be taken, by one man at least. My horse, saddle and bridle, sabre and hat were the losses. Gains (were) scratched hands, half a dozen bruises and a pretty well tired out body. This is a map of the "situation":

(Map drawn and inserted.)

June 12 - Rested today and wrote a letter to father and one to Gilman. On Wednesday I wrote to Baker, Davis and father. Went up to see Walt. He is getting along slowly. Got a letter from father.

June 13 - Nothing of importance today. Eat dinner in the new mess - Baker, Goddy, Crittenden and I. Murdock made up the trouble about my cowardice by saying the last time that he saw me I was stopping my horse nearly half a mile from the corner, when I did not go fifty feet. Owens rode a horse of the same color and he was the one that Murdock saw. It is to bad to have to run the risk of courage and horses too.

June 14 - Three companies went out to Bear Creek today. I was up to the hospital and shaved Walt. While I was there and at work one of the men died. He was buried in the afternoon. Eat dinner or supper with the boys in the old mess.

June 15 - Sent in report today. Nothing of interest. Wrote a letter to Jennie Gilman.

June 16 - Today went to Corinth. Got a few things for mess (cost $1.75). Find that _____ _____ can not be mustered out and I am told Lieutenant Trammell and Grey. I was going to try for a commission. Eat dinner at one of the restaurants on Grey's expense. Burdick put out a bottle of cider. Co. got a negative for a photograph. Came home in an ambulance. It is reported that Colonel Cornyn has gone to Jackson with his force and will burn the place. Wherever I go I always think of Ransom being gone. No one to talk with. It seems harder every day.

June 17 - Made out an inspection return. Made details and kept busy all day. Had a hard storm in the afternoon. I lost my dinner and eat a pie instead. There was a rumor of four cannon being seen in the Kis Mills road. It proved to be government wagons. An order came today for the removal of all refugees. There was a good deal of rebellion but the thing will have to be done.

June 18 - Went up to see Walt. Found him improving. Strained my shoulder and have a bad diarrhea. I tried to get Mrs. Crittenden out of the mess. She cooks for our mess. There came an order for an eight days scout. (I) am out of (a) horse but think I can get one. There were over two hundred men mounted. Major said that he did not want me to go so I staid. Spencer commands and has some forty with him. Wrote a letter to cousin.

June 19 - There was a report today of (a) heavy force of cavalry and artillery advancing on the place. Went to majors mess this morning. Major and I rode out three or four miles to see if there was anything in it. Saw nothing.

June 20 - Nothing today. Got report of yesterday sent back because I put in Company G which belongs to the battalion but is not at this post. I was right (I) know I was but I can suit him.

June 21 - Nothing but read Dickens.

June 22 - Scout got back today. Came near being taken or at least badly whipped. Got twenty prisoners, a few horses but had to burn a wagon and leave three. Walt came down from hospital.

June 23 - Nothing today but a letter from E.A.

June 24 - Read Dickens a little.

June 25 - Raining all the time. Sent in reports today. Walt went to hospital.

June 26 - Got mess started today and drew twenty days rations.

June 27 - Sent in inspection reports.

June 28 - July 1 - Busy all these days making out reports.

July 2 - Letter from father. Busy making out reports.

July 3 - Busy making out reports.

July 4 - Company A of the Yates Sharpshooters got up a good dinner and asked old boys in. It was just as good as they could have done at home. After it was over they tried to get some speaking but did not succeed. In the afternoon they sung songs and finally pushed Fullerton and Anderson and myself on the stand. I did not want to speak, had nothing to say and said nothing. Some of the men from the other companies thought that I praised A Company to much and said to little about the other companies. Came very near having a fight over it and one fellow went to the guard house.

July 5 - One company (A) went out on scout to Burnsville. Just as they were crossing Yellow Creek while they were watering horses and some of the men dismounted, the Rebels came up from the bushes and poured a volley into them. It scattered the men immediately. Some few came direct to camp but the most of them took a round about way - three horses were killed, several wounded, one man was shot dead, another badly wounded and died in the night, two (are) missing (and are) supposed to have been wounded and taken prisoner. The battalion went out immediately but found nothing. Went to Burnsville.
    NOTE: William M. Murphy was the soldier killed in action at Yellow Creek.

July 6 - Vicksburg has been taken. Led Company D, went out about nine o'clock. About twelve a courier came in with the news that Shurtleff was attacked and wanted reenforcements.

July 7 - About one or half after, the battalion got started. The advance found the Rebel pickets posted at the same place that Shurtleff had been fired on. When they fired, major formed a line and waited awhile (and) then fell back beyond the mill and formed another line but they would not attack us. About eight, major advanced again, (and) threw out skirmishers on the hill this side of Patrick's. They found nothing until they came to the creek. Here there was some firing. One of our men (was) wounded and all of them thought one Rebel killed. The major said as long as he thought it safe, then fell back to the mill again. We learned at night that there were some 300 in the swamp and 200 over in Scattertown two miles north. I felt quite sick going without breadfast and no sleep. Major sent me in at noon and I was glad of it. Infantry had gone out to scattertown. Major Johnson had run in on (the) corral and taken one company and quite a lot of horses and Cornyn was enroute after him. At night the teams went out and I went back. They took out a days provisions and I supposed that they were going to stay but when I got there found that they were only waiting for the infantry to come on the cars and then were coming back. As soon as we got back (we) found another order to leave at two o'clock. I staid up all night getting rations, ammunition and giving the orders. I started the men at two but they did not leave much before four.

July 8 - Cornyn came back with captain and two privates killed and eighteen or twenty wounded. The Rebels suffered more than ours. The Alabama was in Iuka and saw three of the dead Rebels. Our boys got in just after dark. The news came in that a heavy force was advancing and the place attacked. It is certain that they have been crossing troops over the Tennessee for some time.

July 9 - Made out reports today. Got a letter from E.A. Forgot to mention receipt of things from on the seventh, and letter from Miss Fisher and Thomas.

July 10 - Nothing of any importance. got letter from cousin.

July 11 - Drill. Got Burnside carbines.

July 12 - Nothing of interest. Sent a letter to Miss Fisher and Thomas.

July 13 - Got a letter from Jennie Gilman. Picked some balckberries while (I) was out looking for place for hospital. George Kellogg appointed as regimental commissary.

July 14 - Had drill in the afternoon. At work on ordnance reports.

July 15 - Bailey sent up work that I could be mustered by making out rolls. Had a spell of down heartedness in the evening thinking over what this war has cost me. It seems harder to bear every day and camp is so practical, (it) cares so little for feelings. You must be like the rest, laugh and talk without feeling like it.

July 16 - Saddled up at nine to cut off the retreat of Biffle who had been whipped at Jackson and was trying to make a junction with Roddey. We went out to Yellow Creek and found ourselves more than twelve hours behind time. The country was better settled than I had seen before. Got into camp at dark. Joe Ford offered me 2nd Lieutenant in his company.

July 17 - Nothing of consequence.

July 18 - Went to Corinth to get mustered, but mustering officer to drunk to work. Got a little colored boy for mess.

July 19 - Made out reports.

July 20 - Nothing different.

July 21 - Wrote letters to Hank Jenner and cousin and E.A.

July 22 - Not much on hand.

July 23 - Whole company went to Corinth to witness the execution of one of Company D who deserted to the enemy some three weeks since. Day (Walt) did not go down, his horse was lame. I had to take his place. We moved around the ground and formed on one side of a square, one side of infantry, on another artillery, the third and the fourth left open. Johnson was brought to the line in a wagon. (A) brass band playing march, and soldiers in front and rear, chaplain with him in the wagon. They walked around the three sides of the square and then back to the center. Johnson was dressed in a white shirt, butternut pants drawn up to his knees and a slouched hat. He did not look up during the whole time and kept a hankerchief over his mouth to conceal his emotions. It had entirely unmanned him. The chaplain said prayers and the order for execution was read to the regiments. I had to read it to the Alabama (men). Some of our own men were detailed to preform the execution. Either from some excitement or want of drill, one or two of the men fired first, but the rest fired before the man fell and almost every ball struck him. He was sitting on his coffin and fell back over it. The balls had taken effect in his neck and breast. The scene was solumn but it did not seem to effect the soldiers that witnessed it. They are a careless set. The men had been captured and enlisted. He was thought to be a doubtful case and along with Woodruff and Brown was examined. Brown and Johnson were allowed to enlist and Woodruff was retained. Brown also deserted taking arms and everything with him.
NOTE: Alex J. Johnson had been ordered shot by General Dodge for deserting. The Brown mentioned was William M. Brown.

Got mustered and bought some things. Major came back immediately with the regiment. Joe Palmer detained me until he got so drunk that they put him in the guard house. I got an order for his release and started home with him. Got to hill and Joe tumbled off dead drunk. We left him and came in. I told major of it but he would not send for him. Captain Burdick was drunk in the morning and major left him at the post picket under guard. I noticed him first at the spring. He would clutch at the rains and weave around so that I thought at times he was going to fall. When he started off he had to clutch the saddle to keep from falling. As soon as I told the companies to close up, I rode forward and asked the major "Have you noticed Captain Burdick? He is so drunk he can hardly sit his horse. If you don't do something with him he will disgrace the whole regiment." He said that he had just then noticed him and asked "What is it best to do?" "Would you leave him under guard?" I said there ought to be something done about it. At the first post his horse turned around with him and I thought he was going to fall but he straightened up and rode on. Doctor Stuart made the remark that Kellogg had held him up for a mile or so. At the picket by the breastworks major left him under arrest. He is a smart man and a good man if he would let liquor alone, but this has ruined him. Most probably he will be dismissed (from) the service for this.

July 24 - Saddled up and off at six en route for Iuka and Bear Creek. Advance ran into the Rebel pickets this side of Iuka and charged them into the place. The order in reference to falling out was given to the companies and there was no trouble from this cause. We found the pickets again on the little stream this side of Bear and again on the ridge. We went down to the flat. Company F deployed and Company B took in after them. There was smart firing for a few minutes. You could hear the bullets whistle and they were just about the right height. When the skirmishers came out they brought a man shot through the body. He was up at the first house. We heard there were six regiments the other side of the creek and the sooner one departed the better. We went down on the Boonville Road, found our picket only after dark. Got into the swamp and run around back and forth about half the night. I was so tired and sleepy I could hardly sit on my horse. Some of the companies got lost. We had to go single file to keep together. The road was nothing but a cattle path and hardly that. Got into camp about three o'clock in the morning.

July 25 - Eat, drank and rested.

July 26 - Cavalry went out to guard the fords on Yellow Creek, one company in each place. 2000 Rebels crossed at Savannah and Dodge is going to try and capture some of them.

July 27 - Made out a morning report and wrote a letter to father. Went to Yellow Creek.

July 28 - Today we are stationed as reserve. Went down the creek and major stationed one company at Billings (old) Ford. At night he sent me to station men at Hubbards Ford. Men were to be taken from Billings Ford (young). Lost the way and went about two miles to far and had to return. Found another ford two miles below the Hubbard and major sent some of Company D to guard it. Did not get around until long after dark. We were at Reynolds Ford and about a mile below us was Company F. Part of them at night went to the ford below Billings (old) and with part of D stood guard two miles above. F was (at) another ford. Company G (was) in charge. The remainder of the troops with the 5th Ohio were at Burnsville and above. The remainder of the troops with the 5th Ohio were at Burnsville and above. The line was nearly 25 miles long. No blanket first night, slept very well but hungry.

July 29 - Some of the fords blockaded and companies thrown together. F came to Reynolds. Boys got some honey. I killed a sheep and lived well on mutton, green corn and honey. Walt came up today and slept more comfortably. No enemy yet in sight. Captured two straglers.

July 30 - Major started to camp with escort of four or five. About half a mile from where we stopped, he was fired into by some 15 or 20 guerrillas and one of the men was shot through the leg and hip, horse killed. One ball through major's hat and one on sabre sheath. We saddled up in a hurry and went down to the place the company was deployed but found nothing. They had broken down the bushes to get a rest and still had only hit one man and the whole squad was not more than six or seven rods from them. Major at first said that he did not want me to go on with him but now he said I might. Staid at Glendale about an hour and then rode back. After dark got all the companies together and left for Chambers Creek, twelve miles. Made a man get up and show us the way. Went to sleep without anything to eat.

July 30 - Spent the day at the creek getting what we could to eat. I cooked some apples in a tin pail and major, Day, Walt and I made a scouting dinner in good shape.

August 1 - Went to Snake Creek to overshot mills about seven miles from Savannah. Two companies of 5th Ohio went with us. Some of the men went above us and some below. Major and I made a supper of mush and sugar. Day went back at Monterey, horse given out.

August 2 - Heard that Forrest was crossing yesterday morning at Chalk Bluffs and major marched there. Found that the Rebels crossed at Swallow Bluff, 14 miles below. Started back and met couriers three miles from Adamsville with orders to go to Yellow Bluff. Swallow Bluff was meant and the major finally decided to go to the ford. The horses are in poor condition. Mine has been sick all the time and today I sent him back and took a mule from Neal and went on. Went nine miles towards Swallow Bluff. The whole distance 25. Found forage and camped.

August 3 - Went to the ford. Met a squad of 1st Tennessee under Lieutenant Smith and he went on with us as a guide. The Rebels had crossed but stragglers were going over all the while but there were guerrillas enough to warn them. Where we stopped to feed, the boys took most all that was at the place. The women claimed to be Union but Smith said it was Secesh. Moved back to the camp of last night and took the rest of the Secesh's corn and some three or four mules. Most of the men through here are Union. They will shake hands with us and offer to guide and go with us anywhere.

August 4 - Went back for home. Got the order at overshot mill. Here there was a Rebel that had been ordered off by General Dodge and was just moving off. I went to work and opened one of his beehives. The boys followed up and soon the thing went up. Camped at the spring north of Monterey. Nothing to eat. I tried to catch a pig, did not get him. Cooked some corn and eat that. Major no better off.

August 5 - Came into camp. Found a letter from Pratt and Gilman.

August 6 - Rested. Wrote up some reports.

August 7 - Nothing of much importance.

August 8 - One of our men (from) Company D was shot by a guerrilla while in swimming just out of the lines. Not dangerous. Got letter from Hopkins. Made out reports.

August 9 - At work on Fri (?) months. Took all the forenoon.

August 10 - Ruled out some line markers.

August ll - August 13 - Office work.

100

August 14 - Went to Corinth. Got some things for new mess. Eat dinner at Captain Carpenters. Got muster roll back from W. Hoffman.

August 15 - Nothing. Got letter from Hank.

August 16 - Sharpshooter boys wanted me to go out in the country with them. Had a lot of watermelons and _____ on a butternut that lied to us about the distance. Got wet.

August 17 - Letter from cousin. Wrote to Hank. Nothing.

August 18 - From August 17 to September 1 regular routine of the office. Nothing of any special interest. Received two letters from Hank. Every night after crowd has left my tent, I get to thinking over the first days of my enlistment and then of Ransoms death. It has taken out the large share of my enjoyment for life. It does not seem to me that he can be dead but will meet me when I go home and so he will if I go home to Heaven. The prospect looks gloomy after father is gone. There will be the children to care for but no one to sympathize with me in any understanding. The place can never be filled, but I believe after the present there will be a glorious future. Time passes so rapidly I shall soon be with them. But while I am waiting, his voice and actions are always before me. I think of him on a scout and how this would suit his disposition. I think of him with every letter I receive. The men I am surrounded by are mostly rough and infidel but my faith does not waver in the least. Sometimes I do things that are not right but this does not affect trust in the Bible and God.

September 1 - Our new arrangements are much more pleasant than the old. Mrs. Crittenden cooks for us and is a very good cook, but one doubtful thing I have noticed, (she) is using the wash dish to cook in, or just as she does any other dish. Paymaster came today. Will pay off the companies tomorrow. Got my discharge papers from the Yates Sharpshooters made out.

September 2 - Paymaster paid me $52. No bounty, but pay due from Sharpshooters settled. Nothing going on of any consequence.

September 3 - September 7 - Nothing of consequence. Went out once on a short scout.

September 8 - The news was brought in today that our men gone south had been attacked on their return near Jacinto. What was left of the batallion went out but the thing was over. The five companies were separated, 3 in the rear and two in advance and the rest of our men followed them. When they came up the Rebels went in every direction. Barnet came in with the (reports), and when they came to find out that the Rebels were not as numerous as they had expected, they put the man under arrest for bringing in a false report, when it was the same that Cameron himself would have brought if he had come in when Barnet did. A case of punishing a private to save an officer.

September 9 - (Not reported.)

September 10 - Sent in semi-weekly (reports). Made out the reports of transportation etc. for Inspector General. Got an order to be ready to move at short notice. Day went into town to get carbines and pistols.

September 11 - Order came this afternoon to move at sundown. I got myself ready but just before night, Fullerton sent over an order for some reports that I could not make out and so (?) major did not go. After dark the train came down with 300 carbines and 400 revolvers. Some of them I issued to troops that were left to bring them up. Day did not come back.

September 12 - Finished up reports. In the afternoon report came in that there was some horses out in the country a few miles. Major got together eighteen or twenty and sent them out under me. The horses were the same that Company F got yesterday. Captain George, Captain Smith and two lieutenants came in with flag of truce. Day came back. Colonel Spencer came to Corinth.

September 13 - Our men came back today. They went out to Bears Creek, fired into the woods two or three times and came back. Went out with flag of truce. George is a blackleg looking fellow, rides a cream colored horse. Cololen Spencer came down. The flag of truce brought in 7 wounded men, arms off, legs off, hands shot and etc. A man in Company E was shot through the head tonight. Accident.

September 14 - The man that was shot yesterday died today.
>   *NOTE:* *This was probably Jacob G. Settlemire who died at Corinth, Mississippi on September 14, 1863.*

September 15 - Colonel Spencer started to Corinth with Captain Shurtleff and two men. Ran into an ambush of fifteen or twenty men and got chased back to camp. The same gang captured two of the Sharpshooters and an ambulance. Captain Shurtleff shot one of them but it is not known how badly.

September 16 - Inspecting Officer came down today and the regiment was paraded for inspection. The regiment made a good show. Books in the office all right.

September 17 - Received a good letter from father, one from Hank and Davis. Answered
fathers.

September 18 - Had an incident in the camp. Jack a sailor soldier in Company F stole some shiskey from commissary department. Major detected him in the act and was going to punish him but he was to drunk.

September 19 - One hundred horses came today. An order came to make Edwards of the 122nd Illinois Infantry a second lieutenant of company. This throws me out. Edwards has been a clerk in Corinth. The company now numbers 31 men.

September 20 - Took a ride with Barker. General Carr came down about noon on train, ordered a scout to Tuscumbia, but it was postponed in order to give a chance for horses to be shod. Had a family jar in the evening. Crittenden got mad at Rolla and was going to send him to Corinth. I told him he was not chief and other plain truths. Ford tells me that the appointment of Edwards is only temporary, that he is to be the 1st lieutenant of the next company raised. Went to Tuscumbia. Three companies went to the creek, drove in the Rebel pickets (and) camped near by all night. Captured 5 prisoners. Lieutenant Tramel brought in 100 men, mostly men for the service. He has been gone about two weeks and captured a lieutenant and six or seven prisoners and a Rebel mail. This was all of any consequence. Crittendon left the mess on the 8th. His wife had gone home. Troops are coming in very fast. This is all the record from the 20th to the 8th of October.

October 8 - Colonel Spencer went to Iuka and all the officers. Austin that I used to know at Hillsdale (Michigan) came over to see me a short time, went out in the country, got a chicken or two and some cabbages and etc. had a good ride.

October 9 - Went over to see Austin. Found Capatain Packard that used to be at Hillsdale and Spring Arbor (Michigan).

October 10 - Went over after chestnuts with Barker. Horses came today from Memphis. I tried one but after I had made the change, Grey said I would have to take it back, very crusty. Got a letter from father and wrote an answer. Booth came back.

October 11 - Traded horses with Captain Tramel and got the Brown that I wanted. Yesterday in the afternoon Barker and I went out in the country and had quite a time. Barker shot at some sheep and the woman that owned them came out and gave us a lecture on the enormity of the sin, but as we did not kill any and then offered to pay for anything that they had to sell, we did not feel very guilty. News came tonight that the Rebels had captured a train that General Sherman came up on.

October 12 - Report of yesterday is contradicted. General Sherman was not captured but took shelter in a stockade at Collierville and the force at that point beat off the Rebels. Got my horse shod. Letter from Hank, a real open hearted letter. Hank is a diamond in the rough.

October 13 - Scout is postponed in order to get two months pay now due. Four companies yet in Iuka.

October 14 - Men came in today. Paymaster arrived in the evening went out to graze my horse in the afternoon. Horse not well, not fit to go on scout.

October 15 - Got two months pay today. Sent home $40. Sent to town by Day for leggins.

October 16 - Crittenden went down early in the morning and took an oven that he had paid for but which had been charged to the mess. Barker went to Company A after it. Got into a row with Crit, knocked tables over and etc. Lieutenant Smith ordered some of his men to arrest him. Barker made a run to Company D quarters. Lieutenant Slaughter followed with a club but stopped before he came to Barker. All of them came down to the office. Captain Chandler in the first place was going to have them arrested but finally concluded not to. The oven he ordered to be brought back. Crit. drew a knife but did not hurt anyone. When we came down to the office Barker picked up a pistol but I got him to put it down. Some of them thought I gave it to him and Smith said that he should prefer charges.

October 17 - Nothing of any consequence except 29 recruits brought in by Company D. Company H got most of them.

October 18 - Thought that Spencer would give me an opportunity to get the order for 2nd lieutenant of H company but he says that he is going to leave it to an election. I do not much care. We start tomorrow and my horse is so lame that he can hardly walk. It is going to be a dangerous trip but if it should turn out disasterous to me, I think it will be my gain. God and Heaven are realities to me and poor as I am I believe that there is home for me after the thing of this.

October 19 - Left camp about 10. My horse was not able to travel and for awhile I thought that I was not (going to be) able to get one, but Mr. Smith gave me his to ride and in that way I got off. Mr. Smiths was not shod on one hind foot and I went up to the shop to get him shod. They only got two shoes on and then the columns started. I saddled and followed up. On the road we passed the ruins of several houses burned by the Jayhawkers in retaliation for the shooting of two of their men from these houses. Camped at Pollards where I drew the potatoes from the oven. Pettis and Steve and I went down to get something to eat. Got some dried beef and chickens. The woman was going to knock Steve over with a club but he got the chicken. Camped there at night and had another time taking things.

October 20 - Went as far as Vinsons (Vincent's) Crossroads today. Wagons all the time behind. At noon Lieutenant Latty and ten of us went to McRaes and found one of his men. McRae was rich. (He) owned a large house, two or three stores, and plantation. On the whole (his was) the best outfit I have seen in the South. Most of their negroes had run away, some were in our camps. Mrs. McRae said she did not want to see them any more. They are pro-slavery and Union. Got several recruits near here. Captured a gun and two uniform coats near here. Stopped to feed at Daniels. He had robbed some of our men and colonel gave them permission to burn his house. Everything was destroyed. It looked rough enough. Where we camped at night was at a Union scouts but when we halted we thought it was Rebel. Corn is very scarce in the country.

October 21 - Country getting worse and worse. Went through a piece of woods about 20 miles with only one or two houses. I tried to keep up the wagons, and did two of them for the most of the forenoon, finally one tipped over and when I started again found that one shoe was off and horse getting lame. Tonight fed again from a Union mans corn, but stopped at a Rebel house. Gray gave reciepts for the stuff. Barker lives with us and tonight had a sheep. We live pretty well.

October 22 - Tonight got to Charley Kaights, stoney and rough country as I ever saw. A detachment was sent out and burned Allens factory, about 120,000 worth of goods. Factory employed 50 hands. Horse getting worse and changed with a sick man that wanted to ride in the wagon. At noon some of Company L went in advance to Underwoods. Got several horses and brandy, negroes and apples. When we started again I secured a horse at the same place. One wagon broke down and was burnt before we reached Kaights. Old Charley lives in a narrow strip of land between two hills so steep that wagons could not go down. How he makes a living I can not see. The strip of land is not more than 20 rods wide. Charley lives in caves outside. Took two wagons (for) government in the afternoon. Were hauling corn.

October 23 - Rained today. Burned the wagons and packed as much stuff as we could on the mules. The rest was left at Charleys beside pistol and cannon ammunition. Quite a number of recruits came in. Intended to get to Jasper but only got within ten miles of the place. Stopped at Lovealls. I was in the advance and Tramel pretended to be Rebel and the man to my understanding was that in reality, but when the column came up they said he was a Union man and placed a guard over the house. Dr. Stewart was left at noon, to sick to ride. In the afternoon met Thristomen. Shook hands and God Bless You. They told us to go ahead. Colonel was sick in the evening. The advance went two miles ahead of the column before any notice of halt was given. Here I got a fine mare and led her back to the column. Also got a coffee pot, a thing we have hard work to get. Slept in a corn crib.

October 24 - Turned back in the morning, a disapointment to most of the men. Raining as usual. Took up Doctor Stewart on the route. In the afternoon met four Rebels almost face to face. They run and the advance with which I was traveling gave them chase but did not catch them. The old man runs pretty well. At Underwoods I filled a bag with apples and chickens and got corn for feed. Went two miles further and there camped for the night. Had a good supper, apple sauce.

October 25 - Started about four o'clock. Guide took us right through the woods. Stopped near to Bull Mountain at Wallace. Caught a chicken also Steve. Eat with colonel and staff. All of us slept under the shed. Sung and talked late into the night. Some of the men went two miles ahead to a house, Wothingtons and played smash generally.

October 26 - Started about six in the morning. Heard that there were plenty of Rebels, 5,000 of them ahead of us at Vinsons (Vincent's) Crossroads. We kept on however and heard that there was only Morelans Battery and so pushed forward. At the crossroads did not find any tracks and thought the thing a hoax. Four or five miles from there we found a squad of six out in the field. They all run. Fed our horses at Pattersons. His wife was a rough woman. Spencer told her we were the children of Israel bringing the plague on them. Colonel left me to guard the cotton. Barker came down to burn it. We went about two miles. I had not got to the front when several shots were fired. I pushed ahead and found the two guns on a little rise of ground and the gunners loading. (Companies) F, B, and G had been deployed to the left of the road, E and A to the right and H was just going in. The road runs north and south. On the right was a narrow field 30 or 40 rods wide for almost half a mile, only broken by a strip of underbrush about 20 rods through. Companies L and D were put into the open field on the right, at first facing to the east and then L faced to the north. I and K were in a similar position on the west of the road. C was rear guard. Pack mules and refugees (were) also to the rear. Their line was also longer than ours and they were outflanking us. The two guns were brought back to the house in the middle of the field. (Companies) E, A, and H were soon driven out and the Rebs began to fire on Companies L and D. They stood the fire for awhile and then retreated. I was letting down the fence at the time they began to fire on Company L and had some trouble to get on my horse. This was the only time that I was in much danger. Orders were sent to B, F, and G to fall back and soon they came tearing. Stenburg was killed, Swift wounded and Chandler killed. Company L was formed again dismounted at the little strip of woods in the center of the field. The Rebels were now in plain view in the corn field but the artillery soon drove them out and the column then fell back the length of the field. The refugees tried to get by and the pack mules were running everywhere. I tried to get the men into shape and some of them would come and some would not. At this place (Companies) D, K, and C were left to check the advance of the Rebels. The pack train and refugees had gone on the wrong road and I went for them. Company I had the advance but the guide was gone. I found him after awhile and the column moved on at a smart trot. Refugees and loose men of all kinds doing their best to get ahead. Colonel and all of us that cared anything for the regiment were trying to get them to fall into the road. I succeeded in keeping some of them from going ahead of the guns. Half a mile southwest of the field and just after the guns had crossed a little brook, the advance was fired into. I told the colonel of it and he came to the front of the column, then took a road going still more to the south. I staid in the rear of the guns, and did what I could to keep the men back. About this time the Rebels charged on the rear and the companies left there gave them a volley that disabled a great many. I did not see it but the Adjutant was there and told me how it was. We crossed an open field and (went) into a swamp. There the men had to get into shape for the bushes were so thick that they could not get ahead. At the end of the swamp was a small stream. The men in front of the guns said: "Up the stream", "Up the stream", and I went ahead of the guns to the place where they ought to come out but after getting into the creek they got tangled and here the guns were left. We then pushed ahead. Only a short distance from this the woods became more open and another rush was made for the front. At this point Captain Shurtliff came ahead, McWright with him, and tried to get the men to halt. He told the colonel the guns had been left. Spencer then drew a pistol and tried to form a line. As soon as I saw him, I whirled my horse and called the men that I knew to help form the line but there was no use. They had heard a few shots in the right and then spread out each side of the colonel and when I turned I could not see him but the men had divided into two streams. The left hand one was headed by the colonels guide and I went with that division. (We) had only gone a short distance when ten volleys were fired from the right and rear of us. Several men are believed to have been killed at this place, Lieutenant Perry among the rest. He and Tramel had both acted bravely in the field, encouraging the men to hold their ground. Captain Tramel and Ford both passed me. Lieutenant Snelling rode with me quite a ways. (I) got separated from him at a bridge that we had to cross. We went right into the woods away from roads of any kind. Had three or four shots fired at us once after leaving the hill. A man (who was) shot through the hand and body rode with us six or seven miles and then stopped at a house. After we had gone fifteen miles, we were only seven from the field from this point. Henry

Kellogg's boy guided us to Iuka. We stopped once to feed and then kept on, having heard that 300 had just gone down looking for us. Three miles from Iuka we halted and fed. It was four o'clock and we had rode 75 miles.

   NOTE: The following soldiers were killed at Vincent's Cross Roads: Marshal H. Byrd, Erasmus D. Chandler, James Mack Cooper, James K. Morphis, James Perry, Phillip A. Stenberg/Sternburg, James C. Swift (died November 1 or 2, 1863), and William Tyler.

October 27 - Went into Iuka in the morning, drew rations and forage for 122 man and horses. Colonel Spencer got into Glendale a little later with about the same number. Dodds not heard from. The old man is used up but quartermaster says I can sell her if she recruits and I got Ned to take care of her. (I) was intending to go to Glendale but train did not go. Slept in the car.

October 28 - Came down in the morning. Pretty hungry, had no supper last night. Rested during the day. Nothing heard from Dodds.

October 29 - Nothing today. Spencer went to Iuka. The boys tell some funny stories of the affair. One man got thrown, and jumped on behind another horse. The fellow in front said: "Oh Lord, do get off", but he could not push him off, nor coax him off and at last said: "Well if anybody is shot in the back it will be you". The colonel told one man to halt or he would blow his brains out. The fellow stopped for a few seconds and then said "It is only a bullet anyway", and away he went.

October 30 - Nothing of any consequence. A few men coming in all the time. Lieutenant Swift still living. Colonel Spencer is to be chief of staff. The sharpshooters are ordered to move. A second major has been appointed, formerly adjutant in the 2nd Iowa. Wrote a letter to father. It is said that the railroad is to be abandoned and the Tennessee used as the base of supplies. Lieutenant colonel heard from at Iuka.

October 31 - Rained last night and all day today. Major Godfrey is a strict disciplinarian, an orderly came very near being put under arrest for failing to bring his detail for patrol at the proper time. Had a game or two of chess with McGaughey. He slept all night with me.

November 1 - Lieutenant Swift reported dead.

November 2 - Nothing of interest.

November 3 - Sharpshooters moved today. They belong in General Dodge's Division and are to be Provost Guard. Willard wanted me to take charge of some express that he was expecting and some of the boys wanted pictures etc. They went out with cheering and in good spirits. Eat dinner at McGaughey's today.

November 4 - Today all the women were ordered to move. This looks like our soon leaving.

107

November 5 - Made out morning reports from the 1st. Had a hard job of it. Received a letter from father. He had noticed a report in the Tribune to the affect that the regiment was either captured or cut to pieces and he was very anxious in consequence.

November 6 - Had something of an excitement. In the afternoon got everything ready to move and two trains came down to take Companies G and C to Corinth. I managed to get the tents and tables on the cars as well as the bunk. It took 23 cars to haul the goods of the regiment and refugees together. Had nothing but overcoat and felt very cold. There were some very amusing scenes. Some of the women wanted their husbands relieved from picket so that they could accompany them to Corinth.

November 7 - Arrived at Corinth about four o'clock. Cold enough. As soon as it was daylight the refugees tumbled out of the cars and began to cook. It looked more like an emigrant train than a regiment of soldiers. (We) were at work all day moving up the things to the camp of the 50th Illinois rather poor quarters but can't be arranged. Eat with the teamsters.

November 8 - Guard mounting was dismounted and a great deal of style about it. Colonel Dodds has several of the men tied up for being absent in town with out leave. He put Lieutenants Gardner and Holly under arrest at Glendale for not having their details made promptly. All details have to be made in writing. Got orders today to be ready to move tomorrow.

November 9 - Packed everything and saw it started to the train. Eat dinner at the restaurant. Rode one of Major Fairfield's horses to Camp Davis (Camp Davies) rather than wait for the train. Had nothing to eat at supper but Booth came around with a can of oysters and this was some help. The stockade at Camp Davis incloses about ten acres, perhaps 12 - and very strong built. The barracks are log and very comfortable, the best I have ever seen. The colonel's quarters are a frame house good enough for home. The adjutant has a room by himself. I have an office and a sleeping room. Two more orderlies are also detailed. Fire places and windows in all the houses, everything comfortable. They had a theatre, bakery, etc., and excellent hospital. Slept without any cover, feet to the fire, cold as the dickens.

November 10 - Train did not come until aftrnoon. Came very near starting before it arrived. Old Gab got supper just at night. Built a fire and got things straightened up in the office.

November 11 - Heavy fatigue details today. Had to assist in guard mounting. Old Gab deserted us and about 8 o'clock I went down to get some information on the subject and found Gab among the missing. He had gone to work for himself. I made the gentleman cook breakfast, but dinner and supper were very slim. Gray made some disturbance about our taking the sutler shop but we kept it.

November 12 - Guard mounting again, better than yesterday. Setphen cooked breakfast. Dinner and supper Scott cooked. Booth is going to take charge of the mess. Got a cook at night after supper. Major Godfrey took his battalion out with one days rations. Lieutenant Hinds came in with ten men. He had enlisted 116 but they did not dare to come on with him. Kaight had been killed and several other men. Some of the stragglers from the fight of the 26th. Major Fairfield came up on the 10th. He asked me today to try to get the place in Company H. I did not care but very little about it. It will extend my time almost seven months. Colonel Spencer asked me if I intended to run. I told him I should if there appeared any desire to have me from the men themselves. The election will take place in a day or two.

November 13 - Nothing but the usual routine.

November 14 - Good cook and things again pretty good shape. Labor pretty confining.

November 15 - Last night a man by the name of Morrison, a citizen, was killed only a quarter of a mile from the picket post. Some of the soldiers most probably. They came to rob but he resisted and (he) gave to them a severe wound with an axe and then they shot him. In the evening firing was heard near Danville. Some men were sent out to investigate. They came upon the 3rd Michigan (Cavalry) in the woods and fired upon them before they knew what force it was. The Michigan men had chased some guerrillas and one of them had turned on them and shot one through the head.

November 16 - Tom Barnet had charges preferred against him today for robbery and was sent to the guard house. He is a systematic horse thief and deserves hanging.

November 17 - Inspection today. Had to make reports for the various branches.

November 18 - Today the four men that were in the gang that killed Morrison were taken near Glendale and they did not try to get away. They had an examination today. They did not shoot until the old man struck at them with an axe while trying to drive them out of the house. Telegraph operator came today.

November 19 - Some of Morrison's children came in again today to identify (the killers). Rebel lieutenant came in this morning, had become tired of Southern life and wanted to go north.

November 20 - Guard not all present. Walt told me that and I had better see to the matter and I replied that I was not a company orderly. Made out a tri-monthly. Paymaster is to be down tomorrow. Mustering officer was to have come today but did not. Captain Ford said that he would have an election, but for some reason did not. Made out some muster-in rolls for colonel. Got $1.00 for them.

November 21 - Report of yesterday came back today incorrect. I had marked one man absent sick in the column of commissioned officers. Paymaster came in the afternoon. Colonel Spencer also.

November 22 - Did not get pay on account of it's being Sunday.

November 23 - Paymaster paid us today. Nothing of any interest.

November 24 - Edwards gave me my order assigning me to duty as second lieutenant (of) H. Captain Wood had an election on sunday and there was no opposition.

November 25 - Went to town on Walt's horse. All of the men that had horses in the regiment went out on scout with Colonel Mizner's men going to Okolona. Bit, belt, hat, etc.

November 26 - November 29 - Nothing but usual routine.

November 30 - Regiment came in and one company of the 3rd Michigan. (They) brought 35 prisoners, had killed some fifteen. They reported a large force at Okolona, New Albany and Tupelo.

December 1 - Nothing but office work. Received a letter from Hank and J.J. Hopkins.

December 2 - Wrote a letter to Hank and sent one to J.J. Had a good ride in the evening. Rebels are reported advancing on Corinth but it is very doubtful and they will hardly dare to attack Corinth although they are 3 to one. Got a letter from Father.

December 3 - Gave invoices to the ladies to buy rations, while Day made out reports.

December 4 - Helped make reports in the evening. Colonel had a couple of girls in his room, gay time. Rebels made an attack on Moscow but were repulsed. Colonel Hatch of the 2nd Iowa (Cavalry) mortally wounded. Reported that Meade had captured __?__ Army Corps, Grant captured 15,000 and had headquarters at Dalton, Georgia. Had no papers or letters, train did not come through.

December 5 - Bought a horse of some refugees $55. Colonel said the horse would be taken by the government. 29 refugees and soldiers came in last night.

December 6 - Lukens came in to the office tonight but we are to work the thing together for a few days. Got a letter from Gilman.

December 7 - Made out some monthlies. Wrote a sesational dispatch on telegraph paper to the effect that Moscow was threatened, and if the Rebels advanced on Corinth we were to evacuate and join General Dodge. The thing spread like wildfire and when I came back from dinner two or three of the companies were getting their things together for a move. Sutler packing, and a disturbance generally. Pettis (sp?) sent a telegraph message to Corinth and sent for a team to draw his cotton from stockade to the railroad. Got a letter from Father. The road is not open to Memphis yet but they bring the mail (by) horseback the distance that the track is torn up.

December 8 - Nothing worth mentioning.

December 9 - Wrote a letter to E.A.

December 10 - (Nothing written.)

December 11 - Wrote out descriptive book for Captain Ford.

December 12 - Went to company. Wrote out ordnance (reports).

December 13 - Read and did nothing in particular.

December 14 - Went out on drill, made one blunder but otherwise got along very well.

December 15 - Nothing. Wrote out December book.

December 16 - Companies B and H went on scout to burnt mills. Captain Ford in command of both companies, and I'm in command of "H". Peck did not go. Started about two o'clock, reached the place about 11 o'clock. Object of expedition to meet Tramel if possible and at least bring one of the men that was wounded and laying at one of the houses. Started back immediately, reached home about 5. Rode nearly 60 miles.

December 17 - Rested today from the trials of war.

December 18 - Officer of the day today not at guard mount. Asked old O.D. if it was guard call that sounded. He said no such call and I went in to breakfast. It was a very cold day but clear and had a good ride at 12 - midnight.

December 19 - Orders came tonight to be ready to move at 8 tomorrow.

December 20 - Hoped that I should be allowed to stay in order to muster, but was detailed as Adjutant and had to saddle up. Got to Corinth and found orders to wait until next day. Murdock said that he would take my place and Major gave me leave to return. Colonel Spencer goes to Pulaski tomorrow. (He) is to be Chief-of-Staff for General Dodge.

December 21 - Wrote out muster and forms.

December 22 - Nothing of any note.

December 23 - Major Fairfield told me something of Southern life that I had never believed before. He said that he had known of a young man being rejected until by passing a night with the ladys maid he satisfied the lady that there was something of the animal in her composition. The major had a mulatto boy that while he was on the plantation and had been made to gratify the animal passions of his masters two daughters. It does not seem possible but the major said that he had seen the girls and had been told of several white women giving birth to black children. The same requests that at the North would be considered positive insults are here generally

111

decided by the consequence of time and place. Major said that when Mrs. Chester went home, some blacklegs made a plan to carry her to some house in Cairo and by the help of some drugs ruin her, and would have done (it) if he had not been along. This is worse than I ever believed possible.

December 24 - Made out some muster rolls. Nothing doing.

December 25 - Christmas! Went to Corinth in the afternoon in company with Lukens. Left out house at colonel's. In the evening went to a party at the refugee camp of which Coe has charge. It was a very silly affair. From here we went to a negro dance in the village. It was the opinion of three of us that the negros had more intelligence and more taste. In reply to a question as to where he worked, one of the boys about fifteen replied, "I do not work for anyone, I am a soldier sir; drummer for the 1st Tennessee". It was spoken with all the pride and smartness that the palest of pale faces could assume. At the refugee camp one of their plays was conducted after this fashion. One of the young girls would take a stand in the middle of the room, the rest would move around keeping time with a song, the words of which were: "There sits a little girl that wants a little boy to keep her awake". After awhile they would kiss all around this concluding the exercises. The only thing that I consider them superior to the negro in is malignantly and readiness to fight.

December 26 - Came home in the forenoon. Rained some today. In the evening, about 8 o'clock got an order to report to Major Cramer who had returned from Tennessee scout as an Adjutant. Slept at Tishomingo House.

December 27 - Got breakfast at restaurant. Some expect to go home but have orders to draw 3 days rations and be in readiness to move at any time. Got orders tonight to be at depot at 7 o'clock. Got mustered today.

December 28 - Had a good bed in the hay last night and woke up in the morning feeling very well. Went to the depot, put our horses on the cars and got on top of them ourselves and rode to Lagrange. Went out two miles from the town and tied our horses to apple trees, once the orchard of a large establishment. Rested until dark and feeding horses. Just at dark mounted up and rode to within four miles of Holly Springs. The road that we traveled had hardly a house and not a rail on the route. It is the richest part of the state, most of the planters having held 80 or a 100 negroes each. Our cavalry burned all the houses.

December 29 - At daylight started towards Collierville. Forrest had more than a days advance on us. General Grierson was in command of the troops, infantry, cavalry and artillery. We had to pass from the rear of the column to the front. It was a a trot of four or five miles. At noon we passed through a small place, Mount Pleasant. Must have been a very pretty place, but now almost entirely destroyed. One of our men had been shot at this place. Camped at night - 1 - miles from Collierville in a swamp. Rained some toward morning. I slept with major and Captain Tramel. (I) mess with them.

December 30 - Today took the road to Lagrange. Passed through Mount Pleasant. Rainy and cold during the day. The rain changed to sleet and it blew cold enough to freeze one through. Some of the men were frost bitten. At night camped 10 miles from Lagrange. Killed a sheep and had some supper. Had to get up at two o'clock to warm my toes. Cold as need be. The coldest weather I ever saw in the South. Ground frozen and water in the roads hard enough to bear a horse.

December 31 - Rode six miles and camped where we could get feed. There has been only our brigade since we started towards Lagrange. A detail was sent into the village for rations. I went over to Mr. Purdues, an old gentleman, rich once owning over 100 negroes. He was very much down in the mouth, the boys having taken all his corn, hogs and meat. The people here are the best, most refined of any in the South. It looks rough to see the country so desolate and so little cultivated. Major came back tight. We got ordrs to be at the depot at 8 o'clock and drew three days rations.

1864

January 1 - Up at daylight and off for town. Did not get the horses on the train until noon. The rest of the brigade remain in Lagrange. Mizner established his headquarters there. Got some breakfast in town. It has been very cold for three days. This is a wealthy place and has been. People cultivated and wealthy. Most of the men rode with the horses going to Corinth. Officers were in the caboose. Cramer to drunk to walk straight. Captain Tramel became so before we got to Corinth. Unloaded at the platform, mounted and started for home. Tramel too drunk to ride decently, went on in advance. After the column got through the swamp, major wanted me to stay and close up. The ambulance was some behind and it did not get up before reaching camp. They came on the jump all the way. These reports are wrong, the regiment left Corinth on Tuesday and returned on Saturday instead of Friday.

January 2 - Nothing.

January 3 - Made out monthly returns and one pay roll. General Tuttle is said to be under arrest for allowing Forrest to retreat south without attacking him.

January 4 - Made out another pay roll and mustered for pay. I hope that the Pay Master will be around soon for money is all gone. The officers had a dance in the evening at headquarters, but I did not go down.

January 5 - Nothing but making rolls and returns.

January 6 - Same.

January 7 - Same.

January 8 - Captain went to Memphis on his way home. Leave of absence for twenty days. A letter from Henry.

January 9 - This morning some of Company "F" were at Danville and got captured. Major Fairfield with 40 men went out to see about it. The Rebels were gone. There were only five of them but they took our men at a disadvantage and captured two of them. I had charge of Company "H" squad.

January 10 - Captain Baker was down here today. Four or five regiments of cavalry were ordered to this department and came through Corinth today. Captain Baker thinks that the 2nd Michigan (Cavalry) is coming. Rode out in the afternoon with Lukens, etc.

January 11 - Finished the ordnance work today. In the afternoon (at) 1 pm all the mounted men were ordered out. They are going to Sulpher Springs. Peck went in command.

January 12 - Went to town, 2nd Michigan not yet come. Passenger train was fired into at Bray's Station and track torn up near Memphis. Scout returned just at evening. Nothing accomplished.

January 13 - Made out clothing roll. Sent old letters home. This morning men ordered to move to Lagrange but countermanded and stay at Camp Davis for awhile.

January 14 - Doing nothing today. In the afternoon rode out with Lukens. Met Latty on the road. He told us to get the McNutt girls and come to the dance at his company. Lukens asked the girls and after awhile they agreed to come. While we were waiting a wagon came by from Alabama. Only one horse, the others had been drown. One young woman was riding behind the wagon. Smart bright looking woman. A good talker and intelligent. This family had moved out because they had nothing to eat. Starvation was looking them in the face and nothing was left there but our lines for provisions. The girls (McNutt) rode over to camp behind us. The horse made it very cully and we got along without trouble. The party was in our mess room. The major gave up his rooms for a dressing room. I danced twice, both times with Mollie. There were only nine other ladies in all. Broke up about one. The girls staid in one of Latty's rooms. The girls are tolerable fair but they never take the trouble to comb their hair and are given to spitting. After I had brought them here Narwood was going to go in and leave me. Of course I objected and pretty soon he was taken sick and left.

January 15 - Carried the girls home. I rode Peck's horse and Mollie rode mine. We had a good ride, tip top. Got a letter from father, and work on W.F.Y. & Pratt. They are shipping siege guns from Corinth and the Quartermaster and Commissary at that place have orders to turn over everything but ten days supply. It looks as if the place was going to be left.

January 16 - Officer of the day today. Filled out the heading of clothing book. Brigade inspector came in today, inspected the regiment. The Third Battalion has orders to go to Lagrange (with) horses, etc. and all the companies. Orders to be ready to move at short notice. Some move of grand importance is on the way.

January 17 - Went to Corinth after horses, got 14. Found Quartermaster (of the) 7th Kansas is to turn over 50 more. They go home to recruit as veterans. Had some trouble in leading the horses out but got them all through. "H" had twenty of them, very fair horses. There appears to be no doubt that Corinth is being evacuated. All government stores are being taken away, sick, etc. There is quite a force being organized in Lagrange. I think that an attempt will be made to occupy Meridan. It rained hard coming home and as I had no coat got wet and chilly, the beginning of a cold spell.

January 18 - Got a good man from the lot drawn yesterday to ride myself. One of L Company took a horse issued to H and intended to keep it. I told the Quartermaster Sergeant to take the horse wherever he could find it. Fishback did not understand the circumstances and was at first inclined to get rathy, but finally concluded that it was all right.

January 19 - Finished the clothing book. In the evening went out to Mr. George's. Colonel Dodd came out too drunk to walk straight. They attempted to get up a dance but the men was so boisterous that they could not do anything at it and the party broke up. The McNutt girls came to our quarters and Peck and I chatted with them until almost 12.

January 20 - Charley Murphy and I rode home with the girls in the morning. Had a very good ride. At night got orders to have an extra set of shoes fitted to the horses. This means marching. It is the very worst part of the year to commence the march, and our men will get sick very fast. I would not care if the march had been delayed until the middle of March.

January 21 - Nothing of importance. At night D and H were ordered out. Went to old Reb breastworks. Davenport and Shurtliff sent me down to Jacinto with a little squad. Found a light in one of the houses. Went to it to see whether the Rebs have been in. Woman said there was a sick woman there. Mac was going to open the door and she began to yell like murder. I thought she was badly frightened but after I had left I wondered that it was a Reb but there was no use in going back.

January 22 - Did nothing but lie about camp. In the evening had a dance at our office. Tore down the partition and had a good time. Colonel Dodd and Cheney and Dr. Smith were a little tight. Don't like that part. Enjoy fun but this is not up to that hardly.

January 23 - Camp moved today, all the dismounted men going to the train. Major Fairfield and the cavalry remained. The train left about 11. In the afternoon I was ordered to Jacinto. Peck and I both went. Just before we got to the place, someone in the woods called to us. Said is a friend. We told him to come out and when he had got to the road he said: "I thought you were Southern cavalry". We mounted him up behind us and came home. Everything was packed and nothing to eat. The McNutt girls had not been allowed to leave but I was too sleepy to talk.

January 24 - In the afternoon got orders to move. An old gentleman came in from Alabama just before we started. He was a mechanic but at six dollars a day could not cloth himself. He was a native of Vermont. After the men had all marched out, a detail was sent back to burn the barracks. It was a grand sight, barracks and stables for 1000 cavalry burning at once. Went to Corinth and camped at the refugee quarters.

January 25 - About 11 the last train left the place and we began to destroy the quarters and public buildings. **We had orders not to take or destroy any private property** and the major was very careful not to have any of the buildings fired but the large government buildings made such a tremendous fire that other buildings caught fire. The Corinth House had burned before we left and the pickets that left town last said that the Tishomingo had also caught. The last warehouse fired burned so fast that one company hardly had time to pass it and the others had to go around a foundry. Before one block of stock had either caught accidently or been set on fire and there is but little left of Corinth. Major was sorry that the buildings had caught but it could not be helped. The barracks, stables and warehouses all burned at the same time and the occasional bursting of shells that had been left around the camps made a scene that was forceful and awful. We camped two miles (illegible).

January 26 - Today we marched two miles beyond Salisbury. Our horses are suffering for want of forage. At Pocahontas we had to about half build a floating bridge, then cross the horses one at a time. Here too the troops were all ready to move. We passed over some very bad road and two of our horses got mired in one place. Had to move slow.

January 27 - Marched into Lagrange about 11. Found our men about 1 1/2 miles from the place. Wrote a letter to father. About 5, had to saddle up and come down town with ten men for patrol duty. Lieutenant moves with ten men in command. Old gentleman asks us to stay all night with him. Was rather afraid that the soldiers might trouble him. We went up and talked with him a little while. Fine old man and pleasant wife.

January 28 - Got relieved about noon. Things are somewhat torn up. Made a shelter out of an old tent cloth and slept well. Read life of Burr by Parton.

January 29 - Today the regiment left those dismounted on the train just at night and the mounted men moved out just after dark some three miles. H Company and D remain in Town and stood picket on the roads. The night was rainy and there was some prospect of a visit from the Rebels but after all they did not trouble us. Forrest is said to be about 15 miles from Moscow.

January 30 - Moved out at daylight out on the Moscow Road. Got to Moscow just at daylight. There were plenty of Butternuts about and as the Wolf River crosses the railroad here. I thought that now the time for a fight had come but they claimed to be citizens and as they had no arms we could not do anything with them. I think they were the same men that fired on the train last night. Got to Collierville about one, 24 miles. Drew some grain and rations. Took one feed for night and next morning and moved through to Germantown, 10 miles further. The country is the best I have seen. Rich farm houses and so much of the land cleared that it looks now (more) like prairie than anything else. Rained some in the night but kept dry under the blankets.

116

January 31 - Went in to Memphis in the forenoon. Found the camp just out of the city. Everything at loose ends. The men had only come in last night. We have no tents of any consequence and this is glum enough. At night it rained like suds, and Peck, Tupper and Shurtliff and I went to one of the houses near by and slept on the porch. I was down in the city in the afternoon to find some company property.

February 1 - Woke up at daylight, pretty well chilled through. In the afternoon tents came. Only 8 wedge tents for our company (and) one wall tent for the officers. Peck was ordered to town with twenty of the men. I saw to putting the tents up. Put up picket rope and got everything in as good a shape as possible. In the evening went to the theatre with Grey, Day, Kellogg and some dozen of (the) officers. Not much of a performance. The Paymaster paid the men today but in consequence of some delinquences in the ordnance report he had been ordered not to pay the officers and not an officer got a cent. Got letters from father and Dans.

February 2 - Opened boxes, read a little and arranged things a little and did a little of everything. Some of our men went to town, came back drunk and there was a prospect for difficulty but it cooled down. The first thing with these Southern men in a quarrel is a knife or a pistol. Plenty of both were drawn but fortunately were not used. Made out monthly return.

February 3 - This morning went to Major Dean's headquarters to get pay for some of the men who did not get pay yesterday. He told me that the rolls were closed and the men will be obliged to wait. Bought a monthly Atlantic and a German lixicon. Don't know whether I can study any or not but I thought I would try it any way. Went to Fort Pickering, a considerable fortification built along the river. The guns were heavy columbiads. Negro troops garrison the fort. I saw Colonel Phillips and his daughters on the sidewalk but did not speak to him. The city looks like home. The people are well dressed, and the civil predominates over the military. On the way back to camp passed a school just dismissed. 15 or 20 young girls were finding their way into the street and about the grounds. I could not help of thinking of old Hillsdale. If we were going to stay here I believe I would try to get acquainted with some of the Memphians. Wrote a letter to Jennie, read a little, etc.

February 4 - In the afternoon took a ride around the city in company with Lukens and Booth. Dead horses are scattered all around the outskirts of the city and the coming summer can not do otherwise than bring a terrible amount of sickness to the city. If they attempt to bury them it will not be half done and the evil will only be checked not remedied. This thing and the condition of the streets with the frequent murders and robberies do not speak in very flattering terms of the post commander. General Veatch has been in command, the name of the present officer I have not learned. We took supper down town and then stayed to (attend) the theatre. There is no other public place of either amusement or interest. No lectures, concerts, operas or exhibitions of any kind. The play was a good one and I enjoyed it. If there was nothing different from the performance of last evening, I can not see that there would be anything injurious in the influence of theatres. Perhaps the dancers ought to be kept in a little closer bounds but as far as I was concerned, my attention was taken up with the ease and grace of the movements full as entirely as it would have been if the dress had been longer. The acting was, some of it, over done but on the whole pretty good. If I was at home, I would have no question of maintaining that the theatre might be a place of improvements as much as a gallery of paintings, yet I do not think I would not go from the fact of so many people being prejudiced against them. With this theatre there are no liquor shops nor side attractions of any kind. It seems to me that the objectors of presenting life under false colors hold equally against the plays. If we throw out Hamlet on the stage we must do the same from Shakespear. The fact is it is only the extraordinary incidents in life that have any power to interest; but the usual occurrences can establish principles and motives as firmly and is just the proposition that they are out of the usual modes for action.

February 5 - Finished Aaron Burr and read some in the Atlantic. Had a ride in the evening.

February 6 - Peck came back today. The battalion under Major Fairfield had been to (the) Coldwater River. Peck and Shurtliff captrued nine prisoners at a party. One Reb chaplain was shot through the knee. Peck got a good saddle and two good horses. Tried my German a little but did not make much headway. Got relieved from Officer of the Day to go on scout on the tomorrow. 5 days trip. This breaks up my plan of attending church tomorrow, a thing I had been promising myself for some time.

February 7 - Did not get off quite as soon as expected but caught up with the column about 11. Found it stuck in a swamp. Major and I rode to the front, 3 miles nearly. Colonel McMillan wanted one company in advance and I went back and sent up Edwards Company (?). It was about two o'clock before we got out of the swamp. Fed at a house where they said there was not an ear of corn on the place. Some of the boys found it in the woods. The road is very good except across the streams. It used to be a plank road. Reached Hernando, 21 miles just after dark. Took some time to find camping ground. I slept in a barn. Had plenty of fodder and corn for our horses and good supper for ourselves. All the business of the town has been burnt. I suppose by soldiers but do no know. The people are all secessionist.

February 8 - Did not leave town before 9, and then waited for infantry. While we were stopping I went into the cemetery. The monuments were, some of them, very costly and the inscriptions appropriate but I noticed that all of them bore the mark of St. Louis. Memphis near as it is had not furnished one. Built a bridge over the Coldwater. The Rebs had tried to cut the first loose but did not have time. Only got twelve miles, two miles from Senatobia. Found the bridge torn up over quite a stream. Could not fix it and fell back to where the brigade was camped. The soldiers were crowding into a house and I ordered them out. Lady asked me to stay. Went in for awhile and she did not recollect me. Wanted to know what business I had. Was very polite when she found that I was the Adjutant of the battalion. Half of the Rebels that tore up the bridge were citizens, 41 in all. There has been a little squad of 5 or 6 in front of us all day but they are mounted on the best of horses and it is impossible to catch them. The roads have been very good with the single exception of the creeks. Fed just beyond the Coldwater. Man begged for his corn but I told him I was afraid that we would have to use about half of it. Found a negro asleep in the woods. Edwards made a good deal of amusement for his company by making him sing and dance. This while country is Rebel to the backbone. All of these small places lest. Hatch had almost entirely destroyed (them) burning all the warehouses and shops.

February 9 - Moved before daylight. Reached the bridge just as soon as it was light enough to distinguish anything. Two companies of infantry went with us. Fixing the bridge was a short job, then the cavalry and most of the infantry moved into Senatobia. At about a mile this side of the place a squad of Rebels, 25 or 30 were waiting for us. I was with the advance and from the move I thought there was too many for the advance, and was getting ready to deploy into the field and then advance. Peck was a little distance in the rear and he called charge. Away we went up on the hill and down the other, and on the second ridge was their line. Peck saw it and told the boys to keep steady, but before they could draw in, the Rebs had fired and then they went again. Our boys shot a few times but no one was hurt. Peck and Turrentine then moved through a mile beyond town skirmishing at each hilltop. One squad of infantry was sent out with them and pickets posted about town. Major and I stopped at a doctors who had two young ladies. Had discussion with the old gentleman, music and chat with the girls, and dinner of turkey and etc. with both. Between one and two (there was) heavy firing on the picket post. I mounted and rode to the other picket post, gave them instructions, then back to town. Peck and the infantry had to fall back. They commenced to fire on the posts on left. We had sent word to Colonel McMillan that 25 of them had camped 4 miles below. He did not send any more until afternoon. One company came up at four and were just in time to give them a parting salute. The Rebs gave back slow and our men fired at them occasionally across the field. The rest of the regiments of infantry came up and stayed awhile and then all marched back across the bridge. Colonel McMillan was going to leave a guard at the bridge but thought it was too far and drew them in to the same position of the night before. Several horses were shot, Peck's with the rest. I heard the balls thud into the trees several times but they were not very close. We could get plenty of shots by just riding out into sight.

February 10 - Kept our position on the road. The pickets fired occasionally all day. They had put the planks down over the Heck Haley but only a few came over. They shot a few times but did not hurt us any. Captain Cameron came up in the evening with 30 men from Memphis. Smith was still there. No other news. He had driven in the 95th (Ohio) pickets thinking them Rebels. I drew three days rations for our regiment and the train was sent back to Memphis. We are to go up the river Coldwater.

February 11 - This morning burned the bridge on the road to Senatobia. Peck went down the river two miles with two companies of infantry. They had partly torn up the bridge when the Rebs charged down on them. The boys took the back track and lay down behind the bank and gave them a shot. Two of their horses were killed and Peck says that he saw one of their men tumble from his horse. In the afternoon we burned _____ another two miles up the stream and then moved on to Burksnort 7.5 miles. Company L took a prisoner, home from Virginia on furlough. His sisters had a wet time over it, cried like everything. Camped at town. The infantry came up just at dark.

February 12 - Boys tore up druse and so forth. Played smash generally. Tore down empty houses to make fires of. None of the boys from our regiment but from the infantry. Colonel issued orders not to touch anything. Moved from Bucksnort to Chulahoma about 15 miles. Heard of our troops at Pigeon Roost at Chulahoma. People told us that (the) 2nd Iowa Cavalry had passed thru in the morning. Got dinner in town and fed horses. (The) infantry came up and then moved out about two miles to Dick Bowens and then camped for the night. Not much water and had to go back to town for corn. Slept like a king. 2nd Iowa came up in the morning.

February 13 - Went to Waytte 10 miles. Miserable country. Captain Cameron rode almost to river before halting his men and when he did halt they began to fire on us. The balls whistled pretty lively but not a man nor a horse was hurt. The men dismounted and fired some but they could not see the Rebels only at first and no one was injured. Infantry came up after an hour or so and sent out skirmishers in place of ours. In the afternoon some of the 7th Illinois (probably 7th Cavalry) came in on an exploratory expedition. At night General Smith came himself with a squad of the 4th regulars. We went out foraging, got plenty of corn but no meat. Old darkey was carrying on the place for his mistress, Mrs. Martin. He got dinner for us. The boys stole the eggs but we had cornbread and milk and this answers very well. One of our men of Company D got shot through the heel accidently.

February 14 - Skirmished some in the morning, then 15 or 20 shots fired with artillery and infantry moved away. Our men staying in their places. At ____ we moved. Fed about ____ at Mr. Cox's 5 miles east of Chulahoma, 10 miles south from Holly Springs. It had been raining all day. There was a handsome lady, two of them at the house. The rest quarters for negroes. Best that I ever saw, good double log houses, well built barn. Cotton gins and all in good shape. None of his negroes had ever left him. He had always cared for them top top. They told me that they would not leave him if they were free but would like to be free. Saw a girl slave red cheeks and auburn hair. I thought the negro woman was her nurse, (she) proved to be her grandmother. Cox was her father. Took 1400 pounds of meat from him. He tried to keep it but McMillan took half he had, receipted for it. Eat pretty near one chicken for my dinner. Started for Waterford, 4 miles. Guide took us out the wrong road up to Holly Springs, 5 miles out of the way. Major was mad as you please. Went to Waterford, found infantry had not been there and then went back to Cox's. The command had camped around. We stopped in Mr. Jeffrie's house. He had gone away and we took one room and managed to sleep comfortably. Company H got two good horses from a brother of Cox's. The man was crazy from whiskey. Said he has lost 400,000 dollars.

February 15 - Moved at daylight. Snelling came in with despatches last night from Memphis and a squad came in from New Albany and then back again. Smith had crossed the Tallahatchie. Snelling started for Memphis again this morning. Stopped raining during the day. At night had a comfortable bed - slept well. On half rations.

February 16 - Moved toward Gaines Mill on the Coldwater and waited for the infantry. On the way down a couple of Rebs (run) into the woods and got their horses. Heard of a guerrilla by the name of Fort that robs wagons and killed two of Smith's men, will be hung if caught. Took some 15 bushels of corn from a woman, she proved to be Union but couldn't help it. Infantry got over the river without trouble. All camped 6 miles south of Collierville.

February 17 - This morning Colonel McMillan gave us the permission to move out and we came into Memphis on the state line road, the same that we had passed over on the route from Corinth. Got into camp about 2 p.m. Captain Ford got back two days ago. Mrs. Fairfield had come down. (I received) letters from father, Hank and J.J.

February 18 - Wrote to father. Went to town and etc.

February 19 - Nothing today. Peck and I went to the village to see about getting some saddles but the expense was too much. Got orders to go out at 3 o'clock tomorrow on the Hernando Road with 25 men.

February 20 - Got off about 4 with 20 men. Went out 17 miles, nothing heard of. Returned and reported to General Buckland. In the evening went to theatre with captain and Lukens and etc. Most miserable performance but there is no other place to go.

February 21 - Went to the city in company with several of the officers. They all were going to the Catholic church and I went with them although I had no wish to hear their senseless muminary. The sermon was only a panicifric with church. No preaching anywhere in the afternoon. Went to three churches in the evening, found them closed and finally went to the Episcopalian. The sermon was very good - practical. The reading from Ezekiel "Are not my ways equal?". I was agreably not disapointed. The minister seemed to believe what he said. In the afternoon had a chat with Mrs. Kellogg who has just come down from the North.

February 22 - This morning went into the convention of Union Tennessee. The chapel was half filled with soldiers and then was not crowded. There is not much Unionism in this part of the state, perhaps enough to get in under the presiden'ts proclamation and hold the office. The voting was very faint, not over 100 men all together.

February 23 - Nothing today. In the evening went to hear Horace Maynard. He is the complete model of the supposed Southerner in eyes, hair and appearance. A very good speaker and as full of abolitionism as any one could expect or ask. It was just in the convention yesterday, every remark looking to overthrow of slavery or cursing it's past influence was applauded. Maynard told how the state had been ruined by slavery compared to Georgia, Tennessee, Kentucky and Ohio. Each one being wealthy and prosperous according as it was free from slavery, just the John Helper style. He advocated the plan of keeping the slaves in the country as proposed by the president but thought that they would follow the Indians and in time the country would be peopled by white men entirely.

February 24 - Nothing today. Got some rolls made out ready to muster the few men that were left but Captain Williams would not muster them on account of two being under age. Had to get the boys some guardians and make out the consent as the orders provide.

February 25 - Peck got in this morning from the scout last night. It was my turn but he went so as to give me a chance to make out rolls. Did not see anything. Used up the whole day until three o'clock in getting the boys mustered. An order to have five days rations and be ready to move immediately came about three. I was ordered out as Adjutant but it made no difference as the captain was going to have me along with the company anyway. Smith was reported to have been badly whipped and the cavalry was ordered out to communicate with him. Roads were dusty. Lieutenant-colonel of the 19th Pennsylvania (Cavalry) was in command. Met the advance of General Smith this side of Germantown and turned back home. 2nd Illinois (Cavalry) major said that they had succeeded in everything they had undertaken and were not whipped at all. Had over 1,000 negroes, about as many mules and had burned corn, cotton without limit. Got back to camp between 11 and 12. Mouth and throat full of dust.

February 26 - This morning Peck and I went over to one of those houses and Peck got permission to make out rolls in one of their rooms. They gave us the parlor and during the day we made out two rolls. Young lady came in occasionally and talked very agreeably and when we left in the evening gave us permission to come again tomorrow and finish the rolls. When we first came in the morning they were expecting company but some way the company did not come. I suppose (it was) a little deceit so that we would not conclude to stay but they felt better satisfied the longer we were there. Went to the theatre again this evening. Miserable performance and I shall not go again until something comes out of more importance than that play. Wouldn't go at all if there was a lecture, a concert or preaching or anything else to use up the evening.

February 27 - Captain Ford went over and read for me. Peck drilled the company. It took me all day to finish the rolls, pretty good ones though.

February 28 - Looked very much like rain but did not. I went to church at the Union Chapel. Not much of an audience and very ordinary sermon but it sounded better to me than anything I have heard in some time. The sermon was one calling Christians to let their light shine. Let the world know their belief by their life and conversation. I tried myself by the standard given and found that I was wanting. (I) am not afraid to state my views and my own hopes and fears and have done so quite often especially when talking with Day. But after all I am afraid of taking hold of the work actively, partly I think because I dread a rebuke on this subject more than I would anything else. Just as a man is more ready to discuss the merits of a simple acquaintance than his wife or father. But this fear can be carried too far and I do not think I have said as much as I could and ought to have said.

February 29 - Raining all last night and all day today. Cold and sleet. Horses (are) all drawn up, no shelter, not half enough feed.

March 1 - Raining and snowing today, could not muster.

March 2 - Cleared off today and company mustered in the afternoon. This morning the snow lay over the whole ground and did not entirely melt off during the day.

March 3 - Read a little. In the evening went to the theatre. Good play and well performed. Paid for it. Day says he can muster out immediately. 7 months yet to expiration of my muster. Looks like a long stretch but will soon go by.

March 4 - Ordered out about 11:00 to Hernando. Three companies went. Major Fairfield in command. Camped four miles this side of Hernando. Did not see anything. Rained some during the day, but cleared at night.

March 5 - Went through Hernando at daylight but did not find any though. Met a boy (who) told us that there had been a force of 150 on the road the day before. They had crossed over into some other road and we will not meet them. Got into camp about two.

March 6 - Took a bath in the city. Peck went to the Horn Lake Creek with the company. Put my little man to a buggy and had a ride in the afternoon. Goes pretty well. No church in the afternoon, went in the evening. Not much of a sermon.

March 7 - Peck tried his horse today and she kicked the dashboard out of the affair and broke the stalls in no time.

March 12 - Nothing up to this time. Been to the theatre and saw representation of the ghost. Very striking scenery but not much of a play. Last night got orders to move with ten days rations. Going to Arkansas. Got away about 8 a.m. Colonel Dodds goes in command and takes every officer in camp but Major Fairfield and Cramer. "H" has out all three of us although only 2/3 of the men. Ferried over the river, took us all day. The old boat had only one of the wheels in working order. Could only take some 20 at a time. Got everything over and moved out after dark to Lakes, 6 miles on the railroad running out to Little Rock. The river makes a bend west and at Lakes is only some 100 rods from the railroad. Here we are to camp and the Irishmen are going to tear up the rails and take them to the river. They are to be used on the portion running from Little Rock to the Arkansas River, which is unfinished. Did not get into came until quite late. I slept in a barn quite comfortably.

March 13 - Peck and I went up with the company to guard railroad hands while they fixed up some trucks which the Rebels had partly destroyed over a year ago. Got them out of the mud and fit to run by 3. I came back to camp. We went out 3 miles. The country is very swampy, the regular cane brake. Cottonwood and ash are the trees of the country. The river is not 20 feet from the top of the banks but every spring comes up enough to flood the whole country. For miles back the trees are not in good condition and are not always to be relied upon. Besides there are bayous into which the water runs during the flood of the river filling the land with innumerable lakes. The houses are all set up enough to keep their floors from the water. Land as might be expected is rich, giving a bale to the acre. Woods are full of game, bear, deer, foxes, turkey and etc. I am told that the country is all ____ back to the St. Francis River, 40 miles. The people look lean and sallow and sick half of the time.

March 14 - Heard of a squad of some guerrillas said to be about 200 hid in the cane break about 5 miles from us. Colonel Dodds took the command but one company and a few pickets and went out 10 miles. (They) did not see anything. Where we stopped for dinner (I) got a bear skin about half size. Just the thing to cover a saddle with.

March 15 - Colonel Dodds took the regiment around thru Marion but only saw a few Rebs. Heard of quite a number still back in the country. Our company guarded the wagons up to the landing which used to be Hopeful, a place of some 3 or 400. It was burned a year ago in retaliation for the destruction of a steamer by a set of guerrillas. 36 houses burned. Pretty cold night and not much to eat but expect something better tomorrow.

March 16 - Waited at the river for the wagons, rations and Colonel Dodds until nearly night, then moved out again to lakes. The rest of the regiment went out in the morning.

March 17 - Went out with the trains or teams ie., two cars drawn by mules. Company "H" and 10 men of F. Took up about half a mile of track and drew it to Lakes.

March 18 - Went down the river to Jones and got 3 loads of corn and good dinner. 5 miles. People all have safeguards and protetion papers but I am inclined to believe them mostly Rebel. Not much principle.

March 19 - Doing nothing today.

March 20 - Made the same trip today again to McNeils where I got the bearskin. Heard there were 200 in the cane brake and F Company with "H" (Captain Ford has gone to camp and I was in command) were sent out as skirmishers. We went about 5 miles through the cane break but saw nothing but the paths the Rebs had made. Perhaps there may have been a 100 in the swamp, not more. At Lorry where H & F stopped for feed, found a can of powder and bread cooked for (the) Rebs, but still they have protection papers. No ____. The day before, Snelling had seen some 20 or 25.

March 21 - Doing nothing today. About 2 p.m. they came in saying they are firing on the picket post. (I) hustled out and got men into line. Snelling's horse was saddled and we started out to the cars where the firing had been. His company followed on foot in a few minutes. He came back saying they had got every man in "K" Company, the one that was guarding the cars. Godfrey got the command strung out on the road, I took a little scout down the road to river and then back to Hopefield. 4 of K came in but 17 of them are gone and the lieutenant with them. They must have been surprised, not having any pickets out or something of the kind. There was but little fighting, doubt very much whether there was any on our side. Major tried to get the boat over today but it was too late. Almost every man in the regiment wanted to follow the Rebs but major wouldn't do it. There were a lot of wagons to be guarded but one of two companies might have been sent with them and the rest left to hunt Hornbeck and his men. On the way to town met Major Cramer coming out to take command. They were both impressed with the idea that the Rebs would attack us. Cramer wanted 4 picket posts, 25 men each and only 160 men out. Peck who has been acting as Adjutant for Godfrey induced him to put out only 10.

March 22 - Was sent out two miles to Marion before daylight. Went out 5 miles but did not see anything. Little scouts were being sent out all day on the same roads. Cheney went to Lakes and Cramer thought him gone and sent Snelling to look him up. He met him coming back. The force that took Hornbach was 60 men and they double quicked the boys 18 miles.

March 23 - Got over the river into camp just at night. Godfrey and Hornbach are both blamed for the disaster - which amounts to the loss of 17 soldiers, 1 lieutenant and their arms and 19 work horses.

March 24 - Going to Decatur at once.

March 25 - Packed everything and got ready to strike tents in the morning. All the men _____ that could be got.

March 26 - Everything was put on the boat except some mules. These will be sent on some other boat. The boat is of course very much crowded. Quite a number of the men are not able to go and it is mere nonsense to take them. Today I was thinking of a year ago. It has passed very quickly and every little curcumstance I remember as well as the day after it took place. I will renew the resolutions I made then and try to make them realities. The cloud that day brought on my life has not cleared away, it never will. Every pleasure is only half enjoyed when I have not one to sympathize in the enjoyment.

March 27 - Major Cramer's horse had the glanders and we threw it overboard. The boat got off just about sunrise. I had no money at all. Lukens bought me a supper and breakfast this morning. Captain Shurtliff bought dinner and supper. The Mississippi is just about the same, nothing but the wide river and low banks.

March 28 - Still on the river, passed today Island #10, New Madrid, Columbus and etc. The fortifications on the island are almost all washed away. Lukens showed me the place where our 64th were camped. Got a letter from father just before I left. Got into Cairo about 11:00.

March 29 - Cheney and Curtis were put in arrest for leaving the boat last night and I was put in command of Company "F". The horses were taken off in the morning and fed (and the) boat (was) cleaned and horses put back. Did not leave till morning.

March 30 - Went up to Paducah and were stopped here in anticipation of Forrest returning. Kept all day. Some little girls on board helped pass away the time very pleasantly. The fight was on Saturday (March 26). Colonel Hicks had about 600 men in the best kind of a fort. The country around is very flat, and if it had not been for the houses there would have been a slaughter, for the guns commanded the whole. After the first attack, Hicks burned their houses some 40 or 50. Some placed the killed as high as 300 but I saw no signs of any such slaughter. 100 would full cover it in my opinion. I saw the place where General Thompson fell. The ground was red with his blood. (He was) struck by a cannon ball and blown entirely in two. He was killed within a few steps of his own door. The city must have been a very handsome one but it is now more than half destroyed. The banks (2) were not robbed. The gun boats drove the Rebs away before they could open the vaults.

March 31 - Got orders to leave (at) once and then countermanded.

April 1 - Up (the) Cumberland. The Tennessee empties just at Paducah, the Cumberland about 20 miles further up at Smithland. The Cumberland is very ____ and no shoals. The banks are high and on the whole I suppose it is like the Hudson.

April 2 - Today passed (Fort) Donelson, now very strongly fortified. The Rebel works are still in sight and the battery where the Rebels had their 128 pounder is very plain. The country is high and full of commanding points for batteries. Reached Clarksville about 8. Went up town a little while, quite a business place.

April 3 - Up to Nashville. The river and country are still the same only more so. I would like to live on the banks of the Cumberland as well as anywhere. Some of the cliffs on the river were at least 500 feet high. Out of money and had to go without supper. Peck went home at Cairo but only got two months pay and said that McGaughey would lend captain and I some money. (We) borrowed and got $10.00 at Cairo but this was gone at Nashville.

April 4 - Went without breakfast. At noon captain gave another 10 and am all right for a few days. Got everything off and men slept on shore. The officers had staterooms and staid on boat. We put up tents here and wait the course of events.

April 5 - Went around town some. Saw some very hard cases. Nothing very tempting to my mind. Colonel Spencer and Dodds came in tonight.

April 6 - Got my horse shod and captain wanted me to go to the Provost Marshalls and get the pistols that one of our men had taken from him when arrested. Found St. Clark, an old college chum in charge of the prisoners. Stayt was close by and Stanley Davis and Jennings. Bradley was in town. Yerkes Fuller and his wife, etc. Had a long talk with the boys. Put on ____ in the afternoon but got off and went up (and) saw them a little while in the evening. Bradley was out too far and I shall not see him as the mounted men go tomorrow and I will have to go with ours. They told me that Van Valkenburg and Pierce had been here only a day or two since. Van is Provost Marshall for the 9th Army Corps and Pierce is assistant. It is almost as good as a furlough to see them. I shall try and get back sometime. These are the first I have seen. Father telegraphed today asking about me. I hardly know what to think of it whenever he is anxious about me which can hardly be the case for he has written in answer to a letter of mine of the 12th. Whether this is the matter or some of them are sick I cannot decide. This day should be marked in white, I have not felt so well in an age.

April 7 - Did not get off as expected.

April 8 - Still in Nashville.

April 9 - Moved this morning. Saw Chaplain Bradley at his regiment. The road was macadamized and tip top. Reached Franklin just at dark. Got a good supper in the village and then Doctor Cheney, Snelling and I went into a house where some young girls were singing and listened to the same for an hour or two.

April 10 - The roads remain the same. Country very fine, it has been settled over 50 years. Reached Columbia at night and camped on the ledge.

April 11 - Today up at 2:00 and on the road. Reached Pulaski before dark. Camped in a miserable place. Handsome little town. The whole road is lined with Northern farms very much like Michigan but more hilly.

April 12 - Laid over all day. 50 of the 100 beef cattle that we drove are left here. Met Frank Kellogg today. He is 2nd lieutenant in a negro regiment.

April 13 - Today went to Elk River. Camped on a government plantation worked by a colonel of an Ohio regiment.

April 14 - (Went) into Athens, left the rest of the cattle and went to our camp 15 miles beyond.

April 15 - Took 42 men and went to Athens after horses. Eat dinner with Tom Kennedy. Got some good horses. Got letter from father and $2 in the evening. Also one from Magie.

April 16 - Wrote letters to Hank and father. Made out company monthly etc.

April 17 - Went to Triana about 14 miles up the river. Took 16 men with me. Did not see anything at all. Commenced to rain before we got back. Most of the regiment was ordered out. Major Fairfield took command. Captain went with the company. I did not go. Some fighting is looked for at Decatur.

April 18 - Various reports came in today of the condition of affairs at Decatur but there was no fighting more than a little skirmishing. Peck came (back) in the evening.

April 19 - Regiment came back today, no one hurt. Rebels came within a couple of miles of the place but did not attack.

April 20 - Made out ordnance return for the quarter.

April 21 - Making out ordnance returns for Major Fairfield.

April 22 - Ditto for Colonel Dodds.

127

April 23 - Went to Decatur. Spent the day with the sergeant, very pleasant time. Got wet a little on the way home. The 64th (Illinois) now has 1000 men and is filled up to 10 companies.

April 24 - April 30 - (Missing)

May 1 - Got into line about 7 but did not move till 10. I was going as far as Stevenson as Adjutant, only went some 4 miles. Went to Madison and got shoe set. Had good camp. General Veatch's etc. are there. Morning _____ (illegible) Brigade the same with the 64th.

May 2 - Off at daylight. The hills beyond Huntsville were in sight all the forenoon. Reached _____ about noon. Pretty place but badly used up by the war. (Illegible)

May 3 - Left in the morning about nine. Lost our way and went some two miles out of the way. We are now in the range of the Cumberland Mountains which rise up on every side of our way. The road is mostly through the valleys but sometimes winds up the rocky side of the mountains. We camped at night (illegible). Colonel and major rode about for an hour finding a place to camp. Got a shoe put on my mare. Captain was sick and I detailed the guards etc.

May 4 - Off at daylight and (got) as far as Woodville. Colonel sent me down. Put the regiment in camp. Waited until afternoon, the brigade came up. I went over to the 64th. The infantry go by train. Our regiment guards the train, 269 wagons. There is rumor of fighting at Dalton. The troops are hurrying to the front. Camped on a stream 4 miles from Larkins. Had a good place to rest in.

May 5 - Captain of artillery wanted to go on last night. He was very much excited because the major had put 2 of his guns with Captain Ford to guard the rear. The major told him to go on if he was willing to do it without orders. He went on. We left about daylight. The roads are through the same rough country. Was comfortably warm. Reached Bellfonte about one and went into camp. The rear of the train got up about five. Rations and forage were issued. Picket fired six shots at something, either horse or rebel. We mounted and had some of the men in line. The farms are barren and uncultivated. A complete picture of desolation.

May 6 - Got a very early start and reached Bridgeport about 4. I was sent on from Bridgeport to hunt (a) campground. Train all came up. 7000 cavalry on the road from Stevenson. Our camping ground was on an island just across from Bridgeport, poor but the country all around Bridgeport has been cleared of timber and nasty enough. Wrote a letter to father.

May 7 - Left the town about 9:00. Marched as far as Shell Mountain Station. There was a ___ (cave) and a stream running from it larger than the St. Joe. We went in a short distance but had no torches and did not explore it any distance. The Rebels had used it to manufacture salt peter from quite extensive works. The cavalry has been traveled for 3 miles. In the afternoon we climbed the mountain. The Tennessee could be seen for miles and the long ridges of mountains looked like easy swells in a prairie country. We were 40 minutes in coming down and did not rest at all. The Rebel works at this point were very strong, commanding what is called the narrows. The roads have been the same - rough.

May 8 - The train was up before we were saddled and our teams got in the rear. Only marched 8 miles but it was the most rocky and hilly road that I ever saw. The mountains came so close to the river that the side had to be blasted to give room for the track. Our wagon road was just below but would probably be overflowed in high water. Dead mules and broken wagons were in sight most of the time. We passed under one bridge 126 feet high. It was put up like the scaffolding of a house, brace and stay nailed. The uprights were ash, oak and pine about 10 inches in diameter and 30 (feet) long. The timber was green. (There was) one upright in the center of each rail and one at each end. We were told that the contractor made $40,000; but some train must go crashing through that bridge before the season is over. We pay for his fortune. They have already been obliged to repair it and (it) was not completed until February. Had a good camping ground by the side of a spring big enough to run a saw mill.

May 9 - Today (we are) along the side of Lookout Mountain and camped at its foot. The mountain is the highest of any in the chain. There is a road that runs around to the top - 6 miles from town. The fortifications at Chattanooga are very strong, too strong to be taken by direct attack. They pointed out to us the position of the Rebels and the route that our men took in getting to the top of the mountain. Two regiments climbed up a cliff so steep that it was not walking but simply climbing. It hardly seems possible that such a place could be taken. The importance of the battle appears when a man once sees the position. The valley in the rear of Chattanooga with two good roads, Little Mill Valley with a branch road and the Memphis and Charleston Railroad were all held by the Rebels. Our supplies had to be taken by a hilly road north of the river and was not half sufficient to supply the army.

May 10 - Began to rain in the morning. I went to the company. Peck went into town and got my horse shod. Our road was a very rough one and during the day we made some 12 miles. We slept in a carpenters shop.

May 11 - Off very early but did not march very far. Dodge has been pushing ahead and is said to be at Resaca. We camped at Gordon's Gap. The train all went over. It began to pass about 3 but did not get over until midnight. The hill was very bad. Occasionally during the day we heard cannonading. Very cold today, need overcoats. My rubber blanket was hardly enough to keep out the cold. We are taking out to the front 400 head of cattle.

May 12 - Reached our destination about noon - Snake (Creek) Gap - Dodge's depot of supplies. dodge with the army is some 5 or six miles from here. Cannonading would be heard occasionally all day. My horse was sick in the forenoon but got better after a little trot, (and) some provisions of Captain Kellogg. There is nothing but hardtack for anyone, nothing but the regular army ration. About 4:00, 5 companies were ordered to saddle and guard train to Ringgold. "H" was one and I went in charge. Peek and captain stayed in camp. Between 3 and 400 wagons. We met on our road two army corps passing around to the position held by Dodge.

Their trains and men were mostly in camp. If they had not been it would have been nearly impossible to have got by, as it was, we got into camp about 1:30. The train had gone out in advance of us and we did not get by it for 6 miles, most of the time on the trot. A good many of the boys lost their haversacks, myself with the rest but one of the boys found it. Once we stopped for trains to pass and I lay down, got to sleep and did not wake up until the company were all gone. The orderly had formed the company thinking that I was on in front. This was two nights with no sleep until after midnight and all day in the saddle. Letter from Hopkins.

May 13 - Up at sunrise and on to Ringgold. Met Major Fairfield and Captain Tramel on the road. Captain brought in 83 men to Decatur. At Ringgold, heard that our troops were in Dalton. In the morning heard cannon and musketry very plain. Our road was only 4 or 5 miles from it. Everyone is confident of victory and encouraged by the news from the East. Wrote a letter to Hopkins. Company loaded train in the evening ready to start tomorrow.

May 14 - Moved out to the gap, our company in the advance. The remainder of the regiment were out camped for the night.

May 15 - Moved up the gap some 4 miles. Halted all day waiting for the train to load which was then to go to the front - 10 miles. The 64th has been in a slight skirmish, Willard wounded.

May 16 - 5 companies went out early in the morning. I went with them. Ford and 4 companies staid to bring up the rear. When we got to McPherson's headquarters found that the Rebels had left and the 64th with all the troops in front of Resaca were crossing the Oostanaula. In Resaca we found some corn and some guns. I saw 150 prisoners but do not know how many were captured. Saw General Thomas pass, fine looking old man, iron grey whiskers, perhaps 50 years old. (He is a) full faced portly man. Major with his men moved up the right and front with the train. I started at the crossroads waiting for Ford. He did not come during the day and at night I went on to the regiment. Troops and trains had been passing all day, one line to Resaca and one to crossing of the Oostanaula. There had been some skirmishing by the 2nd division and Captain Taylor of the 66th Illinois was killed and Colonel Burke wounded. Our men occupy Rome. The Rebs appear to be trying to retard our advance but do not deem anxious to do any fighting.

May 17 - Slight firing in the morning. The 15th Corps passed in advance of the 16th. Did not move our train until nearly sundown, then about 3 miles. Thought we were going into camp, had taken the saddles off and began to get supper, orders came to move. We got ready and waited until about 11 before we moved. Got the coffee pot out again and made supper. In the saddle all night but do not think that we moved very far as the teams were stopping all the while. Did not get into camp until after daybreak. (I) do not feel very well in consequence of slight diarrhea. Burke had to have his leg taken off. Fishback offers me first lieutenant in his company. Major says that he will give me a company in his new regiment or the adjutant but I don't think that I shall do any more soldier(ing) after November. Major Godfrey was mustered as lieutenant colonel.

May 18 - Rested until afternoon and then moved out on the Adairsville Road. Went a few miles and camped at sundown. I climbed up a high point in front of us and could see the long trains, one wagon after the other on three roads for miles, just as far as I could see the roads. A division was camped just at the foot of the hill and our camp fires sent their smoke up through the trees from every direction. Our horses had one feed of clover in the afternoon, the most home institution that I have seen. The Rebs had thrown up some slight breastworks near where we camped and dug a few rifle pits but they were not able to detain us i.e. the advance but a short time. They are expecting a fight at Kingston. Got papers from home.

May 19 - Moved out before breakfast, went to Adairsville. Wagons did not get up but managed to get a little something to eat. The town was almost entirely destroyed. We stopped in the same house that General Polk had used for his headquarters the day before. Moved out again about 2 on the mountain road. It is reported that a brigade of Rebs were captured lying in wait for one of our trains. (They) were taken without firing a shot. There is said to be an official telegram at McPherson's Headquarters announcing the capture of Richmond and general said general staff getting high on the strength of it. What was saved from Richmond is coming to Johnston. More reinforcements are on the way to us. It is hardly possible for them to check us certainly (not) drive us back. Our forces got into Kingston early this morning without a fight. Got very sleepy before our stop at night. The train is stopping so much that it makes it worse than a steady gait. Saw quite a lot of infantry boys tired out that had thrown themselves down by the road, sleeping unconscious of everything.

May 20 - Moved on about a mile and went into camp all day. Took a wash in the brook by our camp. 16th Corps train are at this place about 1/2 mile from Kingston. Trains went to Kingston last night. The Rebs not having torn up the track much south of Kingston and our troops have taken position on the other side of it. The reported capture of Richmond is ours (is false). The armies are in line of battle each receiving reinforcements i.e. the report. Two trains were taken in the capture of Rome. In the afternoon General Dodge sent for the best company that Godfrey had to report to Captain Hickenlooper as a permanent reconoriting party. Our duty will be to accompany him as he rides around making up maps of the country. I suppose that there will be more danger connected with it than guarding (the) wagon train but more pleasant in other respects.

May 21 - Reported to General McPherson's headquarters and about 9 the captain went out. We crossed the hightower, a stream 20 or 30 rods wide on a bridge which the Rebels had failed to burn. Passed beyond the pickets some 5 miles, lower down. Did not see any Rebels but 15 had been on the road only a few minutes (before). We shall be very likely to run into them some day. The river was pretty deep and two of our men got down too low. Their horses went in all over and one was washed off. There was some danger of his drowning for a few moments but (he) finally came out very pale and tired. It is said that we move in two days, no one knows. Lukens came in today. Day has been appointed major in one of the 100 day regiments. Burke has died from the effects of his wound.

May 22 - Letters from father. Rested all day. In readiness to move tomorrow. All sorts of conjectures as to where we will go.

May 23 - Went out today on the same road that we scouted. Out with Hickenlooper. Had a swim in the Hightower. Left the bridge about 8. I left my spurs behind and had to go back for them. Halted at 1:00.

May 24 - Grazed our horses a short time in the morning and then moved on the right of the train. We went up to within 4 miles of Rome and had to come back a piece. Found a crib of nice corn at a Mr. Jones. Fed and took (some) along and he had several 100 sacks marked USA that had been left behind to be filled with corn. The furniture in his house had been good - sofas and centre tables, mirrows - etc. Most of them were destroyed. The regular <u>soldiers</u> do not do this but stragglers with the train. It does not suit my ideas to destroy property in this way. Using corn and supper is all right but smashing a chandelier or sofa only exasperates the people, does no one any good and does not help end the war. The man had fed and furnished liquor to about 50 Rebels 3 days ago and he has a brother (who is) an officer in the Reb army but this does not justify such destruction. Had no meat for breakfast and could get none. G. Kellogg, one of our boys, found a lot hid in the woods and while bringing it in dropped one. Captain had Sanford pick it up and we consider it almost a providential interposition. Just after dark it commenced to rain or rather pour. We stopped to camp and I held my rubber over saddle and blankets until it stopped a little and then made (a) fire. Sanford got supper and we had a good nights rest. It was so dark that we could hardly see a foot before us.

May 25 - Went about 2 miles to the right. Found the road or the country too hilly to get over and came back to the old road about a mile east of Vannirls (Vinings?) and halted until 5 1/2 p.m. Our train got backed up with the 15th Army Corps and did not all leave out until nearly night. 2 companies of the 7th Illinois (Infantry) stopped on the hill with us and one of their captains drank coffee. There was a little saw mill near here built between two hills just far enough apart to place the mill. A very little outlay would give a fall of a 100 feet here. The land yesterday and today has been pine barrens, very rocky with an occasional valley which can be cultivated. Got into the road and went lugging along with the train until late at night and then turned out (on) one side and slept until morning 4 a.m. To increase the beauty of the thing we had a good rain just after dark. I had put some corn in my saddle packets and so had some feed but the rest had nothing.

May 26 - Rebels said to be in rear of us and we moved pretty early. By noon we were within 4 miles of Dallas. Stopped here until night. Boys made a big haul of tobacco. Trains began to move out just about dark and we passed and camped in Dallas. Train was all night getting in. There was a report that some of our men had been killed but they afterwards came in. Cannonading in front of Dallas could be heard very distinctly. The Rebels are making a stand a mile or two from the place.

May 27 - Woke up in the morning by the booming of cannon. The cannonading lasted all day. Skirmishing and occasionally volley firing from daylight until after dark. The Rebels were driven from one ridge but our men were not able to cross the ravine and could not turn either flank on account of the road winding through the mountains in such a shape that they could get an enfilading fire from artillery and musketry upon a column advancing through it. In the ravine between the two hills on which most of the forces were drawn up the Rebs had a strong line of sharp shooters. Two companies of the 64th, A & F were deployed in front of the brigade drawn up with regimental front. Captain Conger was in charge. They were skirmishing all day. "A" lost 3 men killed and several (wounded). The two companies lost 20 killed and wounded. Bob Beatty killed and Spring wounded were all that I knew. Captain Conger was wounded in the side of the neck but not dangerously. Hooker is said to have lost 700 killed and wounded. The total loss cannot be ascertained. Hooker commanded the 14th Corps. About nine o'clock the Rebs raised a yell and charged our line but were met by a volley that sent them back again. What the loss was I did not learn. The musketry was a roar and then a rattle like a dozen snare drums. The Rebs have the advantage. The ridges running in a east and west direction in a kind of lapped shape.

May 28 - Saddled up about 3 a.m. and moved about 5 miles east of Dallas. Country very hilly. Had to go 2 miles to get water for our horses. From the top of the hills the smoke of our campfires could be seen and the whole country to the peaks in the Allatoona Mountains but the country is so wooded that you can get but little idea of the situation.

May 29 - It is said that the Rebs made another charge last night and lost 3,000 in killed, captured and wounded. Not much musketry today. In the afternoon moved out some 8 miles in advance of empty train, going after forage to Kingston. Was just cooking supper, got coffee, ready to eat when the "To Horse" was sounded and taking my cup in my horse, away I went for a few miles further and then lay down and slept until morning. The Rebels seem ready to fight in their present position which is a very strong one.

May 30 - Got into Kingston by noon but only loaded part of the train. Large railroad train went into Chattanooga tonight with wounded from Dallas. Bought 24 small biscuits, paid $1.00. A barrel of flour (would) make a $100.00 worth. Got a few things for the mess and a look at the papers. Sent a letter to father. They are fortifing at this point and I should not be surprised if the army spent the larger part of the summer here.

May 31 - Loaded the train in the morning and left Kingston about 8:00. Our company was in the rear but I was with the colonel. He sent me on to find if the corps had moved. Stopped on the way and fed our horses. Got to old camp about sundown. Our forces occupy Dallas. The line is somewhat further back and the troops are being pushed over to the left, moved rather. The Rebs made some desperate charges night before last but were repulsed every time. General McPherson buried over 300. Our loss has been very heavy. We passed about 150 ambulances and more than this number of wagons filled with the wounded. The whole train of empty wagons going to Kingston had 57 (to?) 60 teams in it. Many were filled with prisoners. There were 5 or 600 wounded men walking. I never saw before such a proportion of men wounded in the arms. It shows how large a share of the fighting has been skirmishing and how heavy it has been. The troops have been skirmishing almost every day for the last 25 at half distance. In the charge made by the Rebs Sunday night, 14 pieces of artillery were brought to bear on them and two regiments that were armed with Spencer and Henry rifles were in front of these. Two regiments alone, 123 were buried. Prisoners say that the governor of Georgia has demanded of Johnston that he fight the battle before reaching Atlanta and not risk the destruction of the city. Found letters for me from Magie and Pratt. Magie is with 2nd Brigade, 1st Division, 5th Army Corps and Pratt is at Lixington, Kentucky.

June 1 - Train came in during the forenoon. Had a good wash. No firing of any importance, some skirmishing. The 16th Corps is moving to the left in which I suppose they intend to advance. I should not be surprised if the heaviest fighting was over but could not tell anything with certainty. Read Paul to the Corinthians in the afternoon. Like to read that way, taking a whole letter or book.

June 2 - Moved this morning pretty early. Our right has been drawn back and the entire pushed out. Where we camped in the forenoon is now the line of battle. 4 companies were put out as skirmishers or videttes and at noon we went out and took their place. We made our headquarters at the bridge we crossed the day we went after forage from Dallas. We are now 3 or 4 miles northeast of Dallas. There had been some slight picket firing before we came and some shelling but none on our line after we came. Pretty heavy firing on the left of our line in the afternoon. Our men (are) throwing up breast works just north of the creek. The persons living in the house here by the bridge left in the morning leaving everything in the house. The infantry went in and took some things such as dishes and etc., but returned most of it when the woman came back at night. (I) dislike so much pilfering. There would not be half as much if the people would stay home.

June 3 - Some sharp skirmishing in the morning by the infantry on our right and shelling on the left. Our men were in the thick underwood and the Rebels did not dare to advance far enough to come within range. The infantry and the cavalry were both firing at very long range. During the forenoon General Veatch moved the troops that were behind the creek back to the east so as to connect with General Sweeny. Dodge's line which can be seen is now fronted west southwest. There are some strong forts and positions along it. It must be nearly at right angles to the general line. The Rebels have cut the trees from in front of their works and they can be seen very plainly. Their heaviest work (in sight) is just about on the extension of Dodge's line south, but we are far enough so that they can not shell to any advantage. Our skirmishers fell back in front of the new line about 2:00. Company I had one horse shot. Just before dark we came back to our camp. (We) fed horses and got supper and then moved northeast about 2 miles. I went back to General Dodge and reported our position. Sometimes I think we are falling back but they report the corps as advancing and perhaps we will move forward by the left. The right is certainly much nearer Kingston than a week ago. We are now 4 or 5 miles east northeast of Dallas. Snelling says that our carbines will throw a ball much further than that of the Spencer gun. Some of the Rebel bullets came nearly a mile and others would fall short of the first pickets. The horse was shot beyond a half mile. Those that fell short were probably musket balls and the others swedge bullets. Our carbines would send a ball as far as their best.

June 4 - Laid in camp all day. Some heavy skirmishing in front of us. Kellogg sick, went to Lookout Mountain. Colonel assigned me to duty in his place. Drew 700 pounds of beef and issued to companies by George Buches help. Will not be likely to have so much night work to do.

June 5 - In camp until nearly night. Reports come in the morning that the Rebels have disappeared from the front and we were to move forward. The news was confirmed and we soon had orders to follow the train on its way to Allatoona. The order was afterward changed to remain with some supplies which had been unloaded. The mules in the supply train are about used up. If they would feed the grain given to 12 mules to 6 they could draw more supplies, have a shorter train and be more convenient (in) every way. Some of them will stall with 5 boxes of hardtack. Nothing of any interest. Watched the trains passing all day.

June 6 - Moved at noon for Ackworth, the teams having taken off the stores. Colonel sent me on with five men to find out General Dodge's position and the train and get rations. Went three miles out of the way found Kellegg but our teams not up. Colonel sent men over on horseback and I took it over to camp 4 miles as best I could. Did not issue being so late. Passed by General Thomas' headquarters, saw the general in front of his tent. He is a heavy, thick man 3 scores old, perhaps four.

June 7 - Issued rations in the morning, some grumbling, our boys have been in camp on full rations and regular work easily. In the afternoon got an order to draw rations to the 11th which I did. Got full rations. Our regiment has been picking up stragglers. Today took up 50 or more. The orders are to put them to work on intrenchments. Most of those taken up I believe to be ignorant of the order which requires that foraging parties etc. be under charge of some officer under the required authority. Officers are served exactly like privates. The straggling ought to be stopped but thousands of innocent men will be severly punished for the carelessness of their officers in not publishing the order. One of the squads taken up just at night said they belonged to the 2nd Michigan (Cavalry). I got one of them to stop, saddled my horse and rode about 4 miles most to their camp when I met Douglas. I talked to him until it was late enough for me to turn back. He was detached at General McCook's Cavalry Division Topographic Engineers. (He) told me that most of Company G were home yet on furlough. He had not returned. Wrote to father and Hank. Had a good supper, since better at headquarters than can (get) in the company.

June 8 - Got an order to draw full rations for 6, 7, and 8. Made out the return, got it approved and after waiting awhile got some crackers and sugar, fresh beef. Fresh beef bothers me more to issue than all the rest. Wrote a letter to Pratt but can't get a stamp. We are to move tomorrow at daylight.

June 9 - As I expected the train did not get off and we are still at camp. Read some in Adam Bede. In the afternoon issued rations. Did not find it so much trouble. General Blair with the 17th Army Corps went into camp between us and the village. It is said that his men are dissatisfied with him. (The) cavalry had a fight ____ of us, six or seven miles. (They) lost 18 killed and wounded.

June 10 - Regiment moved about two miles north of Ackworth so as to be in the rear of the wagons. Colonel made his headquarters at the house of Mr. Sears, the most Yankee Southerner I ever saw. (He) had a little girl (that) looked so much like Nellie that if I had seen her at home I should have picked her up in a minute. There was more life and get up to the whole family than I have ever seen before in the South. More odor of school room. The head was near Atlanta on the railroad. Captain K was gone and I went to the 2nd Division (for) supplies which we were guarding and made arrangements for rations in case we had to stay more than tomorrow.

June 11 - Rained today like suds. In the afternoon went over to see about the rations. Clerk told me that he couldn't let me have them. I told the colonel and he overtook the train at the depot and gave the clerk to understand that he must give me some rations which he did. Train came in during the afternoon. There is something strange in the affection that a soldier gets for a locomotive and train. Everyone flocked to see it and when it went down to Big Shanty 8 miles below and right up to the skirmish line the whole army sent up a roar like a tempest. The railroad now will take supplies right to the camps of the men. News of the nomination came today - Lincoln and Johnson (and) Fremont and Cochran. The last ticket I had not heard of and I do not understand it at all.

June 12 - One company and the teams moved out to Big Shanty in the forenoon. The roads were terrible. (I) drew rations while the quartermaster was hunting campground and issued in the afternoon between the showers. Rained almost all day. Colonel and the remains of the regiment came up about 2:00. Colonel did not like the ground. Some little skirmishing and a little cannonading. The Rebel works and Rebels themselves can be seen very plainly on the mountain (Kenesaw). The position is not thought to be as strong as it was at Dallas. (It) can be turned on either side. We are now only 25 miles from Atlanta. Saw two of our men get soused in a slough of mud and water. (They were) covered completely . (It was) fun for us but very disagreeable for the men. Six of us tried to sleep in a wedge tent. Couldn't make it and I got my blanket, put my head and shoulders under the tent and let my feet run out. It rained pretty fast but I could get the blankets just about so warm and managed to sleep some.

June 13 - Nothing today. The skirmishing continues just about the same. Our troops have also thrown up breastworks. Got my horse shod and went out to graze. Some of the men went to another field and gave me a tramp of a mile for my horse. Heard that Colonel Morrell had got marked with a bullet but not how much. Goerge and B.F. and Kellogg came tonight. George is not able to do duty yet and B.F. goes back to raise a company for Fairfield and so I remain at headquarters. Colonel Godfrey does not like the way Major F. goes to work. This is what I expected if the major tried to get any help from the regiment while this (regiment) was not full. Spencer would like a brigade but Godfrey would like a full regiment. Fairfield will be slow raising the regiment.

June 14 - The army holds just the same position so far as I have heard. Went out to General Dodge's which is close to the line of battle. Got provision return approved and a good look through a glass at the Rebels on the mountain. Could see their signal flag very plainly with a glass. Got three days rations and issued (them).

June 15 - Killed a beef in the morning and issued to the regiment. In the afternoon, went over to our batteries in the 17th Corps with Ford, Tupper and Edwards. Had ten guns in the battery where we were planted in the centre of a wide field about two miles from the Rebels. The Rebels did not return a shot during the afternoon. You could see their passing back and forth without the help of a glass. Once a whole regiment came in sight but the first shell brought half of them to the ground and the rest soon fell back into the woods. There was a fascination about the scene that could hardly be resisted and I hated to leave. Our shells exploded almost every time, a large cloud of smoke marking the spot exactly. Some of the guns were James rifles and some 20-pounder Parrotts. The shell for the James makes a noise something between the whirr of a saw and the noise of a stick going through the air end over end. The Parrotts leave the gun with a noise like the sucking of a piston rod and afterwards have a distinctive and continued whizz. General Thomas was to have made an attack at 2 p.m. but for some reason did not do it. The 17th Corps in the forenoon had moved their left around nearly 3 miles, bringing their line fronting the face of Kenesaw Mountain; while in the morning it was at right angles to it connecting on the right with the 15th Corps which fronted the mountain. This was the extreme left. The 16th Corps was to the right of the 15th. 90 Rebels gave themselves up to the 64th when they advanced, the Rebels shooting at them as they advanced. The 17th Corps captured over 300. We saw them coming on as we were going to the battery. Every one feels confident of success. Generals Logan, McPherson, Blair, Smith and a lot of others were on the hill by the battery. Blair is a reddish whiskered, large, stern, active looking man. McPherson is a black whiskered, heavy set, thoughtful looking man. Logan has long moustaches, (is a) savage looking man and at this time unusually cross on account of the mules having eat off the tail of his black stallion. In the night the Rebels made a charge on our working parties but were repulsed. Our loss has been almost nothing. Got a letter from Barker stating that he had got into difficulty on account of leaving his old regiment after being captured and enlisting in the 1st under an assumed name. (He) had been arrested as a deserter and had the prospect of three years service before him as a conscript. I got up the affidavits of his service in the regiment and his papers and sent them to him but am afraid they will not reach him in time.

June 16 - Went out to the lines in the forenoon. Infantry breastworks somewhat advanced but batteries in same position. Rebels threw a few shells which burst near enough to attract our attention to say the least. Got a letter from J.J.H.

June 17 - Went around the breastworks in the forenoon. Nothing very active. No firing of any consequence. Drew rations for three days and issued.

June 18 - Did not go out today on account of the rain. Colonel was over to the house and sent for mess chest and headquarters stuff. Took it over at noon. People had lost everything as usual. Rained hard all day.

June 19 - Got orders last night to move out to Marietta and left about six. I was with the wagons. Colonel took the regiment thru the battle line of the line of skirmishers until he was in sight of the Rebel line of battle and the skirmishers began to pour it into them and a battery from the mountain began to shell them. They departed as speedily as possible. General Sherman who was in front ordering them to leave. Seems to me like a mistake to have taken the regiment through an infantry skirmish line. They were fortunate not to get hurt though the shells came very near some of them. Watched the shelling all the forenoon. Our troops throwing shells on the hillside and the Rebels from their battery on the summit of the mountain replying occasionally. The infantry moved out across the open field and while they were crossing, the Rebels fired pretty rapidly but no one was hurt. I took a position in the breastworks and could see the Rebel shells 80 rods in front of me. One they threw entirely over us though it must have been nearly if not quite 3 miles. Went out to the regiment which had moved to the left in front of General Dodge's headquarters. Put up tent on brick floor in the woods and then had to take it up and move to the Colonel's selection; no very pleasant work while the rain was coming by small pail fulls.

June 20 - Got ready to draw rations and found Captain Barnes had gone out to the front and the general's headquarters were being moved. Went out to the line trying to find him. Got out to the railroad to where it said 25 miles to Atlanta and to where the ungenerous Rebels began to shoot at me and then turned around. The railroad turns like a letter U, with Big Shanty on the west end of it and the mountain along the east line, the curve of the U being toward the south so that the railroad turns back toward the north. In front of the mountain is a creek along which the railroad runs. Beyond this is a ridge on which the Rebels had fortifications and which we now hold. In front of this ridge is a open field varying from one to two miles in width and three miles in length. Our men had at first thrown up breastworks in the edge of the woods next to Big Shanty but every night they advanced the rifle pits, and at the time the ridge was abandoned we had three lines of breastworks; the first two abandoned and the troops occupying the third at some points, one in front of Dodge. We had thrown up a dozen different lines. From the point in front of General Dodge's new headquarters a complete view of the whole line can be had and the two spurs of the Kenesaw, the position of the Rebel batteries and etc. From the railroad where I was, the shells would whistle over our heads as they were thrown from our battery to the mountain. Some of them came so close that I thought it safe to get down from my horse. Barnes came back after a little and I got the return approved and then went to Captain K for the rations. Just as I got through drawing, an order came to take them back to our camp. (This) occupied the morning before issue, two days rations. Take over in the wagon. We are ordered to Rome where we shall probably stay for awhile. Slept in the kitchen. Floor full of negroes. Colonel ordered teamsters cook to be left. She wanted to go on. Had a small black boy with her, his face all swelled up where she had pounded him. I have noticed as a curious fact that the negro women are more degraded and more brutal than the men.

June 21 - Passed through Acworth. Colonel had me stop and see if there was any forage. Found some damaged. Went to within two miles of the Etowah at Hightower. The road was very bad, one team gave out. It lead over the Allatoona Mountains, passing by Allatoona and following the railroad. Passed a foundry and furnace built in '63 now destroyed. Hills all the way from Acworth to the Etowah. Hills large enough to be called mountains in most countries. Our army by going to

Dallas, secured the river, these mountains, and 16 or 17 miles of railroad which could not have been got in a direct attack. If Sherman can make another such move it will put him on the Chattahoochee.

June 22 - Crossed the Etowah which is strongly fortified and reached Kingston about 11:00 a.m. Got provision return approved and drew rations for 400 men. One day, got no meat. Moved out 4 miles, issued 2 days rations. Had a first class supper, grapes, potatoes and etc. The man living at the house not owning it, had lost everything. Had nothing to eat. He can not get inside the lines for three weeks and if he does not starve before that time it will be a wonder.

June 23 - Moved out about 8:00, giving our horses time to graze before moving. Got into Rome about 11:00 and moved out over the Oostanaula about a mile and a half and went into camp around a big house once owned by the aristocracy. Drew three days rations of post commissary. Wagon stuck in the mud by the bridge and took us all of the time till night unloading, carrying up the hill, and rolling up the wagon. Mud about 8 inches deep but good road once up on level ground. Candles and soap fell out and wagon crushed 12 pounds of candles in a hurry. To late for supper but got some after waiting awhile. Our camp is very pleasantly situated, only the woods are hardly thick enough to shelter the camp. A very good spring (is) in the center of the regiment. The place was owned by Colonel Shorter (the colonel simply a title). The house is quite costly, $10,000, two stories, kitchens and rooms below arranged in the best style. There was at first considerable good furniture in the house but it has been all moved away. The out houses, negro quarters, and stables are substantially built and the grounds covered with all kinds of fruit trees and ornamental shrubbery. It was a handsome place built by a gentleman of taste and immense wealth. The house overlooks Rome and the two rivers with their valleys covered now with ripening wheat. There was a family of squatters in the house when we came but the general had sent them orders to move tomorrow. Oh they are about as miserable a set of the biped race as I ever saw. They were very indignant over the order but commenced to pack. Rome is a very pretty place, one of the handsomest in the South. A wide street runs back from the junction of the two rivers at about equal distances from each. This is the business street of the town. There is a row of trees on each side and one through the center, several fine churches, and a good many fine residences. The town is now mostly deserted, the troops being camped outside and only a few buildings used for offices etc. General Vandever is in command of the troops which comprise the 50th, 57th Illinois and 39th Iowa, the 1st Michigan Battery (B) and our regiment. Another battery of three guns has been dug up from the wells and will be put in position in a few days. They had been apprehensive of a attack for some time and troops were ordered to be ready to fall in at a moments notice. General was very glad that our regiment had arrived. They increased his force besides giving him something to scout with. 30 men had caused the excitement and anticipation of attack by charging upon our picket post.

June 24 - Issued rations in the forenoon. Wrote part of a letter to father. Had a good swim in the Coosa. Splendid dinner, berries etc. People are making a living.

June 25 - Finished the letter to father, it was a long one, written (with) a description of situations etc.

June 26 - Edwards went to church. Would have gone but clothes are too ragged to go inside a church. Wrote a letter to Hopkins.

June 27 - Drew 4 days rations. Hunted all over town and finally found some scales, good ones. Sent team for them. Got rations issued by noon. Went swimming in the afternoon. Swim almost every day.

June 28 - Went swimming again today. Nothing of interest. Pickets have been attacked for two nights or imagined themselves attacked and alarmed the camps. Got some beef killed in the afternoon and issued to the companies.

June 29 - Edwards went to Decatur. Kellogg is to be adjutant while he is gone. Worked a short time on Captain Ford's quartermaster papers. Found some of them gone and had to stop. Had another swim.

June 30 - Read Mrs. Morrants auto or Life of an Actress, a very interesting book and takes a good view of the theatre. Most to good for it presents influence. Got a beef killed, issued in the forenoon.

July 1 - Got rations. Did not have full rations of hardly anything. Issued what we got. Mc. went to Chattanooga.

July 2 - Nothing of any interest. Read Bleak House and went in swimming.

July 3 - Nothing today but a little reading. Would have gone to church but clothes are too bad.

July 4 - The detachment sent out yesterday under Captain Tramel got in this morning. They had captured over 40 horses, killed one captain, captured 10 men. The regiment went over to the village to a review. Only lasted an hour or so. I got some flour and meal. It is very difficult to get rations at this point being so far from the front. The most part of the rations go right through. Spalding went at night and captured a captain home on furlough.

July 5 - Nothing again today except the arrival of the detachment under Major Cramer, nearly 200 strong. Good many of the old mess mates along. Company D numbers themselves some 70 men. Got rations today, full of flour and crackers and sugar, 1 of pork, 2 1/2 beans. Very unfortunate as the men go out tomorrow on 3 days (scout); no coffee, hard on them.

July 6 - Nothing today of interest. Had a swim. Colonel offered me a 1st lieutenant in Company H, 3 years muster. I do not think it will pay to go in. Father is against (it) and so am I although I am sometimes almost tempted to do it, but I believe in my sober moments I am not at all inclined that way. Colonel somewhat astonished that I should not be ready to take it. Peck is to take command of Company D, just raised.

He was not going in again but the temptation was not to be resisted and he has agreed to take the company.

July 7 - Colonel sent me out to look for beef. Found 1 yoke about 3 miles from camp and in all got 18 head. We traveled about 15 miles, went on the Alabama road. The man where I got the oxen was very anxious to keep his oxen, but work oxen are as little advantage to the citizens as anything as we could take in the form of meat. I would make a good tax gatherer however. Went out 5 miles on the Alabama (road) then took across to the Summerville road. Heard of some cattle out 1/2 mile. Stopped at a house and sent out 8 men to bring them in. Snelling went out with me just for the fun but had no detachment along. We had quite a talk with the woman who was very witty and smart and able. The men brought a herd of good cattle and we then went back to camp. The expedition came in, had one man killed belonging to Company A.

July 8 - Killed two of the cattle and issued the meat to the companies. Went in swimming. Nothing of any interest. Got a letter from father.

July 9 - Woman came in today who owned a cow and heifer that I had taken and stated her case to the colonel so that he gave her back the cow. The heifer I had already killed.

July 10 - Killed another beef this morning and issued it. The men do not care much for fresh meat; it is too much trouble to save it and (it) is generally poor and tough. Yesterday having got the remainder of coffee and pork and I wish the people had them back, at least one of pork, the other one could be spared just as well as not. In the afternoon the colonel told me that the regiment was going out for 3 days and of course I had to draw rations. Drew for 5 days. Brown has been relieved by a captain and A.C.S. He would not take back my spoiled part of pork. Gave full rations of everything but coffee. Worked till 9:00 p.m. issuing. An(drew) Scott helped me. Got him detailed so as to keep him from being mixed up in the row in Company F which is disposed to mutiny and refuses to go on duty, their times having expired, some of them nearly 3 months. Colonel sent two of them to the guard house and preferred charges against them. I think they ought to be relieved when their time is up, but an enlisted man will always be the loser in an issue with an officer.

July 11 - Colonel left pretty early. I did nothing of any special value except get a barrel of pork out of the commissary and full rations of coffee for the half. They are not a very pleasant set to deal with.

July 12 - Nothing at all today.

July 13 - Lieutenant Edwards not returned yet. Colonel got back about noon. Did not get but few prisoners but one of them was a colonel on special duty under Governor Brown. Issued the remainder of the rations. Wrote a letter to father.

July 14 - Edwards came back today but did not get the property beyond Chattanooga. This is another disappointment for I am getting more ragged every day. Another letter from father, written in May.

July 15 - Drew rations in forenoon and issued in the afternoon. Edwards brought 65 men through with him. Lieutenant Kellogg left today but he did not know whether he would go to the front before going home or not. Ruf Sparks at the hospital in the forenoon. He was fit for duty and expected to join his regiment in a few days. Our regiment (the 64th) has suffered severely in the fights of the 27th and the 4th. Hinckley (the) adjutant was killed, Captain Gibbons wounded, since died. Hinckley went out to inspect a skirmish line and was going to a rifle pit where Colonel Morrill was when he was shot. Captain Stoner helped him into the pit. Another man on the line, shot in the foot, came to the same place and while he was lying on his side another bullet struck him in the heart and the blood spurted over the colonel, captain and Hinckley and gathered at the bottom of the pit. The colonel lay here all day between these two dead men. The regiment began the march with 750 men and now has less than 300. I don't think there is in the history of the world an account of a campaign as long and as active as this one has been East and West. It can not last much longer. The men are wearing out.

July 16 - Colonel Spencer came today and the army correspondent. I believe it is the intention to have this regiment join Rousseau's command, moving from Decatur. Another big raid and the colonel is not very well but just as schemey as ever. Got some chickens, butter and berries for the mess. Am getting very lazy with nothing to do only every five days. Spoke to colonel about going back to company as captain wished. Colonel would not relieve me at present. Sent a letter to Jennie Gilman. In one of father's letters he speaks of Luce Magee having called on him, a thing that I should like to do, I don't care how soon.

July 17 - Captain Tramel went to Chattanooga today. Colonel Godfrey wanted to go but his application was refused. Nothing else.

July 18 - No clothing today. Got appointment from Spencer as 1st lieutenant, Blaloch 2nd. Peck got his as captain, Shurtleff and Tramel as majors and Edwards as captain. Was told in the evening about a man stripped and shot, a woman hacked with a sabre and lying out in the woods. (They) encountered another tied and whipped, house set on fire, bed burning and child thrown into it and then thrown out on the floor. This is worse than cannibalism but there is no doubt of its truth, the citizens were Union and the wretches who did the work guerrillas.

July 19 - Nothing of any interest.

July 20 - Went to town after rations. While over there darkey told me my father was waiting for me at headquarters. I mounted and started for home. Found him at the window looking a little more grey than formerly but on the whole, full as well if not better than when I left. We had a long talk after affairs in our place and another until noon. In afternoon I had to issue rations. Colonel was glad to see him and a little surprised that a ragamuffin like myself should have as good looking, well dressed, and as intelligent a father as owned me for a son.

July 21 - Passed day with father. Clothing came in the afternoon. Got some pants, boots, stockings, hat, shirts, drawers, and look a little more respectable.

July 22 - Father wanted me to go to the front with him. Went to the general who told me to forward in writing. Sent up the application in form. Seems like home to have father here. Colonel wanted him to speak on Sunday and he promised to do so if he staid. Application returned approved. Tried to get on the cars but failed, just 5 minutes too (late). Guy Smith was also going but both of us were left.

July 23 - Went on horseback to Kingston with mail riders. Father rode Scott's horse, enjoyed the ride very well. At Kingston got dinner at Sanitary Commission and took the down train for Marietta. Reached that place about 5:00. Could find no train going to the river. Went up to town, found that supplies for the 16th Corps were taken thru Rossville nearly 30 miles. This was too much of a walk and there was no train going to either our corps or the 15th. No ambulances and I could not get any horses. Slept at the rooms of the Christian Commission. Showed the works around Kenesaw to father and explained the position of the troops.

July 24 - Got on a train about 10:00 that was expected to go to the front every minute but which did not leave until 2:00 p.m. Before getting on to the train I looked again to the hospitals for ambulances, in the supply depots, for trains, and to the quartermaster for a horse. Could not get any of them, none going out. Put the dispatches from our regiment and from General Vandever in one package and sent them to Captain Barnes. Reached Vining's Station about 5:00. Then had to go on foot to the bridge over (?) miles from here to General Thomas's Headquarters. We were told that it was 7 miles. The Chattahoochee is about the same size as the Etowah at Rome. Where we crossed there had been a permanent bridge put up and the pontoons taken away. We walked 5 miles beyond the river and still found it 3 miles to General Thomas's Headquarters. Stopped at a courier post in a mill. Got some fish off the boys for supper. Slept on some wool, very good bed. Father stood the tramp much better than I expected. The cannonading we could hear very plainly.

July 25 - Started before breakfast. Did not go to the headquarters, but found the 31st Wisconsin. Saw some of the boys from Wayne. The balls were flying around occasionally while we were standing by the works. Charley Bridgeman who was a lieutenant had gone back to the wagons. Went back (and) found him at the wagons, also Eld. Woodworth, chaplain of the regiment. After awhile got some breakfast. While we were waiting (a) man had his hand taken off by a piece of shell, and one was brought in from the 31st where we had been standing. He was shot through the shoulder. Went over to the 5th Wisconsin Battery, 2 miles, and on the way over a shell struck about a rod in front of us and tore up the dirt generally. Did not appear to frighten father any, for myself I thought them close enough. Found McKnight 1st lieutenant of the battery in his tent. Had a chat with him and eat dinner. Had a pretty good meal. The 31st did not understand how to do things, this being their first experience. 5th Wisconsin was in the 14th Corps which had several batteries within a mile and a half of Atlanta. The lines just cross the railroad on the north and swing around to the south nearly to the Macon Road. In the fight of the 22nd (July) the Army of the Tennessee lost very heavily. Colonel Morrill was commanding a brigade and got a wound in the shoulder. General McPhearson was killed by some Rebel skirmishers who had got between the 16th and 17th Corps, the line not being continuous. A colonel said that 2000 Rebels were buried in front of the army when he left. After dinner we walked back to Vinings, a hard walk. I tried to get some supper or something to make it from (out) of the commissary but could not find him. Father saw the sanitary agent. From him we secured a good supper. Slept on the oats under the wood shed. The hospital is the general one for the Army of the Cumberland, of course very large. Two or three regiments of Rousseau were here and full of the account of their raid which was a success, they having torn up over 30 miles of track and destroyed a large quantity of supplies. In the morning father said we may not be together again if I conclude to stay and proposed to pray once with me before he left. It seemed like home and made me think of old times to hear his prayer.

July 26 - One train went by from the bridge but did not stop and we could not get on. A colonel was taking up some of his goods on a wagon and father and I rode in it up to Marietta. Provost Marshall would not give me a pass until I got transportation from the transportation officer. (He) said I ought to have a pass from department headquarters. This delayed me. Train transportation officer gave me a pass without any questions and we got on the 2 1/2 train. Eat dinner with Mr. Pierce the sanitary agent who was formerly a student from H(illsdale). Had quite a talk. Father was pretty tired and thought he would keep on to Chattanooga and not come to Rome. I would not urge him for the living at the best is not very good and not very likely to improve a mans health. I would like to have him stay but think he is running risks all the while. The train stopped until 3:00 and I slept in the car, then slept in a broken one till morning. Could not get out on any train they said (going) to Rome.

July 27 - The train was out to Rome and had not returned yet. Started to come out with some of the boys. Mail carriers ride part of the way and walk part but the provost marshall said that we could not get through, so truned back pretty hungry and made at my ill luck. Found a place where they kept boarders on one side of town and eat dinner. Train with sick and wounded came about 3:00 and I got a ride home. Reported to general and (he) said it was all right. Colonel and lieutenant colonel were disappointed at my not having seen General Dodge, etc.

July 28 - Carried over the letters to the sanitary agent which had been given to me by Pierce and tried to get mustered but the mustering officer would not muster me for the unexpired term of service and I would not muster for three years. Colonel Spencer said that he would get my resignation honorably accepted if I should wish to resign when the company would be mustered out but he may not be able to make the work or he may not be in the service and then I would be bound for the three years. I am not sure either that he would try to get me released. He was very anxious for me to go in again but I refused although I am on the point once of making out the rolls and trusting to his promise to have me released. Captain Ford is going to Nashville tomorrow to see about the payment of troops mustered out of the companies.

144

July 29 - Nothing of any consequence. Colonel wished me to run the company and commissary while the captain was gone.

July 30 - Went to town and drew the rations for next issue. Got the candles, etc. for headquarters, full rations for the men. Paymaster came in afternoon.

July 31 - Got receipt rolls and made out for May and June. Worked all day at it. Paymaster's name (is) Bruce.

      NOTE: This is the beginning of a new diary. Front is inked: F. Wayland Dunn "H" Co. 1st U.S. Cav. Ala. Volunteers.

August 1 - Finished muster and pay rolls and had the men sign them. Sent to the city for the signature of boys in hospital. Paymaster pays up to the 1st of July. Issued 7 days rations.

August 2 - Helped Peck make one roll last night and finished this morning. Company was paid in the afternoon. Paymaster was very accommodating, allowed us (to) change the rolls after they were sent in. Colonel Godfrey got leave to travel to Memphis etc. on recruiting service. He will go home probably. McWorkman had leave of absence and also goes tomorrow.

August 3 - Got pay this morning 869 dollars (?) and immediately paid my debts; Peck 30.70, Tharpe 30, Kellogg 52, Blaloch 30, Sanford 35, and am now square with the exception of Major Fairfield 15. In the afternoon Captain Edwards was taken very sick with something like a congestive chill and we had to rub him for an hour or two to keep the circulation up and keep him from dying. Sergeant Lukens and McGaughey came from Decatur today. Fairfield has about 80 men recruited. I understand that Colonel Spencer is going to stop recruiting for that regiment and break up the organization. That is not using the major right. He is not active enough but his regiment is filling up faster than this did at first. Major does not understand wire pulling, does not confer with Spencer and Spencer does not think he is doing anything. Mc says that he (Mc) has spent over 200 and is now no nearer a command than at first.

August 4 - Nothing of any interest today except from Hank - a tip top good letter which I answered at once.

August 5 - Nothing today. Read Ivanhoe.

August 6 - Drew rations today. Rained and got stuff wet while it was being brought over.

August 7 - Mr. Collins preached in the afternoon, a very good discourse but I found from what little I had seen that a chaplain to be of any value in a regiment must be able to draw the attention of the men.They will not take the same interest in it that they do at home where the church and the public opinion will in some measure regulate their actions. Colonel Spencer got an idea that I was going to study for the ministry. (He) asked me if it was so (and) offered me the chaplaincy of the regiment if I would take it, half joke and half in earnest. There is but little prospect of my being a minister very soon. It is said that precepts without example are very poor preaching and I am far from being a suitable example for a man trying to live a Christian life and the consciousness of unworthiness would be to me as actual a barrier as if everyone was possessed with the same knowledge. The time is coming round again when I am to choose some occupation for a year or so if not for life. The army I feel indisposed to continue in because I do not wish to separate myself from the home influences and from father in such a permanent manner as a 3 year muster would be. Besides this, I do not feel the obligations to stay in the army that I did for entering it and do not care to expose myself to the dangers of soldier life and the hardships (not physical) for the sake of the pay and commission.

August 8 - Issued rations today, only a pound of flour to a man. The first seven days having been issued, he cut off 2 ounces. Got a letter from father, all safe at home.

August 9 - Edwards left for home this morning. More reports come to the regiment of cruelties practiced upon the relatives of men in the regiment. 8 or nine men killed. One member of the regiment had his leg unjointed, was scalped and castrated. This was in retaliation for the shooting of a conscript officer who was shot for the killing of a brother of one of our men. (Bill Sims brother).

August 10 - Received a letter from Day. Snelling gave his horse to General Dodge. It is a very valuable one. The owner is said to have refused $2600 for her at the commencement of the war. He could get $300 for him any day. The company got in at night. Kellogg had succeeded in getting a good supply of vegetables. Took a ride over to town.

August 11 - Got orders to go on 3 days scout. Went over to town just at night to draw the rations for the command. Could not get any meat. Kellogg went after rations after dark.

August 12 - Issued rations in the forenoon. In the afternoon got the company into line after some trouble. Men were scattered so only half the company was here. Finally got 26 men. Went to Cave Springs before halting. Rained and had a poor night of it. Did not get into camp until 11:00.

August 13 - Broke camp about 4 and went from here to Cedartown and then down towards Jacksonville. Got some horses. Winters got a very nice one but before he got to the front Snelling hit him for it. Camped about 9:00, 6 miles from Possum Snout. Had nothing to eat of any consequence, a little green corn, a hendfull of crackers, and a little milk.

August 14 - Charged into Possum Snout with Company "L". Found nothing. Heard of several small squads of Rebel cavalry. Some of the boys found three men that the conscripting bushwackers had killed and not buried. Went to Buchanan. Boys tore the stores open, court house, and smashed things generally. Rebel squad fired into the rear while we was feeding at noon, thought we were going to have a fight but proved to be only a little scouting party. Went two miles further and advance were

146

fired into. Spent some time in looking up the bushwacker but did not find him. Saw a mare out in the field 1/2 a mile from road. Took three of the boys with me. Went over to get her. Man tried to run her off and I shot three times at him, did not hit him. Let down the fence and Simpson followed him (and) caught him at the next fence. Went over the mountains in the direction of the Rome and Vanwert Road. Camped at 8:00 in the pine timber by a little log shanty.

August 15 - Started before daylight. Horses backs getting sore, saddles not been off since we left camp longer than 15 minutes. Went 5 miles through the woods without any road and then struck the Rome Road. "H" had the advance and got several more horses and mules. Heard the Rebels were in waiting for us but did not see any of them. Had a hard rain just before we reached town. All along found plenty of fruit, watermelons, and etc. Boys got to Jayhawking. One man (in) Company L stole a watch which the colonel made him give up. When we got into camp heard that Dalton had been captured and Wheeler was playing hit generally.

August 16 - The reports about Wheeler prove to be exaggerated. Did nothing today.

August 17 - Drew and issued 5 days rations. Got extra coffee on account of going on a scout. Colonel expects to be gone 8 or 10 days. The horses are in very poor condition for such a trip. He wants me to go as commissary and quartermaster.

August 18 - Left camp about nine. Men took 3 days (rations) on mules in addition to what they had in haversacks. Mare's back a little sore and did not like to ride her. Got a substitute horse from the company. All the good horses had riders and I would not take a horse away from a man. Went 15 miles on the Alabama Road without seeing any Rebels and camped about 3:00 pm. Got plenty of oats for the horses and the color cooked supper at the house. The owners of the house had been moved 2 times, once from Tennessee by Bragg where he left a large crop of grain and 300 hogs and again from Rome when the Rebels supplied themselves from the proceeds of his farm. Heard of the 6 men who deserted from Company B day before yesterday. The Rebels got after them and chased them into the next county. Took good care of my horse, washed his back, curried him, and etc. Always take care of my own horse. Niggers can't be trusted to saddle them.

August 19 - Got into Cedar Bluff about 9:00 am. Major Tramel took two companies around another road so as to come into the place from different roads. Major Tramel took two prisoners. One of them had his sister and two or three lady friends. They were very handsome and somewhat aristocratic smart. Colonel asked them about their sweethearts and they told him they were in the army, one a colonel and another a major. They were very anxious to get Steve released but the colonel would not do it but instead proposed to take the women themselves along, making one of them ride behind each of us on our horses. Steve had a letter applying for a furlough and the colonel took him along. We found some salt which was distributed to the companies. Snelling asked the colonel for Steves coat which the colonel made him give up. The girls thought this the extreme of injustice and that was the reason of the colonels doing it, just to hear them talk and cry a little. Miss Butler stood it out until colonel asked her for her major stars which she wore on her collar. She couldn't stand this and broke down completely. Colonel did not press the point. I had no disposition to talk rough but rather dismount and do a little visiting in a peaceable parting. Heard of General Clanton with 600 men going to Little Wills Valley from Cedar Bluff. We went to the Summerville Road as far as Mrs. Price's bridge. Crossed the river about a mile and camped. Rebels fired on the rear guard. Latty chased them a mile or two but they are too well mounted. Got old corn from one building at Mrs. Prices. She thought it very hard (and) wished to know whether I knew what corn was for. I did not know. She informed me that it was to save life so we fed it to the horses. The old lady was very pleasant and talked very fair. Someone had burned a 100 bales of cotton for her. She did not think it was Yanks or Rebs but that it (was) some private enemies. The old man where we camped was disposed to fold his hands and trust to Providence. Got a good supper and comfortable dining hall to eat in. Slept on hall floor. Colonel slept in bed. Rained like suds. Horse improving.

August 20 - Left early. Advanced guard, rather Mc captured an orderly sergeant and one man. Belonged to Wheeler's command. (They) were with him when he captured Dalton but had got leaves of absence and were making their way to the main army. They had four good horses. Charged into Alpine but found nothing but a tip top good dinner which had been prepared for some thrashers. We had taken their horses and they had gone home. It was a stunning dinner, best I've had in a long time. Got some old Long Island watermelons. Came pretty near eating to much. After dinner crossed the region called the Lookout Mountains. It was hard climbing but at the top the view back was magnificent, over range after range of mountains and up a valley 80 miles long. The top of the mountain was a level plain 10 or 15 miles wide and 80 long. Through the center of this (ran) a river large enough so that it could be forded only at a few points. A few citizens live on the mountain. The stream is very romantic and near where we crossed there was a falls 60 feet in height. There are mines of stone, coal and iron. In the afternoon colonel asked Snelling to take the prisoners coats and go ahead to find out where Clanton's force was. I asked him if he did not want to take a prisoner along. He replied yes and so I gave him my pistol and went with him, making 3 Confederates and one captured Yank. We went down the mountain, terrible steep place. At the bottom we found that Weatherspoon and a 100 men had been in the valley during the day and were going to Trenton and then return. We went on to Winston's, a judge and prominent man of the country. He gave us the same information and more besides. While we were waiting, Snelling in the house with one man, and the rest just at the gate holding their horses, the column came in sight. We had not expected them so soon and felt somewhat anxious and just as much relieved when we found who they were. It was amusing to hear the old man and woman come round from Confederate to Union side. The old man claimed to be Confederate when he knew we were Yanks and was sharp enough to ask for some of the coffee we had captured from the Yanks (Rebels?) at Dalton. It was two or three hours before the whole thing was owned up. The judge had been a Union man and in the Succession Convention was one of the 15 that would not sign the ordinance. He said that now he had to make friends with both sides.

August 21 - Went back over the mountain. Got some leather and a fine 3 year old colt when we stopped for dinner. In the afternoon got another very fine one, same age. Rebels fired into our rear once. Crossed the bridge at Price's and went a mile or so beyond where we camped the day before. Tied the horses in the yard. One of the boys turned over a beehive after honey. The bees swarmed out and began to sting the horses and they went crazy. One of mine broke loose, the other I got untied. All the headquarters horses got furious and while Doctor Swaving was trying to get (the) colonel's horse out, he kicked him breaking his leg below the knee.

August 22 - Doctor (was) put in a wagon and taken along. (It was) very painful. Passed over the road where Corporal Johnson of Company A, who took the news of Clanton's movement was shot. Mr. McClance said that the Rebels had about ten men. When they fired, our men returned the fire and three of them dismounted. The Rebels did not go to Johnson, and in the morning McClance sent in the dispatch. Johnson had tried to chew it up but did not have the strength. McClance buried the man and took care of his things until the Rebels came the next day and took them. Two of the boys horses came into the road just as we were passing and we took them along. The men got into camp all right.

August 23 - Drew rations today and issued. Clerk was disposed to find fault but I did not care to explain, as I had the order for the issue.

August 24 - Nothing today of any consequence except paying Hudson $10 for his mare, a fine animal.

August 25 - Nothing today. Little mare trotted in the sulky. I got in the country (and) made time. Got the sulky from a man ten miles out. He said I could have it if I promised to leave it at Mr. Kauffman's. When I told him about giving him a mule when we were going out and he said I could keep the sulky.

August 26 - Wrote letters to father and Jennie and got one from J.J. and Walt. Drove Hudson mare in evening.

August 27 - Wrote letters to J.J. Drew 3 days rations and issued to the regiment in order to supply them with 6 days for the scout which is to start tomorrow. Colonel Spencer has gone to W__tville and Major Cramer is to take command.

August 28 - Did not go as expected, the general ordering the regiment in camp. Chaplain preached in the evening.

August 29 - Drove my little mare in the evening, took like fun.

August 30 - Made out a muster and pay roll in the afternoon. Colonel Dodds is staying at headquarters and they are having gay times.

August 30 - Half sick, but finished another pay roll. Sick all day, but took a ride in the evening. Came near getting sulky kicked to pieces.

September 1 - Nothing worth mentioning.

September 2 - Took a drive in the evening.

149

September 3 - Drew rations for seven days. Full rations of all but meat. Rained before we got to camp but did not do much damage. Issued in the afternoon, 40 behind on flour. Clerk made a mistake of 50 pounds in sugar. News came last night that Atlanta had been evacuated and this morning that Mobile with 10,000 prisoners and 100 pieces of cannon. Most too good to be true.

September 4 - Inspection of the regiment on the drill ground. Thought of going to church but was too late. Ferris and Lieutenant Moe (?) of the 44th colored came over to see me. Did not know them at first ie-could not recall their names. Had a long talk and a ride back to camp with them. Pretty sick at night, too much hard tough bread. Colonel Spencer came tonight.

September 5 - Went to Rome in forenoon and succeeded in getting the 50 pounds of sugar due. Got a barrel of flour. Worked on quartermaster papers in afternoon. Felt miserable all day. Took a dose of salts in the evening.

September 6 - Nothing of interest today.

September 7 - Colonel Spencer, Colonel Dodds, and the adjutant with escort went on flag of truce to Cave Springs and if they can get through, to Jacksonville. Major Cramer told me to act as adjutant while Tupper was gone. Had drill in the afternoon, only a few out. Most of the regiment on duty. At 5:00 had dress parade infantry fashion. Got through the adjutant's part with one or two slight variations. Colonel's party came in the evening. Had only got 10 miles from Cave Springs and found a captain that understood his business and took their dispatches intimating that they were at the end of their march. They found a lieutenant of scouts and got him pretty drunk but obtained but little information from him. Found that a force was kept in Cave Springs large enough so that Tupper thought (that) a 100 men (were) few enough to go to the place. They are mostly boys however from 15 to 18. (They are) armed with Enfield muskets. The Texas Rangers are a lot of horse theives feared as much or nearly as much by the Confederates as by our troops. Their chief business is stealing horses and it is of no importance to whether the horse belongs to a soldier or a citizen nor to what army the soldier may belong.

September 10 - Drew 10 days full rations, 1/2 rations pork, 1/2 beef. Had to wait 3 hours before I could get it loaded. Then had to send back in the afternoon for 2 loads (of) flour. Issued the whole after 2:00 o'clock. Issued very even sugar and coffee, not varying 2 pounds from the draw, flour and pork only 10 or 15. This is very close work in 5600 rations issued for 19 different detachments. Got through just in time for supper and tired enough to be willing to stop. But little left on this issue for headquarters. No mail from the north yet. The road is said to be cut again. Started a letter to Alt Day.

September 11 - Did nothing today. Colonel Spencer and Dodds, Cramer and Flint got on a spree at night. Dodds drunk as a fool, had a regular tear, smashed things generally.

September 12 - Worked on quartermaster papers for the captain. McWorkman and Godfrey came today, had overstaid their time about two weeks in consequence they say of railroad being cut. They are hail fellows and it will be all right.

September 13 - Nothing of any consequence.

September 14 - Got a letter from Mayer Hec (?). Had established himself at H(illsdale College) and is going to study. Trying to put in ____ days into ____.

September 15 - Got letter from father. Says he intended to let the farm but if I wanted he would keep it for me. I hardly know what to do, but I can see nothing better than the farm. I like it tip top, that is a stock farm. I suppose father thinks I ought to be in some other position where my education would be of more use to me than it will on a farm. I feel very certain that he would be best pleased to see me studying for the ministry, but that is out of the question. I am not good enough for a preacher and will not study hoping for improvement. I am sorry that it can't be so for I feel certain that it would please him more than any other occupation. I do not think that there is anything in my outward life in conflict with the Bible's teaching but I have the consciousness of an unworthiness too great to allow me to think of setting up myself as an example. If others did not I never could feel like an honest man knowing myself.

September 16 - Nothing of any consequence. General Clanton's Brigade came to Cave Springs but did not attack Rome although there was some expectation that he would. He planted two pieces of cannon within 2 1/2 miles of the city but only fired two or three shots and those at the skirmish line of the 7th Illinois. Our regiment had a sharp skirmish with their advance in the forenoon, killed one, wounded two and sent in four prisoners. There was a forage train out; Captain Lomax's Company (H) and two companies (of) infantry with Henry rifles (7th Illinois). They had a sharp skirmish and only saved the train by the help of the Henry rifles. They made hobs of the Rebels, heavier than a regiment. We got an order to move personal baggage. It was Cramer's order but was revoked before things were packed.

September 17 - There is some excitement and there are heavy details out in all the roads from our regiment.

September 18 - Nothing today. Took a long ride in the sulky.

September 19 - Wrote a long letter to Hank. Fishback went south after recruits yesterday.

September 20 - Weaver came from Decatur and Lukens and he went to the front, Spencer and Cramer also. Drew five days rations and issued to command. Was short about 20 pounds coffee and other things besides.

September 21 - Fishback returned today, 26 recruits but some of them disposed to join his company. Drew rations for recruits and got full rations of pork for beef rations issued yesterday. Lukens went to the front today. Rained all day and last night.

September 22 - Did nothing today but read papers, did forms and etc.

September 23 - Finished the quartermaster papers and captain sent them away. Lieutenant Moore came over in the afternoon, had been up to Nashville.

September 24 - Moore went back today. River has risen from rains of yesterday and last night so that the bridge can not be crossed on horseback. Could not draw rations in consequence.

September 25 - Read a little today and in the afternoon went out on the Summerville Road to ride. Found myself without a pass and the lieutenant would not let me pass but informed me that I could exercise my horse on the track. Went to town and got a pass from Captain Edwards for five days and then had a good ride.

September 26 - Went to town and drew five days rations, got full of all but salt. Do not understand why they cheat a little on most everything, two or three pounds on coffee, eight or ten on sugar, and all the rest in the same way. There are more swindlers in the army than cells for them in the state prisons. Frank issued the rations in the afternoon.

September 27 - Crossed the river this morning and went up the Costenaula. Found an excellent road level and smooth for a nearly a mile. The little mare did some excellent trotting. Hope I can take her home. Have not yet heard from my application for transportation.

September 28 - Made out muster rolls for our men whose time is out. 20 present and they were mustered out in the afternoon. Worked pretty hard at it and my head ached some when I was through. Troops have been coming in today and yesterday of the 2nd Division of the 16th (Corps) and the 4th of the 17th (Corps). Six or seven regiments came in. I made out the return and Frank went to town and drew ten days rations after the teams got in from foraging. I drew this early for fear that so many regiments coming in Captain's Owens stock might get low in the next two days. (It is) said that the Rebel army has been broken up and a large share of it is going to be stationed at Blue Mountain which is about two days ride from Rome. If this proves true the force now here will be largely increased. It is also reported that Forrest has captured Decatur and two regiments of negro troops. Got a letter from Pratt dated at hospital, Lexigton, Kentucky.

September 29 - Nothing of interest today. It is said today that Athens not Decatur was captured by Forrest. Judge Wright eat dinner at our mess today. He is the father of Colonel Wright who came in some time since. He has been a member of both congress' U.S. and Confederate. He belonged to the opposition party in the last, has been a Union man all the while and is a person of a good deal of intelligence. McWorkman told a pretty good story of a Tennessean at a camp meeting on the Tennessee River after the fall of Donelson, and our gun boats were coming up the river. The leader of the meeting was praying that as the lord dried up the waters of the Red Sea so he would dry up the Tennessee that the enemy might not encompass them. All of them were responding with heardy Amens, but one more earnest than the rest broke out: "Sink 'em Lord G-D d-m 'em Lord, right now". The right now Mc got off in good style. The railroad is said to be cut near Murfreesboro.

September 30 - Made out monthly return and quarterly return of deceased soldiers. Spent some or most of the day in reading "New York - Its Upper Ten and Lower Million", a very interesting book and a good one if the exhilarations to correct living are any criterion of such a book. No news of any interest. General Vandever has gone to Marietta and Edwards went with him. General Corse assumed command.

October 1 - The first day of my last month of soldier experience in the 1st Alabama. I made out the issue tickets and Frank issued the rations. Rode over to town, got a Continental and U.S.S. magazine. Had a ride up the river. The large mare did some very good trotting but not equal to the small one. Was bringing a couple of hams home on the sulky and one of them fell off. Did not notice it for some distance and then some ladies had picked it up. Did not like to ask them for it though I knew they had it. Frank got it. The Nashville Railroad is in the hands of the Rebels and there is no prospect for letters going or coming very soon. Should like to hear from home, hear what disposition he has made of the farm.

October 2 - The recent rains have raised the river so that in the afternoon the Oostenaula was over the ends of the bridge and there was no crossing for horses or wagons. Read Continental, two or three good pieces.

October 3 - River still rising. Detail that went to Kingston yesterday can not get their horses over. Read last of Adam Bede, it is a great book. Had a long talk with Captain Ford about Chile. He says that a fortune could be made there selling reapers, threshers, and fanning mills. Very healthy. Country reapers first introduced into California brought 12 to $1400 and freight only $90. Think it would be a good thing for a man going there to learn ambrotyping. Could make a good thing of it. Captain said that clipper ships made the trip from San Francisco to China in 3 and 4 weeks. Got me into something of a furor to go west. A trip to China or Japan would not be a bad thing. Colonel Spencer took a 100 men and a large boat to Coosaville in the afternoon. Expects, I believe, to capture a squad of guerrillas. Has been raining for a week and is at it again today.

October 4 - The scout returned today, not able to cross the river. In the afternoon news came from Allatoona that the Rebels had taken possession of the road between that place and Marietta and were threating Allatoona. General Corse goes down to Allatoona with all the troops at this place but one brigade. We had orders to move with 3 days rations but the bridge was not finished until after dark and general sent orders for us to remain in camp and if we were wanted he would send for us before 10:00 tomorrow. Colonel said that he wanted me to go and I was not at all sorry. I should like to take part in one fight before I go home that would amount to something. As my time draws near its close instead of dreading to get into a fight I am more anxious than ever to do something worth noting if even it is a little risky. Colonel Spencer is left in command of the place and troops.

October 5 - Got no orders to move but news came that General Corse commenced fighting at 2:00 am. It is said that the Rebel force is quite large, the largest half of Hood's Army, the same that was reported to be at Blue Mountain. In the evening two deserters came in from Cedar Bluff. They said that Wheeler with 8000 men was at Edwards Ferry trying to cross. He had sent heavy details over the Chattanooga which was swimming after boats and rafts for the troops to cross in. These boys saw men of their own regiment and learned that Wheeler had been ordered to Lost Mountain. They boys had furloughs and when they were out they had got passes from local provost marshall for the rest of the time. Every creek and little stream in the country is swimming and it is doubtful whether he will be able to cross. The pontoons broke loose last night and five of them were lost but pontoons were taken from the Etowah to fix it. The Rebels were repulsed at Allatoona and left their dead and wounded. General Sherman crossed the Chattahoochee and Hood (is) falling back to Dallas.

October 6 - Got orders to move at 8:00 and packed things. Went into camp 2 1/2 miles from town, very good camping ground. Men tore things generally getting lumber for barracks. Family had been living here about three months. They had a brother in the 1st Georgia. He used to be a lieutenant in the regiment U.S. only adjutant now. He was a lieutenant in the regiment that Davis was major of and had some difficulty there with him. Davis recalls it and will not give him a field office. Slept in one of the house rooms. Young mulatto here 18 or 19, she has auburn hair. No one at the North would think of her having negro blood in her veins. She dresses neat and looks better than most of the country women.

October 7 - Two pontoons were taken from the bridge to let the drift through, river rising all the while. It is now at least 15 feet higher than a week ago. (We) were not able to get anything from camp. Kellogg put up the tent in the afternoon and I exchanged a couple of barrels (of) spoiled flour. Colonel Stubblefield and Lieutenant Myers were killed at Allatoona.

October 8 - Straightened up tent and put flour in it. General Corse and the troops coming back. The division list 173 killed and 200 wounded. The Rebels lost more heavily. It is said that General Sherman took General French and a whole division prisoners while they were trying to cross the Chattahooche. Stopped them from crossing and is not pursuing the rest of the army. General Wheeler has not been able to cross yet. Before attempting to cross, he tore up about 2 miles of track. The high water washed away the Resaca bridge. It will take two or three days to fix this but tearing up the track does not amount to anything.

October 9 - Nothing of any importance. Colonel Rowett of the 7th Illinois was badly wounded at Allatoona, also Lieutenant Colonel Hanna. Colonel Rowett will not recover. It is a mistake about General French's Division being captured. Hood's Army is crossing the Coosa, at least that is the report.

October 10 - Rations drawn today. Got full of everything, 1/4 salt meat. Issued in the afternoon. Troops coming in quite fast.

October 11 - Several companies out scouting. Rebels standing picket just beyond the old camp. Captain Peck went out on the Summerville Road, jumped in between two divisions and captured a general's horse, another belonging to a major, the general's servant and one soldier, also two other horses. By some blunder the road had not been picketed. A battery of six guns was within 40 rods of them when the capture was made and our boys could hear the orders of the officers to their men very plainly. They did not happen to have any cavalry at that point and Peck got back all right. General Corse paid him a very high compliment. The whole Rebel army is moving northeast and will no doubt attack Resaca.

October 12 - Troops coming in all the while, General Sherman himself in the afternoon. General Garrard's cavalry crossed in the forenoon and about 10:00 attacked the Rebels who were occupying our old camp. They skirmished awhile and finally charged them, driving them 3 or 4 miles. Two Rebels were killed dead, two badly wounded (who) cannot live fell into our hands. Whether they took off any or not can't be known. None of our men (were) touched. There was a brigade of Rebel cavalry. Sill Willard who was wounded at Snake (Creek) Gap came yesterday. The first train from the north in some time. He left again today.

October 13 - Regiment went out to Cave Springs, I went along. General Corse in command went in an ambulance. Struck the Rebel line of skirmishers and pickets about 5 miles from town and drove them about 6 or 7 miles beyond the road leading to the river. They had two pieces of cannon and we used two pieces, 4 more in reserve. Drove them through a piece of timber and then had to follow them over a field a mile and a half wide as far as we went. Our regiment and the 9th (Illinois Mounted Infantry) drove them out of the woods, then the infantry came up and the two regiments went on the flanks over the rockest and hillest ground I ever took a horse over. The Rebels moved their guns four or five times and everytime they moved the cavalry was in their rear, but the field was too wide and too many fences in the way to allow us a charge. Then about 5:00 an order came from Sherman to return to Rome immediately. The infantry were drawn off and our regiment covered the retreat. In the woods some of the companies became scattered but all came out straight. As we left they sent a regiment to follow. Captain Hinds was in the rear and they kept firing whenever they could get a chance. The Rebels charged several times and came up very near. Hinds killed four of their horses, none of ours hurt. When we got half way home found a poor fellow given out. He thought we had an ambulance. When he found that we hadn't he cried like a child. Some of the boys helped him through on their horses. General Kilpatrick came in on the Vanwert Road and rode down to General Corse and if the order for return had not come Kilpatrick was going round in their rear and we were going to gather them. Heard the shells whistle very near a couple of times and once in a while a bullet but in no danger of any consequence. Peck and one company of the 9th went down the river road and had a pretty sharp engagement and one man (was) killed (wounded so that he will die). The expedition showed that all the infantry had crossed the Coosa and were going north.

October 14 - News came today that 30 Rebels were killed and wounded yesterday. Garrard drove them again yesterday. 4th Michigan (Cavalry) made a sabre charge (and) captured two pieces of cannon and 30 prisoners. They (had) one other regiment to help them. Sherman's Army and the cavalry all moved towards Resaca. All sorts of rumors that Resaca was captured, 3000 prisoners taken, and all the bridges burnt between Kingston and Chattanooga, Atlanta evacuated and burned. How much of it is true (I) can't tell. Got a big mail yesterday but no letters for me.

October 15 -Regiment went out today on the Summerville Road. I did not go. Had a fight with the Rebels and drove them. Wheeler's inspector general was wounded and taken. One of our men (was) shot through the arm. His whole command is lying on the other side of a swamp 9 miles from town. Our troops went to this side of the swamp. Had the pleasure of eating the sweet potatoes that he was cooking for his dinner and feeding his corn. A brigade of infantry was along but did not do any fighting. Wheeler is guarding the rear of the army and on the flank between Rome and wagon train crossing at Cedar Bluff and Gadsden. Made out Captain Ford's ordnance returns for the 3rd quarter.

October 16 - Did nothing today but write up my diary. Read a little etc.

October 17 - Got candles for headquarters. No news of any consequence. The Rebels still keeping pickets (on) the other side of the river. Captain Ford pretty sick. Read good number of Harpers.

October 18 -Regiment went out on expedition. Major Tramel went to within one mile of Dirt Town. Colonel Spencer, a brigade of infantry, and the remainder of our regiment went to Coosaville. I drew rations so as to be sure of them. Got full rations of everything. Had a job loading, (used) new men from Company E and it took more work to get them to help than to do it myself. News comes that Hood's Army was beaten in a general engagement at Dalton today but do not know as it is so. Our men found Rebels on both the Alabama and Summerville Roads. Just as the regiment was coming in, a foraging party from town fired their guns off just as they were opposite our camp, saddled up and started out. Major Cramer was coming in just as they were going out and took his command out also. Everybody was somewhat mad when they found that it was a false alarm.

October 19 - Nothing of any special interest today. Several companies (go) out every day.

October 20 - Halped Captain Ford on his papers and divided the ordnance stores and quartermaster (returns).

October 21 - Worked on papers for the captain.

October 22 - Made out muster out rolls for the men. Tried to find out whether I could take my horse home or not. No one could tell me anything about it.

October 23 - Regiment (went) out to Cave Springs (and) stayed all night. Two regiments of infantry alone. Rebels had a division and our men moved in the morning early to escape them. Finished muster out rolls and discharge papers. The men are uncommonly anxious to get out, especially when we consider that they are only one years men. Finished the papers and got everything ready to move tomorrow. Captain Ford is going with them to Nashville to witness their payment and will get pay himself.

October 24 - Went to the mustering out to see if my rolls were right, found them correct. Captain signed them and mustering out in the afternoon. Captain will leave tomorrow.

October 25 - Captain went north with the men today. I went after blanks for ordnance (returns). Could not find any and ruled a set in the afternoon.

October 26 - Worked on captain's papers. In the afternoon sold (the) little mare for $40, saddle and bridle in, to surgeon of the 52nd Illinois, P.F. Arndt, and got his note with order for its payment on Mr. McEnber of Freeport. Sorry to part with her but could not get her home and it is the best I can do.

October 27 - Worked on quartermaster papers for Captain Ford and can not make much headway on account of Godfrey's refusal to receipt for ordnance and the difficulty in getting the inspector to condemn worthless property. Am afraid that all the quartermaster forms are wrong that have been sent on account of the certificate of loss not being sworn to by some enlisted man. Tom Kennedy came in the afternoon.

October 28 - Got a certificate from Day that he had received the ordnance in charge for the commanding officer of the regiment and of captain. Can't do any better. He can make a certified invoice on them. I told colonel that Godfrey refused to receipt for it and he swore that he should or he would make it very uncomfortable for him. Godfrey is not with the regiment but will be in a short time and Spencer does not wish to become responsible as he is soon to be out. Major Fairfield came in the afternoon. He did not know that he was mustered out of the service (and) wished me to straighten up his papers etc. He had made a good deal of money during the past few months taking bounties for recruits.

October 29 - News comes today that our army is to be cut in two and Thomas with the 4th Corps (is) to hold the country north of the Tennessee and Sherman with the remainder of the army (is) to strike for some point in the gulf or sea coast. Communication will be cut in a few days and I am afraid that captain will not get back.
Finished major's papers and made out abstract of expendures to cover the charges against him. He is going back tomorrow.

October 30 - Worked hard on muster and pay rolls. Made them out so as to charge deserters with revolvers. Made out Frank's muster out rolls.

October 31 - Made out my own rolls and in the afternoon mustered out. Colonel said that he would make me brigade commissary if I would stay during the march. The march has some temptation for me but the brigade commissary would only make me responsible for a lot of stores and returns to be made etc. The troops are beginning to move back to the railroad.

157

November 1 - Put captain's papers in order and left him a note explaining matters. Packed his personal baggage to take north with me. Wet and rainy. Colonel said that an order had been issued to stop any further muster out of the troops. McKnight made me a visit in the afternoon and staid all night. The regiment is to be paid tomorrow and then the detachment that goes with Major Shurtleff will start north.

November 2 - Sold my mare to McKnight for $65 with an agreement that if he sold her at $25 advance I should have $20 more. Peck and Lomax are going north on their leaves of absence. In the afternoon McWorkman told me that he knew of a chance to sell my horse. I had already sold her however and it was too late. It is a little doubtful after all whether I could have sold her to a stranger as she had not yet recovered from her bruse. I hated to sell her but am very confident that I could not get her home. I could have got 40 or 50 more if I had not put little mare in the stable and so got her injured. Paid McWorkman 27 dollars to settle accounts and Andrew 23 1/2 which ends my indebtness in the regiment. Smith is going north with us and will give me the clothing purchased for me at Chattanooga and the money that is extra.

November 3 - The regiment was paid today. I could have got 2 months pay by making out two full muster rolls but there were only 3 men to pay and I thought it would not pay. Burdick was drunk as a fool. Godfrey was having him settle his ordnance papers and he got to drunk to finish them. Fishback was in the same condition and it was amusing to see him sign the pay roll. Each of the letters (were) over an inch long and he looking at it was one of the funniest things of the campaign. Got the haversacks, canteens and water proof plankets condemed. He will give a certificate tomorrow that will do to send with the papers. I went to Captain Flint for a similar one but he said that I could make a statement that the stores turned over (were) in the quartermaster and ordnance officer for inspection and the inspector would condemn them for him. Captain came in the afternoon not looking very well. I was glad to see him for I disliked to leave and I can not complete the papers until they do know that he is here. He can use his own judgement. Godfrey came in a great fury day before yesterday saying that there were 10 carbines that he had receipted for which he did not have and wanted me to bring him over the papers so that he could change it. I told him I would see about it but I thought his script receipt for them was out. I examined and found that it was nothing but Dodds and that when he left he had turned over to Godfrey 10 carbines which really belonged to Ford. I told Goefrey that I thought there was an understanding that he (G) was to give Ford a receipt for them. He said not and I told him that I would try and get him a receipt for them in the regiment. I would not have given up the receipt though at all, but would have told him that the papers were finished as they were and captain and he must settle the matter. Hinds said that he would give the receipt if necessary and this saved a difficulty. In the quartermaster (stores) there was a bugle, 100 pounds (of) picket rope, and 3 hatchets short. I explained the whole thing to captain and he said that he thought he could get the receipt from Mc. The captain has been sick all the time he has been gone and is now very ill. Spencer seems to be a great favorite at headquarters and gets the news. He says that all the troops north of Resaca are to stay with Thomas who will have 70,000. The rest, 60,000 under Sherman, are to move in two columns to Savannah.

November 4 - Major Shurtleff got his squad together and we went to the depot in the morning. Could not get on the first train but had the promise of the next one that should come. Did not dare to go back to camp for fear that the train might come. Rained most all day. Slept on the floor upstairs.

November 5 - The train came about 8:00 and we got aboard. It was loaded down with ammunition and hospital stores and it was all we could do to get on. At Kingston we built up some fires and had some coffee. Meat we could not get. There was none to sell and there was such a rush for whiskey that it was impossible to get into the commissary. In the afternoon a train came along and we got on top. The cars were full and we had to ride on some platform cars. It was cold enough and we only got as far as Resaca when we had to stop for down trains and waited all night. It was cold and disagreeable and the cars were so full that we could not lie down to sleep.

November 6 - Went about 10 miles and then waited all day for down trains. A detachment of the 1st Michigan Engineers were on the train. At the station there were some rations for issue to the troops but they would not sell it for love or money. $5.00 we offered for one shoulder of meat. Pettis got a side of bacon by telling the men that had it that major was running the train and wanted the meat. Went to one of the houses and got them to cook some meat and coffee. The track through here has been completely destroyed. The Rebs tore up the rails, piled up the ties and put the rails on top of them, and by burning the ties bent every one of them so that new iron (will have to be) used. The Rebs were issuing sugar cane as part of their rations while doing it. Started just at sundown. Heard that the patrol had been fired on and the men got on the cars in anticipation of the fight. It did not come however and we went to Chattanooga making a long stop at Dalton. Tonight Peck, B.F. and I got into a box car. They tried to make us believe that it was full but we could not see it, especially when the alternative was sleeping out on the railroad car. Got a good sleep by making a bed on the floor of the car between the piles of ammunition; but (by) laying down the rubbers we kept out of the dirt and slept well.

November 7 - Got off the cars about seven and tried to carry the chest to the Crutchfield House. Found it too heavy and gave a darkey a dollar to do the job. Got transportation in the morning and then watched the trains for Smith who got on the train just behind us. He did not come however. At night I made the final work on captain's papers and directed them. This ends the returns but I am afraid that they are not right and told captain so that he understands how they might be wrong. The inspection report ought to go up with the papers. They may send them all back. Got meals at the house $1.00 and after a long labor a room without fire and (a) most miserable bed.

November 8 - Captain was too late for the Knoxville train and so goes on with us as far as Murfreesboro. Smith has not come yet and I left a note with major directing him to express me the $50 to Hillsdale. The train left at 1 1/2. It was loaded with convalescents and (was) very difficult to get on, but Peck showed our transportation orders and I hustled on the baggage and finally (we) go on through. There were hundreds that did not. The conductor at first told us he would not take anyone.

(He) said he would not let us ride on top of the car. At Dechard I was off for supper when the train started and I got left. Enjoyed a bed at the saloon and slept well. Saw several wrecks of trains but nothing so bad as near Kingston, when from Rome to Resaca, there were 5 wrecks of trains. The road through the Cumberlands was wild enough. At Tantallon we had a pusher and steamed up the mountain. Went through two tunnels and steep cuts without number. In a good many places the water was running out the side of the cuts in streams. (There were) subjects for painters without number.

November 9 - Took the first train that came north which proved to be loaded with soldiers. Rode on top most of the time. The inside of the car smelled like a hog pen. Just before night got into a car completely empty, with some officers and had a very comfortable ride to Nashville. At Murfreesboro saw some of the heaviest fortifications of the war. The country from Chattanooga up is level and looks like a good farming country. Got a good supper of oysters at Nashville. Found Peck and Frank registered at the St. Cloud but the clerk said they were out. At 11:00 got him to show me up to their room. Found Frank in bed with a spare room for me.

November 10 - Peck and Lomax got off on the morning train but Frank and I could not get the chest and waited for the noon train. Went to see paymaster but he could not pay under 3 days and (I) made up my mind to go on to Louisville. The afternoon train was loaded with dismounted cavalrymen and they were not taking any passengers, but I put the baggage (on) and then told the adjutant general that my baggage was on and could not be got off so got permission to stand in the aisle. Found a seat after a little (while) and had a comfortable ride to Louisville.

November 11 - Went to paymaster. He would not pay; only to the 30th of June and I could not get any pay. Wrote out my affidavit to send for a certificate of non indebtedness and made the affidavit beore a notary public. Could not get a blank form. Got into Louisville about midnight. Took a room and breakfast at the Galt House, a good house and more reasonable charges than any we had been in. At noon went over (to) the river and took train for Indianapolis. Got in about 11:00. Separate cars for soldiers. Got a bed in a room with six and slept until the 4 o'clock train. Find I am one day ahead. Got into Indianapolis on the 10th instead of the 11th.

November 12 - Got into Hillsdale about 6:00. Folks not up much and waited at hotel until they began to get out. Got breakfast and then went up to Mr. Rices. Found mother and the children. Father had gone to Chicago but would be back on the afternoon train. The folks all glad to see me and father in particular. They had not heard from me in 2 months and were afraid that I had been either captured or killed, the communication being cut has lost the letters.

CHAPTER IX

CAMP-FIRE CHATS

In the book, "Camp-Fire Chats of the Civil War", by Washington Davis, published in 1888, Chapter XXII, there is an interesting story about a soldier in the 1st Alabama Cavalry, USA which states:

"Gathered together this evening - a very comfortable one - the veterans chatted miscellaneously for a time before commencing business. Finally the commander fired up the pipe of peace, and then called the assembly to order. But in his eagerness to preceed with the chats he somehow forgot to pass the pipe around, thereby totally disregarding the traditionary custom of his majesty, the redskin. Since it was the commander who abused the tradition, the comrades each concluded to light a pipe for himself, after which Captain M___k spoke:

In the summer of 1862 our regiment was stationed along the line of railroad from Decatur to Courtland, Alabama. Small parties of us, from time to time, went out foraging on our own account, and on one of these expeditions I had an adventure which had never recurred to my mind until an event which happened a few years after the war recalled it forcibly.

After the cessation of hostilities there was considerable talk through the North of forming colonies to settle in the West and South. Well, I got the 'colony fever' and conceived the idea of getting up a colony to settle in Northern Alabama, probably near our old stamping ground.

With this project in view I went from Chicago to Decatur, Alabama, and from there by rail still further South toward the Black Warrior River. Reaching my journey's end I concluded to return on horseback by a round-about way, and visit some of the back country; so I hired a horse and started out, first gathering information as to where I could find accommodations on the road, for houses and settlers are very scarce in that part of the world, so that it behooves a traveler to get his 'points' before setting out on a journey. My calculation was to reach the house of a certain settler at about seven o'clock in the evening. Seven o'clock came, but no settler's house in sight; - eight o'clock - nine o'clock - ten o'clock, and still no house to be seen.

By this time I was thoroughly convinced that I had lost my way. I was tired out, and my horse was completely jaded. I rode on about an hour, and at last to my supreme delight I spied a light which I made for at once. I found that it proceeded from the window of a log cabin to which I rode up, and dismounting and hitching my horse, I attempted to enter the yard, when three savage dogs with angry growls disputed my further advance. But I finally succeeded in safely reaching the porch. I gave a knock on the door which roused the proprietor of the place whereupon the following dialogue ensued, through the closed door:

'Who's there?'

'A traveler who has lost his way.'

'What do you want?'

'I want accommodation for myself and horse till morning.'

'Well, you can't stay here. I don't keep tavern.'

'How far is it to the next house?'

'Seven miles.'

'It's not possible for me to go seven miles, for my horse is completely tired out.'

'I can't help that; my wife is sick, and I can't have you around.'

'Can't you give me some feed for my horse, and a blanket for myself? I'll sleep on the porch.'

After considerable parleying and urging, this request was finally granted. Soon the door opened and a tall, powerful man emerged, carrying a lantern which he held squarely in my face for a moment in order to get a good look at me, after which he led the way to the stable, where he groomed and fed my horse, and then we returned to the house.

At the porch I halted, expecting him to go in and get me a blanket; but as he entered the door he said:

'Come in, stranger; I want to talk to you.'

I entered the cabin and sat down. He threw a few pine knots upon the smoldering fire and soon a bright blaze illumined the room. Then placing himself squarely in front of me, and giving me a searching look, he demanded in an imperious manner:

'Now, stranger, I want to know who you are, and what is your business in these parts?'

I have already told you that I am a traveler looking for a suitable location to establish a colony from the North.'

'Looking for land, hey" Going to establish a colony? Now, stranger, that story is altogether too thin! Men don't go round at midnight hunting for land. Now tell me the truth - who are you, and what are you after?'

'I have already told you who I am, and my business; and if you don't believe me it is not my fault.'

Again he searchingly eyed me, and then with an earnest emphasis, said:

'Stranger you have been in these parts before!' ·

'Yes.'

'You were a Yankee soldier, then?'

'Yes.'

'In 1862, and stationed near Decatur?'

'Yes.'

'While out foragin' one day with another Yankee you stumbled into Roddy's confederate cavalry camp; but before you were discovered you turned back and escaped?'

'Yes.'

'Just as you left Roddy's camp you met one of Roddy's men with a neck-yoke over his shoulders, and carrying a couple of buckets of water in his hands?'

'Yes.'

'Yor put your pistol to that man's head and forced him to go over a mile to the rear with you to prevent his giving an alarm?'

'Yes.'

'Stranger, *I am that man!'*

It seemed to me, about that time, that he meant business, and intended to settle the old affair there and then. But putting on a bold front, I remarked as unconcernedly as I could:

'Well, you have a mighty good memory.'

'Yes, I remember some things. You bet I knew you the minute I set eyes on you; and I'll remember you as long as I live.'

Meanwhile his wife had made her appearance, and, lighting her corn-cob pipe, seated herself near the fireplace, prepared to enjoy the fun.

I hardly knew what would come next; but, after a pause, the man changed his position and manner, and said:

'Now that I've told you who *you* are I'll tell you more about myself. I staid with Roddy's Cavalry Company for about three months after I saw you, and then my brother and myself deserted and enlisted in the First Alabama Union cavalry regiment, where we staid till the close of the war. After the war we came home; we were obliged to sleep in caves and keep concealed for a long time, as our former companions sought to kill us, and hunted us like wolves. Our lives were in danger every minute - but lately they don't trouble us much.'

'But I say, stranger, how's things up North? Is there going to be another war? We think there will be soon. If there is you may count on me in going in for the *Union!*'

He now brought me out a lunch to which I did ample justice, and then I asked for a blanket that I might go to sleep upon the porch, as agreed.

'No sir,' said he; 'no blanket for you; I've as good a bed as there is in this part of the country, and you are welcome to it!'

After sleeping till morning I found a fine breakfast awaiting me, and that my horse had been already taken care of; and when I started off again my landlord accompanied me for several miles to show me the way.

'That's a good story,' said Colonel Van Buren, of the 192d New York; 'but let me tell an incident that will remind many of you of a hundred similar schemes which the homesick invented to get discharged.......''

This is further proof of how the Union soldiers from Alabama were treated after trying to preserve the Union.

CHAPTER X

ROSTER OF FIRST ALABAMA CAVALRY, US SOLDIERS

Abbott/Abbitt, David D., Pvt., Co. M&L, age 34, EN 12/16/63, Camp Davies, MS, MI 12/29/63, Corinth, MS, was charged in May & June, 1864 with one Remington Revolver which he lost, POW March 10, 1865 at Solomon Grove, NC. Discharged at Camp Chase, OH June 12, 1865 by reason of GO#77. Born Wayne Co., KY.

Abbott, Israil P., Pvt., Co. A, age 18, EN 4/7/65, Stevenson, AL, MI 4/18/65, Nashville, TN, born Walker Co., AL, farmer, died in hospital, Huntsville, AL June 18, 1865 of chronic diarrhea. (Buried in grave #219, Huntsville Cemetery and later reinterred in Grave L-554, Chattanooga National Cemetery.)

Abbott, Lewis W., Pvt./Corp., Co. C, age 23, EN 1/1/63, Corinth, MS, MI 1/20/63, Corinth, MS, born Spartanburg, SC, shoemaker, MO 1/31/64.

Abernathy, John, Pvt., Co. L&A, age 43, EN 10/1/64, Rome, GA., MI 7/19/65, Huntsville, born Lawrence Dist., SC, farmer, MO 10/20/65, Huntsville, AL.

Abner, John, Pvt., Co. A, age 21, EN & MI 10/6/64, Rome, GA, born Cobb Co., AL. KIA at Faison Station, NC 4/9/65.

Abner, William T. (or J.), Pvt., Co. A, age 23, EN & MI 10/6/64, Rome, GA, Born Cobb Co., GA, deserted 11/10/64, Rome, GA. On 4/12/92 the War Dept. denied a request to remove charge of desertion and grant an honorable discharge.

Adair, Francis O., Pvt./Corp., Co. H, age 18, EN & MI 10/10/63, Glendale, MS, MO 10/24/64.
    NOTE: Francis O. Adair was also in Company B, 5th U.S. Cavalry. On February 1, 1898, he filed a Declaration for Invalid Pension while in a Soldiers Home in Los Angeles County, CA. He stated he had been married May 17, 1863 in Winston Co., AL by Perry Shipman but was a widower with no children.

Adair, Nathan, age 46, born Madison Co., GA, wagon maker, EN 12/20/63 at Camp Davies, MS and was rejected by surgeon for broken down constitution.*

Adair, Jasper N., Pvt., Co. H, age 18, EN & MI 12/18/63, Camp Davies, MS, MO 11/23/64, Nashville, TN.

Adams, James M., Pvt., Co. C, age 17, EN 12/1/62, Corinth, MS, MI 12/22/62, Corinth, MS, farmer, born Tishomingo, MS, died 11/28/63 of accidental gunshot wound at Camp Davies, MS.

Adams, James M., Pvt./Corp., Co. G, age 21, EN 4/10/64, Decatur, AL, MI Rome, GA, born Carroll Co., GA, appt. Corp. 5/1/64, POW 3/10/65 at Solomon Grove, NC, paroled at Aikens Landing, VA 3/30/65, MO 10/20/65.

Adams, John Q., Pvt./Corp., Co. C, age 28, EN 12/22/62, MI 12/27/62, Corinth, MS, born Fayette, TN, farmer, died 6/18/63 at Glendale, MS.

Adams, Levi, Pvt./Sgt., Co. K&E, age 20, EN 6/26/62, Limestone Co., AL, transferred from Co. K, 21st Regt. Ohio Vols., farmer, born Johnson, NC, POW 5/1/63, Bluntsville, TN. Died of pneumonia 2/2/64 at Overton Hospital, Memphis, TN. (Buried in Memphis National Cemetery.)

Adams, William C., Pvt., Co. C, age 24, EN 12/22/62, Corinth, MS, MI 12/27/62, Corinth, born MS, AWOL 2/1/63. POW June 1863-Dec. 1863..

Adams, William C., Pvt. Co. G, age 29, EN 3/5/63, Chewalla, TN. Deserted 4/30/63, Chewalla, TN.

Aiken, James B., Pvt., Co. D, EN 1/1/63, Glendale, MS, on duty as company cook.*

Aiken, John, Pvt., Co. D, EN 6/1/63, Glendale, MS.*

Aiken, W.T., Pvt., Co. D, EN 6/1/63, Glendale, MS.*

Akers, Gideon A., Pvt., Co. K, age 24, born Rutherford Co., TN, farmer, EN 12/1/63, Camp Davies, MS, rejected by surgeon on account of physical disability. Traveled 90 miles from his home in Marion Co., AL to Camp Davies, MS to enlist.*

Akers, Meredith T., Pvt., Co. K, age 32, born Rutherford Co., TN, farmer, EN 12/1/63, Camp Davies, MS, rejected by surgeon on account of physical disability. Traveled 90 miles from his home in Marion Co., AL to Camp Davies MS to enlist.*

Aldrich, William C., Pvt., Co. F, EN 10/30/63, Glendale, MS.*

Aldridge, Henry, Pvt., Co. A, age 21, EN 12/25/63, Camp Davies, MS, MI 2/5/64, Memphis, TN, born Walker Co., AL, deserted 11/3/64, Rome, GA with 2 Remington revolvers and saddle, returned for duty 5/1/65, Huntsville, AL.

Alexander, Jeremiah, age 41, born Morgan Co., AL, farmer, EN 12/20/63, Camp Davies, MS, rejected by surgeon on account of chronic neuralgia.*

Alford, Jackson, Pvt., Co. L, age 35, EN & MI 9/1/64, Rome, GA, born St. Clair Co., AL, deserted 11/10/64, Rome, GA.

Allison/Alerson, Jasper M.C., Pvt., Co. D, age 27, EN & MI 6/10/63, Glendale, MS, born Morgan, AL. Was Company Cook in July 1863, MIA 10/26/63, MO 7/27/64, Rome, GA

Allison, Jonathan K., Pvt., Co. H, age 18, EN 5/25/65, Huntsville, AL, MI 10/16/65, Huntsville, AL, born St. Clair Co., AL, MO 10/20/65, Huntsville, AL.

Alvis, David H., Pvt., Co. B, age 18, EN 3/16/64, Decatur, AL, MI, 3/27/64, Decatur, AL, born Jackson Co., AL, WIA Oconee River, GA 11/23/64. MO 10/20/65.

Alvis, Franklin., Pvt., Co. L, EN 9/25/63, Fayette Co., AL, MI 9/25/63, MIA 10/26/63 at Vincent's Crossroads, MS, MO 9/25/64, Rome, GA. One POW record.

Alvis, G.A., Pvt., Co. B, age 38, EN 3/16/64, Decatur, AL, MI 3/27/64, Decatur, born Madison Co., AL. Left sick in Decatur, AL 4/17/64.

Alvis, Henry S., Pvt., Co. B, age 45, EN 3/21/64, Decatur, AL, MI 3/27/64, Decatur, AL, born Madison or Winston Co., AL, MO 10/20/65, Huntsville, AL.
    NOTE: Henry Alvis spent part of the summer of 1864 sick in the Union army field hospital in Decatur, AL. He also spent some time in the field hospital near Chattanooga in the summer of 1865. He had been married to Margaret M. Maynard who died December 3, 1890. He then married Emily Duncan Echols on June 8, 1891 in Cullman Co., AL and they moved near Westpoint in Lawrence Co., TN where he died October 3, 1894. Emily died in 1909 and is buried in the Emeus Cemetery in Cullman, AL.[20]

Alvis, William J., Pvt./Corp., Co. B, age 21, EN 4/2/64, Decatur, AL, MI 4/13/64, Decatur, born Tuscaloosa Co., AL. MO 10/20/65, Huntsville, AL.

Amason, John W. (W.M.C), Pvt., Co. B, age 37, EN 3/9/64 and MI 3/27/64 Decatur, AL, farmer, born Blount, AL, deserted 9/29/64 in Rome, GA, charges later removed, MO 10/20/65, Huntsville, AL. (Muster Roll also shows he was discharged 2/29/64 due to disability.) One POW Record was listed.

Anders, William P., Pvt., Co. G, age 26, EN 4/10/64 Decatur, AL, born Shelby Co., AL, farmer, deserted from Rome, GA, 7/11/64 with arms, saddle blanket and horse, never MO.

Anderson, Charles, Pvt., Co. H, age 18, EN 3/1/65, Stevenson, AL, MI 4/5/65, Nashville, TN, born Dade Co., GA, AWOL 5/8/65, deserted 5/8/65, Huntsville, AL, did not MO.

Anderson, John W., Pvt., Co. B, (cards filed with John W. Amason).

Anderson, Lee M., Pvt., Co. B, age 28, EN 3/31/63, Chewalla, TN, MI 3/31/63, Corinth, MS, deserted, 4/30/63, Chewalla, TN, MO date shown as 1/3/64, Memphis, TN.

Anditon, Samuel, Pvt., Co. F, age 28, EN 10/25/63, Camp Davies, MS, born Marion Co., AL, farmer, discharged 1/15/64 for disability at Camp Davies.

Andors/Andoes, William A., Pvt., Co. C, age 18, EN 2/15/64, Memphis, TN, MI 3/10/64, Memphis, TN, born Green Co., GA, farmer.

Anglin, George W., Pvt., Co. E, Bugler, EN 4/1/63, Glendale, MI 4/30/63, Corinth, MS, MO 3/18/63, Memphis, TN.

Anthoney, William H., Pvt., Co. K, (cards filed with John C. Anthony), age 44, EN 12/25/63, Camp Davies, MS after traveling 100 miles from Marion Co., AL. Born St. Clair Co., AL, farmer, deserted from camp at Memphis, TN 2/21/64 while on guard duty, not apprehended.

Appleton, C., Pvt., Co. K, patient in Gayoso USA Hospital at Memphis, TN Jan & Feb 1864, returned to duty 6/16/64.*

Armor, William L., Pvt., Co. C, age 40, EN 12/1/62, Corinth, MS, MI 12/22/62, Corinth, MS, MO 12/17/63, Memphis, TN.

Armsted, Levin, Pvt., Co. F, in Hospital #14 at Nashville, TN March & April 1865.*

Armstrong, Charles , Pvt., Co. A, age 22, EN 1/12/64, Camp Davies, MS, MI 2/5/64, Memphis, TN, born Bibb Co., AL, died in Gen. Hospital, Larkinsville, AL 8/5/64 of typhoid fever.

Armstrong, James M., Pvt., Co. C, age 21, EN 12/21/62, Corinth, MS, MI 12/22/62, Corinth, MS, born, Marshall, MS, farmer, died 12/9/63, Memphis, TN, pneumonia. (Buried in Memphis National Cemetery.)

Armstrong, William, Pvt., Co. C, sent to hospital at Memphis, TN 10/16/63.*

Arnold, Asbury B., Pvt., Co. H, age 26, EN 10/17/63, Glendale, MS, MI 10/17/63, Glendale, MS, discharged 3/26/64 for disability. Born Marion, IL.

Arick, William C., Pvt., Co. E, term of service expired 3/1/64, Memphis, TN.*

Arrick, M.J., Corp., Co. E, term of service expired 3/1/64, Memphis, TN.*

Arst, John, Pvt., Co. H, on duty as nurse in hospital 10/63.*

Arthur, James, Pvt., Co. A, age 25, EN 2/4/64, Memphis, TN, MI 2/5/64, Memphis, TN, born New York City, NY, farmer, deserted 3/25/64, Memphis, TN with Carbine, pistol, sabre, mule/horse, and equipment.

Aston, A., Pvt., Co. D, absent supposed POW 10/26/63.*

Atkerson, John R., (cards filed with John R. Atkinson) age 28, Pvt., Co. B, EN 2/6/64, Pulaski,, TN, MI 3/11/64, Decatur, AL, born Walker Co., AL, wood corder, deserted 7/10/64, Rome, GA with arms.

Atkins, Martin, Pvt., Co. H, age 40, EN 10/17/63, Glendale, MS, MI 10/17/63, Glendale, MS, POW, 10/26/63, MO 10/24/64, Rome, GA.

Atkins, William C., Pvt/Sgt., Co. H, age 35, EN 10/17/63, Glendale, MS, MI 10/20/63, Glendale, MS, sick in hospital Memphis, TN March & April 1864, MO 10/24/64, Rome, GA.

Atwell, John, Co. F, sick in US General Hospital 4/65.*

Austin, Bryant, Pvt/Corp., Co. D, age 21, EN 4/19/64, Decatur, AL, MI 6/16/64, Decatur, AL, born Franklin, AL, MO 10/20/65, Huntsville, AL. Appointed Corporal July 1, 1864.

Austin, Jasper, Corp/Sgt., Co. E, age 23, EN 12/16/62 and MI 12/16/62, Corinth, MS, MO 12/16/63, Memphis, TN.

Austin, Jesse W., Pvt., Co. L, age 19, EN 9/25/63, Fayette Co., AL, MI 9/25/63, Glendale, MS, farmer, born Fayette Co., AL, died 3/15/64, Overton Military Hospital in Memphis, TN of measles. (May be the Austin buried in Grave 1-14, Memphis National Cemetery.)

Austin, John R., Pvt., Co. D, age 19, EN 4/19/64 and MI 6/16/64, Decatur, AL, born Walker Co., AL, farmer, MO 10/20/65, Huntsville, TN.

Austin, Sanders, Pvt., Co. C, age 25, EN 12/21/62 and MI 12/22/62, Corinth, MS, born Anson, NC, farmer, MO Camp Davies, MS 12/27/63.

Autry, William T., notation stating, "probably belonged to scout or guide not mustered into the service, in Cumberland USA Hospital at Nashville, TN 5/1/64.*

Backard, B.F., absent sick in hospital at Corinth 7/15/65.*

Baggett, Andrew J., Pvt., Co. E, EN 3/1/63, Glendale, MS, MIA 10/23/63 at Vincent's Crossroads, on detached service at Q.M. Dept. at Vicksburg, MS as Teamster 1/25/64, MO 3/18/64.

Baggett, Drury B., Pvt., Co. E, age 40, EN 3/1/63, Glendale, MS, MI 3/1/63, Corinth, MS, deserted 5/63, returned 7/6/63 at Glendale, MS, MO 3/3/64, Memphis, TN.

Baggett, James W., Pvt., Co. E, EN 3/1/63, Glendale, MS, MI 3/1/63, Corinth, MS, deserted 7/9/63, Glendale, MS, POW at Vincent's Crossroads Oct. 26, 1863, MO 3/18/64, Memphis, TN.

Baggett, William F., Pvt., Co. F, absent sick in Louisville, KY 4/30 64.*

Bailey, George M., 1st Lt., Co. D, age 20, EN 5/23/63, Glendale, MS, MI 5/23/63, Corinth, MS, appt. by special order of Brig. Gen.Dodge, MI as 1st Lt., on detached service by order Brig. Gen. Dodge, 7/14/63, MO 5/30/64, Pulaski, TN.

Bain, Alfred A.D., Corp., Co. I, age 25, EN 7/21/62, Huntsville, AL, died 11/8/62, Nashville, TN.

Bain, John D.H., Pvt., Co. I, age 24, EN 7/21/62, Huntsville, AL, born Morgan Co., AL, farmer,. died 12/30/62, Nashville, TN

Baker, Henry M., Pvt., Co. A&D, age 33, EN 1/13/64, Camp Davies, MS, MI 2/5/64, Memphis, TN, born Ash Co., NC, farmer, deserted 5/10/65 from Huntsville, AL with Remington revolver, charges were later removed and he was discharged as of 5/10/65, prepared in War Department January 10, 1927.

Baker, Peter, Pvt., Co. K, age 57 (another MR states age 44), EN 7/24/62, Huntsville, AL, born Jackson Co., TN, farmer, discharged due to disability in Nashville, 1863.

Baker, R., Co. E, absent sick 7/63.*

Baker, William H., Pvt., Co. E, det. service as teamster at Vicksburg, MS 1/25/64, POW 2/65.*

Baker, William J., Pvt., Co. D, age 27, EN 3/15/63, Glendale, MS, deserted 4/23/63, Glendale, MS, on detailed duty as secret scout May & June 1863, POW 6/3/63, MO 3/25/64.

Bakerstaff, John W., Pvt., Co. E, age 36, EN 3/27/63, Glendale, MS, deserted 7/25/63, Glendale, MS, returned from desertion 1/8/64 at Camp Davies, MS, MO 3/3/64, Memphis, TN.

Baley, William B., Pvt., Co. E, age 32, EN 6/24/63, Glendale, MS, deserted 7/9/63 at Glendale, MS.

Ballard, Albert I.(or J.), Pvt., Co. M, age 20, EN 12/9/63, Camp Davies, MS, MI 12/29/63, Corinth, MS, born Pontotoc, MS, farmer, deserted 1/20/64, Camp Davies, MS with Remington revolver (Remarks: lives in Marion Co., AL, supposed to go home).

Ballard, George W., Pvt., Co. G, age 17, EN 5/16/63, Chewalla, TN, MO 11/26/63, Memphis, TN.

Ballard, Levi, G., Pvt., Co. B,H&A, age 18, EN 12/3/63, Camp Davies, MS, MI 2/5/64, Memphis, TN, born Marion Co., AL, farmer, deserted 7/30/65 at Blountsville, AL. (Another Muster and Descriptive Roll shows Levi G. Ballard as age 18, born Marion Co., AL, EN 1/12/65, Huntsville, AL, MI 1/12/65, Nashville, TN, paid $100.00 bounty). A note from the Military Secretary's Office of the War Dept. dated 12/16/64 stated that Levi G. Ballard was not in the military service of the United States in the 1st AL Cav.

Ballew, William H., Pvt., Co. I, age 20, EN 7/21/62, Huntsville, AL, MI 7/21/62 Huntsville, AL, born Polk Co., TN, blacksmith, MIA 4/28/63 at Day's Gap, AL, MO 7/19/65, Nashville, TN.

Balton, Hugh L., (see Bolton, Hugh L.)

Bangers, I.M., Co. L, absent on det. service 10/64.*

Bardon, Michael, Pvt/Corp., Co. C, age 38, EN 12/6/62, Corinth, MS, MI 12/22/62, Corinth, MS, MO 12/17/63, Memphis, TN, born Langford, Ireland.

Barker, Charles F., Sgt., Co. E, age 25, EN 2/1/63 and MI 2/1/63, Corinth, MS, MO 2/5/64, Memphis, TN. (Previously served in Co. A, 1st Kansas Vols, under the name Benjamin P. Curtis.)

Barker, Thomas J., Pvt/1st Sgt., Co. D, age 33, EN 3/5/63, Glendale, MS, MI 3/26/63, Corinth, MS, promoted to 1st Sgt., 11/2/63, born Fayette Co., AL, farmer, MO 3/25/64, Decatur, AL.

Barker, William M., Pvt., Co. C, age 36, EN 1/20/64, Corinth, MS, never MI, deserted 3/3/64, Memphis, TN with Remington revolver, Smith carbine, pistol and holster, born Marion Co., AL, farmer.

Barnes, Morgan C., Pvt., Co. D, age 18, EN 6/26/63 and MI 6/26/63, Glendale, MS, MO 7/27/64, Rome, GA, born Cleveland, NC, farmer.

Barnes, William, Pvt., Co. C, age 25, EN 12/10/62 and MI 3/30/63, Corinth, MS, born Bibb Co., AL, farmer, MO 2/1/64.

Barnett, James, Co. F, det. secret service 8/63.*

Barnett, James W., Pvt., Co. H, age 19, EN 4/1/65, Stevenson, AL, MI 4/5/65, Nashville, TN, born Marshall Co., AL, deserted from Huntsville 5/8/65.

Barnett, Job, Corp., Co. F, age 35, EN 6/27/63, Corinth, MS, MI 8/13/63, Corinth, MS, born Marshall Co., AL, shoemaker, absent with leave at home near Adamsville, TN in July & Aug. 1863, died while POW in Richmond, VA 3/18/64, Bronchitis. (Buried in Richmond National Cemetery, VA.)

Barnett, Lewis, Pvt., Co. E, age 18, EN 2/2/63, Sulphur Springs, MI 3/1/63, Corinth, MS, taken POW between Glendale and Burnsville, MS 6/11/63, paroled at City Point, VA 7/2/63, died at Camp Parole, MD 7/11/63. Residence of widow was shown as Hardin Co., TN.

Barnett, Robert, Co. F, absent POW 4/65.*

Barnett, Thomas, Pvt., Co. B&A, age 18, EN 1/10/63, Glendale, MS, MI 1/22/63, Corinth, MS, transferred to Co. A 10/6/63, absent in arrest at Corinth 11/24/63 for robbery - court proceedings and depositions on microfilm, born Lawrence, AL, farmer, MO 12/22/63, Memphis, TN.
    NOTE: Thomas W. Barnett was married to Mary Elizabeth Moore December 22, 1857 and had six children: Marshall, William, Thomas, Sally, Eletha

and George Moore Barnett. He died in Demopolis, AL and was buried in Prospect, MS.[21]

Barnet, William, Co. F, absent POW, taken by enemy.*

Barny, Francis A., Pvt., Co. B, (cards filed with Francis A. Burney)

Barran/Barren, Joseph M., Sgt., Co. K&A, EN 11/28/62, Glendale, MS, MI 12/31/62, Corinth, MS, discharged 11/7/63, Glendale.

Barraun, George L., died 11/6/63 of smallpox in hospital at Corinth, MS.**

Barren, Thomas A., Pvt., Co. K&A, age 47, EN 11/15/62, Corinth, MS, MI 12/31/62, Corinth, MS, born Jasper Co., GA, died 6/29/63, Glendale, MS.
   NOTE: Testimony of T.A.J. Barren/Barron as published in the *Nashville Daily Union* in Nashville, TN on March 4, 1863, under "Reign of Terror in the South" stated, "I live in Marion County, Alabama. The rebels have burned my house with furniture, beds, bedding, clothing, and etc.; Also, three (3) bales of cotton, two hundred bushels of corn, fodder, etc." Sworn to and subscribed before me at Glendale, Miss., this 24th day of Jan., 1863 and signed by J.W. Stewart.

Barren/Barron, Wiley J., Pvt., Co. K&A, EN 11/28/62, Glendale, MS, MI 12/24/62, Corinth, MS, absent on leave with refugees at Purdy, TN "20 days from 3/7/63", MO 12/22/63, Glendale, MS. Court martialed for horse stealing and larceny on or about 9/14/63 at Glendale.

Barren, William, Pvt., Co. K&A, age 39, EN 12/5/62, Glendale, MS, MI 12/31/62, Corinth, MS, MO 12/22/63.

Barrett, George W., Pvt., Co. A, age 18, EN 1/4/64, Camp Davies, MS, born Lawrence Co., AL, deserted at Camp Davies 1/24/64 with horse, equipment & arms.

Bartholomew, Rion, Pvt., Co. I, discharged 6/28/65 due to disability.*

Bartlett, John, Pvt., Co. F, age 24, EN 4/3/63, Corinth, MS, MI 8/13/63, Corinth, MS, deserted 9/10/63, taken prisoner 9/11/63 near Burnsville, born Wain Co., IL, farmer.

Barton, Gilford M., Pvt., Co. L, age 25, EN 9/25/63, Fayette Co., AL, MI 9/25/63, Glendale, MS, born Hall, GA, farmer, MO 9/28/64, Rome, GA.
   NOTE: Gilford M. Barton was born in January 1841 in Hall Co., GA, and died August 1, 1915 in Tuscaloosa Co., AL. He is buried at Sardis Baptist Cemetery in Winston Co., AL. He married Nancy Jane Weaver in Hall Co., GA.

There were five Barton brothers who served in the 1st Alabama Cavalry, USV: Jonathan, Gilford, James, Madison and William H. and all five served in Company L under Capt. Sanford Tramel and then Captain Edwards. They had three brothers-in-law: F.C. Harris, Jesse D. Hyde and Thomas H. Blackstock who also served in this regiment. In a claim filed by Jonathan Barton with The Southern Claims

Commission after the war, he stated, **"I was threatened, shot at and molested by the rebel soldiers on account of my union principals or sentiments. They burned my still, took one mare, two mules and a buggy, knocked the heads out of my whikey barrels after taking what they wanted, and turned out the balance. They threatened to kill me and burn my dwelling if I did not come in and give up to them. The still house was burned and the mare and two mules and buggy taken by the rebels on the 15th March 1863 at my house...."**

The Commissioners of Claims stated the following about Jonathan Barton: "At the beginning of the war, claimant was a man past 30 years old and well-to-do farmer near Larissa in North Alabama. He talked and voted against secession and had a universal reputation as a Union man. In the earlier part of the war, he did the only thing that a loyal man in his neighborhood could do - harbor and pass along Union men who were making their way to the Federal lines. He was much abused and threatened by the Confederates civil and military and was often a refugee from his home. Much property belonging to him was also taken and destroyed because of his position as a loyalist. When Spencer organized the First Alabama Federal Cavalry in 1863 claimant made his way, with four brothers and three brothers-in-law to the rendezvous and became a sergeant and served one year till honorably discharged. We have made inquiry into this claim and all the evidence and information we have received is to the effect that claimant was a true and notorious Union man from beginning of secession to the end of the war...." Claim was allowed.

Barton, James A., Pvt., Co. L, age 37, EN 9/25/63, Fayette Co., AL, MI 9/25/63, Glendale, MS, born Hall, GA, blacksmith, MO 9/28/64 in Rome, GA.

Barton, John, Pvt., Co. C, age 35, EN 12/21/62, Corinth, MS, MI 12/28/62, Corinth, MS, born Tishomingo, MS, farmer, MO 12/27/63, Camp Davies, MS.

Barton, John, Pvt., Co. L, MIA 10/26/63, sick in hospital at Nashville, TN March & April 1864, on det. service recruiting at Decatur, AL 8/4/64.*

Barton, Jonathan, Sgt., Co. L, age 33, EN 9/25/63, Fayette Co., AL, MI 9/25/63, Glendale, MS, born Hall, GA, farmer, MO 9/28/64, Rome, GA.
    NOTE: Jonathan Marion Barton was born December 26, 1830 and died April 17, 1910 in Winston Co., AL. He was married to Hannah Ann Blackstock and had three brothers and two brothers-in-law who served in this regiment. He is buried at Sardis Baptist Cemetery in Lynn, Winston Co., AL.

Barton, Madison M., Pvt., Co. L, age 26, EN 9/25/63, Fayette Co., AL, MI 9/25/63, Glendale, MS, born Hall Co., GA, farmer, MO 9/28/64, Rome, GA. Reenlisted 11/1/64 in Stevenson, AL, MI 7/19/65 in Huntsville, AL, appt. Sgt. 7/1/65, MO 10/20/65, Huntsville, AL.
    NOTE: Madison Matthew Barton was born 1836 in Hall Co., GA and is buried at Dodd (Cap Baughn) Cemetery near Lynn, Winston Co., AL. He married 1st, Sarah Jane Dodd November 24, 1859 in Hall Co., GA and 2nd, Mariah Duke.[22]

Barton, William H., Pvt., Co. L, age 27, EN 9/25/63, Fayette Co., AL, MI 9/25/63, Glendale, MS, born Hall Co., GA, farmer, POW 10/26/63 at Vincent's Cross Roads,

AL, died at Andersonville, GA 9/1/64 while POW. (Buried in Grave #7524, Andersonville National Cemetery.)

Baswell/Basnell, Andrew G., Pvt., Co. E, EN 3/1/63, Glendale, MS, MI 3/1/63, Corinth, MS, deserted 5/20/63, Glendale, MS, returned from desertion 6/10/63, on detached service as teamster 1/25/64 in Vicksburg, MS, MO 3/18/64, Memphis, TN.

Bates, Hamilton S., Pvt., K&A, age 17, EN 11/1/62, Corinth, MS, MI 12/31/62, Corinth, MS, MO 11/28/63.
> **NOTE:** Hamilton S. Bates was born about 1846 in Marion Co., AL. He married Ellen (?) in 1869 in Arkansas and raised a family of seven children.[23]
> Hamilton died January 18, 1939, at the age of 92, in Central, Sebastion County, Arkansas and is buried in the White Cemetery which is located on the Fort Chaffee Military Reservation.[24]

Bates, John, Pvt., Co. I, age 36, EN 10/1/63, Glendale, MS, MI 10/1/63, MO 7/19/65, Nashville, TN. Served extra duty as nurse and saddler, sick in hospital in Memphis, TN 3/25/64, born in GA.

Bates, Stephen, Pvt., Co. I, age 34, EN 9/30/63, Glendale, MS, born in GA, farmer, MI 10/1/63, sick in hospital in Nashville 4/15/64, MO 7/19/65, Nashville, TN.

Bates, William C., Pvt., Co. K&A, age 46, EN 11/1/62 and MI 12/1/62, Corinth, MS, sick in hospital at Corinth, 3/63, discharged 6/18/63, Glendale, MS due to disability, born Marion Co., AL, farmer.
> **NOTE:** William C. Bates was born about 1817. His wife was Sarah (?) and they were the parents of Hamilton S. Bates, above. Other children were Micajah, born about 1844 in AL; Elizabeth, born about 1848 in AL; William, born about 1849 in AL; George, born about 1853 in TN and John Elbert Bates, born October 7, 1858 in MS. Their last child, Belle, was born about 1865 in Iowa. William died before 1870 and family legend is he was killed by "Bush Wackers" in Missouri after the Civil War.[25]
> Becky Davenport states William C. Bates died September 16, 1867, in Marion Co., IL.

Batey/Battey, William T., Pvt., Co. C, age 18, EN 4/25/64 and MI 4/30/64, Decatur, AL, born Rome, GA, farmer, residence shown as Morgan Co., AL, POW 3/10/65, captured at Solomon Grove, NC, discharged 6/12/65 at Camp Chase, OH.

Baty, John A., Pvt., Co. G, age 18, EN 4/24/64, Mooresville, AL, MI Rome, GA, born Poland (Paulding?) Co., GA, farmer, MO 10/20/65, Huntsville, AL.

Baugh, James P., Pvt., Co. G, age 19, EN 3/10/64, Decatur, AL, MI 4/13/64, Decatur, AL, born Carroll, GA, farmer, company cook Sept. & Oct. 1864, MO 10/20/65, Huntsville, AL

Baughn, John N., Bugler, Co. L, age 24, EN 9/25/63, Fayette Co., AL, MI 9/25/63, Glendale, MS, MO 6/30/65, Nashville, TN.

Baulch, Joseph B., Pvt., Co. C, age 18, EN 1/1/64, Corinth, MS, born Lawrence, TN, farmer, MI 3/10/64, Memphis, TN, deserted 4/24/64 from Mooresville, AL with Remington revolver, sabre, belt, pistol, holster, cartridge and cap box.

Baxter, Richard, Pvt., Co. L, on daily duty as blacksmith 11/63.*

Baxter, William R., Pvt., Co. L&F, age 18, EN 8/1/64, Rome, GA, MI 10/17/64, Rome, Ga, born Cherokee Co., AL, farmer POW 3/10/65 at Solomon Grove, NC, discharged at Camp Chase, OH by reason of G.O. 77, War Dept. 6/12/65.

Bayne, Thomas C., Co. F, absent sick at Memphis, TN 12/63.*

Beach, John, Pvt., Co. D, died April 19, 1863, complaint was pneumonia.**

Beachum, Hugh L., Pvt., Co. C, age 25, EN 1/1/64, Corinth, MS, MI 3/10/64, Memphis, TN, born Marshal, MS, farmer.

Beard, Alfred, Pvt., Co. C, age 18, EN 1/1/64, Corinth, MS, MI 3/10/64, Memphis, TN, born Lincoln Co., TN, farmer, deserted 5/20/64 near Dallas, GA. POW 6/1/64 near Dallas, GA. Charges of desertion were removed 4/16/84 by War Dept. stating he died in prison at Andersonville GA on or about 12/1/64. (Another Muster Roll stated "died in hospital at Anapolis, MD of disease.")

Beard, George R., Pvt., Co. L, age 21, EN 4/7/65, Stevenson, AL, born Lincoln Co., TN, farmer, MI 4/18/65, Nashville, TN, MO 10/20/65, Huntsville, AL.

Beard, John, Pvt., Co. L, age 19, EN 4/7/65, Stevenson, AL, born Lincoln Co., TN, farmer, MI 4/18/65, Nashville, TN, MO 10/20/65, Huntsville, AL.

Beard, Robert E., Pvt., Co. H, age 26, EN 4/1/65, Stevenson, AL, MI 4/18/65, Nashville, TN, born Abbeville Dist., SC, MO 10/20/65, Huntsville, TN.

Beasley, Thomas F., Pvt., Co. I, age 19, EN & MI 8/18/62, Huntsville, AL, sick in hospital in Nashville 11/14/62, MIA at Day's Gap, AL 4/28/63, rejoined Co. 10/24/63, appt. Corp. 1/1/64 by Lt. Col. Dodd, reduced from Corp. 10/1/64 by Col. Spencer, born Shelby Co., AL, farmer, MO 7/19/65, Nashville, TN.

Beasley, William, Pvt., Co. A, age 50, EN 1/1/64, Camp Davies, MS, MI 2/5/64, Memphis, TN, born Abbeville Dist., SC, farmer, deserted 4/11/64 from Mooresville, AL with side arms.

Beasley, William M., 1st Lt., Co. I, age 35, EN 7/21/62, Huntsville, AL, MI 7/21/62, Huntsville, AL, resigned 10/8/62, sick in Hospital #14 in Nashville, TN, discharged 10/16/62.

Beaver, William, Co. F, absent sick in USA Hospital 3/65.*

Belcher, Charles W., Pvt/Sgt, Co. D, age 23, EN 5/20/64, Decatur, AL, born Jefferson, AL, farmer, MI 6/16/64, Decatur, AL, MO 10/20/65, Huntsville, AL.

Belford, S., Co. H, absent sick in Post Hospital at Huntsville, AL 6/5/65.*

Bell, Francis, Pvt., Co. K, age 19, EN 7/24/62, Huntsville, AL, AL, farmer, MI 7/24/62, Huntsville, AL, born Marshall Co., AL, in hospital in Nashville, 10/9/62, discharged 3/14/63 for disability.

Bell, James T., Pvt., Co. K, age 17, EN 10/23/63, born Marion Co., AL (another Muster Roll stated Marshall Co., AL), on detached service 1/24/64 as teamster in Gen. Sherman's expedition, POW in Arkansas near Memphis, TN 3/21/64, died 7/24/64 in hospital at Decatur, AL.

Bell, James, Co. D, on daily duty as teamster 7/63.*

Bell, John, Sgt/Pvt., Co. K, age 28, EN 7/24/62, Huntsville, AL, born Morgan Co., AL, blacksmith, reduced to Pvt. 1/1/63, died in hospital at Rome, GA 8/17/64, typhoid/congestive fever. (Buried in Grave #1234, Marietta National Cemetery.)

Bell, Robert, Pvt., Co. A, age 30, EN & MI 1/20/63, Glendale, MS, MIA Vincent's Cross Roads, MS 10/26/63, died of disease at Andersonville, GA 8/3/64 while POW. (Buried in Grave #4622, Andersonville National Historic Cemetery.)

Bellamy, Nathan P., Pvt/Sgt., Co. C, age 24, EN 2/20/64, Memphis, TN, born Franklin, GA, farmer, MI 3/10/64, Memphis, TN, appt. Sgt. 3/1/64, deserted 11/9/64 in Rome, GA with two revolvers, one Smith Carbine, horse and equipment.

Bennett, William, Pvt., Co. C, age 27, EN 12/24/62, Corinth, MS, born White Co., TN, farmer, MI 12/28/62, Corinth, MS, MO 12/27/63, Camp Davies, MS.

Benson, George W., Sgt/2nd Lt., Co. A&B, age 22, EN 1/12/64, Camp Davies, MS, born Franklin Co., AL, Professor, MI 2/5/64, Memphis, TN, MO 10/20/65, Huntsville, TN.

Bergin, James A., Pvt., Co. M, age 37, EN 11/11/63 and MI 11/11/63, Camp Davies, MS, born Tuscaloosa Co., AL, deserted 10/29/64 with arms, on detached service 11/3/64, deserted 6/1/65from Mooresville, AL.

Berry, Doctor M., Pvt., Co. A&D, age 25, EN 1/10/64, Camp Davies, MS, MI 2/5/64, Memphis, TN, born Marshall Co., AL, farmer, MO 10/20/65, Huntsville, TN.

Berry, Elijah, Pvt., Co. E, EN& MI 3/5/63, Glendale, MS, detailed as teamster in Q.M. Dept. at Vicksburg, MS 1/25/64, MO 3/1/64, Memphis, TN.

Berry, James M., Pvt., Co. D, age 19, EN 4/19/64, Decatur, AL, MI 6/16/64, Decatur, AL, born Blount Co., AL, POW 9/19/63 at Chickamauga, GA, admitted to hospital at Andersonville, GA 5/3/64 where he died 6/17/64. (Buried in Grave #2111, Andersonville National Historic Cemetery.)

Berry, Samuel, Co. L, farmer, EN Sept. (?) Fayette Co., AL by Capt. Tramel.*

Berry, Sylvester, Pvt., Co. L, age 30, EN 9/25/63, Fayette Co., AL, MI 9/25/63, Glendale, MS, deserted 1/10/64 from Camp Davies, returned 1/22/64, MO 9/28/64, Rome, GA.

NOTE: Sylvester Berry was born about 1829 in Limestone Co., AL to William and Sarah Nelson Berry. Other children were: John Nelson, born September 26, 1823 in GA, married Elizabeth Moore, and died March 13, 1883 in Fayette Co., AL; Nancy, born May 15, 1825 in GA, married George Washington Brazil and died November 26, 1906; Elizabeth Ann, born about 1833 in AL, married John Rainey; Henry B., born about 1837 in AL; Robert, born about 1839 in AL; Cinthia, born March 8, 1844 in Fayette Co., AL, married Albert Dobbs and died April 23, 1899 in Fayette Co., AL; William, born June 6, 1842, married Mariah G. Culpepper September 20, 1868 and died June 12, 1913 in Fayette Co., AL; Joshua, born December 6, 1844 and died January 31, 1862; Sarah M., married John Collier February 13, 1845; and Tarpling, born March 16, 1850, married Emma Collier February 12, 1874 in TX and died June 23, 1926 in Pushmataha Co., OK.

Sylvester married Sarah Redman Johnson July 7, 1852 in Fayetteville, Fayette Co., AL, and had the following children: Sherman, Jasper A.; Mathilde Jane, born June 15, 1854, married John Canterbury 1873 in Hardin Co., TN; William Sanford, born January 21, 1856, died February 20, 1922 in Johnston Co., OK; Henry B., born August 10, 1858, died September 24, 1942 in Colorado City, TX, married Martha Estelle Heard; George W., born August 19, 1860, died June 20, 1940 in Pontotoc Co., OK; Emma, born 1864; John F., born 1871; Ulysses L., born October 12, 1873; Lee, born January 25, 1877.

Sylvester's son, Ulysses, married Annie Mae Watson and this union produced thirteen children: Sally Leo, Audy Edmond, Claudy, Sherman Edwin, Fredrick Earl, Roscoe Shelby, Neva Agnes, Carl Darwin, Arzelle, Eula Faye, Maymie, Hazel Argene, and Sherley Berry.

In 1950, Kenneth Foree wrote an article about Ulysses L. Berry entitled *NO RAILROADS RAN TO DALLAS HE SAW.* Due to the faded ink, some of the words are illegible. The article goes something like this: "It's strange how the whirligig of life handles a man at times. It turns him about. It really does. There's U.L. Berry, for instance. Berry, whose initials stand for Ulysses because his father was a soldier under Ulysses S. Grant, has the distinction few living men have. He saw Dallas before the railroads came.

A small man is Berry, who once was five feet ten but who has shrunk a bit by seventy-eight years. He's also slightly stooped but so would you be if you'd followed as many mules as many miles along a cotton row. And a paradoxical sun has burned into him a rich complexion that city life has not removed and bleached his hair, at the same time thinning it down to almost silver wisps on the top of his head. However he is much more active than when he first saw Dallas. Then he was 2 years old. A couple of years back he laid his own concrete sidewalks and built on a front porch.

Berry naturally recalls that glimpse of Dallas through the stories of his parents who were a part of the great westward movement that settled up Texas. Early 1872 it was when his father, Sylvester Berry, his wife, their ten children including Ulysses and possessions and set out from Alabama with one ox wagon. The larger boys walked with the dogs or rode a horse that Sylvester Berry probably owned for he has fought with the Yankees although his brother, Tarp Berry, was a Confederate.

Westward they picked up company, nine ox wagons eventually in all, leaving a war-wrecked land for raw, free Texas. The Berrys were headed for Delta County and a soil blacker'n any slave, deeper'n the ocean, rich as all git out, or so John Collier, a brother-in-law, had written.

They had no intention of staying in Dallas in the first place. But when they saw it they thought less of it.

As they came down the long slope through the post oaks where skyscrapers are now, they saw a shirttail full of houses, mostly log cabins. Down near the end of them they stopped in front of a log saloon and a log store. In a hog wallow in front of the saloon was a big dead dog.

"Howdy," said Sylvester Berry to a knot of men in front of the saloon. "Whar's a good place to camp?"

"Right ahead less'n a quarter." (This is where the ink begins to fade.) "Whar ye frum?"

Shortly, the wagon train moved on .... to the river where they found a wel .... camp ground. They also found some ....else: That big dead dog tied to their .... axle. "I swan," said Sylvester Berry.... "No, leave him thar."

Next day they started out for .... County. No use in fiddling in this on .... town. The oxen slowly climbed in the rise .... Berry stopped them in front of the s.... where stood the same gang of men. .... got down, went back, untied the dead .... and said, "You Texas fellers can't git n.... on an Alabamian."

The Texans grinned. "Come in an' .... set 'um up." They did.

Up by the store and cabins .... Greenville, John Cantebury, brother-in .... gave a pony for forth acres which G....ville n.... month later offered two ponies for the .... acres Cantebury snapped him up. Texa.... lots of acres but not too many ponies.

Up in Delta County they found .... Collier hadn't told the half of it. They f.... 20 acres with brush, planted it to c.... and that fall they had picked 27 bales .... cattle got in one night and ate up .... three more.

But you've got to sell cotton. So Sy....ter Berry and other farmers loaded up ....wagons and started for old Jefferson .... mean sort of young fellow who wouldn't .... his name or where he was from ta.... along. They tried to get shut of him .... and couldn't. One night after they campe.... Indian came in with a load of hides .... and made motions he wanted to sell. The .... young fellow said they oughta kill him ... take his hides. The others said no not a.... But the young fellow grabbed up a gun .... shot the Indian who whooped before he ....

Purty soon there were 100 In.... whooping around the camp. A wrinkled .... one made motions which they said they w.... kill only the killer if someone would .... him out; otherwise all. Finally Mi.... Jackson pointed him out. The Indians p.... him down with forked sticks, then ski.... him alive. Ultimately they cut his head.... put it on a lance and rode away. Sylv.... Berry and the rest yoked up and lit out ....

Father Berry made many trip.... Jefferson, but later he moved his family .... the Nations. He died at Roff in the Ch.... saw Nation in the 90's after son U.L. B.... had married and gone. U.L. farmed .... ranched all over the Nations before .... finally went back to their first love, ... County and its black waxy.

He made twenty-five cotton crops up in that deep soil around Mount Joy until the early 1920's. Then he moved to near New Hope, Dallas County. Why did he leave that black waxy paradise? "Got tired wadin' black mud. When it rained I'd hitch four mules to the front wheels, put a box on it and stop every quarter to punch mud out. At New Hope they had fine roads." That whirligig of time was turning.

It turned further. Berry's family of ten children was already breaking up. George D. Cummings, son-in-law and his wife Leo moved here. Then Sherman came to Dallas to work for Dr. Pepper and Roscoe for the R.B. George Machinery Company, both of them finally forming Berry Brothers Machine and Repair Works.

U.L. Berry moved in to the Big World Store area, quit farming and did some carpentering. By 1945 all of his children but one had been attracted by the magnet of Dallas. Then that whirligig spun again and Berry came back .... to the town he came through seventy-six years ago. But this time didn't find any dead dog in a mudhole in front of a saloon. Gosh! But it was bigger'n all git out."[26]

Berry, William, Corp., Co. D, on det. service recruiting in Decatur, AL 10/64.*

Berryhill, William R.A., Pvt., Co. E, EN 3/1/63, Glendale, MS, MI 3/1/63, Corinth, MS, MO 3/1/64, Memphis, TN.

Besow, George W., Sgt/2nd Lt. (Cards filed with George W. Benson).

Bess, William J., Pvt/Sgt., Co. A, EN & MI 6/25/63, Glendale, MS, promoted to Corp. 7/1/63, MO 12/22/63, Memphis, TN.

Bice/Brice/Price, John C., Pvt., Co. L, age 17, EN 9/25/63, Fayette Co., AL, MI 9/25/63, Glendale, MS, MIA 10/26/63 from Vincent's Crossroads, MS, died 9/11/64 while POW at Andersonville, GA. (POW Record states he died 9/10/64. Buried in Grave #8425, Andersonville National Cemetery.)

Bice, Nathaniel, Pvt/Corp., Co. M, age 45, EN 10/30/63, Glendale, MS, MI 10/30/63, Corinth, MS, born Winston Co., AL, farmer, POW 3/10/65 from Solomon Grove, NC, paroled 3/30/65.

Bickerstaff, John W., Pvt., Co. E, (Cards filed with John W. Bakerstaff)

Biddel, Simeon, Pvt., age 38, EN 3/14/64, Decatur, AL born Walker Co., AL, farmer.

Biford, Perry, Pvt., Co. A (Cards filed with Perry Byford)

Biford, Quiller J., Pvt., Co. A (Cards filed with Quiller J. Byford)

Billinger, John, Pvt., Co. M (Cards filed with John Dillinger)

Billings, Thomas, Pvt., Co. F, age 30, EN 6/30/63, Corinth, MS, MI 8/13/63, Corinth, MS, born McNairy Co., TN, farmer, deserted 7/11/63 from Glendale, MS.

Bird, John A., Pvt., Co. D, age 20, EN & MI 6/1/63, Glendale, MS, born Denton, TN, laborer, MO 6/16/64, Decatur, AL.

Birdsong, Milton M., Pvt., Co. G, age 17, EN 12/14/62, Pocahontis, TN, MI 12/14/62, Corinth, MS, MO 12/26/63, Memphis, TN.

Birt, Henry, Pvt., Co. D, in DeCamp USA General Hospital at David's Island, NY, MO 6/8/65.*

Bishop, Calvin, Pvt., Co. M, age 26, EN 12/2/63, Camp Davies, MS, MI 12/29/63, Corinth, MS, born St. Clair Co., AL, deserted 1/19/64 from Camp Davies. (Note stated he lived in Marion Co., AL)

Bishop, Columbus, Pvt., Co. M, age 18, EN 12/2/62, Camp Davies, MS, MI 12/29/63, Corinth, MS, born Spartanburg Dist., SC, farmer, MO 1/15/65, Savannah, GA.

Bishop, David H., Pvt., Co. M, age 16, EN 12/16/63, Camp Davies, MS, MI 12/16/63, Corinth, MS, born Marion Co., AL, farmer, died in hospital at Camp Davies, MS 1/11/64 of typhoid pneumonia.

Bishop, Francis M., Pvt., Co. C, age 18, EN 11/11/63, Camp Davies, MS, MI 11/11/63, born Marion Co., AL, farmer, MO 1/12/65.

Bishop, James M., Pvt., Co. M, age 44, EN 12/6/63, Camp Davies, MS, MI 12/29/63, Corinth, MS, deserted at Camp Davies, MS 1/13/64 with revolver, Born Bibb Co., AL, farmer.

Bishop, Robert W., Pvt., Co. B, age 37, EN 1/5/63, Glendale, MS, MI 1/22/63, Corinth, MS, born Bibb Co., AL, died 8/3/63 in regimental hospital at Glendale, MS.

Black, J., Co. F, absent sick in USA General Hospital 6/65-9/65.*

Black, William A., Pvt., Co. D, age 28, EN 5/20/64, Decatur, AL, MI 6/16/64, Decatur, AL, born Marshall Co., AL, farmer, MO 10/20/65, Huntsville, AL.

Blackburn, Andrew J., Pvt., Co. M, age 36, EN 10/31/63, Glendale, MS, MI 12/29/63, Corinth, MS, born Wilkes Co., GA, deserted 5/20/65 in Durham, NC with Spencer carbine, horse, saddle & bridle.

Blackstock, Thomas H., Corp., Co. L, EN 9/25/63, Fayette Co., AL, MI 9/25/63, Glendale, MS, MIA 10/26/63, Vincent's Crossroads, MS, died 2/1/64 while POW at Cahawba Prison.

Blackstock, William H., Pvt., Co. L, absent POW 10/26/63.*

Blackwell, John G., Pvt/Sgt., Co. M, age 25, EN 10/31/63, Glendale, MS, MI 10/31/63, Corinth, MS, born Floyd Co., GA, farmer, POW 3/10/65 at Solomon Grove, NC.

Blakeney, Alfred, Pvt., Co. A, age 35, EN 1/23/64, Camp Davies, MS, MI 2/5/64, Memphis, TN, born Chesterfield Dist., SC, farmer, deserted 2/23/64 from Memphis, TN with pistol and sabre.

Blalock, James M., Pvt/2nd Lt., Co. D,H&G, age 28, EN & MI 9/18/63, Glendale, MS for 1 year, reenlisted 7/1/64 in Rome, GA at age 30 for 3 years and promoted to 2nd Lt. and assigned to Co. G, sick in hospital in Savannah, GA 1/20/65, MO 10/20/65, Huntsville, AL.

Blalock, William C., Corp., Co. L (Cards filed with William C. Blaylock)

Blanchard/Blancitt, C., 1st Lt., Co. C, died November 11, 1863.*

Blankenship, Robert S., Pvt., Co. B, age 29, EN 3/12/64, Athens, AL, MI 3/27/64, Decatur, AL, born Shelby Co., AL, farmer, on furlough 4/17/64 to settle family in Pulaski, TN, died 8/25/65, Pulaski, TN.
   NOTE: Was detailed to go to Nashville, TN to look after deserters and while returning to his command under military orders was killed in railroad accident when train fell through bridge at Richland Creek in Giles Co., TN.[27]

Blankenship, William W., Pvt., Co. I, age 22, EN & MI 7/21/62, Huntsville, AL, on leave with wagon train at Nashville, TN 12/27/62, born Winston Co., AL, farmer, died 4/29/64 at Decatur, AL (another record states he died in Nashville, TN).

Blankenship, Zephemiah (Zeffeniah H.), Pvt., Co. I, age 24, EN & MI 7/21/62, Huntsville, born Shelby Co., AL, on leave with wagon train at Nashville, TN 12/27/62, died in hospital at Murfreesboro, TN 4/63.

Blankinship, Jessie, Pvt., Co. G, age 18, EN 3/10/64, Decatur, AL, MI 4/13/64, Decatur, AL, born Lawrence Co., AL, MO 10/20/65, Huntsville, AL.

Blaylock, William C., Corp., Co. L, age 19, EN 9/25/63, Fayette Co., AL, MI 9/25/63, Glendale, MS, born Pickens Co., AL, discharged due to disability January 1864 (one Muster Roll shows a W.C. Blaylock discharged September 1864 in Rome, GA by reason of exp. of term of service. (An enlistment form for William B. Blaylock born in Haywood, NC was in with papers of William C. with same EN date.

Blevins, Armstead E., Pvt., Co. L, age 19, EN 3/1/65, Stevenson, AL, MI 4/18/65, Nashville, TN, born Walker Co., AL, farmer, sick in hospital 4/20/65 in Nashville, TN, MO 10/20/65, Huntsville, AL.

Blevins, Dillard, Pvt., Co. K, age 26, EN & MI 7/24/62, Huntsville, AL, born Walker Co., AL, died in Hospital #14, Nashville, TN 10/17/62 of measles.

Blevins, Jacob J., Sgt/Pvt., Co. K, age 37, EN & MI 7/24/62, Huntsville, AL, born Morgan Co., AL, farmer, discharged 11/22/62 in Nashville, TN for disability.
   NOTE: Jacob Jonathan Blevins was born February 12, 1825 to John and Elizabeth Ryan Blevins. After the war, he moved to Effingham Co., IL and on to

Arkansas. He married Mary Ann Davis in Morgan Co., AL May 8, 1849. Mary Ann died October 9, 1878, and Jacob died February 3, 1901 in Scott Co., AR. He is buried in Cedar Grove Cemetery in Scott Co.[28]

Blevins, John, (No. 1), Pvt., Co. K, age 35, EN & MI 7/24/62, Huntsville, AL, born Morgan Co., AL, farmer, wounded by accidental gun shot from pistol of Wm. H. Hefner 1/6/63, WIA 3/10/65 at Monroe's Crossroads, NC.

Blevins, John, (2), Pvt., Co. K, age 25, EN & MI 7/24/62, Huntsville, AL, born Walker Co., AL, farmer, died in Hospital #8 in Nashville, TN 2/4/63 of typhoid fever. (Buried in Grave E-0436, Nashville National Cemetery.)
NOTE: John was the son of Celia Cranford and Armstead Blevins, Sr. Armstead died March 23, 1882 in Winston Co., AL at age 74 and Celia applied for support based on her son's military service.[29]

Blevins, Nathaniel, Pvt., Co. K, age 39, EN & MI 7/24/62, Huntsville, AL, born Morgan Co., AL, farmer, in hospital at Tuscumbia, AL 4/23/63, died 3/1/64 in Memphis, TN of smallpox. (Buried Grave #1-46, Memphis National Cemetery.)
NOTE: Nathaniel Blevins was born in Morgan Co., AL about 1823. The following is a letter found in Nathaniel's military files:
Thunderbolt, Georgia
Jan 14th, 1865

In compliance with your order dated Sept 1st, 1864, I herewith transmit Final Statements of the Cases of Privates Blevins, Bell, and Huey, Co. K 1st Ala Vol Cav.

It has been impossible to attend to it sooner having been on a active campaign the whole time since the receipt of your letter.

I had furnished Blevins Descriptive Roll when he was sent to the hospital at Memphis, Tenn and the Surgeon in charge had all the necessary documents to render Final Statements. Huey and Bell were left sick at Decatur, Ala without descriptive Rolls. I being a prisoner to the rebels in Arkansas at the time and the Co. being commanded by Lieut. Tupper 1st Ala. Cav.

There are some facts in the case of Blevins to which I would most earnestly invite attention, Viz, he had $211.50 dollars in his pocket when he was sent to the hospital but a few days before his death (March 1st 1864). Our camp was not a half mile from the small pox hospital and we knew of Blevins death next day. But I received no official notice till the 9th. I had to make a written request for it. John Blevins, private Co. K, 1st Ala. Vol. Cav. had called at the hospital before I had received a Statement and ascertained from the clerks that the money of his brother Nathaniel was there but Surgeon Geo. F. Huntingdon was not willing to admit but $101.00 dollars but the clerks had told John Blevins of $201.00. He finally admitted it and the figures on the Inventory he sent me shows a 1 altered to a 2. John Blevins offered to identify himself as brother to the deceased and his legal representative but Surgeon Huntingdon refused to hear the testimony offered on the case and preferred to pay the money over to the paymaster if he has done so his receips were sent up with the papers he should have sent. I reported the facts of the case to the proper authorities at Memphis immediately but was captured by the rebels in Arkansas on the 21st of March and detained there till 24th April by which time the Regt had moved to Decatur, Ala. and it was impossible for me to attend to *it. I intended to prefer charges against Surgeon Huntingdon and have the matter investigated but have had other duties of more importance of the service to attend to. There are the main facts in the case which I can fully prove and if Surgeon Huntingdon has not sent receipts from some Paymaster, I would respectfully ask to be informed of it so that I can prefer charges against Asst. Surgeon Geo. F. Huntingdon and get justice done to a faithful and good soldier.*

Yours respectfully, your obedient servant,
J.H. Hornback, 1st Lieut 1st Ala. Vol. Cav., Comdg Co. K[30]

Blevins, William, Pvt., Co. L, age 25, EN 9/25/63, Fayette Co., AL, MI 9/25/63, Glendale, MS, MIA 10/26/63, sick in hospital in Memphis, TN 2/16/64, MO 6/30/65, Nashville, TN.

Bodkins, Charles W., Pvt., Co. H, age 20, EN 3/1/65, Stevenson, AL, MI 4/18/65, Nashville, TN, born Marion Co., AL, farmer, appt. Sgt. 4/1/65 but reduced to ranks 7/15/65.

Boen, Archie, Pvt., Co. D (Cards filed with Archie Bowen).

Bolding, Augustus M., Pvt., Co. C, age 21, EN 8/24/63, Glendale, MS, MI 9/27/63, Corinth, MS, reduced from Sgt. to Pvt 8/18/64, born Hamilton, TN, MO 8/28/64, Rome, GA.

Bolding, Thomas J., Pvt., Co. C, age 19, EN 8/24/63, Glendale, MS, MI 9/27/63, Corinth, MS, born Franklin Co., AL, MO 9/28/64, Rome, GA.

Bolding, Wyley V., Pvt., Co. C, age 22, EN 1/10/63, Corinth, MS, MI 1/20/63, Corinth, MS, born Ducktown, TN, farmer, MO 1/31/64, Memphis, TN.

Bolen, William, Pvt., Co. M (Cards filed with William Bowlin)

Boling, Ozias D., Pvt., Co. H, age 18, EN 1/1/65, Stevenson, AL, MI 4/5/65, Nashville, TN, born Grundy Co., TN, MO 10/20/65, Huntsville, AL.

Boling/Bolin, William C., Pvt/Sgt., Co. K, age 21, EN 6/26/62, Limestone Co., AL, MI 6/26/62, born Warren Co., TN, transferred from Co. K, 21st Ohio Vols., appt. Sgt 9/1/62, in hospital in Nashville, 9/30/62, KIA 3/10/65 at Monroe's Crossroads, NC .

Bolley, George, Pvt/Teamster, Co. M (Cards filed with George Boxley)

Bolton, Hugh L., Pvt/2nd Lt., Co. L&F, age 22, EN 9/25/63, Fayette Co., AL, MI 9/25/63, Glendale, MS, promoted to 2nd Lt. 7/1/64, (another Muster Roll states he EN & MI in Rome, GA) POW 3/10/65 Monroe's Crossroads, NC, born Pickens, AL, MO 10/20/65, Huntsville, AL.

Bolton, John, Pvt., Co. H, age 27, EN 10/23/63, Glendale, MS, MI 10/23/63, Camp Davies, MS, born in Georgia, died of typhoid fever 8/7/64 in hospital at Rome, GA. (Buried in Grave #1630 in Marietta National Cemetery.)

Bone, James, Pvt., Co. H, age 17, EN 3/1/65, Stevenson, AL, MI 3/5/65, Nashville, TN, born Paulding Co., GA, deserted from Blountsville, AL 9/6/65 with Remington revolver, Colt pistol & sabre.

Booker, William W., Pvt., Co. E, age 29, EN & MI 8/27/63, Glendale, MS, born McNairy Co., TN, POW 10/26/63 Vincent's Crossroads and died 8/13/64 while in prison at Andersonville, GA. (Buried in Grave #5505, Andersonville National Cemetery.

Bookout, Abel, Pvt., Co. H, age 28, EN & MI 9/18/63, Glendale, MS, born Cleveland, NC, farmer, WIA 10/26/63, died 12/18/63 in Memphis, TN of pneumonia. (Buried in Memphis National Cemetery.)

Boon, John W., Pvt., Co. C, age 18, EN 2/15/64, Memphis, TN, MI 3/10/64, Memphis, TN, born Yancy Co., NC, farmer, POW 3/10/65, MO 10/20/65, Huntsville, AL.

Booth, George, Veterinary Surgeon, Co. H&L, age 37, EN & MI 4/13/63, Glendale, MS, promoted from private, 64th IL Inf. Vols., MO 4/12/64.

Borden, Francis M., Pvt., Co. A, age 20, EN 6/12/63, Glendale, MS, MI 6/12/63, Memphis, TN, MO 12/22/63, Memphis, TN.

Borolin, Pvt., Co. L, EN 12/16/63.*

Bostic, William F., Pvt., Co. K, age 21, EN & MI 12/1/63, Camp Davies, MS, on detached service as teamster in Gen. Sherman's expedition 1/24/64, MO 7/19/65, born Cass Co., GA, farmer.
NOTE: William Bostic traveled 90 miles from his home in Marion Co., AL to join the Union army at Camp Davies, MS.

Boswell, Andrew G., (Cards filed with Andrew G. Basnell)

Botkins, Charles W., (Cards filed with Charles W. Bodkins)

Bourland, Gabriel L., Pvt., Co. B, age 35, EN 12/19/62, Glendale, MS, MI 12/31/62, Corinth, MS, on leave 3/28/63 to take his family to Jackson, TN, on leave 6/19/63 to take his family north, born Franklin Co., AL, farmer.
NOTE: Gabriel Lee Bourland was born about 1827 in AL and died in 1913 in Prague, Lincoln Co., OK. He married Milda "Milly" Oliver and according to the 1860 Franklin Co., AL Census, had the following children: John H., 1849; Susan C., 1851; I.A., 1852; Madenia I., 1855; Joseph, 1856 and Walter B. 1859. He also had daughters, Alta and Belle. John Henderson married March 22, 1872 in Salem, Marion Co., IL to Mary Alice Lybarger. Joseph McDonald married July 22, 1879 in Jefferson Co., IL to Paralee A. Youngblood. Walter B. married February 5, 1881 in Jefferson Co., IL to Margaret E. Sweeton.[31]

Bowlin/Bowling, William, Pvt., Co. M, age 18, EN 12/16/63, Camp Davies, MS, MI 12/16/63, Corinth, MS, born Marion Co., AL, farmer, died in hospital at Nashville, TN 4/6/64 of inflamation of lungs.

Bowman, Isaac V., Pvt., Co.H, age 18, EN 4/1/65, Stevenson, AL, MI 4/18/65, Nashville, TN, born Cass Co., GA, farmer, MO 10/20/65, Huntsville, TN.

Bowman, Lorenzo D., Pvt., Co. H, age 44, EN 4/1/65, Stevenson, AL, MI 4/18/65, Nashville, TN, born Gwinnett Co., GA, blacksmith, MO 10/20/65, Huntsville, AL.

Bowman, Robert B., Pvt., Co. H, age 18, EN 4/1/65, Stevenson, AL, MI 4/18/65, Nashville, TN, farmer, born Cass Co., GA, MO 10/20/65, Huntsville, AL.

Bowen, Archie, Pvt., Co. D, age 46, EN 10/14/64, Decatur, AL, MI 11/10/64, Rome, GA, born Kershaw Dist., SC, farmer, KIA Monroe's Crossroads, NC 3/10/65.

Bowland, William, Pvt., Co. E, EN 3/1/63, Glendale, MS, MI 3/1/63, Corinth, MS, MO 3/3/64, Memphis, TN.
NOTE: William Bowland was charged with the murder of Neal Morrison, a citizen of Tishimingo Co., MS, on or about 11/14/63, near Camp Davies, MS. He deserted and was captured by a scouting party near Glendale, MS and returned about 11/18/63. He was alleged to also be in Co. G, 44th IL Inf. as William Bowlin.

Bowyer (See Boyer)

Box, Francis E., Pvt., Co. H, age 25, EN 10/16/63, Glendale, MS, MI 10/16/63, Camp Davies, MS, born Blount Co., AL, farmer, deserted 4/30/64, died 5/17/64 US Gen. Hospital at Jefferson Barracks, MO.

Boxley, George, Teamster/Pvt., Co. M, age 31, EN 8/5/63, Chewalla, TN, MI 8/5/63, Corinth, MS, born Meigs Co., TN, farmer, on duty as nurse in smallpox hospital, Savannah, GA 1/10/65, MO 10/20/65, Huntsville, AL.

Boxley, W., Co. F, absent sick in USA General Hospital.*

Boyd, Doctor T., Pvt., Co. K, age 34, EN & MI 12/21/63, Camp Davies, MS, born Morgan Co., AL, farmer, POW 3/21/64 in AR near Memphis, TN, MO 7/19/65, Nashville, TN. Traveled 150 miles from Walker Co., AL to Camp Davies, MS to enlist.
NOTE: Doctor Tandy Boyd was the son of Hannah James and James Lee Boyd, Sr. and brother of Tillman Boyd, below. He was born May 6, 1829 in Morgan Co., AL and on October 19, 1852 he married Sarah Reid in Walker Co., AL. Sarah was born October 25, 1834 and died November 9, 1904. Children of Tandy and Sarah were: John Daniel, January 12, 1854, died April 4, 1936, married Mary Bell Godfrey; James Wesley, born May 21, 1858, died 1938, married Willie Burrel; Martha Jane, August 8, 1860, died April 23, 1943, married Thomas Clemons; Sarah Ann, April 29, 1866, died October 4, 1937, married John W. Wood and Green

Williams; Joseph Monroe, January 2, 1877, died April 18, 1947, married Ida Childers; and Gereda Elizabeth, September 30, 1870, died about 1880.

In 1862 Doctor Tandy Boyd and several other men including his three brothers, were locked in the Walker County Courthouse until they either joined the Confederate Army or be conscripted. After refusing twice, Doctor T. finally agreed to go and shoe horses for Captain E.J. Rice of the Confederate Army where he remained for five or six days and then escaped. In December 1863 Doctor T. and his brother, Tillman, walked 150 miles from Walker Co., AL to Camp Davies MS where they enlisted in Co. K of the First Alabama Cavalry Volunteers. While on his way to Camp Davies, Doctor T. was repairing his gun lock when the main spring flew out and penetrated his left eye causing him to loose site in that eye. On March 21, 1864 in Arkansas near Memphis, TN, Doctor T. was held prisoner by the Rebels where he was exposed to very cold and rainy weather, without shelter or sufficient food causing him to have liver, kidney, rhetumatism and heart disease. Due to these medical conditions, he was able to draw a pension of twenty dollars per month after the war. During the war he recruited in Walker, Winston and Morgan Counties in AL. Doctor T. died January 11, 1908 and he and his wife, Sarah, are buried in Antioch Cemetery at Bug Tussle near Bremen, AL. Sarah Narcissa Boyd, sister of Doctor T. and Tillman Boyd, married William P. Ramey who was also in Co. K, First AL Cav., U.S.A.[32]

Boyd, Elisha F., Pvt/Sgt., Co. B, age 21, EN 8/1/64, Wedowee, AL, MI 8/1/64, Rome, GA, born Meriwether Co., GA, farmer, died 4/1/65 of wounds received in action at Richland, NC.
    NOTE: Elisha F. Boyd was the son of Alexander Boyd who lived in the Wedowee area of Randolph Co., AL.[33]

Boyd, Joseph, Pvt., Co. I, died August 25, 1863 of fever, "effects delivered to brother", Casualty Sheet was completed at Corinth, MS.**

Boyd, Tilmon S., Pvt., Co. K, age 21, EN & MI 12/21/63, Camp Davies, MS, born Walker Co., AL, farmer, left sick at Ackworth, GA 6/20/64, captured 3/10/65 at Solomon Grove, NC, discharged at Camp Chase, OH 6/12/65. Traveled 150 miles from Walker Co., AL to Camp Davies to enlist.
    NOTE: Tillman S. Boyd was born February 18, 1842 and was a brother of Doctor Tandy Boyd, above. Tillman died May 16, 1915 and is buried at Sulphur Springs Cemetery in Blount Co., AL. He never married. His pension record stated he was captured by the Rebels at Solomon Grove, NC and was forced to walk barefoot in the snow 200 miles from Monroe's Crossroads to Richmond, VA. On March 30, 1865 he was paroled and was discharged in June 1865 at Camp Chase Ohio.[34]

Boyd, Thomas J., (Cards filed with Thomas J. Byrd)

Boyer, Thomas Henry, Pvt., Co. F, age 18, EN 5/23/63, Corinth, MS, MI 8/13/63, Corinth, MS, born Octibbeha Co., MS, died in hospital at Corinth, MS of disease 11/63. (Buried Grave # B-3357, Corinth National Cemetery.)

Bradley, Samuel, Pvt., Co. A, in Overton USA Hospital at Memphis, TN Jan & Feb 1864.*

Bramman, William M. (Cards filed with William M. Branen)

Bramley, Barton, Pvt/Corp., Co. B, age 33, EN 1/20/63, Glendale, MS, MI 1/29/63, Corinth, MS, born Fayette Co., AL, farmer, POW 10/26/63 Vincent's Crossroads, MO 1/22/64, Memphis, TN.

Branen/Branan, William M., Bugler/Pvt., Co. A, age 18, EN 8/1/64, Rome, GA, born Coosa Co., AL, farmer, sick in hospital in Nashville, TN 11/8/64, POW 3/10/65, deserted 10/6/65, charges removed January 10, 1893, MO 10/20/65, Huntsville, AL.

Branhan, Andrew, Pvt., Co. F, in USA Field Hospital at Bridgeport, AL, returned to duty 5/7/64.*

Brannan, William, Pvt., Co. B, age 17, EN 1/16/63, Glendale, MS, MI 1/22/63, Corinth, MS, born Coosa Co., AL, farmer, MO 1/22/64, discharge certificate furnished by War Dept. October 18, 1890.

Brantley, James M., Pvt., Co. H, age 20, EN 1/15/65, Stevenson, AL, MI 4/18/65, Nashville, TN, born Walton Co., GA, MO 10/20/65, Huntsville, AL.

Braswell, J.B., Pvt., Co. L, EN 4/1/64, Mooresville.*

Brasswell, James, Pvt., Co. L, EN 6/1/64, Ackworth, GA.*

Bray, Stephen S., Pvt., Co. L, age 18, EN 9/25/63, Fayette Co., AL, MI 9/25/63, Glendale, MS, born Winston Co., AL, returned from MIA 12/25/63, sick in Nashville, TN 4/2/64, MO 9/28/64, Rome, GA.

Bray, William H., Pvt., Co. L, age 42, EN 9/25/63, Fayette Co., AL, MI 9/25/63, Glendale, MS, born Winston Co., AL, farmer, MIA 10/26/63 at Vincent's Crossroads, deserted 1/2/64 from Camp Davies, MS with revolver, MO 9/29/64, Rome, GA.

Brewer, Sanders, Pvt., Co. C, age 45, EN 12/1/62, Corinth, MS, MI 12/22/62, Corinth, MS, born Anson, NC, farmer, POW 8/9/63 & 10/26/63.

Brewer, William, Pvt., Co. D, age 23, EN 2/1/63, , Glendale, MS, MI 2/4/63, Corinth, MS, born Marion Co., AL, farmer, discharged 7/10/63 due to disability (had measles when he enlisted).

Brice, John C., (See John C. Bice).

Brigman, James N.(R.), Pvt., Co. G, age 27, EN 6/26/63, Chewalla, TN, MI 6/26/63, Corinth, MS, deserted 7/3/63 (could be 7/30/63).

Brigman, Moses, Pvt., Co. G, temporarily attached from 11th IL Cav.

Britnell, William S., Pvt., Co. K&A, age 26, born Franklin Co., AL, farmer, deserted 6/3/63, returned 8/16/63 and was tried and found guilty of desertion. Notation from War Dept., Adj. General's Office dated August 19, 1897, "charges no longer stand", MIA Vincent's Crossroads, MS 10/26/63, MO 10/20/65.

Britton, John, Pvt., Co. K&A, age 45, EN 10/13/62, Corinth, MS, MI 10/14/62, Corinth, MS, born Edgefield, SC, discharged 2/24/63 due to disability - loss of eyes.

Britton, N.H. Pvt., Co. E, discharged, term of service exp. 7/27/64, Rome, GA.*

Brodigan, Peter, Pvt., Co. F, age 28, EN 6/29/63, Corinth, MS, MI 8/13/63, Corinth, MS, born New York City, NY, printer, MIA 10/26/63, Vincent's Crossroads, MO 7/27/64, Rome, GA.

Brogden, Charles J., Pvt/Bugler, Co. K&A, age 30, EN 9/8/62, Corinth, MS, MI 10/1/62, Corinth, MS, born Warren Co., TN, farmer, MO 9/11/63.

Brogdon, Claborne, Pvt., Co. G, age 40, EN 3/2/64, Decatur, AL, MI 4/13/64, Decatur, AL, born Morgan Co., AL, in hospital at Hilton Head, SC 2/6/65, transferred north 3/15/65, transferred to Nashville, TN 4/26/65, MO 10/20/65, Huntsville, AL.

Bromley, Barton, (Cards filed with Barton Bramley)

Bromley, Riley Y., Pvt., Co. K,A&B, age 34, EN 11/5/62, Corinth, MS, MI 12/31/62, Corinth, MS, deserted 12/31/62, MI 1/22/63, Corinth, MS, POW 10/26/63 Vincent's Crossroads, MO 1/22/64.

Bronson, David A., (Cards filed with David A. Brunson)

Bronson, William H., (Cards filed with William H. Brunson)

Brooks, George W., Pvt., Co. A, age 40, EN & MI 8/27/64, Rome, GA, born Henry Co., GA, farmer, died 6/17/65, Huntsville, AL of disease of heart.

Brooks, Henry F., Pvt., Co. K, age 24, EN & MI 7/22/62, Huntsville, AL, born Lauderdale Co., AL, farmer, POW at Rome, GA, 5/23/63, sent to hospital at Camp Chase, OH 5/22/63.

Brooks, James L., Pvt., Co. D, age 30, EN 5/20/64, Decatur, AL, MI 6/16/64, Decatur, AL, born Carroll Co., GA, farmer, MO 10/20/65, Huntsville, AL.

Brooks, John A., Pvt., Co. K, age 28, EN & MI 8/22/64, Huntsville, AL, born Lauderdale, AL, farmer, died in hospital #14 at Nashville, 11/7/62, measles. (Buried in Grave A-5186, Nashville National Cemetery.)

Brooks, John C., Sgt/2nd Lt., temporarily attached from 66th IL Vols.

Brooks, John W., Pvt., Co. E, EN & MI 3/1/63, Glendale, MS, MO 3/3/64, Memphis, TN.

NOTE: John W. Brooks was charged with the murder of Neal Morrison, a citizen of Tishimingo Co., MS, on or about November 14, 1863, also charged with desertion but captured by scouting party near Glendale, MS and returned.

Bross, J.A., Co. E, absent in arrest at Corinth since 11/22/63.*

Brown, Elijah, Pvt., Co. K, age 44, EN 7/24/62, Huntsville, AL., born Lawrence Co., AL, died 10/30/62, Camp Campbell, Nashville, TN. (Buried in Grave B-6968, Nashville National Cemetery.)

Brown, George L., Co. I, on det. service as courier at Reedyville, TN 1/27/63.*

Brown, George S., Co. I, EN 8/1/63, Shelbyville, TN by Lt. Snelling.*

Brown, George S., Co. D, absent on Courier Post Jan & Feb 1863.*

Brown, George W., Pvt., Co. K&A, EN 12/31/62, Corinth, MS, MI 12/31/62, Corinth, MS, MO 12/22/63, Memphis, TN.

Brown, John, Pvt., Co. G, age 36, EN 3/10/64, Decatur, AL, MI 4/13/64, Decatur, AL, born Pike Co., GA, farmer, deserted 11/17/64 from Atlanta, GA with side arms & equipment, returned 8/5/65, Decatur, AL.

Brown, John, Co. F, absent sick in USA General Hospital 5/65.*

Brown, M.V., Pvt., Co. D, EN 6/1/63, Glendale, MS.*

Brown, Merrill, Pvt., Co. K, age 30, EN & MI 7/24/62, Huntsville, AL, born Lawrence Co., AL, farmer, deserted from picket post with arms & horse 11/2/62 in Nashville, TN, not apprehended.

Brown, Robert M., Pvt., Co. F, age 27, EN 5/27/63, Corinth, MS, MI 8/13/63, Corinth, MS, died 9/17/63 at Glendale, MS of disease.

Brown, Robert K., Pvt., Co. B, age 18, EN 1/13/63, Glendale, MS, MI 1/22/63, Corinth, MS, born Marion Co., AL, farmer, deserted 3/9/63 from Glendale, MS, returned 9/15/63, POW 10/26/63 at Vincent's Crossroads, MO 1/22/64, Memphis, TN.

Brown, Spencer R., Pvt., Co. A, EN 5/12/63, Glendale, MS, MI 5/12/63, Corinth, MS, MO 12/22/63, Memphis, TN. (A Spencer R. Brown of 1st AL Cav. died April 1864 and is buried in Grave # B-234, Corinth National Cemetery.)

Brown, William, Pvt/Corp., Co. F, age 20, EN 6/25/63, Memphis, TN, MI, 8/13/63, Corinth, MS, Born Chickasaw Co., MS, WIA 10/26/63 & in hospital at Memphis, TN.

Brown, William, Pvt., Co. K, age 28, EN & MI 7/24/62, Huntsville, AL, born Lawrence Co., AL, farmer, died 12/13/62 in Hospital #14, Nashville, TN of rubeola. (There are two William Browns buried in the Nashville National Cemetery: Wm. F., died 12/12/62, buried in Grave B-6102; and Wm. M., died 12/20/62, buried in Grave N-10742.)

Brown, William E., Pvt., Co. C, age 18, EN 2/15/64, Memphis, TN, MI 3/10/64, Memphis, TN, born Marshall Co., MS, farmer, KIA 4/7/65, Faison's Station, NC, shot by the enemy while a scout.

Brown, William G., Pvt., Co. H, age 18, EN 1/15/65, Huntsville, AL, MI 2/13/65, Nashville, TN, born Walton Co., AL, MO 10/20/65, Huntsville, AL.

Brown, William M., Pvt., Co. D, EN 6/1/63, Glendale, MS, deserted 6/22/63 from Glendale, MS.

Brumley, Barton, (Cards filed with Barton Bramley)

Brumly, J.L., Pvt., Co. G, transferred by order of Col. Mercy 8/24/63.*

Brumley, Riley Y. (Cards filed with Reley Y. Bromley)

Brumly, Larkin J., Pvt., Co. G, temporarily attached from 11th IL Cav.

Brunson, David A., Sgt., Co. L, age 31, EN 9/25/63, Fayette Co., AL, MI 9/25/63, Glendale, MS, born Wilkes, GA, farmer, died 12/28/63 in hospital at Camp Davies, MS of jaundice. (Buried Corinth National Cemetery and classified with unknown dead.)

Brunson, William H., Corp., Co. L, age 23, EN 9/25/63, Fayette Co., AL, MI 9/25/63, Glendale, MS, born Wilkes, GA, farmer, died 12/9/63 at Camp Davies, MS of disease. (Buried Corinth National Cemetery and classified with unknown dead.)

Bryant, Henry, Pvt., Co. F, age 36, EN 3/27/63, Corinth, MS, MI 4/18/63, born Florence, AL, factory worker, AWOL 4/27/63, deserted 7/16/63, Glendale, MS.

Bryant, John A., Pvt., Co. M, age 24, EN 12/7/63 and MI 12/7/63, Camp Davies, MS, born Tippah Co., MS, farmer, in hospital at Mound City, IL 9/15/64, MO 5/31/65.

Bryant, J.H. Pvt., Co. L, EN 12/7/63.*

Buchanan, Thomas S., Pvt., Co. L, age 27, EN 10/15/64, Rome, GA, MI 10/17/64, Rome, GA, born Anderson Dist., SC, deserted at Rome, GA 11/10/64.

Buford/Biford, Jerry, Pvt., Co. A, sick in hospital at Memphis, TN 2/14/64 - 10/64.*

Buford, John H., Pvt., Co. H, age 18, EN 11/26/64, Huntsville, AL, MI 4/5/65, Nashville, TN, born Madison Co., AL, farmer, MO 10/20/65, Huntsville, AL.

Buford, Stanfield, Pvt., Co. H, age 18, EN 11/26/64, Huntsville, AL, born Madison Co., AL, farmer, MO 10/20/65, Huntsville, AL.

Bullen, Robert, Pvt/Saddler, Co. B, age 45, EN 12/17/62, Glendale, MS, born Baychilton, MS, on leave 3/28/63 to take family to Jackson, TN, MO 12/27/63, Camp Davies, MS.

Bullen, Robert (2nd), Pvt., Co. B, age 19, EN 3/2/63, Glendale, MS, POW 10/26/63 from Vincent's Crossroads, MO 1/22/64, Memphis, TN.

Bullen, William C., Pvt., Co. B, age 22, EN 3/2/63, Glendale, MS, MI 3/2/63, Corinth, MS, POW 10/26/63, Vincent's Cross Roads, MO 1/22/64, Memphis, TN.

Bumper, David A., Sgt., Co. L, died December 18, 1863 of billious fever in regimental hospital.*

Bumper, William H., Corp., Co. L, died December 9, 1863 of lung fever in regimental hospital.*

Bunders, J.B., Pvt., Co. H, absent POW 11/63.*

Burden, John H., Pvt., Co. G, age 19, EN 3/10/64, Decatur, AL, MI 4/13/64, Decatur, AL, born Lincoln Co., TN, farmer, sick in hospital at Decatur 5/1/64 through 9/64, MO 10/20/65.

Burdick, Frank Cortez, 1st Lt/Capt., Co. K&A, age 26, EN 6/11/61, Belleville, IL, MI 6/25/61, Caseyville, IL, promoted to Captain 12/18/62, furnished his own horse & equipment, MO 6/16/64, Decatur, AL, Special Order #74 from War Dept. states he was discharged 12/22/63.

NOTE: Frank Burdick was born in 1838 and was the son of Russell Burdick. He was married to Nancy Margaret Feltman. He first enrolled as a private in Co. C, 22nd Regiment of Illinois Volunteers and was discharged 9/8/62. He re-enlisted 9/8/62 in Co. A, 1st AL Vol. Cav. near Bridgeport, AL. He was a clerk, teacher, county clerk and probate judge of Winston Co., AL. He died in 1884.

After Frank Burdick's father, Russell Burdick, died he went to New York City and worked as a clerk in a store. He remained there until he enlisted in the Union Army for service in the Civil War.

He enrolled on June 25, 1861 at Centralia, Illinois as a private in Company C, 22nd Regiment of Illinois Volunteers, later Sgt., commanded by Col. Daugherty, and discharged September 8, 1862. He re-enlisted September 8, 1862 with a commission as 1st LT., Company A, First Alabama Volunteer Cavalry near Bridgeport, Alabama (near Chattanooga, TN), and served until his final discharge as captain on December 22, 1863.

He applied for a pension (#463519) on October 30, 1862, based on a disability. According to his pension papers "he was greatly disabled and was compelled to resign his position as Captain." His widow, Nancy Margaret Feltman

Burdick, and the older children were away from home when he died. She applied for a widow's pension (#292479) on September 26, 1888 which was denied on the grounds that the soldier's death was not the result of military service. The claim was referred for special examination, and several depositions were taken and affidavits obtained.

In April of 1927, Probate Judge John B. Weaver wrote to the U.S. Pension Department on behalf of his "door neighbor" Nancy M. Burdick to inquire if she was not entitled to more than $30.00 per month in pension benefits. A June 13, 1927 response from Winfield Scott indicted she would be entitled to no such increase as she was not the wife of soldier during his period of service.

Fernando "Frank" Cortez Burdick was left behind in the surgeon's tent after having contracted the disabling condition. He was treated by the post surgeon in his tent for 27 (or 37) days, being unable to leave it. Between his illness and apparent paperwork confusion of mustering out of the Illinois regiment to accept a promotion into the First Alabama Cavalry, he somehow wound up being reported "deserted" August 27, 1862, though another roll reports him left sick in Tuscumbia, Alabama on August 27, 1862. A War Department communication dated May 11, 1888 reports "The charges of desertion of August 27, 1862, and on Regtl return for December, 1862, against this man are removed as erroneous."

He received his discharge December 23, 1865 and remained in Alabama which began the Burdick family there. He was a clerk, teacher, county clerk, and probate judge of Winston County; and he assisted in re-establishing postal service in northwest Alabama. See also, petition to Brig. Gen. Wm. Smith on behalf of Fernando "Frank" Cortez Burdick to be appointed Register of Votes, by loyal and true Union Men formerly of the 1st Alabama Cavalry.

Among his friends were the Feltman brothers from Walker County in Alabama. When he obtained his army discharge in 1865 he remained with his Feltman friends and married Nancy Margaret Feltman and they made their home in Winston County, Alabama. Both are buried at the Burdick Family Cemetery near Houston, Alabama which was named for his family and is maintained by the Houston Community.[35]

Burleston/Burlison, James M., Pvt., Co. C, age 18, EN 3/15/64,, Memphis, TN, MI 3/19/64, Memphis, TN, born Calhoun Co., MS, farmer, POW 12/3/64 at Millen, GA, MO 10/20/65, Huntsville, AL. Another Muster Roll shows James M. Burleston EN 3/15/64, Memphis.

Burleston, Pvt., Co. C, absent sick in hospital at Memphis, TN 3/64, absent sick in hospital at Nashville, TN 4/64.*

Burnett, Peyton, Pvt., Co. K, age 27, EN & MI 12/1/63, Camp Davies, MS, born Spartanburg Dist., SC, farmer, POW 3/21/64 in AR, near Memphis, TN, MO 7/19/65, Nashville, TN. Note stated he furnished his own horse which failed 6/15/65 for want of forage and was abandoned. Traveled 90 miles from his home in Marion Co., AL to Camp Davies, MS to enlist.

Burney, Francis A., Pvt., Co. B, age 20, EN 2/10/64, Pulaski, TN, MI 3/27/64, Decatur, AL, born Lauderdale Co., TN, deserted from Rome, GA 3/10/64.

Burns, James L., Sgt. Co. F, age 21, EN 4/3/63, Corinth, MS, MI 8/13/63 Corinth, MS, born Chetannga, GA, farmer, deserted 9/11/63 from Glendale, MS.

Burns, Perry/Berry, Pvt, Co. L, age 18, EN 9/25/63, Fayette Co., AL, MI 9/25/63, Glendale, MS, born Itawamba Co., MS, discharged 2/10/64 for disability.

Burrell, John, Pvt/Sgt., Co. D, age 26, EN 4/19/64,Decatur, AL, MI 6/16/64, Decatur, AL, born Walker Co., AL, farmer, appt. Sgt. 7/1/64, MO 10/20/65, Huntsville, AL.

Burrough, William H., Pvt., Co. H, age 18, EN 3/20/65, Stevenson, AL, MI 4/5/65, Nashville, TN, born Marion Co., TN, farmer, MO 10/20/65, Huntsville, AL.

Burton, H., Pvt., Co. L, nurse in hospital 11/63.*

Butler, H.H., Co. D, absent, supposed deserter 8/63.*

Butler, John C., Pvt., Co. G, age 26, EN 6/15/63, Chewalla, TN, MI 6/15/63, Corinth, MS, deserted 7/3/63.

Butler, Napoleon/Nathan B., Pvt., Co. E, age 21, EN 6/24/63, Glendale, MS, deserted 7/9/63, returned 1/23/64, MO 7/27/64, Rome, GA.

Butler, Nathan H., Pvt., Co. E, age 40, EN 6/24/63, Glendale, MS, deserted 7/9/63, returned 1/23/64, on detached service as teamster 1/25/64 at Vicksburg, MS, MO 7/27/64, Rome, GA.

Butler, William J., Pvt., Co. A, age 32, EN 1/20/64, Camp Davies, MS, MI 2/5/64, Memphis, TN, born Shelby Co., AL, farmer, MO 10/20/65.

Byars/Byers, William A., Corp/Pvt., Co. L, age 19, EN 9/25/63, Fayette Co., AL, MI 9/25/63, Glendale, MS, born Pickens, GA, farmer, MIA 10/26/63 at Vincent's Crossroads, sick in hospital in Memphis, TN 2/8/64, sick in hospital in Nashville, TN 4/2/64, MO 9/28/64..

Byars, John H., Pvt., Co. G, age 21, EN 3/10/64, Decatur, AL, MI 4/13/64, Decatur, AL, born Union Co., GA, farmer, MO 10/20/65, Huntsville, AL.

Byers, Joseph P., Pvt/Sgt., Co. G, age 23, EN 3/10/64, Decatur, AL, MI 4/13/64, Decatur, AL, born Habersham Co., GA, farmer, appt. Sgt. 5/1/64, MO 10/20/65, Huntsville, AL.

Byers, Robert J., Pvt/Sgt., Co. G, age 26, EN 3/10/64, Decatur, AL, MI 4/13/64, Decatur, AL, born Habersham Co., GA, farmer, MO 10/20/65, Huntsville, AL.

Byers, Samuel P., Pvt/Sgt., Co. G, age 33, EN 4/10/64, Decatur, AL, MI Rome, GA, born Habersham Co., GA, farmer, MO 10/20/65, Huntsville, AL.

Byford, Perry, Pvt., Co. A, age 20, EN 12/22/63, Camp Davies, MS, MI 2/5/64, Memphis, TN, born Winston Co., AL, farmer, MO 10/20/65, Huntsville, AL.

Byford, Quiller J., Pvt., Co. A, age 18, EN 12/22/63, Camp Davies, MS, MI 2/5/64, Memphis, TN, born Winston Co., AL, farmer, died 3/1/64 in Gen. Hospital in Memphis, TN of measles/inf. of lungs. (Buried in Memphis National Cemetery.)

Byram, William T.C., Pvt., Co. C, age 23, EN 2/20/63, MI 2/25/63, Corinth, MS, born Tishomingo, MS, farmer, died 8/6/63 at Glendale, MS of disease.

Byrd, H.H., Pvt., Co. E, POW 10/26/63.*

Byrd, Josephus, Pvt., Co. E, age 23, EN & MI 8/27/63, Glendale, MS, farrier, MO 9/28/64, Rome, GA.

Byrd, M.C., Pvt., Co. E, MIA 10/26/63, Vincent's Crossroads.*

Byrd, Marshal H., Pvt., Co. E, age 35, EN & MI 9/1/63, Glendale, MS, born Hardin Co., TN, KIA 10/26/63 at Vincent's Crossroads on Bear Creek.
NOTE: Marshall Byrd married Nancy E. Robertson on January 20, 1848 in Hardin Co., TN and had the following children: James Jackson born June 23, 1850; William A. born July 11, 1852, died August 21, 1866; Susan E.B. born April 8, 1854, died June 12, 1876 and Major H. born April 18, 1856. Marshall's wife, Nancy died January 31, 1862 in Hardin Co., TN. Noel C. Byrd was appt. guardian of minor heirs and affidavit was signed by T.J. Byrd, who was also a member of this regiment.[36]

Byrd, Thomas J., Pvt., Co. E, age 18, EN & MI 10/1/63, Glendale, MS, MO 9/28/64, Rome, GA.

Byrd, William R., Pvt., Co. E, age 26, EN & MI 8/27/63, Glendale, MS, MO 9/28/64, Rome, GA.

Byrum, B., Pvt., Co. D, sick in hospital at Nashville, TN July & August 1864.*

Byrum, Cavaller/Cavileer/Cowden H., age 49, Pvt., Co. D, EN 3/15/63, Corinth, MS, born Madison Co., AL, farmer, sick in refugee camp, Corinth, MS 11/20/63, sick in hospital in Memphis, TN 3/24/64, died 4/21/64 of pneumonia at Adams Gen. Hospital. (Buried Grave # 1-49, Memphis National Cemetery.)

Byrum, Noah D., Pvt., Co. D, POW 1/8/64. *

Byrum, W., Pvt., Co. D, on daily duty as hospital nurse.*

Byrum, William A., Bugler, Co. L, EN 11/14/63.*

Byrone, John T.C., Pvt., Co. C, died in hospital at Glendale, MS 8/6/63.*

Cabaniss, Madison, Pvt., Co. K, age 36, EN & MI 12/1/63, Camp Davies, MS, born Tuscaloosa Co., AL, farmer, deserted. He traveled 90 miles from home in Marion Co., AL to Camp Davies, MS to enlist.

NOTE: Madison Cabaniss was born in 1829 in Tuscaloosa Co., AL and was the brother of Obediah Cabaniss. They were the sons of Peter Randolph Cabaniss, born about 1795 in Nottoway Co., VA, died before 1834 in Tuscaloosa Co., AL, and Catherine Mayfield, born 1806 in SC.[37]

Cabaness, Obediah, Pvt., Co. M, age 30, EN &MI 12/16/63, Camp Davies, MS, born Holmes Co., MS, farmer, deserted 3/18/64 at Memphis TN with Remington revolver & Smith carbine.

NOTE: Obediah Cabiness was born in 1832 in MS and first enlisted in Co. C, 41st AL Inf, CSA on 5/15/62 at Tuscaloosa, AL. Muster Roll of June 30, 1862 states he was absent in hospital at Knoxville, TN, Muster Roll of March & April state he was furloughed from hospital to Marion Co., AL and never returned to his unit. He then enlisted in the Union army. He was charged with desertion by the CSA and found guilty. He was sentenced to be shot to death with musketry. (Some of the men charged had their sentences remitted.) See Madison Cabaniss note about parents.

Cabit, Headley (Cards filed with Headley Coburn)

Cadle, Kinard A., Pvt/Sgt., Co. H, age 23, EN 12/25/64, Rome, GA, MI 12/25/64, Nashville, TN, born Randolph Co., AL, farmer, MO 10/20/65 Huntsville, AL.

Cagh, Charles B., Pvt., Co. A, age 45, EN 12/62, Glendale, MS, deserted 1/24/63.

Cagh, John H., Pvt., Co. A, age 16, EN 12/5/62, Glendale, MS, MI 12/31/62, Corinth, MS, deserted 1/24/63.

Cagle, Albert S., Pvt., Co. A, age 29, EN 1/7/64, Camp Davies, MI 2/5/64, Memphis, TN, born Winston Co., AL, farmer/blacksmith, MO 10/20/65, Huntsville, AL.

Cagle, David C., Pvt., Co. L, age 28, EN 9/25/63, Fayette Co., AL, MI 9/25/63, born Hall Co., GA, farmer, discharged 9/29/64, Rome, GA, reenlisted 12/21/64, Stevenson, AL, MI 12/21/64, Nashville, TN, MO 10/20/65, Huntsville, AL.

NOTE: David Crockett Cagle was born May 11, 1834 in Gainsville, GA. He married Mary Ann Herdon on August 21, 1861 in Alabama. He died May 6, 1923 and is buried in Fanshawe Cemetery, Le Flore Co., OK. His parents were William C. Cagle, born 1797 in NC and Mary (last name unknown) born in 1798 in NC. Children of David and Mary were: James William, born 1863; Sarah T., born 1866; Thomas A., born 1868; Joseph Newton, born 1870; Phillip C., born 1872; Jacob M., born 1874; Otto A., born 1876; Virgil W., born 1879; Mary "Janie" E., born 1881 and Flora C., born 1888. William C. Cagle was the son of Jacob Cagle, born 1766 and died 1850. Jacob was the son of John Cagle, born 1710 and died 1799. John was the son of Leonard Leonhart Kagle who was the original immigrant of this family. He was born in 1684 in Rhenish, Palentine, Germany and arrived in Philadelphia in 1732 and died in 1754.[38]

Cagle, Enoch, Pvt., Co. A, age 23, EN 1/7/64, Camp Davies, MS, MI 2/5/64, Memphis, TN, born Winston Co., AL, farmer, died in Gen. Hospital New Albany, IN 5/3/64 of measles.

Cagle, James, Pvt., Co. A, age 19, EN 10/14/64, Decatur, AL, MI 11/10/64, Rome, GA, born Walker Co., AL, farmer, MO 10/20/65, Huntsville, AL.

Cagle, James R., Pvt., Co. A, age 39, EN 1/7/64, Camp Davies, MS, MI 2/5/64, Memphis, TN, born NC, blacksmith, MO 10/20/65, Huntsville, AL.

Cain, James, Pvt., Co. C, age 18, EN 7/27/63, Glendale, MS, MI 8/15/63, Corinth, MS, born Tishomingo Co., MS, died 3/26/64 at Memphis, TN of smallpox. (Buried in Memphis National Cemetery.)

Cain, William, Pvt., Co. A, age 46, EN 12/22/63, Camp Davies, MS, MI 2/5/64, Memphis, TN, born Buncombe Co., NC, farmer, sick in hospital in Memphis, TN 1/28/64, sick in hospital in Nashville, TN 8/64, sick in hospital at Jefferson Barracks, MO 6/8/65, MO 5/31/65 St. Louis, MO.

Caldwell, Stephen N., (Cards filed with Stephen N. Colwell)

Calvert, Jonathan, Pvt., Co. I, age 27, EN & MI 12/21/63, Camp Davies, MS, born Winston Co., AL, farmer, MO 7/19/65, Nashville, TN.

Calvert, Ralphord, Pvt., Co. I, age 30, EN & MI 8/18/62, Huntsville, AL, born Winston Co., AL, died in Hospital #12, Nashville, TN 11/7/62.

Cameron, Alexander T., Capt. Co. C, age 23, EN 3/30/63, Glendale, MS, MI 3/30/63, Corinth, MS, MO 3/29/64.
   NOTE: Capt. Alexander Cameron requested permission to be absent from his command for 30 days to take the remains of his brother, J.C. Cameron, who was killed in the engagement at Barton Station, AL 4/17/63, to the family burial ground at Ottawa, IL. Leave was approved.
   Alexander Cameron was born in Scotland April 5, 1840 and settled in Ottowa, IL. After the war, he moved to Santa Barbara, CA in 1875 where he was an Attorney. He died December 17, 1877 and his grave is marked with a military headstone & "Co. C, 1st Alabama Cav." He left a widow, Nancy and one child. His obituary describes him as "Lieut. Colonel".

Cameron, J.C., Captain, present detached by S.O. from 64 Illinois & not aggrigated 3/63, KIA 4/17/63 at Battle of Barton Station, AL.*
   NOTE: James C. Cameron, brother to Alexander, above, first enlisted in 64th Regiment Illinois Infantry, Company A., Yates Sharpshooters. He was promoted to captain September 12, 1862. On April 15, 1863, he was detailed by order of Gen. Dodge to command 1st Reg. Alabama Cavalry Volunteers. He was killed in action April 17, 1863 at Bear Creek.[39]

Camp, Alfred B., Pvt., Co. B&E,age 18, EN & MI 8/1/64, Rome, GA, born Chambers, AL, reenlisted 1/1/65, Stevenson, AL, MI 1/1/65, Nashville, TN, MO 10/20/65, Huntsville, AL.

Camp, William A., Pvt/Corp., Co. B, age 19, EN 8/1/64, Wedowee, AL, MI 8/1/64, Rome, GA, born Randolph Co., AL, farrier, promoted to Corp. 6/13/65, MO 10/20/65, Huntsville, AL.

Camp, William M., Pvt. Co. B&E, age 27, EN & MI 8/1/64, Rome, Ga, born Chambers, AL, blacksmith, POW 3/8/65 near Fayetteville, NC, MO 5/30/65, Camp Chase, OH.

Campbell, Adam, Pvt., Co. K, age 24, EN 7/24/62, Huntsville, AL, born Pendleton, SC, farmer, died 10/23(or 24)/62 in hospital #14, Nashville, TN of Rubeola. (Buried in Grave A-5062 in Nashville National Cemetery with death date shown as 12/24/62.)

Campbell, Alexander Pvt., Co. K, age 30, EN & MI 7/24/62 in Huntsville, AL, died 12/5/62 in Hospital #12 in Nashville, TN of bronchitis, born Pendleton Dist., SC, farmer. (Buried in Grave B-5628 in Nashville National Cemetery.
  NOTE: Alexander Campbell was born 1828/1832, married Millie Noles/Knowles in Cass Co., GA December 1, 1848, and they had the following children: Thomas Jefferson, born June 2, 1850; John Robert, born August 3, 1852; Samuel Henry, born November 1854; Sarah Ann, born June 3, 1857; Andrew Jackson, born July 1, 1859 and William Green, born July 1, 1861.[40]

Campbell, Andrew J., Pvt., Co. G, temporarily attached from 11th Illinois Cavalry.

Campbell, Andrew J., Pvt., Co. G (may be same as above), age 22, EN 5/29/63, Chewalla, TN, MI 5/29/63, Corinth, MS, MO 11/26/63, Memphis, TN.

Campbell, Andrew J., Pvt., Co. G, deserted 7/7/63 from Glendale.*

Campbell, George B., Pvt., Co. H, age 43, EN 12/16/64, Stevenson, AL, born Halifax Co., VA, farmer, died in post hospital at Huntsville, 2/15/65 of smallpox.

Campbell, John R., Pvt., Co. K, age 25, EN & MI 7/24/62, Huntsville, AL, born Pendleton Dist., SC, farmer, MIA 4/30/63 at Day's Gap, AL during Streight's Raid, returned 12/1/63, on detached service in Gen. Sherman's expedition 1/24/64, MO 7/19/65, Nashville, TN.
  NOTE: John R. Campbell was born about 1839, married first, Jane Catharine Blevins and had the following children: Flora Ann, born 8/22/1857; Sarah Tayor, born 3/29/1859 and John Nathaniel, born 3/2/1863. After Jane's death March 6, 1863, he married Rachel Blevins November 23, 1864 and had the following children: General Strate, born 12/20/1865; Bird Sherman, born 1/26/1868; Lucretia, born 8/4/1871; Susanah Elizabeth, born 4/3/1876; Alexander, born 5/8/1878 and Henry Jackson, born 10/18/1880. John died October 28, 1908.[41]

Campbell, William, Pvt., Co. M, age 30, EN 8/2/63, Chewalla, TN, MI 8/2/63, Corinth, MS, born White Co., TN, farmer, deserted at Lagrange, TN 1/28/64 with Smith carbine and Colt revolver.

Campbell, William H., Pvt/Corp., Co. D, age 19, EN 5/20/64, Decatur, AL, MI 6/16/64, Decatur, AL, born Jefferson Co., AL, farmer, appt. Corp. 9/1/64, MO 10/20/65, Huntsville, AL.

Canada/Canady, John H., Pvt., Co. F&L, age 18, EN 9/25/63, Fayette Co., AL, MI 9/25/63, Glendale, MS, born Heard Co., GA, sick in hospital in Memphis, TN 2/16/64, MO 9/28/64, Rome, GA. (One Muster Roll shows a John H. Canada as age 32 and EN 9/29/64 in Rome, GA.)

Canada, Russell, (Cards filed with Russell L. Kenedy).

Canady/Canada, Isaac A., Pvt., Co. I&D age 33, EN & MI 8/18/62, Huntsville, AL, born Morgan Co., AL, farmer, died 11/22/62 in Nashville, TN.

Canterbury/Canterberry, Andrew S., Pvt., Co. M, age 44, EN 12/19/63, Camp Davies, MS, MI 12/29/63, Corinth, MS, born Bibb Co., AL, farmer, MO 10/20/65, Huntsville, AL.

Cantrell, Daniel C., Pvt., Co. A, on detached service in Co. M since 2/5/64.*

Cantrell, Dennis C., Pvt/Sgt., Co. D, age 45, EN 2/1/63, Glendale, MS, MI 2/4/63, Corinth, MS, born Spartanburg Dist., SC, farmer, MO 2/4/64, Memphis, TN.

Cantrell, George D., Pvt., Co. C, age 25, EN 2/20/63, Corinth, MS, MI 2/25/63, Corinth, MS, born McMinn Co., TN, farmer, MO 2/20/64, (or 3/26/64), Memphis, TN.

Cantrell, James H., Pvt., Co. D, age 20, EN 2/1/63, Glendale, MS, MI 2/4/63, Corinth, MS, born Spartanburg Dist., SC, farmer, MO 2/4/64, Memphis, TN.

Cantrell, John S., Pvt., Co. D, age 35 (one Muster Roll states age 29 and another one states he was age 24 and born in Lumpkin, GA), farmer, EN 10/26/63, Glendale, MS, MI 10/26/63, Camp Davies, MS, POW at Jacinto, near Corinth, MS 1/18/64, killed by the rebels in Franklin Co., AL on or about 6/18/64 while POW.

Cantrell, Moses B.,Pvt., Co. D, age 25, EN 4/19/64, Decatur, AL, MI 6/16/64, Decatur, AL, born Lumpkin, GA, farmer, POW 12/18/64, supposed to be dead in the field 5/1/65.

Cantrell, Reuben, Pvt., Co. D, age 29, EN 2/1/63, Glendale, MS, MI 2/4/63, Corinth, MS, born Gwinnett, GA, farmer, on leave 3/28/63 to move family to Jackson, TN, in hospital in Corinth, MS 10/12/63, MO 2/4/64, Memphis, TN.

Cantrell, William, Pvt., Co. D, EN 2/1/63, Glendale, MS, MI 2/4/63, Corinth, MS, died of disease 2/20/63 at Glendale, MS.

Cape, Thomas K., Pvt/Sgt., Co. L, age 34, EN 9/25/63, Fayette Co., AL, MI 9/25/63, Glendale, MS, born Hall, GA, farmer, MO 9/28/64, Rome, GA.

Carnelius, William R., Pvt., Co. H, age 19, EN 2/20/65, Huntsville, AL, MI 5/20/65, Nashville, TN, born Blount Co., AL, farmer, MO 10/20/65, Huntsville, AL.

Carpenter, Frazier, E., Pvt., Co. C, age 35, EN 12/18/62, Corinth, MS, MI 12/22/62, Corinth, MS, born Anson Co., NC, farmer, died in hospital at Glendale, MS of disease 8/9/63.

Carroll, Anderson B., Pvt., Co. B, age 20, EN 5/10/63, Glendale, MS, MI 5/10/63, Corinth, MS, POW 10/26/63 Vincent's Crossroads, MO 1/22/64, Memphis, TN.
NOTE: Anderson Bailey Carroll was born January 14, 1843 in Georgia, married Mary Elizabeth Clement on August 8, 1862 in Franklin, AL and died May 4, 1896 in Paducah, McCracken, KY. Mary Elizabeth Clement was the daughter of Eunice C. Sullivan and William Benjamin Clement and she had two brothers, William and Harvey, who also served in the 1st AL Cav., USA. Children of Anderson and Mary were: Joseph N., born November 25, 1863 in AL, died July 25, 1945; John B., born September 30, 1865 in Centralia, IL, died July 4, 1903; James R., born August 28, 1867 in Livingston, KY, died January 23, 1876; William Jefferson, born August 23, 1869 in Livingston, KY, married Maggie Blackwell July 12, 1888 and died July 3, 1957; Mattie Belle, born August 24, 1871, died February 13, 1888; Lyddia R., Born June 7, 1873, died May 7, 1927; Anderson Bailey, born April 23, 1875 in Livingston, KY, died 1958; Mary Elizabeth, born April 23, 1875, died February 20, 1903; Hugh Harvey, born September 28, 1880, died October 15, 1890; Georgie, born August 25, 1883, died March 16, 1884; and Annice Beatrice, born October 31, 1885 in Paducah, Livingston, KY, married John Benton Carroll on April 18, 1903, died March 31, 1981 in Paducah, KY.[42]

Carroll, James K.P., Pvt/Corp., Co. B, age 17, EN 12/23/62, Glendale, MS, MI 12/31/62, Corinth, MS, appt. Corp. 1/22/63, born Floyd, GA, farmer, POW 10/26/63, Vincent's Crossroads, MO 12/27/63, Camp Davies, MS.

Carter, Andrew, Pvt., Co. D, age 18, EN & MI 6/1/63, Glendale, MS, born Lewis, TN, factory hand, MO 6/16/64, Decatur, AL.

Carter, James T., Pvt., Co. D, age 18, EN 11/25/64, Gordon, GA, MI 7/13/65, Huntsville, AL, born Paulding Co., GA, sick in US Gen Hosp. in Savannah, GA, Jan. 65 to March 65.

Carter, John, Pvt/Sgt, Co. A&D, age 18, EN 1/14/64, Camp Davies, MS, MI 2/5/64, Memphis, TN, born Spartanburg Dist., SC, farmer, sick in hospital in Memphis, TN 2/28/64, KIA 10/1/64 near Decatur, AL.
(Buried in Grave N-4516 in Marietta National Cemetery.)

Carter, Samuel L., Pvt., Co. F, age 32 (or 30), farrier, EN 4/5/63, Corinth, MS, MI 8/13/63, Corinth, MS, born Hamilton Co., TN, machinist, MO 4/14/64.

Cartwright, Asberry/Asbury, Pvt., Co. G, age 24, EN 6/8/63, Chewalla, TN, MI 6/8/63, Corinth, MS, deserted 6/19/63, Chewalla, TN.

Caruthers, John, Pvt., Co. E, EN 12/25/62, Chewalla, TN, MI 12/25/62, Corinth, MS, POW 1/20/63 near Chewalla, TN, deserted 3/3/63, Glendale.

Case, Thomas L., Sgt., Co. C, age 29, EN 12/1/62, Corinth, MS, MI 12/22/62, Corinth, MS, born Jefferson Co., AL, on detached detail as horse farrier 9/1/63, MO 12/17/63, Memphis, TN.

Cash, Francis M., Pvt/Sgt., Co. M, age 30, EN 11/11/63, Camp Davies, MS, MI 11/11/63, Corinth, MS, sick in hospital in Madisonville, IN May-Aug. 1864, wife shown as Martha J. Cash and residence as Fayette Co., AL, born Abbeville Dist., SC.

Casteel, James H., Pvt/Corp., Co. K, age 20, EN & MI 8/22/62, Huntsville, AL, born Limestone Co., AL, blacksmith, sent to hospital at Corinth, MS 10/10/63 from accidental pistol shot 9/15/63 at Nashville, TN, appt. Corp. 8/1/64 and Sgt. 1/1/65, WIA 3/10/65 at Monroe's Crossroads, NC.

Castleberry, David, Pvt., Co. E, age 20, EN & MI 5/1/63, Glendale, MS, Sept. 1863 on detached detail as nurse in hospital, 1/25/64, on detached detail as Teamster at Vicksburg, MS, MO 6/15/64.

Castleberry, Solomon, Pvt., Co. E, EN 4/1/63, Glendale, MS, MI 4/1/63, Corinth, MS, 1/25/64 on detail as teamster in Vicksburg, MS, MO 3/8/64 Memphis, TN.

Castlebury/Castleberry, Robert B., Pvt., Co. G, age 32, EN 4/10/64, Decatur, AL, farmer, died in Field Hospital, Army of TN in Chattanooga, TN 6/28/64. (Buried Grave # E-11506, Chattanooga National Cemetery.)

Cathey, John, Pvt/Corp., Co. C, age 18, EN 1/1/64, Corinth, MS, MI 3/10/64, Memphis, TN, born Tishomingo Co., MS, farmer, appt. Corp. 3/1/64, MO 10/20/65, Huntsville, AL.

Caughorn/Caughren, Daniel R., Pvt/Bugler, Co. E, age 17, EN 1/1/63, Chewalla, TN, MI 1/1/63, Corinth, MS, born Pontotoc Co., MS, MO 1/1/64, Memphis, TN, reenlisted 1/1/64, Bugler, Co. A, transferred to Co. M, Memphis, TN 3/9/64, MO 10/20/65, Huntsville, AL.

Cayne, Thomas C., Co. F, sick in hospital at Memphis, TN, wounded 10/26/63.*

Chafin, John H., Sgt/Pvt., Co. B, age 28, EN 1/6/63, Glendale, MS, MI 1/22/63, Corinth, MS, MO 1/22/64.

Chafin, William M., Pvt., Co. B, age 22, EN 1/6/63, Glendale, MS, born Pickens, AL, died 6/28/63, Glendale, MS.

Chalmers, Andrew J. Vet. Surgeon, temporarily attached from 9th Illinois Cavalry.

Chambers, Baily/Bailey Y (or G)., Pvt., Co. B, age 18, EN & MI 9/1/64, Rome, GA, born Edgefield Dist., SC, farmer, MO 10/20/65, Huntsville, AL.

Chambles/Chambers, Elisha, Pvt., Co. A, age 17, EN 9/8/62, Iuka, MS, MI 10/1/62, Corinth, MS, born Franklin Co., AL, deserted 3/30/63 at Glendale, MS, returned 8/16/63, MO 9/16/63, Corinth, MS, reenlisted 2/1/64, Memphis, TN, MI 2/26/64, Memphis, TN, MO 10/20/65, Huntsville, AL.

Chambless, Isaac J., Pvt., Co. A, age 18, EN 10/29/62, MI 12/31/62, Corinth, MS, deserted 3/31/63, returned 8/16/63, MO 11/28/63, Memphis, TN.
   NOTE: Isaac was born in Powderly Texas in April 16, 1811 and married Sarah Ann Fredericks who was born August 24, 1845 and died July 11, 1911. Isaac died November 3, 1913. They are buried in Riverside Cemetery, McLoud, Oklahoma.[43]

Chambles, James M., Pvt., Co. A, EN 10/29/62, Corinth, MS, MI 12/31/62, Corinth, MS, deserted 3/31/63.

Chamness, James M., Pvt/Corp., Co. H, age 18, EN 12/20/64, Stevenson, AL, MI 12/20/64, Nashville, TN, born Calhoun Co., AL, farmer, appt. Corp. 4/1/65, MO 10/20/65.

Chandler, Erasmus D., Capt., Co. E, age 37, EN 9/5/61, Lightsville, IL, MI 10/5/61, Springfield, IL, reenlisted 1/28/63, Corinth, MS, promoted to Captain from Sgt., Co. B, 7th Illinois Cavalry, 1/28/63, KIA Vincent's Crossroads near Bay Springs 10/26/63. (Buried Grave # C-9, Corinth National Cemetery.)

Chaney, Alexander, Pvt., Co. D&E, EN 2/15/63, Glendale, MS, MI 3/13/63, Corinth, MS, deserted 9/6/63, Glendale, MS.

Chaney, Artemus, Pvt., Co. D&E, age 36, EN 2/15/63, Glendale, MS, MI 3/13/63, Corinth, MS, deserted 5/8/63 at Glendale, MS and returned, on duty at Refugee Camp in Corinth 12/28/63, MO 3/1/64, Memphis, TN.

Chaney, John, Pvt., Co. M, age 42, EN 11/20/63, Camp Davies, MS, MI 11/20/63, Corinth, MS, born Fayette Co., AL, farmer, in Hospital #1 in Nashville, TN 6/28/64 and transferred to Totten USA Gen. Hospital in Louisville, KY on 8/2/64, residence shown as Illinois, MO 10/20/65, Huntsville, AL.

Chapman, Joseph A., Pvt., Co. E, age 36, EN 3/1/63, Glendale, MS, MI 3/1/63, Corinth, MS, AWOL for 2 months, MO 3/1/64, Memphis, TN.
   NOTE: After the war, Joseph bought a 40 acre farm in Centralia, Illinois. His first wife was Malinda Bennett and they were married December 1850. Children of this marriage were: Frances Elizabeth, October 10, 1853; Levinia Ann Adaline, April 19, 1856, died January 23, 1859; Martha, August 8, 1859, died November 12, 1865; William Allen, March 3, 1862, died August 16, 1863; Wanda Ann, September 15, 1863, died October 20, 1863. After the death of his first wife, January 5, 1864, he married Celia Ann Gossett on November 5, 1864 in Centralia, Illinois. Celia had been Malinda's nurse during her illness for several years. Children of this marriage

were: James Lafayette, February 16, 1861, died December 30, 1938; John Allen, September 23, 1865; Henry Franklin, March 9, 1868, died April 5, 1943; Nancy Ann, December 12, 1871, died January 19, 1956; Emma L., April 14, 1876, died 1953; Cora L., April 11, 1880, died 1948; and Charles W., August 5, 1885, died April 19, 1950. He died July 14, 1887 and is buried in Ebenezer Cemetery, 8 miles north of Mt. Vernon, IL. Celia died in 1911.[44]

Chastain, James P., Corp/Sgt., Co. K, age 21, EN & MI 7/24/62, Huntsville, AL, born Union Co., GA, farmer, POW 11/5/62, captured in action near Nashville, TN, appt. Sgt. 10/1/62, MIA 10/26/63 at Vincent's Crossroads, MS, paroled at Savannah, GA 11/20/64, sent to hospital at Annapolis, MD 12/4/64 and sent to Wilmington, Del. 1/25/65, MO 7/19/65, Nashville, TN.
NOTE: James K. Polk Chastain was born June 3, 1839 in Marion Co., AL and died May 15, 1901 in Stone Co., MO. He married Martha Emeline Dyke May 10, 1860. His parents were Sarah J. Shelton, born June 10, 1810, died June 17, 1891, and James Edward Chastain, born May 10, 1805 in Haywood Co., NC and died May 17, 1867 in Marion Co., AL. James and Sarah were married October 7, 1825 in Haywood Co., NC.

Cheak, George M., Pvt/Sgt., Co. C, age 18, EN 1/1/64, Corinth, MS, MI 3/10/64, Memphis, TN, born Tishomingo Co., MS, farmer, appt. Sgt. 3/1/64, on duty 9/64-6/65 as Regt. Forage Master in Q.M. Dept., MO 10/20/65, Huntsville, AL.

Cheek, Edmund/Elijah S., Pvt., Co. E, age 23, EN 3/1/63, Corinth, MS, was nurse in post hospital at Corinth 11/22/63, born Green Co., MO, died at smallpox Gen. Hospital in Memphis, TN 2/6/64. (Buried in Memphis National Cemetery.)

Cheek, Elisha, Pvt., Co. A, age 18, EN 1/5/65, Savannah, GA, MI 7/13/65, Huntsville, AL, born Franklin Co., GA, (Discharge states he was born in Cobb Co., GA), farmer, MO 10/20/65, Huntsville, AL.

Cheek, Samuel M., Pvt., Co. A, age 18, EN 10/18/64, Rome, GA, born Hart Co., GA, in arrest at Raleigh, NC 4/20/65 charged with plundering & stealing, MO 10/20/65, Huntsville, AL.

Cheney, N., Co. E, deserted 9/12/63 at Glendale.*

Cheney, William H., 1st Lt., Co. F, age 23, EN & MI 3/23/63, Corinth, MS, resigned 9/2/64.

Chestaine/Chastain, David D., Pvt., Co. A, age 18, EN 1/12/64, Camp Davies, MS, MI 2/5/64, Memphis, TN, born Union Co., GA, farmer, POW 3/10/65 at Solomon Grove, NC, paroled and sent to Camp Chase, OH , MO 6/12/65, Camp Chase, OH.

Childers, Samuel, Pvt., Co. C, age 27, EN 12/1/62, Corinth, MS, born Greenville, SC, 5/63-10/63 on detail as nurse, POW 10/26/63 (no further information on this soldier).

Childress, M. (or W.), Pvt., Co. C, died October 13, 1864 at Charleston, SC

Chowley, Pvt., Co. F, on detached service as orderly in 2nd Q.M. & A.A.G. Depts.*

Clannahan, W.D., Pvt., Co. H, discharged by reason of exp. of term of service 10/25/64, Rome, GA.*

Clark, Daniel C., Corp/Sgt. Co. B&A, age 18 EN 1/20/63, Glendale, MS, appt. Corp. 1/22/63, born Marion Co., AL, farmer, POW 10/26/63 at Vincent's Crossroads, reenlisted 12/23/63, Camp Davies, MS, MI 2/5/64, Memphis, TN, was in USA Gen. Hospital at Hilton Head, SC 12/15/64 of wounds received 11/27/64 at Ball's Ferry, GA, returned to duty 4/22/65, MO 10/20/65, Huntsville, AL.

Clark, George W., Pvt., Co. A, age 19, EN 12/25/63, Camp Davies, MS, MI 2/5/64, Memphis, TN, born Tipton Co., TN, saddler, deserted 2/17/64 in Memphis, TN with Smith carbine & Pistol.

Clark, Jonathan W., Pvt., Co. G, age 36, EN 3/21/64, Decatur, AL, MI 4/13/64, Decatur, AL, born Madison Co., AL, farmer, sick in hospital in Wilmington, NC 3/10/65, MO 10/20/65, Huntsville, AL.

Clark, Martin, Pvt., Co. B, age 18, EN 3/6/64, Decatur, AL, MI 4/13/64, Decatur, AL, born Lawrence Co., TN, farmer, deserted near Chattanooga, TN 5/11/64 with horse, Smith carbine & equipment.

Clayton, John M., Pvt., Co. B, EN 4/10/63, Glendale, MS, absent 6/63 with pass from Brig. Gen. Dodge to take family North, (no further information on this soldier).

Clearman, William D., Pvt., Co. H, age 40, EN & MI 10/17/63, Glendale, MS, MO 10/24/64, Rome, GA.

Clemen, Lewis, Pvt., Co. F, EN 12/6/63.*

Clement, Harvey, Pvt., Co. B, age 19, EN 6/10/63, Glendale, MS, MI 9/8/63, Corinth, MS, MO 1/22/64, Memphis, TN.
        NOTE: John Harvey Clement was the son of Eunice C. Sullivan and William Benjamin Clement. He was born in 1843 in St. Clair Co., AL and married Martha J. Carroll on April 25, 1869.[45]

Clement, William, Pvt., Co. B, age 23, EN 1/6/63, Glendale, MS, MI 1/22/63, Corinth, MS, born Pickens, AL, farmer, POW 10/26/63 at Vincent's Crossroads, MO 1/22/64, Memphis, TN.
        NOTE: William C. Clement was the son of Eunice C. Sullivan and William Benjamin Clement. He was born in 1850 in Franklin Co., AL and married Martha E. Doublin on December 15, 1872.[46]

Clements, Curtis, Pvt., Co. A, age 25, EN 10/5/62, MI 12/31/62, Corinth, MS, born St. Clair Co., AL, died 6/25/63 at Corinth, MS of measles.

Clements/Clemens, Edward, Pvt., Co. L, age 19, EN 9/25/63, Fayette Co., AL, MI 9/25/63, Glendale, MS, born in Georgia, MIA/POW, Vincents Crossroads, MS, 10/26/63, admitted to hospital at Richmond, VA 1/2/64 where he died in C.S. Mil. Prison Hospital 1/25/64 of pneumonia. (Buried in Richmond National Cemetery, VA)

Clements, Peter, Sgt., Co. A, age 22, EN 10/25/62 & MI 12/31/62, Corinth, MS, MO 11/28/63, Memphis, TN.

Clements, Phillip/Phillippe O.(or J.), Pvt., Co. B, age 18, EN 4/12/64, Decatur, AL, MI 4/13/64, Decatur, AL, born Calhoun Co., GA, farmer, left sick in US Gen. Hospital in Decatur, AL 4/17/64, no MO date.

Clements, S.Z./Smith L., Pvt/Corp., Co. B, age 23, EN 4/2/64, Decatur, AL, MI 4/13/64, Decatur, AL, born Walker Co., AL, farmer, deserted 7/16/64 in Rome, GA with Smith carbine & equipment.

Cline, Jacob H., Pvt., Co. A, age 41, EN 1/23/64, Camp Davies, MS, MI 2/5/64, Memphis, TN, born Wayne Co., TN, MO 10/20/65, Huntsville, AL.

Cloar, Andrew J., Pvt., Co. H, age 23, EN & MI 9/13/63, Glendale, MS, sick in hospital at Memphis, TN since 11/10/63, no MO date.

Clutter, William H., assistant surgeon, Co. F&G (no further information on this soldier).

Cobb, Alexander, Pvt., Co. E, EN & MI 2/10/63, Corinth, MS, deserted 3/20/63, Glendale, MS.

Cobb, I.M., Co. F, AWOL 4/29/63.*

Cobit, Headley, (Card filed with Headley Coburn).

Cobleigh, Edward J., 1st Sgt/1st Lt., Co. M&G, promoted from Pvt., Co. L, 15th Illinois Cavalry 5/25/63, EN 11/1/63, Glendale, MS, MI 12/28/63, Camp Davies, MS, on special duty commanding Co. G, 4/15/64, on 2/5/65 he requested leave to visit his home in Northfield, Vermont, leave was granted by Maj. Gen. W.T. Sherman and a second leave was requested, due to health reasons, MO 10/20/65, Huntsville, AL.

Coburn, Headley, Pvt., Co. I, age 18, EN 4/20/63, Murfreesboro, TN, MI 9/28/63, Glendale, MS, born Winston Co., AL, tanner, MO 9/29/64, Rome, GA.
    NOTE: James Headley Coburn was born January 4, 1848 in Lauderdale Co., AL and died October 18, 1934 in Lonoke Co., Arkansas when a team of mules he was driving bolted, throwing him from the wagon which then ran over him and fractured his skull. He is buried in Tomberlin Cemetery in Lonoke County. In 1863 he emigrated from Colbert Co., AL to Murfreesboro, Rutherford Co., TN where he enlisted in the 1st AL Cav. USA and was shown as a Tanner. After the war he returned to Colbert Co., AL where he remained until 1881 when he emigrated to

Lonoke Co., AR and in 1902 he moved to Durant (Oklahoma), Indian Territory. By 1910 he was living in Tomberlins, AR, farming about 400 acres. He married first, Martha June Mayes, August 6, 1865 and had the following children: Mary Lue, May 26, 1866; Robert E., Oct 15, 1869; Eliza Permealia, July 8, 1872; Agnes Elizabeth, April 25, 1876; and Lydia A., Oct. 9, 1878. His wife, Martha, died February 18, 1879 in Colbert Co., AL and James married Julia Fuery/Fiery/Fureigh on December 21, 1879 and they had the following children: Mattie Bell, Oct. 23, 1881; James Franklin, Feb. 3, 1884; John Thomas, Nov. 18, 1885; Minnie L., July 10, 1889; Sallie S., Jan. 22, 1892; Edna E., Dec. 11, 1893; Margrette I., Feb. 7, 1895; Charles Sidney, April 6, 1897; Jerry and Joel, (twins), Sep. 13, 1899; Julia H., July 21, 1902. James had three other sons who died at birth and were not named. After the death of his second wife, Aug. 20, 1910, James married Etha Elizabeth Poteet.[47]

Cochran, Levi, Pvt., Co. K, age 21, EN & MI 8/5/62, Huntsville, AL, born Marion Co., AL, farmer, deserted 10/22/62 from Camp Campbell in Nashville, TN, not apprehended.

Cock, Charles, Sgt/Pvt., Co. B, age 54, EN 1/20/63, Glendale, MS, MI 1/22/63, Corinth, MS, born Lincoln Co., TN, farmer, appt. Sgt., 1/22/63, MO 1/22/64, Memphis, TN.

Cock, Charles C., Pvt., Co. K, age 18, EN & MI 7/24/62, Huntsville, AL, born Fayette Co., AL, farmer, taken prisoner by rebels at Day's Gap, AL 4/30/63, MIA 10/26/63 at Vincent's Crossroads, returned 1/14/64, on detached service 1/24/64 at Vicksburg, MS, captured 3/10/65 at Solomon Grove, NC, paroled POW at Annapolis, MD, discharged at Camp Chase, OH 4/28/65, MO 6/12/65, Camp Chase, OH.

Cock, I., Pvt., Co. H, deserted 10/64 while on detached service.*

Cock, Jeremiah D., Pvt., Co. B, age 17, EN 1/20/63, Glendale, MS, MI 1/22/63, Corinth, MS, born Fayette Co., AL, POW 10/26/63 at Vincent's Crossroads, MO 1/22/64, Memphis, TN.

Coe, Edward D., 2nd Lt., Co. B, age 28, EN 11/1/63, Glendale, MS, MI 11/1/63, Corinth, MS, appt. 2nd Lt. in 1st AL Cav. Vols. from Pvt. in 11th Regt. Illinois Cavalry, Co. I, Vol. by Brig. Gen. G.M. Dodge, Supt. of refugee camp in Corinth, MS 12/14/63.

Coffman, Robert R., Pvt., Co. M, in USA Hospital #3 at Nashville, TN July & August 1864.*

Cohorn, David R., Pvt., Co. M, on detached duty as regimental Bugler 1/65-6/65, returned 6/1/65.*

Cole, John R., Pvt., Co. B, age 27, EN 1/20/63, Glendale, MS, MI 1/22/63, Corinth, MS, born Franklin Co., AL, farmer, POW 10/26/63 at Vincent's Crossroads, MO 1/22/64, Memphis, TN.

Coleman, Edward, Co. B, age 21, born Shelby Co., TN, EN 2/11/64, Pulaski, TN by Lt. Judy.*

Coleman, Thomas C.(or T.M.), Pvt/Corp., Co. B, age 21, EN 2/20/64, Pulaski, TN, MI 3/27/64, Decatur, AL, born Giles Co., TN, farmer, sent to hospital in Rome, GA 10/14/64 after being WIA, MO 10/20/65, Huntsville, AL.

Collier, Allen, Pvt., Co. C, age 21, EN 2/10/63, Corinth, MS, born Tishomingo, MS, farmer, deserted 6/28/63, Glendale, MS.

Collier, George W., Pvt., Co. C, age 32, EN 2/10/63, Corinth, MS, born Perry Co., TN, farrier, no MO date.

Collier, Squire, Pvt., Co. C, age 23, EN 2/10/63, Corinth, MS, born Perry Co., TN, farrier, deserted 6/28/63, Glendale, MS.

Collins, Christopher C., Pvt/Sgt., Co. M, age 18, EN 12/16/63, Camp Davies, MS, MI 12/16/63, Corinth, MS, born Marshall Co., MS, farmer, promoted 12/1/64 for good conduct in the field, MO 10/20/65, Huntsville, AL.

Collins, Volney B., Pvt/Corp., Co. M, age 24, EN 12/16/63, Camp Davies, MS, MI 12/29/63, Corinth, MS, born Spartanburg Dist., SC, farmer, died 1/15/64 at Camp Davies, MS of typhoid pneumonia.

Coltman, J.R., Pvt., Co. H, EN 10/18/63 at Glendale.*

Colwell/Caldwell, Stephen N., Pvt., Co. F, age 18, EN & MI 8/5/64, Rome, GA, born Buncombe Co., NC, sick in Nashville, TN 11/6/64, returned 6/27/65, deserted 10/1/65 at Moulton, AL with Spencer carbine, sabre, saddle and equipment.

Con/Crow, John W., Corp., Co. C, age 27, EN 12/15/62 & MI 12/22/62, Corinth, MS, born Pickens, AL, farmer, died in hospital at Corinth, MS 2/27/63.

Conaway, Andrew J., Pvt., Co. C, age 19, EN 3/22/63, Glendale, MS, MI 4/10/63, Corinth, MS, born Lumpkin Co., GA, farmer, POW 10/26/63 (probably Vincent's Crossroads), returned 11/17/63, MO 3/22/64, Memphis, TN.

Conaway, John E., Pvt., Co. C, age 21, EN 3/22/63, Glendale, MS, MI 4/10/63, Corinth, MS, born Lumpkin, GA, farrier, died in regtl. hospital 1/15/64 of inflamation of tonsils.

Connelin, L., Pvt., Co. H, discharged 10/25/64 by reason of exp. term of service.*

Conner/Comer, Lewis E., Pvt., Co. F, age 36, EN 12/6/63, Camp Davies, MS, MI 2/24/64, Memphis, TN, born Lincoln Co., NC, farmer, detached as scout at Gen. Vandivers Hd.Qrs. Rome, GA, KIA 9/6/64 near Rome, GA.

Connor, Marion/Martin, Pvt., Co. D, age 24, EN 5/10/64, Decatur, AL, born Dekalb Co., AL, farmer, deserted 7/10/65, charges were removed May 4, 1888 by the War Dept., and he was discharged as of 6/30/65.

Cook, Charles J., Pvt., Co. L, age 41, EN 9/25/63, Fayette Co., AL, MI 9/25/63, Glendale, MS, born Union Co., NC, farmer, MIA/POW 10/26/63 at Vincent's Crossroads, died 2/23/64 in Richmond, VA while POW. (Buried in Richmond National Cemetery.)

Cook, Daniel, L., Pvt., Co. A, age 35, EN 1/23/64, Camp Davies, MS, MI 2/5/64, Memphis, TN, born TN, farmer, was charged with assault with intent to commit murder on or about 5/5/65 in NC. He shot John Abernatha, who was also a member of Co. A, during an argument and serously wounded him. MO 10/20/65, Huntsville, AL.

Cook. George L., Pvt., Co. H., age 36, EN & MI 12/13/63, Camp Davies, MS, sick in Nashville, TN 3/26/64, deserted with Remington revolver, no MO date.

Cook, James, Pvt., Co. D, age 18, EN 5/1/64, Decatur, AL, MI 6/16/64, Decatur, AL, born Marion Co., AL, (another Muster Roll states NC), farmer, MO 10/20/65, Huntsville, AL.

Cook, Riley P., Pvt., Co. C, age 32, EN 1/12/63, Corinth, MS, MI 1/20/63, Corinth, MS, born Haywood, NC, farmer, detailed as bugler in August 1863, MO 1/31/64, Memphis, TN.

Cook, Thomas K., Pvt., Co. H, age 36, EN 12/30/64, Stevenson, AL, MI 2/13/65, Nashville, TN, born Wall Co., GA, farmer, MO 10/20/65, Huntsville, AL.
NOTE: Thomas Cook was born in 1828. He married Jane Grizzle and had seven children, all but one born in Georgia. He first enlisted in Atlanta, GA in Co. C, 35th Georgia Inf., CSA and was involved in the battles of Seven Pines (Fir Oaks), Chickahominy (Mechanicsville), Cedar Mountain, Second bull Run, Fredericksburg, Chancellorsville, Gettysburg, The Wilderness, and Spotsylvania. He is reported as deserting at Petersburg on August 26, 1864, signed the oath of allegiance to the USA on October 21, 1864, and sent to prison at Chattanooga, TN. He then enlisted in the First Alabama Cav. USA in December. In 1872 he took his wife and five children and moved to northern Arkansas in a covered wagon. They settled on a farm in Marion County near Yellville. He died between 1876 and 1880 and is buried in Fairview Cemetery near Flippin, AR.[48]

Cook, William W., Pvt., Co. I, age 46, EN 7/21/62, MI 8/18/62, Huntsville, AL, born Wayne Co., NC, blacksmith, sick in hospital at Nashville, TN 10/24/62, MIA 4/28/63 at Day's Gap, AL, MIA after Battle of Cedar Bluff, AL 5/9/63, paroled at City Point, VA 5/23/63, sent to Camp Chase, OH 6/23/63, died 12/1/63 at Camp Davies, MS of ruptured aorta.

Cooksey, Enoch C., Pvt., Co. B, age 28, EN 12/23/62, Glendale, MS, born Warren Co., TN, farmer, died at Seminary Hospital at Corinth, MS of measles 2/22/63. (Buried Grave # B-230, Corinth National Cemetery.)

Cooksey, Martin L., Pvt., Co. C, age 37, EN 12/1/62, Corinth, MS, MI 12/22/62, Corinth, MS, detailed as hospital nurse 5/18/63, sick in Corinth 11/9/63, MO 12/17/63.

Cooly/Cooley, John H., Pvt., Co. A, age 21, EN 9/5/64, Rome, GA, born Cowetta, GA, farmer, on detached service as guide 10/64, POW, captured at Cave Springs, GA 10/2/64, never heard from again.

Cooner, James C., Pvt., Co. G&A, age 28, EN 3/28/64, Decatur, AL, MI 4/13/64, Decatur, AL, born Walker Co., AL, farmer, deserted at Atlanta, GA 11/17/64 with side arms, returned 6/17/65, charge of desertion was removed by War Dept. 4/21/86, MO 10/20/65.

Cooper, James M., Pvt., Co. E, EN 4/1/63, Glendale, MS, MI 4/1/63, Corinth, MS, detailed as teamster in Q.M. Dept. at Vicksburg, MS 1/25/64, MO 3/1/64.

Cooper, Mack (James M.), Pvt., Co. E, EN 4/1/63, Glendale, MS, MI 4/1/63, Corinth, MS, taken prisoner between Glendale & Burnsville, MS 6/11/63, paroled at Richmond, VA 7/3/63, KIA 12/15/63.

Corgan, William W., Sgt/Sgt. Maj., Co. F, age 27, EN 11/25/63, Corinth, MS, MI 2/24/64, Memphis, TN, born Union Co., IL, carpenter, appt. Sgt. Maj. 10/10/64, was on march from Atlanta to Savannah, GA, MO 12/17/64, Savannah, GA.

Corghanny, J.H. (or I.H.), discharged 10/25/64 by reason of exp. of term of service at Rome, GA.*

Corley, Holis M., Co. I (no further information).

Cormich, W., Co. E, AWOL 7/1/63.*

Cornelius, Cargell, Pvt/Corp. Co. H, age 34, EN & MI 10/10/63 Glendale, MS, MO 10/24/64, Rome, GA.

Cornelius, Zion, Pvt., Co. H, age 18, EN 10/19/63, Glendale, MS, MI 10/19/63, Camp Davies, MS, MO 10/24/64, Rome, GA. (Buried in Graves Cemetery near Cleveland, Blount Co., Alabama.)[49]

Cossett, Henry, Pvt., Co. G, temporarily attached from 11th Illinois Cavalry.

Cothern, George W., Pvt., Co. K, age 28, EN 11/1/63, Glendale, MS, MI 11/1/63, Camp Davies, MS, born Henry Co., GA, farmer, on detached service as teamster in Gen. Sherman's expedition 1/24/64, POW, wounded in battle 3/10/65 at Monroe's Crossroads, NC, discharged at Willet's Point, NY 5/16/65 due to disability.
NOTE: George Cothern was born in 1835 in Henry Co., GA and a brother to William R. Cothern. He was wounded twice during the war. After the war he lived in Madison Co., AL before moving to Cross County, AR approximately 1890. He was married three times and had six children. He died in St. Francis Co., AR.[50]

Cothern, Joel A., Pvt., Co. K, age 18, EN & MI 12/1/63, Camp Davies, MS, born Spartanburg Dist., SC, farmer, on detached service as teamster in Gen. Sherman's expedition 1/24/64, left sick at Savannah, GA 1/28/65, in DeCamp USA Gen. Hosp. at David's Island, NY Harbor 3/3/65, discharged at David's Island, NY 6/17/65.

NOTE: Traveled 90 miles from his home in Marion Co., AL to Camp Davies, MS to enlist. He was born in 1845 in Spartanburg District, SC and returned to Marion Co., AL after the war and married Isabella Clementine Wylie. He died in Hempstead Co., AR January 7, 1889.[51]

Cothern, William R., Pvt., Co. K, age 25, EN 11/1/63, Glendale, MS, MI 11/1/63, Camp Davies, MS, born Carroll Co., GA, farmer, MO 7/19/65, Nashville, TN.

NOTE: William Cothern was born in 1838 in Carroll Co., GA. After the war he lived in Madison Co., AL. He was a brother to George Cothern, above, and their brother Collins Cothern served in the 25th Alabama Infantry, CSA, throughout the war.[52]

Cotton, James H., Pvt., Co. M, age 31, EN 12/16/63, Camp Davies, MS, MI 12/16/63, Corinth, MS, born Fayette Co., AL, farmer, died in hospital at Memphis, TN 1/27/64 of measles. (Buried Grave in Memphis National Cemetery.)

Couch, Benjamin, Pvt., Co. L, in USA General Field Hospital at Bridgeport, AL May & June 1864.*

Coughman, Jesse R., Pvt., Co. H, age 19, EN & MI 10/17/63, Glendale, MS, 3/64 & 4/64 sick in hospital in Memphis, TN, 7/64 & 8/64 sick in Hospital #2 in Nashville, TN, MO 10/24/64, Rome, GA.

Counce, John A., Pvt., Co. E, age 45, EN & MI 8/27/63, Glendale, MS. Note from Record & Pension Office states, "evidence on file that this man was discharged on or about 11/30/63, Robert M. Reed having been accepted to serve in his place and stead." (Cards filed with Robert M. Reed, true name of soldier.)

Cowen/Cowan, George W., Pvt., Co. B, age 18, EN 4/1/65, Faisons, NC, born Onslow, NC, farmer, deserted about 6/20/65 in Huntsville, AL.

Cox, Jefferson, M., Pvt., Co. H, age 18, EN 12/25/64, Huntsville, AL, MI 12/25/64, Nashville, TN, born Greenville Dist., SC, farmer, MO 10/20/65.

Cox, Mordecai M., Sgt., Co. A, age 26, EN 12/22/63, Camp Davies, MS, MI 2/6/64, Memphis, TN, born Habersham Co., GA, farmer, MO 10/20/65.

Crabb, William P., Pvt/Corp., Co. C, age 35, EN 12/1/62, Corinth, MS, MI 12/22/62, Corinth, MS, born Giles Co., TN, farmer, appt. Corp. 6/18/63, MO 12/17/63, Memphis, TN.

NOTE: William P. Crabb was born 1829 in Giles Co., TN and had three borthers who served in the C.S.A. His first wife was Elizabeth Horn, born 1828 in TN and died 1878 in Prentiss Co., MS. His father was Joseph Crabb, born 1805. William died in 1893 in Yell Co., AR.[53]

Cramer, Francis L., Major, F&S, age 26, EN 10/22/63, Memphis, TN, MI 10/24/63, Memphis, TN, on leave of absence 3/14/65 because of wounds received 3/10/65 at Monroe's Crossroads during battle between Maj. Gen. Kilpatrick and Maj. Gen. Wade Hampton, appt. Colonel for gallant and meritorious services during the war, MO 10/20/65, Huntsville, AL. (Several pages of correspondence in file.)

Crandell, Levi, Co. M, age 17, born Dark Co., OH, farmer, EN 2/3/64, Memphis, TN by Capt. Lomax.*

Crawford/Cranford, James D. Sr., Pvt., Co. H, age 22, EN & MI 10/17/63, Glendale, MS, MO 10/24/64, Rome, GA.

Crawford/Cranford, James D., Jr. Pvt., Co. H, age 19, EN & MI 10/17/63, Glendale, MS, MO 10/24/64, Rome, GA.

Crawford, John F., Pvt/Corp., Co. H, age 19, EN & MI 9/14/63, Glendale, MS, MO 9/29/64, Rome, GA.

Crawford, Samuel A., Pvt., Co. H, age 25, EN & MI 10/17/63, Glendale, MS, MO 10/24/64, Rome, GA.

Crawford, W.H. Sgt., Co. E, MO, term of service exp. 3/1/64, Memphis, TN.*

Crawford, William L., Pvt., Co. H, age 22, EN & MI 10/17/63, Glendale, MS, POW 10/26/63 (probably at Vincent's Crossroads.)

Creekmore, Brison C., Pvt., Co. A, age 27, EN 9/8/62, Iuka, MS, MI 10/1/62, Corinth, MS, born Wilkes Co., GA, died at Corinth 2/27/63 of disease.

Creel/Creal, John T., Pvt., Co. D, age 19, EN & MI 6/10/63, Glendale, MS, born Bibb, AL, farmer, MO 6/16/64, Decatur, AL.

Creel/Creal, Joshua D., Pvt., Co. D, age 20, EN & MI 6/10/63, Glendale, MS, born Bibb, AL, farmer, MO 6/16/64, Decatur, AL.

Crittenden, William, Corp., Co. A, EN 12/13/62, Glendale, MS, MI 12/31/62, Corinth, MS, 6/63 - 9/63 on duty as saddler, MO 12/22/63.

Crocker, James D., Pvt., Co. D, age 22, EN 5/20/64, Decatur, AL, MI 6/16/64, Decatur, AL, born Jefferson Co., AL, farmer, deserted 7/17/64 with Smith carbine & Remington revolver from Rome, GA.

Crocker, John Y., Corp., Co. G, age 29, EN 11/27/62, Grand Junction, TN, MI 11/27/62, Corinth, MS, MO 11/26/63, Memphis, TN.

Cross, John W., Pvt., Co. B, age 32, EN 6/10/63, Glendale, MS, MI 6/10/63, Corinth, MS, born Perry, AL, POW 10/26/63 at Vincent's Crossroads, MO 6/22/64, Memphis, TN.

Crow, John D., Pvt., Co. K, age 39, EN & MI 12/25/63, Camp Davies, MS, born Morgan Co., AL, farmer, on detached service as teamster in Gen. Sherman's expedition 1/24/64, 3/64 & 4/64 on daily duty as regt. hospital nurse, on recruiting service in TN 11/10/64, MO 7/17/65, Nashville, TN. Traveled 100 miles from Marion Co., AL to Camp Davies, MS to enlist.

Crow, John W., (Cards filed with John W. Con)

Crowley, William R., Pvt., Co. F, age 21, EN 11/20/63, Corinth, MS, MI 2/24/64, Memphis, TN, born Marion Co., AL, farmer, MO 12/17/64, Savannah, GA.

Crumbley, Thomas, Pvt., Co. H, age 22, EN 1/1/65, Huntsville, AL, born Lawrence Dist., SC, died in barracks at Nashville, TN 2/12/65 of smallpox. (Buried in Grave H-09225, Nashville, National Cemetery.)

Crumbly, William W., Pvt/Sgt., Co. H, age 24, EN 2/10/65, Stevenson, AL, MI 2/10/65, Nashville, TN, born Lawrence Dist., SC, farmer, MO 10/20/65, Huntsville, AL.

Cunningham, James P.W., Pvt., Co. F, age 32, EN 12/8/63, Camp Davies, MS, MI 7/27/64, Rome, GA, born Shelby Co., AL, farmer/blacksmith, MO 12/17/64, Savannah, GA.

Cupples, Elijah, Pvt/Sgt., Co. M, age 24, EN 9/14/63, Chewalla, TN, MI 9/14/63, Corinth, MS, born Hardeman Co., TN, farmer, MO 10/20/65, Huntsville, AL.

Curtis, Henry, Sgt/Lt., Co. F, age 23, EN 5/15/63, Memphis, TN, MI 8/13/63, Corinth, MS, born Washington Co., NC, appt. 2nd Lt. from 1st Sgt. 2/5/64. Notation from Record & Pension Office dated 1/24/96, states, "This man under the name William R. Crocker deserted from 30th Reg't Ill. Vols. on or about Apl. 30, 1863 and enlisted in this organization in violation of the 22d (now 50th) Article of War the notation of Dec. 17, 1886 is cancelled." Discharged 9/14/64.

Curtis, Isaac R., Pvt., Co. G, temporarily attached from 11th Illinois Cavalry.

Dagger, George W., Pvt., Co. A, on detached service in Co. D since 2/5/64.*

Daily/Dailey, Green, Pvt., Co. E, EN 4/1/63, Glendale, MS, MI 4/1/63, Corinth, MS, deserted 9/6/63, Glendale, MS.

Daughtery, William, Pvt., Co. G, age 17, EN 7/11/63, Glendale, MS, MI 7/17/63, Corinth, MS, MO 11/26/63, Memphis, TN.

David, (?), Pvt., Co. D, absent sick since 9/8/62 at Nashville, TN.*

Davis, Adam A., Pvt., Co. A, age 36, EN & MI 9/6/64, Rome, GA, born Dekalb Co., GA, shoemaker, sick in Whiteside, TN 10/1/65, discharge furnished 10/29/65.

Davis, Archibald M., Pvt., Co. I&D, age 18, EN & MI 8/18/62, Huntsville, AL, born Blount Co., AL, farmer, died 11/12/62, Hospital #8, Nashville, TN of disease, father listed as William Davis. (Buried in Grave A-4340 in Nashville National Cemetery.)

Davis, Arthur, Pvt., Co. E, age 21, EN 12/13/62, McNairy Co, TN, MI 12/13/62, Corinth, MS, MO 12/17/63, Memphis, TN.

Davis, Bird, Undercook, Co. G, age 18, (Colored), EN 7/1/64, Decatur, AL, MI Rome, GA, born Jackson, MS, served as teamster/wagoner, MO 10/20/65, Huntsville, AL.

Davis, Charles, Pvt/Blacksmith, Co. E, age 33, EN & MI 8/27/63, Glendale, MS, MO 9/28/64, Rome, GA.

Davis, Charles M., Pvt., Co. G, age 24, EN 3/5/63, Chewalla, TN, MI 3/5/63, Corinth, MS, deserted 8/3/63 at Glendale, MS, rejoined & awaited trial, MO 11/26/63.

Davis, Christopher C., Pvt/Sgt, Co. K, age 23, EN & MI 7/27/62, Huntsville, AL, born Marshall, AL, farmer, appt. Sgt. 10/1/62, in hospital at Nashville, TN 12/26/62, discharged for disability 2/18/65, was shown on Descriptive List of Deserters from USA Gen. Hosptial in Mound City, IL 4/15/64.

Davis, George W., Pvt., Co. C, age 24, EN 12/15/63, Corinth, MS, MI 3/10/64, Memphis, TN, born Walker Co., AL, farmer, deserted 10/1/65, Moulton, AL with horse, carbine & equipment, charge of desertion was dismissed 7/31/86 and discharge issued as of 10/1/65.

Davis, Henry/Harvy H., Pvt., Co. D, age 18, EN & MI 5/3/63, Glendale, MS, born Tuscaloosa, AL, farmer, MO 6/16/64, Decatur, AL.

Davis, James, Pvt., Co. E, EN 12/9/62, Nabors Mill, MI 12/9/62, Corinth, MS, taken POW near Chewalla, TN 1/20/63, deserted 3/2/63, Corinth, MS.

Davis, Jeremiah/Jesse B., Pvt., Co. D, age 19, EN & MI 5/3/63, Glendale, MS, born Walker Co., AL, farmer, MO 6/16/64, Decatur, AL.
NOTE: Jesse Davis was born August 18, 1836 in Surry Co., NC. His parents were Joshua Davis, born July 8, 1805 in Wilkes Co., NC and Kisiah Stanfield, born 1813, who were married September 8, 1832 in NC. Joshua died March 30, 1882 in Brown Co., IN and Kisiah died October 2, 2906. Jesse married Margaret Spiegle January 10, 1861 and had the following children: Lou Allen, born November 13, 1861 in Winston Co., AL; Jesse David, born February 12, 1863 (five months after his father died); Sarah, born 1838; Robert, born May 7, 1841; Mason, born December 31, 1842; Lucinda Jane, born June 14, 1846; Roxannah, born June 5, 1847; Martha, born June 7, 1849; and Joseph, Jasper Newton, born May 12, 1852.[54]

Davis, Jesse, Pvt., Co. I, age 25, EN & MI 7/21/62, Huntsville, AL, born Surry Co., NC, died in Hospital #12, Nashville, TN 10/19/62 of disease. (Buried in Grave A-5045 in Nashville National Cemetery.)

Davis, Joseph H., Asst. Surgeon, Co. F&S, EN 8/19/64, Rome, GA, MI 8/19/64, Savannah, GA, MO 10/20/65, Huntsville, AL.

Davis, Mason, Pvt., Co. I (or J), age 20, EN & MI 8/18/62, Huntsville, AL, born Surry Co., NC, farmer, detached as courier at Reedyville, TN 1/27/63, teamster/ambulance driver, MO 7/19/65, Nashville, TN.
   NOTE: Mason was born December 31, 1842 in Surry Co, NC (see Jesse Davis, above, for family information), married 1st, Christen Ann Young November 20, 1870 in Blue Earth Lake, MN and had the following children: Ida Lucinda and Gerome. Married 2nd, Emma Jane Anthony and they had the following children: Jasper Newton, Lemuel, Grant E., Ettie, and Nettie. Mason died December 23, 1917 in Janesville, MN.[55]

Davis, Robert, Pvt., Co. I, age 18, EN & MI 8/18/62, Huntsville, AL, born Surry Co., NC, farmer, died in Hospital #8, Nashville, TN 1/27/63 of typhoid fever. (Buried in Grave B-6554 in Nashville National Cemetery.)

Davis, Thomas P., Pvt., Co. D, age 20, EN 5/1/64, Decatur, AL, born Walker Co., AL, farmer, deserted 5/10/65 from Huntsville, AL, charge of desertion removed 11/7/84 and discharge issued as of 5/10/65.

Davis, William, Pvt., Co. B, age 17, EN 5/1/64, Decatur, AL, MI 5/1/64, Rome, GA, born Roane Co., TN, farmer, KIA 11/23/64, Oconee River, Balls Ferry, GA.

Davis, William, Sgt/Pvt., Co. E, age 28, EN & MI 2/1/63, Corinth, MS, reduced to rank 9/22/63, MO 3/1/64, Memphis, TN.

Davis, William, Undercook, Co. M, (Colored), age 23, EN 1/9/65, Savannah, GA, born Burke Co., GA, farmer, sick in hospital in Decatur, AL 7/15/65, no MO date.

Davis, William C., Pvt., Co. D, age 19, EN & MI 5/3/63, Glendale, MS, born Walker Co., AL, farmer, MO 6/16/64, Decatur, AL.

Davis, William J., Pvt., Co. C, age 20, EN 1/1/64, Corinth, MS, MI 3/10/64, Memphis, TN, blacksmith, born Bibb Co., AL, farmer, MO 10/20/65, Huntsville, AL.

Davis, William T., age 18, born Cincinnati, OH, EN 9/25/63, Stevenson, AL. (This enlistment record was signed by Lt. Irvine of the 28th KY but is in with 1st AL Cav. files.)*

Davis, William W., Pvt., Co. M, in Adams USA General Hospital at Memphis, TN 1/21/64.*
(Both of these may be for the same person.)

Davis, William W., Pvt/Sgt., Co. C, age 26, EN 12/15/63, Corinth, MS, MI 3/10/64, Memphis, TN, born Walker Co., AL, farmer, deserted 10/1/65, Moulton, AL with arms & equipment, charge of desertion was removed 12/26/95 and discharge issued as of 10/1/65.

NOTE: William Wallace Davis was the son of Catherine and William Davis and married Elizabeth Jane Handley in the late 1850's. Their children were: George Washington, William Mack, Andy M., Levi Henry, Mary Elizabeth, Dovie Ann, John Irvin, and Manley Carol. He became a preacher in 1866, served one term as a state representative from Winston Co., AL in 1890, died December 23, 1901 and is buried in Union Grove Cemetery in Winston Co., AL.[56]

Davlin, George W., Pvt/Corp., Co. C, age 18, EN 2/5/64, Memphis, TN, MI 3/10/64, Memphis, TN, born Panola, Texas, drover, appt. Corp. 3/1/64, deserted 11/9/64 with two Colt revolvers, Smith carbine & horse in Rome, GA.

Dawson, Lewis N., Pvt/Corp., Co. G, age 22, EN 3/5/63, Chewalla, TN, MI 3/5/63, Corinth, MS, appt. Corp. 9/1/63, MO 11/26/63, Memphis, TN.

Day, Enos, Pvt., Co. B, age 20, EN 2/16/64, Pulaski, TN, MI 3/27/64, Decatur, AL, born Jackson Co., AL, farmer, MO 10/20/65, Huntsville, AL.

Day, F., Pvt., Co. B, on daily duty as nurse in hospital 4/64.*

Day, Gardner C., Co. B, age 18, born Lawrence Co., TN, EN 2/1/64, Pulaski, TN by Lt. Judy.*

Day, George W., Pvt., Co. I, age 18, EN & MI 8/22/64, Louisville, KY, born Morgan Co., AL, farmer, MO 7/19/65, Nashville, TN.

NOTE: George William Day was the son of David M. Day and Cyrena Dutton, the grandson of Richard Day and the great grandson of both David Day, Jr. and Stephen Penn. He had two uncles in the 1st AL Cav., USA. In 1870 he was living in the Crowdabout Community with his wife, Laura and young son, Lucian.[57]

Day, James H., Sgt/Lt., Co. I&D, age 21, EN & MI 7/21/62, Huntsville, AL, born Morgan Co., AL, reenlisted 10/12/63, Camp Davies, MS, as 2nd Lt. , MO 7/19/65, Nashville, TN.

NOTE: 2nd Lt. James H. Day was the son of Richard Day & Elizabeth Penn, the grandson of David Day, Jr. and Stephen Penn. On March 10, 1865, he was given command of Co. K after its leader was killed in action in NC. After he mustered out of service, he returned to his home community, married Martha Simpson and fathered four children, his first born being named George Spencer Day after Col. George Spencer, commander of the First Alabama Cavalry. James Day died 1/1/81 at the age of 80.[58]

Day, Lionel W., Lt/Adj. F&S, age 24, EN 3/3/63, Corinth MS, MI 3/3/63, Glendale, MS, promoted from Pvt. of 64th Regt. Illinois Vols., Co. A where he had MI 8/10/62 in Springfield, IL, MO 3/2/64, Memphis, TN.

Day, Richard B., Pvt/Corp. Co. I, age 25, EN 8/26/62, Huntsville, AL, MI 8/26/62, Nashville, TN, born Morgan Co., AL, carpenter, appt. 1st Sgt. 9/30/62, detached as courier at Reedyville, TN 1/27/63, MIA 5/2/63 at Cedar Bluff, AL, rejoined 11/10/63, MO 7/19/65.

NOTE: Corporal Richard B. Day was the son of Richard Day and Elizabeth Penn, and the grandson of David Day, Jr. and Stephen Penn. After he mustered out of service he returned to Crowdabout and married Martha Ellen Gibson 10/10/66 and they had six children. He was Justice of the Peace in his community and died February 22, 1923 at the age of 86.[59]

Dean, William J., Sgt., Co. G, age 23, EN 11/27/62, Grand Junction, TN, MI 11/27/62, Corinth, MS, MO 11/26/63, Memphis, TN.

Deaton, James, Pvt., Co. B, age 31, EN 12/20/62, Glendale, MS, MI 12/31/62, Corinth, MS, born Bledsoe, TN, farmer, MO 12/27/63, Camp Davies, MS.

Delk, David M., Pvt., Co. G, temporarily detached from 11th Illinois Cavalry.

DeVaney, James W., Captain, Co. H, age 24, EN & MI 4/1/65, Huntsville, AL, MO 10/20/65, Huntsville, AL.

NOTE: Affidavit from James DeVaney's widow states the following: *"I will write a few lines to inform you of the services of James W. DeVaney. We were married near Bernadotte Fulton Co., Ills Nov 24th 1860 on the 12th day of Sept 1861 he enlisted at Bernadotte In Co G 50th Regt Inft Ills Vol Col M. M. Bain Com Regt said James W. Devaney was 4th Sergeant until the 4th day of March 1863 when he was made 1st Sergeant until the 19th day of May 1864 he was Sergeant Major of the 50th Regt of Ills Vols.*

On the 29th of December 1863 he was discharged at Springfield Ills by reason of re-enlistment as a veteran volunteer. Was sent home with Jacob Fleming to recruit for the Regt they got (9) nine recruits (8) eight new ones and a veteran. They reported to Capt. G.S. Fairwell of the 28th Ills Vols at Macomb Ills. Then about Sept 1864 he was discharged to raise a Co for the 1st Alabama Cav was made Capt of Co. H, 1st Ala. Cav was left at Huntsville Ala until was discharged from the service of the United States on the 20th day of October 1865 at Huntsville Ala. Said James W. DeVaney was born Ross Co Ohio 29th day of October 1840 was five feet nine inches high dark complexion hazel eyes black hair by occupation a farmer and school teacher him nor I ever applied for a pension except me one time when so many was getting I thought I had four small children mabe I could get one but when I said he was killed by accident that was all. Said James W. DeVaney was at Ft. Henry, Ft. Donalson, Shiloh both days had a wounded man shot of his shoulder he was carrying off the battle field. Then he was on the advance on Corinth 28 days in second battle of Corinth he was sunstruck there so he never could work in the hot sun after he came home....Nov 2nd 1865 at Vermont Ills then in the Spring of 1868 we came to Woodson Co Kansas settled on a homestead in 1870 the 17th of Nov he with a party of thirteen more went on a buffalo hunt where he was shot by accidently never got him home I never seen him in June 16, 1874 I married Charles Steffen of Co G 5th Kansas Vol Cav lived with him until death July 24, 1910." (Signed Phebe C. Steffen and dated 16th Day of Feb. A.D. 1911. His death date was shown as Dec. 2, 1870.)[60]

Devine, J., Sgt., Co. H, deserted while on detached service 10/64.*

Deweese, John P., Pvt., Co. A&G, age 25, EN 3/28/64, Decatur, AL, MI 4/13/64, Decatur, AL, born Dallas Co., AL, farmer, deserted 10/28/64 at Decatur, AL with arms and equipment.

Dickenson/Dickinson, Rufus, B., Pvt., Co. G, age 21, EN 3/10/64, Decatur, AL, MI 4/13/64, Decatur, AL, born Marion Co., AL, farmer, MO 10/20/65, Huntsville, AL. (One Muster Roll states he died 5/1/64 in Decatur of disease.)

Dickenson/Dickerson, James, Pvt., Co. F, age 26, EN 11/25/63, Camp Davies, MS, born Harden Co., TN, farmer & mechanic, died 2/15/64 at Vicksburg, MS while on detached service as teamster.

Dickinson, George W., Pvt., Co. L, age 19, EN 3/1/65, Stevenson, AL, MI 4/18/65, Nashville, TN, born Marion Co., AL, farmer, MO 10/20/65, Huntsville, AL.

Dickinson, John H., Pvt., Co. G, age 25, EN 3/10/64, Decatur, AL, MI 4/13/64, Decatur, AL, born Marion Co., AL, farmer, died 5/1/64 in hospital at Decatur, AL.

Digby, Benjamin F., Pvt., Co. B, age 27, EN 12/23/62, Glendale, MS, MI 12/31/62, Corinth, MS, born Bibb Co., AL, POW 4/10/63 & in St. Louis, paroled at City Point, VA 5/5/63, MO 12/27/63, Camp Davies, MS.

Dikes/Dykes, Thomas L., Pvt., Co. L, age 17, EN 9/25/63, Fayette Co., AL, MI 9/25/63, Glendale, MS, born Marion Co., AL, farmer, POW 10/26/63 at Vincent's Crossroads, died 10/2/64 in Charleston, SC.

Dill, James, Pvt., Co. B, age 23, EN 4/7/64, Mooresville, AL, MI 10/17/64, Huntsville, AL, born Walker Co., AL, farmer, deserted 7/10/64 in Rome, GA while on furlough - later found erroneously reported, MO 10/20/65, Huntsville, AL.
   NOTE: James P. Dill was born December 30, 1831 and died August 7, 1918. He is buried in the Shady Grove Primitive Baptist Church Cemetery in Cullman Co., AL near Bugtussel.[61]

Dillard, James T., Co. M, age 38, born Spartanburg Dist., SC, EN 1/14/64, Camp Davies, MS by Capt. Lomax.*

Dillard, Smith, Pvt., Co. B, age 23, EN 12/20/62, Glendale, MS, MI 12/31/62, Corinth, MS, born Spartanburg Dist., SC, farmer, died 3/14/63 at Glendale, MS.

Dillard, William, Pvt., Co. B, age 35, MI 12/31/62, Corinth, MS, born Spartanburg Dist., SC, detailed as teamster and ambulance driver, MO 12/27/63, Camp Davies, MS.

Dillinger/Billinger, John, Pvt., Co. M, age 19, EN 11/19/63, Camp Davies, MS, MI 11/19/63, Corinth, MS, born Lincoln Co., NC, farmer, died 7/18/64 in hospital at Rome, GA. (Buried in Grave #1433 in Marietta National Cemetery.)

Dixon, Wm. Pvt., Co. I, paroled POW at College Green Barracks, Annapolis, MD March & April 1865.*

Dobson, Benjamin P., Pvt/Sgt., Co. B, age 38, EN 8/1/64, Wedowee, AL, MI 8/1/64, Rome, GA, born Macon Co., NC, promoted to Sgt. 6/13/65, MO 10/20/65, Huntsville, AL.

Dodd, Franklin, Pvt., Co. L, age 24, EN 9/25/63, Fayette Co., AL, MI 9/25/63, Glendale, MS, born Walker Co., AL, farmer, died 4/15/64 at Adams USA Gen. Hospital at Memphis, TN. (Buried in Memphis National Cemetery.)
   NOTE: Franklin Dodd married September 24, 1857 to Elizabeth Tucker, daughter of Simeon Tucker who was also in this regiment. Elizabeth was the mother of three children by Franklin; Mary Ann, born September 23, 1858, died March 10, 1930; William Simeon, born April 10, 1861, died August 7, 1949; and Mary Priscilla, born May 24, 1864 and died March 18, 1911. After Franklin's death, Elizabeth married George Washington Webb, Sr. Franklin and John Dodd were brothers.[62]

Dodd, John, Pvt., Co. L, age 18, EN 9/25/63, Fayette Co., AL, MI 9/25/63, Glendale, MS, born Walker Co., AL, farmer, discharged 12/27/63 for debility resulting from deformity of chest which existed from infancy.
   NOTE: John Dodd was born April 4, 1844 to Michael/Mikel and Mary "Polly" Knight Dodd. He married Nancy Elizabeth Ingle, daughter of Andrew Jackson Ingle, September 3, 1868 in Larissa, Winston Co., AL and died March 15, 1928 at Haleyville, Winston Co., AL. Their children were: Mary Elizabeth, born July 28, 1869, died January 12, 1896; Andrew M., born January 27, 1871, died November 28, 1877; Jessie, born September 15, 1872, died December 18, 1875; Jasper N., born August 28, 1874, died September 10, 1914; Nancy Jane, born 1876; Rufus Irving, born June 1, 1879, died December 26, 1909; Virgil Marion, born November 19, 1881, died June 18, 1938; Genia Adling, born October 12, 1884, died June 21, 1908; Emma and Anna (Twins) born October 28, 1886; Nancy Jane, born August 18, 1887, died September 12, 1894; Elzie "Otho", born October 2, 1889, died August 17, 1938 and Alta, born December 15, 1891, died June 21, 1924.[63]

Dodd, John, Pvt., Co. L. age 20, (may be same John Dodd as above), EN 12/23/64, Stevenson, AL, MI 12/23/64, Nashville, TN, born Walker Co., AL, farmer, MO 10/20/65, Huntsville, AL.

Dodd, Wyatt N., Corp., Co. L, age 19, EN 9/25/63, Fayette Co., AL, MI 9/25/63, Glendale, MS, born Walker Co., AL, farmer, MO 9/28/64, Rome, GA.

Dodds, Ozro J., Lt. Col., F&S, age 23, EN 10/9/63, Glendale, MS, appt. from Capt. 81st Ohio Inf., resigned 4/30/64 stating his father was in poor health, their manufacturing business was suffering and needed his immediate and personal attention.

Dodson, John W., Pvt/Corp., Co. H, age 31, EN 12/21/64, Decatur, AL, MI 12/21/64, Nashville, TN, born McMinn Co., TN, farmer, MO 10/20/65, Huntsville, AL.

Donner, Michael, Pvt/Corp., Co. C, age 35, EN 12/6/62, Corinth, MS, MI 12/22/62, Corinth, MS, born Ireland, farmer, in Union USA Hospital in Memphis, TN 10/16/63, MO 12/17/63, Memphis, TN.

Doss, Francis M., Corp/Pvt., Co. A, age 26, EN 1/1/64, Camp Davies, MS, MI 2/5/64, Memphis, TN, born Chickasaw Co., MS, in arrest in prison 4/64 for desertion, charge of desertion was removed 10/6/84 and discharge issued as of 10/1/65.

Douthet/Douthit, William G., Pvt., Co. C, age 51, EN 12/3/62, Corinth, MS, MI 12/22/62, Corinth, MS, born Rowan, NC, school teacher, died 2/17/63 in Corinth, MS.

Downing, Thomas, Pvt., Co. F, term of service exp. 12/17/64 at Savannah, GA.*

Downum/Donnum/Donner, James H., Pvt., Co. F, age 18, EN 11/25/63 Camp Davies, MS, born Marion Co., AL, farmer, on detached service as teamster in Vicksburg, MS 1/25/64, died 4/13/64 at Nashville, TN.

Downum, William T., Pvt., Co. F, age 23, EN 11/25/63, Camp Davies, MS, born Marion Co., AL, farmer, detached as teamster in Vicksburg, MS 1/25/64, in hospital #19, Nashville, TN 3/64, MO 12/17/64.

Doxon, William, POW 3/10/65 from Monroe's Crossroads near Fayetteville, NC and confined at Richmond, VA, paroled 3/29/65 and admitted to hospital 4/1/65.*

Doyle, Joseph C., Pvt., Co. A, age 43, EN & MI 9/6/64, Rome, GA, born Jackson Co., AL, farmer, MO 10/20/65, Huntsville, AL.

Duckett, John T., Pvt., Co. A, age 24, EN 9/8/62, Iuka, MS, MI 10/1/62, Corinth, MS, born McNairy Co., TN, farmer, promoted to Corp. 12/18/62, MO 9/16/63, Corinth, MS.
    NOTE: John T. Duckett was the son of Mahala Massengill and Rignal Odell Duckett. He was born September 14, 1838 and died April 5, 1913 in Whitfield Co., GA. After he mustered out of service he lived in Cairo, IL where he married his first wife, Nancy Wilhoit. His second wife was Mary Chasteen. From 1865-1890, he resided in Cullman, Morgan, Blount, and Cherokee Counties in Alabama. In 1900, he moved to Whitfield Co., GA where he lived the rest of his life and had 11 children.[64]

Dudley, Dean, Pvt., Co. H, died 6/3/63.*

Dugan, K.H. Capt. Co. C, on detached service detailed to go North with refugees 6/20/63.*

Dugan, Richard S., Pvt/Corp., Co. C, age 27, EN 2/20/63, Corinth, MS, MI 2/25/63, Corinth, MS, born McMinn Co., TN, farmer, appt. Corp. 6/10/63, was on detached service 6/20/63 to go North with refugees, died 9/27/63 in hospital at Glendale, MS.

NOTE: Richard Dugan was born July 3, 1836 in Monroe Co., TN and died September 27, 1863. His sister, Minerva Jane Dugan, was born February 5, 1834 in Monroe Co., TN, married to William L. Peoples, who was in Co. E, 1st AL Cav. USA. Minerva died October 26, 1876 in Marion Co., AL. Richard and Minerva were the children of Absalom L. Dugan (1812-1862)and Susannah Sanders, who emigrated to Marion Co., AL from East TN in 1850. They were forced to leave in 1863 because of their Union sympathies and fled to Marion Co., IL.[65]

Dumick, J., Sgt., Co. H, on detached service recruiting in AL 9/64.*

Duncan, John W., Pvt., Co. C, age 28, EN 2/20/63, Corinth, MS, born Perry, AL, farmer, deserted 6/28/63 from Glendale, MS.

Dunn, Francis W, Sgt. Maj/2nd Lt., Co. H (F&S), age 20, EN & MI 5/16/63, Corinth, MS, first EN 8/28/62 in Freedom, IL & MI 8/28/62 at Springfield, IL, MO 10/31/64, Rome, GA.
   NOTE: Francis Wayland Dunn and his brother, Newell Ransom Dunn, both enlisted in the 64th Illinois Infantry in September 1862. Wayland became Sgt. Maj. of the 1st AL Cav. US, May 16, 1863. He was born January 29, 1843 in Wayne, Astabula Co., Ohio, to Ransom Dunn who was a minister and missionary of the Free Will Baptist faith. Newell Ransom Dunn died March 26, 1863. Wayland survived the war and taught at Hillsdale College where his father was president. Wayland died in his sleep December 13, 1874 just before he reached age 32.

Dunn, Fred T., Pvt., Co. G, temporarily attached from 11th Illinois Cavalry.

Dunn, John, Pvt., Co. A, in USA Gen. Field Hospital at Bridgeport, AL 5/64, returned to duty 5/15/64.*

Dunn, Joseph F., Pvt/Sgt., Co. H, age 28, EN & MI 9/18/63, Glendale, MS, reported deserted in Sep. & Oct. 1864.

Dunn, William, Pvt., Co. G, age 25, EN 6/13/63, Chewalla, TN, MI 6/13/63, Corinth, MS, was member of West TN Cav. and sent back to 6th Regt. 6/25/63, 1st US Cav.

Dunn, William D., Pvt., Co. G, age 22, EN 11/27/62, Grand Junction, TN, MI 11/27/62, Corinth, MS, MO 11/26/63, Memphis, TN.

Durm, John, died 8/15/63 at Nashville, TN. (Casualty sheet states he was attached to 1st Middle TN at time of death.)*

Dwyer, William, Pvt., Co. K, age 24, EN 12/13/62, Nashville, TN, MI 9/27/63, Glendale, MS, born Bibb Co., AL, MIA 10/26/63, Vincent's Crossroads, Bay Springs, MS, escaped from Cahaba and went to Winston Co., AL 12/63, returned to duty 11/15/64 as per Record & Pension Office, 3/2/96. Affidavit from Thomas A. McWhirter dated July 3, 1865, stated William Dwyer was taken POW by the enemy with him at Vincent's Crossroads, MS in action 10/26/63 and taken to Cahaba Prison, AL. After remaining there two months they both escaped from prison and started together for their lines at Camp Davies, MS and after traveling six days, William Dwyer became exhausted and unable to travel further when Thomas A. McWhirter left him about 150 miles from their lines. (There are several documents in his file stating how he tried to get back to his regiment but due to weather conditions and his illness he was not able to return until 1/5/64 when he reported to Maj. Shurtleff who was the only officer left as the regiment had gone with Maj. Gen. Sherman.

Dykes, Thomas L., (Cards filed with Thomas L. Dikes).

Eakins, James B., Pvt., Co. D, age 23 (or 28), EN & MI 6/1/63, Glendale, MS, was company cook 10/63, on detached service at refugee Camp in Memphis, TN 2/64, born Marshall Co., AL, farmer, MO 6/16/64, Decatur, AL.

Eakins, John, Pvt., Co. D, age 30, EN & MI 6/1/63, Glendale, MS, born Marshall Co., AL, farmer, MO 6/16/64, Decatur, AL.

Eakins, Robert, Pvt., Co. D, age 31, EN & MI 8/24/63, Glendale, MS, on detached service at refugee camp in Memphis, TN 1/64-3/64, sick in hospital 7/64, born Marshall Co., AL, farmer, MO 9/26/64, Rome, GA.

Eakins, William T., Pvt., Co. D, age 25, EN & MI 6/1/63, Glendale, MS, company cook 4/64, born Marshall Co., AL, farmer, MO 6/16/64, Decatur, AL.

Earnest, David, Pvt., Co. C, absent sick in hospital at Memphis, TN 2/2/64.*

Earnest, Francis D., (Cards filed with Francis D. Ernest)

Earp, Daniel, Pvt., Co. M, age 40, EN & MI 9/5/64, Rome, GA, born Anderson Dist., SC, mechanic, daily duty in Regt. Carpenter Shop, sent to hospital from the front 11/3/63, MO 10/20/65, Huntsville, AL.

East, James M., Pvt., Co. K, age 19, EN 9/8/62, Iuka, MS, MI 10/1/62, Corinth, MS, born Patrick, VA, farmer, MO 9/16/63, Corinth, MS.

Eaton, Lewis Cass, Corp/Sgt., Co. F, EN 4/29/63, Corinth, MS, MI 8/13/63, Corinth, MS, born Whitley Co., KY, farmer, WIA 10/26/63, (probably Vincent's Crossroads), died 11/19/63, at Church Hospital, Memphis, TN. (Buried Grave # 1-41, Memphis National Cemetery.)

Eaton, Monroe, Pvt., Co. C, age 18, EN 12/1/62, Corinth, MS, MI 12/22/62, Corinth, MS, born Cass, NC, farmer, deserted 6/28/63.

Eaves, Dudley F., 2nd Lt., Co. G, age 30, EN 12/8/62, Oxford, MS, MI 12/8/62, Corinth, MS, first appt. 2nd Lt. of MS Rangers by Brig. Gen. C.S. Hamilton 12/8/62, MO 12/7/63, Memphis, TN.

Edgil, John, Co. M. age 36, born Morgan Co., AL, EN 12/20/63, Camp Davies, MS by Capt. Lomax, rejected by surgeon on account of imbecility 12/20/63.*

Edmonds, Emanuel, Pvt., Co. L, age 20, EN 9/25/63, Fayette Co., AL, MI 9/25/63, Glendale, MS, born Georgia, farmer, sick in USA Post Hospital in Corinth 12/5/63, discharged for disability 3/19/64, Memphis, TN, smallpox.

Edwards, Alonson W., 1st Lt/Capt., Co. L (F&S), age 22, promoted to 1st Lt. Co. I, 122nd Regt. Illinois Inf. Vols. 10/18/63, EN 9/18/63, Glendale, MS, promoted to Adjutant 3/2/64, appt. Capt. 7/1/64, in Savannah, GA 12/31/64, MO 6/1/65, Huntsville, AL.

Edwards, James, Pvt., Co. K, age 32, EN & MI 7/24/62, Huntsville, AL, born Morgan Co., AL, farmer, died in hospital at Nashville, TN 1/28/63 of disease. (Buried Grave # B5674, Nashville National Cemetery.)

Elkins, Francis C., Pvt., Co. F, age 22, EN 6/27/63, Corinth, MS, MI 8/13/63, Corinth, MS, born Choctaw Co., MS, farmer, deserted 9/15/63, Glendale, MS, returned 11/11/63, sick in Gayoso USA Hospital, Memphis, TN Jan. & Feb. 1864, MO 7/27/64, Rome, GA.

Elkins, William J., Pvt/Sgt., Co. G, age 21, EN 3/10/64, Decatur, AL, MI 4/13/64, Decatur, AL, born Lawrence Co., AL, farmer, appt. Sgt. 11/1/64, sick in Wilmington, NC 3/10/65.

Elliott, Samuel, Pvt/Sgt., Co. B, age 36, EN 2/4/64, Pulaski, TN, MI 3/27/64, Decatur, AL, born Pall. Co., GA, farmer, MO 10/20/65, Huntsville, AL.

Ellis, Charles, Pvt., Co. D, age 19, EN 4/19/64, Decatur, AL, MI 6/16/64, Decatur, AL, born Branberry, (or Brandon), KY, shoemaker, POW 2/18/65 near Fayetteville, NC, MO 6/13/65, Camp Chase, OH.

Ellis, Isaac R., Saddler/Pvt., Co. F, age 24, EN 3/27/63, Corinth, MS, MI 5/18/63, Corinth, MS, born Crawford Co., IN, shoemaker, POW 2/15/64 from Camp Davies, MS, no MO date.

Ellis, Lorenzo D., Corp/Sgt., Co. F, age 25, EN 6/25/63, Memphis, TN, MI 8/7/63, Corinth MS, born Cocke Co., TN, railroader, MO 7/27/64, Rome, GA.

Ellison, William J., Pvt., Co. H, age 17, EN 4/1/65, Stevenson, AL, MI 4/5/65, Nashville, TN, born Cherokee Co., GA, farmer, died 5/22/65 at hospital in Huntsville, AL of measles. (First buried in Grave 212, Huntsville, Cemetery, later reinterred Grave # L-558, Chattanooga National Cemetery.)

Emerich, George, Sgt., Co. E, transferred from 2nd Illinois Arty. 8/13/63 at Glendale, on detached service recruiting 11/22/63.*

Emmerson/Emerson, John, Pvt., Co. C, age 18, EN 2/1/64, Memphis, TN, MI 3/10/64, Memphis, TN, born McNairy Co., TN, farmer, POW 3/10/65, Monroe's Crossroads, Fayetteville, NC, in Tripler USA Gen. Hospital, Columbus, OH, Mar. & April 1865 where he was discharged 5/29/65, father shown as Arch Emersin.

Emrich/Emerick, George W., 1st Lt. Co. A, age 25, EN 2/4/64, Camp Davies, MS, born Ross Co., OH, WIA 3/10/65, Monroe's Crossroads, sent to Gen. Hosp. Wilmington, NC.

England, Francis Marion, Pvt., Co. K, age 17, EN 11/1/63, Glendale, MS, MI 11/1/63, Camp Davies, MS, born Morgan Co., AL, farmer, sick and sent to hospital in Nashville, TN 4/3/64, sick in Jeffersonville, IN May & June 1864, MO 7/19/65, Nashville, TN.

Entrican, John W., Pvt., Co. G, age 28, EN 3/5/63, Chewalla, TN, MI 3/5/63, Corinth, MS, died at Camp Davies, MS 12/20/63. (Buried Grave B-3495, Corinth National Cemetery.)

Epperson, Sanford J., Pvt., Co. K, age 25, EN 12/1/63, Camp Davies, MS, teamster, born Cherokee Co., AL, MO 7/19/65, Nashville, TN. Note states he traveled 90 miles from his home in Marion Co., AL to Camp Davies, MS to enlist.

Ernest, Francis D., Pvt., Co. C, age 18, EN 12/15/63, Camp Davies, MS, MI 4/30/64, Decatur, AL, born Fayette Co., AL, farmer, MO 10/20/65, Huntsville, AL.
   NOTE: Note in file states Francis D. Earnest died July 25, 1923 at Catalpa, Arkansas and that his widow's name was Sarah.

Ernest, William C., Pvt., Co. A, age 22, EN 1/5/64, Camp Davies, MS, MI 2/5/64, Memphis, TN, born Tuscaloosa Co., AL, farmer, POW 3/10/65, Solomon Grove, NC, sent to Richmond, VA. (A William Ernest of the 1st AL Cav. is buried in Grave A-1979, Corinth National Cemetery.)

Estell, William L., Pvt., Co. M, age 25, EN 12/12/63, Camp Davies, MS, MI 12/29/63, Corinth, MS, born Marion Co., AL, farmer, sick in hospital in Chattanooga, TN 5/22/64, deserted 6/1/65 with Smith carbine, Colt and equipment, died of disease 6/1/65 at Decatur, AL.

Evans, Edmund R., Sgt., Co. K, age 37, EN & MI 7/24/62, Huntsville, AL, born Morgan Co., AL, on recruiting service in TN 11/10/64, died 2/5/65 in hospital at Mooresville, AL of smallpox, one POW Record.

Evins, William C., Pvt., Co. D, age 18, EN 5/12/64, Larkinsville, AL, MI Rome, GA, born Marion Co., AL, POW 3/10/65 at Solomon Grove, NC, paroled in MD.

Ezell, James, Pvt., Co. M, age 18, EN 9/14/63, Chewalla, TN, born McNairy Co., TN, farmer, deserted 10/26/63, Glendale, MS.

Ezell, Thomas L., Pvt., Co. M, age 31, EN 8/9/63, Chewalla, TN, MI 12/29/63, Corinth, MS, born Lauderdale Co., AL, mechanic, died 3/10/64 in hospital at Memphis, TN of smallpox. Receipt in file stated his wife was Mrs. Nancy Ezell. (Buried in Memphis National Cemetery.)

Fagans, William B., Pvt., Co. G, age 18, EN 4/24/64, Mooresville, AL, MI Rome, GA, born Forsythe Co., GA, farmer, MO 10/20/65, Huntsville, AL.

Fairfield, Micajah F., Major, (F&S), age 40, EN 4/22/63, Corinth, MS, appt. from 1st Lt. 15th Illnois Cav., resigned 9/2/64.
NOTE: Major Fairfield was born in Pittsford, Vermont but was a resident of Ottawa, IL where he worked in the lumber industry. He was married and had three children. The 15th IL Cav. was based in TN until March 1863 when they were transferred to Corinth, MS where Gen. Dodge detailed Fairfield to help recruit a regiment of patriotic white Southerners who would fight for restoration of the Union. He took command of the 1st AL Cav. US in April 1863. It was during this duty that he contracted typhoid fever. In September of 1863, the regimental surgeon warned him that the two day scouting missions were doing him physical injustice and that he should no longer expose himself to the heat of the day or night air. He finally resigned and returned to Ottawa, IL but after his physician recommended a change of climate, he moved to Minnesota in 1866 and started a business. He died there in 1872 of tuberculosis. His wife died in 1899 of the same disease.

Farmer/Foman, Simon, undercook, Co. A, (Colored), age 37, EN & MI 10/24/64, Rome, GA, born Spartanburg Dist., SC, teamster, MO 10/20/65, Huntsville, AL.

Faulkner, Frank, Pvt., Co. E, EN 12/25/62, Chewalla, TN, MI 12/28/62, Corinth, MS, died 3/20/63, Corinth, MS.

Faulkner, William, Pvt., Co. H, on daily duty as company cook.*

Feamster, William J., Pvt., Co. A, age 18, EN 1/3/64, Camp Davies, MS, MI 3/5/64, Memphis, TN, born Lowndes Co., MS, farmer, sick in hospital Indianapolis, IN 10/3/64, discharged 11/21/64 at Jeffersonville, IN for disability.

Feltman/Felpman, Benjamin F., Pvt., Co. L, age 20, EN 9/25/63, Fayette Co., AL, MI 9/25/63, Glendale, MS, born Fayette Co., AL, farmer, MO 9/28/64, Rome, GA, reenlisted 3/1/65, Stevenson, AL, MI 4/18/65, Nashville, TN, MO 10/20/65, Huntsville, AL.

Feltman, Isom/Isham B., Pvt., Co. L, age 21, EN 9/25/63, Fayette Co., AL, MI 9/25/63, Glendale, MS, born Fayette Co., AL, farmer, MO 9/28/64, Rome, GA, reenlisted 1/1/65, Stevenson, AL, MI 1/1/65, Nashville, TN, MO 10/20/65, Huntsville, AL.

Felton, Abraham, Pvt., Co. I, age 30, EN & MI 7/21/62, Huntsville, AL, born Paulding Co., GA, school teacher, died 12/22/62 in Hospital #12, Nashville, TN of typhoid fever.

Ferguson, J.C., Pvt., Co. H, EN 10/18/63, Glendale, MS.*

Fielder, Enos T., Pvt., Co. H, age 19, EN 2/17/65, Stevenson, AL, MI 2/19/65, Nashville, TN, born Dekalb Co., GA, farmer, MO 10/20/65, Huntsville, AL.

Fielder, John N., Pvt/Sgt. Co. H, age 18, EN 2/17/65, Stevenson, AL, born Dekalb Co., GA, farmer, MO 10/20/65, Huntsville, AL.

Fields, Isaac, Pvt., Co. D, age 45, EN 5/20/64, Decatur, AL, MI 6/16/64, Decatur, AL, born Jefferson Co., AL, farmer, in USA Gen. Hospital in Savannah, GA 2/1/65, MO 10/20/65, Huntsville, AL.

Fields, William, Pvt., Co. C, EN 12/20/62, Corinth, MS, MI 12/22/62, Corinth, MS.

Files, James L., Pvt., Co. L, killed in action 12/24/63 in Tennessee.*

Files, Jeremiah F., 2nd LT., Co. L&A, age 27, EN 9/25/63, Fayette Co., AL, MI 10/8/63, Glendale, MS, sick in Officer's Hospital at Memphis, TN March & April 1864, resigned 5/13/64 at Snake Gap, GA.
NOTE: In Case No. 116312 of the Southern Claims Commission filed by Jeremiah Files, he states the following: *"From April 1862 until June 1865 I spent my time between Fayette Co., Ala. and the Union lines, and also in the Union lines... My business was a portion of the time recruiting for the Union Army. I crossed quite a number of times between April 1862 and March 1864 for the purpose of getting Union men out of the rebel lines and getting them into the Union lines. I then joined the Union Army at Glendale, Miss., I joined the First Reg. Ala. Cav. Vol. commanded by Col. Geor. E. Spencer and remained with the army until Nov. Folowing on the 24th day of November 1863 I left camp at Camp Davies, Miss. with two other soldiers and came back to Fayette Co., Ala. and got about fifty Union men and reached camp at Camp Davies taking the above mentioned number of Union men with me and reached there on the 13th day of December 1863. I then remained in the Union lines, until the summer of 1864, I then taken up the same occupation gathering Union men for the Union army and was so employed until the surrender. In the summer of 1865, I came back to my farm where I now reside.*

I was threatened by every rebel that knew me with damage to my person and property. I was threatened to be hanged, shot, and even burned, all on account of my Union sentiments. I influenced about five hundred men to go in to the army...

I did not have any relatives in the rebel army except cousins. I had two brothers and two nephews, also two brothers in law and quite a number of cousins in the Union army....."

Files, Jesse, Pvt., Co. L, age 39, EN 9/5/63, Fayette Co., AL, MI 9/25/63, Glendale, MS, born Jefferson Co., AL, farmer, MO 9/28/64, Rome, GA. (One Return states he died of disease in Memphis, 3/4/64.)

Files, Jesse L., Pvt., Co. L, age 17, EN 9/25/63, Fayette Co., AL, MI 9/25/63, Glendale, MS, born Fayette Co., AL, farmer, KIA 12/24/63 at Jack's Creek, TN.

Files, John, Pvt., Co. L, age 18, EN 9/25/63, Fayette Co., AL, MI 9/25/63, Glendale, MS, born Fayette Co., AL, farmer, MO 9/28/64, Rome, GA.

Files, Thomas B., Pvt/Sgt., Co. A, age 24, EN 3/23/63, Glendale, MS, MI 3/24/63, Glendale, MS, promoted to Sgt. 7/1/63, MO 12/22/63, Memphis, TN.

Finch, Francis M., Pvt., Co. B, age 29, EN 7/14/63, Glendale, MS, MI 7/14/63, Corinth, MS, born Spartanburg Dist., SC, farmer, POW 10/26/63, Vincent's Crossroads, MO 1/22/64, Memphis, TN.

Finerty/Finnerty, Thomas W., Corp., Co. K, age 36, EN & MI 7/31/62, Huntsville, AL, born Rockingham, VA, farmer, died 10/20/62 in Hospital #14, Nashville, TN of rubeola.

Finley, James, Pvt., Co. H, age 19, EN 2/20/65, Huntsville, AL, MI 4/5/65, Nashville, TN, born Hawkins Co., TN, AWOL 6/27/65, MO 10/20/65, Huntsville, AL.

Fish, O., Co. F, absent sick in US General Hospital, location not known at this time.*

Fishback, Oliver H., Lt., Co. L&F, age 21, EN 1/7/64, Camp Davies, MS, MI 6/7/64, Memphis, TN, sick in Carlinville, IL 8/18/65, appt. 2nd Lt. from Sgt., 2nd Ills. Lt. Arty.

Fisher, Pleasant P., Pvt., Co. E, EN 3/1/63, Glendale, MS, MI 3/1/63, Corinth, MS, on detached service as teamster in Vicksburg, MS, 1/25/64, MO 3/1/64, Memphis, TN.

Fisher, Thomas J., Pvt., Co. E, EN 3/1/63, Glendale, MS, MI 3/31/63, Corinth, MS, deserted 12/10/63 near Corinth, MS to go to 6th TN Cav.

Fitzpatrick, John C., Pvt., Co. M, age 17, EN 12/8/63, Camp Davies, MS, EN 12/8/63, Corinth, MS, born Itawamba Co., MS, deserted 11/11/64 at Rome, GA with Smith carbine and Remington revolver.

Flannagan, Andrew P., Pvt., Co. G, age 18, EN 4/24/64, Mooresville, AL, MI Rome, GA, born Dekalb Co., AL, farmer, MO 10/20/65, Huntsville, AL.

Flippor, Francis M., Pvt., Co. H, age 18, EN 4/20/65, Huntsville, AL, MI 5/20/65, Nashville, TN, born Jackson Co., AL, farmer, MO 10/20/65, Huntsville, AL.

Flint, Mortimer R., Capt., Co. E, age 27, EN 11/18/63, Camp Davies, MS, promoted from 1st Lt., Co. D, 10th MO Vols. Cav., MO 1/18/65, Savannah, GA.

Floyd, John A., Pvt., Co. C, age 26, EN 7/10/63, Glendale, MS, MI 8/15/63, Corinth, MS, born Henderson, TN, farmer, in Adams USA Gen. Hospital, Memphis, TN 1/20/64, MO 7/27/64, Rome, GA.

Floyd, William D., Sgt. Co. A&F, age 23, EN 1/23/64, Camp Davies, MS, MI 2/5/64, Memphis, TN, born Murray Co., GA, farmer, MO 10/20/65, Huntsville, AL.

Fonsh, James, Co. L, absent on detached service 9/64.*

Ford, James A/N, , Pvt., Co. F, age 34, EN 11/25/63, Camp Davies, MS, MI 2/24/64, Memphis, TN, farmer, born Monroe Co., GA, in Washington USA Gen. Hospital in Memphis, TN Jan. & Feb. 1864, sick in Nashville, TN 4/30/64, sick in USA Gen. Hospital in Madison, Ind. March & April 1865, MO 5/2/65.

NOTE: Records on James A. Ford and John H. Ford are all mixed up together. Anyone wishing to request military records on either soldier, need to request both files.

Ford, John A., Pvt., Co. F, age 25, EN 11/25/63, Camp Davies, MS, MI 2/24/64, Memphis, TN, born Harris Co., GA, farmer, died 9/17/64, Chattanooga, TN. (Buried Grave #E-220, Chattanooga National Cemetery.)

Ford, Joseph, Capt., Co. H, age 30, EN 10/18/63, Glendale, MS, MI 12/28/63, Camp Davies, MS, MO 11/3/64, Rome, GA.

Ford, Joseph M., Pvt., Co. M, age 19, EN 12/25/63, Camp Davies, MS, MI 12/25/63, Corinth, MS, born Henry Co., GA, farmer, sick in Small Pox USA Gen. Hospital in Memphis, TN 2/25/64, sick in Hospital #1, Nashville, TN 6/28/64, sick in Totten USA Gen. Hospital in Louisville, KY July & Aug. 1864, residence shown as Marion Co., AL.

Ford, Michael D., Pvt., Co. G, age 17, EN 7/11/63, Glendale, MS, MI 7/11/63, Corinth, MS, MO 11/26/63, Memphis, TN.

Ford, Richmond, Saddler, Co. K, age 25, EN & MI 12/13/63, Camp Davies, MS, born Dekalb Co., GA, in secret service in AL 11/10/64, MO 7/19/65, Nashville, TN. Note in file states he traveled 300 miles from Randolph Co., AL to Camp Davies, MS to enlist.

Ford, Thomas, Pvt., Co. F, age 23, EN 5/15/63, Memphis, TN, MI 8/13/63, Corinth, MS, born New York City, NY, seaman, POW 10/26/63, Vincent's Crossroads, in hospital at Louisville, KY from wounds received 10/26/63, in DeCamp USA Gen. Hospital at David's Island, NY 10/13/65, right leg amputated, exchanged POW 4/5/65. He stated he was held in prison at Andersonville & Cahawba, AL. (Several documents in his file concerning desertion and assumed name.)

Ford, William, Pvt., Co. M, age 39, EN 9/14/63, Chewalla, TN, born Hardiman Co., TN, farmer, deserted 10/28/63, Glendale, MS.

Forest, Israel, Co. D, discharged for disability at Glendale, MS 4/5/63.*

Forest, Thomas, Co. F, absent with leave in Alabama 11/63.*

Forman, Elijah, Pvt., Co. B, age 23, EN 1/18/63, Glendale, MS, MI 1/22/63, Corinth, MS, born Marshall Co., AL, died 6/4/63, Glendale, MS of valvular disease to the heart.

Forrester, John T., Pvt., Co. M, age 16, EN 9/6/63, Chewalla, TN, MI 9/6/63, Corinth, MS, born Tishamingo Co., MS, deserted at Rome, GA 11/11/64 with Smith carbine & Remington revolver.

Forrister, John, Co. L, on detached service as nurse in hospital at Memphis, TN 1/64.*

Forsythe, Thomas J., Pvt., Co. I, age 30, EN & MI 8/18/62, Huntsville, AL, born Habersham Co., GA, farmer, with wagon train in Nashville, TN 12/27/62, on detached service as courier at Reedyville, TN 1/27/83, MIA 4/28/63 at Days Gap, AL.

Fortner, William D., Pvt., Co. H, Bugler, age 33, EN 9/13/63, Glendale, MS, MO 9/29/64 at Rome, GA.

Foster, John, Pvt., Co. K, age 21, EN & MI 12/13/63, Camp Davies, MS, born Washington Co., IL, farmer, traveled 250 miles from Chattanooga, TN to enlist, on detached service as teamster in Gen. Sherman's expedition 1/24/64, MO 7/19/65.

Foster, Samuel M., Pvt., Co. D, age 18, EN 5/20/64, Decatur, AL, MI 6/16/64, Decatur, AL, born Calhoun Co., AL, farmer, MO 10/20/65, Huntsville, AL.

Foust/Forest, John M., Pvt., Co. L, age 21, EN 9/25/63, Fayette Co., AL, MI 9/25/63, Glendale, MS, detached 10/1/63 as scout for Gen. Dodge, MIA 10/26/63 from Vincent's Crossroads.

Fowler, Israel, Pvt., Co. D, age 19, EN 5/3/63, Glendale, MS, born Marion Co., AL, farmer, died 7/28/63 of disease in the Post Hospital at Corinth, MS. (Buried Grave #A-2190, Corinth National Cemetery.)

Fowler, James, Pvt., Co. H, age 18, EN & MI, 9/13/63, Glendale, MS, MO 9/29/64, Rome, GA.

Fowler, L., Pvt., Co. D, enrolled 5/31/63 at Glendale, MS.*

Fowler, Samuel B., Pvt/Corp., Co. E, age 25, EN & MI 10/4/64, Rome, GA, born Dekalb Co., GA, farmer, promoted to Corp. 10/20/64, MO 10/20/65, Huntsville, AL.

Fowler, William, Pvt., Co. D, age 18, EN 5/3/63, Glendale, MS, born Marion Co., AL, farmer, died 7/4/63 at Corinth, MS of imbecility.

Fowler, William N., Pvt., Co. E, EN 3/1/63, Corinth, MS, deserted 5/1/63, Glendale, MS.

Frambers, Samuel C., Pvt., Co. A, deserted at Memphis, TN 2/4/64.*

Frankes, Peter, Pvt., Co. A, EN 12/15/62, Glendale, MS, MI 12/31/62, Corinth, MS, MO 12/22/63, Memphis, TN.

Franklin, R.J., Pvt., Co. I, absent with leave 9/63.*

Franks, James M., Pvt., Co. A, age 23, EN 12/15/62, Glendale, MS, MI 12/31/62, Corinth, MS, died 2/5/63, Corinth, MS of measles.

Franks, Jeremiah/Jerry, Pvt., Co. A, age 18, EN 12/15/62, Glendale, MS, MI 12/31/62, Corinth, MS, born Marion Co., AL, farmer, MO 12/22/63, Memphis, TN, reenlisted 2/1/64, Memphis, TN, MI 3/10/64, Memphis, TN, sick in USA Gen. Hospital at Savannah, GA 1/23/65, MO 10/20/65, Huntsville, AL.

Franks, William, Pvt., Co. A, age 23, EN 12/15/62, Glendale, MS, MI 12/31/62, Corinth, MS, on detached service at refugee camp in Corinth, 11/29/63, MO 12/22/63, Memphis, TN.

Freehour, W.H., Pvt., Co. E, deserted 5/4/63.*

Freeman, Benjamin F., Pvt., Co. B, age 18, EN 3/18/64, Decatur, AL, MI 4/13/64, Decatur, AL, born Cherokee Co., GA, farmer, left sick in hospital at Savannah, GA 2/3/65, MO 9/9/65 from Washington, DC, residence shown as Walker Co., AL.

Freeman, John, Pvt., Co. I, enlisted 11/1/63 at Glendale, MS, deserted 12/17/63 at Camp Davies, MS.*

Freeman, John, Co. I, age 27, born Cherokee Co., GA, farmer, EN 10/10/63, Glendale, MS.*

Freeman, Robert D., Pvt., Co. F, age 44, EN 6/5/63, Corinth, MS, MI 8/13/63, Corinth, MS, born Choctaw Co., MS, died 9/29/63 at Glendale, MS.

French, (?), Co. A, on detached service as guide 10/64.*

Fresham, William N., Pvt., Co. E, age 18, EN 3/1/63, Corinth MS, MI 3/13/63, Glendale, deserted 6/1/63, Glendale, MS.

Fretwell, Esby, Pvt/Corp., Co. G, age 38, EN 3/21/64, Decatur, AL, MI 4/13/64, Decatur, AL, born Winston Co., AL, farmer, MO 10/20/65, Huntsville, AL.

Fretwell, William W., Pvt., Co. G, age 42, EN 3/21/64, Decatur, AL, MI 4/13/64, Decatur, AL, born Blount, AL, farmer, MO 10/20/65, Huntsville, AL.

Frost, Christopher S., Pvt., Co. H, age 18, EN 10/18/64, Rome, GA, MI 10/16/65, Huntsville, AL, born Walker Co., AL, farmer, in Jefferson USA Gen. Hospital in Jeffersonville, IN 12/15/64, MO 10/20/65, Huntsville, AL.

Froshour, Samuel C., Pvt., Co. A, age 22, EN 12/26/63, Camp Davies, MI 2/5/64, Memphis, TN, born Walker Co., AL, farmer, deserted 2/4/64, Memphis, TN.

Fry, J.H., Pvt., Co. L, discharged 9/29/64 at Rome, GA by reason of expiration of term of service.*

Fry, Thomas W., Pvt., Co. L, age 20, EN 9/25/63, Fayette Co., AL, MI 9/25/63, Glendale, MS, born Forsythe Co., GA, farmer, returned from desertion 12/2/63, MO 9/28/64, Rome, GA.
  NOTE: Thomas Fry was born April 4, 1843 in Forsythe Co., GA and married Mary Laissa Ingle. He died March 17, 1926, Pittsburg Co., OK. His sister, Sarah Fry, married Murry/Murray Ingle, also in this regiment.[66]

Funderburk, Christopher C., Corp., Co. K, age 25, EN & MI 7/24/62, Huntsville, AL, born Rome, GA, farmer, sent to Winston Co., AL to recruit and never heard from since 8/13/62, died 2/21/64 while POW.

Furth, Elmore, Pvt., Co. E, in Gayoso USA Hospital at Memphis, TN Jan & Feb 1864.*

Gaddy, Calvin M., Pvt., Co. E, age 23, EN 12/8/62, Chewalla, TN, MI 12/8/62, Corinth, MS, MO 12/17/63, Memphis, TN.

Gaddy, Stephen H., Pvt., Co. E, age 18, EN 12/8/62, Chewalla, TN, MI 12/8/62, Corinth, MS, MO 12/17/63, Memphis, TN.

Gaggers, G.W., Co. D, EN 12/10/63.*

Gaha, William C., (Cards filed with William C. McGaha)

Gailey, David J., Pvt/Corp., Co. A, age 24, EN 9/8/62, Iuka, MS, MI 10/1/62, Corinth, MS, born Habersham Co., GA, in Washington USA Gen. Hospital in Memphis, TN May & June 1863, MO 9/16/63, Corinth, MS.

Gaines, Charles W., Pvt., Co. H, age 28, EN 12/20/64, Rome, GA, MI 2/13/65, Nashville, TN, born Gwinnet Co., GA, saddler, died 3/8/65 in hospital at Huntsville, AL of smallpox.

Gains, Ralph, Co. E, absent sick 3/63.*

Galaway, Jason, Pvt., Co. B, in USA General Field Hospital at Stevenson, AL Sept & Oct 1863.*

Galbraith, John, Pvt., Co. C, in General Hospital #2 at Louisville, KY Nov & Dec 1865.*

Gallion, John, Pvt., Co. H., in Small Pox USA Hospital at Memphis, TN 3/28/64.*

Galloway, J.C., Pvt., Co. B, in USA General Hospital at Evansville, Indiana Nov & Dec 1863.*

Gallowa, Jason J. (or C.), Pvt., Co. B, in Crittenden USA General Hospital at Louisville, KY 2/10/64.*

Gammill, Joseph E., Sgt., Co. F, age 32, EN 5/23/63, Corinth, MS, MI 8/13/63, Corinth, MS, born Pickens Co., AL, farmer, AWOL 10/1/63.

Gammville, G., Sgt., Co. F, deserted while on furlough 9/24/63.*

Gann, David, Pvt., Co. A, transferred to Co. B, 1st Ala. Cav., 3/1/63 at Glendale, MS.*

Gann, G.W., Co. F, hospital nurse 9/63.*

Gann, Newton E., Co. F, age 27, EN 6/29/63, Corinth, MS, deserted from Glendale, MS 9/20/63.*

Gann/Gan, Newton E., Pvt., Co. F, age 27, EN 6/29/63, Corinth, MS, MI 8/13/63, Corinth, MS, born McNariy Co., TN, died 2/11/64 in Memphis, TN of smallpox. (Buried in Memphis National Cemetery.)

Gann, Smith W., Pvt., Co. F, age 23, EN 11/25/63, Camp Davies, MS, born Marion Co., AL, farmer, in Adams USA Gen. Hospital in Memphis TN 2/17/64, sick in Rome, GA July 1864, MO 12/17/64, Savannah, GA "by reason of being on march from Atlanta to Savannah".

Ganns, David F., Pvt., Co. K&A, age 19, EN 12/11/62, Glendale, MS, MI 12/31/62, Corinth, MS, born Marion Co., AL, died 4/12/63 in camp at Glendale, MS of measles.

Ganns, David J., Pvt., Co. A, absent sick near camp at house.*

Gans, David, Pvt., Co. K, age 36, MI 1/22/63, Corinth, MS, born Newell, TN, farmer, sick at home in AL 3/8/63, sick in refugee camp at Corinth, MS 11/15/63. (No further information on this soldier.)

Garden, Samuel, (Cards filed with Samuel J. Gordon)

Gardner, Charles, Pvt/Bugler, Co. F, age 25, EN 5/25/63, Memphis, TN, MI 8/7/63, Corinth, MS, in confinement at Corinth, MS Nov. & Dec. 1863, born Bourbon Co., KY, butcher, MO 7/27/64, Rome, GA.

Gardner, James, Pvt., Co. I, deserted in Winston Co., AL 10/24/63.*

Gardner, John, Pvt., Co. I, age 21, EN 10/1/63, Glendale, MS, MI 10/1/63, Camp Davies, MS, born Winston Co., AL, farmer, sick in Overton USA Gen. Hospital at Memphis,TN 1/20/64, deserted 10/24/63, rejoined 11/10/63, MO 7/19/65, Nashville, TN.

Gardner, John Q.A., Sgt/Lt., Co. E, age 37, EN 2/1/62, Corinth, MS, promoted from Orderly Sgt. to 2nd Lt. 9/25/63, MO 9/28/64, Rome, GA.

Gardner, William, Corp. Co. I, age 23, EN 11/15/63, Camp Davies, MS, born Winston Co., AL, farmer, appt. Corp. 12/1/63, MO 7/19/65, Nashville, TN.

Garrett, Dorsey, Pvt., Co. D, in Webster USA General Hospital at Memphis, TN March & April 1864.*

Garrett, James, Pvt., Co. H, absent sick in Alabama 10/20/63, ambulance driver March & April 1864.*

Gay, Johnathan, Pvt/Sgt., Co. B, age 25, EN 4/10/64, Decatur, AL, MI 4/13/64, Decatur, AL, born Morgan Co., AL, farmer, appt. Corp. 8/1/64, promoted Sgt. 6/1/65, MO 10/20/65, Huntsville, AL.

Gay, William R., Corp/Sgt. Co. I, age 24, EN & MI 7/21/62, Huntsville, AL, on courier duty at Reedyville, TN 1/27/63, sick in hospital at Murfreesboro, TN 6/24/63, MIA 10/26/63 at Vincent's Crossroads, returned 11/1/63, appt. Sgt. 1/1/64, MO 7/19/65, Huntsville, AL.

Gaylor, Robert, Pvt., Co. M, age 18, EN & MI 9/5/64, Rome, GA, born Cherokee Co., AL, farmer, attached to Foster USA Gen. Hospital at Durham Station, New Berne, NC as nurse, 3/20/65, MO 10/20/65, Huntsville, AL.

Gean, John, Pvt., Co. F, age 29, TN, farmer, EN 7/6/63, Corinth, MS, MI 8/13/63, Corinth, MS, born Clinton Co., TN, deserted 9/20/63 from Glendale, MS.

Gean, Wiley R. (or F), Pvt., Co. F, age 27, EN 7/6/63, Corinth, MS, MI 8/13/63, Corinth, MS, born Louden Co., TN, deserted 9/20/63 from Glendale, MS.

Gean, William R., Pvt., Co. F, age 25, EN 7/6/63, Corinth, MS, MI 8/13/63, Corinth, MS, born Clinton Co., TN, farmer, deserted 9/20/63 from Glendale, MS.

Gear, J.J., Co. F, absent nurse at Corinth, MS 7/63.*

Gentry, John L., Pvt., Co. C, age 26, EN 12/1/62, MI 12/22/62, Corinth, MS, born Shelby Co., AL, farmer, died 6/3/63 in camp at Glendale, MS.

Gerrings, D., Pvt., Co. D, absent sick in Memphis, TN 4/64.*

Ghist, William H., Pvt., Co. A, age 18, EN 9/8/62, Iuka, MS, MI 10/1/62, Corinth, MS, born Marion Co., AL, farmer, MO 9/16/63, Corinth, MS.

Gibbs, Anderson, Pvt., Co. H, age 45, EN & MI 10/17/63, Glendale, MS, MO 10/24/64, Rome, GA.

Gibbs, John W., Pvt/Sgt., Co. H, age 18, EN 5/1/65, Huntsville, AL, MI 5/20/65, Nashville, TN, born Cherokee Co., AL, farmer, appt. Sgt. 7/15/65, MO 10/20/65, Huntsville, AL.

Gibson, Jackson E., Pvt., Co. C, age 23, EN 2/10/63, Corinth, MS, born Gilmore Co., GA, farmer, MO 10/20/65, Huntsville, AL.

Gibson, John, Pvt., Co. K, EN 11/22/63 at Camp Davies, MS.*

Gibson, John H., Pvt., Co. C, age 28, EN 12/6/62, Corinth, MS, MI 12/22/63, Corinth, MS, born Simpson, MS, farmer, died 5/26/63 in hospital at Glendale, MS.

Gibson, M., Pvt., Co. L, EN 10/15/63 at Glendale, MS.*

Gibson, Richard B., Pvt., Co. I, age 21, EN 8/26/62, Huntsville, AL, MI 8/26/62, Nashville, TN, born Morgan Co., AL, farmer, on duty as courier 1/27/63 at Reedyville, TN, MO 7/19/65, Nashville, TN.
        NOTE: Richard Gibson was the son of James W. Gibson and Mary Day and the grandson of John Gibson and of David Day, Jr. He had a number of cousins in Co. I, 1st AL Cav. USA. After the war he returned to his home and married Emily Day and they had seven children. He died June 21, 1925 at age 84.[67]

Gibson, William R., Pvt., Co. D, absent sick in Refugee Camp 11/5/63.*

Gilbreth, George W., Pvt., Co. G, age 18, EN 4/24/64, Mooresville, AL, MI Rome, GA, born Dekalb Co., AL, MO 10/20/65, Huntsville, AL.

Gilbreath, James M., Pvt., Co. H, age 30, EN 3/1/65, Stevenson, AL, MI 4/5/65, Nashville, TN, born Jefferson Co., TN, farmer, MO 10/20/65, Huntsville, AL.

Gillim/Gilliam, David C., Pvt., Co. A, age 19, EN 1/23/64, Camp Davies, MS, MI 2/5/64, Memphis, TN, born Fayette Co., AL, farmer, sick in Gayoso USA Hospital in Memphis, TN 2/14/64, MO 10/20/65.

Ginn, Benjamin F., Pvt., Co. G, age 20, EN 2/20/63, Chewalla, TN, MI 2/20/63, Corinth, MS, sick at Pocahontas, TN 8/25/63, sick at Memphis, TN Oct. 1863, MO 11/26/63, Memphis, TN.

Gird, W.F., Co. F, absent POW 11/63.*

Gist, Sidney C., Pvt., Co. C, EN 1/1/63, Chewalla, TN, deserted 3/18/63 from Glendale, MS.

Glascow, William, Pvt., Co. A, age 22, EN 12/26/63, Camp Davies, MS, MI 2/5/64, Memphis, TN, born Marion Co., AL, farmer, in arrest in prison at Athens, AL, April 1864, charged with desertion, MO 10/20/65, Huntsville, AL.

Glascow, William, Pvt., Co. E, EN 3/6/63, Tishomingo, MS, MI 3//63, Glendale, MS, deserted 4/25/63, Glendale, MS.

Glass, Elisha, Pvt., Co. G, age 19, EN 3/23/64, Decatur, AL, MI 10/16/65, Huntsville, AL, born Marion Co., AL, farmer, sick in hospitals at Chattanooga, TN; Resacca, GA; & Kingston, GA, MO 10/20/65, Huntsville, AL.

Gleen, J., Pvt., Co. B, died 3/9/64 at Richmond, VA.* (This is probably the James H. Glenn, below.)

Glenn, George W., Pvt., Co. I, absent sick in hospital at Memphis, TN 1/20/64.*

Glenn, James F., Pvt., Co. B, age 47, EN 1/13/63, Glendale, MS, MI 1/22/63, Corinth, MS, born Lawrence, SC, farmer, from May-August 1863, he was absent to take his family to Illinois where he died August 10, 1863 in Perry Co.
   NOTE: James F. Glenn was born about 1816 and married Mary Mitchell in Laurens District, SC June 10, 1846. Their children were: David, born July 29, 1851; Ensley H., born June 12, 1857; Rupel P., born June 11, 1860; and Mary J., born January 4, 1863. Affidavits state, *"the soldier, together with about 300 other parties, mostly families of Union men in Alabama, who had joined the Union army, sick and convalescent Union Soldiers, were ordered to go to Illinois by Col. Morrow, who at that time had command. At that point, James F. Glenn, then very sick with chronic diarrhea was among the number..."*[68]

Glenn, James H., Pvt., Co. B, age 18, EN 12/15/62, Glendale, MS, MI 12/31/62, Corinth, MS, born Lawrence, SC, POW at Belle Island, VA, admitted to hospital at Richmond,VA 2/24/64 where he died 3/9/64. (Buried in Richmond National Cemetery.)

Glenn, John W.F., Pvt., Co. I, age 20, EN & MI 12/21/63, Camp Davies, MS, sick in hospital at Memphis, TN 1/20/64, died 6/11/64 at Jefferson Barracks in St. Louis, MO of disease.

Glenn, Mathew H., Pvt., Co. B, age 19, EN 1/13/63, Glendale, MS, born Marion Co., AL, farmer, MI 1/22/63, Corinth, MS, sick in hospital at Corinth, MS 3/26/63, MO 1/22/64, Memphis, TN.

Glover, Silas J., Pvt., Co. D, age 24, EN 5/20/64, Decatur, AL, MI 6/16/64, Decatur, AL, born Jefferson Co., AL, farmer, MO 10/20/65, Huntsville, AL.

Glover, William, Pvt/Corp., Co. G, age 21, EN 3/10/64, Decatur, AL, MI 4/13/64, Decatur, AL, born Montgomery, AL, farmer, deserted 11/17/64 at Atlanta, GA with side arms.

Glover, William J., Pvt/Corp., Co. D, age 22, EN 5/20/64, Decatur, AL, MI 6/16/64, Decatur, AL, born Jefferson Co., AL, farmer, appt. Corp. 12/1/64, MO 10/20/65, Huntsville, AL.

Godfrey, George L., Maj/Lt. Col., (F&S), age 27, EN 10/18/63, Glendale, MS, promoted from Lt. and Adjutant 2nd Iowa Inf. Vols. to Major 10/18/63, promoted to Lt. Col. 5/8/64, was in charge of stores at Savannah, GA 1/19/65, MO 10/20/65, Huntsville, AL.

Godsey, John, Pvt., Co. D, transferred from Co. D to Co. A 7/28/64, Rome, GA.*

Godsey, John J., Pvt/Corp., Co. A, age 18, EN 5/4/64, Decatur, AL, MI Rome, GA, born Morgan Co., AL, farmer, promoted to Corp. 11/1/64, MO 10/20/65, Huntsville, AL.

Godsey, Robert A., Pvt., Co. D, age 22, EN 2/15/63, Glendale, MS, born Morgan Co., AL, farmer, taken POW 4/25/63 during Tuscumbia Raid, deserted 11/26/63 from Camp Davies, MS.

Godwin/Goodwin, Henry K., Pvt., Co. K, age 26, EN 8/25/62, Huntsville, AL, MI 11/1/62, Nashville, TN where he was MI to Co. F, 1st Middle TN Cav., born Cass Co., GA, farmer, POW at Days Gap, AL 5/1/63, paroled 5/13/63 from Richmond, VA, WIA 10/26/63 at Vincent's Crossroads and his right arm was amputated, died 12/9/63 of gangrene in Memphis, TN. (Buried Grave #1-38, Memphis National Cemetery.)

Godwin, James A., Corp., Co. C, in General Hospital #2 at Louisville, KY Nov & Dec 1863.*

Godwin, Samuel J., Pvt., Co. K, age 24, EN 8/25/62, Huntsville, AL, MI 9/25/62, Co. F, 1st Middle TN Cav. Nashville, TN, born Cass Co., GA, farmer, MIA at Crooked Creek, AL 4/30/63, MIA 10/26/63, Vincent's Crossroads, on detached service as teamster in Gen. Sherman's expedition 1/24/64, POW 3/24/64 in AR, near Memphis.

Goff, William T., Pvt., Co. A, age 18, EN 8/1/64, Rome, GA, MI 10/20/64, Rome, GA, born Lawrence Co., AL, POW 9/11/64 near Rome, GA and never heard from again.

Goggiss/Gargis, Meridith, Pvt., Co. E, EN 3/1/63, Glendale, MS, MI 3/6/63, Corinth, MS, deserted 7/63.

Going, Doctor, Pvt/Sgt., Co. D, age 44, EN 3/15/63, Glendale, MS, MI 3/26/63, Corinth, MS, born Pittsylvania, VA, farmer, reduced to ranks 12/3/63, MO 5/18/64, Cairo, IL.

Good, William, Co. F, absent POW 4/65.*

Good, William A., age 29, born Green Co., IN, EN 1/29/64 at Bridgeport, AL.*

Goode, James, Pvt., Co. K, died 3/6/63, Nashville, TN. (Buried in Grave E-0850 in Nashville National Cemetery.)

Goode, John M., Pvt., Co. K, age 30, EN & MI 8/22/62, Huntsville, AL, born Lauderdale Co., AL, POW at Days Gap, AL 5/1/63, paroled 5/13/63 at Richmond,

VA, on detached service as teamster in Gen. Sherman's expedition 1/24/64, died 3/3/64 near Vicksburg, MS of smallpox.

Goodwin, Jas. A., Corp., in USA General Field Hospital at Stevenson, AL Sept. & Oct. 1863.*

Goodwin, James A., Corp., Co. C, in USA General Hospital #2 at Louisville, KY Jan-April 1864.*

Goof, William T., Pvt., Co. F, age 18, EN 6/30/63, Corinth, MS, MI 7/1/63, Corinth, MS, born Lawrence Co., AL, farmer, in arrest at Rome, GA, POW 10/1/64 at Rome, GA.

Gordon, Samuel J., Pvt/Sgt., Co. B, age 22, EN 3/10/64, Decatur, AL, MI 3/27/64, Decatur, AL, born Morgan Co., AL, farmer, WIA 11/23/64, Oconee River, GA, died 12/27/64 in hospital at Hilton Head, SC of wounds rec'd. in Battle of Balls Ferry, GA, buried Sec. 53, Grave #6346, Beaufort National Cemetery, SC.

Gordon, W., Pvt., Co. L, POW 10/26/63 from Vincent's Crossroads near Bay Springs, MS and confined at Richmond, VA, MO 11/2/63 at Mobile, AL.*

Gorley, Samuel, Pvt., Co. K, EN 11/22/63 at Camp Davies, MS.*

Gortney, Lorenzo M., Pvt., Co. C, age 25, EN 1/29/63, Corinth, MS, MI 2/5/63, Corinth, MS, born Franklin, GA, farmer, POW 10/26/63 (probably Vincent's Crossroads), returned 11/2/63, Glendale, MS, MO 1/31/64, Memphis, TN.

Gortney, Marion, Pvt., Co. C, on duty as cook 8/20/63, company cook 9/11/63.*

Goss, Allen L., Pvt., Co. H, age 34, EN 3/20/65, Stevenson, AL, MI 4/5/65, Nashville, TN, born Gwinnett Co., GA, farmer, MO 10/20/65, Huntsville, AL.

Gown, N., Pvt., Co. F, absent sick 3/64.*

Grace, Nathan P., Pvt/Corp., Co. G, age 22, EN 3/21/64, Decatur, AL, MI 4/13/64, Decatur, AL, born Pike Co., GA, farmer, promoted to Corp. 5/1/64, MO 10/20/65, Huntsville, AL.
    NOTE: Nathan Grace was born in May 1842 in GA to John Grace, Sr. and Mary Polly Caldwell. Other children of John & Mary were: John, Jr., Daniel, Richard Y., Thomas, William and Solina Grace. The family moved from Georgia to Walker Co., AL about 1859.[69]

Granger, Henry H., Pvt., Co. M, EN 1/11/64, Camp Davies, MS.*

Granger, William H., Pvt/Sgt., Co. M&A, age 22, EN 1/11/64, Camp Davies, MS, MI 2/5/64, Memphis, TN, born Henry Co., TN, farmer, MO 10/20/65, Huntsville, AL.

Granville, James, Co. F, absent on furlough 8/63.*

Graves, Benjamin, Pvt/Corp., Co. I, age 22, EN & MI 7/21/62, Huntsville, AL, born Monroe Co., TN, sick in hospital at Nashville, TN 12/12/62, POW 11/22/63, sick in hospital at Nashville 4/18/64.

Graves, Ralph, Pvt., Co. E, EN 1/1/63, Corinth, MS, MI 3/13/63, Corinth, MS, deserted 5/1/63.

Gray, William T./Thomas W., Sgt., Co. F, age 20, EN 6/30/63, Corinth, MS, born Fayette Co., TN, farmer, sick in Gayoso USA Hospital at Memphis, TN 4/30/64, MO 7/27/64, Rome, GA.

Gray, William T., Lt. (F&S), age 35, EN 3/16/63, Glendale, MS, promoted from 2nd M. Sgt., 57th Ill. Vol. Inf., first MI 10/1/61 in Chicago, IL, MO 4/30/64, Decatur, AL.

Green, Elijah C., Pvt., Co. M, age 17, EN 12/16/63, Camp Davies, MS, MI 12/23/63, Corinth, MS, born Marion Co., AL, farmer, deserted 4/17/64 at Mooresville, AL with Remington revolver.

Green, Jasper N., Pvt/Sgt., Co. K, age 32, EN 12/1/63, Camp Davies MS, born Marion Co., AL, farmer, sick in hospital at Nashville, TN 11/10/64, appt. Sgt. 1/1/64, MO 7/19/65. Traveled 90 miles from his home in Marion Co., AL to Camp Davies, MS to enlist.

Green, John B., Pvt., Co. H, EN 9/14/63, POW 10/26/63 (probably Vincent's Crossroads).

Green, John J., Pvt., Co. D, age 20, EN 2/15/63, Glendale, MS, MI 3/20/63, Corinth, MS, born Franklin Co., AL, farmer, died 7/25/63 in hospital at Glendale, MS of disease. (Buried Grave A-2067, Corinth National Cemetery.)

Green, Joseph, Pvt., Co. K&A, age 50, EN 11/14/62, Corinth, MS, MI 12/30/62, Corinth, MS, born Montgomery Co., NC, farmer, died 3/2/63, Corinth, MS of disease. (Buried Grave #A-100, Corinth National Cemetery.)

Green, Robert, Pvt., Co. B, age 20, EN 4/4/64, Decatur, AL, MI 4/13/64, Decatur, AL, born Walker Co., AL, farmer, deserted 5/11/64 near Chattanooga, TN with horse, Smith carbine and equipment.

Green Samuel, Pvt., Co. K, age 24, EN & MI 12/1/63, Camp Davies, MS, born Marion Co., AL, farmer, sick in hospital at Nashville, TN 4/3/64, died 7/7/64 in hospital at Decatur, AL. Traveled 90 miles from his home in Marion Co., AL to Camp Davies, MS to enlist. (Buried Grave #B-3241, Corinth National Cemetery.)

Green, Samuel, Pvt., Co. M, age 43, EN 12/16/63, Camp Davies, MS, MI 12/29/63, Corinth, MS, born Madison Co., AL, farmer, died 2/29/64 in Memphis, TN of disease.

Green, William, Pvt., Co. A, in Washington USA Hospital Jan & Feb 1864, died 2/25/64.* (Buried in Memphis National Cemetery.)

Green, William, Pvt/Saddler, Co. H, age 46, EN 9/14/63, Glendale, MS, MO 9/29/64, Rome, GA, died in Washington General Hospital.

Green, William G.B., Co. M, age 20, born Marion Co., AL, farmer, EN 12/16/63, Camp Davies, MS, rejected.*

Green, William R., Pvt., Co. M, age 38, EN 9/9/63, Chewalla, TN, MI 12/29/63, Corinth, MS, born Warren Co., TN, deserted 1/28/64 at Lagrange, TN with Smith carbine and Remington revolver.

Greenhaw, John, Pvt., Co. G, temporarily attached from 11th Illinois Cavalry.

Griffin, Franklin, Pvt., Co. H, age 19, EN 10/29/64, Rome, GA, born Spartanburg Dist., SC, farmer, died 2/10/65 in Post Hospital at Huntsville, AL of smallpox.

Griffin, John, Pvt., Co. A, age 18, EN & MI 9/30/64, Rome, GA, born Cherokee Co., AL, farmer, deserted 4/15/65 at Lincolnton, NC, charges of desertion removed 7/27/89 and discharge issued as of 5/15/65.

Griffin, Rufus M., Pvt., Co. K, age 19, EN 12/6/63, Camp Davies, MS, born Cherokee Co., NC, farmer, traveled 300 miles from his home in Randolph Co., AL to Camp Davies, MS to enlist, MO 7/19/65, Nashville, TN.

Griffin, William, Pvt., Co. E, in USA General Field Hospital at Bridgeport, AL April & June 1864, returned to duty 6/18/64.*

Griffith, Green L., Co. K,

Grimes, William R., Pvt., Co. K, age 18, EN 2/23/64, Memphis, TN, MI 2/26/64, Memphis, TN, born Franklin Co., AL, farmer, sick in hospital at Louisville, KY 4/5/64, MO 10/20/65, Huntsville, AL.

Grimmit/Grimmett, Francis, C., Pvt., Co, I, age 25, EN & MI 8/18/62, Huntsville, AL, born Walker Co., AL, farmer, with wagon train at Nashville, 12/27/62, MIA 10/26/63 at Vincent's Crossroads, rejoined 11/4/63, courier at Reedyville, TN 1/27/63, MO 7/19/65, Nashville, TN.

Grinell, James, Co. D, absent on courier line 2/63.*

Grisham, Green W., Pvt/Corp., Co. K, age 18, EN & MI 8/22/62, Huntsville, AL, born Limestone Co., AL, farmer, POW 5/1/63 at Day's Gap, AL and sent to Richmond, VA, appt. Corp. 1/1/64, POW 3/21/64 in AR near Memphis, TN, left elbow dislocated by fall from horse while on the march in GA 11/28/64, MO 7/19/65, Nashville, TN.
  NOTE: Green Washington Grisham was the son of Louis Cullen Grisham (1820-1853) and Eliza Suzannah Speegle, born January 29, 1825 and died January 7,

1875, and grandson of Thomas Grisham of Duplin Co., NC who moved to Limestone Co., AL in 1801. He was born December 9, 1843 in Athens, AL and died October 18, 1914 in Holland, Arkansas. He was married January 29, 1868 to Georgia Ann Potete/Poteet, who was born September 6, 1852 and died September 5, 1924, and they had 12 children: Fressie, Arthur, Luther, Virgil, Simeon, Rosetta, Lewis Peale, Noble Ernest, Flora, Eva Pearl, Sarah, & Rualla.

There is a Grisham/Gresham family reunion in Athens, AL on Memorial Day Week-end for the descendants of this Thomas Grisham.[70]

Groves, Patterson, Pvt/Sgt., Co. M, age 27, EN 8/2/63, Chewalla, TN, MI 12/29/63, Corinth, MS, born Madison Co., TN, farmer, POW 3/10/65 at Solomon Grove, NC, discharged at Camp Chase, OH 6/10/65.

Guess, William C., Pvt., Co. B, age 18, EN 3/29/64, Decatur, AL, MI 4/13/64, Decatur, AL, born Marion (or Limestone) Co., AL, farmer, MO 10/20/65, Huntsville, AL.

NOTE: William Mack (C.) Guess was born October 24, 1846 in Glen Allen, Fayette Co., AL and was the son of Elijah Martin Guess and Talitha Whitehead. He married Laura Jane Biggers November 5, 1869 in Fayette Co., AL. Laura was the daughter of J.A. Biggers. Children of William and Laura were: Joseph Lute, William Shirley, Daniel Mack, A. Delmer, James Arthur and Andrew Frank Guess. After the war, William moved to Hardin Co., TN and later Lake Co., TN where he died April 29, 1922. Laura died December 8, 1920. She and William are buried in Madie Cemetery near Ridgely, TN.[71]

Guice, James P., Pvt/Corp., Co. G, age 30, EN 3/2/64, Decatur, AL, MI 4/13/64, Decatur, AL, born Franklin Co., AL, farmer, appt. Corp. 7/1/65, MO 10/20/65, Huntsville, AL.

Guin, Asa, Pvt., Co. A, age 28, EN 1/23/64, Camp Davies, MS, MI 2/5/64, Memphis, TN, born Fayette Co., AL, farmer, deserted at Snake Creek Gap 5/15/64.

Guin, Jason, Sgt/Pvt., Co. A, age 32, EN 1/23/64, Camp Davies, MS, MI 2/5/64, Memphis, TN, born Anson Co., NC, farmer, promoted to Sgt. 2/5/64, reduced to ranks 12/30/64, POW 3/10/65, MO 10/20/65, Huntsville, AL.

NOTE: Jason Guin was born about 1822 but stated he was only 32 when he enlisted in the Union army. He was conscripted into the Confederate army. He escaped to Union lines on the underground slave railway, which he had helped set up. He was first a civilian scout, carrying messages between various Union generals and E. Woolsey Peck of Tuscaloosa, leader of the Unionist Cabal. While on a scouting mission he was cornered at E. Woolsey Peck's home but escaped, swimming the Warrior River on his horse, while bullets were flying about him. After the war, Jason was shot twice from ambush, attacked by overwhelming numbers and left for dead. He would have died but for the loyalty of a Negro who lived on his farm. Jason served several terms as sheriff in Sanford/Lamar Co., AL. He died in 1878 of a heart attack.[72]

Guin, Levi, Pvt., Co. A, age 27, EN 1/23/64, Camp Davies, MS, MI 2/5/64, Memphis, TN, born Fayette Co., AL, farmer, died 4/7/64 in Gayoso USA Gen.

Hospital at Memphis, TN of rubeola. (Buried Grave #B-1362, Memphis National Cemetery.)

Guin, Michael, Pvt., Co. M, age 34, EN 12/16/63, Camp Davies, MS, MI 12/29/64, Corinth, MS, born Tuscaloosa Co., AL, farmer, died 3/22/64 in Small Pox USA Hospital in Memphis, TN of smallpox. (Buried Grave #B-1772, Memphis National Cemetery.)

Guin, Rasey, Pvt., Co. A, age 24, EN 1/23/64, Camp Davies, MS, MI 2/5/64, Memphis, TN, born Fayette Co., AL, farmer, deserted 2/23/64, Memphis, TN.

Gundney, (?), Pvt., Co. F, absent sick 3/64.*

Gunn, Simeon, Pvt., Co. C, age 23, EN 12/1/62, Corinth, MS, born Bedford Co., TN, farmer, MO 12/17/63, Memphis, TN.

Gurley, Charles A., Pvt., Co. L, age 22, EN 9/25/63, Fayette Co., AL, MI 9/25/63, Glendale, MS, MO 9/28/64, Rome, GA.

Guthery/Guthrie, Isaac, Pvt., Co. I, age 29, EN & MI 8/18/62, Huntsville, AL, born Walker Co., AL, farmer, on wagon train in Nasville, TN 12/27/62, courier at Reedyville, TN 1/27/63, MIA 5/2/63, Cedar Bluff, AL, died 9/8/64 at Andersonville, GA of scorbutus while POW. (Buried in Grave #8147, Andersonville National Cemetery.)

Guthery/Guthrie, John, Pvt., Co. I, age 18, EN 8/1/63, Shelbyville, TN, MIA 10/26/63 at Vincent's Crossroads, died at home in AL, date not known.

Guthery/Guthrie/Guttery, Marion M., Pvt., Co. I, age 18, EN 8/1/63, Shelbyville, TN, MIA 10/26/63 at Vincent's Crossroads, sent to Baltimore, MD, died 4/20/64 of bronchitis, buried in Grave #764, Pall Cemetery.

Guthery, William, Pvt., Co. I, age 19, EN & MI 7/21/62, Huntsville, AL, born Cherokee Co., AL, farmer, MO 7/19/65, Nashville, TN.

Guthery, William E., Pvt., Co. L, age 17, EN 9/25/63, Fayette Co., AL, MI 9/25/63, Glendale, MS, born Walker Co., AL, farmer, MIA 10/26/63, Vincent's Crossroads, MS, MO 9/28/64, Rome, GA, reenlisted 4/24/65, Huntsville, AL, MI 5/20/65, Nashville, TN, MO 10/20/65, Huntsville, AL.

Guthrey, David, Pvt., Co. B, age 23, EN 3/16/64, Decatur, AL, born Cherokee Co., AL, farmer, left sick in hospital at Decatur, AL 4/17/64, no MO date.

Guthrey, James, Pvt., Co. B, age 18, EN 3/16/64, Decatur, AL, MI 3/27/64, Decatur, AL, born Cherokee Co., AL, farmer, left sick in hospital at Decatur, AL 4/17/64, no MO date. (One note states he died at Andersonville, GA 9/8/64 while another record states that note was cancelled.

Guthrie, Calvin, Pvt., Co. I, age 40, EN 10/17/63, Glendale, MS, died 4/19/64 of disease at Cumberland Gen. Hospital, Nashville, TN. Widow was shown as Rhoda Guttery living at Bassams Gap, AL. (Buried in Grave H-09834 in Nashville National Cemetery.)

Guthrie, G.W., Pvt., Co. D, detached orderly for Gen. Dodge 9/64, detached in North Alabama with Maj. Shurtleff Jan. to March 1865, detached in North Alabama with Capt. Lomax April 1865.*

Guthrie, George W., Pvt., Co. H, age 28, EN 10/10/63, Glendale, MS, POW 10/26/63 (probably at Vincent's Crossroads).

Guthrie, Henry, EN 11/11/64, Rome, GA.*

Guthrie, Lemon/Demon, Pvt., Co. B, age 28, EN 2/4/64, Pulaski, TN, MI 3/27/64, Decatur, AL, born Walker Co., AL, MO 10/20/65, Huntsville, AL.

Guthrie, Robert L., Pvt., Co. B, age 26, EN 3/27/63, Glendale, MS, born Hall, GA, farmer, MO 1/22/64, Memphis, TN.

Guthrie, Seborn, Pvt., Co. B, age 18, EN 2/6/64, Pulaski, TN, MI 3/27/64, Decatur, AL, born Walker Co., AL, farmer, MO 10/20/65, Huntsville, AL.

Guthrie, William B., Pvt/Sgt., Co. B, age 38, EN 2/4/64, Pulaski, TN, MI 3/27/64, Decatur,AL, born Pall, GA, farmer, MO 10/20/65, Huntsville, AL.

Guthry, B., Co. B, absent sick in US General Hospital 2/65.*

Guthry, Jacob J., Pvt., Co. D, age 22, EN 5/1/64, Decatur, AL, MI 6/16/64, Decatur, AL, born Walker Co., AL, farmer, POW 3/10/65 at Solomon Grove, NC, discharged 6/13/65, Camp Chase, OH.

Guthry, John W., Pvt., Co. D, age 26, EN 5/1/64, Decatur, AL, MI 6/16/64, Decatur, AL, born Pontotoc, MS, farmer, MO 10/20/65, Huntsville, AL.

Guttery, Benjamin F., Pvt., Co. L, age 29, EN 9/25/63, Fayette Co., AL, MI 9/25/63, Glendale, MS, MO 9/28/64, Rome, GA.
  NOTE: Benjamin Franklin Guttery was born 27 May 1834 in Old Coffeeville, Yallabusha County, Mississippi. He was the son of Mary Willis and Johnson Guttery, born 12 March 1806 in Georgia, and married 24 November 1824. Johnson Guttery was the son of William Guttery, born in 1775 in South Carolina, and Hannah Johnson. Johnson Guttery died 23 May 1876 and is buried in Townley, Boshell Graveyard, Walker County, Alabama. He was a Primitive Baptist Minister. William Guttery died 7 July 1825.
  In November 1857, Benjamin married Elizabeth Nesmith, born 27 March 1836 , in Lynn, Winston County, Alabama. She died 8 April 1934 in Tennessee. Their children were: Martha Ann, born September 1858 in Alabama; Malinda Maniza, born 1863 in Alabama; Mary Elizabeth, born 1865 in Alabama; William Johnson, born 1 October 1866 in Alabama and died 21 October 1899; John Newton,

born 20 Jan 1868 in Alabama and died 7 April 1950 in Leoma, Lawrence County, Tennessee; Ariminta, born 1870 in Alabama; Benjamin Franklin, born 1872 in Alabama; Robert Martin, born 3 April 1875 in Alabama and died 6 July 1905. Benjamin, Sr. died 10 December 1920 in Five Points, Lawrence County, Tennessee and is buried in Second Creek Cemetery.

On 25 September, 1863, Benjamin was enrolled as a Private of Company "L", 1st Regiment Alabama Cavalry Volunteers for one year, in Fayette County, Alabama. He was discharged at Rome, Georgia on 28 September 1864 by reason of expiration of term of service and paid in full by Maj. Holt, Nashville, Tennessee.

On 30 July 1920, Benjamin filed a Declaration for Pension in Lawrence County, Tennessee. He was 86 years old. His personal description was: Height: 5' 8"; Complexion: Fair; Eyes: Blue; Hair: Light; Occupation: Farmer. Records state that he requires the regular personal aid and attendance of another person on account of the following disabilities: "Old age and his mind is no good, can't take care of himself and has to be watched all the time".

AFFIDAVIT TO ORIGIN OF DISABILITY:

"Andrew D. Mitchell of Thorn Hill, County of Marion, State of Alabama, age 41, Sgt. in Co. L, 1st Regiment Alabama Cavalry Volunteers, states the following:

"On or about 15 or 20th day(s) of June, 1864, while in the line of duty, and without fault or improper conduct on his part, at or near Kingston, State of Georgia said soldier was taken with chronic diarrhea and was sent back to Chattanooga, Tennessee to convalescent camps and I was sent with him and he was verry weak and I was also weak with the same complaint and when we got there we found it was on the bank of the river in a low nasty sickly looking place and we left there just as quick as we could get away and went back to the front for we thoat we would get worse or perhaps dye if we staide there. I never new B.F. Guttery untill we jainde the Army he was sound boddied so far as nowed."

DEPARTMENT OF THE INTERIOR, BUREAU OF PENSION

"11 January, 1889, respectfully returned to the Surgeon General USA for a further search of the records showing the nature of the disabilities for which the within named soldier was treated in General Hospital and convalescent camp at Chattanooga, Tennessee from April to August 1864."

Benjamin Guttery's Death Certificate states he died from "infirmities of old age".[73]

Guttery, Henry, Pvt., Co. L, age 21, EN 9/25/63, Fayette Co., AL, MI 9/25/63, Glendale, MS, born Walker Co., AL, farmer, MO 9/28/64, Rome, GA, reenlisted 9/29/64, Rome, GA, died 12/9/64 of disease in Savannah, GA, buried in Sec. 23, Grave #2070, Beaufort National Cemetery, SC "the bodies in this cemetery were originally buried at various places in and about SC and GA".

Guttery, Henry, Pvt., Co. F, died of disease 11/30/64 in the field, GA.*

Guttery, Robert Pvt., Co. L, age 32, EN 9/25/63, Fayette Co., AL, MI 9/25/63, Glendale, MS, MO 9/28/64, Rome, GA.

Guttery, William, Pvt., Co. L, age 17, EN 9/25/63, Fayette Co., AL, MI 9/25/63, Glendale, MS, returned from MIA 12/25/63, discharged 2/10/64 for disability.

Guyse, Enoch, M., Pvt/Corp., Co. M, age 42, EN 11/29/63, Camp Davies, MS, MI 12/29/63, Corinth, MS, born Buncombe Co., NC, farmer, died 4/17/65 at Grant USA Gen. Hospital, Willett's Point, NY of gun shot wounds in chest and knee which he received in action 3/10/65 at Monroe's Crossroads, NC.

Guyse, George W., Pvt., Co. L, age 19, EN 9/25/63, Fayette Co., AL, MI 9/25/63, Glendale, MS, MO 9/28/64, Rome, GA.
    NOTE: George Guyse was born February 1846 in Fayette Co., AL, married Malinda Cummins December 17, 1861 in Winston Co., AL and had the following children: John, October 10, 1862; Peter, May 8, 1864; William J., February 17, 1867; George P., June 5, 1872 and Emma, October 11, 1874. George died September 24, 1903 of Bright's disease.[74]

Hagood, Mansfield, Pvt., Co. K, in Overton USA General Hospital at Memphis, TN Jan. & Feb. 1864.*

Halcomb/Holcomb, Wiseman, Wagoner, Co. K, age 27, EN & MI 7/24/62, Huntsville, AL, born Marion Co., AL, farmer, died 8/23/62 in hospital at Huntsville, AL of brain fever.
    NOTE: Wiseman Holcomb was born about 1837 (according to the 1850 Marion Co., AL Census) and was the son of David and Nancy Holcomb. David was born about 1798 in GA and Nancy was born about 1810 in SC. Other siblings of Wiseman N. Holcomb were: Pheba and John K, both born 1832 in GA; Caleb, 1836; Abel M., 1838; Green, 18, 1839; Nathan, 1841; Nancy E., 1845; and Thadeus, 1850. The last six children were born in AL. Wiseman is buried in Section 1, Maple Hill Cemetery in Huntsville, AL and currently does not have a grave marker.

Halden/Holden, Jones (Archibald J.), Pvt., Co. G, age 24, EN 3/31/63, Chewalla, TN, MI 4/9/63, Corinth, MS, born Tippah Co., MS, temporarily attached as a scout to Co. C, 18th MO Vols, KIA 8/3/63 in Ripley, MS by gunshot wound to the head.

Halderman, David B., Capt., Co. B, age 28, EN 10/30/63, Glendale, MS, appt. Capt. from 2nd Lt., 122nd Illinois Inf. Vols. 10/30/63 by Gen. G.M. Dodge, MO 9/2/64.

Hale, Nathaniel, Pvt., Co. C, age 27, EN 2/20/63, Corinth, MS, MI 2/25/63, Corinth, MS, born Smith Co., TN, farmer, MO 2/20/64, Memphis, TN.

Hale, Nephthali D., Co. M, age 26, born Smith Co., TN, farmer, EN 12/20/63, Camp Davies, MS, rejected by surgeon on account of phissis palmonalis of superior portion of left lung and disease of antrim of left superior maxolary 12/20/63.*

Hall, Alexander P., Co. A, age 32, born Frederick Co., VA, EN 9/6/64, Rome, GA.*

Hall, Henry J., Pvt., Co. C, age 21, EN 2/20/64, Memphis, TN, MI 3/10/64, Memphis, TN, born Fayette Co., AL, farmer.

Hall, Pinkney D., Pvt/Corp., Co. B, age 18, EN 1/20/63, Glendale, MS, born Franklin Co., AL, farmer, MO 1/22/64, Memphis, TN.

Hall, Richard W., Pvt., Co. A, age 35, EN 12/7/63, Camp Davies, MS, MI 2/5/64, Memphis, TN, born Marion Co., AL, carpenter, POW 3/10/65, deserted 8/25/65 in Decatur, AL with Remington revolver, horse & pistol.

Hall, Samuel M., Pvt., Co. A&D, age 31, EN 1/13/64, Camp Davies, MS, MI 2/5/64, Memphis, TN, born Anderson Dist., SC, farmer, MO 10/20/65, Huntsville, AL.
    NOTE: Samuel McCager Hall was born August 21, 1832 and died December 17, 1928. He is buried in Fairview Cemetery, Hackleburg, Marion Co., AL.

Hall, Thomas J., Pvt., Co. G, age 18, EN 4/10/64, Decatur, AL, MI 4/10/64, Rome, GA, born Marion Co., AL, deserted 11/17/64, Atlanta, GA with side arms.

Hall, William A., Pvt/Com. Sgt., Co. B, age 47, MI 1/22/63, POW 10/26/63 Vincent's Crossroads, born Beaufort, TN, farmer, MO 1/22/64, Memphis, TN.

Hall, W.H., Pvt., Co. A, transferred to Co. D 1st Ala. Cav. 7/19/64, Rome, GA.*

Hall/Hull, William H., Pvt., Co. B, absent without leave 5/10/63.*

Hall, William H., Pvt/Sgt., Co. C, age 21, EN 2/20/64, Memphis, TN, MI 4/30/64, Decatur, AL, born Madison Co., TN, farmer, appt. Corp. 3/1/64, appt. Sgt. 9/1/64.

Halley, J.H. (or I.H.), Co. B, absent on detached service in North Ala. with Maj. Shurtleff 11/9/64.*

Hallmark, Azel T., Pvt., Co. A&B, age 24, EN 1/13/63, Glendale, MS, MIA 7/5/63 at Yellow Creek, MS, confined at Richmond, VA, paroled at City Point, VA 8/29/63, in USA Gen. Hospital at Annapolis, MD 8/30/63, returned to duty 12/2/63, MO 1/29/64, Memphis, TN.
    NOTE: Azael Thompson Hallmark was born about 1835 and was the son of Robert and Gracy Hallmark of Marion Co., AL. He married Margaret Jackson December 8, 1857 in Tishomingo Co., MS. In his pension application he stated he was treated at Annapolis, MD for fever and a gunshot wound in the right thigh that he received on Yellow Creek near Burnsville, MS from the Confederates. He was then captured, sent to Richmond, VA where he was exchanged in August and sent to Annapolis.
    Pension papers state the following: *State of Alabama, Marion County*
    Personally appeared before me, John A. Pope, Judge of Probate for said county and state, A.T. Hallmark, who after being duly sworn deposeth and says that he left the hospital at Annapolis, Maryland on the 2nd day of December 1863, or there about. That he went to Washington City and was there detailed by the Secretary of War to drive a team and there remained about one and a half months, driving a team for the government. The reason as stated to me why I was so detailed was that there not a sufficient number to form a squad that belonged to the Western Army. Then, I was something near a week going from Washington to Memphis, Tennessee. I, there remained about a week before I was or could be mustered out, on account of my Captain's having to rush home to Illinois, I think. I

was discharged on the 29th day of January 1864, and while I was at the hospital at Annapolis, Maryland, I was there treated for fever and wound in the right thigh from gunshot received on Yellow Creek, near Burnsville, Mississippi, from the Confederates. I was then captured and sent to Richmond, Virginia, where I remained till August, about the last. Was exchanged and sent to Annapolis, Maryland.

Sworn to and Subscribed to before me on the 18 day of August 1884.
John H. Pope, Judge of Probate[75]

Hallmark, George N., Pvt., Co. K, age 22, EN & MI 7/24/62, Huntsville, AL, born Fayette Co., AL, farmer, died 11/3/62 in Hospital #14 in Nashville, TN of rubeola followed by typhoid fever.

Hallmark, James W., Pvt., Co. K, age 39, EN & MI 7/24/62, Huntsville, AL, born Jefferson Co., AL, farmer, sent to hospital in Nasvhille, TN 12/26/62, died 2/26/63 in USA Gen. Hospital in Louisville, KY, (Casualty Sheet shows he died 8/17/64.

Hallmark, John M., Pvt., Co. A, age 18, EN 12/22/63, Camp Davies, MS, MI 2/5/64, Memphis, TN, born Fayette Co., AL, farmer, in Washington USA Gen. Hospital at Memphis, TN 2/14/64, deserted 4/17/64 from Mooresville, AL, reported for duty 5/15/65, MO 10/20/65, Huntsville, AL.

Hallmark, Thomas F., Corp., Co. K, age 33, EN & MI 7/24/62, Huntsville, AL, born Fayette Co., AL, discharged 11/14/62 at Nashville, TN of disability by Maj. Gen. Rosecrans.

Hallmark/Halmark, Thomas, Pvt., Co. C, age 23, EN 2/20/63, Corinth, MS, MI 2/25/63, Corinth, MS, born Itawamba Co., MS, farmer, MO 2/10/64, Memphis, TN.

Hally, Joab, Pvt., Co. C, relieved from duty as guide per S.O. #47 dated 8/24/63. (No further information on this soldier.)

Ham, James F., Pvt., Co. F, age 21, EN 8/1/63, Corinth, MS, MI 8/13/63, Corinth, MS, died 8/27/63 at home near Adamsville, TN.

Haman, Andrew, (Cards filed with Andrew J. Homan)

Hamby, Thomas A., (Cards filed with Thomas A. Henby)

Hamilton, H.H., Corp. Co. E, in Small Pox USA General Hospital at St. Louis, MO 2/25/64.*

Hamilton, Haton/Haden M., Pvt., Co. A, age 37, EN 9/8/62, Iuka, MS, MI 10/1/62, Corinth, MS, born Abbeville, SC, farmer, discharged 7/2/63 for disability.

Hamilton, Riley, Pvt., Co. E, EN 12/9/62, Nabors Mill, MI 12/9/63, Corinth, MS, POW 1/20/63 near Chewalla, TN.

Hamilton, William, Pvt., Co. E, age 36, EN & MI 2/1/63, Corinth, MS, MO 2/1/64, Memphis, TN.

Hamilton, William R., Pvt., Co. E, absent POW taken at Chewalla 1/20/63, absent POW 10/63, detached as teamster in Q.M. Dept. at Vicksburg, MS 1/25/64, absent POW 2/64-4/64. (Name also shown as Riley Hamilton & Wm. K. Hamilton.)*

Hamilton, William R., Pvt/Corp., Co. E, age 26, EN 12/9/62, Nashville, TN, MI 3/1/63, Corinth, MS, POW 10/1/63, paroled at Richmond, VA 11/17/63, sick in Marine USA Gen. Hospital in St. Louis, MO 6/13/64, returned to duty 7/1/64, MO 7/24/64, Rome, GA, residence shown as McNairy Co., TN.

Hammill, Hugh, Corp., Co. F, age 20, EN 4/30/63, Corinth, MS, MI 5/18/63, Corinth, MS, born Lauderdale Co., AL, farmer, MO 7/27/64, Rome, GA.

Hammock, Robert B., Pvt., Co. C, age 34, EN 1/5/63, Corinth, MS, MI 1/10/63, Corinth, MS, born Cowetta, GA, in arrest at Corinth 4/63-8/63, MO 1/31/64, Memphis, TN.

Hammond, John A., Pvt., Co. E, EN 2/1/63, Corinth, MS, POW 2/5/63 near Chewalla, TN, deserted 3/16/63 at Chewalla.

Hammonds, Robert, Pvt., Co. B, age 21, EN 1/23/63, Glendale, MS, born Lawrence, SC, died 3/3/63 at Corinth, MS of measles.

Hamner, Clement/Clemand A., Corp/Sgt., Co. D, age 27, EN 9/25/63, Fayette Co., AL, MI 9/25/63, Glendale, MS, MO 9/28/64, Rome, GA.

Hamon, S., Co. D, absent POW 4/65.*

Hampton, Allen, Pvt., Co. F, age 19, EN & MI 8/1/64, Rome, GA, born Floyd Co., GA, farmer, MO 10/20/65, Huntsville, AL.

Hampton, Joseph, Pvt., Co. G, age 19, EN 4/10/64, Decatur, AL, born Marion Co., AL, farmer, MO 10/20/65, Huntsville, AL.

Hampton, Miles, Pvt., Co. I, age 34, EN 11/1/63, Camp Davies, MS, born Oldom, KY, carpenter, served as ambulance driver and cook, MO 7/19/65, Nashville, TN.

Hampton, William H., Pvt., Co. H, age 18, EN 10/16/63, Glendale, MS, MO 10/24/64, Rome, GA.

Hanley, James, Pvt., Co. C, age 24, EN 12/15/63, Camp Davies, MS, MI 3/10/64, Memphis, TN, born Fayette Co., AL, deserted 7/7/64 at Rome, GA with side arms.

Hanson, Eli, (Cards filed with Eli Henson)

Hanson, James A., Pvt., Co. A, age 20, EN 1/11/64, Camp Davies, MS, MI 2/5/64, Memphis, TN, born Walker Co., AL, farmer. (Notation stated this entry was canceled, no further information.)

Harbin, John H., Sgt., Co. L, age 33, EN 9/25/63, Fayette Co., AL, born Anderson Dist., SC, farmer, died 3/16/64 at Overton Hospital in Memphis, TN of measles. (Buried in Memphis National Cemetery.)

Harbison, Charles H., Pvt., Co. I, age 29, EN 12/21/63, Camp Davies, MS, born Morgan Co., AL, sick in Gayoso USA Gen. Hospital in Memphis, TN 3/10/64, MO 7/19/65, Nashville, TN.
   NOTE: Charles Hill Harbison was born February 27, 1833 in Morgan Co., AL and died May 14, 1906 in Good Hope, Cullman Co., AL. He married Mary A. Kinney September 17, 1856. Their children were: Margaret L., born November 1858; Olivia Jane, born 1859, died May 20, 1923 in Walker Co., AL, married Jeremiah Alexander O'Rear; Willis M., born 1864; Nancy, born 1867; Pleasant Wiley, born 1869; George, born 1871; Alice, born 1873; and Sarah Harbison. Charles married second, Mary Elizabeth Crocker, born February 1847 in AL and their children were: Tandy W., born July 1883 and Samuel J., born August 1886. Charles and his three brothers, Matthew, David and Pleasant, were all in the Civil War and Charles was the only one to live to return home. They were the sons of Samuel H. Harbison, Jr., born 1807 in KY, and Eliza Louisa Davis, born 1811 in Madison Co., AL, who were married August 6, 1829 in Morgan Co., AL.[76]

Harbison, David, Pvt., Co. I, age 28, EN 12/21/63, Camp Davies, MS, born Morgan Co., AL, farmer, died 5/3/64 at Gayoso USA Gen. Hospital in Memphis, TN of measles.
   NOTE: David Harbison was born 1835 in Morgan Co., AL and married Emily Calvert July 1856. Emily was born March 22, 1835 in Walker Co., AL and died October 8, 1888 in Cullman Co., AL. (See Charles Harbison, above, for additional family information.)[77]

Harbison, Mathew D., Pvt., Co. I, age 33, EN 12/21/63, Camp Davies, MS, born Morgan Co., AL, farmer, died 7/15/64 at Rome, GA of disease.
   NOTE: Matthew Davis Harbison was born July 15, 1830 in Morgan Co., AL and married Elizabeth Malinda Calvert October 10, 1854. Elizabeth was born in 1831 in Walker Co., AL and died September 20, 1865 in Houston, Winston Co., AL. Their children were: Samuel M., born November 2, 1856 in Walker Co., AL, died July 27, 1934 in Anderson, AL and married Flora Ann Campbell March 7, 1878; James Davis, born July 9, 1855 in Winston Co., AL, married Theadocia Crawford; John D., born December 30, 1858 in Winston Co., AL, died January 28, 1932 in Cullman Co., AL, married Matilda Emma Dye January 26, 1893; Charles Hill, born December 30, 1860 in Trade, Winston Co., AL, died November 28, 1940 in Cullman Co., AL, married Rebecca Mary Lott October 16, 1881; and William Joshua, born August 21, 1863 in Winston Co., AL, died November 2, 1939 in Cullman Co., AL, married Melvina Loraine Roden January 24, 1895. (See Charles Harbison, above, for additional information.)[78]

Harbison, Pleasant M., Pvt., Co. H, age 23, EN 10/16/63, Glendale, MS, sick in Overton USA Gen. Hospital in Memphis, TN 2/64, MO 10/24/64, Rome, GA.

Harden, John L., Pvt., Co. G, age 18, EN 5/6/63, Chewalla, TN, MO 11/26/63, Memphis, TN.

Hardy, Henry, Pvt/Corp., Co. H, age 22, EN 2/1/65, Huntsville, AL, MI 2/13/65, Nashville, TN, born Lawrence Dist., SC, farmer, appt. Corp. 4/1/65, MO 10/20/65, Huntsville, AL.

Hardy, James C., Pvt., Co. H, age 18, EN 10/1/63, Glendale, MS, POW 10/26/63 (probably Vincent's Crossroads).

Hardy, John C., Pvt., Co. H, EN 10/10/63, Glendale, MS, absent sick in AL 10/20/63, sick in hospital at Memphis, TN 2/64, absent sick in Decatur 7/64, absent sick in General Hospital 9/64 & 10/64. (Name also appears as J.W. Hardy & J. H. Hardy.*

Harper, Joseph H., Pvt., Co. L, age 35, EN 9/25/63, Fayette Co., AL, MI Glendale, MS, born Clark Co., GA, farmer, POW 10/26/63, sick in Overton USA Gen. Hospital in Memphis, TN 12/31/63, MO 6/30/65, Nashville, TN.
NOTE: Joseph Harper married Sarah Kelley, sister of the Elizabeth Kelley who married James Jarrett, also a member of this regiment.

Harper, Josiah/James, Pvt., Co. B, age 28, EN 1/20/63, Glendale, MS, MI 1/22/63, Corinth, MS, on detached service as scout 2/8/63, born Smith Co., TN, farmer, MO 1/22/64.

Harper, Robert, Pvt., Co. B, age 38, EN 1/20/63, Glendale, MS, detached on secret service 2/8/63, died 3/8/63 at Corinth, MS of measles.

Harper, Tennessee P., Pvt., Co. K, age 18, EN 6/26/62, Limestone Co., AL, MI 6/26/62, Huntsville, AL, born Walker Co., AL, farmer, died 12/9/63 in Hospital #9 at Nashville, TN. (Buried in Grave C-7159 in Nashville National Cemetery.)
NOTE: Tennessee Polk Harper was the son of Thomas Harper, born 1802 in VA and the sister of Sarah Harper McWhirter. Sarah was the wife of Andrew Ferrier McWhirter and mother of Thomas and George McWhirter who also served in this regiment.

Harris, Anderson B., Pvt., Co. G, age 40, EN 3/5/63, Chewalla, TN, MI 3/5/63, Corinth, MS, discharged - was member of the 1st West TN Cav., sent back to 6th Regt. TN Vol. Cav. 6/25/63.

Harris, Andrew Jackson, Pvt., Co. F, age 24, EN 4/10/63, Corinth, MS, MIA 10/26/63, returned 12/12/63, born Franklin Co., AL, farmer, MO 4/9/64, Decatur, AL.

Harris, Francis C., Pvt/Sgt. Co. L, age 37, EN 9/25/63, Fayette Co., AL, MI 9/25/63, Glendale, MS, born Abbeville, SC, farmer, returned from MIA 12/25/63, promoted to Sgt. 5/1/64, MO 9/28/64, Rome, GA.

NOTE: Francis C. (Gerry) "Frank" Harris was born February 21, 1826 in SC and died March 1, 1897. He is buried at Sardis Baptist Cemetery in Winston Co., AL. He married Delila M. Barton, sister to Jonathan, Gilford and Madison M. Barton.[79]

Harris, M., Co. A, AWOL 4/20/65.*

Harris, Martin V., Pvt/Sgt., Co. K&E, age 28, EN & MI 8/19/64, Rome, GA, born Talapoosa, AL, farmer, promoted to Sgt. 10/20/64, POW Faison's Depot, NC 3/30/65, discharged 6/12/65, Camp Chase, OH.

Harris, N.J., Pvt., Co. F, term of service expired 4/13/64, Mooresville.*

Harris, V., Pvt., Co. F, MIA 10/26/63 at Vincent's Crossroads.*

Harris, William W., Pvt., Co. A, age 19, EN 12/6/63, Camp Davies, MS, MI 2/5/64, Memphis, TN, born Marion Co., AL, farmer, deserted 5/20/65 from Durham's Station, NC.

Harrison, John S., Pvt/Corp., Co. B, age 15, EN 3/15/64, Decatur, AL, MI 3/27/64, Decatur, AL, born Lauderdale Co., AL, farmer, appt. Corp. 8/1/64, MO 10/20/65, Huntsville, AL.

Harry, William F., Pvt., Co. D, age 48, EN 5/4/63, Glendale, MS, born Jasper Co., GA, discharged 7/23/63 for disability.

Hart, J.H., Pvt., Co. L, absent sick in hospital at Memphis, TN 3/64.*

Hartgraves, Hugh, Pvt/Corp., Co. C, age 27, EN 2/20/64, Memphis, TN, MI 3/10/64, Memphis, TN, born Yalobusha Co., MS, farmer, MO 10/20/65, Huntsville, AL.

Harville/Harvel, Warren, Pvt., Co. D, age 46, EN 2/1/63, Glendale, MS, MI 2/4/63, Corinth, MS, born Orange Co., NC, farmer, served as nurse in hospital, MO 2/4/64, Memphis, TN.

Hatfield, Robert S., Pvt., Co. A, age 21, EN 1/9/64, Camp Davies, MS, MI 2/5/64, Memphis, TN, born Tuscaloosa Co., AL, farmer, deserted 4/17/64 from Mooresville, AL.

Hawkins, Jackson, Corp., Co. F, died 10/9/63.*

Haws, John A., Pvt., Co. F, age 31, EN 9/7/63, Camp Davies, MS, MI 2/24/64, Memphis, TN, born Warren Co., NC, farmer, sick in hospital in Nashville, TN 11/6/64, MO 11/23/64, Nashville, TN.

Haygood, Evon E., Pvt., Co. C, age 18, EN 12/15/63, Camp Davies, MS, MI 3/10/64, Memphis, TN, born St. Clair Co., AL, served as nurse in hospital, MO 10/20/65, Huntsville, AL.

Haynes, John W., Pvt., Co. A, age 18, EN 12/22/63, Camp Davies, MS, MI 2/5/64, Memphis, TN, born Cherokee Co., GA, farmer, MO 10/20/65, Huntsville, AL.

Hays, Mansfield, Pvt., Co. K&A, EN 12/15/62, Glendale, MS, MI 12/31/62, Corinth, MS, born Marion Co., AL, died 2/28/63 at Corinth, MS of measles.

Head, William, Pvt., Co. M, age 18, EN 12/16/63, Camp Davies, MS, MI 12/29/63, Corinth, MS, born Marshall Co., MS, farmer, sick in Gayoso USA Gen. Hospital in Memphis, TN 1/1/64, sick in hospital in Savannah, GA 6/23/65, MO 10/20/65, Huntsville, AL.

Healy, William M., Pvt., age 20, EN 2/17/65, Stevenson, AL, MI 2/17/65, Nashville, TN, born Marshall Co., AL, farmer. (No further information).

Heathcock, Andrew J., Pvt., Co. C, age 18, EN 12/20/62, Corinth, MS, MI 12/22/62, Corinth, MS, born Tippah Co., MS, farmer, MO 12/27/63, Camp Davies, MS.

Heathcock, James M., Pvt., Co. C, age 21, EN 12/20/62, Corinth, MS, MI 12/22/62, Corinth, MS, born Tippah Co., MS, farmer, MO 12/27/63, Camp Davies, MS.

Heatherly/Heatherby, James A. (or M.), Pvt., Co. B, age 20, EN & MI 3/27/64, Decatur, AL, born Dekalb Co., AL, farmer, MO 10/20/65, Huntsville, AL.

Heatherly/Heatherby, John W. Pvt., Co. I, age 22, EN 12/21/63, Camp Davies, MS, born Dekalb Co., AL, farmer, MO 7/19/65, Nashville, TN.

Hefley, Robert M., Pvt., Co. G, temporarily attached from 11th Illinois Cavalry.

Hefner, James H., Pvt., Co. K, age 35, EN & MI 7/24/62, Huntsville, AL, born Greenville Dist., SC, farmer, sent to hospital at Annapolis, MD 5/16/63 with mumps, sent to Winston Co., AL on recruiting service 12/17/63, captured at Rome, GA 5/3/65 and confined at Richmond, VA, paroled at City Point, VA 5/15/65, and sent on board steamer en route for the West.

Hefner, William H., Pvt., Co. K, age 20, EN & MI 7/24/62, Huntsville, AL, born Henderson Co., NC, farmer, died 2/12/63 in field hospital at Murfreesboro, TN of pneumonia. (A Washington Hefner is buried in Grave J-3883 in Stone's River National Cemetery in Murfreesboro with same death date.)

Helton, James, Co. B, age 18, born Giles Co., TN, farmer, EN 2/20/64, Pulaski, TN by Lt. Judy.*

Helton, James D. (James E./John D.), Pvt/Sgt., Co. F, age 20, EN 8/1/63, Corinth, MS, appt. Corp. 12/1/63, MO 7/27/64, Rome, GA.

Hemby/Hamby, Thomas A., Pvt., Co. C, age 37, EN 12/20/62, Corinth, MS, born Anson Co., NC, farmer, POW 2/1/63 near Jacinto, paroled at City Point, VA 5/23/63, MO 12/27/63, Camp Davies, MS.

Henderson, George, Pvt., Co. F, age 31 (or 21), EN 5/15/63, Memphis, TN, born Paulding Co., OH, deserted 3/20/64, Memphis, TN, returned and restored to duty, MO 11/3/64, Rome, GA.

Henderson, George, saddler, Co. G&F, age 32, EN 9/1/64, Rome, GA, born Lauderdale Co., AL, farmer, MO 10/20/65, Huntsville, AL.

Hendon, Henry H., Pvt., Co. D, age 18, EN 5/1/64, Decatur, AL, MI 6/16/64, Decatur, AL, born Walker Co., AL, farmer, died 1/15/65 in Hospital #14 in Nashville, TN of measles. (Another roll states he died in Jeffersonville, Indiana 12/22/64.)

Hendon, Jonathan H., Pvt., Co. L, age 21, EN 9/25/63, Fayette Co., AL, born Walker Co., AL, farmer, sick in Adams USA Gen. Hospital in Memphis, TN 3/25/64, MO 9/28/64, Rome, GA.

Hendon, Robert H., Pvt., Co. L, age 26, EN 9/25/63, Fayette Co., AL, born Sumpter, AL, farmer, MIA 10/26/63, Vincent's Crossroads, returned in November, MO 9/28/64, Rome, GA.

Hendricks, Joseph, Pvt., Co. B, age 20, EN 2/2/64, Pulaski, TN, MI 3/27/64, Decatur, AL, born Lauderdale Co., AL, farmer, left sick in hospital in Decatur 4/17/64, no further information.

Hendricks/Hendrix, Moses J., Pvt., Co. L&F, age 45, EN & MI 10/11/64, Rome, GA, born Pickens Dist., SC, (one description states Cherokee Co., AL), farmer, WIA 3/10/65 at Monroe's Crossroads, NC and sent to Berry Houser Hospital at Wilmington, NC (shown on MR at USA Post Hospital at Goldsboro, NC), 3/16/65 and sent on to hospital at Annapolis, MD.)

Hendrick, Moses P., Co. F, age 19, EN 10/11/64, Rome GA (Card filed with Moses J. Hendricks above).

Hendrix, Eli W., Pvt., Co. A, age 18, EN 1/4/64, Camp Davies, MS, born Paulding Co., GA, farmer, deserted 1/24/64 at Camp Davies, MS with horse, arms & equipment.

Henis, G.S., Pvt., Co. B, absent sick in general hospital 11/64.*

Henis, U.L., Pvt., Co. B, absent sick in general hospital 11/64.*

Henley, James, Pvt., Co. C, age 18, EN 2/5/64, Memphis, TN, MI 2/15/64, Memphis, TN, born Shelby Co., AL, farmer, appt. Corp. 3/1/64, reduced to Pvt.,

5/14/65, charges filed against him for drunkeness and disorderly conduct, struck James Canada over the head with revolver. MO 10/20/65, Huntsville, AL.

Henry, John R., Jr., 2nd Lt., Co. I, age 22, EN & MI 7/21/62, Huntsville, AL, died 4/13/63 of wounds received in railroad accident near Murfreesboro, TN.

Henry, Peter, Pvt., Co. F, age 17, EN 5/3/63, Corinth, MS, born Lincoln Co., NC, farmer, POW 10/26/63 at Vincent's Crossroads, died 6/26/64 while in prison at Andersonville, GA. (Buried in Grave #2514, Andersonville National Cemetery.)

Henry, William, Pvt., age 24, born Ohio, EN 10/8/64, Paducah, KY, MI 10/8/64, Paducah, KY, mechanic.
Note states "substitute (white) furnished by Marshall Hobson an enrolled man of Graves Co. 1st Dist of KY. - Preference of organization, 1st Alabama Cav."*

Henry, William, Pvt., Co. F, age 23, EN 5/15/63, Memphis, TN, MI 5/15/63, Corinth, MS, born Rosa Co., OH, machinist, MO 7/27/64, Rome, GA.

Henson, Andrew T., Pvt., Co. M, age 36, EN 9/12/63, Chewalla, TN, born Hardiman Co., TN, farmer, died 11/27/63, Corinth, MS of typhoid pneumonia, buried at post hospital burial ground.

Henson, Eli, Pvt., Co. L&M, age 21, EN 12/1/63, Camp Davies, MS, MI 12/29/63, Corinth, MS, born Walker Co., AL, farmer, MO 1/12/65, Nashville, TN, reenlisted 3/1/65, Stevenson, AL, MI 4/5/65, Nashville, TN, MO 10/20/65, Huntsville, AL.

Henson, John, Pvt., Co. B, age 18, EN 3/28/64, Decatur, born Bladshaw, (?) AL, left sick in hospital at Chattanooga, TN 5/20/64, died 6/11/64 at Totten USA Gen. Hospital in Louisville, KY.

Herndon, J.H., Pvt., Co. L, MIA 10/26/63 at Vincent's Crossroads, absent sick in hospital at Memphis, TN 4/64.*

Herndon/Hurneton/Hernet, James M., Corp/Pvt., Co. A, age 29, EN 1/12/64, Camp Davies, MS, MI 2/5/64, Memphis, TN, born Lumpkin Co., GA, farmer, appt. Corp. 2/5/64, reduced to ranks 12/30/64, MO 10/20/65, Huntsville, AL.

Herndon, James M., Corp., Co. B, age 28, MI 1/22/63, Corinth, MS, appt. Corp 1/22/63, deserted 4/2/63 at Glendale, MS.

Herron/Herrin, David, Pvt., Co. G, age 23, EN 3/21/64, Decatur, AL, MI 4/13/64, Decatur, AL, born LaFayette, AL, farmer, deserted 7/21/65 at Decatur, AL, charges of desertion cancelled 1/8/85 and discharge issued as of 7/21/65.

Herron/Herrin, James, Pvt., Co. K, age 25, EN & MI 7/24/62, Huntsville, AL, born Walker Co., AL, farmer, POW 3/21/64 in AR near Memphis, TN, released 4/29/64, MO 7/19/65, Nashville, TN.

Hewett, William A., Pvt/Sgt., Co. K&A, age 45, EN 12/5/62, Glendale, MS, MI 12/30/62, Corinth, MS, promoted to Sgt. 12/18/62, discharged due to disability (broken constitution) 7/2/63.

Hide, William, Pvt., Co. E, age 25, MI 3/1/63, Corinth, MS, born Hall Co., GA, farmer, deserted 9/6/63.

Higgins, Andrew J., Pvt., Co. B, age 30, EN 4/9/64, Decatur, AL, MI 4/13/64, Decatur, AL, born Cherokee Co., AL, farmer, deserted 9/5/64, Rome, GA, deserted 6/1/65, Huntsville, AL.

Higgins/Haggins, William, Pvt., Co. F, age 33, EN 5/20/63, Memphis, TN, POW 10/26/63 (probably Vincent's Crossroads), POW 1/10/64 from Camp Davies, MS. (Age shown as 23, 33, & 38).

Higgins, William A., Pvt., Co. F, EN 5/30/63, Memphis, MI 8/7/63, Corinth, MS, sick in hospital in Memphis, TN 1/15/64, no further information.

Hightower, John D., Pvt., Co. I, age 22, EN 10/1/63, Glendale, MS, MO 7/19/65, Nashville, TN.
    NOTE: See Marion D. Hightower, below, for family information.

Hightower, Marion D., Pvt., Co. I, age 26, EN & MI 8/18/62, Huntsville, AL, born Pickens Dist., SC, farmer, sick in Hospital #12, Nashville, TN 10/24/62, MIA 5/2/63 at Cedar Bluff, AL, returned 10/10/63, MO 7/19/65, Huntsville, AL.
    NOTE: John C. Hightower was a deputy sheriff in Marshall County, Alabama in the pre-war years. He had married Martha Jordan in their native North Carolina but they had moved to northern Alabama soon after 1830. They had ten children, the youngest being a son named Marshall, born in 1850, the same year Martha died. On Christmas Day of that year John married Margaret Lang Patrick, the widow of James Patrick. Over the next eight years more children were added to the family until John was tragically killed while trying to arrest a criminal. When the war started Margaret Patrick hightower was a widow living in Winston County with thirteen children including two daughters and a son from her marriage to James Patrick. Marion Hightower and his brother, Monroe, were quick to answer the call to arms and join the 1st Alabama Cavalry. Brothers Wilburn and John joined the following year. All four Hightower brothers were assigned to Company I where they served with Thomas Wiley. Of the four brothers, two died during the war years. In addition to the four Hightower Brothers that were her step-sons, Margaret Patrick Hightower had two sons from her first marriage that served in the 1st Alabama, Francis Marion Patrick and William Patrick. Another one of her sons, Henry Greenberry Patrick, served in the Confederate Army.[80]

Hightower, Monroe, Pvt., Co. I, age 19, EN & MI 8/18/62, Huntsville, AL, born Gilmer Co., GA, farmer, died 12/6/62 at Nashville, TN.
    NOTE: See Marion D. Hightower, above, for family information.

Hightower, Wilburn, Pvt., Co. I, age 18, EN 10/17/63, Glendale, MS, died 3/29/64 at Adams USA Gen. Hospital in Memphis, TN of pneumonia. (Buried in Memphis National Cemetery.)
NOTE: See Marion D. Hightower, above, for family information.

Hill, Francis M. (or A. or H.), Pvt., Co. B, age 18, EN 2/27/64, Pulaski, TN, MI 3/27/64, Decatur, AL, born Carroll Co., GA, farmer, left sick in Decatur, AL 4/17/64, no further information.

Hill, Joel, S., Pvt., Co. G, age 19, EN 3/5/63, Chewalla, TN, left sick in Memphis, TN 10/10/63, MO 11/26/63, Memphis, TN.

Hill, I.M. (or J.M.), Co. C, absent POW 3/10/65.*

Hill, John F., Pvt., Co. B, age 19, EN 2/27/64, Pulaski, TN, MI 3/27/64, Decatur, AL, born Carroll Co., GA, farmer, deserted 8/15/64 from Rome, GA with Smith Carbine & equipment, in Hospital #14, Nashville, TN and transferred to Jefferson USA Gen. Hospital, Jeffersonville, IN 11/17/64.

Hill, Richard G., Pvt., Co. D, age 16, admitted to military field hospital in Bridgeport, AL 5/2/64 and died 5/4/64, date of enlistment not determined. Henry H. Hill claimed to be his brother. (Buried Grave #H-10930, Chattanooga National Cemetery.)

Hill, Silas W., Pvt., Co. B, age 40, EN 2/27/64, Pulaski, TN, MI 3/27/64, Decatur, AL, born Clark Co., GA, farmer, left sick in hospital in Decatur, AL 4/17/64, deserted 8/15/64 from Rome, GA with Smith carbine & equipment.

Hillis, John M. (or N), (alias John Phillips) Pvt., Co. C, age 22, EN 4/25/64, Decatur, AL, MI 4/30/64, Decatur, AL, born Lauderdale Co., AL, deserted 6/1/64 from Dallas, GA with Colt revolver, Smith carbine, sabre & equipment, charges later removed when found to be POW, admitted to hospital at Annapolis, MD 2/26/65.

Hinds, Jerome, J., 2nd Lt/Captain, Co. F&A, age 25, EN 4/26/63, Memphis, TN, appt. Captain 2/1/64 by Brig. Gen. G.M. Dodge, MO 10/20/65, Huntsville, AL.
NOTE: Jerome James Hinds was born May 12, 1838 in Fayette County, Illinois and was the son of Simeon Hinds. According to his service record, in September and October 1863, he was absent on detached service per order of General Dodge by instructions of the Secretary of War . On October 1863, he was shown to be recruiting in Alabama by direction of Col. Spencer. In January 1864, he was detached from Company F to Company A by order of Lt. Col. O.J. Dodds. On February 4, 1864, he was appointed Captain of Company A, 1st Alabama Cavalry US Volunteers by authority of the Secretary of War by order of Brig. Gen. G.M. Dodge. In January and February 1865 he was commanding the 2nd Battalion. In April 1865, he was on special duty in the Regiment. On October 2, 1865, he made affidavit that he had rendered all requisite returns relating to public property for which he had been accountable as required by army regulations. He mustered out of service on October 20, 1865 in Huntsville, Alabama.

In a letter written by Major Sanford Tramel from Faison's Depot in North Carolina, dated March 28, 1863, he stated that after he was captured by the enemy and held prisoner, Captain J.J. Hinds took command of the regiment and retained it until he returned. He stated that Capt. Hinds handled the command in a gallant manner during the remainder of the severe and terrible fight.

From 1868-1872, he served as State Representative from Marion Co., AL and later settled in Decatur, AL where he and his brother, Joseph Munroe Hinds, were in the steamboat and mercantile business. They associated these businesses with a stage line. Jerome served as US Marshal for the Southern District of Alabama. He died April 1, 1912 in Philadelphia, Pennsylvania and his remains were returned to Decatur where he is buried in the Decatur City Cemetery by two other Hinds' graves. One is Adolphus L. Hinds, born February 28, 1848 and died June 10, 1864 while serving in the Union Army. The other grave is Albert M. Hinds born September 16, 1850 and died December 1, 1860.

Hinds, Joseph M., 2nd Lt. Co. A, age 22, appt. from Sgt., Co. H, 8th Regt. Illinois Vols. 10/4/64, MO 10/20/65, Huntsville, AL.

NOTE: Joseph Monroe Hinds was the brother of Capt. Jerome J. Hinds (see above), and son of Simeon Hinds. After the war, he garnered a federal appointment as Consul-General for the U.S. in Brazil in 1872 and returned to the U.S. in 1878. He was then appointed U.S. Marshal for the Northern District of Alabama. [81] His daughter, Grace, married George Nathaniel Curzon, Viceory of India and the First Marquis of Kedlestone, after the death of her first husband. Alfred Duggan. Joseph was born January 6, 1842 in Fayette Co., IL and died in Bantangas, Philippine Islands October 18, 1901. He is buried in Section 13, Row 8 in Maple Hill Cemetery in Huntsville, AL with "G.A.R" at the top of his tombstone.

Hinell, (?), gain 12/19/63 enlisted in Co.*

Hinley, R., Co. F, absent recruiting 7/63.*

Hobgood, Benjamin F., Pvt., Co. C, age 25, EN 6/5/63, Glendale, MS, born Anson Co., NC, farmer, MO 7/27/64, Rome, GA.

Hobson, Nathan D., Pvt., Co. A, age 23, EN & MI 10/17/64, Rome, GA, born Greenville, Dist., SC, (or Chattanooga, TN), farmer, wounded and sent to Foster USA Gen. Hospital in New Berne, NC 4/25/65, MO 10/20/65, Huntsville, AL.

Hodges, Charles W., in USA General Field Hospital at Stevenson, AL 10/31/63.*

Hoffman, Henry L., Pvt., Co. C, age 18, EN 1/1/64, Corinth, MS, MI 3/10/64, Memphis, TN, born Georgia, farmer, in Adams USA Gen. Hospital, Memphis, TN 2/15/64, MO 10/20/65, Huntsville, AL.

Hoffman, Robert R., in USA General Hospital #3 in Nashville, TN 9/64, returned to duty 10/11/64.*

Hogan, John A., Sgt/Pvt., Co. A, age 24, EN 12/22/63, Camp Davies, MS, MI 2/5/64, Memphis, TN, born Kirshaw Dist., SC, farmer, reduced to ranks 7/26/64, deserted 11/12/64, Kington, GA with two Remington revolvers.

Hogan, John H., Capt./ (Brevet Lt. Col.), Co. G, age 28, EN 8/6/64, Marietta, GA, on detached service in Chattanooga, TN 8/6/64 as Chief Ordnance Officer, in Atlanta, GA 9/13/64 with office on Peachtree St., discharged 11/30/65.

Hohns, William, Pvt., Co. K, in USA General Hospital at Savannah, GA 2/1/65.*

Holaway, William J., Pvt/Corp., Co. H, age 22, EN 5/1/65, Stevenson, AL, MI 5/20/65, Nashville, TN, born Walker Co., AL, farmer, appt. Corp. 7/1/65, MO 10/20/65, Huntsville, AL.

Holcomb/Hallcomb, James A., Pvt., Co. B, age 22, EN 1/5/63, Glendale, MS, MI 1/22/63, Corinth, MS, born Cherokee, GA, farmer, sick in hospital 2/20/63 at Corinth, MS with measles, deserted 4/18/63 from Glendale, MS, application for removal of charge of desertion was denied 11/3/90.

Holcomb, Wiseman - (See Halcomb, Wiseman)

Holden, Archibald J., Co. G, temporarily attached from 1st AL Cav. to Co. C, 18th Reg't. MO, Inf., died 8/3/63 near Ripley, MS, KIA.*

Holermon/Holermire, Aaron, Pvt/Sgt., Co. H, age 22, EN 10/7/63, Glendale, MS, MO 10/24/64, Rome, GA.

Holland, Andrew J., Corp., Co. C, age 35, EN 12/19/62, Corinth, MS, MI 12/22/62, Corinth, MS, born Lawrence Co., TN, farmer, appt. Corp. 1/1/63, MO 12/27/63, Camp Davies, MS.

Holland, John, Pvt/Corp., Co. M, age 24, EN 8/2/63, Chewalla, TN, MI 12/29/63, Corinth, MS, appt. Corp. 8/21/63, born Hardiman Co., TN, farmer, sick in hospital at Savannah, GA 1/15/65, MO 10/20/65, Huntsville, AL.

Holley, Hardy M., Sgt., Co. C, age 23, EN 12/1/62, Corinth, MS, born Anson Co., NC, farmer, appt. Sgt. 1/1/63, MO 12/17/63, Memphis, TN.

Holley, James D., Pvt/2nd Lt., Co. C, age 31, EN 12/1/62, Corinth, MS, MI as 2nd Lt. 1/25/63, born Anson Co., NC, farmer, MO 1/25/64.

Holley, John N., Pvt., Co. C, age 19, EN 1/1/63, Corinth, MS, born Tishomingo, MS, farmer, POW 4/18/63.

Holley, Pinkney, Pvt., Co. D, age 21, EN 4/19/64, Decatur, AL, MI 6/16/64, Decatur, AL, born Tuscaloosa, AL, farmer, sick in Gen. Hospital 11/64, MO 10/20/65, Huntsville, AL.

Holley, Pleasant, Pvt., Co. G, age 46, EN 3/5/63, Chewalla, TN, on duty as teamster 8/24/63, MO 11/26/63, Memphis, TN.

Holley, William S., Corp., Co. G, age 22, EN 2/14/63, Chewalla, TN, appt. Corp. 4/1/63, MO 11/26/63, Memphis, TN.

Hollingsworth, Samuel, Pvt., Co. H, age 21, EN 4/1/65, Stevenson, AL, MI 4/5/65, Nashville, TN, born Jefferson Co., AL, farmer, MO 10/20/65, Huntsville, AL.

Holloway/Halloway, Isaac W., Pvt., Co. B, age 33, EN 8/1/64, Wedowee, AL, MI 8/1/64, Rome, GA, born Carroll Co., GA, farmer, on special duty 11/10/64, MO 10/20/65, Huntsville, AL.

Holly/Hilly/Kelly, James, Co. C, absent in arrest at Salisbury, NC 5/16/65.*

Holmes, Garnet, Pvt/Corp., Co. E, age 22, EN & MI 9/1/64, Rome, GA, born Carroll Co., GA, farmer, promoted to Corp. 1/1/65, sick in hospital 9/1/65.

Holmes, J.A., Pvt., Co. F, absent sick in US Gen. Hosp. 12/64, absent sick in U.S. Gen. Hosp. 3/65-9/65.*

Holmes, James R., Pvt/Corp., Co. E, age 26, EN & MI 9/1/64, Rome,GA, born Dekalb, GA, farmer, promoted Corp. 1/1/65, MO 10/20/65, Huntsville, AL.

Holmes, John M., Pvt., Co. K, EN 5/4/63, Memphis, TN, MI 9/27/63, Glendale, MS, born Dekalb Co., GA, farmer, MIA 10/26/63, Vincent's Crossroads, returned 11/2/63, on detached service as teamster in Gen. Sherman's expedition 1/24/64 at Vicksburg, MS, left sick in Randolph Co., AL 8/19/64, left sick in Savannah, GA 1/28/65, died in hospital at Savannah 3/27/65. (Buried Sec. 23, Grave #2072, Beaufort National Cemetery, SC.)

Holmes, Joseph, Pvt., Co. B, in USA Gen. Hospital at Savannah, GA 2/1/65.*

Holt, Andrew J., Pvt., Co. M, age 17, EN 12/16/63, Camp Davies, MS, MI 12/29/63, Corinth, MS, born Blount Co., AL, farmer, MO 10/20/65, Huntsville, AL.

Holt, Isaac M., Pvt., Co. M, age 22, EN 10/30/63, Glendale, MS, MI 12/29/63, Corinth, MS, born Winston Co., AL, farmer, died 5/21/64 in hospital at Decatur, AL.

Holt, Jasper C., Pvt., Co. M, age 17, EN 12/16/63, Camp Davies, MS, MI 12/29/63, Corinth, MS, born Blount Co., AL, farmer, MO 10/20/65, Huntsville, AL.

Holt, Oziah N., Pvt., Co. M, age 20, EN 10/30/63, Glendale, MS, MI 12/29/63, Corinth, MS, born Winston Co., AL, farmer, MO 10/20/65, Huntsville, AL.

Holt, Peter F., Corp., Co. L, age 33, EN 9/25/63, Fayette Co., AL, MI 9/25/63, Glendale, MS, MO 9/28/64, Rome, GA.

Holt, Richard, Pvt., Co. A, EN 2/5/64, Memphis, TN.*

Holt, Samuel M., Pvt., Co. A, absent detached in Co. D since 2/5/64.*

Holt, William D., Pvt/Corp., Co. M, age 25, EN 10/30/63, Glendale, MS, MI 12/29/63, Corinth, MS, born Winston Co., AL, farmer, promoted to Corp. 7/1/65 for good conduct in the field, MO 10/20/65, Huntsville, AL.

Homan/Homen/Homes, Andrew J., Pvt., Co. D, age 45, EN 5/1/64, Decatur, AL, MI 6/16/64, Decatur, AL, born Tuscaloosa, AL (or Pendleton Co., SC) farmer, POW 3/10/65 at Solomon Grove near Fayetteville, NC, delivered at Cox's Wharf, VA 3/30/65, reported at College Green Barracks MD 3/31/65 and at Camp Chase, OH 4/5/65, reported to his regiment 5/21/65, died 5/21/65 at post hospital in Stevenson, AL.

Homan/Homen/Homes, William J., Pvt., Co. D, age 18, EN 5/1/64, Decatur, AL, MI 6/16/64, Decatur, AL, born Tuscaloosa, AL, farmer, POW 3/10/65 at Solomon Grove, NC, MO 6/13/65, Camp Chase, OH.

Homes, M., Co. E, absent POW 3/10/65.*

Hood, David A.(or H), Pvt., Co. A, age 19, EN 12/23/63, Camp Davies, MS, MI 2/5/64, Memphis, TN, born Franklin Co., AL, farmer, deserted 4/3/65 from Mt. Olive, NC.

Hood, David A., Pvt., Co. B, age 18, MI 1/22/63, Corinth, MS, born Franklin Co., AL, farmer, MO 1/22/64, Memphis, TN. (May be same as above.)

Hood Dennard, Pvt., Co. A, age 44, EN 10/1/62, Corinth, MS, MI 10/14/62, Corinth, MS, born Jefferson Co., AL, farmer, deserted 12/31/62, sick in hospital at Purdy, TN 3/12/63.

Hood, John, Pvt., Co. A, EN 10/1/62, Corinth, MS, MI 10/14/62, Corinth, MS, deserted 12/31/62.

Hood, John, Corp., Co. B, EN 1/5/63, Glendale, MS, appt. Corp 1/22/63, died 2/24/63 in hospital at Corinth, MS of measles.

Hood, John W. (or M), Pvt., Co. D, age 18, EN 5/1/64, Decatur, AL, MI 6/16/64, Decatur, AL, born Pontotoc, MS, farmer, sick in hospital at Chattanooga, TN 10/7/64, MO 10/20/65, Huntsville, AL.

Hood, Richard, Pvt., Co. A, EN 2/5/64, Memphis, TN.*

Hood, William W., Pvt., Co. B, age 26, EN 1/5/63, Glendale, MS, MI 1/22/63, Corinth, MS, born Jefferson Co., AL, farmer, deserted 4/18/63 from Glendale, MS.

Hooker/Hooks, John A., Pvt., Co. E, EN 2/1/63, Corinth, MS, POW near Chewalla, TN 2/5/63, deserted 3/16/63, Glendale, MS.

Horn, Anderson, Pvt., Co. C, age 32, EN 12/1/62, Corinth, MS, MI 12/22/62, Corinth, MS, born Lawrence Co., TN, farmer, MO 12/17/63, Memphis, TN. (An Anderson Horn died 2/12/64 and is buried in Grave #A-366, Corinth National Cemetery.)

Hornbeck/Hornback, Joseph H., 1st Lt., Co. K, age 39, EN 8/24/61, Wood Co., OH, transferred from Co. K, 21st Ohio Vols. 7/24/62 to 1st Regt. AL Cav. in Huntsville, AL, born Champaign, OH, carpenter, captured 12/31/62 at Stone's River, Murfreesboro, TN, POW 3/21/64 with 15 other men in AR, exchanged POW and reported for duty 6/7/64 at Decatur, AL, WIA 3/10/65, Monroe's Crossroads, NC, suffered gunshot wound to left leg, MO 7/19/65, Nashville, TN.
NOTE: Joseph Hornbeck was born March 12, 1823 in Indiana and died October 4, 1905 in San Bernardino County, CA. His wife was Celicia Amanda Gulick, born November 12, 1826 in Ohio.[82]

Horton, William H., Pvt., Co. H, age 48, EN 1/24/64, Camp Davies, MS, MI 2/5/64, Memphis, TN, born Jackson Co., GA, shoemaker, deserted 4/11/64 from Mooresville, AL with carbine & equipment.

Houston, S.T., Pvt., Co. F, died 9/4/63, Glendale, MS.*

Hovel, Jno., absent sick in Gen. Hospital 11/64.*

Howard, William P., Pvt., Co. G, age 20, EN 3/10/64, Decatur, AL, born Marion Co., AL, farmer, deserted 7/11/64 from Rome, GA with arms & equipment.

Howard, E.F., Pvt., Co. G, in Cumberland USA Hospital at Nashville, TN 7/65 & 8/65.*

Howard, Edward, in prison at Nashville, TN 8/65, his brother was killed by a bushwhacker and he was charged with being an accessory. (Records state he was in the 1st Alabama Cavalry but they were unable to locate enlistment papers.)*

Howell, Marcus, Pvt., Co. L, EN 6/1/64, Ackworth, GA.*

Howell, William C., Pvt., Co. L&M, age 39, EN 12/1/63, Camp Davies, MS, MI 12/29/63, Corinth, MS, on recruiting service in AL 9/15/64, MO 6/30/65, Nashville, TN.

Huddleston, Levi H., Pvt., Co. C, age 25, EN 2/15/64, Memphis, TN, MI 3/10/64, Memphis, TN, born Pike Co., AR, MO 10/20/65, Huntsville, AL.

Hudson, Ephraim, Pvt., Co. G, age 21, EN 4/15/63, Chewalla, TN, on duty as teamster 9/63-11/63, MO 11/26/63, Memphis, TN.

Hudson, James B., Pvt/Sgt., Co. H, age 28, EN 9/14/63, Glendale, MS, promoted to 1st Sgt. 7/1/64, MO 9/29/64, Rome, GA.

Huey, Joseph, Pvt., Co. K, age 25, EN 12/6/63, Camp Davies, MS, born Dekalb Co., GA, farmer, served as teamster and Regimental wagon master, MO 7/19/65, Nashville, TN. Traveled 300 miles from his home in Randolph Co., AL to Camp Davies, MS to enlist.

Huey, Thomas, Pvt., Co. K, age 36, EN 12/6/63, Camp Davies, MS, born Dekalb Co., GA, farmer, on duty guarding ordnance at Memphis, TN 3/64, died 7/21/64 in Cumberland USA Hospital at Nashville, TN. Traveled 300 miles from his home in Randolph Co., AL to Camp Davies, MS to enlist. (Buried in Grave J-13787 in Nashville National Cemetery.)

Huff, Elias, Pvt., Co. H, age 17, EN 10/16/63, Camp Davies, MS, MI 2/24/64, Memphis, TN, born Missouri, farmer, in Small Pox USA Hospital in Memphis, TN 1/17/64, MO 10/24/64, Rome, GA.
(Henry C. Peck signed consent as guardian of Elias Huff.)

Huffman, Henry S., (Cards filed with Henry S. Hoffman)

Hughes, David M., Pvt., Co. D, age 21, EN 5/1/64, Decatur, AL, MI 6/16/64, Decatur, AL, born Walker Co., AL, farmer, MO 10/20/65, Huntsville, AL.

Hughes, Eli P., Pvt., Co. I, age 18, EN & MI 8/18/62, Huntsville, AL, born Madison Co., AL, farmer, MIA 4/28/63 at Day's Gap, rejoined 11/10/63, detached as courier at Reedyville, TN 1/27/63, also served as blacksmith and ambulance driver, MO 7/9/65, Nashville, TN.

Hughes, George R., Pvt., Co. L, age 18, EN & MI 9/25/63, Fayette Co., AL, born Walker Co., AL, farmer, MO 9/28/64, Rome, GA.

Hughes, George S., Corp., Co. I, age 24, EN & MI 7/21/62, Huntsville, AL, born Madison Co., AL, farmer, detached as courier at Reedyville, TN 1/27/63, MIA 5/3/63 at Day's Gap, Cedar Bluff, AL, rejoined 8/1/63, MO 7/19/65, Nashville, TN.
  NOTE: George S. Hughes was born November 18, 1838, married Margrette E. Dutton, January 12, 1867 and had the following children: Edmon Albert, born November 1, 1867; George Luther, born May 1, 1869; John, born January 15, 1871; Malissie Francis, born May 29, 1873; Willie Edna, born September 20, 1876; and Mary Emily, born February 12, 1884.[83]

Hughes, John B., Corp., Co. I, age 27, EN & MI 7/21/62, Huntsville, AL, born Madison Co., AL, carpenter, MIA 5/20/63 at Day's Gap, Cedar Bluff, AL, rejoined 11/10/63.

Hughs, I. (or J.), Co. D, AWOL 10/64.*

Huld, (?), Co. A, absent detached recruiting at Decatur, AL 10/64.*

Humphry/Humphries, John L., Pvt., Co. B, age 18, EN 4/7/64, Decatur, AL, MI 4/13/64, Decatur, AL, born Blount Co., AL (or Marshall Co.), farmer, in hospital at

Decatur 4/30/64, POW 3/10/65, Monroe's Crossroads, NC, discharged 6/13/65 at Camp Chase, OH.

Hunt, James T., Pvt., Co. H, age 21, EN 1/26/65, Huntsville, AL, MI 2/13/65, Nashville, TN, born Madison Co., AL, farmer, deserted 5/2/65 at Huntsville, AL.

Hunt, William T.(or F. or A.), Pvt., Co. E, age 18, EN 11/13/63, Camp Davies, MS, MI 11/13/63, Rome, GA, born Bowling Green, KY, farmer, MO 12/16/64, Savannah, GA.

Hunter, Henry C., Pvt., Co. I, age 33, EN 12/21/63, Camp Davies, MS, born in TN, farmer, sent to Jefferson Gen. Hospital in Jeffersonville, IN 1/1/65 from Hospital #3 in Nashville, TN with typhoid fever, returned to duty 1/26/65, MO 7/19/65, Nashville, TN.

Hunter, John, Pvt., Co. G, age 18, EN 5/6/63, Chewalla, TN, in USA Post Hospital at Corinth, MS 11/63, MO 11/26/63, Memphis, TN.

Hunter, Thomas T., Pvt., Co. F, age 30, EN 4/6/63, Corinth, MS, born Nash Co., NC, farmer, sick in Post Hospital at Corinth, MS 6/20/63, died 8/31/63 at Corinth. (Buried Grave #A-2131, Corinth National Cemetery.)

Hurst, Billington Sanders, Pvt., Co. K, age 50, EN 12/13/63, Camp Davies, MS, born Columbia Co., GA, farmer, in USA Field Hospital at Rome, GA 7/12/64, returned to duty 9/1/64, sent to Nashville, TN sick 11/10/64, left sick at Mt. Olive, NC 4/9/65, MO 8/7/65, Washington, DC. Traveled 200 miles from his home in St. Claire Co., AL to Camp Davies, MS to enlist.
    NOTE: Billington S. Hurst was born in 1813 in Columbia Co., GA and married Elizabeth McCallum August 1, 1834. Their son, Hugh McCallum Hurst, born in 1834, joined the 19th Louisiana, CSA. Billington told Hugh that he was on the wrong side fighting for the wrong reasons. Although he survived the war, his experience cost him everything including his family and land. He had bought 360 acres of land in St. Clair Co. near present day Moody, and no record of any slaves has been found. At age 50, Billington rode 210 miles through Rebel lines from his home in St. Clair Co., AL to Camp Davies, MS to join the Union army. He was in USA Field Hospital at Rome, GA on July 12, 1864, with a broken collar bone caused when his horse was shot out from under him while charging Rebels. After the war, he returned home to Alabama, gathered his belongings and left, never to be spoken of again by his family. He remarried in 1867 in Jefferson Co., AL to a widow named Jane Crump.[84]

Hurston, Samuel B., Pvt., Co. M, age 22, EN 12/20/63, Camp Davies, MS, born Lauderdale Co., AL, rejected by surgeon for epilepsy 12/20/63.

Hutchingson, Joseph, Pvt., Co. A, in USA Gen. Hospital #2 at Annapolis, MD 5/2/64, returned to duty 8/12/64.*

Hutto, Aaron, Pvt/Sgt., Co. B, age 32, EN 1/18/63, Glendale, MS, MI 1/22/63, Corinth, MS, born Lexington, SC, mechanic, appt. Sgt. 3/1/63, MO 1/22/64, Memphis, TN.

Hyde, Holland W., Pvt., Co. D, age 33, EN 5/1/64, Decatur, AL, born Hall Co., GA, farmer, deserted 5/10/65 from Huntsville, AL, never MI, sent out on recruiting service by Col. Spencer and never returned.

Hyde/Hide, Jesse D., Pvt., Co. M&L, age 37, EN 12/1/63, Camp Davies, MS, MI 12/29/63, Corinth, MS, on duty as regimental carpenter, MO 1/12/65, Nashville, TN.
  NOTE: Jessee Daniel Hyde was born June 11, 1825 in GA and died May 10, 1883 in AL. He is buried at Sardis Baptist Church Cemetery in Lynn, Winston Co., AL. He married Sarah Jarome Barton on September 3, 1850 in GA.[85]

Hyde/Hide, William, Pvt., Co. D, age 25, EN 5/1/64, Decatur, AL, born Hall Co., GA, farmer, deserted 5/10/65 from Huntsville, AL with Remington revolver & equipment, never MI.

Hyfield, Robert H., Pvt/Sgt., Co. H, age 23, EN 10/16/63, Glendale, MS, appt. Sgt. 1/1/64, MO 10/24/64, Rome, GA.

Inghram, John W., Pvt., Co. A, age 23, EN 3/23/63, Glendale, MS, MI 3/24/63, Glendale, MS, born Calhoun Co., AL, discharged 7/16/63 for disability.

Ingle, Murray, Pvt., Co. L, age 25, EN 9/25/63, Fayette Co., AL, born Fayette Co., AL, farmer, returned from MIA 12/25/63, died 7/31/64 at Rome, GA of congestive fever. (Buried in Grave #1518 in Marietta National Cemetery.)
  NOTE: Murray Ingle was born about 1838. He, along with his brothers, John and Robert Milburn Ingle, were rounded up by the Alabama Partisan Rangers and taken to Jasper, Alabama along with hundreds of other men and forced to join Co. A, 13th Alabama Partisan Rangers, CSA on September 6, 1862. By the time the regiment left for Columbus, MS on October 31, 1862, they were shown as deserters. Murray had enlisted in the 1st AL Cav. USA on September 25, 1863. He married Sarah Catherine Fry in 1860 and had two daughters. After Robert Milburn "Doc" Ingle deserted the CSA, he joined Co. A, 1st Mississippi Mounted Rifles, USA on December 30, 1863.[86]

Ingle, Peter, Co. M, age 18, born Itawamba Co., MS, farmer, EN 12/16/63, Camp Davies, MS by Capt. Lomax. *

Ingle, Wm., Co. L, absent with leave 10/63.*

Ingram, James J., Pvt., Co. I, age 23, EN & MI 8/18/62, Huntsville, AL, born Carroll Co., GA, farmer, with wagon train in Nashville, TN 12/27/62, sick in hospital at Memphis, TN 10/12/63, POW 11/22/63, sick in hospital at Nashville, TN 11/10/64, MO 7/19/65, Nashville, TN.

Inman, Arthur, Pvt., Co. B, age 18, EN 1/13/63, Glendale, MS, MI 1/22/63, Corinth, MS, born Talladega, AL, farmer, died 3/26/63, Corinth, MS of measles. (Certificate of Death states he was age 50.)

Inman, Henderson, Pvt., Co. B, age 16, EN 6/10/63, Glendale, MS, MO 1/22/64, Memphis, TN.

Inman, Henry, Pvt., Co. K, age 51 (or 45), EN & MI 7/21/62, Huntsville, AL, born Lincoln Co., TN, farmer, died 12/1/62 in Hospital #8, Nashville, TN.

Inman, John, Pvt., Co. B, age 50, EN 1/13/63, Glendale, MS, MI 1/22/63, Corinth, MS, born Newberry, SC, farmer, sick in refugee camp at Corinth 12/15/63, MO 1/22/64, Memphis, TN. (One MO Roll states he was 18 years of age.)

Irby, John M., Pvt., Co. G, age 21, EN 2/15/63, Chewalla, TN, POW 4/10/63, MIA 10/26/63 from Vincent's Crossroads, MO 11/26/63, Memphis, TN.

Irby, Joseph A., Pvt., Co. G, age 18, EN 2/15/63, Chewalla, TN, POW 4/10/63, MO 11/26/63, Memphis, TN. (Notation states "see also Co. B, 1st Miss. Mt'd Rifles.)

Irven/Irvin, Edward F., Pvt., Co. H, age 19, EN 3/1/65, Stevenson, AL, MI 4/5/65, Nashville, TN, born Marshall Co., AL, in confinement at Nashville, TN 5/1/65 for manslaughter.

Irwin, Benjamin F., Corp/Sgt., Co. A, age 19, EN 1/1/64, Camp Davies, MS, MI 2/5/64, Memphis, TN, born Henry Co., MO, carpenter, promoted to Sgt. 7/3/64, MO 10/20/65, Huntsville, AL.

Ivey, Charles V., Pvt., Co. D, age 20, EN 5/1/64, Decatur, AL, MI 6/16/64, Decatur, AL, born Marshall Co., AL, farmer, MO 10/20/65, Huntsville, AL.

Ivey, Young M., Pvt., Co. L, age 21, EN 4/7/65, Stevenson, AL, MI 4/18/65, Nashville, TN, born Walker Co., AL, MO 10/20/65, Huntsville, AL.

Jackson, Alfred, Pvt., Co. L, deserted 11/11/64 from Rome, GA.*

Jackson Benjamin F., Pvt., Co. L, age 23, EN 4/7/65, Stevenson, AL, MI 4/18/65, Nashville, TN, born Walker Co., AL, farmer, MO 10/20/65, Huntsville, AL.

Jackson, Emmanuel, Pvt., Co. F, age 25, EN 6/16/63, Corinth, MS, born Tuscaloosa, AL, farmer, MO 7/27/64, Rome, GA.

Jackson, Joseph, Pvt., Co. L, age 43, EN 3/1/65, Stevenson, AL, MI 4/18/65, Nashville, TN, born Newton Co., GA, farmer, MO 10/20/65, Huntsville, AL.

Jackson, Joseph M., Pvt., Co. B&A, age 20, EN 1/13/63, Glendale, MS, MI 1/22/63, Corinth, MS, born Cherokee Co., GA, KIA 7/5/63 at Glendale, MS.

Jackson, Nicholas W., Pvt., Co. B, age 23, EN 2/5/64, Pulaski, TN, MI 3/27/64, Decatur, AL, born Limestone Co., AL, farmer, deserted March 29, 1864 from Decatur, AL.

Jackson, Samuel H., Pvt., Co. B, age 31, EN 8/4/63, Glendale, MS, born SC, MO 1/22/64, Memphis, TN.

Jackson, Stith, Co. B. (No further information).*

Jackson, William H., Pvt., in USA Gen. Hospital at Annapolis, MD 3/24/64, returned to duty 7/19/64.*

Jackson, William A., Pvt., Co. D, age 34, EN& MI 6/1/63, Glendale, MS, born Hall Co., GA, discharged 1/4/64 for disability "near blind".
   NOTE: William A. "Billy" Jackson was born in August 1828 in Hall Co., GA. His first wife was Martha Canaday and they had the following children: William Tyre, born May 8, 1850; Luther Greenbury, born August 8, 1852; and Leonard Jackson, born April 7, 1855. Martha died in May 1857 and in 1860, William married Hannah Hollon Grissom and had the following children: Sarah Adeline, Andrew, John, Aaron, Robert and Marion A. Jackson. William A. died June 23, 1910 and is buried at Wesley's Chapel Methodist Church Cemetery in West Lauderdale Co., AL. [87]

Jaggers, Benjamin F., Pvt., Co. I, age 30, EN & MI 8/18/62, Huntsville, AL, born Morgan Co., AL, farmer, died 10/16/62 in Hospital #14, Nashville, TN of measles. (Buried in Grave A-4518 in Nashville National Cemetery with death date shown as 10/17/62.)

Jaggers, George W., Pvt/Saddler Sgt., Co. A&D, age 31, EN 12/10/63, Camp Davies, MS, MI 2/5/64, Memphis, TN, born Marion Co., AL, appt. Sgt. from Co. Saddler 11/1/64 by order of Col. Spencer, appt. Saddler Sgt. 8/1/65, MO 10/20/65, Huntsville, AL.

Jaggers, James W., Pvt/Sgt., Co. I, age 19, EN & MI 7/21/62, Huntsville, AL, born Morgan Co., AL, farmer, on wagon train at Nashville, TN 12/27/62, appt. Corp. 11/1/63, appt. Sgt. 1/1/64, on courier service at Reedyville, TN 1/63, POW 3/10/65 from Monroe's Crossroads, Solomon Grove, NC, paroled at Camp Chase, OH, MO 7/19/65, Nashville, TN.

James, Francis H., Pvt., Co. G, age 19, EN 6/26/63, Chewalla, TN, MO 11/26/63, Memphis, TN.

James, Jesse, Pvt., Co. I, age 22, EN 10/1/63, Glendale, MS, born Lawrence Co., AL, farmer, POW 11/27/63, sick in hospital in Nashville, TN 4/15/64, MO 7/19/65, Nashville, TN.
   NOTE: Jesse James was the son Ann Cottingham and Pleasant James (born 1809 in TN), who married September 29, 1826 in Lawrence Co., AL. Pleasant and Laban (father of Williah H. James, below)

were brothers and sons of Laban James, born 1769 in North Carolina and died after 1860 in Winston Co., AL. Other children were: Jesse, born 1814; Sarah B; James, born 1817, died August 29, 1868 in Walker Co., AL; Solomon, born 1825 in AL and Charles James, born 1828 in AL.[88]

James, James/Jefferson H., Pvt., Co. G, age 16, EN 4/16/63, Chewalla, TN, MO 11/26/63, Memphis, TN.

James, Joseph, Pvt., Co. E, EN 3/10/63, Glendale, MS, MI 3/17/63, Corinth, MS, died 6/24/63 at Glendale, MS of typhoid fever.

James, William H., Pvt., Co. I, age 21, EN 11/10/63, Camp Davies, MS, born Lawrence Co., AL, farmer, died 7/13/64 in Hospital #3, Nashville, TN, residence shown as Winston Co., AL. (Buried in Grave H-09946 in Nashville National Cemetery.)
NOTE: William H. James was born about 1842 in Lawrence Co., AL. He was the son of Mary Crawley and Laban James, born 1814 in TN, who married January 30, 1840 in Lawrence County. See Jesse James above for additional family information. [89]

James, William F., Corp/Sgt., Co. G, age 33, EN & MI 3/7/63, Chewalla, TN, appt. Corp. 4/1/63, promoted to Sgt. 9/1/63, MO 11/26/63, Memphis, TN.

James, William R., Pvt., Co. A, absent sick in hospital at Nashville, TN 8/64.*

Jarrett, James, Pvt., Co. H. age 25, EN & MI 9/20/63, Glendale, MS, absent sick 10/20/63, on duty as teamster Jan. & Feb. 1864, MO 9/29/64, Rome, GA.
NOTE: James "Jim" Jarrett was born April 4, 1838 in Fairfield Dist., SC and died January 23, 1918 in Davidson Co., TN. He married 1st, about 1858, Elizabeth "Lizzie" Kelley, born November 10, 1841 in Elbert Co., GA, died sometime before 1870 in Robertson Co., TN. She was the daughter of Margaret Menervia Scales (1810-1877) and Barnabas Kelley (1810-1887). James and Elizabeth had the following children: Nancy Adeline; James Henry, born January 3, 1862 in TN and Elizabeth Matilda Jane, born September 30, 1865 in TN. He married 2nd, Fidelia Rhodes in Robertson Co., TN and she died October 22, 1913. Other children of James were: Mary Ada, born September 30, 1871; William, born August 6, 1873; George, born November 6, 1875 and Charlie Davis Jarrett, born December 20, 1870. In a form completed by James April 1, 1915, he stated that his children Elizabeth, Mary and Charlie were dead. He also stated in his pension application that he was the brother-in-law of Joseph Harper, also a soldier in the First Alabama Cavalry US Volunteers.[90]

Jason, (?), Sgt., Co. A, on detached service recruiting 9/64.*

Jefferson, John Rufus, Bugler, Co. A.
NOTE: John R. Jefferson was born October 17, 1844 in Talladega, AL, married Lidia Etta Allman in 1875 in Ashville, AL, died December 11, 1925 and is buried in East Walker Cemetery in Dora, AL. He was the son of Lidia Tines and Campbell Jefferson who were married November 28, 1843 in Ashville, AL. Children

of John and Lidia were: Daisy Ethel, Wes, Van, Thomas Campbell, Joe, Ellen, Mittie and Mattie.[91]

Jeffryes, John, Pvt., Co. C, age 23, EN 1/4/63, Corinth, MS, MI 1/11/63, Corinth, MS, born Franklin Co., AL, farmer, detailed as blacksmith 8/63-12/63, MO 1/31/64, Memphis, TN.

Jenkins, George C., 2nd Lt., Co. M, age 22, promoted from Corp. Co. B, 2nd Illinois Vet. Light Art'y, appt. 2nd Lt. 8/15/64, WIA 3/10/65 at Monroe's Crossroads, gunshot wounds to right foot and left arm, returned 7/25/65, MO 10/20/65, Huntsville, AL. (Several pieces of correspondence on microfilm.)
   NOTE: George C. Jenkins was born in Ross County, Ohio. In a letter to John Gardner dated April 13, 1900, he wrote , *"I was agreeable surprised a short time ago on receipt of a copy of your newsy little paper - 'The Anchor.' It refreshed my memory of tried experiences of my own in Winston during the Civil War of 1861 to 1865 where Comrades Bartin, Emerick and my self enjoyed such a lovely time circulating around the many rock houses and caves beating up recruits for the Old Loyal 1st Ala. Cav. I never shall forget the events of that expedition. Six of us left our Lines at Camp Davis on the evening of Dec. 19th '63, rode thro' the woods until dark, where we took the main road and kept it until day dawned next morning. We stopped at the home of a Union man 76 miles south-east of our starting place - Camp Davis. We stayed there rested and slept during the day; and when darkness came again we mounted our refreshed horses and on we went for another night's ride; and passed the next several days resting in some thickets, and the nights we passed in wandering our way thro the mountain paths of North Alabama. When we struck the Biler road we discovered several bands of Confederate Cavalrymen so we divided our forces, Jim Medlin and two Comrades struck out east, while Comrades Barton, Emerick and myself beat south. On that memorable cold New Years day we ate dinner at Comrade Barton's residence in the Black Swamp Beat on Splunge Creek. I shall never forget the good freezing out we got new years evening when Barton got so dreadful cold we could hardly keep him on his horse, and finally he came bewildered and we were lost and freezing mid the snow which had made the paths invisible. We finally came to an isolated field after going around this lonely field several times our horses struck the trail leading from it and followed it down the mountain to Kelly's tanyard. Barton then knew where we were and as Kelly was a Reb we went a mile or so south of Kelly's and stopped until day again. At the cabin of a good old Loyalist by the name of Weaver, the possession of fire-warmth was never welcomed by no mortal more heartily than it was by me that night at Mr. Weavers. My feet and fingers were almost frozen off. We laid down on a bed and slept while Mr. Weaver stayed out in the cold and kept guard about half way between his cabin and his neighbors where some Confederate Cavalry men were enjoying their New Year dance. His loyal wife, God bless her, cooked us a warm breakfast and at day we started to Barton 5 miles south. Hiding our horses in the thickets on Splunge Creek we reached Mr. Bartons some before noon, his wife cooking us a warm and refreshing dinner, and after dining, we went to the brush until dark, then we returned back to the house where we enjoyed a peaceful nights sleep in a house this being the only night we slept all night in a house, after this, rock houses were our resting places during the day and the roads and trails were kept warm through the night. A cave not far from Taylor's store was our*

headquarters and we recruited as far south as Vince Rodens in Walker County near Jasper, and if old Tid Walker or any of his family are living I guess they will remember the visit we paid them one night when we captured old Tid, his musket, and mule, but I can't go into full details about this visit to old Tids. I often wonder if any of these old boys are living yet. After the war I married and have raised and educated a family of six children, but for the past ten years the disabilities from my wounds and four and half years service in the war has almost overcome my vigor and ambition. I am almost worn out. Oh! how I would like to visit those old mountain cabins in old Black Swamp, but I shall only hope on for the opportunity but fear my hope will never be realized. I frequently hear from Hinds and a few others of my old Comrades, if there are any of them left in Winston, I offer them my best wishes; and would like to see them. I also offer my kindest regards to any and all of the Confederates that I fought so long and hard, God bless them all! The animosity I once held against them is all gone now, and in its place dwells in my heart, a feeling of respect akin to the fraternal love that I have for my old Comrades. What natin (sic) has ever developed better and truer patriotism than our own beloved United States - North and South? I am as proud to day of the records of the brave Confederates as I am my Comrades whom I fought with. With kind regards to any and all, I am yours truly, Geo. C. Jenkins."

Jervett, James, Pvt., Co. H, discharged by reason of expiration of term of service 9/29/64, Rome, GA.*

Jester, John, Pvt., Co. F, age 18, EN & MI 11/1/64, Rome, GA, born Polk Co., GA, farmer, MO 10/20/65, Huntsville, AL.

Jester, Joseph, Pvt., Co. F, age 18, EN & MI 8/5/64, Rome, GA, born Polk Co., GA, farmer, sick in Nashville, TN 11/6/64, returned 1/27/65, MO 10/20/65, Huntsville, AL.

Jett, Isaac, Pvt., Co. I, age 23, EN & MI 8/18/62, Huntsville, AL, born Jackson Co., AL, farmer, died 12/13/62, Nashville, TN of intermittent fever. (A James W. Jett with same death date is buried in Grave C-7114, Nashville National Cemetery.)

Jett, James, Pvt., Co. I, age 28, EN & MI 8/18/62, Huntsville, AL, born Jackson Co., AL, farmer, detached as courier at Reedyville, TN 6/27/63, captured at Day's Gap 5/1/63, paroled at City Point, VA 5/14/63, MIA 10/26/63, Vincent's Crossroads, MO 7/19/65, Nashville, TN.

Jett, James M., Pvt., Co. G, age 18, EN 3/10/64, Decatur, AL, MI 4/13/64, Decatur, AL, born Blount Co., AL, farmer, MO 10/20/65, Huntsville, AL.

Jett, John, Pvt., Co. I, age 25, EN & MI 8/18/62, Huntsville, AL, born Jackson Co., AL, farmer, on courier post at Reedyville, TN 1/27/63, MIA 5/3/63 from Battle of Cedar Bluff, AL, returned 8/1/63, MO 7/19/65, Nashville, TN.

Jobe, Ambrose, Pvt., Co. G, returned to Reg't (11th Ills. Cav.) 11/24/63 at Camp Davies.*

Jobe, Presley D., Corp., Co. G, temporarily attached from 11th Illinois Cavalry.

John, Thomas, Pvt., Co. B, deserted at TN 10/31/64.*

Johnson, Adrian, Pvt., Co. F, age 48, EN 7/1/64, Rome, GA, MI 8/1/64, Rome, GA, born Jackson Co., GA, farmer, detached in Chattanooga, TN 11/11/64 by order of Maj. Gen. Sherman, in Foster USA Gen. Hospital, New Berne, NC March & April 1865, MO 10/20/65, Huntsville, AL.

Johnson, Alex J., Pvt., Co. D, EN 6/1/63, Glendale, MS, deserted 6/19/63 while on pickett duty.
   NOTE: Letter dated 7/22/63 at Corinth, MS by order of Brig. Gen. G.M. Dodge states the following, *"Brigade Commanders will report their commands at 8 1/2 A.M. Thursday, July 23, (1863) on the parade ground east of Corinth, to witness the execution of A.J. Johnson, 1st Ala. Cavalry. - A staff officer will assign brigades their position as they arrive on the ground".*
   On February 2, 1977, *The Daily Corinthian*, Corinth, MS stated the following: *"During the Federal occupation of Corinth a deserter was court martialed and shot on July 23, 1863. According to the Corinth Chanticleer, an occupation newspaper": "Last Thursday the citizens and soldiers of Corinth were permitted to witness one of those awfully impressive spectacles which are the ligitimate result of crime when visited with retributive justice.... A private of Company D, 1st Alabama Cavalry had been found guilty by a military commission of deserting the service of the United States and joining her armed enemies. The place of execution was the parade ground some half mile southeast of town.... After the troops were stationed the prisoner was brought into the square from the right...in front of him his coffin was borne by four soldiers. He was attended by the Chaplain of the 81st Ohio... At precisely 23 minutes past nine, the band sounded the funeral dirge...The chaplain offered prayer and the order for the execution was read as ordered by Brigadier General G.M. Dodge. At four minutes past ten o'clock the order to fire was given after which the troops were marched past the corpse so that troops might have the opportunity of seeing the doom of a deserter. At the time of his desertion the soldier was posted as a vidette (sentry) near the post of Glendale, Mississippi. His last request was to see his photograph which had been taken the morning of the execution. This was denied but he was told that the picture would be sent to his wife."*[92]

Johnson, C., Pvt., Co. D, EN 6/1/63, Glendale, MS.*

Johnson, Christopher C., Pvt., Co. H, age 18, EN 12/21/64, Stevenson, AL, MI 2/13/65, Nashville, TN, born Jackson Co., AL, farmer, MO 10/20/65.

Johnson, Columbus W., Pvt., Co. F, age 18, EN 12/14/63, Camp Davies, MS, born Tishomingo Co., MS, farmer, POW 2/15/64 while on detached service as teamster near Vicksburg, MS, died 6/15/64 at Andersonville, GA. (Buried in Grave #1996, Andersonville National Cemetery.)

Johnson, Ephraim/Ephriam, Pvt/Corp., Co. A, age 20, EN 1/14/64, Camp Davies, MS, MI 2/5/64, Memphis, TN, born Maury Co., TN, farmer, promoted Corp. 9/1/64, MO 10/20/65, Huntsville, AL.

Johnson, G., Pvt., Co. F&D, deserted at Glendale, MS 6/63, absent with leave 11/1/64.*

Johnson, George W., Pvt., Co. I, age 25, EN & MI 7/24/62, Huntsville, AL, born Giles Co., TN, farmer, with wagon train in Nashville, TN 12/27/62, in Army of the Cumberland Hospital at Murfreesboro, TN 3/15/63, Hospital #13 in Nashville, TN 7/25/63, transferred to Hospital #7 in Louisville, KY, returned to duty 9/11/63, POW 11/22/63.

Johnson, Henry, Pvt., Co. A, age 35, EN 9/8/62, Iuka, MS, MI 10/1/62, Corinth, MS, born NC, farmer, promoted to Corp. 12/18/62, no MO date.

Johnson, Jacob C., Pvt., Co. A, age 35, EN 1/25/64, Camp Davies, MS, MI 2/5/64, Memphis, TN, born Lauderdale Co., AL, farmer, deserted 2/23/64, Memphis, TN.

Johnson, James/John, Pvt. Co. H, age 25, EN 10/17/63, Glendale, MS, blacksmith, in Adams USA Hospital in Memphis, TN 2/20/64, deserted while on detached service recruiting in AL.

Johnson James P., Corp., Co. F, age 19, EN 5/23/63, Corinth, MS, born Marion Co., AL, KIA 7/25/63 near Bear Creek, AL.

Johnson, James W., Pvt., Co. C, age 18, EN 12/15/63, Corinth, MS, born Tishomingo Co., MS, farmer, died 3/1/64 in hospital at Memphis, TN of smallpox. (Buried in Memphis National Cemetery.)

Johnson, John, Pvt., Co. B, age 18, EN 2/21/63, Glendale, MS, deserted 3/6/63 from Glendale.

Johnson, John, Pvt., Co. I, age 22, EN 10/17/63, Glendale, MS, died 7/31/64 at Rome, GA. (Buried in Grave #1498 in Marietta National Cemetery.)

Johnson, John B., Pvt/Sgt., Co. G, age 23, EN 3/10/64, Decatur, AL, MI 4/13/64, Decatur, AL, born Lawrence Co., AL, promoted to Sgt. 5/1/64, on detached service as nurse in hospital at Wilmington, NC in March 1865, MO 10/20/65, Huntsville, AL.

Johnson, Joseph, Pvt., Co. A, deserted 2/26/64 at Memphis, TN.*

Johnson, Leonard S., Sgt/Pvt., Co. F, age 22, EN & MI 5/23/63, Corinth, MS, born Marion Co., AL, reduced to ranks 9/15/63, detached on secret service Jan. 1864, deserted 4/10/64 from Nashville, TN, restored to duty 5/23/64, MO 7/27/64, Rome, GA.

Johnson, Mitchell/Michell C., Pvt/Corp., Co. A, age 22, EN 1/14/64, Camp Davies, MS, MI 2/5/64, Memphis, TN, born Marion Co., AL, farmer, KIA 8/20/64 at Coosaville, GA. (Buried Grave #F-991, Marietta National Cemetery.)

Johnson, Moses L., Pvt., Co. L, age 34, EN 9/25/63, Fayette Co., AL, MI 10/21/63, Glendale, MS, born Fayette Co., AL, farmer, discharged 2/10/64 due to disability "chronic pleurisy". (This file is out of order on microfilm and filed after William A. Jones.)

Johnson, N., Co. F, absent sick in US Gen. Hospital 5/65.*

Johnson, Noah, Pvt., Co. D, age 36, EN 3/15/63, Glendale, MS, MI 3/20/63, Corinth, MS, born Spartanburg, SC, died 9/20/63 in Gen. Hospital at Corinth, MS of "dropsy".

Johnson, Robert, Pvt., Co. C, age 39, EN 12/6/62, MI 12/22/62, born Spartanburg, SC, farmer, MO 12/17/63, Memphis, TN.

Johnson, Robert B., Pvt., Co. B, age 40, EN 2/21/63, Glendale, MS, deserted 3/6/63 at Glendale, MS.

Johnson, Ruben G., Pvt/Corp., Co. L, age 38, EN 9/25/63, Fayette Co., AL, MI 9/25/63, Glendale, MS, born Fayette Co., AL, farmer, promoted to Corp. 12/29/63, MO 9/28/64, Rome, GA.

Johnson, Samuel, Pvt., Co. F, age 25, EN 5/15/63, Memphis, TN, MI 8/13/63, Corinth, MS, born Philadelphia, PA, MIA 10/26/63, teamster, deserted 4/8/64 at Nashville, TN, returned 6/10/64 at Dallas, GA, listed as escaped Federal Prisoner 1/5/64, MO 7/27/64, Rome, GA.

Johnson, Thomas, Pvt., Co. B, age 24, EN 3/29/64, Decatur, AL, born Blount (or Tuscaloosa) Co., AL, farmer, deserted while on furlough 4/15/64 at Mooresville, AL.

Johnson, Wiley L. (or S.), Pvt., Co. D, age 20, EN 5/1/64, Decatur, AL, MI 6/16/64, Decatur, AL, born Shelby Co., AL, farmer, discharged 11/5/64 due to disability, "mental faculties impaired, epilepsy caused by wounds of the face and head received while in the rebel army 5/16/63".

Johnson, William, Pvt., Co. E, EN 4/1/63, Corinth, MS, deserted 4/10/63 near Corinth, MS.

Johnson, William, Pvt., Co. F, age 19, EN 11/1/63, Glendale, MS, MI 2/24/64, Memphis, TN, born Cincinnati, OH, farmer, in confinement at Memphis, TN 4/30/64, MO 11/3/64, Rome, GA. (Notation in file states, "This man, under the name Charles Crigar, deserted from Co. F, 5th Reg't Ohio Cav. Vols in October 1863 and enlisted in this organization in violation of the 22nd (now 50th) Article of War".

Johnson, William, Pvt., Co. G, age 18, EN 12/12/62, Pocohontas, TN, deserted 5/1/63.

Johnson, William, Pvt., Co. G, age 21, EN 3/21/64, Decatur, AL, MI 4/13/64, Decatur, AL, born Lawrence Co., AL, farmer, MO 10/20/65, Huntsville, AL.

Johnston, William, Co. M, age 46, born Spartanburg Dist., SC, farmer, EN 11/15/63, Camp Davies, MS, rejected due to disability.*

Jones, Columbus, S., Pvt., Co. G, age 19, EN 3/16/63, Chewalla, TN, MO 11/26/63, Memphis, TN, (Notation in file states, "see also Co. B, 1st Miss. Mtd Rifles).

Jones, Enoch D., Pvt., Co. H, age 45, EN 10/16/63, Glendale, MS, deserted 2/5/64 at Memphis, TN.

Jones, Franklin R.W., Sgt., Co. G, temporarily attached from 11th Illinois Cavalry.
   NOTE: Franklin Jones was born about 1812 in TN and married Mary Hall, February 6, 1833 in Blount Co., AL. Their children were: Melinda, married Losson Wileman; Mary Ann, married William C.J.A. Jones; Susan, married Isaac James; Elizabeth, married John Lee; Louvisa, married John W. Stephenson; Nancy, married Hamilton Stephenson; Daniel F. (died young); and Martha Rebecca, married James P. Tedford. Franklin's 2nd wife was Elizabeth Wildman/Wileman and their children were: Leonard; Wiley, married Julia A. Woodruff; Robert, married Mary Lucinda Stephenson; Manervia; Asbury, married Lydia Eliza Bille Deemer. On November 11, 1869, he married Nancy Rackley in Blount Co., AL.[93]

Jones, George W., Pvt., Co. G, age 17, EN 2/15/63, Chewalla, TN, MI 2/15/63, Corinth, MS, on duty as hospital nurse 8/5/63, MO 11/26/63, Memphis, TN.

Jones, J., Pvt., Co. F, EN 9/20/63 at Glendale, MS.*

Jones, Jackson J., Pvt., Co. C, age 38, EN 12/15/63, Memphis, TN, MI 3/10/64, Memphis, TN, born Fayette Co., AL, farmer, deserted 7/8/64, Rome, GA with Colt revolver & equipment.

Jones, James/John F., Pvt., Co. K, age 18, EN & MI 7/24/62, Huntsville, AL, born Gilmore Co., GA, sick in hospital in Nashville, TN 12/26/62, left sick at the house of Mr. Sims in Winston Co., AL 10/23/63, died 5/10/64 while POW at Andersonville, GA. (Buried in Grave #996, Andersonville National Cemetery.)

Jones, Jefferson, Pvt., Co. C, age 38, EN 12/6/62, Corinth, MS, MI 12/22/62, Corinth, MS, born Walker Co., AL, farmer, MO 12/17/63, Memphis, TN.

Jones, Jeremiah B., Pvt., Co. H, age 26, EN 10/6/63, Glendale, MS, sick in Overton USA Gen. Hospital in Memphis, TN 2/22/64, detached on recruiting service in AL 5/1/64, MO 2/7/65, Nashville, TN.
   NOTE: Jeremiah L.P. Jones (military records state Jeremiah B.) was born August 28, 1837 and died October 19, 1890. He is buried in Brushy Creek Cemetery in Cullman Co., AL. He was first married to Amanda Filylend Speegle,

born December 29, 1834, died May 30, 1887, daughter of Daniel Speegle. Their children were: William Vardie Columbus Jones, born February 17, 1859, died March 15, 1929, buried at Minor Hill, TN, married first, Mary Tubbs and second, Amanda Ann Chapman, born October 5, 1864, died February 2, 1912, buried at Phil Campbell, AL; Louis H.L. Jones, born August 13, 1860, died July 4, 1931, married Susan Ann Long, born February 18, 1862, died October 12, 1952; Zuriann Jones, married William H. Murphy. Jeremiah's second wife was Bettie Ann Speegle, born May 25, 1864, died June 24, 1891, daughter of Sallie Beasley and Michael Speegle. Children from this second marriage were: Arthur, born September 22, 1888, killed when thrown from a horse, buried at Brushy Creek Cemetery; Jeremiah L., born February 18, 1891, died June 19, 1891.

Children of William Vardie Columbus Jones and Mary Tubbs: Absalom Peter, James Albert and Ella S., who married Wylie Springer. Children by his second wife, Amanda: Christina Carniler, who married Luke Coleman; William H.H., died as an infant; Houston A., died as an infant; Mary Lula Elizabeth, married Bill Springer; Henry Clay, married Mary Magdalena Davis; Marandy Beatrice, married Clem Malone; Winnie Catherine, married Wheeler Musgrove; Alice Naomi, married John Green; Annie O., married Turner Williams; Iona, married a Todd; Thomas Marrow Jackson, died as an infant; Leonard Jones, died as a young boy; and Lily, who was a twin to Leonard.

Children of Henry Clay Jones and Mary Davis: Ona May, married 1st Arlie Lee Rose and second Lawrence White; James Aubrey, married Lillian Verlie White; Betsy Beatrice, married Wallace Ezell; and Thomas Calvin Jones, married Virginia McMullins.

Brothers of Jeremiah L.P. Jones were: William B., Thomas J.L., Jesse L., and J.F. Marion Jones.[94]

Jones, John B., Pvt., Co. K, age 20, EN & MI 7/12/62, Decatur, AL, born Morgan Co., AL, died 1/28/63 in hospital at Nashville, TN of pneumonia. (Buried in Grave B-5921 in Nashville National Cemetery.)

Jones, John R., Pvt., Co. E, deserted 4/1/63 near Glendale, MS.

Jones, John W., Pvt., Co. I, POW 3/10/65 from Monroe's Crossroads near Fayetteville, NC and confined at Richmond, VA.*

Jones, Joshua A., Pvt., Co. C, age 37, EN 12/20/62, Corinth, MS, MI 12/22/62, Corinth, MS, born Dallas Co., AL, farmer, died 5/27/63 in camp at Glendale, MS. (Buried Grave #A-2334, Corinth National Cemetery.)

Jones, Mathew, Pvt., Co. C, age 33, EN 6/25/63, Glendale, MS, MI 8/15/63, Corinth, MS, born Anson Co., NC, miller, died 4/2/64 in hospital at Memphis, TN of smallpox. (Buried in Memphis National Cemetery.)

Jones, McDonald, Pvt., Co. K, age 28, EN & MI 7/12/62, Decatur, AL, born Morgan Co., AL, farmer, died 9/9/62 in Hospital #8 in Nashville, TN of typhoid fever. Wife shown as Mary E. Jones in Summerville, AL and stated she was with him when he died. (A Thomas Jones with death date 9/7/62 is buried in Grave A-4010 in Nashville National Cemetery.)

Jones, Sydney A., Sgt/Pvt., Co. A, age 28, EN 1/1/64, Camp Davies, MS, MI 2/5/64, Memphis, TN, born Green Co., AL, deserted 4/1/64 in Mooresville, AL with arms and equipment.

Jones, T., Co. A, POW 3/10/65.*

Jones, Thomas H., Capt. Co. I, age 24, EN & MI 7/21/62, Huntsville, AL, sick in Hospital #8 in Nashville, TN 9/10/62, discharged 1/21/63 due to disability.

Jones, W., Pvt., Co. F, EN 9/20/63 at Glendale, MS.*

Jones, William B., Pvt/Sgt., Co. B, age 40, EN 2/6/64, Pulaski, TN, MI 3/27/64, Decatur, AL, born Morgan Co., AL, WIA 11/23/64 at Balls Ferry, Oconee River, GA, sent to USA Hospital at Hilton Head, SC, returned to duty 2/14/65, appt. Sgt. 3/28/64, MO 10/20/65, Huntsville, AL.

Jones, William A., Pvt/Sgt., Co. C, age 38, EN 5/10/63, Glendale, MS, MI 8/15/63, Corinth, MS, born Lauderdale Co., AL, farmer, appt. Sgt. 12/19/63, MO 7/27/64, Rome, GA.

Jones, William G.T., Pvt., Co. C, age 17, EN 7/16/63, Glendale, MS, MI 8/15/63, Corinth, MS, born Walker Co., AL, farmer, POW 2/15/64 from Corinth, MS, paroled at Savannah, GA 11/30/64, MO 10/20/65, Huntsville, AL.

Jones, William F., Pvt/Corp., Co. B, age 29, EN 3/11/63, Glendale, MS, born Morgan Co., AL, farmer, POW 10/26/63 from Vincent's Crossroads, MO 1/22/64, Memphis, TN.

Jones, William H.F., Corp., Co. A, age 32, EN 1/1/64, Camp Davies, MS, MI 2/5/64, Memphis, TN, born Green Co., AL, farmer, on detached service recruiting 5/17/64, MO 10/20/65, Huntsville, AL.

Jones, William M., Pvt., Co. G, age 18, EN 4/12/63, Chewalla, TN, MO 11/26/63, Memphis, TN.

Jones, William R., Pvt/Sgt., Co. H, age 30, EN & MI 9/13/64, Louisville, KY, born SC, farmer, appt. Sgt. 4/1/65, MO 10/20/65, Huntsville, AL.

Jordan, George, Pvt., Co. L, age 44, EN & MI 11/1/64, Rome, GA, born Greenville, Dist., SC, farmer, sick at Stevenson, AL 11/8/64, MO 10/20/65, Huntsville, AL.

Jordan, John A., Pvt., Co. A, age 22, EN 12/13/62, Glendale, MS, MI 12/31/62, Corinth, MS, deserted 12/31/62.

Jordon, John S.,(Jas. S.) Pvt., Co. F, age 22, EN 3/30/63, Corinth, deserted 4/17/63 from Glendale, MS.

Jordon/Jordan, Joseph J., Pvt., Co. F, deserted 4/10/63 from Glendale, MS, arrested 4/20/64 at Metropolis, Illnois, reward $30.00.*

Jordon/Jourdan, William T., Pvt., Co. E, age 18, EN & MI 9/1/64, Rome, GA, born Dekalb Co., GA, died 7/24/65 in camp at Moulton, AL of intermittent fever.

Keith, James, Pvt., Co. H, age 22, EN 3/1/65, Stevenson, AL, MI 4/5/65 Nashville, TN, born Jackson Co., AL, MO 10/20/65, Huntsville, AL.

Keith, M., Pvt., Co. G, POW 3/10/65 from Monroe's Crossroads near Fayetteville, NC and confined at Richmond, VA.*

Kelley, Lewis, Pvt., Co. H, age 33, EN 10/10/63, Glendale, MS, served as company cook, MO 10/24/64, Rome, GA.
    NOTE: Lewis Kelley was born November 30, 1831 in McMinn Co., TN, married Elizabeth J. Hood October 11, 1850 in Gilmer Co., GA. and had the following children: Mary J., born July 20, 1851, married March 24, 1878 to Willaim Smith; Malinda C., born January 24, 1853, married September 21, 1873 to James M. Lumpkins; John Daniel, born October 28, 1854, married Harriet A. Grinnell and Mary E. Baugus, died May 1, 1912 in Fresno, CA; Nancy Caroline, born January 18, 1857, died December 24, 1858 in Double Springs, AL; William W., born January 10, 1859, married Bettie Smith and V. Elizabeth Smith; Thomas J., born February 18, 1861, married November 17, 1881 to F.L.J. "Lufatha" Smith; James M., born November 5, 1862, married May 24, 1888 to Mary L. Fleeman; Richard Sherman, born June 11, 1866, married December 24, 1890 to Eula Lee Jordon, died July 1, 1952 in Lawrenceburg, TN; Sarah Ann, born March 1, 1868, married March 11, 1891 to W.F. "Frank" Wall; Andrew Benjamin, born February 5, 1870, died January 11, 1887; Christopher Columbus "Lum", born January 18, 1872, married August 10, 1892 to Sallie L. Crook, died June 13, 1952; Josiah M. "Mannie", born January 26, 1874, married December 1898 to Emma A. "Lena" McLean; Jonah M.L.F., born January 18, 1876, married December 28, 1898 to Susie McLean. Lewis Kelley died March 11, 1922 in Lawrence Co., TN.[95]

Kelley, Samuel G., Pvt/Sgt., Co. F, age 20, EN 8/1/64, Rome, GA, MI 10/17/64, Rome, GA, born Chester Dist., SC, farmer, POW 4/10/65, returned 4/21/65, appt. 2nd Sgt. 10/1/64, MO 10/20/65, Huntsville, AL.

Kelley, William M., Pvt., Co. F, age 23, EN 3/27/63, Corinth, MS, born Harden Co., TN, farmer, deserted 7/18/63 from Glendale, MS.

Kellogg, Benjamin F. (Frank W.), Sgt., F&S, age 20, EN & MI 11/1/63, Glendale, MS, promoted from Pvt., Co. A, 64th Ill. Vol. Inf., MO 10/31/64, Rome, GA.

Kellogg, George W., 1st Lt., F&S, age 29, EN 7/8/63, Glendale, MS, promoted from Pvt. 64th Ill. Inf. Vols.

Kelly, Alford M., Pvt., Co. A, age 18, EN & MI 9/23/64, Rome, GA, born Polk Co., GA, farmer, deserted 11/10/64, Rome, GA with pistol and equipment.

Kemp, William (J.W.), Pvt., Co. I, age 23, EN 11/11/63, Camp Davies, MS, deserted 1/7/65, Camp Davies, MS, (one MR states he died of disease at home, later found to be erroneous), charge of desertion removed 10/8/69 by War Dept. and discharged as of 7/19/65.

Kendricks, Elisha E., Pvt., Co. M, age 17, EN & MI 10/17/64, Rome, GA, born Chattooga Co., GA, farmer, served as regimental teamster, MO 10/20/65, Huntsville, AL.

Kenedy, Russell L., Pvt., Co. M, age 17, EN 12/11/63, Camp Davies, MS, MI 12/29/63, Corinth, MS, born Marion Co., AL, farmer, MO 12/17/64, Savannah, GA.

Kennedy, (?), Pvt., Co. E, (1st Reg't Middle Tenn. Cav.),absent sick at Triune 12/28/62.*

Kennedy, Artemus, Pvt., Co. K, age 25, EN & MI 8/5/62, Huntsville, AL, born Morgan Co., AL, farmer, sick in hospital at Nashville, TN 10/19/62, died 3/30/63, Murfreesboro, TN. (Buried in Grave O-5634 in Stone's River National Cemetery in Murfreesboro, TN.)

Kennedy, James J., Pvt., Co. A, age 26, EN 11/25/62, Glendale, MS, MI 12/31/62, Corinth, MS, MO 12/22/63, Memphis, TN.
     NOTE: James J. Kennedy was the son of David Stephenson Kennedy, born 1797 in TN, died October 1, 1862 in Marion Co., AL, and Elizabeth Littrell, born 1800, died October 1, 1862 in Marion Co., AL and the brother of William S. Kennedy, below. He married Malinda Jones (1840-1910) and had the following children: Maude A., Joseph P., Thomas A., Mary Ella, Eva A., Charalotty D., Jennie M., and Benjamen F. Kennedy. James was born April 4, 1835 in Marion Co., AL, married February 11, 1865 in Marion, IL and died December 12, 1905 in Marion, IL.
     According to the *Nashville Daily Union* dated March 4, 1863, David Stephenson Kennedy was "hanged to death, old and loyal citizen of Marion County, Alabama". He was hanged by Confederate Forces commanded by Colonel Phillip D. Roddy.[96]

Kennedy, Simpson W. (or C.), Pvt., Co. A, age 36, EN & MI 2/2/63, Glendale, MS, MO 12/22/63, Memphis, TN.

Kennedy, William S., Sgt., Co. A, age 41, EN 10/25/62, Corinth, MS, MI 12/31/62, Corinth, MS, promoted to 5th Sgt. 12/18/62, born Franklin Co., AL, discharged 6/28/63 due to disability, "chronic hepatitis and hypertrophy of the spleen. He has not got a sound organ in his body".
     NOTE: William S. Kennedy was the son of David Stephenson Kennedy (1797-1862) and and his 1st wife, Elizabeth Littrell (1800-1862). William was born December 1821 in Franklin Co., AL, married January 18, 1844 in Marion Co., AL and died April 6, 1906 in Douglas Co., MO. He married Rebecca Burleson and had the following children: David, 1845; Elizabeth, born 1846, married Will Clack; Sarah, born 1848; Nancy, born 1849, married George Hughes; Finus S., born 1851 and Martha Jane, born 1855 and married Benjamin Dillbeck. William's 2nd wife was Martha J. Burleson.[97] (See James J. Kennedy, above, for more family information.)

Key, George W., Pvt., Co. C, age 18, EN 2/1/64, Memphis, TN, MI 3/10/64, Memphis, TN, born Tishomingo Co., MS, farmer, deserted 3/20/64 from Memphis with Colt revolver and equipment.

Kidwell, William, Pvt., Co. B, age 38, EN 2/2/64, Pulaski, TN, born Madison Co., AL, farmer, no MO date.

Kilburn, Elijah A., Pvt., Co. D, EN 3/15/63, Glendale, MS, MI 3/20/63, Corinth, MS, deserted 6/3/63, from Glendale, MS.

Kilgo, George, Pvt., Co. I, age 41, EN & MI 10/10/63, Glendale, MS, born Waldon, LA (or VA), on detached service as scout 12/18/63, deserted 6/18/64 from Decatur, AL, charges of desertion removed by War Dept. and discharged as of 6/18/64.

Kilgore, Thomas R., Pvt., Co. A, age 24, EN 3/23/63, Glendale, MS, MI 3/24/63, Glendale, MS, born Walker Co., AL, died 7/1/63 in hospital at Glendale of intermittent fever. (Buried Grave #A-2064, Corinth National Cemetery.)

Killingsworth, James M., Blacksmith, Co. K, age 31, EN 12/25/63, Camp Davies, MS, born Tuscaloosa Co., AL, MO 7/19/65, Nashville, TN. Traveled 100 miles from Marion Co., AL to enlist.

Kilpatrick, William, Pvt., Co. I, age 25, EN & MI 7/21/62, Huntsville, AL, born Walker Co., AL, farmer, sick in hospital at Nashville, TN 12/24/62, no MO date. Discharge issued by War Dept. 6/11/72 as of 2/4/63 on surgeon's cert. of disability.
   NOTE: William married Hannah Blevins or or about December 18, 1858 in Winston Co., AL and apparently only had one child, Mary K., born May 4, 1861. William died April 15, 1863 in KY.[98]

Kimbrough, J.H. (or Jas. W. or Joseph W.), Pvt., Co. B, age 23, EN 3/6/64, Athens, AL, MI 3/27/64, Decatur, AL, born Franklin Co., AL, farmer, deserted 5/18/64 from Decatur, AL with Smith Carbine & equipment, deserted 7/28/64 from Rome, GA.

Kimbrough, John B., Pvt., Co. M, age 21, EN 11/18/63, Camp Davies, MS, born Franklin Co., AL, MO 12/27/64, Savannah, GA.
   NOTE: John Kimbrough was born in 1842 and was the son of Pleasant Kimbrough from Jefferson Co., TN. He first married Sarah R. Pate who died June 4, 1863. He married Rachel Vina Dickinson on July 16, 1867 in Thorn Hill (Marion Co.) AL, where they lived until his death October 14, 1891, and had the following children: Sarah J., born 1871; James Henry, born 1873; John Wesley, born 1876; David F., born 1878; Mary F., born 1880; Benjamin Harrison, born 1889; and a posthumous daughter, Ireny Levina, born 1892. John is buried in New Hope Cemetery in eastern Marion County and has a militry headstone. He was on the march from Atlanta to Savannah, GA.[99]

Kindrick, William A., Pvt., Co. M, age 18, EN 8/30/64, Chattooga Co., GA, MI 8/30/64, Rome, GA, born Chattooga Co., GA, POW 3/10/65 at Solomon Grove, NC, MO 6/13/65, Camp Chase, OH.

King, Berryman, Pvt., Co. I, age 44, EN 10/17/63, Glendale, MS, born Franklin Co., GA, farmer, died 3/11/64 in Memphis, TN.

King, B.P. (Benj. P.), Pvt., Co. B, age 18, EN 3/9/64, Decatur, AL, MI 3/27/64, Decatur, AL, born Blount Co., AL, farmer, deserted 6/28/64 Smoke Creek Gap, GA, near Chattanooga, TN with horse, Smith carbine & equipment.

King, John, Capt. Co. D, present, detached from Ford's Ind. Lt. Cavalry, Ill Vols. 3/63.*

King, John, Pvt., Co. E, EN 9/1/63, Glendale, MS, MI 10/6/63, Glendale, MS, POW 10/26/63 at Vincent's Crossroads, returned 1/25/64.

King, Livingston B., Pvt., Co. M, age 25, EN 12/3/63, Camp Davies, MS, MI 12/29/63, Corinth, MS, born Pickens Co., AL, clerk, on duty as clerk in hospital 1/64, MO 12/28/64, Memphis, TN.

King, Samuel D., Pvt., Co. M, age 39, EN 12/4/63, Camp Davies, MS, MI 12/29/63, Corinth, MS, born Buncombe Co., NC, gunsmith, died 1/19/64, Camp Davies of typhoid pneumonia. (Buried Grave #B-3362, Corinth National Cemetery.)

King, Thomas A., Pvt., Co. M&K, age 28, EN 12/3/63, Camp Davies, MS, MI 12/29/63, Corinth, MS, born Pickens Co., AL, shoemaker, MO 12/17/64, Savannah, GA.

King, William, Pvt., Co. A, absent sick in Gen. Hospital at Memphis.*

King, William F., Pvt., Co. M, age 37, EN 12/2/63, Camp Davies, MS, MI 12/29/63, Corinth, MS, born Pickens Co., AL, farmer, sick in hospital at Nashville, TN 11/4/64, MO 1/12/65, Nashville, TN.

Kingsley, Samuel J., Pvt., Co. E, age 53, EN & MI 2/1/63, Corinth, MS, born Union Dist., SC, on duty as nurse in hospital 3/1/63 to 9/63, discharged 10/14/63 at Glendale, MS due to disability, "chronic inflammation of the kidneys, broken down constitition and old age".

Kingsley, William, Pvt., Co. E, age 38, EN & MI 2/1/63, Corinth, MS, sick in Washington USA Hospital at Memphis, TN 9/1/63, MO 2/1/64, Memphis, TN.

Kingsley, William J., Pvt., Co. E, EN & MI 2/1/63, Corinth, MS, died 3/20/63 at Corinth, MS.

Kirkendall, Samuel S., Pvt., Co. G, age 18, EN 3/5/63, Chewalla, TN, WIA 10/26/63, MO 11/26/63, Memphis, TN.

Kirkland, Jefferson W. (or N.), age 18, EN 3/10/64, Decatur, AL, MI 4/13/64, Decatur, AL, born McMinn Co., TN, farmer, MO 10/20/65, Huntsville, AL.

Kirkman, Thomas P., Pvt/Corp., Co. F, age 18, EN 6/29/63, Corinth, MS, MI 7/1/63, Corinth, MS, born Henderson Co., TN, farmer, MO 7/27/64, Rome, GA.

Kirkman, William F., Pvt/Corp., Co. F, age 38, EN 6/29/63, Corinth, MS, MI 7/1/63, Corinth, MS, born Randolph Co., NC, farmer, on detail as teamster at Vicksburg, MS 1/25/64, MO 7/27/64, Rome, GA.

Knabb, S.H., Pvt., Co. F, gain from MIA 11/8/63.*

Knight, Benjamin P., Pvt., Co. L, age 35, EN 9/25/63, Fayette Co., AL, born Walker Co., AL, farmer, died 2/21/64 in Memphis, TN of smallpox.

Knight, James J., Pvt., Co. D, age 23, EN 5/1/64, Decatur, AL, MI 6/16/64, Decatur, AL, born Carroll Co., GA, farmer, deserted 5/10/65 from Huntsville, AL while on recruiting service.

Knight, Pinkney L., Pvt., Co. M, age 18, EN 9/16/63, Chewalla, TN, born McNairy Co., TN, farmer, deserted 10/23/63, Glendale, MS.

Knighton, David/Daniel J., Pvt., Co. A, age 35, EN & MI 9/6/64, Rome, GA, born Chesterfield Dist., SC, carpenter, in hospital at Savannah, GA 2/1/65, MO 10/20/65, Huntsville, AL.

Knighton, Joseph J., Pvt., Co. A, age 26, EN & MI 9/6/64, Rome, GA, born Chesterfield Dist., SC, carpenter, deserted 11/7/64, Rome, GA with horse, saddle, arms and equipment.

Lacefield, Thomas J., Pvt., Co. H, age 23, EN 1/16/65, Huntsville, AL, MI 2/13/65, Nashville, TN, born Limestone Co., AL, farmer, deserted 5/8/65, Huntsville, AL.

Ladfred, John W., Sgt., Co. G, age 20, EN 4/6/63, Chewalla, TN, MO 11/26/63, Memphis, TN.

Lake, Elisha, Pvt., Co. B, age 18, EN & MI 9/1/64, Rome, GA, born Randolph Co., AL, POW 3/10/65, Monroe's Cross Roads, NC, discharged 6/13/65, Camp Chase, OH.

Lake, Wiley J., Pvt., Co. B, age 24, EN 8/1/64, Wedowee, AL, MI 8/1/64, Rome, GA, born Randolph Co., AL, farmer, MO 10/20/65, Huntsville, AL.

Lamar, William L., (Cards filed with William L. Tanner)

Lambert, Hiram M., Pvt., Co. A, age 18, EN 1/14/64, Camp Davies, MS, MI 2/5/64, Memphis, TN, born Harris Co., GA, farmer, sick in hospital at Jeffersonville, IN 8/1/64 with typhoid fever, discharged at Quincy, IL 6/28/65 in compliance with telegram orders.

Lambert, J., Co. A, killed near Cave Spring, GA 7/17/64.*

Lambert, James, Pvt., Co. E, age 20, EN 6/6/63, Glendale, MS, deserted 7/20/63, charges of desertion removed, POW 8/6/63, paroled at City Point, VA 3/15/64, MO 7/27/64, Rome, GA.

Lambert, John, Pvt., Co. E, age 18, EN 6/16/63, Glendale, MS, deserted 7/20/63 from Glendale, MS, POW 8/6/63, paroled 3/15/64 at City Point, VA, MO 7/27/64, Rome, GA, residence shown as Tishomingo Co., MS with James Lambert as nearest relative.

Lambert, Joseph, Pvt., Co. K&A, age 30, EN 10/29/62, Corinth, MS, MI 12/31/62, Corinth, MS, born Henry Co., GA, discharged 3/26/63 at Corinth due to disability, chronic rheumatism.

Lambert, Techer, Pvt., Co. E, age 19, EN 7/1/63, Glendale, MS, MI 7/12/63, Corinth, MS, on detached service as teamster 1/25/64 in Vicksburg, MS, MO 9/28/64, Rome, GA.

Lambert, Walton E., Pvt., Co. M, age 21, EN 11/23/63, Camp Davies, MS, born Talapoosa Co., AL, farmer, deserted 11/26/63 from Camp Davies while on scout.

Lambert, William J., Corp., Co. A, age 20, EN 1/12/64, Camp Davies, MS, MI 2/5/64, Memphis, TN, born Muscogee Co., GA, farmer, appt. Corp. 2/5/64, KIA 7/7/64 (or 7/15) near Cave Springs, GA.

Lambert, Wilson, Pvt., Co. K&A, age 34, EN 10/29/62, Corinth, MS, born Henry Co., GA, died 12/1/62 of disease at Corinth, MS.

Landtroop, Stith, J., Pvt., Co. B, age 16, EN 2/6/64, Pulaski, TN, MI 3/27/64, Decatur, AL, born Limestone Co., AL, farmer, deserted 8/15/64 from Rome, GA with Smith carbine and equipment.

Laniar, Benjamin F., Pvt/Corp., Co. B, age 37, EN 2/5/64, Pulaski, TN, MI 3/27/64, Decatur, AL, born Giles Co., TN, farmer, sick in hospital at Decatur 4/25/64, deserted from Decatur 5/18/64 with Smith carbine and equipment.

Lanker, William M., Pvt., Co. A, discharged 6/20/65 at Quincey, Illinois S.O. dated 3/5/65.*

Lankford, Alexander J., Pvt., Co. I, age 31, EN & MI 7/21/62, Huntsville, AL, MO 7/19/65, Nashville, TN.

Lansford, Michael/Mickael, Pvt., Co. D, age 32, EN 10/12/63, Glendale, MS, MI 10/12/63, Camp Davies, MS, born Buncombe Co., NC, farmer, died 8/15/64 in hospital at Rome, GA of disease. (Buried Grave #C-170, Marietta National Cemetery.)

Lansan, John, Pvt., age 18, EN 4/23/64, Decatur, AL, born Marshall Co., AL, farmer. (Notation states "name not taken up on rolls of regt.", no further information.

Latty, John, Lt./ Capt., Co. C, age 27, EN 12/1/62, Corinth, MS, MI 12/22/62, Corinth, MS, detached from 57th Reg. Ill. Vol. Inf., WIA 3/10/65, near Fayetteville, NC, (severe gunshot wound to left arm), MO 10/20/65, Huntsville, AL.

Lawrence, Alexander, Pvt., Co. A, age 19, EN 9/8/62, Iuka, MS, MI 10/1/62, Corinth, MS, born Fayette Co., AL, farmer, MO 9/16/63, Corinth, MS.

Lawrence/Laurence, Elisha R., Pvt., Co. I, age 25, EN & MI 8/18/62 (or 7/21/62), Huntsville, AL, born Morgan Co., AL, farmer, deserted 10/11/62, Nashville, TN, returned 7/1/65, MO 7/19/65, Nashville, TN.

NOTE: Descendants of Elisha state the name is spelled 'Laurence'. The Book, *Progressive Men of Bannock, Bear Lake, Bingham, Fremont and Oneida Counties, Idaho"*, by Andrew Jenson, states the following: "Elisha R. Laurence - A gallant soldier when the integrity of the Union was in danger and fighting valiantly in its defense, enduring the hardships of the march, the heat of the battle and the terrible sufferings of prison life, and bearing all with fortitude and manly courage, and an enterprising man of productive industry when war smoothed its wrinkled front, boldly challenging the frontier to oppose his energy all its difficulties, Elisha R. Laurence of Whitney, typifies in his character and career the best elements of American citizenship, and is justly esteemed as one of the leading men in his section of the country. He is a native of Morgan Co., Ala., where he was born on September 19, 1837, the son of Orson and Arabella (Allen) Laurence, natives of North Carolina. His father was a planter in Alabama and remained there until a short time before his death, when, on account of failing health, he went to make his home with a daughter in Arkansas where he died in 1883. His wife died in Alabama some years before his removal from the state. Their son, Elisha grew to manhood and was educated in his native county, and in July, 1862, being opposed to disunion, he made his way through the Confederate lines and joined the Federal army at Huntsville, Ala., as a member of the First Alabama Infantry, which was afterward changed into a cavalry regiment. It was assigned to the command of General Buell and saw hard service under him. Mr. Laurence was captured a number of times and was confined in a number of Southern prisons. He rejoined his regiment after each exchange and was transferred to the Army of the Potomac under General Grant. In the concluding campaigns of that organization he took an active part. In July, 1865, he was mustered out of the service at Nashville, Tenn., and returned to his Alabama home, where he engaged in farming until 1872. In 1869 he was baptized into the Mormon communion, and in the spring of 1872 came to Utah. After a short residence at Ogden he came north to where Whitney now stands and settled on land two miles south of Preston, where there was only one other family, there being also but two at the site of Whitney. For four years he farmed his land, and in 1876 he sold it and homesteaded on the ranch he now occupies, which is in Whitney precinct and located three miles southeast of Preston..... He is a stanch Republican in political faith and is deeply and earnestly interested in the success of his party, but steadfastly refuses all efforts to get him to accept public office..... Mr. Laurence was married, in 1857 in Blount County, Ala. to Miss Sarah Williford and has three children as the fruit of the union, (James) Orson, William and Mary. She died in 1865 and was buried in Morgan County, Ala., and in 1868 he married a second wife in Blount County, that state, Miss Mary Ann Ratliff, by whom also he had three children, Sarah, N. Abby and Caroline. The second Mrs. Laurence passed away in 1878 and was buried at Franklin, Idaho. Subsequently he contracted a third marriage, his choice this time being Miss Mary Jane Wall, also a native of Alabama. They have eleven children, Ruth, Elisha, Henry, Francis, Violet, Hartwell, Myrtle, Orla, Vane, Uriel and Delva, all bright and interesting children and popular members of their social circles."

Subsequent to the publishing of the above biography, E. R. Laurence moved to Mesa Arizona in 1902 and lived there for one and one half years. Following that he moved his family to the Stockton area of California. E.R. Laurence died on 16 December 1916 in Bellota, San Jauquin Co., CA aged 79 years. [100]

Lawrence, Jesse, Pvt/Corp., Co. K&A, age 26, EN 9/8/62, Iuka, MS, MI 10/1/62, Corinth, MS, promoted to Corp. 12/18/62, on leave in Jackson, TN 5/63, MO 9/16/63, Corinth, MS.

Lawrence, William F.A., Pvt., Co. K, age 38, EN & MI 8/18/62, Huntsville, AL, born Green Co., GA, farmer, died 9/26/62 in Hospital #14, Nashville, TN of rubeola. (Buried in Grave A-5018 Nashville National Cemetery with death date 9/27/62 and name William T.A. Lawrence.)

Lawrence, William A., Pvt., Co. K&A, EN 9/8/62, Iuka, MS, MI 10/1/62, Corinth, MS, born Fayette Co., AL, farmer, MO 9/16/63, Corinth, MS.

Lawson, Goolder, (Cards filed with Goulder Losson)

Lawson, Patmon, Pvt. Co. A&G, age 32, EN 3/28/64, Decatur, AL, MI 4/13/64, Decatur, AL, born Walker Co., AL, farmer, deserted 10/28/64 while on recruiting service.

Lay, Hardy C., Pvt., Co. A, EN 3/23/63, Glendale, MS, MI 3/24/63, Glendale, MS, MIA 10/26/63 at Vincent's Crossroads, MS, returned 12/28/63, MO as of 12/22/63 due to MO of his company.
NOTE: Hardy C. Lay was born May 2, 1830 in Hamilton Co., TN and died August 28, 1907 and is buried in Livingston Chapel Cemetery in Cullman Co., AL. He married Lucinda Pike June 16, 1862 and had the following children: William, born October 17, 1862, married Ophelia Barnett and died 1931; Lewis, born February 18, 1865, married Dora Barnett; Joseph Canady, born September 1866, married Nancy White; Monroe, born October 14, 1868; married Jane Stricklin; Martha Ann, born December 5, 1870, married Henry Striklin; Mary Jane, born 1869, married John Jacobs; Alexander, born February 1876; Jackson, born September 12, 1879. [101]

Lay, Lewis A., Pvt., Co. I, age 38, EN & MI 7/21/62, Huntsville, AL, born Winston Co., AL, farmer, sick at Tuscumbia, AL 4/19/63, MO 7/19/65.
NOTE: Lewis Lay was born June 1, 1824 in Grainger Co., TN. He married Eunice Calvert who was born October 31, 1816, and had the following children: John, 1848; James, 1851; Alexander, 1854; Martha, 1855; Joseph C., 1857; and Mary Jane, 1859. Lewis and Eunice are both buried in the Old Bethel Baptist Cemetery in Winston Co., AL. [102]

Lay, Robert, Co. B, absent sick in USA General Hospital 5/65.*

Lay, Thomas H., Pvt., Co. E, age 36, EN 4/1/63, Glendale, MS, MI 4/5/63, Corinth, MS, detached on secret service 11/22/63, on duty as nurse in hospital at Memphis, TN 1/64, MO 3/1/64, Memphis, TN.
NOTE: Thomas Lay was born May 2, 1830 in Hamilton Co., TN. He married Rebecca Calvert in 1848 in Walker Co., AL and had the following children: Sarah Ann, 1849; Martha J., 1850; Reuben H., 1855; Mary S., 1859; and Elijah K., 1861. He married second, Jane McKey. Thomas died May 4, 1909. Thomas and Rebecca are both buried in Old Bethel Baptist Cemetery in Winston Co., AL [103]

Leadford, William C., Pvt/Bugler, Co. H, age 18, EN 3/1/65, Stevenson, AL, MI 4/5/65, Nashville, TN, born Jackson Co., NC, farmer, appt. Bugler 4/1/65, MO 10/20/65, Huntsville, AL. (Notation in file states, "For service of this man prior to his enlistment in this organization see record of David Moss, Co. K, 13th Tenn. Cavalry."

Leavens, Jesse L., Pvt., Co. E, EN 11/9/64, Rome, GA.*

Leay, J.M., Pvt., Co. E, POW 8/6/63, POW 10/26/63, POW 3/10/65.*

Lee, George W., Pvt., Co. A, age 19, EN & MI 9/23/64, Rome, GA, born Campbell Co., GA, farmer, deserted 11/10/64 from Rome, GA with pistol and sabre belt.

Lee, James E., Corp/Pvt., Co. A, age 24, EN 1/1/64, Camp Davies, MS, MI 2/5/64, Memphis, TN, born Dekalb Co., GA, farmer, appt. Corp. 2/5/64, promoted to Sgt. 11/1/64, in arrest at Raleigh, NC 4/20/65 for plundering & stealing, deserted 4/25/65, reduced to ranks 5/31/65, charge of desertion removed 5/1/86 and discharge issued as of 9/25/65.

Lees, William, Pvt., Co. D, age 26, EN 4/25/63, Glendale, MS, MI 4/28/63, Corinth, MS, born Pickens, AL, farmer, reduced to ranks from Corp. 12/3/63, MO 6/16/64, Decatur, AL.

Leesmith, Jeremiah A., Pvt., Co., H, age 18, EN 4/1/65, Stevenson, AL, MI 4/5/65, Nashville, TN, born Blount Co., AL, farmer, no MO date.

Legett, William T., Corp., Co. F, age 27, EN 6/29/63, Corinth, MS, sick at Louisville, KY 10/26/63, in Washington Park USA Hospital in Cincinnati, OH 10/31/63, discharged for disability 7/4/64 due to gunshot wound to left knee joint recieved in action at Yellow Creek, TN 7/29/63, left thigh amputated. He asked not to be discharged as he had a large family dependant on his wages for support. Lt. Cheney wrote a letter 3/27/64 from "on board Steamer Westmorland, Memphis" stating the above.

Lemmons, James, Pvt., Co. H, age 18, EN 3/1/65, Stevenson, AL, MI 4/18/65, Nashville, TN, born McMinn Co., TN, farmer, MO 10/20/65, Huntsville, AL.

Lennard, Michael, Pvt., Co. D, on duty as company cook 7/64.*

Lent, (?), Co. A, absent on furlough.*

Lentz, Abraham J., Pvt/Sgt., Co. K, age 32, EN & MI 8/22/62, Huntsville, AL, born Limestone Co., AL, wagonmaker, appt. Sgt. 8/1/64, WIA 3/10/65 at Monroe's Crossroads, NC, MO 7/19/65, Nashville, TN.
NOTE: Abraham was born June 1, 1830, married Mary Ann York, daughter of John and Mary York, on January 30, 1855 in Limestone Co., AL and died April 1, 1871. His parents were Solomon and Sarah Lentze. He is buried in Lentzville Cemetery in Limestone Co., AL.[104]

Lentz, John P., Pvt., Co. K, age 18, EN & MI 8/22/62, Huntsville, AL, born Lauderdale Co., AL, farmer, died 10/21/62 in Hospital #14, Nashville, TN of rubeola.

Lenyard, H.C., Pvt., Co. I, absent sick in hospital.*

Lerock, P., Pvt., Co. D, died 5/1/63 at Glendale, MS.*

Lewis, Abijah H., Pvt., Co. B, age 21, EN 12/20/62, Glendale, MS, MI 12/31/62, Corinth, MS, born Marion Co., AL, farmer, POW 10/26/63 at Vincent's Crossroads, MO 12/27/63, Camp Davies, MS.

Lewis, Hosea H., Pvt., Co. B, age 22, EN 12/20/62, Glendale, MS, MI 12/31/62, Corinth, MS, born Coosa Co., AL, farmer, POW 10/26/63 at Vincent's Crossroads, MO 12/27/63, Camp Davies, MS.

Lewis, Isaiah, Pvt., Co. A, age 40, EN 12/7/63, Camp Davies, MS, MI 2/5/64, Memphis, TN, born Marion Co., AL, farmer, died 10/22/64 in Gen. Hospital in Columbia, TN (there are four different death dates shown), (this name is out of order on microfilm, filed after Prior Lewis).

Lewis, Jasper, Pvt., Co. F, age 34, EN 6/15/63, Corinth, MS, born Choctaw Co., MS, farmer, deserted 8/27/63 from Glendale, MS.

Lewis, Noah, Pvt., Co. A, absent sick in hospital, died 11/1/64 at Rome, GA of disease.*

Lewis, Peter, Pvt., Co. D, EN 3/1/63, Glendale, MS, MI 3/20/63, Corinth, MS, died 4/15/63 in Post Hospital at Corinth, MS of "continued fever".

Lewis, Prior, Pvt., Co. B, age 18, EN 3/10/63, Glendale, MS, MI 8/7/63, Corinth, MS, born Marion Co., AL, farmer, POW 10/26/63, at Vincent's Crossroads, MO 1/22/64, Memphis, TN.

Lewis, William W., Pvt., Co. M, age 20, EN 11/1/63, Glendale, MS, MI 12/29/63, Corinth, MS, born Coosa Co., AL, farmer, sick in Adams USA Hospital at Memphis, TN 1/10/64, returned to duty 4/20/64, MO 10/20/65, Huntsville, AL.

Light, David C., Pvt., Co. H, age 25, EN 12/10/64 Stevenson, AL, MI 4/5/65, Nashville, TN, born Stanley Co., NC, farmer, MO 10/20/65, Huntsville, AL.

Lindley, Jonathan, Pvt., Co. L, age 40, EN 9/25/63, Fayette Co., AL, MI 9/25/63, Glendale, MS, POW 10/26/63 from Vincent's Crossroads, discharged 9/29/64, ex. of term of service, no MO date.
NOTE: Jonathan Thomas "Jott" Lindley was born April 10, 1820 in Carroll Co., GA and is thought to have died October 26, 1863 at Vincent's Crossroads. He married Sarah Elizabeth Knight on January 7, 1846. Elizabeth was born about 1827 in Carroll Co., GA and died from consumption in Walker Co., AL in November 1860 in the Holygrove Community. Their children were: George W., born May 13, 1848, married 1st, Margaret Ann Lay, 2nd, Josie Monroe, and died in May 1929 in Winston Co., AL; Sarah "Sully", born August 5, 1849; Daniel J., born December 16, 1854, married 1st, Elizabeth Hendon, 2nd Roxie Nichcoles, died April 20, 1926 in Marion Co., AL; William M., born July 25, 1856; and Jesse A., born August 5, 1861, married Alice A. Burleson January 24, 1876 in Fayette Co., AL and died in Houston, MS, supposedly over 100 years old.[105]

Lindley, William, Pvt., Co. C, AWOL 3/10/63, deserted 6/63, never mustered in the service and was dropped from the payrolls without being marked deserted.*

Lindsey/Lindsay, Hiram, Pvt., Co. B, age 23, EN 12/23/62, Glendale, MS, MI 12/31/62, Corinth, MS, MO 12/27/63, Camp Davies, MS.

Lindsey/Lindsay, Irving/Irvin, Pvt., Co. B, age 23, EN 1/5/63, Glendale, MS, MI 1/22/63, Corinth, MS, born Marion Co., AL, farmer, sick in hospital at Corinth 2/63 with measles, MO 1/22/64, Memphis, TN.

Lindsey/Lindsay, John, Sgt., Co. F, age 30, EN 8/20/63, Glendale, MS, MI 2/24/64, Memphis, TN, born Lauderdale Co., AL, farmer, appt. Sgt. 12/1/63, gained from MIA 11/15/63, MO 9/28/64, Rome, GA.

Lindsey/Lindsay, Martin L., Pvt., Co. M, age 25, EN 12/12/63, Camp Davies, MS, MI 12/29/63, Corinth, MS, born Fayette Co., AL, farmer, served as company cook, deserted 3/18/64 from Memphis, TN with Remington revolver & Smith carbine.

Lindsey/Lindsley, William R., Pvt., Co. B, age 18, EN 12/20/62, Glendale, MS, MI 12/31/62, Corinth, MS, MO 12/27/63, Camp Davies, MS.

Linley/Lindley, James R., Pvt., Co. E, age 36, (MO Roll shows age 29), EN & MI 10/4/64, Rome, GA, born Walton Co., GA, farmer, MO 10/20/65, Huntsville, AL.
NOTE: James Robert Lindley was born in 1828 to Thomas and Sarah Elizabeth New Lindley, originally from Laurens Co., SC. The family moved to Randolph Co., AL in 1848, but James remained in Carroll Co., GA where he married Elizabeth about 1849 and then emigrated to Randolph Co. They had the following children: William Franklin, Thomas M., Nancy Ann, Amos, James Pinkney, and Sherman. James was wounded twice during the war for which he later received a pension. After the war was over, James, his brother Thomas Mark and several other

men from Randolph Co. were forced to live in the surrounding woods for about three weeks due to the animosity between the USA and CSA soldiers. Their families finally convinced their neighbors to leave them alone. Elizabeth died in 1879, leaving James with a small child. He then married Lavinia Halpin Mize who was the widow of James Robert Mize, nephew of James. Lavinia died June 8, 1909 and is buried at Union Hill Church Cemetery.[106]

Linley, John, Pvt., Co. E, age 18, EN & MI 10/4/64, Rome, GA, born Campbell Co., GA, farmer, MO 10/20/65, Huntsville, AL.

Linley/Lindley, Thomas, Pvt/Corp., Co. E, age 29, EN & MI 10/4/64, Rome, GA, born Walton Co., GA, farmer, promoted to Corp. 10/20/64, POW 3/31/65 near Faison's Station, NC, MO 6/12/65, Camp Chase, OH.
NOTE: Thomas Mark Lindley was born November 15, 1834 and moved with his family to Randolph Co., AL in 1848 where he married Rosanne Elizabeth Susan Ball in April 1856. After the war he returned to Randolph Co. and became a preacher. He was the first pastor of Wesly's Chapel Christian Church and Mandy's Chapel Methodist Church. After Elizabeth "Betsy" died January 7, 1906, Thomas married Sarah Smith. Thomas is buried at Mandy's Chapel Cemetery in Randolph Co., AL.[107]

Little, C., Sgt., Co. L, died 3/20/64 of disease at Memphis, TN.*

Little, James E., Pvt/Corp., Co. G, age 32, EN 3/5/63, Chewalla, TN, appt. Corp. 9/1/63, MO 11/26/63, Memphis, TN.

Little, P., Co. E, AWOL 7/20/63.*

Livingston, Aaron, Pvt., Co. I, age 20, EN 10/1/63, Glendale, MS, born Winston Co., AL, POW 3/10/65, Solomon Grove, NC, MO 6/12/65, Camp Chase, OH.

Lockheart/Lockhard, Thomas J., Pvt., Co. D, age 21, EN 5/1/64, Decatur, AL, MI 6/16/64, Decatur, AL, born Morgan Co., AL, farmer, MO 10/20/65, Huntsville, AL.

Loftis, Lemuel, Pvt., Co. H, EN 10/18/63, Glendale, MS, POW 10/26/63, no further information.

Logan, Alexander, Pvt., Co. B, age 37, EN 1/16/63, Glendale, MS, MI 1/22/63, Corinth, MS, born Fayette Co., AL, farmer, died 2/11/63 in hospital at Corinth, MS of measles, brother shown as J.C. Logan.

Logan, Andrew, Pvt/Sgt., Co. K, age 30, EN & MI 7/24/62, Huntsville, AL, born Fayette Co., AL, farmer, appt. Sgt. 11/1/63, sick in hospital at Nashville, TN 12/26/62, POW 5/3/63, paroled at City Point, VA 5/15/63, discharged 7/19/65 while sick in hospital.
NOTE: Andrew was born December 5, 1831 in Marion Co., AL to Virginia McCaleb and Robert Logan. He married Cathren Cothern on March 12, 1876. Children were: Rhoda, born November 25, 1876; Mary Jane, born September 27, 1878; Margaret Ann, born March 25, 1881; James Pickens, born March 15,

1883; Cathren Jane, born March 29, 1885; Fannie Bell, born January 22, 1887 and Andrew Lincoln, born January 22, 1891. Andrew's father was born 1840 in Stokes Co., NC and purchased land in Marion Co., AL sometime before 1860.

During the Civil War, Andrew voluntarily enlisted in Company K, 1st Regiment Alabama Cavalry Union Army commanded by Col. George E. Spencer on 24 July 1862 in Huntsville, Alabama. On 12 August 1862, he was mustered into Captain David Smith's Company at Huntsville.

From 1 November 1862 until January 1863, he was in Hospital #13 in Nashville, Tennessee with typhoid fever. After he was discharged from the hospital he was assigned on 1 February 1863 to Company E, 1st Regiment of Middle Tennessee Cavalry.

He was captured at Rome, Georgia on 3 May 1863 and confined at Richmond, Virginia on 9 May 1863. He was paroled at City Point, Virginia on 15 May 1863 and reported to Camp Parole, MA on 18 May 1863. He was sent to C.C.O. on 19 May 1863 and then reassigned to Company K, 1st Alabama Cavalry on 9 June 1863 which was commanded by Col. Spencer. He was promoted to Sergeant 1 November 1863 by order of Col. Spencer and was on daily duty as commanding Sergeant of Company K until June of 1865.

On 15 June 1865, Andrew entered Hospital #4 in Nashville, Tennessee with symptoms of malaria and mumps that he had contracted at Huntsville, Alabama. After being in the hospital 20 days, he was released upon request, since he was not fit for service, but desired to be mustered out with the Regiment in order to be assisted home by his comrades.

Sgt. Andrew Logan was honorably discharged with the rank of Sergeant on 19 July 1865 at Nashville, Tennessee by reason of termination of the war.[108]

Logan, Andrew J., Co. M, age 40, born Franklin Co., AL, wagon maker, EN 12/11/63, Camp Davies, MS, rejected by surgeon on account of consumption of left lung.*

Logan, David, Pvt., Co. K, age 17, EN 1/1/64, Camp Davies, MS, born Fayette Co., AL, farmer, traveled 100 miles from Marion Co., AL to enlist, deserted 1/17/64 from Camp Davies, not apprehended.

Logan, James M., Pvt., Co. K, age 27, EN & MI 7/1/62, Limestone Co., AL, born Fayette Co., AL, farmer, transferred from Co. K, 21st R.O.V. died 12/24/62 in Hospital #4, Nashville, TN of pneumonia.

Logan, John C., Pvt., Co. B, age 35, EN 1/16/63, Glendale, MS, MI 1/22/63, Corinth, MS, born Fayette Co., AL, farmer, MO 1/22/64, Memphis, TN.

Logan, Preston, Co. M, age 18, born Franklin Co., AL, farmer, EN 12/11/63, Camp Davies, MS, rejected by surgeon on account of general disability.*

Logan, Robert G.W., Pvt., Co. M, age 20, EN 12/11/63, Camp Davies, MS, MI 12/29/63, Corinth, MS, born Franklin Co., AL, farmer, sick in Overton USA Hospital at Memphis, TN 2/1/64, MO 10/20/65, Huntsville, AL.

Logan, Robert H., Pvt., Co. B, age 22, EN 1/16/63, Glendale, MS, MI 1/22/63, Corinth, MS, born Fayette Co., AL, farmer, POW 10/26/63 from Vincent's Crossroads, MO 1/22/64, Memphis,TN.
NOTE: Robert Henry Logan was the son of Robert "Bob" and Virginia Jane "Jennie" Logan. He was born June 22, 1840 in Fayette Co., AL and on October 10, 1867, he married Mary Elizabeth Matthews at the home of her parents in Lamar Co., AL. Robert died June 21, 1884 in Marion Co., AL after his clothes were caught in the belt of a threshing machine and pulled him in the machine. He is buried at White House Church of Christ Cemetery just out of Haleyville.[109]

Logan, White, Pvt/Corp., Co. B, age 21, EN 1/16/63, Glendale, MS, MI 1/22/63, Corinth, MS, born Fayette Co., AL, farmer, appt. Corp. 1/22/63, MO 1/22/64, Memphis, TN.

Logan, William G., Pvt., Co. A, age 38, EN & MI 9/6/64, Rome, GA, born York Dist, SC, farmer, deserted 11/10/64 from Rome, GA with revolver & sabre belt.

Loggins, Charles C., Pvt., Co. D, age 18, EN 5/20/64, Decatur, AL, MI 6/16/64, Decatur, AL, born Walker Co., AL, farmer, MO 10/20/65, Huntsville, AL.

Lomax, John, Capt., Co. M, age 51, EN 7/20/63, Glendale, MS, MI 12/28/63, Camp Davies, MS, requested leave 9/19/64 while at Rome, GA to visit family in Missouri, MO 10/20/65, Huntsville, AL.

Lomax, William M., Pvt/Hospital Steward, F&S, age 23, EN 5/15/64, Memphis, TN, MI 5/19/64, Memphis, TN, born Linn Co., MO, student, MO 10/20/65, Huntsville, AL.

Long, John, Pvt., Co. D, EN 6/1/63, Glendale, MS, deserted 6/10/63 from Glendale, MS.

Looney, Anderson M., Sgt., Co. I, age 30, EN & MI 7/21/62, Huntsville, AL, born Lawrence Co., AL, farmer, appt. Sgt. 7/21/62, reduced to ranks 9/12/62, appt. Sgt. 3/1/63, MO 7/19/65, Nashville, TN.

Losson, Goulder, Pvt., Co. G, age 18, EN 3/21/64, Decatur, AL, MI 4/13/64, Decatur, AL, born Walker Co., AL, farmer, MO 10/20/65, Huntsville, AL.

Lott, George W., Pvt., Co. I, age 23, EN & MI 7/21/62, Huntsville, AL, born Morgan Co., AL, farmer, sick in hospital at Nashville, TN 10/24/62, sick in hospital at Murfreesboro, TN 3/15/63, MO 7/19/65, Nashville, TN.

Lott, Simeon H., Pvt., Co. K, age 18, EN & MI 7/12/62, Decatur, AL, born Morgan Co., AL, farmer, died 10/23/62 in Hospital #14, Nashville, TN of rubeola.

Lovell, Jerry, Pvt., Co. C, age 18, EN 1/1/64, Corinth, MS, MI 3/10/64 Memphis, TN, born St. Claire Co., AL, farmer, deserted 3/20/64, Memphis, TN with Remington revolver, Smith Carbine & equipment.

Lovett, Andrew J., Pvt., Co. A, age 31, EN & MI 1/27/63, Glendale, MS, born Marion Co., AL, died 3/19/63 at Corinth, MS of measles, brother shown as Ashley H. Lovett. (Buried Grave A-2069, Corinth National Cemetery.)

Lovett, Archibald B., Pvt., Co. A, age 34, EN & MI 1/27/63, Glendale, MS, born Winston Co., AL, died 3/4/63 at Corinth, MS of measles, brother shown as Ashley H. Lovett. (Buried Grave A-2067, Corinth National Cemetery.)

Lovett, Ashley H., Pvt., Co. A&M, age 25, EN 9/8/62, Iuka, MS, MI 10/1/62, Corinth, MS, born Winston Co., AL, teamster, promoted to Sgt. 12/18/62, MO 9/16/63, Corinth, MS reenlisted 12/4/63, Camp Davies, MS, MI 12/29/63, Corinth, MS, MO 7/13/65, Huntsville, AL.
   NOTE: Ashley Lovett, being the only on of the three brothers to survive the war, was born December 5, 1835 in Winston Co., AL. He married Nancy Elizabeth Dickerson on August 5, 1866 in Marion Co., AL and had the following children: William A., born June 1, 1867; Alfred, born December 13, 1868; Frances M., born January 31, 1873; Andrew J., born November 26, 1874; Martha E., born March 10, 1877; James H., born February 16, 1879; Horace A., born February 16, 1879; Fountain Erascus, born September 29, 1883; Sarah Rebecca, born September 10, 1866; Louida, born April 19, 1890; George Washington, born August 16, 1892.
   After the war, Ashley farmed in Winston Co., AL where he died in Haleyville on August 19, 1918, having been married for over 50 years. His wife, Nancy, died August 31, 1934.[110]

Lovey, John, Pvt., Co. B, absent sick in General Hospital 11/64.*

Lovoon/Lovin, William W., Pvt., Co. E, age 19, EN & MI 9/1/64, Rome, GA, born Newton, GA, farmer, died 2/18/65 at Savannah, GA, was first buried Laurel Grove Cemetery in Savannah, Grave #5.

Low, Hudson, Pvt., Co. F, age 17, EN 6/25/63, Memphis, TN, born Davis Co., MO, farmer, deserted 10/1/63 from Corinth, MS with Remington revolver.

Lowrey/Lowry, James C., Sgt., Co. A, age 37, EN 1/10/64, Camp Davies, MS, MI 2/5/64, Memphis, TN, born Surry Co., NC, farmer, appt. Sgt. 2/5/64, KIA 4/15/65 near Huntsville, AL.
   NOTE: James Lowry married Nancy Utley July 28, 1857 in Morgan Co., AL and had the following children: Thomas L., born June 18, 1858; Mary E., born September 15, 1860; and Jesse Sherman, born November 22, 1865. Apparently James had been married earlier, as an affidavit in Nancy's pension papers states, "The said James C. Lowry left one child named Celia A. by a former marriage, who was nineteen years old in November 1867." According to the 1860 Lawrence Co., AL Census, Celia was living with James and Nancy Lowry. Nancy J. Lowry died October 8, 1907.[111]

Lowrimore, James, Corp/Sgt., Co. K, age 32, EN & MI 6/26/62, Limestone Co., AL, born Morgan Co., AL, transferred from Co. K, 21st Ohio Vols., appt. Sgt. 1/1/64, in hospital at Nashville, TN 12/26/62, MIA at Vincent's Crossroads, returned

11/2/63, POW 3/21/64 in AR near Memphis, TN, died 8/3/64 in hospital at Huntsville, AL from gunshot wound received at Paint Rock Creek, AL by guerrillas.

Lowrimore, Jesse, Co. A, age 26, born Fayette Co., AL, farmer, EN 9/8/62, Iuka, MS.*

Lowrimore, John, Pvt., Co. K, age 32, EN 6/14/64, Camp Davies, MS, born Morgan Co., AL, POW 3/21/64, paroled 4/30/64, MO 7/19/65, Rome, GA.

Lowrimore, Thomas J., Pvt., Co. A, age 23, EN 9/8/62, Iuka, MS, MI 10/1/62, Corinth, MS, born Fayette Co., AL, farmer, MO 9/16/63, Corinth, MS.

Lowrimore, William G., Pvt/Blacksmith, Co. K&A, age 30, EN & MI 10/1/62, Corinth, MS, MO 12/22/63, Memphis, TN. (Notation in file states, "see also Co. E, 1st TN Lt. Arty."

Lowrimore, William P., Pvt., Co. K, age 18, EN 6/26/62, Limestone Co., AL, transferred from Co. K, 21st Ohio Vols., born Fayette Co., AL, farmer, on detached service as teamster in Sherman's expedition 1/24/64 at Vicksburg, MS, POW 3/21/64, promoted to Corp. 1/1/65, MO 6/30/65, Nashville, TN.

Lowry (See Lowery).

Lowry, William W. (or B.), Pvt/Sgt., Co. B, age 29, EN 3/12/64, Athens, AL, MI 3/27/64, Decatur, AL, born Carroll Co., GA, farmer, POW 3/10/65, Monroe's Crossroads, MO 6/13/65 at Camp Chase, OH.

Lucas, Uriah D., Pvt., Co. M, age 24, EN 8/25/63, Chewalla, TN, MI 12/29/63, Corinth, MS, born Fayette Co., AL, farmer, MO 10/20/65, Huntsville, AL.

Lucher, Enoth F., (Cards filed with Enoth F. Tucker)

Lukins, James N., Lt., Co. C&D, age 25, detached from Co. A, 64th Ill. Inf. Vol., Actg. Sgt. Maj., EN 2/1/64, Memphis, TN, MO 10/20/65, Huntsville, AL.

Lukins, Thomas W., Sgt. Maj., F&S, (no further information).

Lumens, G., Pvt., Co. H, on duty as cook in ord. office 11/63.*

Lumley/Lumly, Nathan M., Pvt/Corp., Co. G, age 18, EN 6/26/63, Chewalla, TN, appt. Corp. 9/1/63, MO 11/26/63, Memphis, TN.

Lurtey, I. (or J.), Pvt., Co. B, absent sick in Gen. Hospital 10/64.*

Lyang, J.M., Co. B, absent sick in hospital 3/65.*

Mabry/Mayberry, Alberry W., Pvt., Co. I, age 20, EN & MI 8/18/62, Huntsville, AL, born Lumpkin Co., GA, farmer, with wagon train in Nashville, TN 12/27/62, on detail as courier at Reedyville, TN 1/27/63, WIA 11/22/63 near Camp Davies, MS, died 1/4/64 of wounds received in action.

Mabry/Mayberry, James P., Corp., Co. I, age 25, EN & MI 7/21/62, Huntsville, AL, born Lumpkin Co., GA, farmer, MIA 4/28/63 at Day's Gap, AL, rejoined Co. 10/2/63, POW 11/22/63 near Camp Davies, MS, delivered at Jacksonville, AL 4/28/65, arrived at Annapolis, MD 5/15/65 and sent to Camp Chase, OH 5/17/65, MO 6/12/65, Camp Chase, OH.

Mabry, Little T., Pvt., Co. I, age 18, EN & MI 8/18/62, Huntsville, AL, born Lumpkin Co., GA, farmer, on duty as courier at Reedyville, TN 1/27/63, MIA 4/28/63, Day's Gap, AL, rejoined Co. 10/2/63, MIA 10/26/63 at Vincent's Crossroads, MO 7/19/65, Nashville, TN.

Mabry, William, Pvt., Co. B, age 28, EN 7/11/63, Glendale, MS, born Pickens Co., AL, farmer, MO 1/22/64, Memphis, TN.

Mace, James, Pvt., Co. H, age 18, EN 10/17/63, Glendale, MS, POW 10/26/63, MO 10/24/64, Rome, GA.

Mack, Josiah, Pvt., Co. F, absent POW 10/26/63.*

Madison, Green B., Pvt., Co. L, age 18, EN 9/25/63, Fayette Co., AL, MI 9/25/63, Glendale, MS, born Fayette Co., AL, farmer, MO 9/28/64, Rome, GA.

Madison, James A., Pvt., Co. H, age 18, EN 3/1/65, Stevenson, AL, MI 4/5/65, Nashville, TN, born Spartanburg Dist., SC, farmer, MO 10/20/65, Huntsville, AL.

Madison, James K., Pvt., Co. L, age 18, EN & MI 9/25/63, Glendale, MS, born Fayette Co., AL, farmer, sick in Cumberland USA Gen. Hospital in Nashville, TN 12/31/63, MO 9/28/64, Rome, GA.

Madison, John/James Pvt., Co. D, age 22, EN 5/1/64, Decatur, AL, MI 6/16/64, Decatur, AL, born Tuscaloosa, AL, farmer, wounded and in hospital at Hilton Head, SC 11/26/64, in USA Gen. Hospital at Beaufort, SC 12/20/64, WIA in Nashville, TN 5/10/65, MO 5/19/65 from McDougall USA Gen. Hospital at Ft. Schuyler, NY.

Magen/McGaugh/McGane, Richard L., Pvt., Co. L, age 18, EN 3/1/65, Stevenson, AL, MI 4/18/65, Nashville, TN, born Walker Co., AL, farmer, MO 10/20/65, Huntsville, AL.

Mahan, Alexander, Pvt., Co. C, age 28, EN 2/12/63, Corinth, MS, MI 2/20/63, Corinth, MS, deserted 6/28/63 from Glendale, MS, returned 10/10/63, MO 2/12/64, Memphis, TN.

Mahan, Henry, Pvt., Co. C, age 30, EN 2/12/63, Corinth, MS, MI 2/20/63, Corinth, MS, born Pickens, AL, farmer, deserted 6/28/63 from Glendale, MS.

Mai, G., Pvt., Co. H, EN 10/30/63 at Glendale, MS.*

Maise, James, Pvt., Co. E, on daily duty as teamster 10/64.*

Malany, John, Pvt., Co. D, in Gayoso USA Gen. Hospital at Memphis, TN 1/64-4/64. *

Mallard, John B., Pvt., Co. L, age 18, EN 6/1/64, Decatur, AL, MI 6/28/64, Rome, GA, born Lincoln Co., TN, farmer, MIA 10/26/63 from Vincent's Crossroads, MS, MIA/POW 8/14/64 near Buchanan, GA.

Maloy, Hugh R., Pvt/Corp., Co. M, age 33, EN 12/12/63, Camp Davies, MS, MI 12/29/63, Corinth, MS, born Marion Co., AL, farmer, appt. Corp. 12/12/63, died 4/1/64 in hospital at Memphis, TN of smallpox. (Buried in Memphis National Cemetery.)

Mandly/Manly, John, Pvt., Co. B, age 18, EN 3/3/64, Pulaski, TN, born Winston Co., AL, farmer, deserted 8/15/64, Rome, GA with Smith carbine and equipment, charges of desertion were removed 2/14/87 by War Dept. and discharge issued as of 8/15/64. (Notation states, "for subsequent service of this man see Co. I, 4th Tenn. Mtd. Infy."

Maness, Daniel, Pvt., Co. H, age 19, EN 4/1/65, Stevenson, AL, MI 4/18/65, Nashville, TN, born Polk Co., GA, farmer, MO 10/20/65, Huntsville, AL.

Mangrum, George S., Pvt., Co. H, age 18, EN 3/1/65, Stevenson, AL, MI 4/5/65, Nashville, TN, born Dade Co., GA, farmer, MO 10/20/65, Huntsville, AL.

Manker, Henry C., Sgt., F&S, no further information.

Manscil/Mansil, James J., Pvt., Co. A, age 30, EN 6/12/63, Glendale, MS, on secret service in AL 10/24/63, MO 12/22/63, Memphis, TN.

Manuel, James R., Pvt/Sgt., Co. C, age 28, EN 1/5/63, Corinth, MS, POW 1/10/63 while on a scout, appt. Sgt. 4/18/63, MO 1/31/64, Memphis, TN.

Mark, Joseph H. (or A.), Pvt., Co. F, age 20, EN 9/7/63, Camp Davies, MS, MI 2/24/64, Memphis, TN, born Chambers Co., AL, MIA 10/26/63, returned 11/3/63, sick in hospital at Nashville, TN 11/6/64, MO 11/20/64, Nashville, TN, age shown as 26 on MO Roll.

Martin, Daniel, Pvt., Co. K, age 54, EN & MI 7/24/62, Huntsville, AL, born Hawkins Co., TN, occupation shown as "turner of wood", died 11/12/62 in Hospital #14, Nashville, TN of rubeola. (An Eli Martin is buried in Grave A-4495 in Nashville National Cemetery with death date 11/16/62.)

Martin, James, Pvt., Co. F, age 19, EN 5/1/63, Memphis, TN, MI 8/13/63, Corinth, MS, born Fayette Co., TN, farmer. (Notation states he was a substitute furnished by D.J. Foster, an enrolled man of Trigg Co. 1st Dist. of KY." MO 7/27/64, Rome, GA.

Martin, James F., (Cards filed with James F. Morton).

Martin, Jesse B., Pvt/Corp., Co. D, EN 2/1/63, Glendale, MS, MI 2/4/63, Corinth, MS, sick in Union USA Hospital at Memphis, TN Sept. & Oct. 1863, MO 2/4/64, Memphis, TN.

Martin, John, Pvt., Co. F, age 29, EN 7/6/63, Corinth, MS, born Franklin Co., TN, farmer, deserted 9/20/63 from Glendale, MS.

Martin, John M., Pvt., Co. C, age 35, EN 1/1/64, Corinth, MS, MI 3/10/64, Memphis, TN, born Abbeville, SC, farmer, deserted 3/20/64 from Memphis, TN with Colt revolver, carbine & horse, in arrest 10/64, deserted 10/1/65 from Moulton, AL.

Martin, Joseph R., Pvt/Blacksmith, Co. K, age 34, EN 12/21/63, Camp Davies, MS, born Morgan Co., AL, farmer, on detached service as teamster in Sherman's expedition in Vicksburg, MS 1/24/64, POW 3/21/64, MO 7/19/65, Nashville, TN. Traveled 150 miles from Walker Co., AL to Camp Davies to enlist.

Martin, Lewis, Pvt., Co. D, age 19, EN 5/1/64, Decatur, AL, MI 6/16/64, Decatur, AL, born Raleigh, NC, farmer, POW 2/6/65, in arrest at Memphis, TN 7/1/65, MO 10/20/65, Huntsville, AL.

Martin, Lewis W., Pvt., Co. C, age 18, EN 1/1/64, Camp Davies, MS, MI 1/5/64, Corinth, MS, born Abbeville, SC, farmer, no MO date.

Martin, Nathaniel G. (or J.), Pvt., Co. K, age 25, EN & MI 8/22/62, Huntsville, AL, born Lawrence Co., AL, farmer, died 12/26/62 in Hospital #14, Nashville, TN. (Buried in Grave B-6418 in Nashville, National Cemetery.)

Martin, Thomas E., Pvt., Co. C, age 21, EN 12/1/62, Corinth, MS, MI 12/22/62, Corinth, MS, born Abbeville, SC, farmer, MO 12/17/63, Memphis, TN.

Massey, James, Pvt/Bugler, Co. H, age 16, EN 9/30/63, Glendale, MS, on daily duty as Bugler, MO 9/29/64, Rome, GA.

Massey, Thomas C.(or R.), Pvt., Co. H, age 36, EN 10/1/63, Glendale, MS, MI 10/6/63, Glendale, MS, deserted 11/1/63, Glendale, MS.

Master, Daniel H., Co. G, AWOL 10/30/63.*

Masters, George F., Pvt., Co. G, age 33, EN 11/27/62, Grand Junction, TN, MO 11/26/63, Memphis, TN.

Masterson, John H., Pvt., Co. D, age 19, EN 3/5/63, Glendale, MS, MI 3/20/63, Corinth, MS, born Lawrence Co., AL, farmer, discharged 7/2/63, Glendale, MS due to disability.

Mathews, James, Pvt., Co. A, age 47, EN 9/8/62, Iuka, MS, MI 10/1/62, Corinth, MS, born SC, died 10/21/62 (or 9/8/62), at Corinth.

Mathis, Jesse, Pvt., Co. D, age 48, EN 3/5/63, Glendale, MS, MI 3/26/63, Corinth, MS, born NC, died 9/19/63 in Gen. Hospital at Corinth, MS of "dropsy".

Matterso, I. (or J.), Co. B, absent POW 3/10/65.*

Mattison, James, (Cards filed with James Madison).

Mattison, Kenneth/Hunith D., Pvt., Co. I, age 31, EN 9/22/63, Memphis, TN, born Edwards S. Canada, MO 9/28/64, Rome, GA.

Mattox, Henry P. (or J.), Pvt., Co. A, age 28, EN 1/29/64, Camp Davies, MS, MI 3/5/64, Memphis, TN, born Fayette Co., AL, died 5/6/64 in Gayoso USA Gen. Hospital at Memphis, TN of measles. (Buried in Memphis National Cemetery.)

Mauldin, William, Corp. Co. G, age 22 (or 31), EN 3/10/64, Decatur, AL, born Marion Co., AL, farmer, died 5/14/64 in USA Gen. Field Hospital at Bridgeport, AL. (Buried Grave #H-406, Chattanooga National Cemetery.)

Mayfield, Charner Hopkins , Pvt., Co. A, age 28, EN 10/29/62, MI 12/31/62, Corinth, MS, promoted to Corp. 12/18/62, deserted 3/31/63, reenlisted 1/25/64, Camp Davies, MS, MI 2/5/64, Memphis, TN, born Blount Co., AL, MO 10/20/65, Huntsville, AL. (Buried in Belgreen Cemetery, Franklin Co., AL.)

Mayfield, Milton L., Pvt., Co. H&L, age 23, EN 9/3/63, Glendale, MS, MO 9/29/64, Rome, GA, reenlisted 12/1/64, Stevenson, AL, KIA 3/10/65 in Winston Co., AL, buried near Natural Bridge, AL, Mayfield's Branch.

Mayfield, Reed C., Pvt., Co. H, age 18, EN 9/2/63, Glendale, MS, in Overton USA Hospital at Memphis, TN 12/31/63, MO 2/7/65, Nashville, TN. (Buried in Belgreen Cemetery, Franklin Co., AL.)

Mayfield, Thomas R., Pvt., Co. A&H, age 19, EN 10/23/62, MI 12/31/62, Corinth, MS, deserted 5/31/63, rejoined 9/2/63, Glendale, MS, MO 9/29/64, Rome, GA. (Buried in Belgreen Cemetery, Franklin Co., AL.)

Mayfield, William H., Pvt., Co. H, age 26, EN 10/29/62, MI 12/31/62, Corinth, MS, deserted 5/31/63, rejoined 9/2/63, Glendale, MS, deserted while on detached service 10/64. (Buried in Osborne Hill Cemetery, Colbert Co., AL.)

Maze, George, Wagoner, Co. A, age 23, EN 6/20/63, Glendale, MS, MO 12/22/63, Memphis, TN.

McAlister, James W., Pvt., Co. G, age 25, EN 7/17/63, Glendale, MS, MO 11/26/63, Memphis, TN. Service also alleged in Co. E, 1st Tenn. Lt. Arty., daily duty as hospital nurse 9/20/63.

McAller, James, Pvt., age 45, MI 4/13/64, Decatur, AL, born York Dist., SC, farmer.

McAllison, Jasper, Pvt., Co. D, on daily duty as company cook, POW 10/26/63, discharged 7/28/64 at Rome, GA, term of service expired. (Name also shown as J.C. McAllison & J. McAlister.)*

McAlroy, T., Pvt., Co. D, EN 6/1/63 at Glendale, MS.*

McArthur, James S. (or L.), Pvt., Co. B, age 38, EN 12/16/62, Glendale, MS, MI 1/22/63, Corinth, MS, born Coosa Co., AL, farmer, on secret service in AL 2/8/63, no MO date.

McBride, James H., Pvt., Co. A, age 50, EN 9/8/62, Iuka, MS, MI 10/1/62, Corinth, MS, born Bibb Co., NC, farmer, discharged 7/3/63 due to disability, "eyesight and old age".

McCain, Richard, Pvt., Co. I, age 18, EN 10/10/63, Glendale, MS, born Heard Co., GA, farmer, MO 7/19/65, Nashville, TN.

McCall, Thomas, Corp., Co. G, died of disease at Bethel 7/11/63.*

McCall, Thomas J., Pvt., Co. G, temporarily detached from 11th Illinois Cavalry.

McCarver, Felix, T., Pvt., Co. G, age 17, EN 12/13/62, Pocohontas, TN, MO 11/26/63, Memphis, TN.

McCarver, Isaac A., Pvt., Co. G, age 21, EN 4/6/63, Chewalla, TN, wounded 11/63 and in Corinth Hospital, MO 11/26/63, Memphis, TN.

McElroy, Andrew, (Cards filed with Andrew J. McCroy).

McElroy, F., Pvt., Co. D, discharged 7/22/63 at Glendale, MS.*

McClellan, James, Pvt., Co. B&A, age 21, EN 7/1/64, Wedowee, AL, born Cherokee, AL, transferred to Rome, GA 9/15/64.

McClellan, Riley, Pvt., Co. H, age 19, EN 4/1/65, Stevenson, AL, MI 4/5/65, Nashville, TN, born Bradley Co., TN, farmer, appt. Corp. 4/1/65, reduced to ranks 7/1/65 for AWOL, deserted 8/1/65 from Blountsville, AL with Colt pistol, Smith carbine and equipment.

McClung, Vinyard, Pvt., Co. D, age 35, EN 3/5/63, Glendale, MS, MI 3/20/63, Corinth, MS, served as company cook, MO 3/25/64, Decatur, AL.

McCluskey, Joseph, Pvt., Co. I, age 30, EN & MI 8/18/62 (or 7/21/62), Huntsville, AL, born Lawrence Co., AL, farmer, sick in Hospital #3 at Nashville, TN 10/24/62, sick at Murfreesboro, TN 5/3/63, MO 5/20/65 in accordance with telegraphic instuctions from the War Dept.

McCredie, Nelson A., Pvt/Corp., Co. M, age 28, EN 10/14/64, Decatur, AL, MI 11/10/64, Rome, GA, born Bradley Co., TN, farmer, promoted to Corp. 7/1/65 "for good conduct in field", MO 10/20/65, Huntsville, AL.

McCreless, William A., Pvt/Corp., Co. E, age 18, EN & MI 9/1/64, Rome, GA, born Randolph Co., AL, farmer, promoted to Corp. 1/1/65, MO 10/20/65, Huntsville, AL.

McCroy/McElroyMcLeroy, Andrew J. (Alexander J.), Pvt., Co. B, age 18, EN 8/1/64, Wedowee, AL, MI 8/1/64, Rome, GA, born Carroll Co., GA, farmer, POW 3/10/65, Monroe's Crossroads, NC, sent to Camp Chase, OH.

McCron/McKleroy/McCroy, John M.(or C.), Pvt., Co. B, age 26, EN 8/1/64, Wedowee, AL, MI 8/1/64, Rome, GA, born Paulding Co., GA, farmer, (another MR states he enlisted 9/1/64 in Stevenson, AL & MI 4/5/65 in Nashville, TN), sent from hospital at Cartersville, GA to hospital at Nashville, TN 11/12/64, MO 10/20/65, Huntsville, AL.

McCulloch, Leroy M., Pvt., Co. K, age 19, EN & MI 7/31/62, Huntsville, AL, born Lawrence Co., AL, farmer, died 11/22/62 in Hospital #14, Nashville, TN of rubeola. (Buried in Grave B-5863 in Nashville National Cemetery.)

McCulloch, Samuel, Pvt., Co. K, age 45, EN & MI 7/31/62, Huntsville, AL, born Lincoln Co., TN, farmer, died 10/23/62, in Hospital #14, Nashville, TN of rubeola. (Buried in Grave B-6986 in Nashville National Cemetery with death date shown as 10/24/62.)

McCulloch, Thomas D. (or B.), Pvt., Co. K, age 26, EN & MI 7/31/62, Huntsville, AL, born Lawrence Co., AL, farmer, wounded POW from Day's Gap, AL 4/30/63, died 2/26/64 in C.S. Military prison hospital in Richmond, VA.

McCullough, Joseph E., Pvt., Co. D, age 22, EN 3/15/63, Glendale, MS, MI 4/28/63, Corinth, MS, born Marion (?) Co., AL, deserted 6/12/63 from Glendale, MS, killed 6/12/63 by guerrillas while on secret scout 15 miles from Glendale, MS.

McDade, Thomas E., Pvt., Co. F, age 34, EN 5/23/63, Corinth, MS, born Madison Co., AL, farmer, deserted 7/16/63, Glendale, MS.

McDavitt, Virgil, Lt./Asst. Surgeon, F&S, age 34, EN 8/15/63, Glendale, MS, "appointed from citizen", MO 8/15/64, Memphis, TN. (There is quite a bit of controversy about this physician in files.)

McDonald, Leonard B., Pvt/Sgt., Co. G, age 27, EN 3/10/64, Decatur, AL, MI 4/13/64, Decatur, AL, born Jefferson Co., AL, farmer, promoted Sgt. 5/1/64, MO 10/20/65, Huntsville, AL.

McDonald, Miles H., Pvt., Co. B, EN 3/11/63, Glendale, MS, died 5/11/63 in hospital at Corinth, MS.

McDonald, William, Pvt., Co. F, age 27, EN 5/15/63, Memphis, TN, born Cape Vinson, NY, sailor, died 3/14/64, Memphis, TN of gunshot wound.

McDonald, William B., Pvt/Corp., Co. B, age 22, EN 3/11/63, Glendale, MS, MO 1/22/64, Memphis, TN.

McElroy, Thompson, Pvt., Co. D, age 60, EN 5/4/63, Glendale, MS, born Madison Co., GA, discharged 7/17/63 for disability, "hernia".

McGaha, Gille W., Pvt/Sgt., Co. H, age 35, EN 7/28/63, Glendale, MS, MO 7/27/64, Rome, GA, (MO Roll states he was age 25).

McGaha, William C., Pvt/Sgt., Co. H, age 33, EN 7/28/63, Glendale, MS, in Adams USA Hospital at Memphis, TN 1/20/64, returned to duty 3/27/64, MO 7/27/64, Rome, GA.

McGane/McGaugh, Richard, (Cards filed with Richard L. Magen).

McGanghey, James B., Hospital Steward/Lt., Co. H, age 20, EN 4/2/63, Corinth, MS, promoted from Pvt. in Co. A, 10th MO Inf. Vols. where he first EN 1/11/62 in Herman, MO and MI 1/13/62 at High Hill, MO, MO 10/20/65, Huntsville, AL.

McGough, Joseph, Pvt., Co. A, age 21, EN 9/8/62, Iuka, MS, MI 10/1/62, Corinth, MS, born Bibb Co., NC, farmer, died 1/25/63 at Corinth.

McGowen, James, Pvt., Co. K&A, age 21, EN 12/15/62, MI 12/31/62, Corinth, MS, MO 12/22/63, Memphis, TN.
   NOTE: James Aumbers McGowan was born February 18, 1842 in Marion Co., AL. On March 4, 1869 he married Martha E. Bozeman who was born in September 1840 and they raised a family of four sons and three daughters. James died December 26, 1899 and Martha died July 10, 1925. They are buried in the Guin Cemetery in Marion Co., AL. Their children were: Thomas Jurden, born December 29, 1869, died September 20, 1952; William Walker, born May 1, 1872, married Idellia M. Stanford, daughter of George E. and Arena Stanford in 1895 and died October 13, 1926; James Franklin, born 1874; Faithey Jane, born 1876; Samuel Newton, born 1878; Mary Elizabeth, born 1880; and Sarah Francis, born 1882 and married Virgil Taylor.[112]

McHallis, John, Pvt., Co. C, in USA Gen. Hospital #1 at Annapolis, MD 2/22/65.*

McHimes, (?), Pvt., Co. C, on daily duty as teamster.*

McKain, Richard, (Cards filed with Richard McCarn).

McKemie/McKamie, Alfred, Pvt., Co. H, age 44, EN 5/8/65, Huntsville, AL, MI 5/20/65, Nashville, TN, born Madison Co., AL, farmer, sick in hospital at Huntsville, AL 7/19/65, MO 8/15/65 Nashville, TN.

McKinney/McKenna, Amos, Under Cook, Co. C, (Colored), age 20, EN 12/15/63, Corinth, MS, MI Rome, GA, born Chester Co. Dist., SC, farmer, teamster with Regtl. Q.M., MO 10/20/65, Huntsville, AL.

McKinney, James, Pvt., Co. C, on daily duty as reg't teamster.*

McKinney, Thomas J. (or P.), Pvt., Co. A, age 18, EN 1/3/64, Camp Davies, MS, MI 2/5/64, Memphis, TN, born Franklin Co., AL, farmer, died 4/10/64 at Washington USA Hospital at Memphis, TN of rubeola. (Buried in Memphis National Cemetery.)

McKnabb, John, Pvt., Co. K, age 28, EN & MI 7/31/62, Huntsville, AL, born Lancashire, England, farmer, deserted from Columbus, OH 5/22/63, captured 3/10/65 at Solomon Grove, NC, paroled POW at Annapolis, MD, MO 7/19/65, Nashville, TN, charges of desertion removed 10/6/86 stating he was captured at Rome, GA 5/3/63 and confined at Richmond, VA 5/9/63, rejoined company 9/23/63, captured and again confined at Richmond, VA.

McKnable, Pat/John, Co. K, restored to duty 2/28/64 after being AWOL with loss of pay from 5/63 to 9/23/63, signed by Lt. Col. Dodd.*

McLarty, Robert W., Sgt., Co. F, age 25, EN 4/13/63, Corinth, MS, born Cobb Co., GA, farmer, MO 4/12/64, Decatur, AL.

McLarty, William A., Corp/Sgt., Co. F, age 28, EN 4/13/63, Corinth, MS, born Mecklenburg Co., NC, mechanic, MO 4/12/64, Decatur, AL.

McMunn, Birdwell, Pvt/Corp., Co. D&I, age 18, EN & MI 8/5/62, Huntsville, AL, born Marshall Co., AL, farmer, appt. Corp. 10/1/64, on courier post at Reedyville, TN, 1/27/63, MO 7/19/65, Nashville, TN.

McMurrey, Jacob R., Pvt/Sgt., Co. D, age 21, EN & MI 7/1/63, Glendale, MS, born Blount Co., AL, farmer, promoted to Corp. 12/3/63, MO 7/27/64, Rome, GA.

McQuiddy, Henry C., Capt. Co. I, MI by Adj. Gen. of the Army at Nashville, TN 1/21/63, appt. Capt. 2/14/63 from Co. F, 1st Middle TN Cav., POW 5/3/63, Cedar Bluff, AL, confined at Richmond, VA.

McRae, William A., Sgt/Sgt. Maj., Co. C&F, age 22, EN 1/1/63, Corinth, MS, MI 12/22/63, Corinth, MS, born Pickens Co., AL, farmer, MO 12/17/63, Memphis, TN, reenlisted 1/1/64, Corinth, MS, MI 3/10/64, Memphis, TN.

McRay, John H., Pvt., Co. D, in USA Gen. Hospital at Jefferson Barracks, MO Jan. & Feb. 1864.*

McRay, John H., Pvt., Co. C, died 3/14/64 at Jefferson Barracks, MO.*

McVay, Riley, Pvt., Co. G, loss 7/28/63 at Glendale by order to return to his reg't.(1st US Cav.).*

McVey, Joseph A., Pvt., Co. G, age 17, EN 1/13/63, Chewalla, TN, discharged, was a member of the 1st West Tenn. Cav. and sent back by order of Col. Miller of 18th MO Vol.

McWasher, (?), Corp., Co. B, POW 7/65.*

McWorkman, Daniel, Lt. Co. L, age 34, EN 3/2/64, Memphis, TN, promoted from Pvt., 2nd Iowa Inf. Vol., MO 10/20/65, Huntsville, AL.

McWhirter, Andrew F., Pvt., Co. K, age 44, EN & MI 7/24/62, Huntsville, AL, born Warren Co., TN, farmer, died 10/23/62 in Hospital #14, Nashville, TN of rubeola. (Buried in Grave B-6918 in Nashville National Cemetery.)
NOTE: Andrew Ferrier McWhirter was born November 13, 1821 to Elizabeth Robinson and Alexander Hamilton McCandless McWhirter. He married Sarah Harper on June 7, 1842 in Warren Co., TN and had the following children: Thomas Andrew, born July 10, 1843, (see below); George Washington, born 1844, (see below); Andrew Jackson, born June 23, 1847, married Nancy Jane Whitehead, died February 28, 1922; Robert, born 1848; William Hamilton, born July 19, 1852, married Sara Jane Hallmark and Sally Worthy, died March 17, 1907; Mary Caroline, born May 17, 1855, married George Washington Harbin, died December 15, 1934 in Wood, TX; John M., born February 1858, married Georgia Ann O'Mary. Andrew and Sarah emigrated to Walker Co., AL around 1843. By 1850, they were living in Marion Co., AL. Andrew's widow not only lost a husband and son in the Civil War, but she lost at least one brother, Tennessee Polk Harper.

McWhorter/McWhirter, A.J., Servt., Co. K, in Adams USA Gen. Hospital in Memphis, TN in March 1864, returned to duty 3/27/64. No further information shown.
NOTE: This could be Andrew Jackson McWhirter, son of Andrew Ferrier McWhirter, who had two other sons in this regiment. A.J. McWhirter was a Primitive Baptist Preacher and is the great grandfather of the author.

McWhirter, George Washington, Pvt., Co. K, age 18, EN & MI 7/24/62, Huntsville, AL, born Walker Co., AL, farmer, died 10/8/62 in Hospital #14 in Nashville, TN of rubeola. (Died 15 days before his father died and is buried in Grave A-4367 in Nashville National Cemetery.)

McWhirter, Thomas A., Pvt., Co. K, age 19, EN & MI 7/24/62, Huntsville, AL, born Walker Co., AL, on courier post in Jan. & Feb. 1863, on detached duty at Vicksburg MS 1/24/64, served as orderly at regimental headquarters, wounded POW at the Battle of Vincent's Crossroads 10/26/63, escaped on or about 2/15/64 and walked back to Decatur, AL to find the regiment gone, again captured on or about 4/15/65 at Faun's Station, NC, paroled POW at Annapolis, MD, wounded in skirmish at Richland, NC 4/1/65.
NOTE: Thomas Andrew McWhirter was born July 10, 1843, married Mary Jane Hallmark, daughter of George Hallmark, on February 13, 1866 and had the following children: Sarah Elizabeth, born December 18, 1866, married Benjamin Franklin Miles and died November 13, 1935 in Marion Co., AL; Nancy Mahaley,

born 1872, married Thomas Head July 28, 1887; Susan Angeline, born February 10, 1874, married William Curtis Sexton June 29, 1890 and died January 29, 1921 in Marion Co., AL. Thomas and Mary Jane had several children who died in infancy. Thomas died August 22, 1917 and is buried in the old Poplar Springs Primitive Baptist Church Cemetery in Marion Co., AL. Mary Jane died August 1, 1904.

McWorkman, (?), Pvt., Co. F, absent on det. duty as orderly for Gen. Veach.*

McWright, Malin/Melan/Matan, Pvt/Sgt., Co. D, age 45, EN 4/25/63, Glendale, MS, MI 4/28/63, Corinth, MS, MO 6/16/64, Decatur, AL.

Meadows, James H., Corp., Co. B, age 46, EN 3/16/64, MI 4/13/64, Decatur, AL, born West Dist., SC, farmer, deserted 8/15/65 from Courtland, AL, charges of desertion removed 8/23/87 and discharge issued as of 8/15/65.

Medicks, H.J., Pvt., Co. A, absent sick in Gen. Hospital at Memphis, TN 4/64.*

Meeker, J.J., Pvt., Co. H, discharged 10/25/64 at Rome, GA by reason of exp. of term of service.*

Medlin, James P., Pvt/Sgt., Co. A&M, age 22, EN 1/11/64, Camp Davies, MS, MI 2/5/64, Memphis, TN, born Cooper Co., MO, Clerk, POW 3/10/65 at Solomon Grove, NC, discharged 6/12/65, Camp Chase, OH.

Mellen, Johnathan/Jonathan, Pvt., Co. G, age 26, EN 2/15/63, Chewalla, TN, MO 11/26/63, Memphis, TN, (Notation states, "see also 1st Miss. Mtd. Rifles".

Melton, Charles D., Pvt., Co. F, discharged 7/27/64 at Rome, GA, term of service expired.*

Melton, William H., Pvt., Co. C, age 23, EN 2/15/64, Memphis, TN, MI 3/10/64, Memphis, TN, born Franklin, IL, farmer, MO 10/20/65, Huntsville, AL.

Meradith, David E., Pvt., Co. F, age 31, EN 5/23/63, Corinth, MS, born Dallas Co., AL, farmer, deserted 7/16/63 from Glendale, MS.

Merrit, Robert, Pvt., Co. M, age 37, EN 9/12/63, Chewalla, MI 12/29/63, Corinth, MS, born Montgomery Co., NC, farmer, MO 10/20/65, Huntsville, AL.

Messer, Henry A.J., Pvt., Co. H, age 20, EN 5/10/65, Huntsville, AL, MI 5/20/65, Nashville, TN, born Jackson Co., AL, farmer, deserted 10/1/65 from Blountsville, AL with Colt pistol.

Messer, Jesse, Pvt., Co. H, age 18, EN 4/20/65, Huntsville, AL, MI 5/20/65, Nashville, TN, born Jackson Co., AL, farmer, MO 10/20/65, Huntsville, AL.

Messer, John W., Pvt., Co. C, age 19, EN 1/28/63, Corinth, MS, MI 2/1/63, Corinth, MS, born Henry Co., GA, farmer, sick in hospital at Memphis, TN 12/18/63, MO 1/31/64, Memphis, TN.

Messer, William, Pvt., Co. H, age 42, EN 5/1/65, Huntsville, AL, MI 5/20/65, Nashville, TN, born Hawkins Co., TN, farmer, MO 10/20/65, Huntsville, AL.

Michales, J.L., Pvt., Co. D, supposed to be dead in the field 5/1/65.*

Michls, J.S., Pvt., Co. D, absent POW 10/26/63.*

Mickle, George T., Pvt., Co. B, in USA Gen. Hospital Near Troy, NC July & Aug. 1865, transferred to Gen. Hospital at Louisville, KY 7/11/65.*

Mickle, J.F., Co. B, age 18, born Randolph Co., AL, farmer, EN 8/1/64, Wedowee, AL.*

Mickle, Thomas F., Pvt., Co. B, age 18, EN 8/1/64, Wedowee, AL, MI 8/1/64, Rome, GA, born Randolph Co., AL, farmer, in hospital at Wilmington, NC 4/9/65, MO 10/20/65.

Milam, Jessie, Pvt., Co. A, age 22, EN 8/1/64, Rome, GA, MI 10/20/64, Rome, GA, born Hardin Co., TN, farmer, died 1/20/65 at Savannah, GA.

Miles, Benjamin R., Pvt., Co. B, EN 1/20/63, Glendale, MS, MI 1/22/63, Corinth, MS, died 4/27/63 at Post Hospital at Corinth of typhoid pneumonia.

Miles, William H., Pvt., Co. K, age 20, EN & MI 7/24/62, Huntsville, AL, born Lincoln Co., TN, farmer, died 10/14/62 (or 10/15), in Hospital #14, Nashville, TN of rubeola. (Buried in Grave B-5659 in Nashville National Cemetery with death date shown as 10/15/62.)

Miles, William W., Pvt., Co. B, age 35, EN 1/20/63, Glendale, MS, MI 1/22/63, Corinth, MS, born Lincoln, Co., TN, farmer, died 5/26/63 at regimental hospital at Corinth, MS of typhoid fever.

Miles, Woodruff, Pvt., Co. B, age 26, EN 1/20/63, Glendale, MS, MI 1/22/63, Corinth, MS, born St. Clair Co., AL, discharged 7/27/63 at Glendale, MS due to disability.
NOTE: Woodruff Miles married Matilda C. Cocks in Marion Co., AL on November 14, 1861 at her father's house and they were married by Parson Franklin Creel. Children (who were living in 1898) were: Mary C., born June 20, 1862; Benjamin W., born July 23, 1864; William C., born July 3, 1867; Andrew J., born November 21, 1871; and Arrena A., born July 17, 1878. In his Declaration for Original Invalid Pension, Woodruff stated, "I was sent to Corinth Miss to the 2d Iowa Hospital Feb 20/63 and about May 24/63 back to my Regmtl Hospital Glendale Miss and remained under care of Surgeon until discharged for 'Disease of the Lungs' from a relapse of the Measles contracted at Glendale. I am able to follow my occupation about 1/3 of my time. I claim a Pension on Disease of the Lungs."
William was the son of William and Mary Miles and was born in Lincoln Co., TN. He died January 23, 1915 of "cancer and lung trouble" and is buried in the

Miles Cemetery near Stricklin, AL. Matilda died September 30, 1922. Woodruff's brother, Calvin, served in the Confederate army.[113]

Miligan, James M., Pvt., Co. B, age 18, EN 3/16/64, Decatur, AL, MI 3/27/64, Decatur, AL, born Blount Co., AL, farmer, left sick in hospital at Decatur, AL 4/17/64, died 4/28/64. (Buried Grave #B-3230, Corinth National Cemetery.)

Miller, John, Pvt., Co. B, age 32, EN 1/20/63, Glendale, MS, MI 1/22/63, Corinth, MS, deserted 2/28/63 while on scout, returned 12/11/63, no MO date.

Miller, John, Pvt., Co. F, age 32, EN 9/1/63, Corinth, MS, born Londow, Germany, MIA 10/26/63 from Vincent's Crossroads, sick at Louisville, KY 1/10/64, returned from POW 5/2/64 and sent to hospital 5/5/64, no further information.

Miller, Mark S., Pvt., Co, I, age 32, EN 12/21/63, Camp Davies, MS, born Carroll Co., GA, farmer, deserted 1/18/64 from Camp Davies, MS.

Miller, Rilley, Pvt., Co. M, age 29, EN 12/15/63, Camp Davies, MS, MI 12/29/63, Corinth, MS, born Hall Co., GA, farmer, deserted 6/1/65 while on recruiting service in AL, with Smith carbine, horse and equipment, application to remove charge of desertion was denied 1/15/89 by War Dept., later removed February 1, 1905 and discharge issued as of May 31, 1864.

Milligan, William, Pvt., Co. H, age 18, EN 12/20/64, Huntsville, AL, MI 2/15/65, Nashville, TN, born Morgan Co., AL, farmer, MO 10/20/65, Huntsville, AL.

Milligan, William K., Pvt., Co. I, age 21, EN & MI 8/18/62, Huntsville, AL, died 12/27/62 (or 12/1) in Hospital #6 at Nashville, TN of pneumonia. (Buried in Grave A-4351 in Nashville National Cemetery and death date shown as 12/1/62.)

Milligan, William W., Co. I, age 21, born Morgan Co., AL, farmer, EN 7/21/62, Huntsville, AL.*

Milligan, William W., Pvt., Co. I, EN & MI 7/21/62, Huntsville, AL, deserted 9/14/62, Nashville, TN.

Milliner, Jefferson M., Pvt., Co. B, age 26, EN 12/17/62, Glendale, MS, MI 12/31/62, Corinth, MS, born Marshall Co., AL, farmer, absent with leave to take family North June, 1863, MO 12/27/63, Camp Davies, MS. (MO Roll states he was age 35.)

Milling, J.B., Pvt., Co. H, on daily duty as company cook.*

Millins/Mullins, J.M. (or I.M.), Pvt., Co. H, EN 10/2/63 at Glendale, MS.*

Mills, Britton L. (R.S & R.L Mills), Pvt., Co. E, EN 4/1/63, Glendale, MS, on detached service as teamster 1/25/64 at Vicksburg, MS, MO 3/1/64, Memphis TN.

Mills, Johnathan, Pvt., Co. E, EN 3/1/63, Glendale, MS, MI 4/1/63, Corinth, MS, on detached service as teamster 1/25/64 at Vicksburg, MS, also served as nurse in hospital, MO 3/1/64, Memphis, TN.

Mills, Jonathan R., Pvt., Co. I, age 21, EN & MI 8/6/62, Huntsville, AL, deserted 10/30/62 at Nashville, TN.

Mills, Simeon, Pvt., Co. E, EN 4/1/63, Glendale, MS, MI 4/1/63, Corinth, MS, on detached service as teamster 1/25/64 at Vicksburg, MS, MO 3/1/63, Memphis, TN.

Mills, Stephen H., Pvt., Co. F, age 19, EN 7/16/63, Corinth, MS, born Tishomingo Co., MS, farmer, POW 9/63, died 4/3/64 at Overton USA Hospital at Memphis, TN. (Buried in Memphis National Cemetery.)

Mills, Zacharia, Pvt., Co. E, EN 3/1/63, Glendale, MS, MI 4/1/63, Corinth, MS, on detached service as teamster 1/25/64 at Vicksburg, MS, MO 3/1/64, Memphis, TN.

Milum, Jesse M., Pvt., Co. F, age 20, EN 5/27/63, Corinth, MS, MI 6/1/63, Corinth, MS, born East TN, farmer, deserted 2/1/64 from Camp Davies, MS, MO 11/3/64, Rome, GA.

Minton, E.L., Co. F, absent sick in hospital at Memphis, TN 10/29/63.*

Mitchell, Andrew D., Pvt/Sgt., Co. L, age 17, EN 9/25/63, Fayette Co., AL, MI 9/25/63, Glendale, MS, born Forsythe Co., GA, farmer, promoted to Sgt. 5/1/64, MO 9/28/64 at Rome, GA, reenlisted 2/18/65, Stevenson, AL, MI 2/18/65, Nashville, TN, MO 10/20/65, Huntsville, AL.
   NOTE: Andrew D. Mitchell was born November 28, 1846 and died November 3, 1931.
   The following is a speech writen and given by Andrew D. Mitchell September 22, 1910, to a group of Veterans. Some of the words are illegible:
   "As you all know comrades I was one of those soldiers who faut in the war of 1861 to 1865. We are veterans and our white hairs tell that. Our feeling tell us that and as we look over the crowds here today we old Soldiers ralize the fact without being told that. Our days of fighting are past that our days of rest and peace from the gun are hear and that we shold every one of us come together on all Suitable occasions to pres each other's hands and look back and around us; to look back and see if that for which we fought honestly and truly, that for which we left our dead comrades upon the bare pine forests of the South - whether it remains secure to us and whether we may now sleep in rest and peace.
   Every man be he American, English, French or German was as much interested that America slould be free land-to-day free from Maine to Texas and from Florida to Oregon - as you who are living here in your homes in Alabama. We fought for mankind. We fought for all the earth and for all civilization and now stand preminent among the nations of the earth with a glorious past, a magnificent present and future at which we may all rejoice.
   Anybody can fight with a stranger, anybody can shoot an Indian down and it is not a very hard thing to pull the trigger on a foreigner; but when we came to shoot each other, when we had to go to fight these Southern friends of ours, and

sometimes fight in our own streets, that called for nerve, and the highest kind of nerve; and that is what I want the citizens to bear in mind when he lookes at soldiers in this country. They went out, fought, and conquered, and when it was done they stopped and went home. The war has passed and a new generation has grown up, young men capable of doing as much as those who fought. From the simple mechanic and farmer we can secure as capable men for putting on the Blue and buckling on the cartridge belt and taking a rifle and if their hearts be in the right place, and their heads ordinarily clear they can go on the field and be as good men as Sheridan, Sherman or Grant ever were.

We have 50 million such people in America and the work is not yet done. I do not think there are any more civil wars before us, but we must be prepared for what God brings, and be true to ourselves, our country, and our God."

Mitchell, David, Pvt., Co. K&A, age 32, EN 9/8/62, Iuka, MS, MI 10/1/62, Corinth, MS, born York, SC, farmer, MO 9/16/63, Corinth, MS.

Mitchell, Ephraim, Co. A, absent with leave in AL 8/63.*

Mitchell, Eldon/Elden C., Pvt/Corp., Co. L, age 19, EN 9/25/63, Fayette Co., AL, born Walton Co., GA, farmer, promoted to Corp. 12/9/63, died 1/17/64 at regimental hospital at Camp Davies, MS. (Buried Grave #B-3494, Corinth National Cemetery.)

Mitchell, Francis/Frank M., Pvt., Co. B&A, age 30, EN 1/13/63, Glendale, MS, MI 1/22/63, Corinth, MS, born St. Clair Co., AL, died 7/31/63 at Glendale, MS. (Buried Grave #A-2063, Corinth National Cemetery.)
      NOTE: Francis Mitchell married Mary K. Hallmark on or about December 30, 1855 at Robert Hallmark's in Marion Co., AL. Their children were: Martha Malinda, born October 2, 1856 and John Marion, born March 30, 1858. Francis was born about 1832 in SC (military records state St. Clair Co., AL) and was the son of James and Melinda South. (See William H. Mitchell.)[114]

Mitchell, Henry F., Pvt/Corp., Co. E, age 38, EN & MI 10/4/64, Rome, GA, born Walton Co., GA, farmer, promoted to Corp. 10/20/64, MO 10/20/65, Huntsville, AL.

Mitchell, John, Pvt., Co. B&A, age 33, EN 1/6/63, Glendale, MS, MI 1/22/63, Corinth, MS, MO 12/22/63, Memphis, TN.

Mitchell, John A., Pvt., Co. A, age 23, EN 7/8/63, Glendale, MS, MIA at Vincent's Crossroads, MS 10/26/63, MO 12/22/63, Memphis, TN.

Mitchell, John C., Pvt., Co. I&A, age 18, EN & MI 8/26/62, Huntsville, AL, born Morgan Co., AL, farmer, died 10/8/62 in Hospital #14, Nashville, TN. (Buried in Grave A-4566 in Nashville National Cemetery.)

Mitchell, John D., Pvt., Co. B&A, age 24, MI 1/22/63, Corinth, MS, MIA at Vincent's Crossroads, MS 10/26/63, returned 11/19/63, died 8/4/64 at Andersonville,

GA while POW. (Buried Grave #4718, Andersonville National Cemetery.) (See Francis M. and William H. Mitchell for further information on family.)

Mitchell, Leroy P., Pvt., Co. B, age 30, EN 3/3/63, Glendale, MS, deserted 6/2/63 from Glendale, MS.

Mitchell, Logan B., Pvt., Co. D, age 28, EN 4/25/63, Glendale, MS, MI 4/28/63, Corinth, MS, born Blount Co., AL, farmer, POW 6/3/63 while on secret scout, escaped 12/15/63, MIA 2/10/64, discharged as of 4/25/64.

Mitchell, Lorenzo, Pvt., Co. D, EN 3/15/63, Glendale, MS, MI 3/26/63, Corinth, MS, deserted 6/3/63 from Glendale, MS, POW 4/64, no further information.

Mitchell, Samuel M., Pvt., Co. D, age 25, EN 7/17/63, Glendale, MS, born York, SC, farmer, MO 7/27/64, Rome, GA.

Mitchell, Samuel M., Pvt/Corp., Co. L, age 20, EN 9/25/63, Fayette Co., MS, born Walton Co., GA, sick in Post Hospital at Memphis, TN 10/24/63, MO 9/28/64, Rome, GA, reenlisted 3/1/65, Stevenson, AL, MI 4/18/65, Nashville, TN, appt. Corp. 7/1/65, MO 10/20/65, Huntsville, AL.

Mitchell, Thomas, Pvt., Co. E, EN 12/25/62, Chewalla, TN, MI 12/25/62, Corinth, MS, POW 2/20/63 near Chewalla, TN, deserted 5/13/63, Glendale, MS, no further information.

Mitchell, William, (George S.) Pvt., Co. H, age 18, EN 4/1/65, Stevenson, AL, MI 4/5/65, Nashville, TN, born Marshall Co., AL, farmer, MO 10/20/65, Huntsville, AL.

Mitchell, William H., Pvt., Co. K&A, age 32, EN 9/8/62, Iuka, MS, MI 10/1/62, Corinth, MS, born Lawrence, SC, farmer, daily duty as teamster, MO 9/16/63, Corinth, MS.
   NOTE: William H. Mitchell was the son of James and Melinda South Mitchell who moved to Marion Co., AL sometime before 1840. James was the son of John and Anna Mitchell of Laurens Co., SC. According to a book, *"Genealogical Notes on the South Family"*, written by Mrs. Christine Gee, Melinda's grandparents were William South and Catherine Daniel.
   William and his brothers, John and Francis Marion Mitchell, all served in the 1st AL Cav. Union army. His Declaration for an Original Invalid Pension stated that while in the service and in the line of duty he was a teamster and while in a retreat from Yellow Creek, MS, his team became frightened and ran away. He, in attempting to stop them, was injured in his right leg. An affidavit states William's first wife was Louisa.[115]

Mize, Isaac, Pvt., Co. E, age 19, EN & MI 10/4/64, Rome, GA, born Walton Co., GA, farmer, MO 10/20/65, Huntsville, AL.
   NOTE: Isaac Austin Mize was born December 25, 1843 to Reuben and Sarah Lindley Mize, married Nancy Elizabeth Young in Randolph Co., AL on January 13, 1868 and died April 6, 1912. He is buried at Union Hill Congregational Methodist Church in Randolph Co., AL. Nancy died April 16, 1926 and is also

buried at Union Hill. Their children were: Edward Sherman, born & died June 21, 1869; John Thomas, born May 6, 1870, died September 18, 1938; George David, born March 15, 1872, died 1954; James Robert, born March 31, 1873, died December 9, 1937; Annie L., born November 9, 1874, died May 28, 1964; Nancy Ellen, born September 30, 1876, died May 17, 1928; Martha, born December 17, 1877, died December 21, 1877; William Boss, born April 14, 1878, died December 15, 1954; Oscar Austin, born January 12, 1880, died October 17, 1880; Joseph Oliver, born March 16, 1882, died 1971; Isaac Spencer, born August 3, 1883, died June 6, 1966; Ida Bell, born September 11, 1890, died October 17, 1931; Charles O., born August 31, 1893, died May 10, 1971; Jesse Houston, born November 2, 1895, died June 19, 1947.[116]

Mize, James R., Pvt., Co. E, age 27, EN & MI 10/4/64, Rome, GA, born Walton Co., Ga, farmer, on daily duty as teamster 9/6/64, KIA 3/10/65 at Monroe's Crossroads, NC.
   NOTE: James Robert Mize was born in 1837 to Reuben and Sarah Lindley Mize, married Lavinia Halpin in Randolph Co., AL about 1859 and was killed in the skirmish at Monroe's Cross Roads, NC. Their children were; Nancy; Sarah; and James Frances (a daughter).[117]

Monahan, O.B. (or P.B.), Pvt., Co. B, age 21, EN 3/29/64, Decatur, AL, MI 4/13/64, Decatur, AL, born Blount Co., AL, farmer, deserted 6/15/64, Decatur, AL with arms and equipment, in arrest for desertion July & Aug. 1864, sent to hospital at Rome, GA 10/1/64, MO 10/20/65, Huntsville, AL.

Monroe, Perry D., Pvt., Co. H, age 18, EN 4/25/65, Huntsville, AL, MI 5/20/65, Nashville, TN, born Pickens Co., GA, farmer, deserted 9/10/65 from Blountsville, AL with 2 Colt pistols and equipment.

Montgomery, Thomas, Pvt., Co. F, age 21, EN 5/15/63, Corinth, MS, born Greenville Dist., SC, farmer, deserted 7/16/63 from Glendale, MS.

Moody, Samuel, Pvt., Co. H, age 18, EN 3/1/65, Stevenson, AL, MI 4/5/65, Nashville, TN, born Chattooga Co., GA, farmer, died 7/31/65 in Post Hospital at Huntsville, AL of typhoid fever, originally buried in grave #230, Huntsville, Cemetery. (Reinterred Grave #L-504, Chattanooga National Cemetery.)

Moon, W.B., (Cards filed with William B. Moore).

Mooney, George W., Pvt., Co. H, EN 1/16/65, Huntsville, AL, born Bledsoe Co., TN, farmer, in Granger USA Hospital at Huntsville, AL 2/9/65, died 5/1/65 at Madison Station, AL of typnoid fever.

Mooney, Henry, Pvt/Corp., Co. E&K, age 21, EN & MI 7/12/64, Decatur, AL, born Marshall Co., AL, farmer, left in hospital at Murfreesboro, TN when Co. marched to accompany Col. Streight's expedition to AL 4/7/63, on detached service as teamster in Sherman's expedition 1/24/64, in arrest at Savannah, GA 12/3/64, promoted to Corp. 1/1/65, MO 7/19/65, Nashville, TN.

Mooney, I. (or J.), Pvt., Co. E, absent sick in hospital.*

Mooney, Peter C., Pvt., Co. K, age 18, EN & MI 7/12/62, Decatur, AL, born Walker Co., AL, farmer, died 11/17/62 in Hospital #14 at Nashville, TN of rubeola. (An Isaac Mooney is buried in Grave A-4836 in Nashville National Cemetery with death date shown as 10/12/62.)

Moore, Dallas H., Pvt., Co. H, age 20, EN 3/1/65, Stevenson, AL, MI 4/5/65, Nashville,TN, born Madison Co., AL, farmer, sick in Post Hospital at Huntsville, AL 5/10/65, no further information.

Moore, Elie, Pvt., Co. G, temporarily attached from 11th Illinois Cavalry.

Moore/More, E.P., Co. E, on daily duty as orderly Sgt. 4/64.*

Moore, Hamilton K., Pvt/Sgt., Co. E, age 44, EN & MI 9/1/64, Rome, GA, born Jasper Co., GA, farmer, promoted to Sgt. 10/20/64, MO 10/20/65, Huntsville, AL.

Moore/More, H.E., Pvt., Co. G, transferred by order of Col. Mercy 8/24/63.*

Moore, Hansel E., Farrier, Co. G, temporarily attached from 11th Illinois Cavalry.

Moore, J., Co. F, absent POW 10/26/63.*

Moore, James M., Sgt., Co. L, age 17, EN 6/8/63, Chewalla, TN, deserted 6/19/63 from Chewalla.
    NOTE: The cards for these two soldiers (James Moore) are filed together .
Moore, James, Pvt., Co. A, age 28, EN 12/1/63, Camp Davies, MS, MI 3/1/64, Memphis, TN, born Walker Co., AL, farmer, died 4/11/64 in Memphis, TN. (Buried in Memphis National Cemetery.)

Moore, John, Pvt., Co. G, (No further information).

Moore, John G., Pvt., Co. M, age 24, EN 12/16/63, Camp Davies, MS, MI 12/29/63, Corinth, MS, born Fayette Co., AL, farmer, POW 3/10/65 at Solomon Grove, NC, in Tripler USA Hospital at Columbus, OH 5/28/65, MO 6/12/65, Camp Chase, OH. Residence shown as Haleyville, Marion Co., AL.

Moore, John P., Pvt/Lt., Co. E, age 26, EN 11/13/63, Camp Davies, MS, MI 11/13/63, Rome, GA, born Mobile, AL, farmer, promoted to Ord. Sgt. 3/4/64, appt. Sgt. Maj. 7/1/64, discharged to accept appt. as 1st Lt. 10/10/64, reenlisted 10/10/64, Rome, GA, MO 10/20/65, Huntsville, AL.

Moore, Samuel P., Pvt/Corp., Co. L, age 17, EN 9/25/63, Fayette Co., AL, born Walker Co., AL, farmer, MO 9/28/64, Rome, GA.

Moore, William B., Pvt., Co. B, age 18, EN 2/27/64, Pulaski, TN, MI 3/27/64, Decatur, AL, born Montgomery Co., SC, farmer, left sick between Huntsville, AL and Chattanooga, TN 6/15/64, deserted 8/1/64 , deserted 6/1/65 while on leave of absence.

Moore, William R., Pvt., Co. G, temporarily attached from 11th Illinois Cavalry.

Morbin, John H., Sgt., Co. L, died 3/16/64 at Memphis, TN.*

Morgan, John, Pvt., Co. K, age 26, EN & MI 7/24/62, Huntsville, AL, born Morgan Co., AL, sick in hospital at Nashville, TN 12/26/62, discharged 2/14/63 at Nashville due to disability.

Morgan, Nathaniel, Pvt., Co. C, in Jefferson USA Hospital at Jeffersonville, Ind. 11/63-3/64.*

Morphis, Fleet J., Pvt., Co. G, age 18, EN 12/14/62, Pocohontas, TN, sick in hospital at Memphis, TN 10/10/63, MO 11/26/63, Memphis, TN.
NOTE: Fleet Joseph Morphis was born February 1, 1844 in McNairy Co., TN. On November 24, 1872 he married Mary Elizabeth Miller in Saulsbury, TN and had the following children: Sarah Percilla, March 22, 1874; Charles M., December 9, 1875; Mary E., September 2, 1881; Joseph E., March 2, 1884; George A., January 25, 1886; Rachel E., February 25, 1889; Claudy M., April 19, 1893; twins, Essie and Ivy, November 13, 1895. Fleet lived in Posy Co., Indiana from February 4, 1864 until March 2, 1868 when he return to McNairy Co., TN. He later lived in St. Andrews, FL. He is buried in the Kirk Cemetery just off State Hwy. 57 between Ramer and Pocahontas, TN.[118]

Morphis, James K., Pvt/Corp., Co. G, age 21, EN 11/27/62, Grand Junction, TN, MI 4/9/63, Corinth, MS, born McNairy Co., TN, farmer, KIA 10/26/63 at Vincent's Crossroads near Bay Springs, MS.

Morris, G., Pvt., Co. E, deserted 2/20/63.*

Morris, George, Pvt., Co. D, EN 6/2/63, Glendale, MS, deserted 6/16/63 from Glendale, MS.

Morris, J.N., Co. E, absent on det. duty Co. M.*

Morris, James D., Pvt., Co. D,E&C, absent on detached service 8/63, on daily duty recruiting 9/63 & 10/63, transferred to Co. C, Memphis, TN 3/3/63.*

Morris, John D., Corp/Sgt., Co. C, age 24, EN & MI 3/1/63, Corinth, MS, born Henderson, TN, farmer, appt. Corp. 4/10/63, appt. Sgt. 12/19/63, MO 3/1/64, Memphis, TN.

Morris, Joseph D., Pvt/Lt., Co. E&M, age 30, EN 1/1/63, McNairy Co., TN, MI 1/1/63, Corinth, MS, appt. 2nd Lt. 12/1/63 by Brig. Gen. G.M. Dodge, resigned 8/5/64.

Morris/Norris, Phillip, Pvt., Co. L, died 3/18/64 at Memphis, TN of diptheria.*

Morris, Richard N., Pvt., Co. H, age 35, EN 9/18/63, Glendale, MS, POW 10/26/63, (probably from Vincent's Crossroads), sick at Gayoso USA Hospital in Memphis and transferred as guard at Webster USA Hospital at Memphis, TN 3/9/64 while convalescing, MO 9/29/64, Rome, GA.

Morris, Samuel J., Pvt., Co. E, EN 2/15/63, Sulphur Springs, POW 2/15/63 near Glendale, MS, deserted 3/25/63 from Glendale, MS.

Morris, W.H., Pvt., Co. L, discharged 9/29/64 at Rome, GA by reason of exp. of term of service.*

Morris, W.G., Co. E, absent on det. service recruiting 11/22/63.*

Morris, William B., Pvt., Co. H, age 18, EN 9/30/63, Glendale, MS, MO 9/29/64, Rome, GA.

Morrison, John G., Reg. Carpenter, Co. A, age 50, EN 5/1/63, Glendale, MS, MO 12/22/63, Memphis, TN.

Morrow, John, Pvt., Co. B, age 22, EN 4/11/64, MI 4/18/64, Decatur, AL, born Walker Co., AL, farmer, served as cook in hospital, deserted 7/10/64 from Rome, GA with arms & equipment.

Morrow, Thomas J., Pvt., Co. I, age 22, EN 12/21/63, Camp Davies, MS, born Calhoun Co., AL, in Overton USA Hospital at Memphis, TN 1/15/64 from gunshot wound to right foot, in McDougall USA Hospital at Ft. Schuyler, NY 4/8/65 from wounds received at Silver Creek, NC 3/10/65, discharged 6/10/65 due to disability.

Morton, Frank, Sgt., Co. B, absent sick in hospital 4/6/63.*

Morton, James F. (or M.), Sgt/Hospital Steward, Co. B&C (F&S), age 38, EN 1/15/64, Memphis, TN, MI 1/22/63, Memphis, TN, in charge of regimental sick at Nashville, TN 11/3/64, born Marion Co., AL, physician, MO 10/20/65, Huntsville, AL.

Morton, James H., Pvt., Co. C, EN 3/15/64 at Memphis, TN, loss by promotion 4/6/64 at Mooresville.*

Mosher, W.C., Co. B, POW 3/10/65.*

Moss, John L., Pvt., Co. B, age 18, EN 3/9/64, Decatur, AL, MI 3/27/64, Decatur, AL, born Hall Co., GA, farmer, left sick in Rome, GA 11/10/64, sent to hospital in Nashville, TN 11/10/64, MO 10/20/65, Huntsville, AL.

Moss, Joseph L., Pvt., Co. B, in USA Field Hospital at Rome, GA 6/20/64, returned to duty 9/12/64.*

Motes/Moatis, George F., Pvt/Blacksmith, Co. F, age 21, EN 11/25/63, Camp Davies, MS, MI 2/24/64, Memphis, TN, born Edgefield Dist., SC, farmer, on det. duty as blacksmith at Rome, GA 8/64, MO 12/17/64, Savannah, GA "by reason of being on march from Atlanta to Savannah, GA."

Mott, Josuah, Pvt., Co. F, age 25, EN 4/13/63, Corinth, MS, MI 5/18/63, Corinth, MS, born Dauphin, Co., PA, railroader, MIA 5/29/63 from Florence, AL, paroled POW at Camp Benton, St. Louis, POW 10/26/63 from Vincent's Crossroads, sick in Nashville, TN 11/6/64.

Mullins, James B., Pvt., Co. H, age 25, EN 10/22/63, Glendale, MS, MO 10/24/64, Rome, GA.

Mullins, John H., Pvt/Corp., Co. H, age 18, EN 10/22/63, Glendale, MS, MO 10/24/64, Rome, GA.

Mullins, Marcus L. (or D.), Pvt., Co. H, age 17, EN 12/22/63, Camp Davies, MS, MI 2/24/64, Memphis, TN, born Walker Co., AL, farmer, served as Co. cook and orderly, MO 4/5/65, Nashville, TN. (J.B. Mullins signed affidavit that he was the legal guardian of Marcus L. Mullins.)

Murdock, Albert E., Lt., Co. E, age 23, EN & MI 2/1/63, Corinth, MS, promoted to 2nd Lt. 2/28/63, promoted to 1st Lt. 9/25/63, MO 3/1/64, Louisville, KY.

Murdock, William, Pvt., Co. H, age 18, EN 12/24/64, Stevenson, AL, MI 12/24/64, Nashville, TN, born Chatooga Co., GA, farmer, MO 10/20/65, Huntsville, AL.

Murphey, Charles, Pvt., Co. C, age 23, EN 3/25/63, Corinth, MS, MI 4/10/63, born Posy Co., IN, farmer, on leave in Illinois 7/22/63. No MO date shown.

Murphree, James M., Pvt., Co. I, age 17, EN & MI 7/21/62, Huntsville, AL, born Rhea Co., TN, farmer, on det. duty as courier at Reedyville, TN 1/27/63, also served at stable guard, MO 7/19/65, Nashville, TN.

Murphree, James H., Pvt/Sgt., Co. I, age 44, EN & MI 7/21/62, Huntsville, AL, born Blount Co., AL, farmer, POW 5/3/63, paroled 5/15/63 at City Point, VA, KIA 12/24/63 at Jack's Creek, TN near Jackson.

Murphy/Murphree, James D.D. (or P.D.), Pvt., Co. B, age 19, EN & MI 9/1/64, Rome, GA, born Randolph Co., AL, farmer, POW 3/10/65 from Monroe's Crossroads, NC, MO 6/13/65, Camp Chase, OH.

Murphree, Joseph/John J., Pvt., Co. H, age 18, EN 3/1/65, Huntsville, AL, MI 5/20/65, Nashville, TN, born Marshall Co., AL, MO 10/20/65, Huntsville, AL.

Murphy/Murphree, Joseph, Pvt., Co. B, age 18, EN 3/28/64, Decatur, AL, MI 4/13/64, Decatur, AL, born Blount Co., (or Marion Co.), AL, left sick in hospital at Savannah, GA 6/15/64, ret. to duty 3/4/65, MO 10/20/65, Huntsville, AL.

Murphy, William B., Sgt., Co. F, absent on det. duty as scout by order of Gen. Dodge.*

Murphy/Murphree, William M., Pvt., Co. A, EN 3/23/63, MI 3/24/63, Glendale, MS, KIA 7/5/63 at Yellow Creek, MS.

Murphy/Murphree, William P., Sgt/Pvt., Co. F, age 34, EN 4/10/63, Corinth, MS, born Shelby Co., AL, farmer, MO 4/9/64, Decatur, AL.

Muse, Nathan B., Pvt., Co. G, age 25, EN 3/31/63, Chewalla, TN, detached 8/24/63 to act as guide for Co. C, 18th Reg. MO Vol., MO 11/26/63, Memphis, TN. (Notation in file states, *"Dropped Nov. 1, 63 Burnesville, Miss. member of 11 th Ill Cav erroneously taken up on Co. Rolls temporarily assigned to Co. as scout by order Genl Dodge."*

Myers, Howell, Pvt., Co. G, age 18, EN 3/21/64, Decatur, AL, MI 4/13/64, Decatur, AL, born Coosa Co., AL, farmer, POW 3/10/65 from Monroe's Crossroads, NC, MO 6/12/65, Camp Chase, OH.

Myers, Samuel, Pvt., Co. A&B, age 22, EN 12/3/63, Camp Davies, MS, MI 2/5/64, Memphis, TN, born Marshall Co., TN, farmer, POW 8/22/64, MO 10/20/65, Huntsville, AL.

Myers, Samuel M., Pvt., Co. A, enlisted 2/5/64, Memphis, TN, absent POW 8/21/64, MIA 9/3/64 from Rollinwell, AL.*

Myers, Thomas L., Pvt., Co. B, age 27, EN 12/17/62, Glendale, MS, MI 12/31/62, Corinth, MS, born Lincoln Co., TN, det. as cook in hospital, POW 10/26/63 from Vincent's Crossroads, MO 12/27/63, Camp Davies, MS.

Myrick, John, Pvt., Co. D, age 22, EN 5/20/64, Decatur, AL, MI 6/16/64, Decatur, AL, born Jefferson Co., AL, farmer, served as farrier, MO 10/20/65, Huntsville, AL.

Nabors, William, (Cards filed with William Neighbors).

Nagle, Patrick, Pvt., Co. A&B, age 40, EN 1/6/63, Glendale, MS, MI 1/22/63, Corinth, MS, sick in Union USA Hospital at Memphis, TN 10/63, MO 12/22/63, Memphis, TN.

Nail, Julius/Julian, Pvt., Co. D, age 39, EN 5/20/64, Decatur, AL, MI 6/16/64, Decatur, AL, born Rhea Co., TN, farmer, MO 10/20/65, Huntsville, AL.

Nanny, Andrew J., Pvt., Co. C, age 20, EN 2/15/64, Memphis, TN, MI 5/10/64, Memphis, TN, born Rutherford Co., NC, farmer, wounded and in hospital at Hilton Head, (Beaufort), SC 12/9/64, sent to McDougall USA Hospital, Ft. Schuyler, NY 1/29/65, MO 10/20/65, Huntsville, AL.

Napps, William B., Pvt/Sgt., Co. K, age 28, EN & MI 7/31/62, Huntsville, AL, born Limestone Co., AL, appt. Sgt., 1/1/63, WIA in skirmish at Mitchell's farm near

Danville, MS 11/22/63, POW 3/21/64 near Memphis, TN, released 4/29/64 at Collier Ridge, Ark., MO 7/19/65, Nashville, TN.

Neal, Charles B., Pvt., Co. E, MI 3/10/63, Corinth, MS, served as orderly, died 6/24/63 in hospital at Corinth, MS. (Buried Corinth National Cemetery and classified with unknown dead.)

Neal, Duncan, Pvt., Co. E, age 22, EN 12/9/62, Nabors Mill, TN, MI 12/9/62, Corinth, MS, POW 10/1/63, escaped near Richmond, VA, det. as teamster at Vicksburg, MS 1/25/64, MO 6/15/64, Decatur, AL.

Neal, Green P., Pvt., Co. H, age 28, EN 11/12/63, Camp Davies, MS, MO 11/23/64, Nashville, TN.

Neal, James M., Sgt., Co. E, age 38, EN 3/1/63, Glendale, MS, MI 3/1/63, Corinth, MS, promoted to Corp. 3/1/63, MO 3/1/64, Memphis, TN.

Neehard, J.W., Pvt., Co. B, AWOL 4/64.*

Neighbors/Nabors, William, Pvt., Co. E, EN 3/1/63, Glendale, MS, MI 3/18/63, Corinth, MS, on detached service as teamster 1/25/64 at Vicksburg, MS, MO 3/1/64, Memphis, TN.
    NOTE: William Neighbors is buried in Elmwood Cemetery in Centralia, Illinois. [119]

Neil, George W., Pvt., Co. K, POW 4/29/64 at Mooresville, reported from MIA 11/2/62.*

Neil, T., Co. D, detached in north AL with Capt. Lomax.*

Neiley, William, Corp., Co. H, age 20, EN 1/17/65, Stevenson, AL, MI 2/19/65, Nashville, TN, born Marshall Co., AL, farmer, MO 10/20/65, Huntsville, AL.

Nelson, Barron D., Pvt., Co. H, age 19, EN 3/1/65, Stevenson, AL, MI 4/5/65, Nashville, TN, born Tallapoosa Co., AL, farmer, sick in Post Hospital at Huntsville, AL 6/5/65, discharged 12/4/65 due to disability.

Nelson, John, Pvt., Co. M, detached on duty at Brig H.Q. since 2/14/65.*

Nelson, Thomas M., Pvt., Co. I, age 25, EN & MI 8/26/62, Huntsville, AL, born Morgan Co., AL, farmer, died 10/29/62 in Hospital #14 in Nashville, TN of rubeola. (Buried in Grave B-5786 in Nashville National Cemetery.)

Nesmith, Alexander, Pvt., Co. L, age 31, EN 9/25/63, Fayette Co., AL, MI 9/25/63, Glendale, MS, on daily duty as teamster 4/27/64, MO 9/28/64, Rome, GA.

Nesmith, Jeremiah A., Pvt., Co. H, age 18, EN 4/1/65, Stevenson, AL, MI 4/5/65, Nashville, TN, born Blount Co., AL, farmer, MO 10/20/65, Huntsville, AL.

NOTE: One of John B. Nesmith's MI cards mixed in with records of Jeremiah Nesmith.

Nesmith, John B., Pvt., Co. I, age 50, EN & MI 7/21/62, Huntsville, AL, born Roane Co., TN, farmer, died 12/25/62 in hospital at Nashville, TN.

Nesmith, William R., Pvt/Sgt., Co. I, age 24, EN & MI 7/21/62, Huntsville, AL, born Morgan Co., AL, farmer, MIA 10/26/63 from Vincent's Crossroads, MS, rejoined Co. 11/2/63 at Glendale, served as Co. cook, wagoner, & scout, appt. Sgt. 10/1/64, MO 7/19/65, Nashville, TN.

Newland, Clay, Corp., Co. G, age 17, EN 11/27/62, Grand Junction, TN, appt. Corp. 4/1/63, MO 11/26/63, Memphis, TN.

Newland, Hugh, Pvt., Co. G, age 18, EN 6/1/63, Chewalla, TN, MI 3/10/64, Memphis, TN, born Hardeman Co., TN, farmer, KIA 3/31/65 near Faison's Station, NC while on picket duty.

Newman, Benjamin T.(or F.), Pvt., Co. E, EN 1/10/63, Nabors Mill, TN, MI 1/15/63, Corinth, MS, deserted 2/12/63 near Corinth, MS.

Newton, G.E., Co. F, absent sick in hospital at Corinth, MS 10/18/63.*

Niblett, William J.(or G.), Pvt., Co. M, age 19, EN & MI 8/30/64, Rome, GA, born Polk Co., GA, farmer, sent to McDougall USA Hospital, Ft. Schuyler, NY 4/8/65 from Newbern, NC, discharged due to disability 5/16/65.

Nichols, Alfred, Pvt., Co. A, age 43, EN 6/12/63, Glendale, MS, MO 12/22/63, Memphis, TN.

Nichols, Arthur S., Pvt., Co. K&A, age 26, EN 12/15/62, Glendale, MS, MI 12/31/62, Corinth, MS, MO 12/22/63, Memphis, TN.
    NOTE: Arthur Sine Nichols was born in 1837, married Alsey E. Lynch September 22, 1867 at Martins Mills, Wayne Co., TN and died March 18, 1886 in Marion Co., AL. Alsey died November 4, 1899. (This information was printed in the Wayne County Historian, Vol. 3, No. 1, p. 35, contributed by Jerry W. Murphy, who states correct marriage date is September 22, 1868.)

Nichols, Benjamin B., Pvt/Bugler, Co. K&A, age 21, EN 12/5/62, Glendale, MS, MI 12/31/62, Corinth, MS, MO 12/22/63, Memphis, TN.
    NOTE: Benjamin was the son of Mary "Polly" Claxton Smith and William Hedgepeth Nichols.[120]

Nichols, P.S., Pvt., Co. D, absent on detached service.

Nichols, David L., Pvt., Co. K&A, age 45, EN 9/8/62, Iuka, MS, MI 10/1/62, Corinth, MS, born Franklin Co., AL, died 7/2/63, Glendale, MS. (Certificate of death shows him to be age 30.)

Nichols, Edward, Pvt., Co. H, age 18, EN 1/15/65, Stevenson, AL, MI 1/15/65, Nashville, TN, born St. Claire Co., AL, farmer, died 5/1/65 at Hospital in Huntsville, AL of rubeola/smallpox.

Nichols/Nicholas, General Morgan, Pvt., Co. D, EN 2/1/63, Glendale, MS, MI 2/4/63, Corinth, MS, died 4/3/63, Glendale, MS. (See Benjamin Nichols for family information.)

Nichols, Isaac J., Pvt., Co. K&A, age 23, EN 9/8/62, Iuka, MS, MI 10/1/62, Corinth, MS, born Marion Co., AL, farmer, discharged July 2, 1863 due to disability, lost use of his right hand.
    NOTE: Isaac was born June 26, 1840 in Marion Co., AL, married Margaret G. West June 11, 1865 at Martins Mills, Wayne Co., TN and died February 28, 1915 in Stantonville, McNairy Co., TN. Children of Isaac and Margaret according to her Widow's Pension #896.766 filed March 31, 1915, were: Mary C., born March 19, 1867 (line drawn through name); John T.G., born July 20, 1869; Margaret L.E., born September 15, 1872 (line drawn through name); James W.R., born February 25, 1874 (line drawn through name); Arthur F., born March 5, 1876; Andrew J., born December 26, 1877; Nancy C., born August 23, 1879; Martha E. and William L. (twins) born September 8, 1882; and Isaac N., born June 10, 1885. Margaret West Nichols was born 1848 and died June 21, 1927 at Parkin, AR.
    Additional information on Isaac states, "*Was unfit for the duties of a soldier by reason of his right hand being crippled before entering service. Loosing the use of his right hand by having the forefingers injured and the three external metacarpal bones severed by an ax passing transversely across the hand.*"[121]

Nichols, Jacob L. (Joab S.), Pvt., Co. D, age 24, EN 2/1/63, Glendale, MS, MI 2/4/63, Corinth, MS, deserted 4/26/63 from Glendale, MS. (Jacob L. and Joab Nichols may be the same person, however, they have different EN & MI dates. Records of both names state "captured by the enemy 5/15/64" Original record showing card numbers states "cards withdrawn and filed with Jasper Nichols, Co. B, where they probably belong, June 20, 1902.")
    NOTE: Jacob was the son of Nancy and John L. Nichols and on November 22, 1860, he married Patience Hallmark, daughter of Robert Hallmark, at the home of Thomas Hallmark in Marion Co., AL. Their children were: Leanna Evaline, born January 2, 1863 and Gracy Elizabeth, born August 24, 1865 Jacob died June 30, 1870 in Wayne Co., TN.
    Additional information states, "*Soldier received chest wound while in a skirmish with Rebel Troops.*" Jacob stated, "*This wound in my right breast will be the cause of my death; it has effected and obstructed my breathing ever since I received it.*"[122]

Nichols, James F., Pvt., Co. K&A, EN 11/28/62, Glendale, MS, MI 12/31/62, Corinth, MS, died 2/17/63 at Corinth, MS. (See Jasper Nichols for family information.)

Nichols, Jasper, Pvt., Co. B, age 22, EN 1/5/63, Glendale, MS, MI 1/22/63, Corinth, MS, born Marion Co., AL, POW 10/26/63 from Vincent's Crossroads, MS, died 6/14/65 at Jeffersonville, IN.

NOTE: Jasper was the son of Jushua L. and Elizabeth Cochran Nichols. His brother, James F. Nichols also served in this regiment.

The following was found among his military papers:

Paducah, Kentucky - April 18, 1865

This certifies that I have carefully examined J.N. Nichols, Private, Company B, First Regiment, Alabama Cavalry, who is now here on furlough from the U.S. General Hospital, Maryland, (Said furlough to expire the 23 inst), and find him unable to travel to said hospital on account of emaciation and general debility, contracted while incarcerated in a rebel prison at Florence, South Carolina. I furthermore decalre my belief that he will not be able to report in person in a less period of time than thirty (30) days from present date.

J.M. Ball, Surgeon, 44 (illegible) Paducah, Kentucky[123]

Nichols, Joab S., EN 9/13/63, Glendale, MS, MI 9/13/63, Camp Davies, MS, detached on secret service 10/2/63, captured 5/15/64 in Marion Co., AL.

Nichols, Larry L., Pvt., Co. K&A, age 19, EN 9/8/62, Iuka, MS, MI 10/1/62, Corinth, MS, born Marion Co., AL, farmer, MO 9/16/63, Corinth, MS.

NOTE: Larry was the son of Nancy and John L. Nichols and was born December 30, 1843 at Bexar, Marion Co., AL. He married Nancy Ann Wiginton January 4, 1866 in Wayne Co., TN and died October 19, 1932 in Hamilton, Marion Co., AL. Nancy was born August 12, 1843. Pension papers state they had the following children: Sintha Evaline, born December 6, 1866; William Lafayett, born October 1869; John Thomas, born December 6, 1871; Richard Franklin, born July 14, 1873; Sena, born October 15, 1875; Julia Ann, born December 29, 1877; Nancy Ann, born March 6, 1880; Marion Alonzo, born December 23, 1882; Mary Jane, born January 27, 1885; Lorenzo Dow, born July 27, 1887 and Sarah.[124]

Nichols, Stephen, Pvt., Co. M, age 18, EN 11/22/63, Camp Davies, MS, MI 12/29/63, Corinth, MS, born Lawrence Co., AL, in Adams USA Hospital at Memphis, TN 3/25/64, returned to duty 6/26/64, wounded 3/18/65, in McDougall USA Hospital at Ft. Schuyler, NY 4/8/65, discharged 7/7/65 due to disability.

NOTE: Stephen H. Nichols lived at Booneville, MS from 1865-1892 and at Wilsonville, Cocke Co., TN from 1892-1893. He died August 22, 1935 in Ripley Co., MI. He was the son of James R. Nichols, a Mexican War pensioner who lived at Lawrence Co., AL and Prentiss Co., MS. Stephen was the grandson of William Nichols, a Revolutionary War pensioner from Montgomery Co., NC where he was born in 1765 and married Elizabeth Trent on October 4, 1800. He then moved to Lincoln Co., TN and on to Lawrence Co., AL where he died May 16, 1838. His widow then married Robert Barrett who died December 24, 1850.

Nigger, Bill, Co. M, absent April 1865.*

Nine, T.C., Co. F, absent sick in Memphis, TN 10/1/63.*

Nix, William, Pvt., Co. E, age 24, EN 3/1/63, Glendale, MS, MI 3/18/63, Corinth, MS, in confinement at Corinth 11/22/63 charged with desertion and murder of Neal Morrison, a citizen of Tishomingo Co., MS, MO 3/1/64, Memphis, TN.

Noles, John T., Pvt., Co. K, age 19, EN & MI 7/24/62, Huntsville, AL, wounded POW at Blountsville, AL 5/1/63, born NC, in USA Hospital at Annapolis, MD 7/3/63, returned to duty 8/20/64, MO 7/19/65.

Noris, George W., Pvt., Co. A, age 18, EN 3/11/64, Memphis, TN, born Winston Co., AL, farmer, died 4/17/64 in Gayoso USA General Hospital at Memphis TN. (Buried in Memphis National Cemetery.)

Norman, Cicero, Pvt., Co. D, age 18, EN 12/20/64, Savannah, GA, born Washington Co., NC, farmer, deserted 5/10/65 with Remington revolver while on recruiting service in Huntsville, AL.

Norris, George W., Pvt., Co. K, age 17, born Walker Co., AL, farmer, EN 2/26/64, Memphis, TN, did not bear the surgeon's examination.*

Norris, J., Pvt., Co. A, absent on furlough 9/64.*

Norris/Morris, Phillip, Pvt., Co. L, age 18, EN 9/25/63, Fayette Co., AL, born Walker Co., AL, farmer, died 3/11/64 in Overton USA Hospital at Memphis, TN of diptheria. (Buried Grave in Memphis National Cemetery.)

Norris, Reuben, Pvt/Corp., Co. M, age 28, EN 11/4/63, Glendale, MS, MI 12/29/63, Corinth, MS, born Walker Co., AL, farmer, MO 10/20/65, Huntsville, AL.

Norris, William H., Pvt., Co. L, age 20, EN 9/25/63, Fayette Co., AL, MO 9/24/64, Rome, GA, reenlisted 11/1/64, Stevenson, AL, MI 4/18/65, Nashville, TN, born Walker Co., AL, MO 10/20/65, Huntsville, AL.

Norris, William Y.(N.Y.), Pvt/Farrier, Co. E, EN 4/1/63, Glendale, MS, MI 4/1/63, Corinth, MS, MO 3/1/64, Memphis, TN.

Norwood, Daniel L., Corp., Co. C, age 21, EN 12/12/62, Corinth, MS, MI 12/22/62, Corinth, MS, born Morgan Co., AL, farmer, appt. Corp. 1/1/63, MO 12/17/63, Memphis, TN.

Norwood, Samuel, Pvt/Teamster, Co. B, age 36, EN 12/23/62, Glendale, MS, MI 12/31/62, Corinth, MS, appt. wagoner 3/1/63, MO 12/27/63, Camp Davies, MS.

Noy, Robert, Pvt., Co. B, age 18, EN 3/29/64, Decatur, AL, born Marion Co., AL, left sick in hospital at Decatur 4/17/64. No MO date shown.

Null, Francis M., Sgt., Co. G, age 24, EN 6/16/63, Chewalla, TN, appt. Sgt. 8/1/63, MO 11/26/63, Memphis, TN.

Nutty, James, Pvt., Co. K, age 37, born Hawkins Co., TN, farmer, EN 12/13/63, Camp Davies, MS. Traveled 250 miles from Chattanooga, TN to Camp Davies, MS. Rejected on account of physical disability by regimental surgeon.*

Oden, Andrew J., Pvt., Co. I, age 25, EN & MI 7/21/62, Huntsville, AL, born Morgan Co., AL, with wagon train at Nashville, 12/27/62, died 1/6/63 in Hospital #14, Nashville, TN. (Buried in Grave G-8013 in Nashville National Cemetery with death date shown as 1/21/63.)

Oden, Hezakiah, Pvt/Sgt., Co. A, age 21, EN & MI 3/8/63, Glendale, MS, born Morgan Co., AL, farmer, MO 8/22/63, Memphis, TN, reenlisted 1/18/64, Camp Davies, MS, MI 2/5/64, Memphis, TN, MO 10/20/65, Huntsville, AL.

Oden, John A., Pvt/Corp., Co. A, age 20, EN 3/8/63, Glendale, MS, born Cherokee Co., AL, farmer, promoted to Corp. 9/16/63, MO 12/22/63, Memphis, TN, reenlisted 2/23/64, Memphis, TN, MI 2/26/64, Memphis, TN, MO 10/20/65, Huntsville, AL.

Oden, William D., Pvt., Co. I, age 22, EN & MI 7/21/62, Huntsville, AL, born Morgan Co., AL, farmer, with wagon train in Nashville, TN 12/27/62, died 3/20/63 in hospital at Murfreesboro, TN.

Oden, William J., Pvt., Co. A, age 18, EN 1/18/64, Camp Davies, MS, MI 2/5/64, Memphis, TN, born Morgan Co., AL, farmer, deserted 5/15/64 at Snake Creek Gap, GA, reported 5/10/64, MO 10/20/65, Huntsville, AL.

Oden, William N., Pvt., Co. B, age 18, EN 3/16/64, Decatur, AL, MI 3/27/64, Decatur, AL, born Winston (or Madison) Co., AL, farmer, MO 10/20/65, Huntsville, AL.

O'Linger, Daniel, Co. G, age 23, EN 5/6/64, Decatur, AL, born Lawrence Co., AL, farmer.*

Olson, Gabriel, Pvt., Co. A, age 43, EN 1/24/64, Camp Davies, MS, MI 2/5/64, Memphis, TN, born Steronagh Norway, Minister, in Small Pox USA Hospital at Memphis, TN 2/28/64, returned to reg. 3/17/64, deserted 3/22/64 with carbine, Remington revolver & equipment.

Orrick, Madison J. (or I.), Corp. Co. E, age 34, EN 3/1/63, Glendale, MS, MI 3/1/63, Corinth, MS, MO 3/1/64, Memphis, TN.

Orrick, William C., Pvt., Co. E, age 36, EN 3/6/63, Corinth, MS, MI 3/6/63, Corinth, MS, MO 3/1/64, Memphis, TN.

Osborn/Ozbirn, Fountain William S., Pvt., Co. K&A, age 37, EN 9/8/62, Iuka, MS, MI 10/1/62, Corinth, MS, born Jefferson Co., AL, farmer, died 7/10/63 in hospital at Corinth, MS.
   NOTE: Fountain W.S., George W.L., Chesley F.M. and Newton H. Ozbirn (family spelling) were brothers and sons of Pleasant Ozbirn and their sister,

315

Letha Elizabeth, married Jasper M.C. Allison who was also in this regiment and two other brothers were in the C.S.A. Chesley, James and Foutain were married to three Arnold sisters.[125]

Osborn/Ozbirn, George Washington Lafayette, Pvt., Co. A, age 36, EN 12/22/63, Camp Davies, MS, MI 2/5/64, Memphis, TN, born Perry Co., AL, farmer, sick in hospital at Rome, GA 10/27/64, MO 10/20/65, Huntsville, AL.

Osborne, Elick/Alex, Pvt., Co. G, age 18, EN 4/10/64, Decatur, AL, born Marion Co., AL, died 7/1/64 in hospital at Rome, GA. One MR states he was age 34. (Buried Grave #C-1505, Marietta National Cemetery.)

Osburn/Ozbirn, Chesley Francis Marion, Pvt., Co. D, EN 1/25/63, Glendale, MS, MI 2/4/63, Corinth, MS, died 3/14/64 at Glendale, MS.

Osburn/Ozbirn, Newton Hubbard, Pvt., Co. D, EN 1/26/63, Glendale, MS, MI 2/4/63, Corinth, MS, deserted 4/20/63 from Glendale, MS, POW 10/26/63, returned 12/25/63. No MO date.

Osburn/Ozbirn, William L., Pvt., Co. D, EN 1/25/63, Glendale, MS, MI 2/4/63, Corinth, MS, sick in hospital at Jackson, TN 4/3/63, sent to hospital at Corinth 7/20/63 where he died 9/25/63.

Osborn, William, Pvt., Co. A, died 6/26/63 at Corinth, MS.*

O'Singer, Daniel, Pvt., Co. G, absent sick at Decatur, AL since 5/1/64.*

Overton, John K.P., Pvt., Co. H, age 18, EN 12/22/64, Rome, GA, MI 2/13/65, Nashville, TN, born Fayette Co., GA, farmer, MO 10/20/65, Huntsville, AL.

Overton, William H., Pvt., Co. H, age 21, EN 12/20/64, Rome, GA, MI 2/13/65, Nashville, TN, born Fayette Co., GA, MO 10/20/65, Huntsville, AL.

Owen, George T., Pvt., Co. C, age 18, EN 4/25/64, Decatur, AL, MI 4/30/64, Decatur, AL, born Lawrence Co., AL, farmer, POW 3/10/65 from Monroe's Crossroads, NC near Fayetteville, MO 7/12/65, Camp Chase, OH.

Owens, John, Pvt., Co. E, EN & MI 3/6/63, Corinth, MS, in Small Pox USA Hospital at Memphis, TN 2/29/64, MO 3/1/64, Memphis, TN.

Owens, John T. (or J.), Pvt., Co. G, age 38, EN & MI 6/16/64, Decatur, AL, born Spartanburg Dist., SC, farmer, deserted 7/11/64 from Rome, GA.

Ozbirn, (see Osburn)

Pace, Andrew J., Pvt., Co. M, age 18, EN 12/28/63, Camp Davies, MS, MI 12/29/63, Corinth, MS, born Coffee Co., GA, farmer, died 2/12/64 in Adams USA Hospital at Memphis, TN of measles. (Buried in Memphis National Cemetery.)

Pace, Gideon W., Pvt., Co. A, age 41, EN 9/8/62, Iuka, MS, MI 10/1/62, Corinth, MS, born Rutherford Co., NC, farmer, MO 9/16/63, Corinth, MS.

Pace, Tandie W., Pvt., Co. K&A, age 27, EN 9/8/62, Iuka, MS, MI 10/1/62, Corinth, MS, born Lawrence Co., AL, discharged 7/2/63 due to disability. (One record states age 37.)

Pace, William R., Pvt., Co. A, age 18, EN 9/8/62, Iuka, MS, MI 10/1/62, Corinth, MS, born Lawrence Co., AL, farmer, MO 9/16/63, Corinth, MS.

Packard, R., Pvt., Co. D, teamster.*

Page, M., Co. D, absent sick in US General Hospital.*

Page, R.G., Co. D, AWOL 5/1/63.*

Page, Thomas C., Pvt., Co. D, EN 2/1/63, Glendale, MS, MI 2/4/63, Corinth, MS, deserted 5/1/63 from Glendale, MS.

Page, William C., Pvt., Co. D, age 20, EN 4/7/63, Glendale, MS, MI 4/28/63, Corinth, MS, deserted 5/1/63 from Glendale, MS, returned 10/4/63, POW 5/3/64, MO 4/7/64, Memphis, TN.

Palmer, Joseph M., Pvt., Co. A, age 39, EN 10/1/62 & MI 10/14/62, Corinth, MS, MO 10/19/63, Lagrange, TN.
   NOTE: Joseph M. Palmer married Permela Mitchell and had one daughter, Elizabeth Palmer, who married Mathew H. Glenn. Joseph was born in 1827 and died July 21, 1900 in Marion Co., AL. He is buried in the Mt. Zion Cemetery north of Hamilton, AL.[126]

Pannell, Jeremiah J., Pvt., Co. M, age 18, EN 12/9/63, Camp Davies, MS, MI 12/29/63, Corinth, MS, born Itawamba Co., MS, deserted 1/13/64 from Camp Davies, MS and went home to Marion Co., AL.

Pannel/Pennel, Jonathan, Pvt., Co. A, age 40, EN 1/22/64, Camp Davies, MS, MI 2/5/64, Memphis, TN, born Fairfield Dist., SC, farmer, deserted 4/17/64 from Mooresville, AL with arms & equipment.

Pannell, William, Pvt., Co. M, age 43, EN 12/9/63, Camp Davies, MS, MI 12/29/63, Corinth, MS, born Maury Co., TN, farmer, deserted 1/13/64 from Camp Davies, MS and went home to Marion Co., AL.

Panter/Painter, Richard, Blacksmith, Co. L, age 28, EN 9/25/63, Fayette Co., AL, MI 9/25/63, Glendale, MS, born Fayette Co., AL, farmer, MO 9/28/64, Rome, GA.

Panter/Painter, Rufus, Pvt., Co. L, age 19, EN 9/25/63, Fayette Co., AL, MI 9/25/63, Glendale, MS, born Fayette Co., AL, farmer, POW 10/26/63 from Vincent's Crossroads, MS, died 8/15/64 at Andersonville, GA while POW. (Buried in grave #5763, Andersonville National Cemetery.)

Paris, Noah, Pvt., Co. L, age 40, EN 9/25/63, Fayette Co., AL, MI 9/25/63, Glendale, MS, POW 10/26/63 from Vincent's Crossroads, MO 9/28/64, Rome, GA.

Parish, James R. (or K.), Pvt., Co. M, age 18, EN 12/26/63, Camp Davies, MS, MI 12/29/63, Corinth, MS, born Tishomingo Co., MS, farmer, deserted 1/29/64 from Lagrange, TN with Smith carbine & Colt revolver, "went to the enemy".

Park, Ambrose, Bugler, Co. G, temporarily attached from 11th Illinois Cavalry.

Park, John F., Pvt., Co. G, temporarily attached from 11th Illinois Cavalry.

Park, Madison G., Pvt., Co. G, age 19, EN 3/5/63, Chewalla, TN, MO 11/26/63, Memphis, TN.

Parker, Charles, Pvt/Corp., Co. E, age 22, EN 3/1/63, Glendale, MS, MI 3/1/63, Corinth, MS, promoted to Corp. 8/1/63, MO 3/1/64, Memphis, TN.

Parker, Henry H. (or N.), Pvt., Co. B, EN 4/5/64 & MI 4/13/64, Decatur, AL, born Walker Co., AL, farmer, deserted 5/11/64 near Chattanooga, TN with Smith carbine, horse & equipment. (POW Record states he was captured at Fort Pillow, TN 4/12/64, paroled and sent on board Steamer "Platte Valley" to hospital at Mound City, IL.)

Parker, Isaac A.J., 1st Lt., Co. G, age 22, EN 11/27/62, Grand Junction, TN, had been promoted 1st Lt. of Miss Rangers, MO 12/7/63, Memphis, TN.

Parker, James, Pvt., Co. F, in USA General Field Hospital at Bridgeport, AL March & April 1864.*

Parker, John A., Pvt., Co. E, age 20, EN 7/1/63, Glendale, MS, MI 7/11/63, Glendale, MS, served as teamster, MO 7/27/64, Rome, GA.
     NOTE: John Anderson Parker is buried in Evergreen Methodist Church Cemetery in Morgan Co., AL. He married Martha L.W. Stringer and was the brother of Sevier C. and William C. Parker.

Parker, John H., Pvt., Co. A, EN 12/5/62, Glendale, MS, MI 12/31/62, Corinth, MS, born Itawamba Co., MS, served as teamster, captured by the enemy while on scout service, returned 6/17/63, died 12/1/63, death certificate signed at Camp Davies, MS.

Parker, Pleasant A. (or L.), Pvt., Co. D, age 20, EN 3/15/63, Glendale, MS, MI 3/26/63, Corinth, MS, died 8/5/63 in hospital at Glendale, MS.

Parker, P.S., Co. D, nurse in hospital 5/63, absent sick in hospital at Corinth, 4/1/63.*

Parker, Sevier C., Pvt., Co. E, age 18, EN 7/1/63, Glendale, MS, on detached service as teamster 1/25/64 at Vicksburg, MS, MO 7/27/64, Rome, GA.

Parker, William C., Pvt/Corp., Co. E, age 35, EN 7/1/63, Glendale, MS, promoted to Corp. 9/5/63, MO 7/27/64, Rome, GA.

Parker, William C., Pvt., Co. G, absent sick in decatur, AL since 5/1/64.*

Parker, William M., Pvt., Co. B, age 22, EN 4/5/64, & MI 4/13/64, Decatur, AL, born Walker (or Blount) Co., AL, farmer, deserted 5/11/64 near Chattanooga, TN with horse, Smith carbine & equipment.

Parkerson, Richard, Pvt., Co. E, EN 12/26/62, Chewalla, TN, MI 12/26/62, Corinth, MS, age 45, MO 12/17/63, Memphis, TN.

Parkes, L.L., age 22, EN 4/5/64 & MI 4/13/64, Decatur, AL, born Walker Co., AL, farmer. No further information.

Parkhill, Luther M., Pvt/Sgt., Co. A, age 40, EN 9/8/62, Iuka, MS, MI 10/1/62, Corinth, MS, born Marshall Co., AL, farmer, promoted to duty Sgt. 5/1/63 and to M. Sgt. 7/1/63, MO 9/16/63, Corinth, MS.

Parkhill, William L., Pvt/Corp., Co. A, age 17, EN 9/8/62, Iuka, MS, MI 10/1/62, Corinth, MS, born Marshall Co., AL, promoted to Corp. 12/18/62, MO 9/16/63, Corinth, MS.

Parrett, Jno. B., Pvt., Co. F, absent POW 11/64.*

Parson, Raymond, Pvt., Co. C, age 49, EN 12/15/62 & MI 12/22/62, Corinth, MS, born Wilkins, NC, KIA 4/2/63 near Glendale, MS.

Parton, J.R., Pvt., Co. K, absent sick, wounded 3/4/65.*

Parton, James W., Pvt., Co. K, EN & MI 8/22/62, Huntsville, AL, born Limestone Co., AL, farmer, sick in hospital at Nashville, TN 11/3/62, POW 2/15/65 from Lancaster, SC, paroled POW at Annapolis, MD 3/4/65, MO 6/13/65, Camp Chase, OH.

Patrick, Francis, Pvt., Co. I, age 18, EN 10/17/63, Glendale, MS, born Marshall Co., AL, farmer, MO 7/19/65, Nashville, TN.
   NOTE: Francis Marion Patrick was the son of Margaret Lang and James Patrick. He returned to Alabama after the war and married Avilla Jane West in Marshall County on October 20, 1867. He and his brother, William, chose to fight for the Union cause while their brother, Henry Greenberry Patrick, chose to fight for the Confederacy.[127]

Patrick, William, Pvt., Co. I, age 29, EN 10/18/63, Glendale, MS, born Marshall Co., AL, farmer, died 3/21/64 at Overton Hospital at Memphis, TN of typhoid fever. (Buried in Memphis National Cemetery.)
   NOTE: See Francis Patrick, above, for family information.

Patterson, David, Pvt., Co. B, age 18, EN 3/16/64 & MI 3/27/64, Decatur, AL, born Green Co., TN, farmer, died 5/2/64 at Post Hospital at Decatur, AL of measles.

Patterson, James M., Pvt., Co. F, age 40, EN 10/5/63, Corinth, MS, born Lawrence Co., TN, farmer, on detached duty as teamster 1/25/64 at Vicksburg, MS, MO 10/25/64, Rome, GA.

Patterson, John, Co. F, absent with leave 4/65.*

Patterson, T., Co. B, sick in hospital 3/65.*

Patterson, William A., Pvt., Co. K, age 33, EN & MI 8/25/62, Huntsville, AL, born Morgan Co., AL, farmer, POW 10/26/63 from Vincent's Crossroads, served as brigade teamster, died 8/26/64 at Andersonville, GA while POW. (Buried in grave #6886, Andersonville National Cemetery.)

Payne, James S., Pvt., Co. D, age 35, EN 5/20/64 & MI 6/16/64, Decatur, AL, born Carroll, NC, MO 10/20/65, Huntsville, AL.

Payne, Thomas C., Pvt., Co. F, age 26, EN 3/27/63, Corinth, MS, born Wayne Co., TN, farmer, served as Co. Cook, MO 3/26/64, Decatur, AL.

Payne, William C., Pvt., Co. D, absent sick in hospital at Memphis, TN 3/64.*

Peak, James, Pvt., Co. I, age 31, EN & MI 7/21/62, Huntsville, AL, born Walker Co., AL, farmer, sick in hospital at Murfreesboro, TN 2/14/63, on det. duty as scout 12/18/63, POW 3/10/65 from Monroe's Crossroads near Fayetteville, NC, MO 7/3/65, Annapolis, MD.

Peak, Samuel, Pvt., Co. I, age 23, EN & MI 7/21/62, Huntsville, AL, born Walker Co., AL, farmer, with wagon train at Nashville, TN 12/27/62, POW from Day's Gap, AL 5/63, confined to Richmond, VA 5/9/63, paroled at City Point, VA 5/14/63 and sent to Camp Chase, OH, (This POW Record is mixed in with William W. Peak.), MO 7/31/65, Nashville, TN.

Peak, William W., Pvt., Co. M, age 16, EN 11/10/63, Camp Davies, MS, MI 12/29/63, Corinth, MS, born Macon Co., GA, farmer, sick in hospital at Memphis, TN 2/22/64, returned to duty 3/28/64, MO 10/20/65, Huntsville, AL.

Pease, David A., 1st Lt., Co. G, age 27, EN 4/3/64, Bridgeport, AL, MI 4/13/64, Decatur, AL, born Hamilton, OH, farmer, on detached service as recruiting officer at Decatur, AL 4/3/64, resigned 9/15/64 because of his mother being sick and not expected to recover and his father suffering from apoplexy.

Peek, Henry C., 1st Lt/Capt., Co. H&D, age 26, EN 7/11/63, Glendale, MS, requested leave 3/25/64 to visit aged parents in Illinois, MO 6/30/64 to accept appt. as Capt., reenlisted 7/1/64, Rome GA, MO 10/20/65, Huntsville, AL.
    NOTE: Henry Clay Peek was born October 12, 1837 in Vermont. His parents were Lucretia Lamb and John Peek. Lucretia was a sister to the wife of John

Deere who founded the tractor company out of his blacksmith shop. Siblings of Henry were: Samuel, William, George Janette, Melona, John and Horace Peek. In 1864, while on leave, Henry married a school teacher by the name of Adeline S. Chase on November 28, 1864. Adeline was born in Rochester, NY in 1839. Henry was elected sheriff of Ogle County, Illinois in 1874 and re-elected four times. He and Adeline had five children: Harry, Elizabeth, Carlton, Burton and George. Adeline died in 1889 and in 1892, Henry married Julia Waterbury. Julia died in 1923 and Henry died December 9, 1924. Henry is buried in Riverview Cemetery in Ogle County, Illinois. [128]

Hdqrs. Fourth Division, fifteenth Army Corps, Savannah, GA, January 15, 1865, "...at 3 a.m. of the morning of the 10th Captain Peek, of the First Alabama Cavalry, brought in some prisoners belonging to Walthall's and Loring's division, of Stewart Corps. The captain having gallantly assaulted the enemy's outpost, drive them into their reserve; they in turn fell back into the main body, creating great commotion and confusion, under cover of which the captain made his escape, bringing with him quite a squad of prisoners, from whom I obtained positive information of the locality of Hood's different corps...." [129]

On March 28, 1865, Maj. S. Tramel wrote from Faison's Depot, NC, "Captain Peek deserves special mention for his gallant daring and coolness during this struggle. The loss of the regiment in the affairs was 4 men killed, 27 wounded, and 41 missing." [130]

Peers/Pierce, John S.M., Pvt., Co. K, age 15, EN 11/21/63, Camp Davies, MS, born VA, farmer, deserted 12/9/63 with horse & equipment, not apprehended.

Pell, C., Pvt., Co. D, sick in hospital 7/64.*

Pell/Pill, James, Pvt., Co. D, age 19, EN 3/5/63, Glendale, MS, MI 4/28/63, Corinth, MS, born Rayburn Co., GA, farmer, served as teamster, sick in Adams USA Hospital at Memphis, TN 3/24/64, MO 6/30/64, Memphis, TN.

Pell, William, Pvt., Co. I, age 30, EN & MI 7/21/62, Huntsville, AL, born Rayburn Co., GA, farmer, with wagon train at Nashville, TN 12/27/62, POW 4/28/63 from Day's Gap, AL, rejoined Co. 9/23/63, KIA 12/24/63 at Jack's Creek, TN. (Buried Grave #A-327, Corinth National Cemetery.)

Penn, F., Pvt., Co. D, absent on detached service with train since 12/26/62, absent sick in hospital June & July 1863.*

Penn, George W., Pvt., Co. I, age 18, EN 1/15/64, Camp Davies, MS, MI 2/26/64, Memphis, TN, born Morgan Co., AL, farmer, died 3/14/64 in Overton USA Hospital at Memphis, TN of inflammation of the brain. (Buried in Memphis National Cemetery.)

NOTE: George, John and Stephen Penn were brothers and sons of John Penn and Elizabeth Day, grandsons of Stephen Penn and David Day. They were cousins to James, Pleasant and Richard Penn who also served in this regiment. [131]

Penn, James, Pvt., Co. I, age 21, EN & MI 8/26/62, Huntsville, AL, born Morgan Co., AL, farmer, with wagon train at Nashville, TN 12/27/62, MIA 4/28/63 from Day's Gap, AL, sick in hospital at Annapolis, MD 5/63. No MO date.
NOTE: James, Pleasant and Richard Penn were brothers and sons of Stephen C. Penn and Esther Hettie Day and grandsons of Stephen Penn and David Day, Jr. They were cousins to George, John and Stephen Penn who also served in this regiment. After the war James married Sallie Pettus.[132]

Penn, John B., Pvt., Co. I, age 23, EN 1/15/64, Camp Davies, MS, MI 2/26/64, Memphis, TN, born Morgan Co., AL, farmer, MO 7/19/65, Nashville, TN.

Penn, Pleasant, Pvt., Co. I, age 19, EN & MI 8/26/62, Huntsville, AL, born Morgan Co., AL, farmer, died 2/7/63 at Murfreesboro, TN.

Penn, Richard W., Pvt., Co. I, age 25, EN & MI 8/26/62, Huntsville, AL, born Morgan Co., AL, farmer, deserted 10/24/62 from Nashville, TN, returned 7/1/65, charge of desertion removed because he was POW 10/24/62 and confined to a rebel prison at Moulton, AL.
NOTE: Richard Penn was living with his widowed sister, Jane Penn Ford and her four children and working on her farm at the time of his enlistment. He married Mary Emily Simpson and died December 4, 1901.[133]

Penn, Stephen W., Pvt., Co. I, age 21, EN 1/15/64, Camp Davies, MS, MI 2/26/64, Memphis, TN, born Morgan Co., AL, farmer, MO 7/19/65, Nashville, TN.
NOTE: Stephen Penn died June 7, 1920 at age 77.[134]

Pennington, Abner, Pvt., Co. H, age 26, EN 10/18/63, Glendale, MS, MI 2/24/64, Memphis, TN, born Fayette Co., AL, farmer, POW 10/26/63, MO 10/24/64, Rome, GA.

Pennington, Franklin, Pvt., Co. H, age 33, EN 10/17/63, Glendale, MS, in Small Pox USA Hospital at Memphis, TN 3/27/64, discharged 3/24/64 for disability resulting in a horse injury before entering service.

Pennington, James, Co. H, sick in Nashville, TN since 3/26/64.*

Pennington, Irvin/Jerome, Pvt., Co. H, age 35, EN 10/17/63, Glendale, MS, MO 10/24/64, Rome, GA.

Pennington, John, Pvt., Co. H, age 36, EN 12/1/63, Camp Davies, MS, admitted to Post Hospital at Decatur, AL 5/1/64, transferred 6/25/64 to Cumberland Hospital at Nashville, TN and on to Louisville, KY 8/27/64, MO 2/7/65, Nashville, TN.

Pennington, T., Pvt., Co. H, discharged by reason of exp. of term of service 10/25/64 at Rome, GA.*

Peoples, Francis "Frank" Mark, Pvt/Corp., Co. E, age 28, EN & MI 2/17/63, Corinth, MS, in charge of Co. kitchen, MO 3/1/64, Memphis, TN.

NOTE: Francis Peoples, brother of William L. Peoples, below, was born January 11, 1835 in McMinn Co., TN and died September 4, 1889 in Marion Co., IL, where he had been forced to flee because of his Union sympathies. He married Cordelia McRaven on May 20, 1886 in Marion Co., IL.[135]

Peoples, Waddell, Pvt., Co. E, in Overton USA Hospital at Memphis, TN Jan. & Feb. 1864.*

Peoples, William L., Pvt., Co. E, EN & MI 2/17/63, Corinth, MS, MO 3/1/64, Memphis, TN.
NOTE: William Peoples was born July 15, 1842 in McMinn Co., TN and died August 26, 1911 in Marion Co., IL, where he had been forced to flee due to his Union sympathies. He married Minerva Jane Dugan, sister of Richard S. Dugan, on February 9, 1862 in Marion Co., AL. Minerva was born February 5, 1834 in Monroe Co., TN and died October 26, 1876 in Marion Co., IL. They had 5 children, only 2 of whom lived beyond childhood: Andrew Jackson Peoples, born February 28, 1867 and Minerva Jane Peoples, born October 25, 1876. William L. Peoples was a brother to Francis M. Peoples, above and they were sons of James and Rachel McBride Peoples.[136]

Peotl, F., Pvt., Co. L, MIA 10/26/63 at Vincent's Crossroads.*

Perkins, A.R., Pvt., Co. D, stationed at Benton Barracks, MO 2/29/64. No further information.

Perkins, John H., Pvt., Co. H, age 26, EN 3/1/65, Stevenson, AL, MI 4/5/65, Nashville, TN, born Lumpkin Co., GA, farmer, deserted 6/1/65 from Huntsville, AL.

Perkins, William, Pvt., Co. E, EN 12/15/62, Chewalla, TN, MI 12/15/62, Corinth, MS, POW 1/20/63 near Chewalla, TN, deserted 3/2/63 from Corinth, MS.

Perrett, Isaac R., Pvt., Co. F, age 21, EN 7/20/63, Corinth, MS, born Madison Co., AL, farmer, detached as teamster 1/25/64 at Vicksburg, MS, died 4/12/64 in Cumberland USA Hospital at Nashville, TN, father shown as L.B. Perrett and address before enlistment was Pike Co., AL.

Perrett, John R., Pvt., Co. F, age 30 (or 20), EN 7/20/63 & MI 8/7/63, Corinth, MS, born Maury Co., TN, farmer, POW 10/26/63 from Vincent's Crossroads, paroled at Mobile, AL 11/2/63, on duty as teamster 1/25/64 at Vicksburg, MS, admitted to hospital at Andersonville, GA 5/31/64 where he died 6/26/64 while POW. (Buried in grave #2504, Andersonville National Cemetery.)

Perrett, R., Co. F, POW since 10/26/63.*

Perry, D., Pvt., Co. E, term of service expired 3/1/64, Memphis, TN.*

Perry, George W., Pvt/Sgt., Co. D, age 19, EN 5/1/64 & MI 6/16/64, Decatur, AL, born St. Clair Co., AL, in arrest at Nashville, TN 7/1/65, for "highway robbery", several peices of correspondence regarding this matter is in the file and they (Geo W.

Perry, T.S. Perry & L.W. Martin) finally proved they were in camp when robbery was committed, MO 10/20/65, Huntsville, AL.

Perry, J., Co. D, absent sick in US General Hospital.*

Perry, James, 1st Lt., Co. L, age 25, EN 9/25/63, Glendale, MS, promoted from Pvt., Co. C, 2nd Iowa Inf. Vols, KIA 10/26/63 at Vincent's Crossroads, MS.

Perry, James, Sgt., Co. E, transferred from 2nd Iowa Inf. 8/18/63 at Glendale, MS.*

Perry, Riley, Co. F, absent on secret service in Corinth, MS.*

Perry, Thomas S., Pvt., Co. D, age 23, EN 5/1/64 & MI 6/16/64, Decatur, AL, born St. Clair, Co., AL, farmer, in arrest 7/1/65 (see George Perry above), in USA Hospital at Savannah, GA 2/1/65, MO 10/20/65, Huntsville, AL.

Perry, William R., Sgt., Co. F, age 25, EN 5/23/63, Corinth, MS, born Wyatte (?) Co., MS, farmer, deserted 12/15/63 from Camp Davies, MS with Smith carbine, Remington revolver and equipment.

Peter, Henry, Pvt., Co. F, POW 10/26/63.* (This may be Peter Henry.)

Petis, H., POW 3/65.*

Pettus, Egbert J., Pvt., Co. I, age 21, EN & MI 7/21/62, Huntsville, AL, died 11/27/62 in Hospital #14 at Nashville, TN. (Buried in Grave C-7060 in Nashville National Cemetery as Egbert L. Pettis.)

Phenthorn/ Phenthom, F.M., Sgt., Co. F, term of service expired 4/13/64, Mooresville.*

Philips/Phillips, Elijah M., Pvt., Co. C, EN 1/3/63 & MI 1/10/63, Corinth, MS, born McNairy Co., TN, farmer, deserted 8/6/63 from Glendale, MS.

Phillips, E., Co. B, absent sick in US General Hospital.*

Phillips, John, Pvt., Co. C, POW in GA 5/64 and sent to Richmond, VA from Salisbury, NC, paroled 2/24/65.*

Phillips, John R., Sgt., Co. L, age 26, EN 9/25/63, Fayette Co., AL, MI 9/25/63, Glendale, MS, born Marion Co., AL, farmer, sick in Overton USA Hospital at Memphis, TN 1/3/64, sick in Cumberland Hospital at Nashville, TN 4/2/64, MO 6/30/65, Nashville, TN.
        NOTE: John Robert Phillips was born October 18, 1837 in Surry Co., NC, died April 25, 1925 in Bear Creek, AL and was the son of John Spencer Phillips, born March 25, 1810 in Surry Co., NC, died December 21, 1844 in Jonesville, Surry Co., NC, and Susan Hastings, born 1818 in NC, died June 16, 1882 at Thorn Hill, Marion Co., AL, who were married December 12, 1836. On August 23, 1855, John R. Phillips married Mahala Rebecca Ballew in Fannin Co., GA.

Mahala was born January 7, 1837 in Wilkes Co., NC and died March 22, 1867 in Thorn Hill, AL. Children of John and Mahala Phillips are: Salome, born May 20, 1856 in Cherokee Co., NC, died 1863 in Thorn Hill, AL; Eliza, born May 26, 1857 in Cherokee Co., NC, died June 8, 1956 in Seagraves, TX, married James Jackson Coats; John Spencer, born August 20, 1858 in Cherokee Co., NC and died as an infant; Susan Esther, born January 12, 1860 at Thorn Hill, AL, died February 20, 1902 at Bear Creek, AL, married Ben Howell; Martha Jane, born November 23, 1861 at Thorn Hill, AL, died 1943 at Florence, AL, married Charles Little Haley; Olmedo, born January 31, 1864 at Thorn Hill, AL, died June 1, 1946 at Phil Campbell, AL, married Annetta Gertrude Ingram; and Arminda Cenora, born January 15, 1867 at Thorn Hill, AL, died April 10, 1867 at Thorn Hill, AL.

In 1867 John R. Phillips married Mary Evelyn Roberts, born January 10, 1846, died May 26, 1931 at Bear Creek, AL and was buried beside her husband in Bear Creek Cemetery. Children of John and Mary are: Isabella Cenorah, born March 29, 1868, died July 24, 1934 at Tuscaloosa, AL, married Dr. Charles Emil Scharnagel; Virgin Ann, born December 3, 1869, died November 9, 1933 at Ft. Worth, TX, married Joseph Charles Srygley; Victoria, born November 27, 1871, died August 27, 1949 at Haleyville, AL, married Samuel Kennedy Wilson; James Pickens, born August 4, 1874, died July 17, 1951 at Bear Creek, AL, married Lucy Elizabeth Flippo; Wendell Veteo, born December 14, 1876, died January 17, 1934 at Deland, FL, married Rose Josephine Martin; John Robert Phillips, Jr., born September 12, 1879, died March 21, 1902 at Bear Creek, AL, never married; Oscar Wilde, born October 10, 1882, died June 24, 1953 at Bear Creek, AL, married Nina Fairless; Micajah Phillips, born December 25, 1885, died January 16, 1886; Lucien Lowery, born November 19, 1888 at Haleyville, AL, died September 30, 1962, married Lessie Hatcher. Other children were born at Thorn Hill, AL.[137]

Phillips, Thomas, Pvt., Co. E, age 44, EN & MI 9/1/64, Rome, GA, born Jackson Co., GA, farmer, sent to hospital at Decatur, AL 11/5/64, died in hospital at Stevenson, AL on or about 4/1/65.

NOTE: Thomas T. Phillips was born in 1834 in Georgia. He married Helen Callisto Bowen, daughter of Samuel H. and Marcia Dearing Bowen, in Randolph Co., AL August 18, 1859 and had four children: Sarah Clementine, born June 25, 1860, Elizabeth K. Delphia, born November 2, 1861, William F., born April 16, 1863, and Samuel H. Phillips, born May 1, 1865.[138]

Phillips, William L., Pvt., Co. K, age 31, EN & MI 8/5/62, Huntsville, AL, born Greenville Dist., SC, farmer, on daily duty as teamster, POW 5/3/63, "was surrendered near Rome, GA with Col. Streight's command", paroled at Richmond, VA 12/27/63, died in hospital at Alexandria, VA 5/21/65 from "overdose of cyanurat of potassium", wife shown as Salelina/Sebena and residence, High Town, Forsythe, GA, buried U.S. Military Cemetery, Alexandria, VA, grave #3035.

Pickle, Robert, Blacksmith, Co. B, age 26, EN 5/11/63, Glendale, MS, POW 10/26/63 from Vincent's Crossroads, MO 1/22/64, Memphis, TN.

Pierce, Charles, Pvt., Co. B, age 18, EN 2/13/64, Pulaski, TN, MI 4/13/64, Decatur, AL, born Giles Co., TN, farmer, MO 10/20/65, Huntsville, AL.

Pierce, Frederick F., Pvt., Co. D, blacksmith 2/64.*

Pierce, John A., Pvt., Co. A, age 29, EN 1/23/64, Camp Davies, MS, born Upton Co., GA, farmer, deserted 1/23/64 from Camp Davies with arms and equipment.

Pierce, Loron/Loren W., Capt., Co. F, EN 3/19/63, Corinth, MS, promoted from Pvt., Co. C, 2nd Iowa Inf. Vols, in arrest at Memphis, TN 10/18/63, dishonorably dismissed 8/13/64 for AWOL, habitual drunkeness, disobedience of orders, and "assault with intent to kill", offered to dismiss charges if he would resign and he failed to do so within the time limit given him.

Pierce, Uphratus C., Pvt., Co. H, age 18, EN 11/30/64, Stevenson, AL, MI 4/5/65, Nashville, TN, born Coweta Co., GA, farmer, run over and killed by train 5/29/65 in Huntsville, AL.

Pike, John F., Pvt., Co. A, age 25, EN 3/23/63 & MI 3/24/63 at Glendale, MS, MIA 7/5/63 from Yellow Creek, died 1/31/64 at Richmond, VA while POW. (Buried in Richmond National Cemetery, VA.)

Pike, Philip C., Pvt., Co. A, age 18, EN 1/11/64, Camp Davies, MS, MI 2/5/64, Memphis, TN, born Walker Co., AL, farmer, in arrest in prison at Athens, AL 4/64, for desertion, MO 10/20/65, Huntsville, AL.

Pike, William G., Pvt/Corp., Co. A, age 23, EN 3/23/63 & MI 3/24/63, Glendale, MS, promoted to Corp. 9/16/63.

Piles, J.L., Pvt., Co. L, absent with leave 11/25/63.*

Pittman, William, Pvt., Co. G, temporarily attached from 11th Illinois Cavalry.

Pitts, John B., Co. F, age 46, born Lawrence Dist., SC, farmer, no EN or MI date, died 4/14/64 in Hospital #19 at Nashville, TN of measles, wife shown as Melissa and residence as Pikeville, AL. (Buried in Grave H-10019, Nashville National Cemetery.)

Pleinis/Pleissis, William, absent with leave 10/63.*

Plott, Tilmon, Sgt., Co. L, age 39, EN 9/25/63, Fayette Co., AL, MI 9/25/63, Glendale, MS, POW 10/26/63 from Vincent's Crossroads. No further information.
      NOTE: Tillmon Plott is buried in Hargrove Church Cemetary in Pickens County, AL.

Poe, Jessee, Pvt., Co. G, age 18, EN 3/10/64 & MI 4/13/64, Decatur, AL, born Jefferson Co., AL, farmer, sick in hospital at Decatur, AL 9/28/65, MO 10/20/65, Huntsville, AL.

Poe, Robert, Co. G, age 28, born Jefferson Co., AL, farmer, EN 4/10/64, Decatur, AL.*

Poe, Wiley, Pvt., Co. G, age 22, EN 3/10/64 & MI 4/13/64, Decatur, AL, born Jefferson Co., AL, farmer, MO 10/20/65, Huntsville, AL.

Pointer, William T., Pvt/Sgt., Co. H, age 28, EN 12/25/64, Rome, GA, MI 12/25/64, Nashville, TN, born Clark Co., GA, appt. 1st Sgt. 4/1/65, MO 10/20/65, Huntsville, AL.

Pollard, Aaron B., Pvt., Co. A, age 18, EN & MI 10/6/64, Rome, GA, born Cherokee Co., AL, farmer, WIA 2/20/65 and sent to hospital at Wilmington, NC, MO 10/20/65, Huntsville, AL.

Pollard, James R., Pvt/Corp., Co. B, age 19, EN & MI 9/1/64, Rome, GA, born Fayette Co., GA, farmer, promoted to Corp. 6/1/65, in hospital at Decatur, AL 9/1/65, discharge furnished 11/15/65.

Pollard, Thomas L., Pvt., Co. E, age 31, EN 5/1/63, Glendale, MS, served as nurse and cook in regimental hospital, MO 6/15/64, Decatur, AL.

Pollard, William F. (or S.), Pvt., Co. B, age 20, EN 8/1/64, Wedowee, AL, MI 8/1/64, Rome, GA, born Fayette Co., GA, farmer, served as blacksmith, sent to hospital at Savannah, GA 1/15/65, died in Post Hospital at Goldsboro, NC 5/11/65.

Pollman/Rollman, John, Pvt., Co. F, on detached service at Refugee Camp at Memphis, TN 4/64.*

Pool, Thomas, Pvt., Co. M, age 18, (Colored), EN & MI 9/1/64, Rome, GA, born Cherokee Co., AL, farmer, died 7/24/65 from accidental gunshot through the head at Courtland, AL. (Buried Grave #B-3326, Corinth National Cemetery.)

Poole/Pool, Joel J., Pvt., Co. E, age 44, (Colored), EN & MI 9/1/64, Rome, GA, born Jasper, GA, blacksmith, WIA 3/10/65 at Monroe's Crossroads, NC, slight gunshot wound to left ankle.

Pope, James, Sgt., Co. I, age 30, EN 10/17/63, Glendale, MS, born Cobb Co., GA, farmer, appt. Corp. 11/1/63 and Sgt. 12/7/63, MO 7/19/65, Nashville, TN.

Portis/Portico/Portice, George Franklin, Pvt., Co. G, age 19, EN 3/5/63, Chewalla, TN, MI 6/1/63, Corinth, MS, deserted 7/2/63 from at Glendale, MS.

Pose, H.C., Pvt., Co. B, on extra daily duty as scout.*

Post, William, Pvt., Co. D, EN 2/1/63, Glendale, MS, MI 2/4/63, Corinth, MS, blacksmith, MO 2/4/64, Memphis, TN.

Potter, John, Pvt/Corp., Co. H, age 23, EN 12/22/64, Stevenson, AL, MI 12/22/64, Nashville, TN, born Dekalb Co., AL, farmer, appt. Corp. 4/1/65, MO 10/20/65, Huntsville, AL.
 NOTE: John also served in Co. C, 1st AL Vidette Cav. USA. He married Louisa Cooper of Valley Head, AL and had five children: Mary Elizabeth,

born April 3, 1869, married James Denney; Samuel Franklin, born October 24, 1873, married Ruth Elizabeth Collins; Tennessee H., born May 3, 1877, married James Wilce Collins; Doria Elizabeth, born March 22, 1882, married Charles Churchill Collins; and Alice P., born April 3, 1884. Louisa died July 1885 in Kimball, TN and on April 28, 1895, John married Anna Bridget Nelson who died March 5, 1901. On December 10, 1904, John married Josie A. Baker who died June 30, 1916. John stated he was kidnapped by the Confederate Army and taken by force in the Georgia State Troops under Captain Howe. He died November 6, 1910 and is buried at Lasater Cemetery near Jasper, TN.[139]

Pounders, James B., Pvt., Co. H, age 18, EN 7/28/63, Glendale, MS, POW 10/26/63 from Vincent's Crossroads near Bay Springs, MS, sent to prison at Andersonville, GA 7/25/64 where he died 8/8/64. (Buried in grave #5077, Andersonville National Cemetery.)

Pounders, Thomas R., Pvt., Co. B, age 28, EN 2/9/64, Pulaski, TN, MI 3/27/64, Decatur, AL, born Limestone Co., AL, occupation shown as "cotton mark", promoted to Sgt. 7/1/64, reduced from Sgt. to ranks 8/1/64, MO 10/20/65, Huntsville, AL.

Powell, Benjamin H., Pvt., Co. I, age 23, EN & MI 8/18/62, Huntsville, AL, born GA, farmer, MIA 4/28/63 from Day's Gap, AL, sick at Indianapolis 4/27/63, in hospital at Rome, GA 7/26/64, MO 7/19/65, Nashville, TN.

Powell, Jasper N., Pvt., Co. I, in Union USA Hospital at Memphis, TN Sept. & Oct. 1863.*

Powell, Joshua M., Corp. Co. I, in USA General Hospital at Savannah, GA 4/65, returned to duty during the month.*

Powell, Joshua P., Pvt., Co. K, age 21, EN & MI 8/22/62, Huntsville, AL, born Gilmore Co., GA, MIA 4/30/63 from Crooked Creek, Days Gap, AL, murdered by rebels at Summerville, AL 5/2/63. (There is a Pvt. J.P. Powell from AL buried in Grave N-4539 in Marietta National Cemetery.)

Powell, Newton J., Pvt/Corp., Co. I, age 26, EN & MI 8/18/62, Huntsville, AL, born in GA, with wagon train at Nashville, TN 12/27/62 as teamster, sick in hospital at Memphis, TN 10/12/63, appt. Corp. 1/1/64, sick in hospital at Savannah, GA 1/15/65, MO 7/19/65, Nashville, TN.

Powell, Pinkney, Pvt., Co. I, EN & MI 8/18/62, Huntsville, AL, with wagon train at Nashville, TN 12/27/62, on courier post at Reedyville, TN 1/27/63. No further information.

Powell, Tilmon, Pvt., Co. I, age 25, EN & MI 8/18/62, Huntsville, AL, born in GA, farmer, with wagon train in Nashville, TN 12/27/62, sick in Hospital #14 in Nashville, MIA 4/28/63 from Day's Gap, AL, escaped and returned 6/1/65, MO 7/19/65, Nashville, TN.

Powell, William J., Pvt., Co. K, discharged 6/12/65 at Camp Chase, OH 4/28/65.*

Pratt, Ira F., 2nd M. Sgt., (F&S), age 26, EN 10/28/63, Glendale, MS, appt. from Co. H, 57th Illinois Inf. Vols., MO 10/20/65, Huntsville, AL.

Prentice, James S., Pvt., Co. D, age 21, EN 6/1/63, Glendale, MS, died 1/8/64 in hospital at Camp Davies, MS of disease contracted before entering service.

Preshour, W.N., Co. E, AWOL to be dropped as deserted after 5/63.*

Prestidge, Anderson, Pvt., Co. D, EN 2/1/63, Glendale, MS, MI 2/4/63, Corinth, MS, deserted 3/22/63 at Glendale, later found to be POW while on scout.

Prestidge, George, Pvt., Co. D, EN 2/1/63, Glendale, MS, MI 2/4/63, Corinth, MS, deserted 3/22/63 at Glendale, MS. No further information. (See Anderson Prestidge).

Prestidge, John, Pvt., Co. D, EN 2/1/63, Glendale, MS, MI 2/4/63, Corinth, MS, deserted 3/22/63 at Glendale, MS. No further information.

Prewett, Francis M., Pvt., Co. A, age 25, EN & MI 3/3/63, Glendale, MS, deserted 3/31/63 at Glendale.

Price, Frederick, Pvt., Co. G, age 18, EN 8/13/63, Glendale, MS. MO 11/26/63, Memphis, TN.

Price, Frederick F., Pvt., Co. C, age 43, EN 7/1/63, Glendale, MS, MI 2/24/64, Memphis, TN, born Rutherford Co., NC, farmer, MO 7/27/64, Rome, GA.

Price, Gabriel E., Pvt/Corp., Co. C, age 22, EN 2/15/64, Memphis, TN, MI 3/10/64, Memphis, TN, born Wayne, NC, farmer, deserted 5/30/64 near Dallas, GA with Colt revolver, Smith carbine, and horse, captured 5/64, exchanged at Savannah, GA or Charleston, SC in Nov. or Dec. 1864, paroled POW from Annapolis, MD 12/24/64, died in USA Hospital at Annapolis 1/1/65, originally buried in grave #285, Ash Grove US Cemetery.

Price, Howard, Pvt., Co. C, age 21, EN 1/15/63, Corinth, MS, deserted 6/28/63 from Glendale, MS.

Price/Prince, John A., Pvt., Co. D, EN 2/1/63, Glendale, MS, MI 2/4/63, Corinth, MS, in hospital at Memphis, TN 10/26/63, in Marine USA Hospital at St. Louis, MO 11/27/63, returned to duty 1/26/64, in Adams USA Hospital at Memphis, TN 4/19/64, died 5/10/64 from gangrene. (Buried Grave #1-42, Memphis National Cemetery.)

Price, John C., Pvt., Co. L, POW and died 9/11/64 at Andersonville, GA. (Buried in Grave #8425, Andersonville National Cemetery.)

Price, Wilkerson/William P., Pvt., Co. G, age 24, EN 4/28/64, Mooresville, AL, MI Rome, GA, born Lee Co., VA, deserted 11/10/64 at Rome, GA with horse, arms & equipment while on scout.

Prince, John J., Pvt., Co. B, age 18, EN 8/1/64, Wedowee, AL, MI 8/1/64, Rome, GA, born Randolph Co., AL, farmer, left sick in hospital at Savannah, GA 1/15/65, MO 10/20/65, Huntsville, AL.

Pugh, George W., Pvt., Co. K, EN 11/10/63, Camp Davies, MS, died 3/19/64 in Small Pox USA Hospital in Memphis, TN of smallpox. (Buried in Memphis National Cemetery.)

Pugh, Nathan, Pvt., Co. K, age 47, EN 11/10/63, Camp Davies, MS, born Chester Dist., SC, farmer, sent to hospital at Hilton Head, SC 12/18/64, in hospital at Savannah, GA 2/1/65, returned to duty 3/24/65, MO 7/19/65, Nashville, TN.

Pullem, John, Pvt., Co. F, age 25, EN 4/13/63, Corinth, MS, MI 5/18/63, Corinth, MS, born Jackson Co., TN, farmer, on det. duty at refugee camp in Memphis, TN, 3/20/64, admitted to hospital in Memphis 3/15/64 with smallpox, returned to duty 4/8/64, discharged 4/13/64.

Putnam/Pitman, John R., Pvt., Co. K, age 21, EN & MI 8/23/62, Huntsville, AL, born Lawrence Co., AL, MIA 12/31/62 at Battle of Stone's River, Murfreesboro, TN, reported deserted, cleared of desertion and restored to duty 6/1/65, MO 7/19/65, Nashville, TN.

Raburn, John R., Sgt., Co. G, age 26, EN 12/13/62, Pocahontas, TN, appt. Sgt. 4/1/63, POW 10/26/63 from Vincent's Crossroads, paroled at Mobile, AL 11/2/63, MO 11/26/63, Memphis, TN.

Raburn, John F., (Cards filed with John F. Reyburn).

Raby, James F.M., (Cards filed with James F.M. Raley).

Rackard/Rikard/Rachord, John H., Pvt., Co. D, age 18, EN 6/1/63, Glendale, MS, wounded and sent to hospital at Memphis, TN 1/31/64, died from wounds 2/28/64 in Adams USA Hospital at Memphis. (Buried in Memphis National Cemetery.)

Rackard/Rikard, Robert F., Pvt., Co. D, age 21, EN 6/1/63, Glendale, MS, MO 6/16/64, Decatur, AL.

Reavis/Raevis, John J., Pvt., Co. L, age 17, EN 9/25/63, Fayette Co., AL, born Cherokee Co., GA, farmer, died 2/9/64 in Adams USA Hospital at Memphis, TN of measles. (Buried Grave in Memphis National Cemetery.)

Rainey, William, Pvt., Co. G, temporarily attached from 11th Illinois Cavalry.

Raley/Raby, James F.M., Pvt., Co. A, age 36, EN 7/12/63, Glendale, MS, MIA 10/26/63, returned 1/14/64. No MO date.

Raley, William M., Corp. Co. A, age 32, EN 7/11/63, Glendale, MS, promoted to Corp. 9/16/63, MO 12/22/63, Memphis, TN.

Rambo, William, Pvt., Co. E, EN 2/6/63, Trenton, TN, MI 2/6/63, Corinth, MS, deserted 5/1/63, Glendale, MS.

Ramey, John L., Pvt., Co. K, age 23, EN & MI 7/24/62, Huntsville, AL, born Chatooga, GA, farmer, POW 5/3/63 from Cedar Bluff, GA, paroled POW exchanged 5/25/63 from City Point, VA, on detached service as teamster in Sherman's expedition 1/24/64 at Vicksburg, MS, MO 7/19/65, Nashville, TN.
NOTE: John L. Ramey was a brother of William P. Ramey, below.

Ramey, William P., Pvt., Co. K, age 34, EN & MI 7/24/62, Huntsville, AL, born Hall Co., GA, farmer, MIA 4/30/63 from Rhine's Creek, Day's Gap, AL, returned 12/21/63, WIA 3/10/65 and sent to Annapolis, MD, MO 5/30/65, New York, NY. (Notation in file dated August 30, 1887 states, "This man was cut off from his command by the rebel forces April 30, 1863, went home and remained in the mountains until Dec. 21, 1863, when he rejoined his command".
NOTE: William P. Ramey married Sarah Narcissa who was a sister of Doctor T. and Tillman Boyd who were also in this regiment. Dates on his headstone state he was born November 1827 and died April 1872. He is buried in Kimbler Cemetery, just south of Cove City, Crawford Co., AR. Sarah's daughter by her first husband was married to John L. Ramey, brother of William P. Ramey.[140]

Ramsey/Raney, William, Corp., Co. K, age 44, EN & MI 7/24/62, Huntsville, AL, born Lincoln Co., TN, farmer, in battle near Nashville, TN 11/5/64, in Battle of Stone's River, TN, in skirmish at Neelysbend near Nashville, 10/20/62, in hospital at Murfreesboro, TN 3/7/63, sick in Goldsboro, NC 4/9/65, discharged 6/28/65 due to disability.

Randolph, Simeon, Co. M, age 42, born Morgan Co., AL, farmer, EN 11/30/63, Camp Davies, MS, released by surgeon's certificate on incompetency before mustered in.*

Ransom, William, Co. E, absent on courier line 2/63.*

Rape, Charles L., Pvt., Co. E, age 18, EN & MI 9/1/64, Rome, GA, born Henry Co., GA, farmer, deserted 9/1/65 from Moulton, AL, charges removed 7/23/84 and discharged as of 9/1/65.

Ray/Roy, Alexander R., Pvt., Co. L, age 18, EN 4/7/65, Stevenson, AL, MI 4/18/65, Nashville, TN, born Tallapoosa Co., AL, farmer, died 5/17/65 in Post Hospital at Huntsville, AL of typhoid fever, originally buried   grave #211 at Huntsville Cemetery. (Reinterred Grave #L-543, Chattanooga National Cemetery.)

Ray, Clemond R., Co. L, age 18, born Tallaposa Co., AL, farmer, EN 4/17/65, Stevenson, AL, died in hospital at Huntsville, AL 5/17/65.*

Ray, Francis, Pvt., Co. B, age 36, EN 2/6/64, Pulaski, TN, MI 3/27/64, Decatur, AL, born Giles Co., TN, farmer, detailed at nurse in hospital at Decatur, AL, deserted 7/16/64 from Rome, GA with Smith carbine and equipment.

Rayborn, John F., (Cards filed with John F. Reyburn).

Rayborn, Thomas C., Pvt., Co. A, age 17, EN 9/8/62, Iuka, MS, MI 10/1/62, Corinth, MS, born McMinn Co., TN, died 4/12/63 at Corinth, MS of measles/typhoid fever.

Rayburn, Noah D., age 24, EN 2/1/63, Glendale, MS, EN 2/4/63, Corinth, MS, born Franklin Co., AL, farmer, sick in hospital at Jackson, TN 3/4/65, MIA 3/20/63 in Franklin Co., AL while on secret scout, notation in file states he is supposed to be dead in the field 5/1/65, no further information.

Read, John, Under Cook, Co. C, (Colored), age 40, EN 12/1/64, Monticello, GA, MI 10/17/65, Huntsville, AL, born Jasper Co., GA, farmer, MO 10/20/65, Huntsville, AL.

Reall, William, Pvt., Co. K, in Gayoso USA Hospital at Memphis, TN Jan. & Feb. 1864.*

Reddish, Thomas J., Pvt., Co. C, age 26, EN 1/20/63, Corinth, MS, MI 1/20/63, Corinth, MS, born Fayette Co., AL, farmer, died 5/29/63 in regimental hospital at Glendale, MS.

Reddish, William J., Pvt., Co. C, age 20, EN & MI 1/20/63, Corinth, MS, born Fayette Co., AL, farmer, discharged 9/15/63 due to total disability.

Redmond, William A., Pvt., Co. C, age 25, EN 7/11/63, Glendale, MS, MIA 10/26/63 from Vincent's Crossroads, MS, died 10/13/64 at Andersonville, GA while POW. (Buried in grave #10900, Andersonville National Cemetery.)

Redus, David R., Pvt., Co. B, age 35, EN 12/14/62, Glendale, MS, born Marion Co., AL, farmer, served as teamster, nurse and blacksmith, MO 12/27/63, Camp Davies, MS.

Redus, William D., Sgt., Co. E, age 24, EN & MI 2/1/63, Corinth, MS, MO 2/1/64, Memphis, TN.
    NOTE: William D. Redus is buried in Elmwood Cemetery in Centralia, Illinois.[141]

Reed, Aaron L., Pvt., Co. G, age 33, EN 6/11/63, Chewalla, TN, WIA and in hospital at Memphis, TN 10/26/63, MO 11/26/63, Memphis, TN.

Reed, Annias/Ananias S., Pvt., Co. C, age 38, EN 7/25/63, Glendale, MS, MI 12/18/63, Memphis, TN, deserted 8/13/63 from Glendale, WIA and in hospital at Memphis, TN 10/26/63, deserted 4/24/64 and returned 5/23/64, MO 7/27/64, Rome, GA.

Reed, David B., Pvt., Co. E, EN 2/28/63, Sulphur Springs, MI 3/1/63, Corinth, MS, POW between Glendale & Burnsville, MS 6/11/63, POW 10/26/63 from Vincent's Crossroads, died 1/26/64 of pneumonia while POW at Cahaba Prison in AL. (Buried in Grave K-3670, Marietta National Cemetery.)

Reed, Finis E., Pvt., Co. G, temporarily attached from 11th Illinois Cavalry.

Reed, Francis M., Pvt., Co. E, age 24, EN 8/7/63, Glendale, MS, MI 8/27/63, Corinth, MS, born McNairy Co., TN, POW 10/26/63 from Vincent's Crossroads, died 7/29/63 while POW at Cahaba Prison in AL.

Reed, James L., Pvt/Bugler, Co. D, EN 2/1/63, Glendale, MS, MI 2/4/63, Corinth, MS, deserted 4/30/63 from Glendale, MO 2/4/64, Memphis, TN.

Reed, James M., Pvt/Sgt., Co. E, EN 2/28/63, Sulphur Springs, MI Corinth, MS, POW 6/11/63 between Glendale & Burnsville, MS, died 7/29/63 at Benton Barracks, MO of typhoid fever, originally buried in block 6, grave #68. (Certificate for Government Undertakers at St. Louis, MO was in charge of burial.) (Buried Jefferson Barracks, MO.)

Reed, John A., Pvt., Co. E, age 28, EN 8/27/63, Glendale, MS, MI 8/27/63, Corinth, MS, MO 9/28/64, Rome, GA.

Reed, John H., Capt. Co. G, age 38, EN 1/16/63, LaGrange, TN, appt. Capt. from Miss. Rifles 1/16/63, discharged 1/3/64.

Reed, Lovick H., Pvt., Co. D, EN 2/1/63, Glendale, MS, MI 2/4/63, Corinth, MS, MO 2/4/64, Memphis, TN.

Reed, Q.B., Pvt., Co. E, detached - detailed as teamster in Q.M. Dept. at Vicksburg, MS 1/25/64.*

Reed, Robert M., (alias John A. Counce), Pvt., Co. E, age 45, EN & MI 8/27/63, Corinth, MS, MO 9/28/64, Rome, GA. Notation in file states he took the place of John A. Counce and assumed his name.

Reed, Samuel M., Pvt., Co. D, EN 2/1/63, Glendale, MS, MI 2/4/63, Corinth, MS, MO 2/4/64, Memphis, TN.

Reed, Samuel G., Pvt., Co. G, temporarily attached from 11th Illinois Cavalry.

Reed, Thomas, Pvt., died 3/16/63 at Corinth, MS, wife's residence shown as Marion Co., AL.*

Reed, William D., Pvt/Sgt., Co. E, age 35, EN 8/27/63, Glendale, MS, promoted to Com. Sgt. 3/1/64, MO 9/28/64, Rome, GA.

Reedus (See Redus)

Reeves, Archibald, Pvt/Sgt., Co. E, age 44, EN & MI 9/1/64, Rome, GA, born Walton Co., GA, farmer, promoted to Sgt. 1/1/65. No MO date.

Reeves, Josiah C., Pvt., Co. H, age 18, EN 1/15/65, Stevenson, AL, MI 1/15/65, Nashville, TN, born Cobb Co., GA, farmer, MO 10/20/65, Huntsville, AL.

Reeves/Reaves, Thomas, Pvt., Co. E, age 18, EN & MI 8/1/64, Rome, GA, born Newton Co., GA, farmer, POW 3/10/65 from Blackney's Crossroads, SC, MO 6/13/65, Camp Chase, OH. (Buried Fairview Cemetery in League City Texas with a military headstone.)[142]

Reid, John L., Pvt/Sgt., Co. I, age 28, EN & MI 7/21/62, Huntsville, AL, on courier post at Reedyville, TN 1/27/63, promoted Sgt. 11/1/63, on furlough in Illinois 12/18/63, sick in hospital at Memphis, TN 1/28/64, sick in hospital at Rome, GA 7/64, MO 7/19/65, Nashville, TN.

Reid, Jonathan, Pvt., Co. I, age 54, EN 12/21/63, Camp Davies, MS, died 1/18/64 at Camp Davies, MS of typhoid fever.

Reily, J., Pvt., Co. A, absent with leave in Alabama 10/24/63.*

Remington, J., Sgt., Co. H, on detached service in Refugee Camp 2/64.*

Renno/Reno, William F., Pvt., Co. I, age 28, EN 7/21/62, Huntsville, AL, born Jefferson Co., AL, farmer, sick in hospital at Nashville, TN 12/12/62, discharged 3/2/63 due to disability by order of Gen. Roscrans.
Certificate of Disability is mixed in with files of John Reynolds and states he was born in Coffee Co., AL.

Reny, W.R., Co. F, detached on secret service.*

Reyburn, John F., Pvt., Co. D, age 18, EN 6/1/63, Glendale, MS, POW 10/26/63 from Vincent's Crossroads, returned 12/63, sick in hospital at Memphis, TN 2/27/64, MO 6/16/64, Decatur, AL.
(Buried Kirk Cemetery, Hwy 57 West, McNairy Co., TN.)[143]

Reynolds, John H.,(J.A. & J.R.), Pvt/Corp., Co. C, age 40, EN 1/1/64, Corinth, MS, MI 3/10/64, Memphis, TN, born Richmond, VA, farmer, discharge furnished as of 10/20/65.

Reynolds, Memory C., Pvt., Co. H, age 36, EN 2/1/65, Stevenson, AL, MI 4/5/65, Nashville, TN, born Greenville Dist., SC, farmer, MO 10/20/65, Huntsville, AL.

Reynolds, Pleasant/Pleasenton, Pvt., Co. C, age 21, EN 12/15/62, Corinth, MS, born Franklin Co., AL, POW 10/26/63. No further information.

Rhoads, William W., (Cards filed with William W. Roads).

Rhone, John R., Pvt., Co. K, age 40, EN & MI 7/24/62, Huntsville, AL, born Walton Co., GA, died 10/15/62 of rubeola in Hospital #14, Nashville, TN.

Ribourn, E.A., Co. D, AWOL June & July 1863.*

Ricard, James M., Pvt., Co. B, age 18, EN 1/1/63, Glendale, MS, MI 1/22/63, Corinth, MS, served as nurse in hospital, MO 1/22/64, Memphis, TN.

Rice, F.F., Pvt., Co. D, EN 7/1/63 at Glendale, MS.*

Rich, John R., Pvt/Sgt., Co. L, age 18, EN & MI 8/1/64, Rome, GA, born Cherokee Co., AL, farmer, appt. 1st Sgt. 7/1/65, MO 10/20/65, Huntsville, AL.

Richards, John G., Pvt., Co. K&A, age 43, EN 12/5/62, Glendale, MS, MI 12/31/62, Corinth, MS, born Lawrence, SC, farmer, died 5/3/63 (or 4/27/63), at hospital in Corinth, MS.

Richards, Thornton M., Pvt., Co. G, age 18, EN 3/10/64 & MI 4/13/64, Decatur, AL, born Cass Co., GA, sick in hospital at Decatur, AL 5/1/64. No further information.

Richardson, C. Madison, Pvt., Co. G, age 18, EN 6/8/63, Chewalla, TN, deserted 6/20/63, from Chewalla.

Richardson/Richards, John W., Corp., Co. M, age 20, EN 9/18/63, Chewalla, TN, MI 12/29/63, Corinth, MS, born Tishomingo Co., MS, farmer, sick in hospital at Memphis, TN 1/28/64, POW 3/10/65 Blakely Crossroads, SC, discharged 6/26/65 from Camp Chase, OH.

Richardson, Thomas (L.T./T.S.), Pvt., Co. B, age 18, EN 4/7/64 & MI 4/13/64, Decatur, AL, born Cherokee Co., SC, farmer, left sick in hospital at Decatur, AL 4/17/64, MO 10/20/65, Huntsville, AL.

Rickets, Brazilla/Barzilla, Pvt/Corp., Co. C, age 29, EN 1/20/63 & MI 1/25/63, Corinth, MS, born Henderson, TN, farmer, appt. Corp. 4/10/63, appt. Sgt. 12/19/63, MO 1/31/64, Memphis, TN.

Rickets, William, Pvt/Corp., Co. H, age 21, EN 3/1/65, Stevenson, AL, MI 4/5/65, Nashville, TN, born Haywood Co., NC, farmer, appt. Corp. 4/1/65, deserted 9/6/65 from Blountsville, AL with 2 Colt pistols, sabre & equipment.

Ricord, William S., Pvt., Co. B, age 34, EN 3/1/63, Glendale, MS, born Newberry, SC, farmer, discharged 12/12/63 due to disability. (Age shown as 18, 34, & 38).

Riddles, Thomas S., Pvt., Co. K, age 29, EN & MI 7/24/62, Huntsville AL, born Madison Co., AL, farmer, on courier post 1/27/63 at Reedyville, TN, MO 7/19/65, Nashville, TN.

Riedis/Redus, George F., Pvt/Sgt., Co. M, age 25, EN 12/12/63, Camp Davies, MS, MI 12/19/63, Corinth, MS, born Marion Co., AL, farmer, appt. Sgt. 2/1/64, died 3/14/64 in hospital at Memphis, TN of typhoid pneumonia.

Riggett, William, Co. F, absent sick in US General Hospital 4/65.*

Riggs, George, Pvt., Co. G, age 18, EN 4/24/64, Mooresville, AL, born Franklin Co., AL, farmer, died 5/14/64 of measles in hospital at Bridgeport, AL. (Buried Grave H-577, Chattanooga National Cemetery.)

Riggs, James A., Pvt., Co. K, age 18, EN & MI 7/24/62, Huntsville, AL, (or 7/12/62 in Decatur, AL), born Morgan Co., AL, farmer, died 12/13/62 in Hospital #12 at Nashville, TN. (Buried in Grave B-6201 in Nashville National Cemetery.)

Riggs, John W., Pvt/Corp., Co. G, age 24, EN 4/12/64, Decatur, AL, MI Rome, GA, born Morgan Co., AL, farmer, appt. Corp. 7/1/65, MO 10/20/65, Huntsville, AL.

Rickard, (Cards filed with Rackard).

Rikard, William F., Pvt., Co. A, age 18, EN 1/9/64, Camp Davies, MS, MI 2/5/64, born Franklin Co., AL, farmer, sick in hospital at Savannah, GA 2/5/65, returned to duty 4/11/65, MO 10/20/65, Huntsville, AL.

Riley, James, Pvt., Co. F, age 32, EN 5/25/63, Memphis, TN, MI 8/7/63, Corinth, MS, born Marsels(?), France, machinist, deserted 10/28/63 from Glendale, MS, returned 7/8/64, MO 10/25/64, Rome, GA.

Riley, John, Pvt., Co. C, deserted 12/26/63 from Nashville, TN, General Hospital #2 (Union Prisoner).*

Riley, John, Pvt., Co. F, straggler, 11/63, Glendale, MS, arrested 4/7/64, Louisville, KY, no voucher issued from this office. States he is a paroled prisoner.*

Riley, John, Pvt., Co. F, arrested 4/17/64 at the Shoals, White River, Ind. by Phil Brown (citizen), delivered at this office April 18, 1864. He having stolen a horse. He states he was taken prisoner by the rebels near Iuka, MS.*

Ringsley, William J., Pvt., Co. E, died 4/1/63 of typhoid pneumonia.*

Ripley, Francis M., Pvt., Co. A, age 27, EN & MI 9/6/64, Rome, GA, born Calhoun Co., AL, POW 3/27/65 near Faison's Depot, Mount Olive, NC. No further information.

Ringold, H.C., Pvt., Co. H, on daily duty as company cook.*

Rivers, Emery, Under Cook, Co. E, (Colored), age 28, EN & MI 10/1/64, Rome, GA, born Gainsville, GA, farmer, also served as teamster, MO 10/20/65, Huntsville, AL. (MO Roll states age 19).

Roach, Jonathan, Pvt., Co. M, age 47, EN 11/18/63, Camp Davies, MS, MI 12/29/63, Corinth, MS, born Cherokee Co., NC, farmer, POW 12/5/63 from LaGrange, TN, MO 5/20/65, Nashville, TN.

Roach, Joseph, Pvt., Co. M, age 17, EN 10/30/63, Glendale, MS, MI 12/29/63, Corinth, MS, born Winston Co., AL, farmer, MO 10/20/65, Huntsville, AL.

Roads, William W., Pvt., Co. C, age 24, EN & MI 3/10/64, Memphis, TN, born Henderson Co., TN, farmer, deserted 3/20/64 from Memphis with Remington revolver and equipment.

Roberson, Daniel R., Pvt., Co. H, age 35, EN 10/17/63, Glendale, MS, sick in Adams USA Hospital at Memphis, TN 1/20/64, returned to duty 4/9/64, MO 10/24/64, Rome, GA.

Roberson/Robinson/Robertson, William N., Pvt., Co. F, age 31, EN 6/27/63 & MI 7/21/63, Corinth, MS, born St. Clair Co., AL, farmer, sick in Gayoso USA Hospital at Memphis, TN 2/15/64, MO 7/2/64.

Roberts, A.G., Pvt., Co. D, deserted 12/1/63.*

Roberts, Henry M., Corp/Pvt., Co. B, age 18, EN 1/5/63, Glendale, MS, MI 1/22/63, Corinth, MS, appt. Corp. 1/22/63, MO 1/22/64, Memphis, TN.

Roberts, Isaac, Under Cook, Co. M, (Colored), age 21, EN 1/9/65, Savannah, GA, MI 10/16/65, Huntsville, AL, born Chatham Co., GA, teamster, farmer, MO 10/20/65, Huntsville, AL.

Robertson, A.R., Pvt., Co. H, on daily duty as company cook.*

Robertson, J.H., Co. F, absent sick in US General Hospital June 1865-August 1865, "absent sick in US General Hospital whereabouts not known at this time 9/65."*

Robertson, Mathew, Pvt., Co. E, age 44, EN & MI 10/4/64, Rome, GA, born Henry Co., GA, farmer, in hospital 9/1/65, no discharge furnished.

Robertson, R.B., Pvt., Co. H, discharged by reason of expiration of term of service 10/25/64, Rome, GA.*

Robertson, William C.S., Pvt., Co. E, age 18, EN & MI 9/1/64, Rome, GA, born Heard, GA, farmer, MO 10/20/65, Huntsville, AL.

Robins, William M., Pvt., Co. L, age 32, EN 4/7/65, Stevenson, AL, MI 4/18/65, Nashville, TN, born Walker Co., AL, farmer, MO 10/20/65, Huntsville, AL.

Robinson, John B., Pvt., Co. B, age 18, EN 2/6/64, Pulaski, TN, MI 3/27/64, Decatur, AL, born Franklin Co., AL, farmer, in hospital at Wilmington, NC 3/15/65, MO 10/20/65, Huntsville, AL.

Robison/Robinson, George, Pvt., Co. D, EN 2/15/63, Glendale, MS, born Marion Co., AL, sick in hospital at Jackson, TN 4/7/63, died 11/9/63 in Corinth, MS from measles.

Robison/Robinson, James, Pvt., Co. D, EN 2/15/63, Glendale, MS, died 6/15/63 at Refugee Camp at Jackson, TN.

Robison/Robinson, John, Pvt., Co. D, EN 2/1/63, Glendale, MS, died 5/15/63 at Refugee Camp at Jackson, TN.

Robison/Robinson, William, Pvt., Co. D, age 18, EN 2/15/63, Glendale, MS, MI 3/28/63, Corinth, MS, born Marion Co., AL, sick in Refugee Camp at Corinth 4/7/63, discharged 12/29/63 due to disability.

Rocklan, J.M., Pvt., Co. D, absent sick in Gen. Hospital 7/18/63.*

Roden, Raven/Rowen M., Pvt., Co. D, EN 2/1/63, Glendale, MS, MI 2/4/63, Corinth, MS, deserted 3/22/63 from Glendale.

Roden, Vincent S., Pvt., Co. L, in Adams USA Hospital at Memphis, TN 2/9/64, returned to duty 3/27/64.
No further information.

Roden, H., Pvt., Co. A, absent with leave in Alabama 10/24/63.*

Roden, R.M., Co. D, AWOL 3/22/63.*

Rogers/Rodgers, Augustus P., Pvt., Co. G, age 23, EN 4/13/63, Chewalla, TN, born Tippah Co., MS, farmer, died 6/13/63 in hospital at Corinth, MS.

Rogers/Rodgers, George J., Pvt., Co. G, age 18, EN 5/12/63, Chewalla, TN, deserted 6/25/63 from Glendale, MS.

Rogers, George W., Pvt., Co. G, age 16, EN 4/15/63, Chewalla, TN, MO 11/26/63, Memphis, TN.

Rogers, James M., Sr., Pvt., Co. G, age 43, EN 5/7/63, Chewalla, TN, MO 11/26/63, Memphis, TN.

Rogers, James M., Jr., Pvt., Co. G, age 17, EN 5/17/63, Chewalla, TN, MO 11/26/63, Memphis, TN.

Rogers, Jefferson, Pvt., Co. G, absent sick at Chewalla, TN 7/3/63, deserted 9/1/63 at Glendale, MS.*

Rogers, Julius M.(J.W.), Pvt., Co. D, EN 4/25/63, Glendale, MS, MI 4/28/63, Corinth, MS, born Buncombe, NC, WIA 10/26/63 and sent to hospital at Memphis, TN, discharged 6/18/64.

Rogers, M., Pvt., Co. G, POW 2/1/64 from Corinth, MS and paroled 3/3/65.*

Rogers, Robert C., Pvt., Co. D, EN 4/26/63, Glendale, MS, MI 4/28/64, Corinth, MS, POW 6/3/63, shot while prisoner by order of Roddy, CSA. (Died July 4, 1863, buried Grave #B-3330, Corinth National Cemetery.)

Roler/Roller, Christopher C., Pvt., Co. B, captured May 1864, exchanged POW delivered at Savannah, GA Nov or Dec 1864, mustered for US Bounty, discharged 5/64 by reason of exp. of service, captured before leaving his post or station of the regiment.*

Roller, Columbus C., Pvt., Co. B, age 38, EN 12/15/62, Glendale, MS, MI 12/31/62, Corinth, MS, POW 10/26/63 from Vincent's Crossroads, MS, MO 12/27/63, Camp Davies, MS.
    NOTE: Christopher Columbus Roller was born about 1825 in AL and first married Catherine Jane Nichols, sister of James and Jasper Nichols who also served in this regiment. After her death he married Catherine Stout in Wayne Co., TN and moved to Bell Co., TX in the late 1800's and is buried at Temple, TX.[144]

Rollin, William, Co. C, absent in arrest at Corinth, MS since 11/22/63.*

Rollins, George W., Pvt., Co. K&A, age 20, EN 11/5/62 & MI 12/31/62, Corinth, MS, MO 11/28/63, Memphis, TN.

Rollins, John H., Pvt/Bugler, Co. K&A, age 23, EN 11/5/62 & MI 12/31/62, Corinth, MS, MO 11/28/63, Memphis, TN.

Romines, William L., Pvt., Co. L, age 18, EN 10/17/63, Glendale, MS, born Morgan Co., AL, farmer, on detached service as Prov. Guard at Hd. Qtrs. 16th AC, MO 7/19/65, Nashville, TN.

Rose, A.C. Pvt., Co. B, age 42, EN 2/23/64 Pulaski, TN, MI 3/27/64, Decatur, AL, born Habersham Co., GA, blacksmith, detached as scout for Gen. Dodge 3/28/64, deserted 6/1/65 while on scout.

Ross, John W., Pvt., Co. F, age 23, EN 9/15/63, Glendale, MS, MI 7/27/64, Rome, GA, born Tippah Co., MS, deserted 10/24/64 from Rome, GA with arms, horse, saddle & equipment.

Ross, William J. (or James W./James M.), Pvt., Co. E, EN & MI 2/1/63, Corinth, MS, on detached service as teamster at Vicksburg, MS 1/25/64, MO 3/1/64, Memphis, TN.

Rowell, William J., Pvt., Co. K, age 38, EN & MI 7/24/62, Huntsville, AL, born Randolph Co., AL, farmer, left in Marion Co., AL recruiting 10/24/63, on detached service as teamster in Sherman's expedition at Vicksburg, MS 1/24/64, POW 3/10/65 from Monroe's Crossroads, near Fayetteville, NC, discharged 6/12/65 at Camp Chase, OH.

Rowland, James W., Pvt., Co. G, temporarily attached from 11th Illinois Cavalry.

Rowland, John H., Pvt., Co. G, temporarily attached from 11th Illinois Cavalry.

Rowland, William T., Sgt., Co. G, temporarily attached from 11th Illinois Cavalry.

Rumage, Calvin/Charles L., Pvt., Co. H, age 29, EN 10/17/63, Glendale, MS, POW 10/26/63 from Vincent's Crossroads, near Bay Springs, MS, paroled at Mobile, AL 11/2/63. No MO date.

Rumage, Francis, Pvt., Co. H, age 21, EN 10/17/63, Glendale, MS, MO 10/24/64, Rome, GA.

Rumage, John D., Pvt., Co. H, age 34 (or 44), EN 10/17/63, Glendale, MS, MI 2/24/63, Memphis, TN, born Maury Co., TN, farmer, deserted 11/21/63 from Camp Davies, MS, released from arrest and returned to duty, sick at Evansville, Indiana 5/15/64, MO 10/24/64, Rome, GA. (Letter in file states he enlisted without being discharged from 7th Regt. Cav., Kansas Vols.

Russell, George W., Pvt., Co. K, age 31, EN & MI 7/31/62, Huntsville, AL, born Morgan Co., AL, farmer, died 11/23/62 in camp at Nashville, TN after discharge for disability was issued. (Buried in Grave A-5223 in Nashville National Cemetery.)

Russell, J., Pvt., Co. D, EN 4/19/64, Decatur, AL.*

Russell, I.B., Co. F, absent POW 3/10/65.*

Russell, James J., Pvt., Co. K, age 25, EN & MI 7/31/62, Huntsville, AL, born Morgan Co., AL, farmer, died 10/27/62 in Hospital #6 in Nashville, TN of pneumonia/measles. (Buried in Grave C-7110 in Nashville National Cemetery with death date shown as 11/2/62.)

Russell, Jeremiah, Pvt., Co. K, age 44, EN & MI 7/31/62, Huntsville, AL, born Madison, GA, farmer, died 9/13/62 in Hospital #8 at Nashville, TN. (Buried in Grave A-4788 in Nashville National Cemetery.)

Russell, John, Pvt., age 19, EN 4/10/65, Stevenson, AL, MI 4/18/65, Nashville, TN, born Knox Co., GA, farmer. No further information.

Russell, John F., Pvt., Co. K, age 34, EN & MI 7/31/62, Huntsville, AL, born Morgan Co., AL, farmer, sent to hospital at Richmond, VA 5/12/62 while POW, paroled POW 5/13/63, died 5/19/63 at Richmond. (Buried in Richmond National Cemetery, VA.)

Russell, Josiah, Pvt., Co. K, age 21, EN & MI 7/31/62, Huntsville, AL, born Forsyth, GA, farmer, died 6/11/63 at Camp Chase, OH of double pneumonia.

Rymer, James, Blacksmith, Co. G, temporarily attached from 11th Illinois Cavalry.

Rymer, Joel S., Pvt., Co. G, absent sick in hospital at Memphis, TN 10/63.*

Safford, (?), Co. A, absent sick in General Hospital 10/64.*

Sagle, David C., Co. L, absent with leave 10/18/63.*

Salyers, William W., Pvt/Sgt., Co. B, age 24, EN 3/10/64 & MI 3/27/64, Decatur, AL, born Union Co., AR, farmer, promoted to 1st Sgt. 7/22/65, MO 10/20/65, Huntsville, AL.

Sanderson, Jasper N., Pvt/Sgt., Co. A&K, age 21, EN 10/13/62 & MI 10/14/62, Corinth, MS, promoted to Sgt. 7/1/63, MO 10/19/63, LaGrange, TN or Glendale, MS.

Sanderson, John/James M., Pvt., Co. D, age 23, EN 2/15/63, Glendale, MS, MI 4/28/63, Corinth, MS, born Marion Co., AL, admitted to Gayoso Hospital at Memphis, TN 1/25/64, returned to duty 4/21/64, was readmitted 4/23/64 and died 6/14/64 of inflammation of the brain. (Buried in Memphis National Cemetery.)

Sandlin, Daniel J., Co. I, age 27, born Morgan Co., AL, farmer, EN 10/10/63, Glendale, MS.*

Sandlin, Jesse, Co. I, age 23, born Morgan Co., AL, farmer, EN 10/10/63, Glendale, MS.*

Sandlin, Jesse, Pvt., Co. I, EN 2/1/64 at Memphis, TN, deserted 3/1/64 from Memphis, TN.*

Sanford, J., Pvt., Co. D, on daily duty as teamster 11/63.*

Sanford, Michael, Pvt., Co. D, in Cumberland USA Hospital at Nashville, TN March & April 1864.*

Sanford, N., Pvt., Co. D, on daily duty as teamster.*

Sanford, William A., Sgt. Co. E, age 25, EN 3/1/63, Glendale, MS, MI 3/1/63, Corinth, MS, wounded 10/26/63 at Vincent's Crossroads and in hospital at Memphis, TN, MO 3/1/64, Memphis, TN.

Sanner, William M., Pvt., Co. G, age 17, EN 7/11/63, Glendale, MS, MO 11/26/63, Memphis, TN.

Sansing, James, Pvt., Co. H, died 2/5/63 of pneumonia at Huntsville, AL.*

Sasser, John B., Pvt., Co. G, temporarily attached from 11th Illinois Cavalry.

Sasett, Thomas, Pvt., Co. D, company cook 4/64.*

Saulter, R., Pvt., Co. L, absent POW 10/26/63.*

Savage, Temple F., Sgt., Co. E, age 26, EN & MI 2/1/63, Corinth, MS, MO 2/1/64, Memphis, TN.

Sawyer, Thomas J., Pvt., Co. D, age 32, EN 8/24/63, Glendale, MS, MI 8/24/63, Corinth, MS, born Richland, SC, farmer, MO 9/24/64, Rome, GA.

Scott, Andrew J., Bugler, Co. F, age 18, EN 6/15/63, Corinth, MS, MI 7/1/63, Corinth, MS, born Tishomingo Co., MS, farmer, MO 7/27/64, Rome, GA.

Scott, George W.C., Sgt., Co. B, age 38, EN 12/23/62, Glendale, MS, appt. Com. Sgt. 1/22/63, deserted 2/28/63, from Glendale, MS.

Scott, John B., Pvt., Co. H, age 43, EN 12/20/64, Stevenson, AL, MI 2/13/65, Nashville, TN, born Spartanburg Dist., SC, farmer, died 5/28/65 in Post Hospital at Huntsville, AL of measles, buried in grave #214 at Huntsville, Cemetery. Residence shown as Jackson Co., AL. (Reinterred Grave #L-528, Chattanooga National Cemetery.)

Scott, Joseph R., Sgt., Co. B, age 21, EN 12/23/62, Glendale, MS, MI 12/31/62, Corinth, MS, appt. Sgt. 1/22/63, MO 12/27/63, Camp Davies, MS.

Scott, Stephen A., Lt/Pvt., Co. B, age 34, EN 12/23/62, Glendale, MS, MI 12/31/62, Corinth, MS, deserted 2/28/63, returned 9/15/63, POW 10/26/63 from Vincent's Crossroads, , MO 12/27/63, Camp Davies, MS.
    NOTE: Stephen Abijah Scott was born April 4, 1828 in Marion Co., AL to Peter Martin Scott and Jane Williams. He married about 1851 to Margaret Ann Davis, daughter of Magness Davis and Beda Joiner. Margaret was born October 30, 1828 in Lauderdale Co., AL and died May 20, 1908 in Jones Co., TX. Their children were: William Joseph, January 25, 1852; Beda Jane, March 24, 1854; Peter Magness, February 15, 1856; John Belford, April 24, 1858; Sarah Izella, February 29, 1860; Laura Fidella, 1862; Stephen Abijah, Jr., 1864; Edith Elizabeth, May 2, 1866; Martha Adline Lou, January 15, 1869; and Ulysses S. "Liss" Scott, June 14, 1873. Stephen died February 1, 1910 in Jones Co., TX after the load shifted on his hay wagon and he was run over. He is buried in Mount Hope Cemetery, Anson, Jones Co., TX.
    The Western Enterprise Newspaper in Jones Co., TX, dated August 31, 1933, gives an account by Edith Elizabeth Scott on the type of house they built after arriving in TX. She stated they rode to Texas in wagons pulled by mules and took several head of cattle, chickens and enough provisions to last two years.
"Father put up an adobe building. It was shinnery logs and dirt. Mortar was made of clay. We had a stick and dirt chimney. The fireplace was of shinnery logs, plastered inside and out with clay. Mother looked up the chimney every night to see if it was afire. It did catch fire several times but it was easily put out. Maybe I should tell more about how the dug-out was built. They dug down four or five feet in the ground making nice walls on either side for a good-sized room. It must have been a good-sized room because it was our living room, dining room and kitchen, and though we were a large family, I do not remember that we seemed crowded.

Well, after the dirt walls were finished, the dug-out was lined with shinnery or black-jack logs. These were built up above the ground for several feet, and the roof was put on. This roof was of split logs, with the smooth side down for a ceiling. The cracks were chinked with grass and mortar. Dirt was put over the roof also, about 6 to 12 inches."[145]

Scroggins, George/John W., Pvt., Co. B, age 18, EN 3/18/64 & MI 3/27/64, Decatur, AL, born Blount Co., AL, farmer, deserted 5/11/64 near Chattanooga, TN with horse, Smith carbine and equipment, deserted 8/15/64 from Rome, GA with Smith carbine and equipment.

Seay, John M., Pvt., Co. E, age 31, EN 8/27/63, Glendale, MS, POW 10/26/63 from Vincent's Crossroads. Notation in file states, "Enlisted in Co. K, 50 Tenn C.S.A. while a prisoner of war; recaptured 5/20/64, while in arms against the U.S. confined at Rock Island, Ill. date not stated where he enlisted in the U.S. Navy. June 19, 1864."

Seftis, S., Pvt., Co. H, absent POW 10/26/63.*

Segar, Thomas J., Pvt., Co. D, absent sick in General Hospital at Memphis, TN 2/1/64.*

Seigle, David, Pvt., Co. D, absent sick in hospital at Nashville, TN 1/63, discharged 2/4/63 at Nashville due to disability.*

Self, Allen J., Pvt., Co. I, age 18, EN & MI 7/21/62, Huntsville, AL, born Walker Co., AL, died 9/3/62 in Hospital #9 at Nashville, TN.

Self, Allen R., Pvt., Co. I, age 49, EN & MI 7/21/62, Huntsville, AL, born Bledsoe Co., TN, farmer, died 10/10/62 in Howard Hospital #4 at Nashville, TN. (Buried in Grave A-4186 in Nashville National Cemetery.)

Self, Benjamin H., Corp., Co. A, age 33, EN 1/1/64, Camp Davies, MS, MI 2/5/64, Memphis, TN, born Jefferson Co., AL, farmer, MO 10/20/65, Huntsville, AL.

Self, Carter H., Pvt., Co. I, age 21, EN 12/21/63, Camp Davies, MS, MO 7/19/65, Nashville, TN.

Self, James T., Pvt., Co. I, age 32, EN 12/21/63, Camp Davies, MS, died 12/3/64 in Stevenson, AL.
        NOTE: James was born about 1833 in Clay, Jefferson Co., AL, married about 1853 to Rebecca (?) and was the son of Nathaniel and Parmelia Loggins Self.

Self, Martin D., Pvt., Co. I, age 20, EN & MI 7/21/62, Huntsville, AL, born Blount Co., AL, farmer, died 10/27/62 in Nashville, TN. (Buried in Grave A-4671 in Nashville National Cemetery.) (Brother to Matthew G. Self, Sr., below.)

Self, Matthew G., Pvt., Co. I, age 26, EN & MI 7/21/62, Huntsville, AL, born Blount Co., AL, farmer, died 10/28/62 in Nashville, TN of acute bronchitis, buried grave #2572, Collys Hill Cemetery. (Location of this old cemetery is unknown, however, there is a M.G. Self buried in Grave A-4768 in Nashville National Cemetery with death date shown as 1/11/63.)

    NOTE: Matthew Gilbert Self was born about 1836 to Allen R. and Nancy Holloway Self and married Adella H. Speegle on August 14, 1853 in Winston Co., AL. Their children were: Winifred Green, born August 15, 1854; David Allen, born February 2, 1856, died December 7, 1896; Louisa A., born February 10, 1858; Jesse Howard, born December 29, 1859, died January 15, 1902; Chesley Sylvanus, born January 14, 1861; and Matthew Gilbert, Jr., born March 14, 1863, died February 7, 1902.[146]

Sellars/Sellers, Richard C., Pvt., Co. C, age 26, EN 1/1/64, Corinth, MS, MI 3/10/64, Memphis, TN, born Carroll Co., TN, farmer, deserted 3/3/64 from Memphis, TN with Remington revolver, Colt pistol & equipment, returned 3/9/64. No further information.

Sellers, Calvin, Pvt., Co. C, age 24, EN 2/1/64, Corinth, MS, born Decatur, TN, farmer, deserted 3/3/64 from Memphis, TN with Remington revolver & equipment, MO 12/27/63, Camp Davies, MS.

Sellers, Hardy, Corp/Sgt., Co. C, age 40, EN 12/1/62 & MI 12/22/62, Corinth, MS, born Perry Co., TN, appt. Corp. 1/1/63, appt. Sgt. 6/10/63, MO 12/17/63, Memphis, TN.

Selvery/Selvey, William H., Pvt., Co. I, age 22, EN & MI 8/26/62, Huntsville, AL, born Lumpkin Co., GA, farmer, MIA 12/29/62 after action at Stone's River, TN, sick in hospital at Nashville, TN 12/30/62. No further information.

Sems, James, teamster, Co. F, deserted 8/27/63 at Glendale, MS.*

Senyard/Sinyard, Henry C., Pvt., Co. I, age 36, EN 10/17/63, Glendale, MS, POW 11/22/63, sick in hospital at Decatur, AL 5/1/64, died on or about 8/24/64 in hospital at Nashville, TN.

    NOTE: Henry Sinyard, Jr. was born about 1827 in Hall Co., GA and married Katherine Mary Ann Tucker, February 6, 1848 in Paulding Co., GA. He was the son of Henry C. Sinyard, Sr., born 19 September 1801 in Pendleton Dist., SC and Dicy Hulsey, born about 1802 in Pendleton Dist. Henry, Jr. migrated to Winston Co., AL with the Tucker family in the early 1860's. His strong abolitionist views led him to become a Union soldier. Children of Henry, Jr. and Katherine Tucker were: Reuben S., born 13 January 1849; William Simpson, born 13 January 1849; Henry, born 1852, died 1863/64; Martha, born 1855, died 1863/64; Mary, born 1857, died 1863/63; and Lucinda, born 1858, died 1863/64. All children were born in Paulding Co., GA.[147]

Settlemires/Suttlemire, David, Pvt., Co. G, age 15, EN 5/4/63, Chewalla, TN, in Union, Church and Overton Hospitals at Memphis, TN between 10/10/63 and 12/29/63 with gunshot wound, severely wounded at Battle of Vincent's Crossroads, discharged 6/3/64, Memphis, TN.

Settlemires/Suttlemire, Gabriel M., Pvt., Co. G, age 17, EN 4/13/63, Chewalla, TN, MO 11/26/63, Memphis, TN.

Settlemires/Suttlemire, Jacob G., Pvt., Co. G, age 43, EN 4/12/63, Chewalla, TN, died 9/14/63 in hospital at Corinth, MS.

Settlemires/Suttlemire, John W., Pvt., Co. G, age 19, EN 5/4/63, Chewalla, TN, MO 11/26/63, Memphis, TN.

Settlemires/Suttlemire, McKinsy, Pvt., Co. G, age 27, EN 3/6/63, Chewalla, TN, rejected by Surgeon Smith and discharged 5/1/63.

Shafer/Shaffer, William B. (W.H.)., Pvt., Co. I, age 18, EN & MI 7/21/62, Huntsville, AL, born Morgan Co., AL, farmer, sick in Hospital #12 at Nashville, TN 9/8/62, died 4/26/63 at Nashville, TN of disease.
Address shown as Summerville, AL and father shown as John Shaffer. (Buried in Grave E-0248 in Nashville National Cemetery.)

Shaffer, John W., Pvt., Co. B, age 44, EN 3/15/64 & MI 3/27/64, Decatur, AL, born Greene Co., TN, farmer, in hospital at Savannah, GA 2/5/65, MO 10/20/65, Huntsville, AL.

Shakle, James K.P., Pvt/Sgt., Co. B, age 18, EN 12/23/62, Glendale, MS, MI 12/31/62, Corinth, MS, appt. Corp. 3/1/63, POW 10/26/63 from Vincent's Crossroads, MO 12/27/63, Camp Davies, MS.

Shanon/Sharon/Shawn, Owen, Under Cook, Co. G, (Colored), age 24, EN 11/4/64, Rome, GA, MI 10/16/65, Huntsville, AL, born Duplin Co., NC, servant, also served as teamster, MO 10/20/65, Huntsville, AL.

Sharp, William H., Pvt/Sgt., Co. M, age 18, EN 11/1/63, Glendale, MS, MI 12/29/63, Corinth, MS, born Marion Co., AL, farmer, promoted to Corp. 8/6/64 and to Sgt. 7/1/65 for good conduct in the field, MO 10/20/65, Huntsville, AL.

Sharpton, Daniel, Pvt., Co. G, age 40, EN 3/28/64 & MI 4/13/64, Decatur, AL, born Edgefield Dist., SC, farmer, died 9/9/64, previous address shown as Winston Co., AL and wife, Elizabeth Sharpton. (Buried in Grave F-3616 in Nashville National Cemetery.)

Sharpton, Joel T., (Cards filed with Joel T. Shopton).

Sharpton, William, Pvt., Co. G, age 18, EN 3/28/64 & MI 4/13/64, Decatur, AL, born Gwinnett Co., GA, farmer, sick in hospital at Savannah, GA 2/5/65, returned to duty 3/10/65, MO 10/20/65, Huntsville, AL.

Shatts, William Thornton, (Cards filed with William T. Shots).

Shaw, George W., Pvt., Co. F, age 46, EN 4/8/63, Corinth, MS, born Hall Co., GA, farmer, served as nurse in hospital, MO 4/7/64, Decatur, AL.

Shaw, John A.W., Pvt., Co. A, age 27, EN 9/8/62, Iuka, MS, MI 10/1/62, Corinth, MS, born Lincoln Co., NC, farmer, MO 9/16/63, Corinth, MS.

Shaw, John W., Pvt., Co. G, age 32, EN 5/7/63, Chewalla, TN, sick in hospital at Corinth, MS 7/26/63, served as asst. blacksmith, deserted 11/18/63 from Memphis, TN.

Shay, John O., Pvt/Sgt., Co. B, age 23, EN 2/22/64, Pulaski, TN, MI 3/27/64, Decatur, AL, born Lawrence Co., TN, farmer, appt. Sgt. 8/1/64, sent to hospital at Savannah, GA from Sister's Ferry, GA, MO 10/20/65, Huntsville, AL.

Sheets, John T., Corp., Co. I, age 21, EN & MI 7/21/62, Huntsville, AL, died 10/1/62 in Hospital #14 in Nashville, TN. (Buried in Grave A-4139 in Nashville National Cemetery as John J. Sheets and death date shown as 10/2/62.)

Shefen/Shefer, John, Pvt., Co. B, on daily duty as nurse in hospital.*

Shehorn/Shellborne, Peter Elisha, (P.L.), Pvt., Co. C, age 18, EN & MI 3/10/64, Memphis, TN, born Tishomingo Co., MS, farmer, died 6/7/64 in Hospital #11at Nashville, TN of measles/smallpox. (Buried Grave #Q-59, Nashville National Cemetery.)

Shelton, David, Pvt., Co. I, age 18, EN 10/17/63, Glendale, MS, born Floyd Co., GA, farmer, MO 7/19/65, Nashville, TN.

Shelton, Walter, Pvt., Co. B, age 23, EN & MI 3/27/64, Decatur, AL, born Floyd Co., GA, farmer, left sick in hospital at Decatur, AL 4/17/64, discharge furnished on MO of organization.

Sinyard, Henry C., filed under Henry C. Senyard

Shook, Henry, Pvt., Co. C, age 36, EN 2/20/63 & MI 2/26/63, Corinth, MS, born Green Co., AL, farmer, discharged 7/16/63 due to disability.

Shook, Marcus L., Pvt., Co. C, age 19 (or 16), EN 2/20/63 & MI 2/25/63, Corinth, MS, MO 2/20/64, Memphis, TN.

Shook, Michael, Pvt., Co. C, age 28, EN 12/3/63 & MI 12/22/63, Corinth, MS, born Green Co., AL, farmer, MO 12/17/63, Memphis, TN.

Shook, Noah S., Pvt., Co. C, age 21, EN 2/20/63 & MI 2/25/63, Corinth, MS, born Tishomingo Co., MS, POW 6/28/63. No further information.

Shopton/Sharpton, Joel T. (or G.), Pvt., Co. G, age 18, EN 3/28 64 & MI 4/13/64, Decatur, AL, born Gwinnett Co., GA, farmer, died 5/18/64 in hospital at Bridgeport, AL of measles, buried in grave #243 at Field Hospital Burial Plot. (Reinterred Grave #H-548, Chattanooga National Cemetery.)

Shopton, William, (Cards filed with William Sharpton).

Short, James J., Pvt., Co. H, age 18, EN 5/15/65, Huntsville, AL, MI 5/20/65, Nashville, TN, born Walker Co., AL, farmer, sick in hospital at Huntsville, AL 7/19/65, MO at Post Hospital 8/15/65.

Shots, Jabez G., Pvt/Sgt., Co. D, EN 2/1/63, Glendale, MS, MI 2/4/63, Corinth, MS, deserted 3/23/63 from Glendale, sick in hospital at Corinth 7/7/63, promoted to Sgt. 12/3/63, MO 2/4/64, Memphis, TN.

Shots, William, Co. D, AWOL 3/23/63, not heard from.*

Shots, William P., Pvt., Co. D, EN 2/1/63, Glendale, MS, MI 2/4/63, Corinth, MS, deserted 4/20/63 from Glendale.

Shots, William Thornton., Pvt., Co. D, EN 2/1/63, Glendale, MS, MI 2/4/63, Corinth, MS, deserted 4/20/63 from Glendale, MO 2/4/64, Memphis, TN. (This is possibly the same person as above.)

Shott, George W., Pvt., Co. F, nurse in regimental hospital 12/63.*

Shotts, George S.C., Sgt., Co. B, age 20, EN 12/23/62, Glendale, MS, MI 12/31/62, Corinth, MS, appt. Sgt. 1/22/63, POW 10/26/63 from Vincent's Crossroads, MO 12/27/63, Camp Davies, MS.

Shoubert/Shobert/Shoeburt, David J. (or I or C.), Pvt., Co. L, age 22, EN 9/25/63, Fayette Co., AL, MI 9/25/63, Glendale, MS, born St. Clair Co., AL, farmer, sick in hospital at Memphis, TN 2/26/64, sick in hospital at Jeffersonville, IN 7/16/64, MO 9/28/64, Rome, GA.

Shuffield, Marcus N., Pvt., Co. M, age 19, EN & MI 10/9/64, Rome, GA, born Paulding Co., GA, farmer, deserted 11/8/64 from Rome, GA with horse, Smith carbine, Colt revolver & equipment.

Shurtleff, Jude H., Capt/Major, Co. D, (F&S), age 27, EN 5/1/63, Glendale, MS, MI 5/1/63, Corinth, MS, promoted from 1st Sgt., Co. A, 57th Illinois Inf., appt. Major 7/1/64, Topograph Engineer, resigned 6/21/65.
NOTE: Jude Hamilton Shurtleff was born near Buffalo, NY on January 6, 1834 and was the third child of Chester Ballew Shurtleff and Miranda Adams. He enlisted October 9, 1861 in Company A, 57th IL Inf. in Mendota, IL and was mustered into service December 26, 1861 in Chicago, IL and was an engineer by trade. After the war, Jude returned to IL, married Mary Jane Wyrick on December 23, 1866, and emigrated to Vermillion, SD in 1870. He also lived in Yankton and Parker. He had a mail and passenger stageline from Yankton to Sioux Falls and was a county commissioner. His children were: William Arthur, born October 7, 1867 in Mendota, IL; Julia Imus, born October 12, 1868 in Mendota, IL; and Sidney Hamilton, born December 19, 1876 in Hurley, SD. He died in Parker, SD on June 30, 1924. The funeral was on July 3rd with the local Grand Army of the Republic as the Honor Guard and Sons of Union Veterans as pallbearers. The services were

conducted by his son, Sidney Hamilton. Burial was in Rosehill Cemetery, Parker, SD.[148]

Sides, John M., Pvt., Co. G, age 18, EN 3/21/64, & MI 4/13/64, Decatur, AL, born Walker Co., AL, farmer, died 6/6/64 in Post. Hospital at Decatur, AL of fever.

Sides, John R., Pvt., Co. G, age 18, EN 3/21/64 & MI 4/13/64, Decatur, AL, born Walker Co., AL, farmer, died 5/23/64 in Post Hospital at Decatur, AL of fever.

Sides, William A., Pvt., Co. A, age 18, EN 1/11/64, Camp Davies, MS, MI 2/5/64, Memphis, TN, born Atalla Co., MS, farmer, sick in hospital Jeffersonville, IN 6/22/64, MO 10/20/65, Huntsville, AL.

Sikes, Josiah A., Pvt., Co. E, age 46, EN & MI 9/1/64, Rome, GA, born Monroe Co., GA, farmer, deserted 8/3/65 from Moulton, AL with arms, horse and equipment, charges of desertion removed 4/17/73 by War Dept. and discharge issued as of 6/28/65.

Sikes, William M. (or W.), Pvt., Co. E, age 18, EN & MI 9/1/64, Rome, GA, born Troope Co., GA, farmer, MO 10/20/65, Huntsville, AL.

Sillivan, Eli, Pvt., Co. B, age 46, EN 12/20/62, Glendale, MS, MI 12/31/62, Corinth, MS, camp cook, MO 12/27/63, Camp Davies, MS.

Simes, (?), Co. A, detached recruiting in Decatur, AL 10/64.*

Simes, H.H. (or I.), Pvt., Co. D, on extra daily duty 10/64.*

Simes/Sims, Robert M., Pvt/Sgt., Co. F, age 20, EN 8/1/64, & MI 10/17/64, Rome, GA, born Yazoo Co., MS, farmer, appt. Sgt. 7/1/65, MO 10/20/65, Huntsville, AL.

Simms, William R., Pvt., Co. A, EN 2/23/64 in Memphis, TN.*

Simpson, Alexander, Pvt., Co. H, age 31, EN 12/23/64, Decatur, AL, MI 2/13/65, Nashville, TN, born Buchanan Co., TN, carpenter, sick in hospital at Huntsville, AL 5/10/65, MO 10/20/65, Huntsville, AL.

Simpson, John W., Pvt., Co. B, age 43, EN 2/3/64, Pulaski, TN, MI 3/27/64, Decatur AL, born Lawrence Co., TN, farmer, sent to hospital in Nashville, TN 11/10/64 from Rome, GA, deserted 10/1/65 from Courtland, AL, charge of desertion removed 9/13/91 by War Dept. and discharge issued as of 10/1/65.

Simpson, Thomas B., Pvt., Co. D, EN 5/1/64, Decatur, AL, born Tuscaloosa Co., AL, farmer, deserted 7/10/65 from Huntsville, AL.

Simpson/Simson, Wiley, Pvt., Co. H, age 23, EN 10/16/63, Glendale, MS, MO 10/24/64, Rome, GA.

Sims/Simms, George W., Pvt., Co. H, age 25, EN 10/16/63, Glendale, MS, MO 10/24/64, Rome, GA.

Sims, William, Pvt/Corp., Co. H, age 38, EN 10/17/63, Glendale, MS, MO 10/24/64, Rome, GA.

Singleton, William, Undercook, Co. C, (Colored), age 36, EN 12/1/64, Monticello, GA, MI 10/17/65, Huntsville, AL, born Thompson Co., GA, farmer, MO 10/20/65, Huntsville, AL.

Sisson, Joseph F., Pvt., Co. H, age 38, EN 9/13/63, Glendale, MS, MO 9/29/64, Rome, GA.

Sisson, Oliver B., Pvt., Co. H, age 22, EN 9/14/63, Glendale, MS, POW 10/26/63 from Vincent's Crossroads, died 9/13/64 at Andersonville, GA while POW. (Buried in Grave #8728, Andersonville National Cemetery.)

Sisson, Thomas, Pvt., Co. H, age 25, EN 9/13/63, Glendale, MS, deserted 11/1/64 from Glendale, MS.

Sisson, William R. (or K.), Pvt., Co. H, age 40, EN 9/17/63, Glendale, MS, deserted while on detached service at Refugee Camp at Memphis, TN.

Sitton, Mikiel, Co. L, no EN or MI date, died 11/18/63 at Post Hospital in Corinth, MS.

Skinner, John, Pvt/Corp., Co. G, age 34, EN & MI 4/10/64, Rome, GA, born Coweta Co., GA, farmer, deserted 8/28/65 from Decatur, AL, charges of desertion removed 3/15/89 stating he rejoined his company 8/29/65, MO 10/20/65, Huntsville, AL.

Skinner, Richard J., Pvt., Co. G, age 22, EN 10/14/64, Decatur, AL, MI 11/10/64, Rome, GA, born Randolph Co., AL, farmer, MO 10/20/65, Huntsville, AL.

Slaughter, George W., Lt., Co. K&A, age 26, EN 12/5/62, Glendale, MS, promoted to 2nd Lt. 12/18/62, MO 12/17/63, Memphis, TN.

Smalling, Ezekiel, Pvt/Sgt., Co. A, age 18, EN 9/8/62, Iuka, MS, MI 10/1/62, Corinth, MS, born Morgan Co., AL, farmer, promoted to Corp. 5/1/63, MO 9/16/63, Corinth, MS.

Smalling, George W., Pvt., Co. B, age 18, EN 3/22/64 & MI 3/27/64, Decatur, AL, born Morgan Co., AL, WIA 11/23/64 at Oconee River, Balls Ferry, GA, died 1/4/65 Beaufort, SC. (Buried in Sec. 53, Grave #6357, Beaufort National Cemetery.)

Smalling, John P., Pvt/Corp., Co. A, age 22, EN & MI 3/30/63, Glendale, MS, promoted to Corp. 7/1/63, MO 12/22/63, Memphis, TN.

Smallwood, G.M., Pvt., Co. F, absent at home near Corinth, MS 9/63, absent left sick at home 10/10/63.*

Smallwood, Joseph G., Pvt., Co. C, age 24, EN 5/1/64, Decatur, AL, MI 10/17/65, Huntsville, AL, born Pike Co., IL, farmer, on detached service recruiting in AL 5/1/64, MO 10/20/65, Huntsville, AL.

Smith, Abner, Pvt/Sgt., Co. H, age 35, EN 10/17/63, Glendale, MS, promoted to Sgt. 7/1/64, sick in hospital at Rome, GA 7/20/64, MO 10/24/64, Rome, GA.

Smith, Andrew J., Pvt/Corp., Co. G, age 22, EN 3/10/64 & MI 4/13/64, Decatur, AL, born MS, deserted 11/13/64 from Rome, GA with arms, horse & equipment while on scout, reduced to ranks for disobedience of orders and neglect of duties, "did not accompany the regiment when it was expecting to meet the enemy".

Smith, Allen, Sgt., Co. K, age 68, EN 6/26/62, Limestone Co., AL, born Pitt Co., NC, transferred from Co. K, 21st Ohio Vols., blacksmith, died 10/15/62 in Hospital #14 at Nashville, TN of rubeola. (Buried in Grave #A-4748, Nashville National Cemetery with death date shown as 10/14/62.)

Smith, Dallas B., Lt., Co. E, age 20, EN & MI 1/1/65, Savannah, GA, born Randolph Co., AL, clerk, on special duty commanding 1/23/65, MO 10/20/65, Huntsville, AL.

Smith, Daniel, Pvt., Co. H, EN 10/18/63 at Glendale, MS, absent sick in hospital at Memphis 2/10/64, died of disease 8/6/64 at Decatur, AL.* (Buried Grave #E-109, Corinth National Cemetery.)

Smith, Daniel M., Pvt/Sgt., Co. I, age 35, EN & MI 7/21/62, Huntsville, AL, born Gwinnett, GA, farmer, appt. Sgt. 9/1/63, on furlough in Illinois 12/18/63, MO 7/19/65, Nashville, TN.

Smith, David, Pvt., Co. H, age 29, EN 10/17/63, Glendale, MS, born Fayette Co., AL, died 7/10/64 at home.

Smith, David D., Capt. Co. K, age 37, EN & MI 7/24/62, Huntsville, AL, transferred from Co. F, 21st Ohio Vols., born Henry Co., GA, farmer, POW 5/3/63 while on Streight's Raid and sent to Richmond, VA, died 4/18/65 of pneumonia at Officers USA Hospital in Annapolis, MD, originally buried in Grave #1720 (or 1744) at Ash Grove US Cemetery, wife shown as living in Marion Co., GA.
    NOTE: David D. Smith married Sarah (?) on September 15, 1849 in Alabama and had the following children: William, 1851; Martha, 1853; Nancy, 1858; and John, 1861. Sarah died in Centralia, Marion Co., IL on June 7, 1866.[149]
    David was captured by the enemy while on Col. Streight's Raid May 3, 1863 and died of pneumonia April 18, 1865 while prisoner in Annapolis, Maryland.
    The following letter written by David D. Smith, while he was a POW, was found at the National Archives by Robert L. Willett, Jr. and he has so graciously shared it.
    "Libby Prison Richmond Var Decr 13th 63

Dear Wife

this will inform you that my health is excellent & I hope it may reach you & the children enjoying a like blessing. I know that you must have had a hard time of it though I am satisfied that you endured it with chrystian fortitude. twenty months seperation from you & the children without communication has been the hardest trial of my life not knowing where you were or what you were doing though you must be aware that I never dispair when I think I am wright. I want you await arival with the utmost composure as the same God rules in Libby who rules the whole universe. I have prayed that justice might take place in my own cause as well as all others. I pray Almighty God to give you fortitude to bear up under the tryals & troubles of this cruel & unnatural war & grace to save you in the world to come. you cannot be too carful in teaching the children the importance of religion & morality. I think that you had better get John or Andrew to go with you to Illinois (?) with you & teach school. write me soon. your affectionate Husband D.D. Smith to Wife Sarah H.(?) Smith"[150]

Smith, Edmond, Pvt., Co. M, age 44, EN & MI 9/5/64, Rome, GA, born Hall Co., GA, farmer, deserted 9/30/65 from Courtland, AL, charges of desertion removed 10/29/92 by War Dept. and discharge issued as of 9/20/65.

Smith, Frank, Pvt., Co. E, in Webster USA Hospital at Memphis, TN 2/1/64.*

Smith, Guy H., Sgt. Maj., (F&S), appt. from 9th Illinois Cav. at Memphis, TN 2/6/64.

Smith, Henry F., Pvt., Co. H, age 18, EN 11/10/63, Camp Davies, MS, born Fayette Co., AL, sick in hospital at Memphis, TN 2/14/64, died 6/25/64 at Decatur, AL "at home".

Smith, Henry H. (or M.), Pvt., Co. B, age 26, EN 1/16/63, Glendale, MS, MI 1/22/63, Corinth, MS, born Habersham Co., GA, farmer, died 2/10/63, Corinth, MS of measles.

Smith, Henry H., Pvt., Co. K, age 23, EN 6/26/62, Limestone Co., AL, born Fayette Co., AL, farmer, captured by guerrillas near Nashville, TN 9/22/62, deserted from camp at Nashville, TN 9/22/62.

Smith, James, Pvt., Co. H, died 7/6/64 of typhoid fever in Post Hospital at Decatur, AL.* (Buried Grave #B-3225, Corinth National Cemetery.)

Smith, James, Pvt., Co. C, age 26, EN 2/15/64 & MI 3/10/64, Memphis, TN, born Spartanburg, SC, farmer, MO 10/20/65, Huntsville, AL.

Smith, James, Pvt., Co. D, age 21, EN 5/1/64 & MI 6/16/64, Decatur, AL, born Walker Co., AL, farmer, served as company cook, MO 10/20/65, Huntsville, AL.

Smith, James D., Pvt/Sgt., Co. A, age 23, EN & MI 9/6/64, Rome, GA, born Cobb Co., GA, farmer, promoted to Sgt. 10/7/64, left sick near Atlanta, GA 11/15/64, MO 10/20/65, Huntsville, AL.

Smith, James M., Lt., Co. A, age 38, EN 11/30/62, Glendale, MS, MI 12/31/62, Corinth, MS, promoted to 1st Lt. 12/18/62, MO 12/22/63, Memphis, TN.

Smith, James M., Sgt., Co. K, age 38, EN & MI 7/24/62, Huntsville, AL, born Greenville, SC, farmer, discharged 10/30/62 at Nashville, TN due to disability.

Smith, Jasper N., Pvt., Co. G, age 22, EN 3/10/64 & MI 4/13/64, Decatur, AL, born Habersham Co., GA, farmer, deserted 11/17/64 from Atlanta, GA with side arms, request for removal of desertion denied 4/27/88 by War Dept.

Smith, John A., Pvt., Co. M, age 21, EN 9/30/64, Rome, GA, born Cass Co., GA, farmer, on detached duty recruiting in AL 10/5/64, deserted 6/1/65 with Smith carbine, Colt revolver and equipment.

Smith, John M., Pvt., Co. K, age 19, EN 6/26/62, Limestone Co., AL, transferred to Co. K 7/18/62, born Fayette Co., AL, died 10/31/62 in Hospital #14 at Nashville, TN of rubeola. (M.J. Smith buried in Grave #A-5227 in Nashville National Cemetery with death date shown as 10/28/62.) (See Matthew J. Smith for parents of this soldier.)

Smith, John O.D., Sgt/Lt., Co. K&B, age 29, EN 11/1/63, Glendale, MS, born Meriwether Co., GA, student of law, appt. Sgt. 11/1/63, appt. 1st Lt. 4/23/64, left sick in Savannah, GA 1/11/65, MO 10/20/65, Huntsville, AL.

Smith, Jno. W., Pvt., Co. A, recruiting since 5/1/64.*

Smith, Lewis G., Pvt., Co. H, age 36, EN 10/28/64, Rome, GA, born Cherokee Co., AL, farmer, deserted 1/8/65 from Stevenson, AL.

Smith, Martin V.(or B.), Pvt., Co. E, EN 2/1/62, Corinth, MS, deserted 5/20/63 from Glendale, MS, returned 6/10/63, on detached service as teamster 1/25/64 in Vicksburg, MS, MO 3/1/64, Memphis, TN.

Smith, Matthew J., Corp., Co. K, age 21, EN 6/26/62, Limestone Co., AL, transferred from Co. K, 21st Ohio Vols., born Fayette Co., AL, farmer, died 10/28/62 in Hospital #14 at Nashville, TN of rubeola. (Buried in Grave #A-5227 in Nashville National Cemetery.)
    NOTE: Matthew was born in 1841 to Daniel and Nancy Holcombe Smith and was a brother to John M. Smith, above.[151]

Smith, Starling/Starbury M., Pvt., Co. A, POW at Hunt's Mill, AL 9/25/63, paroled 5/8/64.

Smith, Stephen Compton., Lt/Asst. Surgeon, age 49, EN 12/14/63, Camp Davies, MS, in arrest 3/64, dismissed and given honorable discharge 1/11/64. No further information.

Smith, Thomas, Pvt., Co. F, EN 9/20/63 at Glendale, MS.*

Smith, Thomas J., Pvt/Corp., Co. A, age 22, EN 1/15/64, Camp Davies, MS, MI 2/5/64, Memphis, TN, born Putnam Co., GA, transferred 8/1/64 to Rome, GA, MO 10/20/65, Huntsville, AL.

Smith, William, Pvt., Co. M, age 34, EN & MI 8/28/64, Rome, GA, born Walton Co., GA, blacksmith, on detached service at refugee home in Clarksville, TN 2/15/64, MO 10/20/65, Huntsville, AL.

Smith, William/Wiley W., Pvt/Sgt., Co. C, age 18, EN 1/1/64, Corinth, MS, MI 3/10/64, Memphis, TN, born Hart Co., GA, shoemaker, promoted to 1st Sgt. 8/1/64, MO 10/20/65, Huntsville, AL.

Smithers, Jessee, Pvt., Co. H, age 34, EN 7/28/63, Glendale, MS, MO 7/27/64, Rome, GA. (Buried in Kilbeck Cemetery in Scott Co., TN.)

Smithson, John G., Pvt., Co. B, age 18, EN 2/5/64, Pulaski, TN, MI 3/23/64, Decatur, AL, born Williamson Co., TN, farmer, left sick in hospital at Decatur, AL 4/17/64, deserted 8/15/64 from Rome, GA with Smith carbine and equipment.

Snelling, David R., Pvt/Lt., Co. I, age 25, EN & MI 8/5/62, Huntsville, AL, assigned command of Co. 11/8/62, relieved 2/15/63, commanded Gen. Sherman's escort, MO 7/19/65, Nashville, TN.

Snelling, John A., Lt., Co. D, age 31, EN 3/7/63, Glendale, MS, promoted to 2nd Lt., from 15 Ill. Cav. Vols., also served in Co. H, 11th Ill. Inf. Vols., MO 8/26/64, Chattanooga, TN.

Snelson/Smelser, Adam, Pvt., Co. F, age 19, died 5/21/64 at Bridgeport, AL, effects given to his sister, Rebecca Smelsen.* (Buried Grave #H-604, Chattanooga National Cemetery.)

Snodgrass, Francis W., Pvt., F&S, age 18, EN 8/1/64 & MI 10/17/64, Rome, GA, born Cherokee Co., AL, farmer, MO 10/20/65, Huntsville, AL.

Snow, Thomas W., Pvt., Co. A, age 28, EN & MI 3/23/63, Glendale, MS, served as nurse in hospital, MO 12/22/63, Memphis, TN.

Solris, H., Pvt., Co. B, absent sick in general hospital.*

Sonner, William, (Cards filed with William M. Sanner).

Southern, Andrew J., Pvt., Co. D, age 18, EN 5/28/63 & MI 5/28/63, Glendale, MS, MO 6/16/64, Decatur, AL.

Spain, Storex S., Pvt., Co. H, age 25, EN 10/10/63, Glendale, MS, sick in Overton Hospital at Memphis, TN 2/64, deserted while on detached service recruiting in AL, later found desertion erroneously reported, charges of desertion removed 10/19/81 and discharged as of 10/24/64 by War Dept.

NOTE: Strax/Storex Shundy Spain was born in Tishomingo Co., MS and married Eliza Harper September 15, 1855 at George Harper's house in Marion Co., AL. He died July 28, 1865 near Mooresville, AL. Their children were: Pensia J., born August 10, 1856; Samuel D., born October 12, 1858; Mary E., born December 27, 1859; Mima R., born March 1, 1861; Charlotte M., born August 10, 1862; and Frances C., born May 10, 1864.

Spalding, John A., Sgt/Lt., Co. C, age 26, EN & MI 2/20/64, Memphis, TN, promoted from Pvt., Co. H, 57th Ill. Inf. Vols., MO 10/20/65, Huntsville, AL.

Sparks, Coleman, Pvt., Co. D, EN 3/15/63, Glendale, MS, MI 4/28/63, Corinth, MS, died 6/24/63 in hospital at Glendale, MS.

Sparks, Thomas J., Pvt., Co. H, age 18, EN 9/25/63, Glendale, MS, sick in hospital at Memphis, TN 2/29/64, MO 9/29/64, Rome, GA.

Spearman, Asbury, Pvt/Corp., Co. E, age 24, EN & MI 2/1/63, Corinth, MS, promoted to Corp. 8/1/63, MO 2/1/64, Memphis, TN.

Spears, David C., Pvt., Co. B, age 23, EN & MI 8/1/64, Rome, GA, born Randolph Co., AL, farmer, POW from Faison's Station, NC 3/30/65, deserted 3/30/65 from Faison's Station, NC, charges of desertion removed 6/6/89 by War Dept. stating, "he is supposed to have been killed or to have died while in the hands of the enemy on or about March 30th 1865."

Spears, Pleasant C., Pvt., Co. A, age 19, EN 2/25/63, Glendale, MS, MO 12/22/63, Memphis, TN.

Speedle, (?), Pvt., Co. D, absent sick since 12/12/62 at Nashville, TN.*

Speegle, Andrew A., Corp., Co. K, age 26, EN & MI 7/24/62, Huntsville, AL, born Morgan Co., AL, farmer, sick in hospital at Huntsville, AL 8/25/62, captured from hospital 10/29/62, died 12/5/62 (or 1863) at Paducah, KY of typhoid pneumonia. (Buried Section D, Grave # 3868 Mound City National Cemetery in Mound City, IL with death date shown as December 5, 1863.)

Speegle, Carroll K., Pvt., Co. I, age 23, EN & MI 7/21/62, Huntsville, AL, born Morgan Co., AL, farmer, died 10/8/62 in Hospital #8, Nashville, TN, wife shown as Eunice Speegle, Walker Co., AL. (Buried in Grave #A-4707 Nashville, National Cemetery.)

Speegle, D.H., Pvt., Co. H, (1st Regt. Middle TN Cav.), in USA General Hospital at Annapolis, MD 5/17/63.*

Speegle, David H., Pvt., Co. I, age 20, EN & MI 7/21/62, Huntsville, AL, born Morgan Co., AL, sick in hospital at Nashville, TN 10/24/62, POW 3/31/63 from Readyville, TN, (another MR states he was captured from Cripple Creek, MS), paroled at City Point, VA 4/12/63, discharged due to disability.

Speegle, David K. (Cards filed with David K. Spugh).

Speegle Thomas C., Pvt., Co. I, age 19, EN & MI 7/21/62, Huntsville, AL, born Morgan Co., AL, farmer, died 11/2/62 at Nashville, TN. (Buried Grave # B6921, Nashville National Cemetery.)

Speegler, David H., Co. D, (1st Regt. Middle TN Cav.), deserted 12/30/63 from Camp Chase OH.*

Spence, Julius, Pvt., Co. B, age 36, MI 1/22/63, Corinth, MS, born Newberry, SC, farmer, died 9/16/63 in Post Hospital at Corinth, MS.

Spencer, George Eliphaz, Colonel (F&S), age 28, EN 7/30/63, Corinth, MS, MI & commissioned 9/11/63, on detached service with Gen. Dodge at Pulaski, TN 12/9/63, commanding 3rd Brig., 3rd Cav. Div. M.D.M. by order of Gen. Kilpatrick, appt. Brevet Brig. Gen 3/13/65 for gallant and meritorious services during the campaign through Georgia and the Carolinas, resigned 7/5/65.
    NOTE: In July 1863, Capt. Spencer, who was the Chief-of-Staff of Brig. Gen. Grenville M. Dodge, asked permission to be transferred to the First Alabama Cavalry which did not have a permanent commander. His request was granted and he took formal command September 11, 1863 in Corinth, MS. After the war he moved to Decatur, AL and began practicing law. He served as register in bankruptcy court and two terms as senator. His first wife, Bella Zilfa, an Englishwoman, was an author and wrote *Ora, the Lost wife*, in 1866 and *Surface and Depth* in 1867. She died in Tuscaloosa, AL in 1867 and ten years later Spencer married Mrs. Loring Nunez, niece and namesake of Maj. Gen. William W. Loring, CSA. Spencer spent some time in Nevada as a rancher and died February 19, 1893 in Washington, DC.

Spencer, Thomas J.(or H.), Lt., Co. K, age 20, EN 4/30/61, Detroit, MI, born Detroit, MI, student, MI 8/20/62, transferred from Loomis Battery 8/20/62, acting Ord. Officer on Gen. Rosecran's staff 2/6/63, 15th A.C., on staff duty in 15th Army Corps, MO 9/15/65.

Spots, W.P., Co. D, AWOL 5/1/63.*

Spradlin, John M., Pvt., Co. F, age 23, EN 5/27/63, Corinth, MS, born Fayette Co., GA, farmer, deserted 9/10/63 from Glendale, MS.

Spriggins, A.J., Pvt., Co. D, absent on furlough 8/20/64.*

Spugh/Speegle, David K., Pvt/Corp., Co. A, EN 10/18/62 & MI 10/24/62, Corinth, MS, promoted to 1st Corp. 12/18/62, MO 10/31/63, Lagrange, TN.

Stacks, James M., Pvt., Co. H, age 18, EN 9/29/63, Glendale, MS, MO 9/29/64, Rome, GA.

Stallings, J., Co. B, absent sick in US General Hospital.*

Stallings, James P., Pvt., Co. F, EN 11/20/63, Corinth, MS, deserted 12/15/63 from Camp Davies, MS with horse, Smith Carbine, Remington revolver and equipment.

Stallings, John P., Pvt., Co. F, age 18, EN & MI 5/23/63 Corinth, MS, born Choctaw Co., MS, farmer, returned from MIA 11/19/63, detached as teamster at Vicksburg, MS 1/25/64, sick at home in Illinois while on furlough 9/63, MO 7/27/64, Rome, GA.

Stallings, Micajah, Pvt., Co. B, age 18, EN & MI 9/1/64, Rome, GA, born Randolph Co., AL, farmer, POW 3/10/65 at Monroe's Crossroads near Fayetteville, NC, discharged 6/12/65 from Camp Chase. OH.
NOTE: Micajah was born in 1846 and died May 28, 1899 in Greenwood, AR. He married Mary Matilda Crow, born 1844, died June 15, 1896, and had the following children: William Browning, born August 5, 1869,, died March 4, 1941; Amanda Elizabeth, born September 29, 1871, died November 1, 1893; GreenBerry, born August 19, 1873, died June 12, 1953; Dica, born October 25, 1875, died March 30, 1900; Robert Paine, born November 1, 1881, died 1964; and Lucy Matilda, born May 21, 1884, died November 13, 1953. Micajah's second wife was Cora Cantrell.[152]

Stallings, William J.(or G.), Pvt., Co. B, age 41, EN & MI 9/1/64, Rome, GA, born Jasper Co., GA, on daily duty as blacksmith, in hospital at Decatur, AL when discharge was issued 11/13/65.

Stallings, William J.(or W.), Pvt., Co. E, age 22, EN & MI 9/1/64, Rome, GA, born Randolph Co., AL, farmer, WIA & POW 3/10/65 at Monroe's Crossroads, NC, in Grant USA Hospital at Willet's Point, NY 3/25/65, discharged 5/21/65 due to disability.

Stancill, Francis/Marion M., Pvt., Co. I, age 33, EN & MI 7/21/62, Huntsville, AL, born Pickens Dist., SC, on daily duty as hospital nurse, farmer, MIA 4/28/63 from Day's Gap, Cedar Bluff, AL, returned 10/10/63, POW 3/10/65 from Solomon Grove, NC, MO 6/13/65, Camp Chase, OH.

Stanton, Edward L. (or S.)., Bugler, Co. F, age 18, EN 5/5/63 & MI 5/18/63, Corinth, MS, born Limestone Co., AL, farmer, WIA 10/26/63 and in hospital at Memphis, TN, MO 7/27/64 from Rome, GA.

Stanton, Elijah A., Pvt., Co. I, age 20, EN & MI 8/5/62, Huntsville, AL, born Morgan Co., AL, farmer, died 11/9/62 in Hospital #12 at Nashville, TN.

Stanton, Harvey, Pvt., Co. D, age 53, EN 5/1/63, Glendale, MS, born New York, carpenter, served as hospital nurse and cook, sick in hospital at Corinth, MS 7/13/63, discharged 10/14/63 due to disability, "fractured spine".

Stanton, John, Pvt., Co. I, age 21, EN & MI 7/21/62, Huntsville, AL, born Walker Co., AL, farmer, died 10/26/62 in Hospital #14 at Nashville, TN. (Buried in Grave #A-4359 in Nashville National Cemetery.)

Stanton, Robert, Co. F, absent POW taken by enemy.*

Stark, Robert, Pvt., Co. K, age 23, EN 12/13/63, Camp Davies, MS, born Fayette Co., AL, farmer, POW 3/21/64 in AR near Memphis, TN, MO 7/19/65, Nashville, TN. Traveled 200 miles from his home in St. Clair Co., AL to enlist.

Stark, William W., Pvt., Co. K, age 36, born Fayette Co., AL, farmer, EN 12/13/63, Camp Davies, MS, traveled 200 miles from his home in St. Clair Co., AL to Camp Davies to enlist, rejected on account of physical disability by regimental surgeon.*

Statum/Statom, James A., Pvt., Co. D, age 28, EN & MI 8/24/63, Glendale, MS, born Franklin Co., TN, sick in refugee camp at Corinth, MS 11/20/63, detached at refugee camp at Memphis, TN 3/64, died 5/18/64 in hospital at Decatur, AL.

Stearns, D., Co. B, absent POW 3/65.*

Steel, Richard A., Pvt., Co. K&A, age 51, EN 9/8/62, Iuka, MS, MI 10/1/62, Corinth, MS, born Rutherford Co., NC, blacksmith, MO 9/16/63, Corinth, MS.

Steele, George D., Pvt., Co. H, age 18, EN 2/10/65, Stevenson, AL, MI 2/13/65, Nashville, TN, born Jackson Co., AL, farmer, MO 10/20/65, Huntsville, AL.

Steele, Ransom, Pvt., Co. H, age 18, EN 12/21/64, Stevenson, AL, MI 2/13/65, Nashville, TN, born Jackson Co., AL, farmer, MO 10/20/65, Huntsville, AL.

Stephens, Calvin S., Pvt., Co. H, age 18, EN 5/1/65, Huntsville, AL, MI 5/20/65, Nashville, AL, born York Dist., SC, MO 10/20/65, Huntsville, AL.

Stephens, David, Corp/Pvt., Co. G, temporarily attached from 11th Illinois Cavalry.

Stephens, Thomas P.D. (or R.D.), Pvt., Co. G, temporarily attached from 11th Illinois Cavalry.

Stephens, William T., Pvt., Co. H, age 19, EN 5/1/65, Huntsville, AL, MI 5/20/65, Nashville, TN, born York Dist., SC, farmer, MO 10/20/65, Huntsville, AL.

Stephenson, Joseph H. (or J.), Pvt., Co. I, age 26, EN & MI 7/21/62, Huntsville, AL, born Morgan Co., AL, farmer, died 11/17/62 in Hospital #8 at Nashville, TN. (Buried in Grave #A-5124 at Nashville National Cemetery.)
   NOTE: Joseph Stephenson was born in 1836 in Morgan Co., AL. One record indicates he died November 17, 1862 while another states December 27, 1862. He was the son of Alexander and Mary Stephenson. Joseph married Rachel Blevens, daughter of James and Rachel Blevins. Children of Joseph and Rachel were: Joseph Hamilton, born November 19, 1862 in Winston Co., AL, died February 23, 1942 in Winston Co., AL, married Sarah Lou Vestie Ann Ford, born July 1866, died January 15, 1899; and Mary S. Stephenson, born January 21, 1861, married Samuel J. Calvert.

Other siblings of Joseph were: Mary, born 1843; Calvin, born 1844; Mary, born 1846; Jane, born 1848; Alexander, born 1850; Martha, born 1850; John, born 1852; Hamilton, born 1854; Cicero, born 1856; and Johnny, born February 12, 1860. Joseph's father, Alexander, was born 1822 in AL and was the son of Adam K. Stephenson, born 1784 in SC, and Hester/Easter Alexander, born 1785 in TN. Hester's father was Jeremiah Alexander, born July 4, 1763 in MD and died January 26, 1847 in Walker Co., AL, and was a Revolutionary War soldier. Other children of Jeremiah Alexander were: Letisha, born 1800 in TN, married Martin O'Rear, died 1876 in Walker Co., AL; Abagail, married James Randolph; John; and Martha, married July 18, 1822 in Morgan Co., AL to David H. Inman.[153]

Sterling, John, Pvt., Co. B, age 20, EN 3/22/64 & MI 3/27/64, Decatur, AL, born Blount Co., AL, farmer, left sick in hospital at Decatur 4/17/64, MO 10/20/65, Huntsville, AL.

Sterling, John T., Pvt., Co. E, in Jefferson USA Hospital at Jeffersonville, IN July & August 1864.*

Sterling, Josiah, Pvt., Co. B, age 24, EN 3/22/64 & MI 3/27/64, Decatur, AL, born Blount Co., AL, farmer, died 4/25/65 in hospital at Decatur AL. (Buried Grave #B-3235, Corinth National Cemetery.)

Sterling, Silas, Pvt., Co. C, age 18, EN 4/25/64 & MI 4/30/64, Decatur, AL, born Blount Co., AL, farmer, residence shown as Lawrence Co., AL, MO 10/20/65, Huntsville, AL.

Sternberg/Stenberg/Sternburg, Phillip A., Lt/Capt., Co. B, age 38, EN 12/27/62 & MI 12/31/62, Glendale, MS, promoted from Sgt. Co. F, 64th Illinois Inv. Vols., first EN 10/4/61 in Welmington, IL, KIA 10/26/63 at Vincent's Crossroads, MS. (Buried in Corinth National Cemetery.)

Stevens, Bray S., Co. L, absent with leave 10/63.*

Stevens, Debso/Debro, Pvt., temporarily attached from 18th MO Inf. 7/4/63 at Chewalla, TN.*

Stevenson, George W., Pvt., Co. A, absent sick in Memphis, TN.*

Stevenson, William, Pvt., Co. E, age 46, EN 8/27/63, Glendale, MS, accidentally shot & killed in quarters 9/15/63.

Stevenson, William B., Pvt., Co. D, age 23, EN & MI 6/1/63 Glendale, MS, on daily duty as hospital nurse, MO 6/16/64, Decatur, AL.

Steward, D., Co. A, absent POW 3/10/65.*

Steward/Stewart, Jasper S., Pvt., Co. D, age 20, EN 2/15/63, Glendale, MS, MI 4/28/63, Corinth, MS, on daily duty as teamster, MO 6/16/64, Decatur, AL.

Stewart, Andrew J., Pvt., Co. I, age 34, EN & MI 7/21/62, Huntsville, AL, born Walker Co., AL, died 10/27/62 in Hospital #12 at Nashville, TN of hepatitis. (Buried in Grave #C-7088 in Nashville National Cemetery.)

Stewart, Andrew J., Pvt., Co. C, age 18, EN 1/1/64, Corinth, MS, MI 3/10/64, Memphis, TN, born Tippah Co., MS, farmer, in confinement at Decatur, AL 7/3/65 and in Huntsville, AL 7/10/65, MO 10/20/65, Huntsville, AL. No further information.

Stewart, George W., Pvt/Corp., Co. A, age 23, EN 12/22/62, Camp Davies, MS, MI 2/5/65, Memphis, TN, born Walker Co., AL, farmer, WIA 11/23/64 at Ball's Ferry and in hospital at Hilton Head, SC, transferred to DeCamp USA Hospital at David's Island, NY 1/65, discharged due to disability 6/14/65, gunshot wound to left thigh.

Stewart, John W., Asst. Surgeon, (F&S), age 28, EN & MI 8/19/64, Rome, GA, on duty in 5th KY Cav. 1/21/65 and 3rd Brig, 3rd Cav. Div. 4/18/65, MO 10/20/65, Huntsville, AL, residence shown as Randolph, AL.

Stewart, Jonathan M., Pvt., Co. K, age 28, EN 5/4/63, Murfreesboro, TN, MI 9/27/63 Glendale, MS, born Pike Co., GA, farmer, WIA 3/10/65 at Monroe's Crossroads, NC and sent to Annapolis, MD, gunshot wound to both thighs, MO with Co. 7/19/65.

Stewart, Lemuel L., Pvt., Co. A, age 19, EN 12/22/63, Camp Davies, MS, MI 2/5/64, Memphis, TN, born Walker Co., AL, farmer, in arrest in prison 4/64 for desertion & trying to take U.S. arms & ammunition to the enemy, POW 3/10/65 from Monroe's Crossroads at Solomon Grove, NC, MO 10/20/65, Huntsville, AL.

Stewart, Michael, Pvt., Co. L, died 11/15/63 at Corinth, MS of smallpox.*

Stewart, W., Co. B, absent sick in hospital.*

Stillman, Charles L (or S.), Pvt., Co. H, EN 10/18/63, Glendale, MS, rejected on Surgeon's examination.

Stillman, C.P., Pvt., Co. H, discharged for disability 11/10/63 from Camp Chase, OH.*

Stinert, F.M., Co. L, absent POW 3/65.*

Stockton, Robert G., Pvt., Co. F, age 35, EN 4/10/63, Corinth, MS, born Shelby Co., TN, farmer, POW 10/26/63, returned 12/12/63, detached as teamster at Vicksburg, MS 1/25/64, MO 4/9/64, Decatur, AL.

Stockton, William C., Pvt., Co. B, age 34, EN 12/19/62, Glendale, MS, born Warren Co., TN, farmer, absent 3/28/63 to take family to Jackson, TN because "they were in a suffering and destitute condition having been dispoiled (sic) of all their property by the rebels and their houses burned." Sick at Jackson, TN 4/25/63, was cut off from his camp by the enemy and had to stay in woods, discharged due to disability 7/24/63.

Stoddard, John W., Pvt., Co. B, in USA Field Hospital at Rome, GA 8/12/64, returned to duty 9/12/64.*

Stokes, John, Pvt., Co. A, died of disease in hospital at Nashville, TN 9/25/64.*

Stokes, John W., Pvt., Co. A, age 18, EN 12/22/63, Camp Davies, MS, MI 2/5/64, Memphis, TN, born Winston Co., AL, farmer, sick in Gayoso USA Hospital at Memphis, TN 2/12/64, died 4/25/64 at Nashville, TN of rubeola, nearest relative shown as Wm. Stokes, Washington Co., AL. (Buried in Grave #J-13610 in Nashville National Cemetery.)

Stone, Burzealy, Pvt., Co. D, age 19, EN 6/26/63 & MI 6/26/63, Glendale, MS, born Marion Co., AL, farmer, in Adams USA Hospital at Memphis, TN 3/14/64, MO 7/27/64, Rome, GA.

Stone, John H., Pvt., Co. C, age 18, EN 1/15/64, Corinth, MS, MI 3/19/64, Memphis, TN, born Tippah Co., MS, farmer, POW 3/10/65 from Monroe's Crossroads near Fayetteville, NC, and confined at Richmond,VA, discharged 6/12/65 from Camp Chase, OH.

Stone, John H., Pvt., Co. G, age 16, EN 6/26/63, Chewalla, TN, MO 11/26/63, Memphis, TN.

Stone, William H., Pvt/Corp., Co. G, age 16, EN 12/15/62, Pocahontas, TN, appt. Corp. 9/1/63, served as orderly and hospital nurse, MO 11/26/63, Memphis, TN.

Stone, W.J., Co. D, absent sick in hospital 8/63.*

Stone, William J. (James M. & James W.), Corp., Co. E, age 28, EN 3/1/63, Glendale, MS, MI 3/1/63, Corinth, MS, MO 3/1/64, Memphis, TN.

Stout, Daniel D., Pvt., Co. K&A, age 25, EN 12/13/62, Glendale, MS, MI 12/31/62, Corinth, MS, deserted 12/31/62.

Stout, John M., Pvt., Co. F, age 24, EN 6/29/63, Corinth, MS, born Madison Co., TN, farmer, died 11/15/63 in Post Hospital at Corinth, "date of death as alleged 12/11/63".

Stout, John S., Corp., Co. B, age 19, EN 12/23/62, Glendale, MS, detailed for special service as scout appt. Corp. 1/22/63, MO 1/22/64, Memphis, TN.

Stout, William H., Pvt., Co. F, age 23, EN 6/29/63 & MI 7/1/63, Corinth, MS, born Madison Co., TN, farmer, detached as teamster at Vicksburg, MS 1/25/64, MO 7/27/64, Rome, GA.

Stoveall/Stovall, James, Pvt., Co. E, EN 4/1/63, Glendale, MS, MI 4/1/63, Corinth, MS, served as Co. cook, MO 3/1/64, Memphis, TN.

Stover, Abraham, Pvt., Co. I, EN 8/18/62, Huntsville, AL, MI 9/27/62, Nashville, TN, died 12/18/63 at Corinth, MS.

Stover, David, Pvt., Co. A, in Joe Holt USA Hospital 8/26/64.*

Stover, Obadiah, Pvt., Co. I, age 58, EN & MI 7/21/62, Huntsville, AL, born Lawrence Co., AL, farmer, sick in hospital at Nashville, TN 12/12/62, POW 11/22/63, transferred 10/7/64 to Invalid Reserve Corps, 152nd Co. 2nd Batt.

Strain, James D.W., Pvt., Co. K, age 19, EN 12/6/63, Camp Davies, MS, born Lancaster Dist., SC, farmer, POW 3/21/64 in AR near Memphis, TN, MO 7/19/65, Nashville, TN. Traveled 300 miles from his home in Randolph Co., AL to Camp Davies, MS to enlist.

Strait, Hiram W., Lt., Co. B, age 36, EN 2/1/64, Pulaski, TN, MI 3/27/64, Decatur, AL, born Franklin Co., AL, appt. from Pvt., Co. E, 64th IN Inf. Vols., resigned 9/29/64.

Strickland/Strickling, Elijah B., Pvt/Sgt., Co. E, age 21, EN & MI 10/4/64, Rome, GA, born Randolph Co., AL, farmer, promoted to Corp. 10/20/64 and to Sgt. 1/1/65, MO 10/20/65, Huntsville, AL.

Strickland/Strickling, Thomas, Pvt., Co. E, age 44, EN & MI 9/1/64, Rome, GA, born Jasper Co., GA, farmer, MO 10/20/65, Huntsville, AL.

Stricklin, James K. (or R.), Pvt., Co. K, age 20, EN 1/14/64, born in TN, in Hospital #3 at Vicksburg, MS 2/27/64, MO 7/19/65, Nashville, TN.

Stringer, James, Sgt., Co. I, age 49, EN & MI 7/21/62, Huntsville, AL, died 10/30/62 in Hospital #8, Nashville, TN. (Buried in Grave #B-6771 in Nashville National Cemetery as S. Stringer.)

Stringfellow, William M., Pvt., Co. C, age 18, EN 3/1/64 and MI 3/10/64, Memphis, TN, born Tippah Co., MS, farmer, on daily duty as teamster, POW 3/10/65 from Monroe's Crossroads near Fayetteville, NC, discharged 6/12/65 from Camp Chase, OH.

Stroud, Carl/Carrol/Charles A., Pvt., Co. F, age 18, EN 5/15/63, Corinth, MS, born Wayne Co., TN, farmer, detached as teamster at Vicksburg, MS 1/25/64, died 3/30/64 in Adams USA Hospital in Memphis, TN. (Buried in Memphis National Cemetery.)

Stuart, Absalom B., Major/Surgeon, (F&S), age 33, EN & MI 4/2/63, Glendale, MS, detached from 10th MO Inf., resigned 1/20/64 & accepted by Maj. Gen. Sherman.

Stuart, J.M., Pvt., Co. F, died 11/15/63. No further information. (This was filed with wrong soldier.)

Stuart, William H., Co. F, absent POW 10/26/63.*

Stubblefield, Joseph, Pvt., Co. I, age 35, EN 10/1/63, Glendale, MS, born Buncombe Co., NC, farmer, on daily duty as regimental blacksmith, MO 7/19/65, Nashville, TN.

Stubbs, W, Pvt., Co. I, died 8/4/64 at Andersonville, GA of bronchitis. (Buried in Grave #4731, Andersonville National Cemetery.)

Studdard, Andrew, Pvt., Co. A, age 25, EN & MI 3/23/63, Glendale, MS, MO 12/22/63, Memphis, TN.

Studdard, Nathaniel, Pvt., Co. A, age 20, MO 12/22/63, Memphis, TN. No further information.

Studerd/Stodard, William, Pvt., Co. B, age 18, EN & MI 8/1/64, Rome, GA, born Floyd Co., GA, farmer, sent to hospital at Rome, GA 10/1/64, deserted 6/15/65 from Chattanooga, TN, charges of desertion removed 11/4/89 by War Dept. and discharged as of 6/15/65.

Stuttam, Jas, Pvt., Co. D, detached at Refugee Camp at Memphis, TN 2/64.*

Style, John, Co. D, detached as scout by Gen. Dodge 10/64.*

Suit/Suits, John W., Pvt., Co. A, age 31, EN 1/14/64, Camp Davies, MS, MI 2/5/64, Memphis, TN, born Blount Co., TN, on detached service recruiting in AL, MO 10/20/65, Huntsville, AL.

Sullivan, John W., Pvt., Co. H, age 21, EN 5/15/65, Huntsville, AL, EN 5/20/65, Nashville, TN, born Walker Co., AL, farmer, MO 10/20/65, Huntsville, AL.

Sumner, Henry T., Capt., Co. B, MI 1/22/63 as Capt., had originally EN 10/23/61 at Nashville, TN, resigned 7/29/65 due to the illness of his wife and children.

Sunyers, H., Corp., Co. H, discharged by reason of expiration of term of service 10/25/64, Rome, GA.*

Suttlemire, (Cards filed with Settlemires).

Sutton, James, Pvt., Co. F&E, age 18, EN 3/31/63, Corinth, MS, born Jackson Co., AL, farmer, deserted 7/12/63 from Glendale, MS.

Sutton, John, Pvt., Co. F&E, age 29, EN 3/31/63, Corinth, MS, born Jackson Co., AL, farmer, sick at home 6/6/63, deserted 7/12/63 from Corinth, MS.

Sutton, M., Pvt., Co. L, died 11/15/63 of disease in Post Hospital at Corinth, MS.*

Sutton, T., Pvt., Co. E, supposed deserted 6/18/63.*

Swan, Lambert W., Pvt., Co. I, age 18, EN & MI 7/21/62, Huntsville, AL, born Walker Co., AL, farmer, died 11/7/62 in Hospital #14 at Nashville, TN of rubeola.

Swan, William L., Sgt/Pvt., Co. I, age 45, EN & MI 7/21/62, Huntsville, AL, born Pendleton Dist., SC, farmer, POW 5/1/63 from Day's Gap, AL and confined at Richmond, VA, paroled 5/14/63 at City Point, VA, appt. Sgt. 3/1/63, reduced from Sgt. 12/7/63, MO 7/19/65, Nashville, TN.

Swaving, John G.C. (or G.E.), Surgeon (F&S), age 41, EN & MI 1/24/64, Memphis, TN, detached to 2nd Iowa Cav. 1/26/64, suffered fracture of left leg during action at Moulton, AL, POW 3/10/65 from Monroe's Crossroads near Fayetteville, NC, MO 10/20/65, Huntsville, AL.

Sweat/Sweet, Christopher, Pvt., Co. D, age 38, EN 5/20/64 & MI 6/16/64, Decatur, AL, born Abbeville, SC, farmer, POW 3/10/65 from Monroe's Crossroads near Fayetteville, NC and confined at Richmond, VA, MO 6/13/65 from Camp Chase, OH.

Sweat, James, Pvt., Co. D, POW 3/10/65 at Solemn Grove, NC, paroled POW 4/10/65, Camp Chase, OH.*

Sweat, John, Pvt., Co. C, age 23, EN 3/18/63, Glendale, MS, MI 4/10/63, Corinth, MS, born St. Clair Co., AL, farmer, served as Co. farrier, POW 3/15/64, MO 10/20/65, Huntsville, AL.

Sweat, Joseph C., Pvt., Co. D, furnished transportation from Nashville, TN to Louisville, KY 4/28/65, on furlough.*

Sweat, L.T.S., Pvt., Co. C, in Adams USA Hospital at Memphis 3/64, returned to duty 3/19/64.*

Sweat, Thomas J. (or J. Thomas), Pvt., Co. C, age 18, EN 1/1/64, Corinth, MS, MI 3/10/64, Memphis, TN, born St. Clair Co., AL, farmer. No MO date.

Sweet, Lewis, Pvt., Co. C, in Adams USA Hospital at Memphis 2/6/64.*

Swift, James C., Lt., Co. B, EN 3/25/63 & MI Glendale, MS, promoted from Com. Sgt. 15 Ill. Cav. Co. L, WIA 10/26/63 at Vincent's Crossroads and died 11/2/63.

Swim, Aaron H., Pvt/Corp., Co. D, age 36, EN 8/1/63, Glendale, MS, born Hall Co., GA, promoted to Corp. 12/3/63, died 3/12/64 at Overton USA Hospital at Memphis, TN of typhoid fever. (Buried in Memphis National Cemetery.)

Swindle, Elijah J., Pvt., Co. H, age 40, EN 9/23/63, Glendale, MS, on daily duty as blacksmith, MO 9/29/64, Rome, GA.

Tacket, Lewis W., Pvt., Co. C, age 28, EN 12/15/63 & MI 12/22/63, Corinth, MS, reenlisted 1/1/64, Corinth, MS, born Franklin Co., AL, farmer, deserted 3/20/64 from Memphis, TN.

Tacket, Abner W., Pvt., Co. H, age 21, EN 10/17/63, Corinth, MS, MO 10/24/64, Rome, GA.

Tanner, John W., Pvt., Co. A, age 19, EN & MI 10/6/64, Rome, GA, born Harrison Co., GA, farmer.
Notation from Record & Pension Office 4/5/99 states, "In the absence of any record evidence of this man's muster into service, he is not regarded by this Department as having been in the military service of the United States in this organization".

Tanner, Silas, Pvt., Co. L, age 18, EN 9/1/64 & MI 9/17/64, Rome, GA, born Cherokee Co., AL, farmer, deserted 11/10/64 from Rome, GA.

Tanner, William L., Pvt., Co. B, age 30, EN 1/13/63 & MI 1/22/63, Corinth, MS, born Iredell, NC, farmer, sick in hospital at Corinth with measles 2/63, sick at Jackson, TN 5/10/63, discharged 7/24/63 due to disability - dislocation of both ankles and left knee.

Tarrer (See Taver)

Tarver, John, (Cards filed with John Taver).

Tary, Nicholas M., (Cards filed with Nicholas M. Terry).

Tate, John T., Pvt., Co. M, age 17, EN & MI 10/28/64, Rome, GA, born Rutherford Co., NC, farmer, on daily duty as orderly, MO 10/20/65, Huntsville, AL.

Tate, William A. (or H.), Pvt., Co. B, age 21, EN 2/19/64, Pulaski, TN, MI 3/27/64, Decatur, AL, born Marion Co., AL, farmer, on daily duty as teamster, WIA 2/8/65 at Pine Log Bridge and died 2/12/65 at Aiken, SC.

Taver, John, Pvt., Co. B, age 18, EN 3/10/64 & MI 3/27/64, Decatur, AL, born Blount Co., AL, farmer, died in hospital at Decatur, AL 4/8/64 of measles. (Buried Grave #B-3299, Corinth National Cemetery.)

Taylor, Allen J., Pvt., Co. C, age 23, EN 10/30/63, Glendale, MS, MI 12/12/63, Memphis, TN, born Marion Co., AL, farmer, in Adams USA Hospital at Memphis 1/20/64, returned to duty 4/26/64, on recruiting service in AL 5/1/64, MO 10/20/65, Huntsville, AL.

Taylor, Andrew J., Pvt., Co. M&L, age 25, EN 9/25/63, Glendale, MS, MI 12/29/63, Corinth, MS, on recruiting service in AL 1/20/64, discharge issued as of 5/1/64.

Taylor, Charles A., Pvt., Co. M&L, age 28, EN 10/12/63, Glendale, MS, MI 12/29/63, Corinth, MS, returned from MIA 12/25/63, on recruiting service in AL 1/20/64, discharge issued as of 5/1/64.

Taylor, Granville, Pvt., Co. L, age 42, EN 9/25/63, Fayette Co., AL, MO 9/28/64, Rome, GA.

Taylor, Hiram, Pvt/Corp., Co. C, age 20, EN & MI 10/30/63, Glendale, MS, born Marion Co., AL, farmer, appt. Corp. 12/19/63, died 1/10/64 at regimental hospital of measles.

Taylor, James, Pvt., Co. D, absent on detached service 12/64, on detached service in North Alabama with Capt. Lomax 4/65.*

Taylor, James, Pvt/Corp., Co. C, age 26, EN 12/23/62 & MI 12/25/62, Corinth, MS, MO 12/27/63, Camp Davies, MS, reenlisted 1/1/64, Corinth, MS, MI 3/19/64, Memphis, TN, born Marion Co., AL, appt. Corp. 3/1/64 & Sgt. 7/1/64, MO 10/20/65, Huntsville, AL.

Taylor, John, Pvt., Co. A, age 20, EN 12/10/62, Glendale, MS, MI 12/31/62, Corinth, MS, served as hospital nurse, POW 3/10/65, MO 12/22/63, Memphis TN.

Taylor, John J., Pvt., Co. A, age 18, EN 2/23/64 & MI 2/26/64, Memphis, TN, born Franklin Co., AL, farmer, POW 3/10/65 from Monroe's Crossroads near Fayetteville, NC, paroled and sent to Camp Chase, OH where he MO 6/12/65.

Taylor, John R., Pvt., Co. C, age 24, EN 12/1/62 & MI 12/22/62, Corinth, MS, born Blount Co., AL, farmer, POW 4/14/63 from Glendale, MS and confined at Richmond, VA, paroled at City Point, VA 5/5/63, died 8/9/63 in hospital at Glendale, MS.

Taylor, John W., Pvt., Co. D, absent at Refugee Camp in Corinth 6/18/63, on detached service in Illinois with refugees by order of Gen. Dodge.*

Taylor, Jonathan, Pvt., Co. A, age 36, EN 12/5/62, Glendale, MS, MI 12/31/62, Corinth, MS, MO 12/22/63, Memphis, TN.

Taylor, Joseph P., Pvt/Sgt., Co. M, age 30, EN 11/10/63, Camp Davies, MS, MI 12/29/63, Corinth, MS, born Henderson Co., NC, farmer, appt. 2nd M. Sgt. 11/10/63, "killed 8/8/64 by rebels while on scout at Stone's River near Morgan Co., AL".

Taylor, Josiah, Pvt., Co. H, age 21, EN 12/19/64, Rome, GA, MI 2/13/65, Nashville, TN, born Pickens Dist., SC, farmer, deserted 6/13/65 from Huntsville, AL.

Taylor, Martin, age 20, born TN, farmer, EN & MI 10/6/64, Paducah, KY. Note states, "Preference of organization 1st Alabama Cav. substitute (white) furnished by Sidney C. Moore an enrolled man of Webster Co. 1st Dist of KY."*

Taylor, Nathan, Pvt., Co. A, age 27, EN 12/17/62, Glendale, MS, MI 12/31/62, Corinth, MS, MO 12/22/63, Memphis, TN.

Taylor, Simeon, Pvt., Co. G, age 22, EN 3/21/64 & MI 4/13/64, Decatur, AL, born Morgan Co., AL, farmer, died 7/30/64 in hospital at Rome, GA. (Buried Grave #C-53, Marietta National Cemetery.)
   NOTE: Simeon Taylor was born about 1841 in Morgan Co., AL and was a brother to Warren Taylor. They were sons of Isaac Rylie Taylor, born March 12, 1817 and Louisa Stovall, born about 1817.
Isaac was the son of Robert Taylor, born about 1794 and Mary White, born November 8, 1794. Mary was the daughter of Armajer and Absellah White. Simeon died in Texas.

Taylor, Thomas, Pvt., Co. A, age 20, EN 1/25/64, Camp Davies, MS, MI 2/5/64, Memphis, TN, born Spartanburg Dist., SC, farmer, deserted 5/15/64 at Snake's Creek Gap, GA with arms and equipment.

Taylor, Thomas L., Pvt., Co. C, age 22, EN 12/1/62 & MI 12/22/62, Corinth, MS, born Blount Co., AL, farmer, MO 12/17/63, Memphis, TN.

Taylor, Warren, Pvt., Co. G, age 19, EN 3/21/64, Decatur, AL, born Walker Co., AL, farmer, died 5/19/64 at Decatur, AL.
   NOTE: Warren Taylor was born about 1843 in Walker Co., AL. See Simeon Taylor, above, for family information.

Taylor, W.J., Pvt., Co. L, MIA 10/26/63 at Vincent's Crossroads.*

Teal, Jordan, Pvt., Co. D, age 45, EN 5/1/64 & MI 6/16/64, Decatur, AL, born Anson Co., NC, farmer, sick in Hospital #2 at Nashville, TN 11/29/64, MO 10/20/65, Huntsville, AL.

Tease, Joseph, Pvt., Co. E, EN 4/1/63, Glendale, MS, MI 4/1/63, Corinth, MS, deserted 9/6/63 from Glendale.

Tease, Reese, Pvt., Co. E, EN 4/1/63, Glendale, MS, MI 4/1/63, Corinth, MS, deserted 9/6/63 from Glendale.

Tedford, Thomas J., Pvt., Co. I&D, age 44, EN & MI 7/21/62, Huntsville, AL, born Lawrence Co., AL, farmer, died 11/22/62 at Nashville, TN.

Teide, F., Co. D, absent sick in US General Hospital 4/65.*

Tenant/Tennant, Charles W., Pvt., Co. E, age 25, EN 10/1/64 & MI 11/10/64, Rome, GA, born Butts Co., GA, farmer, MO 10/20/65, Huntsville, AL.

Tenant/Tennant, John, Pvt., Co. E, age 18, EN & MI 9/1/64, Rome, GA, born Campbell, GA, farmer, MO 10/20/65, Huntsville, AL.

Tennison, John C., Pvt/Corp., Co. H, age 26, EN 10/17/63, Glendale, MS, MO 10/24/64, Rome, GA.

Terry, Archibald, Pvt., Co. M, age 45, EN & MI 9/16/64, Rome, GA, born Elbert Co., GA, farmer, deserted 11/11/64 from Rome, GA with Smith carbine, Colt revolver and equipment.

Terry, David, Pvt., Co. E, age 42, EN 3/1/63, Glendale, MS, MI 3/10/63, Corinth, MS, in confinement at Corinth 11/22/63 charged with murder of Neal Morrison and desertion, MO 3/1/64, Memphis, TN.

Terry, Garland, Under Cook, (Colored), age 34, EN & MI 9/1/64, Rome, GA, born Garnett (Garrard?) Co., KY, servant, also served as teamster.

Terry, James H., Pvt., Co. F, age 22, EN 4/1/63, Corinth, MS, born Itawamba Co., MS, farmer, deserted 7/16/63 from Glendale, MS.

Terry, John, Pvt., Co. B, age 46, EN 2/19/64, Pulaski, TN, MI 3/27/64, Decatur, AL, born Marion Co., AL, farmer, deserted 7/4/64 from Decatur, AL with arms and equipment.

Terry, Nicholas M., Pvt., Co. A, age 35, EN 6/20/63, Glendale, MS, served as hospital nurse, MO 12/22/63, Memphis, TN.

Terry, William R., Pvt., Co. F, gain from MIA 11/17/63.*

Thacker, Thomas F., Pvt., Co. B, age 18, EN 2/13/64, Pulaski, TN, MI 3/27/64, Decatur, AL, born Giles Co., TN, farmer, died 4/22/64 in regimental hospital at Mooresville, AL.

Themster, William, Pvt., Co. A, absent on furlough 9/64.*

Thise, Hiram, Pvt., Co. B, age 24, MI 1/22/63, Corinth, MS, deserted 2/28/63 from Glendale, MS.

Thomas, J., Pvt., Co. B, AWOL 10/64.*

Thomas, J.J., Pvt., Co. D, POW 3/10/65 near Fayetteville, NC and confined at Richmond, VA, paroled 3/30/65.*

Thomas, Lewis C.(L.H.), Pvt., Co. E, age 28, EN & MI 2/8/63, Corinth, MS, deserted 2/12/63.

Thomas, P., Pvt., Co. E, absent sick in US General Hospital 2/65.*

Thomas, William, Pvt., Co. A, age 19, EN 1/4/64 & died 1/16/64 at Camp Davies, MS of lung disease.

Thompson, Edward, Pvt., Co. C, age 38, EN 3/1/64 & MI 3/10/64, Memphis, TN, born Columbia, NY, carpenter, deserted 5/1/65 from Savannah, GA with 2 Colt revolvers, horse and equipment.

Thompson, John S., Pvt., Co. A, age 23, EN 12/17/62, Glendale, MS, deserted 12/31/62.

Thompson, Johnathan O., Pvt., Co. G, age 45, EN 1/7/63, Lagrange, TN, on daily duty as teamster, MO 11/26/63, Memphis, TN.
    NOTE: In 1840, Jonathan Obediah Thompson was living in Fayette Co., AL with a wife, son and daughter. At some time after that he lived around LaGrange, TN and by 1860, was living in Tippah Co., MS with eight children, all born in TN. His home was in Jonesborough, about 10 miles north of Ripley. He was discharged from the Army with a severe case of bronchitis. After the war he moved with his family to Illinois where they rented farms and did farm work for others. Around 1873 the family moved to Gainsville, Ozark Co., MO where he died January 21, 1904.[154]

Thompson, Lewis, Pvt., Co. C, age 34, EN 9/1/63, Glendale, MS, MI 9/27/63, Corinth, MS, born Williamson Co., TN, deserted 3/20/64 from Memphis, TN with Remington revolver and equipment.

Thompson, Nathan, Pvt., Co. L, age 41, EN 9/25/63, Fayette Co., AL, died 10/20/63 in regimental hospital at Glendale, MS of pneumonia.

Thompson, Robert L., Pvt., Co. G, age 48, EN 5/6/63, Chewalla, TN, appt. saddler 5/6/63, MO 11/26/63, Memphis, TN.

Thompson, William, Pvt., Co. L, EN 12/26/63.*

Thompson, William, Pvt., Co. M, age 22, EN 12/26/63, Camp Davies, MS, MI 12/29/63, Corinth, MS, born Marion Co., AL, farmer, MO 10/20/65, Huntsville, AL.

Thompson, W.L., Pvt., Co. L, died 10/19/63 in regimental hospital.*

Thornhill, James B. (or P.), Pvt., Co. H, age 18, EN 12/20/64, Huntsville, AL, MI 2/13/65, Nashville, TN, born Jackson Co., AL, farmer, deserted 5/2/65 from Huntsville.

Thornton, Henry M., Pvt/Sgt., Co. A, age 28, EN 3/23/63 & MI 3/24/63, Glendale, MS, promoted to Sgt. 7/1/63, died 12/3/63 in hospital at Corinth, MS.

Thornton, James, Pvt., Co. F, age 35, EN 6/10/64 & MI 10/17/64, Rome, GA, born Polk Co., GA, farmer, MO 10/20/65, Huntsville, AL.

Thornton, James M., Pvt., Co. A, age 38, EN 3/23/63 & MI 3/24/63, Glendale, MS, on daily duty as teamster, MO 12/22/63, Memphis, TN.

Thornton, Martin V., Pvt., Co. K, age 19, EN & MI 7/8/62, Decatur, AL, born Fayette Co., AL, farmer, died 11/10/62 in Hospital #12 at Nashville, TN of rubeola. (Buried in Grave #B-5715 at Nashville National Cemetery.)

Thrasher, Francis M., Pvt/Sgt., Co. K&E, age 31, EN & MI 8/19/64, Rome, GA, born Gwinnett Co., GA, blacksmith, promoted to Sgt. 10/20/64, MO 10/20/65, Huntsville, AL.

Thrasher, Marion, Sgt., Co. E, absent with leave 6/20/65, absent with leave 7/20/65.*

Thrasher, William D. (or G.), Pvt., Co. K, EN 5/4/63, Murfreesboro, TN, MI 9/27/63, Glendale, MS, born Franklin Co., GA, farmer, POW 3/10/65 from Monroe's Crossroads, NC and cofined at Richmond, VA, paroled and discharged 6/12/65, Camp Chase, OH.

Tidwell, Benjamin F., Bugler, Co. A, age 25, EN 1/13/64, Camp Davies, MS, MI 2/5/64, Memphis, TN, born Dekalb Co., AL, farmer, appt. Bugler 3/9/64, MO 10/20/65, Huntsville, AL.

Tidwell, Micajah, age 19, EN 4/3/64 & MI 4/13/64, Decatur, AL, born Lauderdale Co., AL, farmer, died 6/26/64 at Decatur, AL of typhoid fever, originally buried in Grave #23 Soldier's Cemetery at the Post.

Tidwell, Peter, Pvt/Corp., Co. B, age 19, EN 3/11/63, Glendale, MS, MI 8/7/63, Corinth, MS, MO 1/22/64, Memphis, TN.

Tidwell, Peter S., Sgt/Pvt., Co. L, age 31, EN & MI 9/25/63, Fayette Co., AL, born Blount Co., AL, farmer, on daily duty as hospital nurse, MO 9/28/64, Rome, GA.
    NOTE: Peter Starnes Tidwell was the son of Mark Jones Tidwell and Eleanor Starnes who married December 28, 1803 in Chester Co., SC. Peter first married Margaret (?) in Marshall Co., AL. After her death he married Eliza Clark about 1842.

Tidwell, Simeon, Pvt., Co. B, age 38, EN 4/11/64 & MI 4/13/64, Decatur, AL, born Walker Co., AL, farmer, deserted 7/16/64 from Rome, GA with Smith carbine and equipment. Notation from Record and Pension Office dated December 6, 1902 states he enlisted 3/27/65 in Co. B, 10th Reg't. MO. Cav. in violation of the 22nd (now 50th) Article of War.

Tidwell, Thomas E., Pvt., Co. B, age 24, EN 3/9/64 & MI 3/27/64, Decatur, AL, born Blount Co., AL, farmer, deserted 7/16/64 from Rome, GA with Smith carbine and equipment.

Tidwell, William, Pvt., Co. B, age 38, EN 2/2/64, Pulaski, TN, born Madison Co., AL, farmer, deserted 3/20/64 from Decatur, AL.

Tidwell, William G., Pvt., Co. A, age 22, EN 1/15/64, Camp Davies, MS, MI 2/5/64, Memphis, TN, born Marion Co., AL, farmer, MO 10/20/65, Huntsville, AL.

Notation from War Dept. dated March 5, 1891 states, "This man deserted from Co. E, 7th Reg't. Illinois Cavalry date unknown and enlisted in this orgination in violation of the 22nd (now 50th) Article of War. This office cannot recognize the legality of this enlistment nor any claim for service rendered thereunder. The law views him as in a continuous state of desertion during the whole period of this enlistment."

Tillman, P., Pvt., Co. L, absent POW since 10/26/63.*

Tilly/Tiley, I. (or J.), Co. D, on detached service in North Alabama with Maj. Shurtliff 3/65.*

Tindal, James M., Pvt., Co. G, age 31, EN 3/16/64 & MI 4/13/64, Decatur, AL, born Limestone Co., AL, farmer, deserted 11/17/64 from Atlanta, GA with side arms, returned 6/17/65, request for removal of charge of desertion denied as he did not return in a resonable time.

Tittle, Clinton, Sgt., Co. L, age 36, EN 9/25/63, Fayette Co., AL, born Walker Co., AL, farmer, died 3/20/64 in Overton USA Hospital at Memphis, TN. (Buried Grave #1-44, Memphis National Cemetery.)
    NOTE: Clinton D. Tittle was was born in 1828 in Walker Co., AL, and was the son of James Tittle, born 1796 in SC. He married Lydia Dodd, daughter of Berry Dodd and Mary "Polly" Sheffield on January 5, 1851 in Hancock Co., AL. Lydia was born in 1828 in Larissa, Walker Co., AL and died in 1895 in Larissa. Their children were: Oscar, born October 4, 1851 in Winston Co., AL, died July 4, 1933, married Martha Harper, born August 20, 1850, died January 4, 1890; James, born September 21, 1853, died 1872; Jonas, born 1853, died 1872; Mary E., born October 14, 1855, died April 22, 1930; Lydia Catherine, born May 17, 1858, died 1887; William Carroll, born May 17, 1858 (twin to Lydia); Sarah Margaret, born October 8, 1861; and Andrew Clinton Tittle.[155]

Tittle, James S., Sgt., Co. L, age 36, EN 9/25/63, Fayette Co., AL, died 12/16/63 at regimental hospital at Camp Davies, MS of typhoid fever.

Tittle, Peter, Pvt., Co. E, EN 4/1/63, Glendale, MS, MI 4/1/63, Corinth, MS, on daily duty as teamster 1/25/64 at Vicksburg, MS, also served as hospital nurse, MO 3/1/64, Memphis, TN.

Tolbert, Silas, Pvt., Co. H, age 18, EN 3/1/65, Stevenson, AL, born Carroll Co., GA, farmer, died 3/25/65 in Post Hospital at Stevenson, AL of pneumonia.

Tomb/Toombs, Nicholas, Pvt., Co. C, age 22, EN 2/25/63 & MI 2/28/63, Corinth, MS, born Nelson Co., VA, shoemaker, MO 2/25/64, Memphis, TN.

Tompkins, John C., Corp/Pvt., Co. A, age 28, EN 1/1/64, Camp Davies, MS, MI 2/5/64, Memphis, TN, born Franklin Co., AL, farmer, appt. Corp. 2/5/64, reduced to ranks 3/31/65, on detached service recruiting in AL 5/1/64, POW 3/10/65 from Monroe's Crossroads, NC, MO 10/20/65, Huntsville, AL.

Tompkins, John W., arrested in Franklin, TN 3/21/65 for desertion.*

Toner, Benjamin F., Corp., Co. B, deserted with arms 7/18/64 from Rome, GA.*

Towns, William B., Pvt., Co. M, age 18, EN & MI 10/9/64, Rome, GA, born Wilkes Co., GA, farmer, deserted 12/14/64 from Savannah, GA with Smith carbine, Remington revolver, horse & equipment.

Tramel, Sanford, Lt/Major, Co. E&L (F&S), age 25, EN 12/5/62, Corinth, MS, promoted from Sgt. 18th MO Inf. Vols. having enrolled 9/17/61 at Trenton, MO, promoted to Capt. in Co. L 9/25/63, in arrest 1/8/64 concerning a general court martial, promoted to Major 7/1/64, MO 10/20/65, Huntsville, AL.

Tramner, C.A., Pvt., Co. L, on daily duty as teamster 3/64.*

Traylor, William, Pvt/Sgt., Co. E, age 19, EN & MI 9/1/64, Rome, GA, born Randolph Co., AL, farmer, promoted to Sgt. 10/20/64, MO 10/20/65, Huntsville, AL.

Treadaway, William/Wade H., Pvt., Co. E, age 29, EN 4/1/63, Glendale, MS, MI 4/1/63, Corinth, MS, on daily duty as company cook, MO 3/1/64, Memphis, TN.

Treadway/Treadaway, Henry G., Pvt/Corp., Co. A, age 27, EN & MI 2/9/63, Glendale, MS, promoted Corp. 7/1/63, MO 12/22/63, Memphis, TN.

Trettwell, Esby, (Cards filed with Esby Fretwell).

Treutham, Frasure M., Sgt., Co. F, age 30, EN 4/30/63, Corinth, MS, born Campbell Co., GA, mechanic, MO 4/12/64, Decatur, AL.

Trice, Joseph A., Pvt., Co. D, age 23, EN 10/14/64, Decatur, AL, MI 11/10/64, Rome, GA, born Marshall Co., AL, farmer, MO 10/20/65, Huntsville, AL.

Trotter, Josiah, Pvt., Co. C, age 22, EN 7/1/63, Glendale, MS, MI 8/15/63, Corinth, MS, born Pickens Dist., SC, farmer, died 3/28/64 in Overton USA Hospital at Memphis, TN of smallpox. (Buried Memphis National Cemetery.)

Truelove, George A., Pvt., Co. E, age 21, EN & MI 2/16/63, Corinth, MS, born Cumberland Co., NC, farmer, died 11/17/63 in Adams USA Hospital at Memphis, TN of pneumonia.

Truelove, Herbert A., Pvt., Co. E, age 48, EN & MI 2/16/63, Corinth, MS, on daily duty as blacksmith, MO 3/1/64, Memphis, TN.

Truin, Benjamin F., Co. A, detached recruiting since 5/17/64, (dated 8/64).*

Tub, I.F., Co. D, absent sick in US General Hospital 3/65.*

Tuck, John F., Pvt., Co. F, MIA 10/26/63.*

Tuck/Tucker, Richard D. (or A.), Pvt., Co. F, age 26, EN 5/1/63, Boliver, TN, MI 8/13/63, Corinth, MS, born Madison Co., AL, farmer, POW 10/26/63 from Vincent's Crossroads, MS.

Tuck, Robert, Pvt., Co. F, age 30, EN 5/1/63, Boliver TN, born Madison Co., AL, farmer, POW 10/26/63 from Vincent's Crossroads, returned from MIA 11/8/63, died 7/2/64 near Chattanooga, TN of apoplexy.

Tucker, Daniel, Pvt., Co. L, age 33, EN 9/25/63, Fayette Co., AL, died 3/11/64 at Washington USA Hospital in Memphis, TN of measles. (Buried Grave #1-28, Memphis National Cemetery.)

Tucker, Edward B., Pvt., Co. F, age 24, EN 4/13/63 & MI 4/18/63, Corinth, MS, deserted 4/21/63 from Glendale, MS.

Tucker, Enoch F., Pvt., Co. F, age 18, EN 11/14/63, Camp Davies, MS, MI 2/24/64, Memphis, TN, born Hardin Co., TN, farmer, sick in Nashville, TN 11/6/64, MO 11/23/64, Nashville, TN.
    NOTE: Enoch Tucker is buried in the White Sulphur Cemetery, Pickwick, Hardin Co., TN. The cemetery is located inside the Pickwick Landing State Park.[156]

Tucker, Greenbury, Pvt., Co. K, age 15, EN 11/1/63, Glendale, MS, born Fayette Co., AL, farmer, POW 3/21/64 in AR near Memphis, TN, paroled 4/30/64, MO 7/19/65, Nashville, TN.

Tucker, Henry, Pvt., Co. B, age 20, EN 3/11/63, Glendale, MS, born Marion Co., AL, farmer, MO 1/22/64, Memphis, TN.

Tucker, Jack, Co. F, absent sick in US General Hospital 3/65.*

Tucker, Jesse, Pvt., Co. L, age 18, EN & MI 9/25/63, Fayette Co., AL, MO 9/28/64, Rome, GA.

Tucker, John J., Pvt., Co. H, age 18, EN 10/17/63, Glendale, MS, MO 10/24/64, Rome, GA.

Tucker, Richard, (Cards filed with Richard Tuck).

Tucker, Simeon, Pvt/Sgt., Co. E&K, age 45, EN & MI 7/8/62, Decatur, AL, born Jasper Co., GA, farmer, appt. Corp. 11/1/63 and Sgt. 1/1/65, POW 3/21/64 in AR near Memphis, TN, released 4/30/64, MO 7/19/65, Nashville, TN.

Tune, James A., Pvt., Co. A, age 43, EN 1/14/64, Camp Davies, MS, MI 2/5/64, Memphis, TN, born Abbeville Dist., SC, farmer, in confinement at Athens, AL where he died 6/1/64 in military prison, charged with deserting and taking US arms and ammunition to the enemy, charges against him were removed by War Dept. June 7, 1988.

Tupper, Francis W., 1st Lt. & Adj., Co. B,D&K, (F&S), age 24, EN 11/20/63, Camp Davies, MS, on detached service as Supt. of Refugee Camp 12/14/63, granted leave 2/23/64 to visit Helena, AR, appt. Adjutant 7/1/64, severly wounded 12/9/64 and sent to USA Hospital at Hilton Head, SC, in Officers USA Hospital at Beaufort, SC 12/20/64, returned to duty 3/22/65, MO 5/15/65 due to wounds received in action. Surgeon's Certificate states "amputation right thigh lower third, result of torpedo wound received near Savannah, GA", permitted to go North.

Turner, Levi, Pvt., Co. A, absent sick in hospital at Memphis, TN.*

Turner, Thomas A., Pvt., Co. G, age 19, EN 2/15/63, Chewalla, TN, on daily duty as company cook, MO 11/26/63, Memphis, TN.

Turner, W.S., Co. A, absent POW 3/10/65.*

Turrentine, Martin F., Pvt., Co. I, age 22, EN & MI 8/26/62, Huntsville, AL, born Morgan Co., AL, farmer, died 12/19/62 in Nashville, TN. (Buried in Grave #B-5931 at Nashville National Cemetery under name of Turntine.)
    NOTE: Martin F. Turrentine was the son of James W. Turrentine, a veteran of the War of 1812 and was a cousin to Martin J. Turrentine.[157]

Turrentine, Martin J., Wagoner, Co. I&K, age 52, EN & MI 7/21/62, Huntsville, AL, born Morgan Co., AL, farmer, on duty as ambulance driver 2/63, sick in hospital at Tuscumbia, AL 4/30/63, died 7/21/63 at Duquom (?), Illinois.
    NOTE: Martin J. Turrentine was the son of James S. Turrentine and Anner Wilson and grandson of John Turrentine. He married Seany Day September 28, 1839. At the time he enlisted in this regiment he was 52 years old and had nine living children, the youngest being only one-year old.[158]

Turrentine, Richard J. Corp/Lt., Co. E,I&D, age 21, EN & MI 7/21/62, Huntsville, AL, born Morgan Co., AL, farmer, promoted to Sgt. 8/12/63 and 2nd Lt. 10/1/64, MO 10/20/65, Huntsville, AL.
    NOTE: Richard was the son of Martin J. Turrentine and Seany Day and grandson of James S. Turrentine and David Day, Jr. He and his father enlisted in this regiment on the same day. After the war, he married Sarah Dutton and had a son, Stephen Henry. Richard died in 1868 at age 27 and is buried in the Turrentine Cemetery.[159]

Tylor, James, Pvt., Co. D, detached as scout by order of Maj. Gen. Dodge 1/65, detached service in North Alabama with Maj. Shurtleff.*

Tyler, Jasper F., Pvt., Co. D, age 21, EN 2/1/63, Glendale, MS, MI 2/4/63, Corinth, MS, discharged 7/2/63 due to disability - chronic bronchitis.

Tyler, John W., Pvt., Co. D, age 23, EN 2/1/63, Glendale, MS, MI 2/4/63, Corinth, MS, born Jefferson Co., AL, farmer, sick at Refugee Camp at Corinth, sent to Illinois with refugee families 7/10/63, discharge issued February 23, 1882 as of 7/2/63 due to disability.

NOTE: John Washington Tyler was born April 10, 1839. He moved to Illinois after the war, settled in Hamilton County and married Lorina Decanter, daughter of Ezekiel Decanter. He died October 10, 1905 and is buried in Sneed Cemetery in Hamilton County.[160]

Tyler, Thomas, Pvt., Co. D, absent on detached service in Decatur, AL.*

Tyler, Wiley S., Pvt., Co. K, age 24, EN & MI 7/24/62, Huntsville, AL, deserted 8/23/62 from Huntsville, AL, returned 10/23/63, died 8/30/64 in 2nd Div. USA Field Hospital at Rome, GA. (Buried Grave# C-1226, Marietta National Cemetery.)

Tyler, William G. (or J.), Pvt., Co. D, EN 2/1/63, Glendale, MS, MI 2/4/63, Corinth, MS, KIA 10/26/63 at Vincent's Crossroads near Bay Springs, MS. (Buried Grave #B-264, Corinth National Cemetery.)

Ullry, Gun, Pvt., Co. H, absent sick in Nashville.*

Urham/Urban, Cosander/Casander/Arthene, Pvt., Co. B, age 36, EN 2/3/64, Pulaski, TN, MI 4/13/64, Decatur, AL, born Lauderdale Co., AL, farmer, deserted 4/13/64 from Mooresville, AL.

Ussery/Ursery, James, Pvt., Co. F, age 16, EN 5/15/63, Bolivar, TN, MI 8/17/63, Corinth, MS, born Henderson Co., TN, farmer, MO 7/27/64, Rome, GA.

Utley, Daniel, Pvt., Co. H, discharged 9/29/64 at Rome, GA by reason of exp. of term of service.*

Uttly/Uttley, George W., Pvt., Co. H, age 18, EN 9/2/63, Glendale, MS, born Morgan Co., AL, farmer, died 6/25/64 at home in Decatur, AL.

Uttly/Uttley, John F., Pvt., Co. H, age 30, EN 9/2/63, Glendale, MS, MO 9/29/64, Rome, GA.

Uttly/Uttley, Samuel, Pvt., Co. H, age 23, EN 9/2/63, Glendale, MS, MO 9/29/64, Rome, GA.

Vail, James J., Pvt/Sgt., Co. A, age 21, EN & MI 2/19/63, Glendale, MS, promoted to Sgt. 9/16/63, MO 12/22/63, Memphis, TN.

Vanhoose, Lewis V. (R.V.), Pvt., Co. C, age 18, EN 8/30/63, Glendale, MS, MI 9/29/63, Corinth, MS, born Tishomingo Co., MS, farmer, POW 2/28/64 from Canton, MS, confined at Richmond, VA, died 6/5/65 in USA Hospital at Annapolis, MD of scorbutus & double pneumonia, originally buried in Grave #1370 at Ash Grove US Cemetery.

Vanhose/Vanhoose, Robert F., Sgt., Co. C, age 24, EN 12/1/62 & MI 12/22/62, Corinth, MS, born Tishomingo Co., MS, farmer, appt. Sgt. 1/1/63, reenlisted 12/15/63, Corinth, MS, MI 4/29/64, Decatur, AL, KIA 3/10/65 at Monroe's Crossroads near Fayetteville, NC.

Vanhose/Vanhoose, William Y., Pvt., Co. C, age 17, EN 7/1/63, Glendale, MS, MI 8/15/63, Corinth, MS, born Tishomingo Co., MS, farmer, MO 7/27/64, Rome, GA.
    NOTE: William Young Van Hoose was born April 1846 in Tishomingo Co., MS. His first wife was Adeline Wright and he later married Sarah Ann Whitehurst in February 1874. Sarah was born October 14, 1858 in Tishomingo Co., MS, and they had two sons; John Alfred, born May 18, 1874 in Corinth, MS, died August 14, 1949 in Longview, TX, and James MacDonald, born October 8, 1883 in Corinth, MS, died May 3, 1953 in Bridgeport, TX. William died March 29, 1885 in Tishomingo Co., MS. Sarah married twice after his death and died in October 29, 1933 in Bridgeport, Wise Co., TX.[161]

Vaughn, Willis A., Pvt., Co. H, age 40, EN 9/14/63, Glendale, MS, on daily duty as teamster, MO 9/29/64, Rome, GA.

Vest, George W., Pvt., Co. K, age 32, EN & MI 7/24/62, Huntsville, AL, born Morgan Co., AL, farmer, deserted from picket post in Nashville, TN 11/2/62, returned 4/29/64 at Mooresville, AL and restored to duty, had been captured by the enemy and held POW until his escape, MO 7/19/65, Nashville, TN.
    NOTE: George W. Vest and William A. Vest were sons of James Vest, born 1791 in GA, married Sallie Harvey in 1809, and died in 1868 in Winston Co., AL. George and William enlisted in the 1st AL Cav. USA, while their brother, James J. Vest, enlisted in an Arkansas Confederate regiment. George was born September 19, 1828 in Morgan Co., AL and died April 3, 1901 in Cullman, AL. Other children of James and Sallie Vest were: Albert, Lucy, Martha Nancy and John Vest.[162]

Vest, Henry K. (name also appears as H.B., R.R., & H.P.), Pvt., Co. B, age 30, MI 3/12/64, Athens, AL, MI 3/27/64, Decatur, AL, born Morgan Co., AL, farmer, left sick in hospital at Savannah, GA 1/13/65, discharged 6/8/65 from DeCamp USA Hospital at David's Island, NY.
    NOTE: Henry K. Vest was the son of James Vest and his second wife, Margaret Canady. He was the brother of Jonathan Vest and half-brother of William A. and George W. Vest of the 1st AL Cav. USA and James J. Vest who fought for the Confederacy.

Vest, Jonathan, Pvt/Sgt., Co. B, age 21, EN 3/12/64, Athens, AL, MI 3/27/64, Decatur, AL, born Winston Co., AL, farmer, on furlough 5/1/64 to settle his family in TN, appt. Corp. 8/1/64, sent to hospital at Rome, GA 10/1/64, died 1/19/65 in Joe Holt USA Hospital at Jeffersonville, IN of typhoid pneumonia.
    NOTE: Jonathan Vest was the son of James Vest and his second wife, Margaret Canady and the brother of Henry K. Vest, above.

Vest, William A. (name also appears as W.W., & Wm. H.), Pvt., Co. B, age 37, EN 4/6/64 & MI 4/13/64, Decatur, AL, born Morgan Co., AL, farmer, left sick at Kingston, GA 5/22/64, left sick in hospital at Chattanooga, TN 1/20/65, returned to duty 8/5/65, MO 10/20/65, Huntsville, AL.

NOTE: William A. Vest was the son of James and Sallie Harvey Vest, (see George W. Vest above.) He was born February 14, 1827 in Morgan Co., AL and died July 30, 1899 in AL.

Viar, Pleasant W., Pvt., Co. E, EN & MI 2/8/63, Corinth, MS, deserted 3/20/63 from Glendale, MS.

Vickers, John, Pvt., Co. H, age 18, EN 3/20/65, Stevenson, AL, MI 4/5/65, Nashville, TN, born Lauderdale Co., AL, farmer, MO 10/20/65, Huntsville, AL.

Vincent, John, Pvt., Co. C, age 34, EN 12/13/62, Corinth, MS, born Lawrence Co., TN, farmer, on daily duty as company cook, MO 12/17/63, Memphis, TN.

Vines, John J., Pvt., Co. D, age 18, EN 5/20/64 & MI 6/16/64, Decatur, AL, born Jefferson Co., AL, farmer, KIA 3/10/65 at Monroe's Crossroads, NC.

Vines, William J., Pvt/Sgt., Co. G, age 22, EN 4/10/64, Decatur, AL, MI Rome, GA, born Pontotoc Co., MS, farmer, appt. Sgt. 5/1/64, MO 10/20/65, Huntsville, AL.

Vinson, William M., Pvt., Co. C, age 18, EN 2/20/63 & MI 2/25/63, Corinth, MS, born Franklin Co., AL, farmer, POW 10/26/63 from Vincent's Crossroads, returned 11/28/63, MO 2/20/64, Memphis, TN.

Waddle, John H., Pvt., Co. H, age 17, EN 1/15/65, Huntsville, AL, MI 2/13/65, Nashville, TN, born Gordon Co., GA, farmer, MO 10/20/65, Huntsville, AL.

Waddle, John R., Pvt/Sgt., Co. H, age 42, EN 2/20/65, Huntsville, AL, MI 4/5/65, Nashville, TN, born Spartanburg Dist., SC, farmer, appt. Sgt. 4/1/65, MO 10/20/65, Huntsville, AL.

Wade, William, Pvt., Co. K&A, age 22, EN 11/28/62 Glendale, MS, MI 12/31/62, Corinth, MS, MO 12/22/63, Memphis, TN.

Wakefield, John W., Pvt., Co. G, age 18, EN 3/21/64 & MI 4/13/64, Decatur, AL, born Walker Co., AL, farmer, MO 10/20/65, Huntsville, AL.

Waldon, Lewis, Pvt., Co. C, age 31, EN 12/20/62 & MI 12/22/62, Corinth, MS, born Anson Co., NC, farmer, MO 12/27/63, Camp Davies, MS.

Waldrep, Pinckney, Pvt., Co. H, age 26, EN 12/1/63, Camp Davies, MS, born SC, killed 7/14/64 by accidental gunshot wound, carbine accidentally discharged. (Buried Grave #F-5439, Marietta National Cemetery.)

Waldrip/Wauldrup, William C., Pvt., Co. F, age 43, EN 11/1/63, Glendale, MS, born Lauderdale Co., AL, farmer, deserted 3/20/64 from Memphis, TN.

Waldron, Stephen, Pvt., Co. C, (Colored), EN 12/15/64 at Monticello, GA on daily duty as company cook.*

Waldrup, J., Pvt., Co. H, on daily duty as ambulance driver.*

Walker, Albert S., Pvt/Sgt., Co. H, age 18, EN 12/24/64, Rome, GA, MI 2/13/65, Nashville, TN, born Lumpkin Co., GA, farmer, appt. Sgt. 4/1/65, MO 10/20/65, Huntsville, AL.

Walker, Buckner, Pvt., Co. D, age 18, EN 11/16/63, Glendale, MS, MI 11/16/63, Camp Davies, MS, born Union Co., GA, farmer, sick in Adams USA Hospital at Memphis, TN 2/17/64, returned to duty 4/20/64, MO 12/19/64 from Savannah, GA.

Walker/Waker, Isaac, Pvt., Co. D, age 22, EN & MI 11/16/63, Camp Davies, MS, born Lumpkin Co., GA, farmer, sent to Washington USA Hospital at Memphis, TN 2/14/64, sick in hospital at Chattanooga, TN 11/6/64, MO 10/20/65, Huntsville, AL.

Walker, James, Pvt/Sgt., Co. D, age 22, EN 2/1/63, Glendale, MS, MI 2/4/63, Corinth, MS, on daily duty as teamster, promoted to Sgt. 12/3/63, MO 2/4/64, Memphis, TN.

Walker, James H., Pvt., Co. F, absent sick in Memphis, TN 2/64.*

Walker, John, Pvt., Co. D, on daily duty as teamster 5/63, daily duty as company cook 10/64, absent sick in US General Hospital 12/64-6/65.*

Walker, John Franklin, Pvt., Co. G, age 18, EN 4/24/64, Mooresville, AL, MI Rome, GA, born Dekalb Co., AL, farmer, POW 3/10/65 from Bartholomew Gr., NC (Monroe's Crossroads) and confined at Richmond, VA, paroled 3/30/65 and sent to Camp Chase, OH, deserted 10/1/65 from Decatur, AL, charges of desertion were removed 1/18/88 and discharge issued as of 10/1/65.

Walker/Waker, Jonathan, Pvt/Corp., Co. D, EN 2/1/63, Glendale, MS, MI 2/4/63, Corinth, MS, promoted to Corp. 12/3/63, MO 2/4/64, Memphis, TN.

Walker, Jonathan, Pvt., Co. I, age 21, EN & MI 7/21/62, Huntsville, AL, born Rutherford Co., NC, farmer, sick in hospital at Nashville, TN 1/15/63, on detached service as scout 8/4/64, POW 3/10/65 from Monroe's Crossroads near Fayetteville, NC, MO 7/19/65, Nashville, TN.

Walker, Robert J., Pvt., Co. H, age 33, EN 4/1/65, Stevenson, AL, MI 4/5/65, Nashville, TN, born Pike Co., GA, carpenter, sick in St. Clair Co., AL 6/1/65. No further information.

Walker, Memory, Pvt., Co. M, age 28, EN 12/7/63, Camp Davies, MS, MI 12/29/63, Corinth, MS, born Lumpkin Co., GA, on daily duty as blacksmith, sick in USA Hospital at Beaufort, SC 4/7/65, MO 10/20/65, Huntsville, AL.

Walker, Robert H., Pvt/Blacksmith, Co. M, age 24, EN 11/19/63, Camp Davies, MS, born Forsythe Co., GA, blacksmith, MO 10/20/65, Huntsville, AL.

Walker, S., Pvt., Co. B, absent sick in general hospital 10/64.*

Walker, T.F., Pvt., Co. G, sick in Gayoso USA Hospital at Memphis, TN Jan. & Feb. 1864.*

Walker, William H., Pvt., Co. F, age 25, EN 4/13/63, Corinth, MS, born Franklin Co., AL, farmer, on daily duty as mail carrier, died (Casualty Sheet states 2/27/64 & MR states 3/17/64) at Memphis, TN of smallpox. (Buried Grave #1-26, Memphis National Cemetery.)

Walker, William, Pvt., Co. I, age 45, EN 12/14/63, Camp Davies, MS, sick in hospital at Nashville, TN 11/20/64, discharge issued 6/24/68 as of 7/19/65.

Walker, William F., Pvt/Corp., Co. M, age 32, EN 5/21/64, Kingston, GA, MI Rome, GA, born St. Clair Co., AL, appt. Corp. 9/20/65, MO 10/20/65, Huntsville, AL.

Walker, William R., Pvt., Co. A, absent sick in hospital at Nashville, TN 8/64.*

Walks, James, Pvt., Co. I, detached as scout 9/64.*

Wall, Alexander, Co. A, age 32, born Fred. City, VA, mason, EN 9/6/64, Rome, GA.*

Wall, John, Pvt., Co. A, EN 11/1/64, Rome, GA, died 11/15/64 near Atlanta, GA.

Wallace, Littleton/Lyttleton, Pvt., Co. B, age 21, EN 1/18/63, Glendale, MS, MI 1/22/63, Corinth, MS, POW 10/26/63 from Vincent's Crossroads, MO 1/22/64, Memphis, TN.

Wallace, Luther, Pvt., Co. B, died 2/23/65 at Savannah, GA, originally buried in Laurel Grove Cemetery.* (May be Robert L. Wallace, below.)

Wallace, Madison M. (Thomas W.M.), Pvt., Co. D&I, age 21, EN & MI 8/26/62, Huntsville, AL, born Morgan Co., AL, farmer, deserted 10/27/63 from Nashville TN, rejoined 4/18/64 and awaiting trial, MO 7/19/65, Nashville, TN.
    NOTE: Thomas William Madison Wallace was the son of Thomas Wallace and Jane Hackworth and grandson of Joel Wallace who was a captain in the NC Militia during the Revolutionary War. He was born about 1841 in Morgan Co., AL.[163]

Wallace, Robert L., Pvt., Co. B, age 16, EN 8/1/64, Wedowee, AL, MI 8/1/64, Rome, GA, born Carroll Co., AL, farmer, left sick in hospital at Savannah, GA 1/21/65 and died 2/12/65, originally buried in Lot 1624, Row 3, Grave 2 at Laurel Grove Cemetery.

Wallard, John, Pvt., Co. L, EN 6/1/64, Ackworth, GA.*

Walling, John H., Corp., Co. C, age 22, EN 12/1/62, & MI 12/22/62, Corinth, MS, born Madison Co., AL, farmer, appt. Corp. 1/1/63, MO 12/17/63, Memphis, TN.

Walls, James F., Pvt/Corp., Co. H, age 25, EN 10/17/63, Glendale, MS, on detached service at Refugee Camp 1/10/64, promoted to Corp. 7/1/64, MO 10/24/64, Rome, GA.

Walls, M.F., Corp., Co. H, discharged by reason of expiration of term of service 10/25/64, Rome, GA.*

Walpool, James H., Pvt., Co. H, age 18, EN 1/23/65, Huntsville, AL, MI 2/13/65, Nashville, TN, born Limestone Co., AL, farmer, paid $100.00 Bounty and deserted 5/8/65 from Huntsville, AL.

Walters, Eli, Pvt., Co. G, age 18, EN 3/10/64 & MI 4/13/64, Decatur, AL, born Cobb Co., GA, farmer, MO 10/20/65, Huntsville, AL.

Walters, J.M., Pvt., Co. B, absent POW 11/64.*

Walton, Stephen, Under Cook, Co. C, (Colored), age 26, EN 12/1/64, Monticello, GA, MI 10/17/65, Huntsville, AL, born Laurens Co., GA, farmer, sick in hospital at Raleigh, NC 5/4/65, MO 10/20/65, Huntsville, AL. (Name also appears as S.C. Walter, & Stephen Waller.)

Warbington, Dilmus, Pvt., Co. C, age 23, EN 12/15/62 & MI 12/22/62, Corinth, MS, born Gwinnett Co., GA, farmer, MO 12/17/63, Memphis, TN.
   NOTE: Dilmus Lafayette Warbington was born June 16, 1840 in GA to Jeffersin Warbington, a school teacher, and Melvina Ward, daughter of Anderson Ward who was born August 10, 1813 in TN, died January 24, 1883 in Harville, Butler Co., MO and Lulis Meridon.

Ward, Anderson, Pvt/Corp., Co. L&M, age 39, EN 12/1/63, Camp Davies, MS, MI 12/29/63, Corinth, MS, on detached service recruiting in AL 9/15/64, MO 6/30/65, Nashville, TN.
   NOTE: Anderson was born in March 1826 in GA and died October 15, 1905 in Winston Co., AL. On March 10, 1844, he married Winnie Catherine Durham in Cherokee Co., GA. After the war he served as postmaster in what is now Haleyville, AL in 1883 and 1886.[164]

Ward, John W., Pvt., Co. D, age 20, EN 12/20/64, Millen/Ogeechee, GA, born Cherokee, NC, farmer, MIA 2/6/65, supposed to be dead in the field 5/1/65. No further information.

Ward, Robert B., Pvt., Co. B, age 30, sick in Northern hospital 6/1/63, deserted 7/63 from Glendale, MS, arrested 3/7/64 in Duquoin, IL "Reward $30.00). No further information.

Ward, William, Pvt., Co. D, absent sick in hospital 7/64.*

Ward, William H., Pvt., Co. M&L, age 18, EN 12/1/63, Camp Davies, MS, MI 12/29/63, Corinth, MS, born Cherokee Co., GA, farmer, died 3/18/64 in Gayoso USA Hospital at Memphis, TN of measles. (Buried Grave #1-24, Memphis National Cemetery.)

Wardlow, Joseph, Corp., Co. E, EN & MI 3/1/63, Glendale, MS, died 7/10/63 at Glendale, MS.

Warfield, (?), Co. A, absent on furlough 10/64.*

Warner, James, Pvt., Co. B, sick in USA General Hospital at Louisville, KY Nov. & Dec. 1863.*

Warner, John, Co. D, discharged 4/5/63 due to disability at Glendale, MS.*

Warren, H., Co. D, absent sick in hospital at Corinth 4/10/63.*

Warren, J., Pvt., Co. C, sick at Jefferson USA Hospital at Jeffersonville, IN. 3/1/64.*

Warren, James A., Pvt., Co. C, sick at Jefferson USA Hospital at Jeffersonville, IN March & April 1864.*

Warron, John, Pvt., age 32, MI 4/13/64, Decatur, AL, born Walker Co., AL, farmer. No further information.

Washer, William G. (or C. or E.), Pvt/Corp., Co. B, age 31, EN 2/27/64, Pulaski, TN, MI 3/27/64, Decatur, AL, born Lawrence Co., AL, farmer, appt. Corp. 3/28/64, POW 3/18/65 near Fayetteville, NC.

Waters, Eli, (Cards filed with Eli Walters).

Waters, Henry H., Lt/Capt., age 25, EN & MI 4/1/63, Corinth, MS, MO 4/10/64 in Memphis, TN for promotion, EN 4/11/64, Memphis, TN. No further information.

Watson, G.W., Co. B, absent POW 3/65.*

Watson, James M., Pvt., Co. B, age 18, EN 3/10/64 & MI 3/27/64, Decatur, AL, born Morgan Co., AL, farmer, POW 11/23/64 from Oconee River, Ball's Ferry, GA, confined at Richmond, VA, discharged 6/13/65 from Camp Chase, OH.

Watts, J.W., Pvt., Co. D, EN 6/10/63 at Glendale, MS, POW 10/26/63.*

Watts, John W., Pvt., Co. D, age 26, EN & MI 6/10/63, Glendale, MS, MIA 10/26/63 from Vincent's Crossroads near Bay Springs, MS, MO 6/16/64, Decatur, AL.

Watts, William, Pvt., Co. D, EN 2/1/63, Glendale, MS, MI 2/4/63, Corinth, MS, deserted 2/25/63 from Glendale, POW 3/2/63, on detached service at Refugee Camp in Memphis, TN 1/64, MO 2/4/64, Memphis, TN.

Wattson/Watson, James, Pvt., Co. H, age 19, EN 3/1/65, Stevenson, AL, MI 4/5/65, Nashville, TN, born Hall Co., GA, farmer, on detached service in Huntsville, AL as blacksmith 7/6/65, deserted 8/30/65 from Blountsville, AL with Colt pistol, Smith carbine & equipment.

Weaver, Henry, Pvt., Co. H, age 19, EN 3/1/65, Stevenson, AL, MI 4/5/65, Nashville, TN, born Calhoun Co., AL, farmer, MO 10/20/65, Huntsville, AL.

Weaver, James R., Pvt/Sgt., Co. C, age 41, EN 12/1/62 & MI 12/22/62, Corinth, MS, born Giles Co., TN, blacksmith, appt. Sgt. 4/10/63, died 6/10/63 in hospital at Corinth, MS.

Weaver, Jessie/Jesse, Pvt., Co. C, age 25, EN 12/8/62 & MI 12/22/62, Corinth, MS, born Jackson Co., AL, farmer, MO 12/17/63, Memphis, TN.

Webb, Hardy, Pvt., Co. E, age 26, EN 3/1/63, Glendale, MS, MI 3/1/63, Corinth, MS, MO 3/1/64, Memphis, TN.

Webb, James E., Pvt., Co. M, age 36, EN 12/5/63, Camp Davies, MS, MI 12/29/63, Corinth, MS, born Marion Co., AL, farmer, deserted 5/29/64 while on leave with Smith carbine and Colt revolver. Notation from War Dept. dated 8/29/76 states, "Dishonorably discharged the service August 17th 1876 to date from May 29, 1864, with loss of all pay, bounty, and allowances."

Webb, John, Sgt., Co. B, age 18, EN 1/1/63, Glendale, MS, MI 1/22/63, Corinth, MS, appt. Sgt. 1/22/63, MO 1/22/64, Memphis, TN.

Wedgeworth, T.M., Co. B, (No further information).*

Welch, Henry C., Pvt/Sgt., Co. I, age 19, EN & MI 7/21/62, Huntsville, AL, born Morgan Co., AL, farmer, with wagon train at Nashville, TN 12/27/62, on detached service as courier at Reedyville, TN 1/27/63, MIA 5/3/63 from Battle of Cedar Bluff, AL and confined at Richmond, VA, rejoined 8/2/63, appt. Sgt. 10/1/63, KIA 12/24/63 at Jack's Creek near Jackson, TN.

Welch, William, Pvt., Co. D, KIA 12/24/63 at Jack's Creek, TN.*

West, Ephraim B., Capt. Co. B, age 24, EN 2/1/64, Pulaski, TN, MI 3/27/64, Decatur, AL, born Hurde, GA, farmer, appt. Capt. 4/12/64, MO 10/20/65, Huntsville, AL.

West, Green B., Farrier, Co. L, age 42, EN 9/25/63, Fayette Co., AL, born Walker Co., AL, farmer, died 3/19/64 in Overton USA Hospital at Memphis, TN of measles/pneumonia.

West, John B., Pvt., Co. L, age 42, EN 9/25/63, Fayette Co., AL, born Fayette Co., AL, farmer, served as hospital nurse, died 6/29/64 in Cumberland USA Hospital at Nashville, TN. Wife shown as Jane West of Nashville, TN.

West, Moses, Pvt., Co. B, age 25, EN 3/21/64 & MI 3/27/64, Decatur, AL, born Lawrence Co., TN, farmer, POW 3/10/65 from Monroe's Crossroads near Fayetteville, NC and confined at Richmond, VA, paroled 5/30/65 from Aiken's Landing, VA, discharged 6/12/65 from Camp Chase, OH.

West, Simon/Simeon, Under Cook, Co. M, (Colored), age 26, EN & MI 9/1/64, Rome, GA, born Polk Co., GA, farmer, also served as teamster, deserted 7/27/65 from Courtland, AL, charge of desertion removed 1/19/86 and discharge issued as of 6/15/65.

West, Zachariah F. (or T.), Pvt., Co. H, age 18, EN 3/1/65, Stevenson, AL, MI 4/5/65, Nashville, TN, born Morgan Co., AL, farmer, deserted 5/10/65 from Huntsville, AL.

Whaley, Charles, Pvt., Co. A, EN & MI 8/29/64, Rome, GA. No further information.

Whaley, Joseph E., Co. A, age 18, born Tishomingo Co., MS, farmer, EN 12/15/63, Camp Davies, MS, deserted from Memphis, TN 2/1/64.*

Whaley, Joseph W., Pvt., Co. A, EN 2/1/64, Memphis, TN, deserted 2/29/64 from Memphis.

Wheeler, James H. (or F.), Corp., Co. L, age 36, EN 9/25/63, Fayette Co., AL, MI 9/25/63, Glendale, MS, sick in Adams USA Hospital at Memphis, TN 12/15/63, MO 9/28/64, Rome, GA.

Wheeler, Joel A., Pvt., Co. A, age 18, EN & MI 9/6/64, Rome, GA, born Calhoun Co., AL, MO 10/20/65, Huntsville, AL.

Whisenant, Peter E., Pvt/Sgt., Co. A&K, age 46, EN 12/11/62, Glendale, MS, MI 12/31/62, Corinth, MS, on detached service at Refugee Camp in Corinth, MS 11/29/63, MO 12/22/63, Memphis, TN.

White, Andrew, Pvt., Co. C, enlisted but not mustered, rejected on examination of surgeon.*

White, Hugh P., Pvt., Co. A, age 25, EN 1/3/64, Camp Davies, MS, MI 2/5/64, Memphis, TN, born Fayette Co., AL, farmer, MO 10/20/65, Huntsville, AL.

White, J., Pvt., Co. I, POW 3/10/65 near Fayetteville, NC and confined at Richmond, VA, paroled 3/30/65.*

White, Jackson W., Sgt., detached for duty as orderly at Hd. Qrs. 12/16/64.*

White, James J., Pvt., Co. K, age 27, born St. Clair Co., AL, farmer, EN 12/21/63, Camp Davies, MS, traveled 150 miles from Walker Co., AL to enlist, rejected by regimental surgeon.*

White, James L., Pvt., Co. H, age 23, EN 4/20/65, Huntsville, AL, born Union Par. LA, deserted 5/12/65 from Huntsville.

White, James P., Bugler, Co. K, age 15, EN 11/31/63, Camp Davies, MS, born AL, deserted 12/9/63 from Camp Davies with horse and equipment, not apprehended.

White, John W., Pvt., Co. F, age 20, EN 5/15/63, Memphis, TN, MI 8/7/63, Corinth, MS, born Philadelphia, PA, clerk, POW 1/10/64 from Camp Davies, MS while sick, delivered at Savannah, GA 12/1/64. Correspondence in file concerning charges against John White for violation of 9th and 6th Articles of War, refused to obey orders and threatened an officer.

White, John, Pvt., Co. K, age 15, EN 11/21/63, Camp Davies, MS, deserted 12/9/63 from Camp Davies with horse and equipment.

Whitehead, Drury Cox, Pvt., Co. B, age 33, EN 1/16/63, Glendale, MS, POW 10/26/63 from Vincent's Crossroads, MO 1/22/64, Memphis, TN.
NOTE: Drury H. Cox Whitehead was born September 5, 1831 in Lauderdale Co., AL and was the youngest son of Archibald and Nancy Smith Whitehead. In 1852 he married Mary Jane Anthony and they made their home in the Fayette/Marion Co., AL area where they raised thirteen children. He was arrested by Confederate Conscript Officers but later escaped and joined the 1st AL Cav. US. He died April 2, 1914 at age 83 and is buried in the Morris Family Cemetery near Glen Allen, Fayette Co., AL.[165]

Whitehead, Ephram, Pvt., Co. K&A, age 32, EN 9/8/62, Iuka, MS, MI 10/1/62, Corinth, MS, born Shelby Co., AL, farmer, MO 9/16/63, Corinth, MS.

Whitehead, George W., Pvt., Co. K, age 17, EN 12/25/63, Camp Davies, MS, born Marion Co., AL, farmer, sick in Adams USA Hospital at Memphis, TN 2/19/64, returned to duty 4/6/64, MO 7/19/65, Nashville, TN. Traveled 100 miles from Marion Co., AL to Camp Davies, MS to enlist.
NOTE: George was born July 4, 1846 at Glen Allen, AL and died February 15, 1937 at Littleville, Winston Co., AL. He first married Mary Jane Tidwell, daughter of Andrew J. Tidwell, on February 7, 1868 in Fayette Co., AL and had seven children: Martha Alice, born 1869; Margaret Lorena, born 1871; William Andrew "Bud", born September 29, 1872, married Ida Carr December 9, 1894, died July 10, 1935; Andrew J., born 1875; Isadora "Icey", born 1876, married George Gaskin; James, born February 17, 1877, died March 13, 1877; and Mary O., born August 20, 1878, died September 17, 1878. After Many Jane's death George married Jane Herren, daughter of Aaron Herren, about 1880 and had the following children: Archiball W., born November 16, 1880, married Sarah Collier, died March 26, 1922; Charity, born April 17, 1882, married Luther Wise, died November 13, 1930; Luciller (Drucilla), born December 5, 1883, married Griffin Bailey; John Thomas, born April 7, 1887, married Fleddie Hamby, died July 30, 1968; Jessie Green, born February 10, 1888, married Scular Robinson, died July 1, 1938; George Harrison, born October 19, 1889, died October 20, 1918; Armendia Missouri, born April 13, 1891, married Lonnie Batchelor; Ollie Mae, born March 29, 1893, married

Port Mahall, died September 20, 1945; Dolly Jane, born May 20, 1895, married Dozier Engel, died June 1, 1988; and Joseph McKinley, born February 28, 1898, married Pearl Hipp, died November 2, 1925. George is buried in Littleville Cemetery, two miles east of Haleyville, AL.[166]

Whitehead, Joseph P., Pvt., Co. B, age 22, EN 3/11/63, Glendale, MS, detailed as scout 3/24/63. No further information.

Whitehurst, Felix G., Pvt., Co. D, age 32, EN & MI 4/30/63, Glendale, MS, sick in Refugee Camp at Corinth, MS, 11/20/63, MO 6/16/64, Decatur, AL.
 NOTE: Felix, Frederick and Simon Whitehurst were brothers and sons of Benjamin G.L. Whitehurst of Tishomingo Co., MS. Benjamin was born in Pitt Co., NC and died in Prentiss Co., MS and was the son of Arthur Whitehurst, Sr., a Revolutionary War soldier. Benjamin had seven sons and four of them served in the 6th Tennessee. Felix was born December 10, 1856 in NC and married Martha Hindricks in Tishomingo Co., MS and had two sons, John born 1858 and James born 1860.[167]

Whitehurst, Frederick W., Pvt., Co. C, age 21, EN 12/1/62 & MI 12/22/62, Corinth, MS, born Jackson Co., AL, farmer, MO 12/17/63, Memphis, TN.

Whitehurst, Simon A., Sgt., Co. C, age 25, EN 12/1/62 & MI 12/22/62, Corinth, MS, born Haywood Co., TN, appt. Sgt. 1/1/63, died 1/16/64 in Regimental Hospital.
 NOTE: Simon Ashbury Whitehurst was born in 1838 in Haywood Co., TN. On September 5, 1860, he married Mary Hill in Tishomingo Co., MS. (See Felix Whitehurst for more family information.)[168]

Whitley, Henry, Pvt., Co. L, age 18, EN 9/25/63, Fayette Co., AL, MI 9/25/63, Glendale, MS, born Cherokee Co., GA, farmer, in Overton USA Hospital at Memphis, TN 2/24/64, MO 9/28/64, Rome, GA.

Whitley, John C., Pvt., Co. G, temporarily attached from 11th Illinois Cavalry.

Whitley/Whitly, Jasper, Pvt., Co. A, age 25, EN 3/22/63 & MI 5/12/63, Glendale, MS, MO 12/22/63, Memphis, TN.

Whitley, William T. (or F.), Pvt., Co. G, temporarily attached from 11th Illinois Cavalry.

Whitly, J.C., Pvt., Co. G, transferred 8/24/63 by order of Col. Mercy.*

Whittaker, James, Pvt., Co. F, age 16, EN 4/29/63 & MI 5/18/63, Corinth, MS, born Tishomingo Co., MS, farmer, detached as teamster in Vicksburg, MS 1/25/64, MO 7/27/64, Rome, Ga.

Whitten/Whiton, William, Pvt., Co. D, age 38, EN 12/10/64, Millen/Ogeeche, GA, born Clark Co., GA, farmer, deserted 1/15/65 from Savannah, GA with arms and equipment.

Wicks, Thomas, Pvt., Co. H, age 19, admitted to hospital at Richmond, VA 1/26/64 while POW and died 3/2/64.*

Wideman, William, Pvt., Co. M, age 45, EN 12/16/63, Camp Davies, MS, MI 12/29/63, Corinth, MS, born Blount Co., AL, farmer, deserted 1/8/64 from Camp Davies with Colt revolver and went home to Winston Co., AL.

Wigginton, Anthony, Pvt., Co. M, age 23, EN 12/9/63, Camp Davies, MS, MI 12/29/63, Corinth, MS, born Blount Co., AL, farmer, deserted 1/20/64 from Camp Davies with Remington Revolver and supposed to have gone home to Marion Co., AL.

Wigginton, James, Pvt., Co. A, age 18, EN 9/8/62, Iuka, MS, MI 10/1/62, Corinth, MS, born Marion Co., AL, farmer, MO 9/16/63, Corinth, MS.

Wigginton, James M., Corp/Pvt., Co. B, age 28, MI 12/31/62, Corinth, MS, deserted 3/9/63 from Glendale, MS, charges of desertion removed 12/17/85 by War Dept. and discharge issued as of 3/9/63.

Wigginton, John K.G., Sgt, Co. B, age 37, EN 12/23/62, Glendale, MS, MI 12/31/62, Corinth, MS, appt. Sgt. 1/22/63, reduced to Duty Sgt. 3/1/63, POW 10/26/63 from Vincent's Crossroads, MO 12/27/63, Camp Davies, MS.

Wigginton, Lafayette, Pvt., Co. A&K, age 20, EN 9/8/62, Iuka, MS, MI 10/1/62, Corinth, MS, born Marion Co., AL, farmer, MO 9/16/63, Corinth, MS.

Wigginton, Lorenzo, Pvt., Co. M, age 20, EN 12/3/63, Camp Davies, MS, MI 12/29/63, Corinth, MS, born Itawamba Co., MS, farmer, deserted 1/20/64 from Camp Davies with Colt revolver and supposed to have gone home to Marion Co., AL.

Wigginton, Martin, Pvt., Co. B, age 25, EN 3/2/63, Glendale, MS, deserted 3/13/63 from Glendale.

Wiley, Benjamin F., Corp., Co. E, age 24, EN & MI 2/1/63, Corinth, MS, MO 2/1/64, Memphis, TN.

Wiley, Thomas, (see Thomas Wyley).

Wilhelms, James, (Cards filed with James Williams).

Wilhite, J.J., Pvt., Co. G, age 18, EN 3/22/64 & MI 3/27/64, decatur, AL, born Morgan Co., AL, farmer, MO 10/20/65, Huntsville, AL.
 NOTE: John Jarman Wilhite was born April 21, 1846 in Wilhite's Cove, Morgan Co., AL and died February 27, 1923 in Lacon, Morgan Co., AL. He was the son of Alfred McCoy Wilhite and Elizabeth C. Morris. On October 30, 1866, he married Nancy Adaline Basham, born December 18, 1849 in Basham's Gap, Morgan Co., AL and died February 22, 1890. Their children were: Serrepta A., born August 13, 1867, died July 5, 1869; Leonodos Spurgeon, born August 13, 1870, died March

7, 1895; Elizabeth, born April 27, 1872, died April 25, 1956; Lola U., born September 21, 1874; Dora Mae, born March 9, 1877, died June 6, 1909; Sarah Ida, born June 13, 1879, died March 1, 1963; Zula B., born February 21, 1882, died May 11, 1971; James Alford, born June 1, 1884, died November 19, 1968; Myrtle Alice, born August 30, 1886; and Beulah M., born August 25, 1889. After Nancy's death, John married Virginia Walling on September 14, 1890 and had the following children: Anna Pearl, born December 1, 1891; Thomas Monroe, born July 14, 1893; and Leslie J., born June 17, 1896.[169]

Wilhite, Ezekiel, Pvt., Co. K, age 21, EN & MI 8/22/62, Huntsville, AL, born Morgan Co., AL, farmer, deserted 11/22/62 from Nashville, TN while at picket post #11, not apprehended.

Wilhite, Jackson W., Pvt/Sgt., Co. D&I, age 42, EN & MI 7/21/62, Huntsville, AL, born Winston Co., AL, farmer, sick in Hospital #8, Nashville, TN 10/24/62, POW 5/1/63 from Day's Gap, AL and confined at Richmond, VA, paroled at City Point, VA 5/14/63, appt. Sgt. 11/1/63, MO 7/19/65, Nashville, TN.

Wilhite, James C., Co. H, age 18, born Morgan Co., AL, farmer, EN 6/1/65, Huntsville, AL, deserted from Huntsville, AL 6/10/65.*

Wilhite/Willhite, James C., Pvt., Co. H, age 18, EN 6/1/65, Huntsville, AL, born Morgan Co., AL, farmer, deserted 6/10/65 from Huntsville.

Wilhite, John P.(James P.), Sgt., Co. D&I, age 43, EN & MI 7/21/62, Huntsville, AL, sick in Hospital #8 at Nashville, TN 10/24/62, died 1/6/63 at Louisville, KY.

Wilis, William S., Pvt., Co. C, age 18, EN & MI 9/15/64, Rome, GA, born Gordon Co., GA, farmer, POW 4/3/65 (or 4/28/65 or 3/31/65) from Faison's Station, NC and confined at Richmond, VA, discharged 6/12/65, Camp Chase, OH.

Williams, Alexander C., Pvt., Co. A, age 18, EN 1/3/64, Camp Davies, MS, MI 2/5/64, Memphis, TN, born SC, in Gayoso USA Hospital at Memphis, TN 2/14/64, returned to duty 7/22/64, MO 10/20/65, Huntsville, AL.
    NOTE: Alexander Campbell "Bud" Williams and his brother, Joe, were the sons of John E. Williams of Virginia. He was really only 16 years old and his brother was 14 when they enlisted in this regiment. After the war they returned home to Huntsville, Alabama but found themselves living in a Confederate "hotbed", which was not a popular place to be after wearing the Union Blue. They finally settled in Bethel Springs, TN where Alexander opened a store in the 1870's and later moved to Rose Creek. He remained a Union loyalist and staunch Republican all his life and was an active member of the GAR Chapter at Sandy Flats until his death in 1918.[170]

Williams, Andrew J., Under Cook, Co. I, (Colored), age 27, EN & MI 9/1/64, Rome, GA, born Montgomery, AL, MO 7/19/65, Nashville, TN.

Williams, Benjamin, Pvt., Co. M, age 36, EN 12/16/63, Camp Davies, MS, MI 12/29/63, Corinth, MS, born Montgomery Co., AL, farmer, deserted 1/8/64 from

Camp Davies with Colt revolver and went home to Walker Co., AL returned 3/20/65, MO 10/20/65, Huntsville, AL.

Williams/Williamson, Charles, Pvt., Co. F, age 26, EN 5/21/63 & MI 8/7/63, Corinth, MS, farmer, POW 10/26/63 from Vincent's Crossroads, still listed as POW when company MO.

Williams, Daniel, Pvt., Co. H, age 27, EN 7/28/63 & MI 9/27/63, Glendale, MS, died 1/7/64 in Adams USA Hospital at Memphis, TN. (Buried Grave #1-39, Memphis National Cemetery.)

Williams, Franklin, Cook, Co. K, age 22, EN 12/21/63, Camp Davies, MS, born Walker Co., AL, deserted 1/15/64 from Camp Davies with Colt revolver and equipment returned 4/30/64, deserted 6/30/64 from Chattanooga, TN and not apprehended. Traveled 150 miles from Walker Co., AL to enlist.

Williams, Frederick, Pvt., Co. C, age 21, EN 1/8/63 & MI 2/1/63, Corinth, MS, born Whitfield, GA, farmer, deserted 8/6/63 from Glendale, MS.

Williams, George B. (or T.), Pvt., Co. A, died 5/15/64 in Field Hospital at Bridgeport, AL.* (Buried Grave #H-578, Chattanooga National Cemetery.)

Williams, George W., Pvt., Co. G, age 18, EN 7/11/63, Glendale, MS, MO 11/26/63, Memphis, TN.

Williams, George W., Pvt., Co. I, age 18, EN 11/10/63, Camp Davies, MS, farmer, died 3/29/64 in Overton USA Hospital at Memphis, TN. (Buried Grave #1-23, Memphis National Cemetery.)

Williams, Green, Pvt., Co. B, age 49, EN 1/20/63, Glendale, MS, MI 1/22/63, Corinth, MS, appt. Sgt. 4/1/63, MO 1/22/64, Memphis, TN.

Williams, Henry B., Pvt., Co. E, EN & MI 2/8/63, Corinth, MS, deserted 3/20/63 from Glendale, MS.

Williams, Isaac A., Pvt., Co. B, age 28, EN 4/6/64 & MI 4/13/64, Decatur, AL, in arrest 12/4/64 under charge of pillaging house and assult with weapon, MO 10/20/65, Huntsville, AL. (MO Roll states age 37.)

Williams, Jack, Co. I, on daily duty as regimental teamster 5/65.*

Williams, J.W.T., (Cards filed with J.W.T. Williamson).

Williams, James/Frank, Pvt/Sgt., Co. A (F&S), age 27, EN 5/15/63, Memphis, TN, born Cincinnati, OH, saddler, appt. Saddler Sgt. 10/31/63, deserted 4/1/64 from hospital at Memphis, TN while under arrest, returned to duty and reenlisted & MI 7/6/64, Rome, GA, deserted 7/19/65 from Huntsville, AL, charge of desertion removed 3/24/92 by War Dept. and discharge issued as of 7/19/65. Note states, "See also Francis Carroll, Co. B, 7th MO Vols."

Williams, James, Pvt., Co. G, age 17, EN 12/29/62, Pocahontas, TN, MO 11/26/63, Memphis, TN.

Williams, Jessy, Co. F, absent sick in US General Hospital 3/65.*

Williams, Joel, Pvt., Co. G, absent sick at Decatur, AL 5/1/64 & 9/64.*

Williams, J.M., Co. B, absent sick in hospital 3/65.*

Williams, Joel W., Corp/Sgt., Co. E, age 35, EN & MI 2/1/63, Corinth, MS, promoted to Sgt. 9/22/63, MO 2/1/64, Memphis, TN.

Williams, John, (Cards filed with John Wilson).

Williams, John, Pvt., Co. A, absent sick in General Hospital at Memphis, TN 9/64.*

Williams, John, Pvt., Co. K, age 20, EN 12/21/63, Camp Davies, MS, born Walker Co., AL, farmer, deserted 1/15/64 from Camp Davies with Colt revolver and equipment, reported 8/2/64 at Rome, GA and put in confinement, escaped 8/5/64 and not apprehended. Traveled 150 miles from Walker Co., AL to Camp Davies, MS to enlist.

Williams, Joseph J.N. (or J.J.), Pvt., Co. A, age 18, EN 1/3/64, Camp Davies, MS, MI 2/5/64, Memphis, TN, born Calhoun Co., AL, farmer. From 1/64-12/65 he was sick in hospital at Memphis, Nashville, and Louisville, KY, (hypertrophy of heart, gunshot wound of the chest), 1/65 in Convalescent Barracks No. 1 in Louisville, nearest relatives shown as Jane & Franklin Williams and residence Franklin, TN, MO 10/20/65, Huntsville, AL.

Williams, Luther M., Pvt., Co. C, age 21, EN 2/15/64 & MI 3/10/64, Memphis, TN, born Carroll Co., TN, farmer, sick in hospital at Chattanooga 9/29/64, discharged from hospital at Mound City, IL 5/11/65 due to disability, mother shown as Elizabeth Williams and residence Manlysville, Henry Co., TN.

Williams, Marion, Pvt., Co. B, age 21, EN 1/20/63, Glendale, MS, MI 1/22/63, Corinth, MS, deserted 5/25/63 from Glendale, MS.

Williams, Riley, Pvt., Co. I, age 25, EN & MI 7/21/62, Huntsville, AL, born Walker Co., AL, farmer, with wagon train at Nashville, TN 12/27/62, MIA 4/28/63 from Day's Gap, AL and confined at Richmond, VA 7/25/63, admitted to hospital at Annapolis, MD 9/30/63, sent to Camp Chase, OH 10/18/63 where he died 1/25/64 of smallpox.

Williams, Stephen, Corp/Pvt., Co. B, age 23, EN 1/20/63, Glendale, MS, appt. Corp. 1/22/63, deserted 2/28/63 while on scout, returned 12/11/63.

Williams, Wesley, Pvt/Lt., Co. A&K, age 40, EN 10/13/62 & MI 10/14/62, Corinth, MS, promoted to 1st Lt. 1/1/63, relieved from duty 4/10/63 by Brig. Gen. G.M. Dodge, no further information.
NOTE: Testimony of Wesley Williams, Headquarters "Yates S.S.", Glendale, Miss. Jan 24, 1863:
"I live in Marion County, Alabama. At some time in October, I left my home and came to the Union lines, since which time I have been back a number of times to my old neighborhood for recruits to fill up the Alabama Calvary now at Glendale; on or about the 1st of October, 1862, the rebels burned my cotton, amounting to about 2000 pounds, and since I left home they have burned my house, furniture, and clothes; at the same time, they also burned 10,000 pounds of cotton belonging to my brother, Green Williams and the house and property of Joseph Posner; they also carried away the clothing of Parson Benjamen Avery, and family; they also took from my nephew Reuben Williams, one horse, saddle & bridle; David Kennedy, an old and loyal citizen, they hanged to death, burned his house, and destroyed his property; the house of J. Barron was also burned." Signed, Wesley Williams.[171]

Williams, William C., Pvt., Co. B, age 18, EN 3/19/64 & MI 4/13/64, Decatur, AL, born Winston Co., AL, farmer, MO 10/20/65, Huntsville, AL.

Williamson, David Jackson, Pvt., Co. E, age 20, EN 8/19/64 in Randolph Co., AL, MI 11/10/64, Rome, GA, born Cowetta Co., GA, farmer, MO 10/20/65, Huntsville, AL. (MO Roll states age 27.)

Williamson, J.W.F, Pvt., Co. B, age 18, EN 3/22/64 & MI 3/27/64, Decatur, AL, born Cass Co., GA, farmer, deserted 5/19/64 from Decatur, AL with Smith carbine and equipment.

Willis, John, Pvt., Co. A, age 18, EN 1/4/64, Camp Davies, MS, MI 2/5/64, Memphis, TN, born Tishomingo Co., MS, farmer, MO 10/20/65, Huntsville, AL.

Willis, William, Pvt., Co. E, age 19, EN & MI 8/27/63, Glendale, MS, on detached service as teamster 1/25/64 at Vicksburg, MS, died 4/18/64 at Ft. Donelson of smallpox.

Willom, C.H. Pvt., age 23, EN 4/6/64 & MI 4/13/64, Decatur, AL, born Rhea Co., TN, farmer, no further information.

Willum, Jesse, Pvt., Co. F, deserted 1/1/64 from Camp Davies, MS.*

Wilson, Baron D., Pvt., Co. H, in Cumberland USA Hospital at Nashville, TN Sept. & Oct. 1865.*

Wilson, Charles M., Pvt., Co. K, age 29, EN 12/21/63, Camp Davies, MS, born Marshall Co., AL, farmer, died 2/19/64 in camp at Memphis, TN of congestion of the brain. Traveled 120 miles from Walker Co., AL to Camp Davies, MS to enlist.

Wilson, George W., (1st), Pvt., Co. M, age 18, EN 12/20/63, Camp Davies, MS, MI 12/29/63, Corinth, MS, born Cherokee Co., GA, farmer, MO 10/20/65, Huntsville, AL.

Wilson, George W., (2nd), Pvt., Co. M, age 24, EN 10/14/64, Decatur, AL, MI 11/10/64, Rome, GA, born Rayborn Co., GA, farmer, MO 10/20/65, Huntsville, AL.

Wilson, Hugh M., Pvt/Corp., Co. H, age 28, EN 11/12/63, Camp Davies, MS, on daily duty as company cook, MO 11/23/64, Nashville, TN.

Wilson, James, Pvt., Co. K, temporarily attached from 5th Tennessee Cavalry.

Wilson, John, Pvt., Co. F, age 23, EN 5/15/63 & MI 8/7/63, Corinth, MS, born Winston Co., AL, farmer, POW 1/20/63 from Vincent's Crossroads. No further information.

Wilson, John, Pvt., Co. M, age 21, EN 10/14/64, Decatur, AL, MI 11/10/64, Rome, GA, born Rayborn Co., GA, farmer, MO 10/20/65, Huntsville, AL.

Wilson, John T., Pvt., Co. E, EN & MI 4/1/63, Corinth, MS, deserted 4/1/63 from Glendale, MS.

Wilson, Josiah, Pvt/Sgt., Co. A&D, age 21, EN 1/14/64, Camp Davies, MS, MI 2/5/64, Memphis, TN, born Spartanburg Dist., SC, farmer, appt. Sgt. 7/1/64, POW 3/10/65, MO 10/20/65, Huntsville, AL.
   NOTE: Josiah Wilson was born December 18, 1842 in Spartanburg Co., SC and married February 21, 1867 to Tabitha Tate. He was the son of Abisha and Elizabeth Brooks Wilson. He first joined the 28th AL Cav. CSA and later joined the 1st AL Cav. USA. He died September 4, 1890 and is buried in Jefferson Co., AL.[172]

Wilson, William W., Pvt/Sgt., Co. M, age 39, EN 12/20/63, Camp Davies, MS, MI 12/29/63, Corinth, MS, born Hall Co., GA, farmer, promoted to Sgt. from Corp. 8/6/64, MO 10/20/65, Huntsville, AL.

Wilton, Mark S., Pvt., Co. I, age 32, EN 12/23/63, Camp Davies MS, deserted 1/18/64, Camp Davies.

Winder, John T., Pvt/Corp., Co. K, age 20, EN & MI 7/24/62, Huntsville, AL, born Tippah Co., MS, farmer, appt. Corp. 1/1/64, MO 7/19/65, Nashville, TN.

Wingul/Wingo, Henry C., Pvt., Co. H, age 17, EN 9/14/63, Glendale, MS, MO 9/29/64, Rome, GA.

Winsett, Thomas, Pvt., Co. B, age 25, EN 1/8/63, Glendale, MS, MI 1/22/63, Corinth, MS, deserted 5/11/63 from Glendale.

Winters, Samuel, Pvt., Co. H, age 18, EN 10/17/63, Glendale, MS, in hospital at Memphis, TN wounded 10/63, in USA Field Hospital at Rome, GA 6/26/64, MO 10/24/64, Rome, GA.

Winters, Willis, Pvt., Co. H, age 18, EN 10/15/63, Glendale, MS, MO 10/24/64, Rome, GA.

Wofford, William, Pvt., Co. A, age 18, EN 12/22/63, Camp Davies, MS, MI 2/5/64, Memphis, TN, MO 10/20/65, Huntsville, AL.

Wolf/Wolfe, Leonard/Lenard, Lt., Co. H, age 23, EN 4/1/65, Huntsville, AL, sick in Louisville, KY 10/1/65. No MO date.

Wolfe, James R., Pvt., Co. I, age 48, EN & MI 7/21/62, Huntsville, AL, born Barren Co., KY, farmer, sick in hospital at Nashville, TN 4/19/63, discharged 9/28/63 due to disability.

Wood, J., Co. D, absent POW 3/65.*

Wood, James M., Pvt., Co. M, age 28, EN & MI 8/28/64, Rome, GA, born Onslow Co., NC, farmer, deserted 5/20/65 from Durham's Station, NC with arms, horse and equipment.

Wood, James N.(or M.), Pvt., Co. F, age 20, EN 11/25/63, Camp Davies, MS, MI 7/27/64, Rome, GA, born Marion Co., AL, farmer, MO 12/17/64 "before Savannah, GA."

Wood, James O., Pvt., Co. G, age 19, EN 3/10/64 & MI 4/13/64, Decatur, AL, born Marion Co., AL, farmer, on daily duty as teamster, MO 10/20/65, Huntsville, AL.

Wood, J.W., Pvt., Co. D, on daily duty as company cook, absent sick in US Hospital 12/64.*

Wood, Joseph R., Pvt., Co. K, age 19, EN & MI 7/24/62, Huntsville, AL, born Blount Co., AL, farmer, died 10/17/62 in Hospital #14 at Nashville, TN of rubeola. (Buried in Grave #A-4280 at Nashville National Cemetery as J.A. Woods.)

Wood, Robert C., Pvt., Co. M, age 44, EN 12/16/63, Camp Davies, MS, MI 12/29/63, Corinth, MS, born Marion Co., AL, farmer, MO 10/20/65, Huntsville, AL.

Wood, William A., Pvt., Co. D, age 27, EN 5/20/64 & MI 6/16/64, Decatur, AL, born Jefferson Co., AL, farmer, WIA 10/15/64 and died 10/28/64 in field hospital at Rome, GA. (Buried Grave #C-1448, Marietta National Cemetery.)

Wood, William B., Pvt/Corp., Co. G, age 27, EN 9/4/64, Decatur, AL, MI 11/10/64, Rome, GA, born Dekalb Co., GA, farmer, promoted to Corp. 11/20/64, on detached service at Wilmington, NC as nurse in hospital 3/65, MO 10/20/65, Huntsville, AL.

Woodall, Ervin/Erving M., Corp. Co. K, age 25, EN & MI 8/23/62, Huntsville, AL, born Morgan Co., AL, farmer, on recruiting service in TN 11/10/64, detached as courier 1/27/63 at Reedyville, TN, appt. Corp. 11/1/62, POW 5/1/63 from Day's Gap, AL and confined at Richmond, VA, paroled at City Point, VA 5/14/63 and sent to Camp Chase, OH, MO 7/19/65, Nashville, TN. Wife shown as Margrett Woodall.

Woodall, Jonathan M., Pvt., Co. K, absent sick 11/10/64.*

Woodall, Joseph, Pvt., Co. B, age 33, EN 2/27/64, Pulaski, TN, MI 3/27/64, Decatur, AL, born Dekalb Co., GA, farmer, sent to Nashville, TN 11/1/64 from Rome, GA sick, MO 10/20/65, Huntsville, AL.

Woodall, William E., Pvt., Co. K, age 32, EN & MI 8/23/62, Huntsville, AL, born Morgan Co., AL, farmer, died 10/4/62 (or 10/9/62) in Hospital #15 at Nashville, TN of rubeola. (Buried Grave # A4999, Nashville National Cemetery.)

Woodall, William J. Pvt., Co. K, age 18, EN 5/1/64 & MI 6/16/64, Decatur, AL, born Morgan Co., AL, farmer,sick in hospital at Nashville, TN 11/10/64, MO 7/19/65, Nashville, TN.

Woodford, Evilyn S., Pvt/Lt., Co. C, age 24, EN 3/1/64 & MI 3/10/64, Memphis, TN, born Matagorda, TX, merchant, appt. Sgt. 3/1/64, EN & MI 8/15/64, Rome, GA as 2nd Lt., MO 10/20/65, Huntsville, AL.

Woodam/Woodham, William, Pvt., Co. B, age 18, EN & MI 9/1/64, Rome, GA, born Upson Co., GA, farmer, MO 10/20/65, Huntsville, AL.

Woodruff, Samuel, Co. D, on daily duty as cook.*

Woody, Daniel, Pvt., Co. C (or K), died 8/16/65 at Huntsville, AL of disease.*

Woolbright/Woodright, James M., Pvt., Co. D, age 19, EN & MI 6/24/63, Glendale, MS, born Marion Co., AL, farmer, on daily duty as company cook, MO 9/28/64, Rome, GA.

Woolbright, Samuel, Pvt/Blacksmith, Co. D, EN 2/1/63, Glendale, MS, MI 2/4/63, Corinth, MS, served as blacksmith, company cook and teamster, MO 2/4/64, Memphis, TN.

Wooley, Benjamin F., Pvt., Co. B, age 20, EN 4/12/64 & MI 4/13/64, Decatur, AL, born Fayette Co., AL, farmer, on daily duty as teamster, left sick in hospital at Savannah, GA 1/18/64, MO 10/20/65, Huntsville, AL. (MO Roll states age 40.) (Correspondence in file relating to charges of assault.)

Woolridge, William, Pvt/Corp., Co. B, age 27, EN 1/6/63, Glendale, MS, MI 1/22/63, Corinth, MS, appt. Corp. 3/1/63, POW 10/26/63, Vincent's Crossroads near Bay Springs, MS, MO 1/22/64, Memphis, TN.

Wooly, William T., Pvt., Co. K, age 18, EN & MI 6/26/62, Limestone Co., AL, born Marion Co., AL, farmer, in hospital at Nashville, TN 12/26/62, sent to hospital at Annapolis, MD 5/16/63, on detached service as teamster in Gen. Sherman's expedition at Vicksburg, MS 1/24/64, fell from train between cars near Marietta, GA 9/28/64 and killed in line of duty while in route from East Point, GA to Rome, GA.

Wooster, Daniel H., Sgt., Co. G, temporarily attached from 11th Illinois Cavalry.

Wooster, Daniel R., Sgt., temporarily attached 7/4/63 Chewalla, TN 18th Reg. MO Inf. from 1st AL Cav.*

Wooster, James P., Pvt., Co. G, temporarily attached from 11th Illinois Cavalry.

Wooten, Charles W., Co. G, Notation in files dated 11/21/88 states he was admitted to hospital at Bridgeport, AL 5/7/64, died 5/25/64 of measles, originally buried 5/26/64 in Grave #250 at Field Hospital Burial Plot. (Reinterred Grave #H-479, Chattanooga National Cemetery.)

Wortham, James H., Pvt., Co. C, age 18, EN 12/15/62 & MI 12/22/62, Corinth, MS, MO 12/27/63, Camp Davies, MS.
   NOTE: These two entries may be same soldier.
Worthom, James H., Pvt., Co. C, age 19, EN 1/1/64, Corinth, MS, born Marshall Co., MS, farmer, died 1/11/64 at Camp Davies, MS of diphtheria.

Wray, George W., Pvt., Co. G, age 22, EN 11/27/62, Grand Junction, TN, MO 11/26/63, Memphis, TN.
(Buried in Kirk Cemetery, Western McNairy Co., TN.)[173]

Wray, Monroe, Pvt., Co. G, age 21, EN 3/6/63, Chewalla, TN, MO 11/26/63, Memphis, TN. (Notation from Record and Pension Office dated December 16, 1901 states discharge is erroneous.)

Wray, Washington, Pvt., Co. G, age 39, EN 3/6/63, Chewalla, TN, MO 11/26/63, Memphis, TN.

Wright, Asa J., Pvt., Co. E&A, age 18, EN & MI 9/1/64, Rome, GA, born Randolph Co., AL, farmer, deserted 9/1/65 from Moulton, AL. Notation from War Dept. dated November 14, 1884 states charge of desertion is removed, dishonorable discharge canceled and discharge issued as of 9/1/65.

Wright, James A., Pvt., Co. H, age 18, EN 1/1/65, Stevenson, AL, MI 2/13/65, Nashville, TN, born Cherokee Co., GA, farmer, MO 10/20/65, Huntsville, AL.

Wright, James H., Pvt., Co. E&A, age 18, EN & MI 9/1/64, Rome, GA, born Cobb Co., GA, farmer, deserted 9/1/65 from Moulton, AL. Notation from War Dept. dated November 14, 1884 states charge of desertion is removed, dishonorable discharge canceled and discharge issued as of 9/1/65.

Wright, John N. (or M.), Pvt., Co. B, age 21, EN 3/25/64 & MI 3/27/65, Decatur, AL, born Walker Co., AL, farmer, reduced to ranks 7/22/65, MO 10/20/65, Huntsville, AL.

Wright, Joseph B. (or V.), Pvt., Co. B, age 18, EN 2/5/64, Pulaski, TN, MI 3/27/64, Decatur, AL, born Lawrence Co., AL, farmer, died 4/8/64 in hospital at Decatur, AL. (Buried Grave #B-3231, Corinth National Cemetery.)

Wright, Robert, Pvt., Co. L, age 33, EN 9/25/63, Fayette Co., AL, MI 9/25/63, Glendale, MS, born Walker Co., AL, farmer, MO 9/28/64, Rome, GA.

Wright, Williamson W., Pvt., Co. E, age 27 (or 47), EN & MI 9/1/64, Rome, GA, born Oglethorpe Co., GA, farmer, deserted 9/1/65 from Moulton, AL. Notation from War Dept. dated 7/24/84 states charge of desertion is removed, dishonorable discharge canceled and discharge issued as of 9/1/65.

Wry, C.V., Co. D, detached recruiting in Decatur, AL.*

Wyatt, John, Pvt., Co. D, absent POW 2/9/63.*

Wyatt/Wyott, Josiah, Pvt., Co. F, absent paroled POW 3/64.*

Wyatt, William, Pvt., Co. D, age 18, EN & MI 8/20/63, Glendale, MS, born Jefferson Co., AL, farmer, POW 3/12/64 in MS, enlisted in 10th TN CSA while POW at Andersonville, GA, charged with desertion, supposed to be dead in the field 5/1/65. It is unclear what happened to this soldier.

Wyley, Thomas J., Pvt., Co. I, age 19, EN & MI 7/21/62, Huntsville, AL, born Madison Co., AL, farmer, on detached service as courier at Reedyville, TN 1/27/63, MO 7/19/65, Nashville, TN.
    NOTE: Thomas Jefferson Wiley, the William Wiley family, and the Hightower Brothers were among some of the earliest settlers in the northern portion of Alabama just south of the Tennessee River having established residence there sometime before 1820. William was 43 years old when his son Thomas Jefferson Wiley was born in Morgan County Alabama in 1843. William died when Thomas was only about twelve years old, and when the Civil War started he was living in Winston County near the communtiy of Houston with his mother, Jane, a widow with eight children still at home. Thomas was the oldest son and soon joined many other young men in the area and volunteered for military service in support of maintaining the Union by joining the 1st Alabama Cavalry and during the war years, formulated a relationship with the Hightower family that would last the rest of his life. About 1867 the families of Thomas Wiley and Marion Hightower decided to move to Arkansas and settled in Scott County near the community of Boothe. Several other families from the northern Alabama area, including Jacob Blevins, also settled in this area. Thomas and Martha had six children that lived to adulthood, the three oldest all being sons that became Baptist ministers. John Wiley served various churches in Arkansas. William Sherman Wiley and James Marshall Wiley served most of their ministry in Oklahoma, beginning when it was still Indian Territory. Martha Hightower Wiley died on March 18, 1886. After Martha's passing Thomas

married Alice McDonald Hogan, but this marriage was short lived as Thomas died May 8, 1888. His obituary stated he was always proud of his military service and had his discharge papers with him at the time of his death. Both Thomas and Martha are buried in the Wiley Cemetery in Scott County, Arkansas. Alice Hogan Wiley died several years later in Fort Smith, Arkansas.[174]

Wyres/Wiers, John A., Pvt., Co. G, age 21, EN 3/10/64 & MI 4/13/64, Decatur, AL, born Bibb Co., AL, farmer, on daily duty as teamster, MO 10/20/65, Huntsville, AL.
NOTE: John A. Wyers was born March 16, 1844 to Frederick and Sophia Stockman Wyers who were married August 17, 1836 in Perry Co., AL. John Married Mary Elizabeth Davis about 1868 in Walker Co., AL. Mary died March 23, 1916 and John died October 1, 1916.

Yarbear, Albert M., Pvt., Co. D, age 37, EN & MI 11/30/63, Camp Davies, MS, born Houston Co., GA, farmer, in hospital at Nashville, TN 10/17/64, MO 6/30/65, Nashville, TN. (Name also appears as A.M. Yonlow, A. Yarbro, A. Yarbour, A. Yonborn & Albert Yerber.)

Yarborough, Joshua P., Pvt/Corp., Co. D, age 37, EN 5/1/64 & MI 6/16/64, Decatur, AL, born Chester Dist., SC, farmer, promoted to Corp. 9/1/64, MO 10/20/65, Huntsville, AL.

Yarbrough, Francis M., Pvt., Co. E, age 29, EN & MI 10/4/64, Rome, GA, born Chambers Co., AL, farmer, on daily duty as teamster, MO 10/20/65, Huntsville, AL.

Yew/Yow, Henry M., Pvt., Co. B, age 17, EN & MI 12/31/62, Corinth, MS, sick in hospital at Corinth 2/20/63, MO 12/27/63, Camp Davies, MS.

York, Marion L., Blacksmith, Co. K, age 23, EN & MI 8/22/62, Huntsville, AL, born Giles Co., TN, blacksmith, died 12/2/62 in Hospital #8 at Nashville, TN of rubeola. (Buried Grave # A4868, Nashville National Cemetery.)
NOTE: Marion York married Mary Ann Perry Lentz December 12, 1854 in Limetone Co., AL. Mary Ann was a cousin to Abraham J. Lentz who was also in Co. K of this regiment. Marion had three brothers who fought for the Confederacy, Andrew Jackson York, Charles Franklin York and Presley Polk York.[175]

York, Wesley C., Pvt/Corp., Co. E, age 42, EN 9/13/63, Glendale, MS, MI 9/3/63, Corinth, MS, on recruiting service in AL 4/16/63, MO 9/28/64, Rome, GA.

Young, Anderson, Pvt/Sgt., Co. M, age 27, EN 9/7/63, Chewalla, TN, MI 12/29/63, Corinth, MS, born Fentress Co., TN, farmer, on daily duty as wagonmaster, MO 10/20/65, Huntsville, AL.

Young, Isaac, Pvt., Co. M, age 35, EN 9/7/63, Chewalla, TN, MI 12/29/63, Corinth, MS, born Dekalb Co., TN, farmer, MO 10/20/65, Huntsville, AL.

Young, John W., Pvt., Co. G, age 25, EN 3/10/64 & MI 4/13/64, Decatur, AL, born Madison Co., AL, farmer, died 9/14/64 in hospital at Decatur, AL.

Young, William W., Pvt., Co. K, age 23, EN 10/4/63, Glendale, MS, born Madison Co., AL, farmer, sent to Winston Co., AL recruiting 1/12/64 and did not return, restored to duty 9/14/64, sick in hospital at Goldsboro, NC 4/8/65, MO 7/19/65, Nashville, TN.

****

* Miscellaneous card extracts found at the end of Roll #10, Microcopy 276, Compiled Service Records of First Regiment Alabama Cavalry Volunteers. There are also some miscellaneous papers which include POW records, letters concerning destruction of property by rebels, various medical records, etc.

The roster of soldiers is in alphabetical order, therefore is not indexed. There are many other surnames listed in **"NOTES"** under the soldiers' names which include maiden names of spouses, mothers, children's spouses, etc. Anyone searching for family members should read the notes for all soldiers as many of the soldiers married sisters and daughters of other soldiers. It is surprising how many of these soldiers and their families are connected in some way.

Any derivative of a surname should be checked as many names were spelled as they sounded.

ABBREVIATIONS USED IN ROSTER

EN - Enlisted
MI - Mustered In
MO - Mustered Out
FS - Field Service/Staff
KIA -Killed In Action
MIA-Missing In Action
WIA-Wounded In Action

[1] Appplication for Widow's Army Pension filed by Sarah Harper McWhirter, January 26, 1806. (Another application filed in 1871 stated they were married in 1842.)

[2] 1850 Marion County, Alabama Census.

[3] Territorial Papers of Alabama, Alabama Department of Archives and History, Montgomery, Alabama.

[4] History of North Alabama Including Marion County, by: Dr. John Mitchell Allman, III, taught at Northwest Community College in Hamilton, Alabama June 11-12, 1993, attended by the author.

[5] Acts of the Alabama Territorial and State Legislatures, published and manuscript; Alabama Department or Archives and History, Montgomery, Alabama.

[6] History of North Alabama, by: Dr. John M. Allman, III. Printed with permission.

[7] Autobiography of Union soldier, John R. Phillips.

[8] The History of Mecklenburg Co., NC, 1740-1900, by J.B. Alexander.

[9] History of Wilson County, Tennessee.

[10] McMillan, *Alabama Confederate Reader.*

[11] Microcopy Number 276, National Archives Microfilm Publications, Compiled service records of Volunteer Union Soldiers who served in Organizations from the state of Alabama.

[12] O.R., I, XVI.

[13] O.R. I, Vol. XVI/1.

[14] O.R. I, Vol. XVI/1.

[15] Detachment Muster Roll dated September 24, 1862 in Nashville, TN, Record of Events.

[16] F&S Regimental Return dated February, 1865 from the field in SC.

[17] Regimental Return for the Month of March, 1865.

[18] Ibid.

[19] *The Prison Camp at Andersonville,* A National Park Civil War Series, text by William G. Burnett.

[20] Courtesy of descendant, Robin Sterling.

[21] Courtesy of descendant Joe Douthit.

22 Courtesy of James E. Gilbert.
23 Courtesy of descendant Silver F. Smith.
24 Courtesy of Becky Davenport.
25 Ibid.
26 Courtesy of Sohnie Fredrick Hill.
27 Notation from War Dept., Adjutant General's Office, June 30, 1874.
28 Courtesy of descendant Robin Sterling.
29 Ibid.
30 Ibid.
31 Courtesy of Greg Bourland.
32 Courtesy of Vicki Corrick.
33 Courtesy of Erlene Boyd.
34 Courtesy of Vicki Corrick.
35 Courtesy of Sallie Cox.
36 Courtesy of descendant Bettie Byrd Hickman.
37 Courtesy of descendant Jim Payne.
38 Courtesy of Louis Cagle.
39 Courtesy of Robert L. Willett.
40 Courtesy of descendant Rhett Campbell.
41 Ibid.
42 Courtesy of descendand Vicki Ruth Ebbert.
43 Courtesy of Linda Worley.
44 Courtesy of Michael R. Sloat.
45 Courtesy of Vicki Ruth Ebbert.
46 Ibid.
47 Courtesy of John Kopp.
48 Courtesy of descendant Gary W. Long.
49 Courtesy of descendant Christopher G. Tanner.
50 Courtesy of descendant John W. Cothern.
51 Ibid.
52 Ibid
53 Courtesy of descendant Mary Ellen Ledford.
54 Courtesy of Carolyn Wright.
55 Ibid.
56 Courtesy of descendant Bill Davis.
57 Sellers, Henry G., Jr., *Some Union Soldiers From a Place Called Crowdabout.*
58 Ibid.
59 Ibid.
60 Courtesy of Johnny L.T.N. Potter.
61 Courtesy of descendant James Quinn.
62 Courtesy of Patricia Ann Dodd Greathouse.
63 Courtesy of Patricia Dodd Greathouse.
64 Courtesy of descendant Wilma Duckett Morgan.
65 Courtesy of Richard Dugan.
66 Courtesy of Nancy Fry.
67 Sellers, Henry G., Jr., *Some Union Soldiers From a Place Called Crowdabout.*
68 Courtesy of Jimmie Nell Nichols Meadors.
69 Courtesy of James Grace.
70 Courtesy of descendant Michael J. Woodruff.

[71] Courtesy of descendant Joel Mize.
[72] Courtesy of descendants Joe Young Guin and Judge J. Foy Guin.
[73] Courtesy of descendant Kathryn Heilman.
[74] Courtesy of Lester Guyse.
[75] Courtesy of descendant Jimmie Nell Nichols Meadors.
[76] Courtesy of Becky Sullins.
[77] Ibid
[78] Ibid.
[79] Courtesy of James E. Gilbert.
[80] Courtesy of Clyde H. Wiley.
[81] Ibid.
[82] Courtesy of Dick Wolfer.
[83] Courtesy of J. Roper.
[84] Courtesy of descendant Robert Hurst.
[85] Courtesy of James E. Gilbert.
[86] Courtesy of Floyd H. Lawson.
[87] Courtesy of Bryan Summerhill.
[88] Courtesy of Chuck James.
[89] Ibid
[90] Courtesy of Phil Henson.
[91] Courtesy of Col. Gerald R. Jefferson.
[92] Researched by John and Sarah Anderson.
[93] Courtesy of Reita Jones Burress.
[94] Courtesy of Doris James.
[95] Courtesy of descendant Dan Sniffin.
[96] Courtesy of Paula Clack.
[97] Ibid
[98] Declaration for Widow's Pension.
[99] Courtesy of Catherine Stiles.
[100] Courtesy of Jeffrey L. Laurence.
[101] Courtesy of Carlyine Gibson Pierce.
[102] Ibid.
[103] Ibid.
[104] Courtesy of Laura Flanagan and Norma Miller.
[105] Courtesy of Carlyine Gibson Pierce.
[106] Courtesy of Robert P. Lindley, Jr.
[107] Ibid.
[108] Courtesy of Lynda McKinley.
[109] Courtesy of McDavid Franks.
[110] Courtesy of Sallie Cox.
[111] Courtesy of Dr. Mary Jo Brazelton.
[112] Courtesy of John McGowen.
[113] Military and Pension records furnished by Johnny Hickman.
[114] Courtesy of Jimmie Nell Nichols Meadors.
[115] Ibid.
[116] Courtesy of Robert P. Lindley, Jr.
[117] Ibid.
[118] Military and Pension records courtesy of Roger K. Howell.
[119] Courtesy of Melinda Mason.

[120] Courtesy of Jimmie Nell Nichols Meadors.
[121] Wayne Co., TN *Historian*, Vol. 3, No. 1, p. 35 & 36, contributed by Jerry Murphy.
[122] Ibid, p. 36.
[123] Courtesy of Jimmie Nell Nichols Meadors.
[124] Wayne Co., TN *Historian*, Vol. 3, No. 1, p. 36, contributed by Jerry W. Murphy.
[125] Courtesy of descendant Bill Pickford.
[126] Courtesy of Jerry Feltman.
[127] Courtesy of Clyde H. Wiley.
[128] Courtesy of Charles Stanley, taken from ISGS Quarterly 26:4 (Winter 1994), p. 242-243.
[129] *War of the Rebellion*, Series 1-Vol. XXXIX, part 1, p. 768.
[130] Ibid, Vol. XLVII, p. 897.
[131] Sellers, Henry G., Jr., *Some Union Soldiers From a Place Called Crowdabout.*
[132] Ibid.
[133] Ibid.
[134] Ibid.
[135] Courtesy of Richard Dugan.
[136] Ibid.
[137] Courtesy of Don Umphrey.
[138] Courtesy of David Cofield.
[139] Courtesy of descendant Johnny L.T.N. Potter.
[140] Courtesy of Vicki Corrick.
[141] Courtesy of Melinda Mason.
[142] Courtesy of Danial F. Lisarelli.
[143] Courtesy of Roger Howell.
[144] Courtesy of Jimmie Nell Nichols Meadors.
[145] Courtesy of Elsie Ward Jones.
[146] Courtesy of Larry R. Brown.
[147] Courtesy of Donald W. Sinyard.
[148] Courtesy of Charles and Lil Shurtleff.
[149] Copied at National Archives by Robert Willett.
[150] Courtesy of Robert L. Willett.
[151] Courtesy of Carlon Knight.
[152] Courtesy of Mary Ellen May.
[153] Courtesy of Victoria Moss.
[154] Courtesy of Vernard A. Thompson.
[155] Courtesy of Patricia Dodd Greathouse.
[156] Courtesy of William Appling.
[157] Sellers, Henry G., Jr., *Some Union Soldiers From a Place Called Crowdabout.*
[158] Ibid.
[159] Ibid.
[160] Courtesy of descendant Greg Brenner.
[161] Courtesy of Alfred Van Hoose.
[162] Courtesy of William J. Shelton.
[163] Sellers, Henry G., Jr., *Some Union Soldiers From a Place Called Crowdabout.*
[164] Courtesy of Sandy Ward Stewart.
[165] Courtesy of descendant Wanda J. Wilson.

[166] Courtesy of descendant Joel Mize.
[167] Courtesy of Dale Johnson.
[168] Ibid.
[169] Courtesy of descendant Anne Miller.
[170] Courtesy of Alexander's son, Waldemar Williams.
[171] Courtesy of Paula Clack.
[172] Courtesy of descendant E.D. Wilson.
[173] Courtesy of Roger Howell.
[174] Courtesy of descendant Clyde H. Wiley.
[175] Courtesy of Norma Miller.

Abbott, Israil P.	77		Box, Francis E.	78
Adams, James M.	73		Brooks, George	77
Adams, John Q.	76		Brooks, John A.	82
Adams, Levi	79		Brown, Elijah	82
Allen's Division	50, 52, 57		Brown, Robert M.	76
Andrews, James	63		Brown, William	82
Armstrong, James	79		Brunner, Lt.	43
Atkins, Gen.	51, 56		Bruns, Capt.	43
Austin, Jessie W.	79		Brunson, David A.	73
Bain, Alfred A.D.	82		Buell, Gen.	6, 9
Bain, John D.H.	82		Bumper, David A.	87
Bane, Col.	27, 31, 44		Bumper, Corp. Wm. H.	87
Barnett, Job	78		Butler's Division	52, 57
Barnes, Lt.	31		Byford, Quiller J.	79
Barraun, George L.	74		Byram, William T.C.	76
Barteau's Command	48		Byrd, Marshall H.	18, 87
Barton, Madison	9		Byrom, Cavaller	79
Barton, Widow	45		Cagle, Enoch	85
Barton, William H.	71		Cain, James	79
Baxter,s Command	46		Calvert, Ralphord	82
Beach, John	87		Cameron, Capt.	28, 41, 43
Beard, Alfred	71		Campbell, Adam	82
Bell, John	85		Campbell, Alexander	82
Bell, Robert	71		Campbell, Anna	5
Berry, James M.	71		Campbell, George B.	77
Bice/Price, John C.	71		Canady, Isaac A.	82
Bishop, David H.	73		Cantrell, John S. (2)	76
Bishop, Robert W.	76		Cantrell, William	76
Blackstock, Thomas W.	73		Carpenter, Capt.	31
Blanchard/Blanchitt, W.C.	87		Carpenter, Frazier E.	76
Blankenship, Robert S.	87		Carter, John	75
Blankenship, William W.	75		Castlebury, Robert B.	73
Blevins, Dillard	82		Chafin, William M.	76
Blevins, John (#2)	82		Chalmers, Gen.	30
Blevins, Nathaniel	79		Chandler, Capt.	18
Boling, William C.	12		Chandler, Erasmus D.	87
Bolton, H.L.	25		Cheatham's Command	57
Bolton, John	86		Cheek, Maj. C.T.	49, 50
Booker, William W.	71		Cheek, Edmond/Elijah S.	79
Bookout, Abel	79		Childress, M.	73
Bowen, Archie	13, 81		Clark, Maj. Gen. John	66
Bowen, Lt. Col.	41, 43, 45,		Clements, Curtis	74
46, 48, 49			Clements/Clemens, Ed	79
Bowlin/Bowling, Wm.	82		Cole, Henry	65
Boyer, Thomas H.	74		Collins, Volney	73
Boyd, Elisha F.	85		Comer, Lewis	86
Boyd, Joseph	74		Conaway, John E.	87

Knight, Benjamin P.	80	McKinney, Thomas	80
Krebs, Edward	43, 44	McMillian, Col	24
Lambert, William J.	73	McRay, John H.	78
Lambert, Wilson	74	McWhirter, A.J.	3
Lansford/Lunsford, M.	86	McWhirter, Andrew F.	1, 3, 5, 83
Latty, Capt.	50, 54, 56		
Lawrence, William F.A.	83	McWhirter, George M.	3
Lawson, Col.	32, 36	McWhirter, George W.	83
Lee, Gen. Robert E.	65, 68	McWhirter, T.A.	3
Lentz, John P.	83	McWhirter, W.H.	3
Lerock, P.	77	Mersy, Col.	47
Lewis, Isaiah	74	Milam, Jesse	86
Lewis, Noah	86	Miles, Benjamin R.	75
Lewis, Peter	74	Miles, William H.	83
Lincoln, Abraham	4, 7, 59	Miles, William W.	75
Little, C.	80	Milligan, James M.	75
Logan, Alexander	74	Milligan, William K.	83
Logan, James M.	83	Mills, Stephen H.	80
Lomax, John	26	Mitchell, Adj.	52
Lott, Simeon H.	83	Mitchell, Gen.	57
Lovett, Andrew J.	74	Mitchell, Eldon C.	73
Lovett, Archibald	74	Mitchell, Francis M.	77
Lovin/Lovoon, Wm. W.	86	Mitchell, John C.	83
Lowrimore, James	77	Mitchell, John D.	71
Lowry, James C.	77	Mize, James C.	13
Luther, Martin	59	Mize, James R.	81
Lytle, Capt.	9	Moody, Samuel	78
Mabry/Maberry, Alberry	73, 87	Mooney, George W.	78, 79
Maloy, Hugh	80	Mooney, Peter	83
Marion, Francis	1	Moore, James	8
Marsh, Dr.	31	Moore, John P.	56
Martin, Daniel	83	Morbin, John H.	80
Martin, Nathaniel G.	83	Morphis, James K.	87
Matthews, James	75	Murphree, James H.	21, 78
Mattox/Maddox, Henry	80	Murphy, William M.	87
Mathis, Jesse	75	Naughton, Capt. P.	42, 43
Mauldin/Madlin, Wm.	72	Neal, Charles B.	75
Mayfield, Milton	87	Nelson, Thomas M.	83
McCall, Corp. Thomas	72	Newland, Hugh	76
McClellan, Gen. George	65	Nichols, David	77
McColloch, Leroy	83	Nichols, Edward	78
McCreden, Col.	17	Nichols, General Morgan	77
McCullough, Capt. P.	42	Nichols, James F.	75
McCulloch, Samuel	83	Nichols, Jasper	78
McCullough, Joseph	77	Norris, George W.	80
McCullough, Thomas D.	79	Norris/Morris, Phillip	80
McDonald, Miles	75	Oden, Andrew J.	83
McDonald, William	80	Oden, William D.	82
McGough, Joseph	75	Offutt, Capt. Andrew	53

Vines, John J.	13, 81
Waldrep/Waldress, P.	88
Walker, William H.	81
Wall, John	71
Wallace, Robert L.	86
Ward, John W.	88
Ward, William H.	81
Wardlow, Joseph	77
Washington	4
Way, Lt. Col.	51
Weaver, James R.	75
Welch, Henry C.	21, 78
Welch, William	78
Welker, Capt.	44
West, Geeen B.	81
West, John	88
West, John B.	85
Wheeler, Gen. Joe	13, 10, 54, 56, 60
Whipple, Gen. Wm. D.	41
Whitehurst, Simeon A.	88
Wicks, Thomas	85
Wilder, S.	66
Wilhite, John	79
Williams, Capt.	14
Williams, Daniel	81
Williams, George B.	72
Williams, George W.	81
Williams, Riley	73
Willis, William	76, 88
Wilson, Charles M.	81
Wood, Joseph R.	85
Wood, William	86
Woodall, William E.	85
Woodward	33
Woody, Daniel	78
Wooly, William T.	71
Wooten/Whorton, C.W.	72
Wooten, Charles W.	72
Worthom, James H.	73
Wright, Capt. D.L.	32
Wright, Joseph B.	76
Yates, Parson	48
York, Marion L.	85
Young, John W.	76

Made in United States
Troutdale, OR
02/10/2024

17572280R00246